QUALITY MANAGEMENT FOR INFORMATION
AND LIBRARY MANAGERS

 **THE ASSOCIATION FOR INFORMATION MANAGEMENT**

Aslib, The Association for Information Management, has some two thousand corporate members worldwide. It actively promotes better management of information resources.

Aslib lobbies on all aspects of the management of and legislation concerning information. It provides consultancy and information services, professional development training, conferences, specialist recruitment, and the Aslib Internet Programme and publishes primary and secondary journals, conference proceedings, directories and monographs.

Further information about Aslib can be obtained from:

Aslib, The Association for Information Management, Information House, 20–24 Old Street
London EC1V 9AP, United Kingdom. Tel: +44 171 253 4488, Fax: +44 171 430 0514.
Email: aslib@aslib.co.uk WWW: http://www.aslib.co.uk/aslib/

QUALITY MANAGEMENT FOR INFORMATION AND LIBRARY MANAGERS

❖

Peter Brophy and Kate Coulling

Published by
Aslib Gower
Gower House
Croft Road
Aldershot
Hampshire GU11 3HR
England

Gower
Old Post Road
Brookfield
Vermont 05036
USA

Reprinted 1996, 1997

British Library Cataloguing in Publication Data

Brophy, Peter
Quality Management for Information and
Library Managers
I. Title II. Coulling, Kate
025.1

ISBN 0-566-07725-6

Library of Congress Cataloging-in-Publication Data

Brophy, Peter, 1950-

Quality management for information and library managers / Peter Brophy & Kate Coulling.
p.   cm.
Includes index.
ISBN 0-566-07725-6 (cloth)
1. Library administration-Great Britain.   2. Information Services-Great Britain-Administration.   3. Total quality management-Great Britain.   I. Coulling, Kate.
II. Title.
Z678.8.G7876 1996   95-23338
025.1'0941-dc20   CIP

Typeset in Garamond Light by Poole Typesetting (Wessex) Limited, Bournemouth and

Printed and bound in Great Britain by
Biddles Ltd, Guildford and King's Lynn

CONTENTS

❖

LIST OF FIGURES

ACKNOWLEDGEMENTS

The authors would like to thank the staff of the University of Central Lancashire Library and of the University's Centre for Research in Library & Information Management for their involvement, constructive criticism and help with the practical quality initiatives which provided the real-life experience on which this book has been based. For our over-enthusiasm, and for the irritation of having to work with those who believe they have 'seen the light', we can only apologize. The support of the British Library Research and Development Department for research in the field of quality management and libraries is also gratefully acknowledged.

Small sections of Chapters 7 and 9, concerning the development of mission statements in libraries, appeared previously in *The British Journal of Academic Librarianship* and the agreement of the publisher, Taylor-Graham, to their use in this volume is hereby acknowledged.

PB and KC
Preston
January 1995

PART I

INTRODUCTION TO QUALITY CONCEPTS

❖

1

WHY DOES QUALITY MATTER?

'Easy to recognise ... difficult to define': so starts the UK Library Association's answer to the question 'What is quality?' (Library Association: Colleges of Further and Higher Education Group, 1994). Who would argue? Quality is universally regarded as a good thing – indeed even that statement is almost tautological. We speak of a 'quality product' and mean that it performs its function well. We talk of 'quality services' and mean that they not only meet our expectations but even exceed them, providing not just the service we need but doing so attractively, employing friendly staff in a welcoming atmosphere. Everywhere we are exhorted to seek quality – yet rarely are we offered a clear definition of what is meant. At the same time we can all too easily recognize it by its absence, when products break or malfunction or those serving us are rude or indifferent. Therein lies an important clue. It is when we, as users, consumers or customers, find our needs and wants unmet, our expectations frustrated, that we complain of poor quality. When things go wrong, assuming it is not due to what the insurance companies call acts of God, we know that somewhere down the line quality has been neglected. As Pirsig (1974) put it in *Zen and the Art of Motorcycle Maintenance,* 'though Quality cannot be defined, you know what it is'.

When the *Challenger* space shuttle exploded on launch in 1986, killing all seven astronauts on board, it appeared at first that it was indeed one of those rare acts of God, a tragic combination of almost impossible coincidences in an incredibly complex system operating at the very leading edge of technology. Only later did it emerge that the fault in the solid fuel booster rockets which caused the accident had been known for at least a year, yet no effective procedure existed to stop the launch. When two trains collided head-on on a single-track line in southern England in 1994, it emerged that the correct preventative equipment had been identified following another crash five years earlier – but had not been installed. After Union Carbide's pesticide plant in Bhopal in India released a cloud of toxic gas across the city it emerged that the safety system consisted of three employees armed with hose-pipes while a similar plant in the United States was equipped with towers which automatically washed down any escaping gas. The technology to prevent the disaster was tried and tested, but it had not been installed.

What links each of these tragedies is that none of them was unavoidable. The solution which would have prevented each accident was known but for one reason or another was not implemented. Each represented a failure to take quality seriously, the adoption of a 'good enough' approach which was patently not good enough in the event. In each case lives were lost as a result.

Such spectacular failures are rare, and they hit the headlines because of their rarity. Failures in service industries tend not to be as spectacular (although the theft of millions of pounds worth of bearer bonds when an unaccompanied messenger was attacked in the City of London is an exception). The quality record of services such as libraries and information services is more often well hidden from view and of less impact. But the failures are real none the less. To recognize such failures is to begin to address the issue of quality, and this leads us back to definitions of the concept itself.

While we may all be able to give examples of what we mean by quality there are numerous ambiguities and confusions surrounding the idea. One of the key reference books on the subject, the *Gower Handbook of Quality Management*, remarks that the word quality must have been used more often in the last ten years than in the preceding ten centuries (Price, 1990). Libraries and information services are not immune from this problem. A great deal has been and is being written about 'quality library services' and 'quality information services' yet often there appears to be little to connect these accounts apart from a genuine desire to provide a good service and an equal inclination to use the latest buzz words. The danger, of course, is that the word will become so overused and abused as to lose all meaning. That would be a pity, not least because quality management is a valued and well used approach among what are generally acknowledged as the best run, most efficient and most successful industrial and commercial companies – and quality management is finding its way into public services too. Libraries and information services have much to gain from participation in the quality management movement.

THE QUALITY AGENDA

The concept of quality came on to the public agenda in Western countries in the 1970s with the realization that Japan in particular had found a way to improve vastly its economic standing within a few short decades. Japan, defeated in the Second World War and with its industrial base largely destroyed, was at first a synonym for poor-value products: toys which were quickly broken, cars which broke down and rusted, electrical goods that failed the moment the all-too-short warranty period was over. The remarkable improvements made by Japanese manufacturers can be seen by examining two products: motorcycles and television sets.

In 1965 the Japanese held about 2 per cent of the world motorcycle market while the UK share, which had at one time been much higher, had declined to about 12 per cent. Over the next ten years the Japanese increased their share to about 10 per cent, while the UK share dropped only marginally. The really spectacular change came between 1975 and 1980. By the end of that period the UK contribution had all but disappeared while the Japanese had captured 80 per cent of the total market. Household names like Norton and Triumph had disappeared into receivership while Hondas and Suzukis were seen everywhere. A similar pattern occurred in the manufacture of television sets. In 1965 the UK held over 15 per cent of the market while Japanese manufacturers accounted for less than 5 per cent. By 1980 the UK share had declined and comprised about 5 per cent of the market while Japan had around 40 per cent.

There were a number of reasons for these events and it would be simplistic to claim that a single cause could be found which would fully explain the whole episode. However, one of the key elements was quite clearly the ability of Japanese manufacturers to deliver products which were what their customers wanted: well designed, reliable, immediately available and at a reasonable cost.

A 1983 survey demonstrated these contrasts starkly (Garvin, 1983). The study looked at the performance of eleven US and seven Japanese companies over a two-year period. The results speak for themselves. The average rate of defects per unit on the production line was 63.5 per cent for US firms, 0.95 per cent for the Japanese. The average rate of defect after delivery, within the warranty period, was 10.5 per cent for the former, 0.6 per cent for the latter. Warranty costs for US firms varied between 1.8 per cent and 5.2 per cent of sales income; for the Japanese it was an average of 0.6 per cent. The lessons are obvious.

QUALITY DEFINED

The ideas behind quality management are essentially everyday concepts – applied common sense – and everyday actions help to illustrate the key ideas behind the word quality. When you get up in the morning, you choose to wear clothes which are suitable for what you expect to be doing during the day – casual, formal, new, old. In effect this is a 'quality assessment' exercise: in deciding which clothes are most suitable for what you will be doing you are recognizing that their suitability is related to your purposes. That, in essence, is what quality means. Before we can legitimately give the tag 'quality' to anything, we have first to have thought through what it is that the product or service is to be used for. You will already have given some kind of quality recognition to your clothes by buying them in the first place – unless it is the horrendously unsuitable socks Granny gave you for Christmas, in which case you will have made your judgement on their quality as soon as her back was turned. Your quality assessment will have various criteria, some related to fashion, some to whether or not they fit, some to comfort, some to whether they are hard wearing, and so on.

This brings in a second idea which is allied to the quality–purpose linkage: quality for one person is not necessarily quality for another. You may hate those socks: I may think they are wonderful. So we get a quality–purpose–customer relationship underlying our definition of the term. In reality, we all learn this idea early in life, of course, and we carry it through life with us: the concept of objects having purposes for which they are fitted and the corollary that there are also purposes for which they are not fitted (although some might think it unfortunate that the innocence which led to the observation that 'to a small boy with a hammer, everything looks like a nail' has to be lost). The concept of choice, the freedom we all have in democratic societies to decide what it is that suits our purposes, our predispositions, our concerns, our preferences, is another side of the same basic idea about the word quality: so it becomes, when used properly, a statement that the essential product–customer–purpose linkage has been established. Fundamentally, quality is concerned with meeting the wants and needs of customers.

It is through this kind of consideration that the early pioneers of quality management arrived at one of the key and enduring definitions of quality which is found throughout the literature and permeates quality management practice across the world: 'Quality is fitness for purpose'.

The British Standard 4778, 1987 (and its international equivalent, ISO 8402, 1986) offers the following definition:

> The totality of features and characteristics of a product or service that bear on its ability to satisfy stated or implied needs.

Feigenbaum (1983), a key writer on quality management whose work will be considered in the next chapter, offered this alternative:

> (Quality is) the total composite product and service characteristics of marketing, engineering, manufacture, and maintenance through which the product and service in use will meet the expectation of the customer.

To drive the point home to its managers, the Ford Motor Company used the following definition (quoted in Lascelles and Dale, 1993):

> Quality is defined by the customer. The customer wants products and services that throughout their life meet his or her needs and expectations at a cost that represents value.

Tann (1993) suggested, in a paper concerned with the application of the ISO 9000 quality assurance standard to libraries (the standard itself is described in Chapter 3), that fitness for purpose would include:

- knowing the customer's needs – stated and/or implied;
- designing a service to meet them on or off the premises;
- faultless delivery of service;
- suitable facilities – car park, café, library, crèche;
- good accommodation – seating, lighting, heating, toilets;
- good 'housekeeping';
- reliable equipment – computers, videos;
- efficient administration – welcome, queries answered efficiently and effectively;
- helpful, courteous staff;
- efficient back-up service;
- monitoring and evaluation including customer expectations, complaints, recommendations for improvement; and
- feedback loops to build-in improvement procedures and/or checking that improvements are put in place.

Leaving aside for the moment the question of whether 'customer' is always the correct terminology, and whether 'client', 'user' or any other term is more appropriate, the key issue is that quality becomes a meaningful concept only when it is indissolubly linked to the aim of total customer satisfaction. It does not matter whether the context is an industrial company involved in heavy engineering, a government department preparing legislation, a library lending books, an airline offering inter-continental travel, an insurance company selling policies (or peace of mind) or a personnel department offering advice internally within a local authority. All have to meet customer needs.

A frequent area of confusion arises from the difference between quality and grade, and it is linked to the common idea that we only get quality if we are prepared to pay for it. While it is perfectly true that customers are frequently willing to pay more for a product with additional features or a premium service with enhanced characteristics, this is a high-grade rather than a quality product. The quality product or service is one which meets the specified requirements of the customer in a consistent fashion. A recent review of ball-point pens revealed that if the customer simply wants a writing device which is reliable and does not clog too much, the humble Bic Biro retailing at less than 20 pence is a very high-quality product. But if the customer amends the specification to say that he also wants a pen that is aesthetically unusual and refillable, then the Bic is not the answer. However, an expensive, beautifully designed and aesthetically pleasing pen, bought to be both an artefact and an efficient writing instrument but which frequently clogs is high grade, but it is not displaying quality.

This is an extremely important distinction, because it demonstrates that quality can be achieved in any organizational setting and with any product or service. What is needed is a clear definition of what the product or service is intended to achieve, agreement with the customers that this will meet their needs and consistent delivery at the agreed price or cost. Sometimes, especially in the public service context, limitations may have to be placed on the service which is offered in that not every customer need can be met: public libraries cannot necessarily expect to be book suppliers, information providers, child-care agencies, schools, leisure centres, counselling services, video shops, restaurants and social services departments within the kind of resource base which they can normally command. The pursuit of quality very often means restricting the range of activity in order that what *is* done, is done well.

It is interesting that a considerable number of studies in the business sector have shown that there is no necessary relationship between price and quality. For example, Gerstner (1985) surveyed 145 different products but failed to uncover any such relationship. A number of other studies have demonstrated that quality, rather than cost, is the most significant factor in achieving success in the business environment. For example, in the European market, Van Nievelt (1989) demonstrated that there is a positive correlation between high customer perceived value and large market share.

We will consider the formal definition of quality and its implications further in the next chapter, but the key issues for the present discussion are these:

O   quality is achieved when customer needs are met;
O   quality is central to all organizations, not an optional extra;
O   quality is not dependent on high price or high levels of resourcing.

The relationship between quality and standards is also worth exploring. It is some-times assumed that if an external body sets, and then raises, standards, then quality will be improved. There is truth in this insofar as the standards reflect the customers' requirements. Thus, an obvious example would be the Consumers' Association, with its publication *Which?*, where the idea is to test products against what are perceived as criteria important to the consumer. A considerable amount has been achieved by this approach, especially where it has achieved a threshold level of acceptance among the public at large and hence been forced on the attention of the producers. The quality of cars has been raised partly because of this consumer-led approach. However, there are two dangers with this method. First, it assumes that standards do indeed reflect the needs of the customers, which is often very far from the case. Second, it assumes that the standards cannot be manipulated by the producers. An example of the problem would be the continu-ous rise in the proportion of first-class honours degrees awarded by UK universities over the last few decades. Does that mean that quality has been raised? Or is the level of attainment (the standard) needed to achieve a first-class honours degree being lowered? And in any case, does the standard actually relate to what the customers (students, employers, etc.) want? The argument can be alluring. The then Secretary of State for Education and Science, Kenneth Clarke, remarked:

> The statistics speak for themselves, with the proportion of graduates in PCFC (Polytechnic and Colleges Funding Council) sector institutions gaining first and upper seconds having risen alongside the surge in student numbers. There are plenty of examples from HMI (Her Majesty's Inspectorate) to show how increasing numbers need not adversely affect quality – quite the reverse (quoted in Harvey and Green, 1993).

The introduction by the UK Government of the *Citizen's Charter* in 1991 has produced an emphasis on standards as a way of guaranteeing quality. This will be considered in Chapter 13.

Quality has sometimes been associated with notions of acquiring something special or 'high class' and therefore in some sense exclusive: not everyone can afford it or has the right of access to it. In a more class conscious society than we now have (although the vestiges are very evident) this idea was very prevalent. Access to Oxford or Cambridge was somehow equated with 'quality', for example, based on tradition and limited access, rather than on outputs or outcomes of an Oxbridge education: thankfully that situation is now changing. Measurement of quality in this conception is virtually impossible, and quality improvement has nothing to do with improvement of internal processes or end products and services. There remains a sense in which 'quality' is used to mean 'superior'. A favourite marketing ploy is to implant the idea that a product is subtly different from its competitors in providing what is called higher or better quality, as no more than an appeal to snobbery or elitism. In Britain there even used to be an expression 'the quality' which referred to the upper classes in what was a notoriously class-conscious society. 'The quality' were one's betters in every possible way!

QUALITY CHAINS

In Chapter 4 we will consider the customer perspective in greater detail, but it is important at the outset to recognize that organizations have internal as well as external customers: the end-user of the service is at the end of a chain of interactions within the organization which involves staff providing products and services to each other. The processes which lead in a library, for example, from a book being requested through its purchase and processing to its finally being made available to a borrower involve a series of internal supplier/customer interactions.

The professional librarian may decide to order the book in the first instance on the basis of either an earlier request or an assessment of likely demand. He or she then becomes the customer of the acquisitions department which is to arrange for the item in question to be purchased. In turn the acquisitions department becomes the customer of an external supplier. When the book is delivered, the acquisitions department supplies it to the cataloguer – another customer/supplier relationship. Each department of the library will in turn be the customer and the supplier as the book travels down the chain until eventually the circulation department supplies it to the end user, the external customer.

In Chapter 4 we will consider the internal customer in greater detail but here we can note that the sequence of customer/supplier relationships is referred to as the 'quality chain'. This concept gives a significantly different outlook on quality because it brings home the reasons for everyone being involved in quality: the next person in each chain (and many staff will be involved in more than one chain) is the customer. In each relationship we can ask the fundamental quality management questions: is the supplier meeting the customer's requirements?; is the product or service supplied meeting the purpose for which it was intended? As with all chains, the strength of the whole is determined by the weakest link, which is why the quality management literature is as concerned with the internal processes of the organization as with the direct relationship with the external customer. In a library, if the acquisitions department buys the wrong book, the end-user is unlikely to be satisfied even if the circulation department offers the highest levels of service. In all quality organizations everyone relies on everyone else. Furthermore, the recognition and identification of the quality chain are among the first steps in managing quality, since they enable management to ask the key questions about the product or service being produced in every part and at every level of the organization. Every section, and every employee, can be asked, or can ask themselves:

○ Who are my customers?
○ What are their requirements?
○ How do I find out about their requirements – and how do I know when their requirements change?
○ How do I know whether or not I am meeting their requirements?
○ What prevents me meeting their requirements – and what can I do about it?

One of the temptations, of course, particularly if staff are poorly motivated, is to concentrate on the last question and turn out negative answers: 'I don't have the resources to meet their requirements and there's nothing I can do!' Yet experience shows that, even when there are severe constraints, quality management can produce remarkable results. Take the case of British Airways. In 1981 it made a loss of £137 million and was clearly in a bad way. One view said that there was not much it could do but try to survive and minimize losses. It had to cope with enormous constraints: its aircraft were the same as everyone else's, except for minor differences such as colour schemes; it had to use the same airport facilities as all the other airlines; it got caught up in air traffic control delays just as often as everyone else; it operated in a highly competitive business in which price-cutting was unlikely to be a serious long-term option; and government regulation, particularly governmental protection for each national 'flag carrier', made nonsense of normal competition. Sir Colin Marshall, then BA Deputy Chairman, told the story of how BA was turned into the world's most profitable and most popular airline:

> the successes we have had in recent years derive primarily from our staff and their attitudes to what needed to be done. Whether in the cabin, behind the check-in desk, on the baggage ramps, in the cargo shed, at the service desk or on the ubiquitous telephone, our people have seen quickly and effectively what implications are to be drawn from an ever-increasingly competitive world, and often they have made major changes in working style and attitudes which our customers have noted favourably. (Marshall, 1991)

Note that the involvement of *all* staff at *all* stages of the operation was needed to achieve this breakthrough: the quality chain had to be transformed from start to finish.

THE EVOLUTION OF QUALITY MANAGEMENT

In Chapter 2 we will consider how the concepts of quality management have developed by examining the work of the quality gurus: key figures who have been influential through the development and application of new understandings of quality. Before doing so, however, it is useful to examine the evolution of quality management and in particular the stages that organizations may pass through as they shift from a lack of awareness of quality to full implementation of total quality management.

LACK OF CONCERN FOR QUALITY

The starting point for many, though not all, organizations is a straightforward lack of concern with quality: the concept is either unrecognized or thought to be of little or no relevance to the business. Typically, such organizations provide a 'directed' product or service in which the customer is left to take it or leave it and there is little or no concern with whether customer needs are being met. The professions are perhaps the last bastion of this approach, and it is not unknown for libraries to operate in this mode. The professionals decide on the service to be delivered (or maybe the service that users can come and get), it is delivered, and that is that. No serious attempt is made to check whether the service was appropriate from the customer's viewpoint. It is not unknown for health services, for example, to process individuals as if they were on a production line and send them away without any real reassurance about their condition – is a hospital which tells a patient to go to his or her general practitioner in ten days' time for the results of tests really meeting its customers' needs? The shop assistant who is clearly annoyed at being interrupted by a customer is displaying the same attitude in different circumstances.

Moore (1992) characterized this approach as the 'ABC Approach to Consumer Service' (Another Bloody Customer):

> all too often we are made to feel that simply by being a customer we are trespassing upon someone's leisure time; or making their life unnecessarily complicated. In some cases, usually in shops selling computers or hi-fi equipment, we are made to feel that, as customers, we fail to come up to the intellectual level of the people serving us.

Libraries and information services are not immune from this approach. Professional skills can be misused to force users into a predetermined mould, and especially in education there is always a temptation to teach instead of promote learning, losing in the process the active involvement of the customer.

INSPECTION

Although most commonly encountered in the manufacturing sector, inspection as the most basic level of quality management can also be found in services. Inspection assumes that some sort of criteria have been laid down to determine whether or not a product is acceptable. It may be applied at various stages of the process. For example, a library may inspect new books arriving from suppliers to check that they are the titles actually ordered. Any which have been wrongly delivered are returned for replacement but no further action is taken to prevent recurrence of the problem in the next batch. Similarly, during processing there may be a check to ensure that a spine label with the correct classification number has been attached to the spine of each book – and in some libraries even the height of the spine label from the base of the spine may be checked. In industrial organizations it is not uncommon to find that specific staff have been appointed to undertake the inspection function and, while this would be uncommon in libraries and information services, it is often a specific, identified task for one or more members of staff.

Inspection is less practical in those parts of the organization where there is direct interaction with the customer, as in the case of many services, since the customer is involved directly in the process of delivery. Very often in these areas it is only when the customer complains that it becomes apparent that something has gone wrong.

QUALITY CONTROL

The next stage of quality management assumes that there is a real concern with the quality of the service or product and that procedures have been put in place to exercise control over the output. In a typical, again manufacturing, context, specific quality control procedures would be put in place at each stage of the process. For example, incoming components and raw materials would be subject to inspection, possibly using statistical procedures, intermediate products would be tested, data on conformance to specification would be logged, and there would be some feedback of information to those responsible for processes. In a service context, such as librarianship and information science, quality control would usually be based on:

○   the detection of errors in internal processes, such as checking of book purchase requests, incoming books and journals, and invoices;

○   control of non-conformance at the point of delivery, for example through customer complaints procedures that enable errors or failures to be caught and action taken to rectify them.

Lascelles and Dale (1993) observe that 'inspection and quality control are based on detection type activities … In the main, (they) are short on scientific analysis, planning and measurement'.

QUALITY ASSURANCE

The key difference between quality control and quality assurance is that the latter involves planning and designing quality into all the processes involved in delivering the service or product to the customer, coupled with the systematic use of quality data throughout the organization. In brief, there is a shift from the concept of inspecting quality failures *out* to designing quality *in*: prevention rather than cure. So in a quality assurance system, any failures will not only be corrected when they occur but will also result in the redesign of the system or procedure which enabled the failure to occur in the first instance. In general, quality assurance will also involve the use of specific quality management tools such as statistical process control, control charts and Ishikawa diagrams. These are described in Chapter 7.

TOTAL QUALITY MANAGEMENT

The final stage of quality management is known as TQM, or total quality management. TQM will be described in detail in Chapter 7, but briefly it can be differentiated from quality assurance in the following ways:

○   TQM requires total commitment by senior management, and by all staff, over the long term.

○   TQM involves complete dedication to meeting customers' requirements.

○   TQM is based on teamwork and partnerships and seeks to break down inter-departmental or sectional barriers and replace confrontation with co-operation and partnership.

○   TQM explicitly recognizes that there are internal and external customers and that proper recognition of all customers' requirements is needed if external customers are to receive quality products or services.

○   TQM will involve a long-term commitment to training and development for all staff.

Above all, TQM is based on the idea that in every part of the organization quality must become a way of life, the natural way to do things. Everyone will seek continuously to improve all the products and services – internal or external – which they produce. The aim will move from meeting specifications to 100 per cent customer satisfaction and on to customer delight (see below). Furthermore, the TQM organization will 'benchmark' itself against the best of its competitors. Such benchmarking, which we describe in Chapter 7, not only looks to numerical or financial comparisons, but also seeks to identify the best way to do things, the cultural variances between organizations and the small differences in customer relationships that mark the line between success and failure.

DELIGHTING THE CUSTOMER

Many organizations are attempting to go beyond meeting customer needs and satisfying customer expectations to providing that little bit extra that can result in *delighted* customers through service that goes beyond what they expected. Of course, it is difficult to define exactly how this can be achieved, and there are grave dangers that some approaches can be counter-productive – the heartily disliked 'Have a nice day!' syndrome being a typical example, where staff are trained to treat every customer as little more than a unit of production. However, there is equally great value in trying to find ways in which service providers can quite genuinely go beyond the basic meeting of needs. Very often, 'delight' can be engendered by relatively small touches, but always it relates to a customer focus and to a dedication that is almost an obsession with quality. The shop or bank – or it could be library – which allows its staff time to acknowledge customers' individual needs, or to greet them with a smile, may offer a point of human contact which is unexpected, unrelated to the service itself and welcome in an age of the impersonal. Exceeding expectations, however it is achieved, is the way to customer delight.

THE IMPERATIVE OF CHANGE

Federal Express, the international parcel and package delivery service, won the prestigious Malcolm Baldridge National Quality Award in 1990. (We consider the major quality awards in detail in Chapter 6 since they offer a systematic audit of the requirements to be met if a company is to gain international recognition for its quality management.) Fred Smith, Chairman of Federal Express, referred to the award as 'a licence to practise' (Sandelands, 1994, p. 38), but he also referred to it as a starting point for yet further quality improvement, for otherwise all the benefits of the company's drive for total quality management would be lost. Every one of the company's 340 senior staff is required to undertake nine days quality training *each year*. Edith Kelly, the President of Internal Audit and Quality Assurance for the company is on record as saying, 'We know that, to stay on top of our industry, we must keep pushing for improvement and step up our quality leadership efforts'. The aim is to give 100 per cent customer satisfaction, measured by achievement against 12 separate indicators which were identified by asking customers what caused them to be dissatisfied: late deliveries, late pick-ups, damaged packages, errors in invoices and so on. The aggregate score is the Service Quality Indicator and the aim is to achieve a score of zero, representing no customer dissatisfaction, but then to go on to maintain that score by adjusting the service offered to meet the changing requirements of the customers. So, not only must the quality company treat quality as an ongoing imperative, it must also recognize that customers' ever-changing demands mean that yesterday's quality is not necessarily today's. Keeping customer satisfaction as an overarching aim implies that it is necessary to keep checking that requirements are being met, and changing processes and systems to keep in step with, or ahead of, user demand.

The Japanese approach to change is summarized in the word *kaizen*, which may be translated as 'continuous improvement' (Imai, 1986). Some observers would rate Imai among the leading gurus for his work on this concept and on the means of achieving ongoing gradual quality improvement through empowering and enabling all employees to be participants in the process. *Kaizen* is a concept based on the perception that not only must there be an emphasis on the continuous improvement of existing products and services, but that as the world changes, and as people change, so those products and services must develop if customer requirements are to continue to be met. Handy (1994) refers to this as 'second curve thinking' which means that to remain successful we have to find new products, new services, new ways of doing things, new things to do, before the still-successful old equivalents start to decline. It is while we are successful that *kaizen* should be applied.

QUALITY AND SERVICES

Much of the literature of quality management is based on experience drawn from industrial organizations and particularly from the manufacture of tangible products which are, at a later stage, delivered to the end-user. In recent years there has been a welcome broadening of quality management into services and it is noteworthy that several service companies have been award winners in the national quality awards. With this broadening of applications has come a recognition that some aspects of quality management need to be approached somewhat differently in services. Obviously, such new understanding is particularly relevant to libraries and information services.

A key observation is that in services there is usually a direct interaction between the customer and the service. Restaurants, consultants, hospitals, banks, libraries and buses have in common the immediacy of contact between the provider and the customer. The difference between this model and that of a product-based organization can be over-stressed since even heavy industries incorporate some service functions and there is still a customer interface even if it is somewhat distant from the organization. However, a service organization, because of the immediacy of the interface, finds itself dynamically redefining the product. The fact that the customer requirement can be modified as part of the service delivery process is both a challenge and an opportunity.

Management of services, because of both the immediacy and the dynamic nature of the customer interface, is very much concentrated on the management of this interface. In fact this merely emphasizes the importance of quality management to services, since quality management is itself focused on the customer and hence on the interface between the customer and the organization.

Services have some unique characteristics which need to be considered, and which arise because of the way that the customer interaction takes place. Each of these characteristics can influence the application of quality management.

CO-PRODUCERS

Customers are participants in the service, because they can alter the product being delivered and the way in which it is delivered in response to the situation as it develops. This can work both ways: a customer may reduce demand because of some unforeseen factor, for example when the transaction takes longer than expected and the customer cuts it short by giving up. On the other hand, the transaction may be extended, as when customers discover an additional feature of the service which was previously unknown to them. In supermarkets, this is the reason for having confectionery and magazines displayed near check-outs. This self-service aspect is becoming more pronounced in libraries: nearly all now operate on a self-service basis as far as book selection is concerned and facilities such as self-service issue systems are becoming quite common. The parallel with banking is an apt one. Just as a wide range of bank services which used to be available by queuing at a counter in the bank are now available 24 hours a day from automatic teller machines, so library services are shifting towards self-service concepts. Information technology thus enables services to move from customer–employee relationships to customer–service direct interaction. It is helpful when analysing these customer–service interactions to think of the customer as being in part an (unpaid) employee. People deliver services to themselves. This has enormous implications for improving quality provided that the sense of participation and ability to influence design and delivery that would be taken for granted by other employees is nurtured.

The complexity of the customer relationship in services is reflected in the varying terminology which is used. There are good reasons for being wary of the term 'customer' in services, and particularly in libraries and information services, since it can carry with it too passive a connotation. So we may prefer 'user', 'client', 'reader', 'citizen', 'visitor', 'member'. Other services have their favoured terminology: 'patient', 'subject', 'guest', 'beneficiary', 'subscriber' and so on. Each term carries with it a recognition that the relationship is not passive and that the customer (we continue to use that term for convenience) is involved in the service and its delivery. Although some of the debate as to whether libraries have users, readers, members or customers is sterile, there are important considerations and assumptions underlying each alternative. Interestingly, a survey at the University of Central Lancashire Library in 1992 revealed that the customers themselves preferred to be known as 'users' (Brophy, 1993b).

Recognition of the involvement of customers in service industries has led to the coining of the term 'co-producers' to describe the participation of the customer in the service delivery. This idea is now widespread in the quality management literature, and helps to overcome some of the difficulties of applying concepts which were previously manufacturing industry based. For example, there is an interesting debate in education at the present time about how quality can best be defined when the consumer is not just receiving a service but is intimately involved in the process itself. Harvey and Green (1993) point out that 'unlike many other services where the producer is doing something *for* the consumer, in the education of students the provider is doing something *to* the consumer … Education is not a service *for* a customer but an ongoing process of transformation *of* the participant'. They suggest that quality needs to be considered in terms of 'enhancing the participant' and 'empowering the participant': the former measured in terms of the value added (an example would be a student with poor pre-entry qualifications and skills who achieves a first-class honours degree), the second by linking participant feedback to policy making, by guaranteeing minimum standards of provision, by enabling participants to select the actual service/product mix they receive and by enhancing their skills, especially their ability to choose critically. In the higher education context, this second approach might work by explicit links between student satisfaction and university decision making, by a meaningful commitment to minimum standards, by permitting a wide choice of courses or introducing a 'learning contract', and by ensuring that while students are at university their critical abilities are developed as they 'learn for life'.

SERVICE VOLATILITY

Services, as such, cannot be stored. This may seem an odd assertion to make about libraries and information services, which have always relied heavily on the storage of texts and now increasingly on the storage of data in electronic forms. However, it is the customer interaction with those stores which provides the key service issue: a library with no users is, unless it is pursuing an historical archive mission, of little value. The point about service volatility is that unused capacity cannot be re-used. For a library, a day spent by a book sitting untouched yet available for loan on the library's shelves is a day wasted, and a day that cannot be recovered. The book may be borrowed the following day, and every other day for years to come, but that particular occurrence is unrecoverable. The parallels in other services are more familiar: a hotel room which is empty overnight is a lost service opportunity, as is a spare seat on a bus, train or aeroplane. Hotels base assessment of their performance on occupancy rates and often adjust their pricing structures accordingly. So, occupancy rates are a key measure of value when a hotel or chain comes on the market. It is interesting to examine libraries and information services from the same perspective. A library with a loanable stock of 100,000 items would get maximum usage if every one of those items was out on loan simultaneously and each time an item came back another user arrived to take it out again. In-house and reference use makes the real equation more complex, of course, but the concept is an interesting one because it illustrates the mismatch between demand and capacity in most libraries. Furthermore, since most libraries have an excess of demand over capacity for some services (i.e. some books), it illustrates that there is a serious mismatch between the service being offered and that being demanded. This leads to the next point.

NON-SUBSTITUTABILITY

Some services are able to offer substitution of one 'product' for another. A restaurant may offer an alternative menu which is perfectly acceptable to customers if their first choice is unavailable, although some compensation may be needed to retain satisfaction. Some services can offer partial substitutability: most people do not object to being offered a different seat on an aircraft from their first choice, but do object to being offered a seat on another flight leaving at another time and certainly will not accept a seat on a flight to another destination. Libraries and information services usually display partial substitutability. Some customers want one precise product: a student requires a particular book taken from a reading list and will not accept any other title. A public library user wants the latest best-seller and will not accept a 'similar' title. There is limited substitutability, of course, in that it is rare for users to demand a particular copy of a title, so stocking multiple copies offers one way to increase service capability. Many readers will also accept another title, especially if they are seeking information on a topic rather than looking for a known title. But even this is limited. The user checking the boiling-point of ethanol is not very impressed to be told that for methanol.

OWNERSHIP AND COMPETITION

Manufacturers of products have an array of legal protection to enable them to produce something which is unique, patent and copyright law being obvious examples. Services find it much more difficult to differentiate themselves from their competitors as far as the basic 'product' is concerned. There is a question of monopoly provision, of course, especially for libraries. Few libraries have direct competitors: academic libraries enjoy a monopoly of library provision within their parent organizations; public libraries are not challenged by private-sector 'public libraries' (yet); special libraries tend to be sole suppliers in their industrial or commercial organization. However, there is very considerable indirect competition. Public libraries compete with bookshops and video stores even if studies show that the public uses all of them. All libraries face competition from the emerging global information providers which offer information delivery direct to the user.

It is instructive to consider how service organizations in other fields react to these issues. Banks, for example, do not have a monopoly over the supply of cash. They therefore take steps to differentiate their service on other grounds, by giving added value. This may be through increased convenience – the 24-hour ATM for example or telephone banking – although none seems yet to have taken a leaf out of the pizza industry's book and developed a home delivery cash service. The environment inside a bank branch is important and forms part of the image that is being portrayed and hence differentiates the bank from its competitors. Bank services may or may not be price sensitive, so banks have to take a view on their charges and interest rates in comparison with their competitors. Finally, banks have to keep one eye on their competitors from other fields, as for example when the building societies start to move beyond their traditional mortgage businesses and into the banks' territory.

MULTIPLE INTERACTIONS

Although it is not always true, typically customers interact with services time and time again. Once a customer has signed up with a bank, he or she will use its services on a regular basis. Each individual interaction will affect the customer's perception of the service. Jan Carlzon, the then president of SAS, the Scandinavian Airlines Systems, put it this way:

> Last year, each of our 10 million customers came into contact with approximately five SAS employees, and this contact lasted an average of 15 seconds each time. Thus SAS is 'created' 50 million times a year, 15 seconds at a time. These 50 million 'moments of truth' are the moments that ultimately determine whether SAS will succeed or fail as a company. (Carlzon, 1987)

The same principle can be applied to libraries and information services. Every time a student enters a university library and goes to the shelves it is a moment of truth. When he or she takes a book to the service counter there is another moment of truth. When the photocopying service is used there is yet another moment of truth. Even leaving the library through an electronic security system can become a moment of truth to the nervous or guilty. The University of Central Lancashire Library is typical of the service offered in a medium-sized UK university: about 650,000 customer entrances are recorded each year. The typical visit generates two or three interactions with different services, so there are upwards of 2 million moments of truth in the library each year. The cumulative effect of all those interactions will spell out both customer satisfaction and customer expectations.

PROCESSES AS PRODUCTS

In manufacturing, it is customary for the production process to be considered separately from the delivery of the product to the customer. The process of producing personal stereos, cars or breakfast cereal is not self-contained in that in the best companies it will be reappraised continuously and re-engineered to ensure that the product is in line with customer requirements, is reliable, consistently produced and so on. Nevertheless, there is a definite demarcation between that process and the customer interaction whereby the product is delivered. In most industries the organization which actually makes the products will not be the same as the one which sells and delivers them: Sony does not sell through Sony-owned personal stereo shops; Ford does not run most Ford dealerships; Kellogg's does not operate breakfast cereal shops.

For services the picture is rather different. Although they will usually have a supporting infrastructure which acquires the basic product, as for example the library which has an acquisitions department, in essence the service product *is* the process. So, when the quality management literature focuses, as it does, on the need to get the process itself right, it is necessary for services to draw together both the process and the product delivery to see them as a whole. This reinforces the notion that, for services, managing the process is part of managing the customer interface.

NON PROFIT-MAKING SERVICES

Many libraries and information services are not profit-making concerns, and there are clearly issues which loom larger in such organizations than in those who see making profits for shareholders as a primary *raison d'être*. It is easy to overstress these differences, however, and to turn them into excuses for inaction. As we have seen already, quality is not inextricably linked to resource levels, and the cost of quality is as real in services, including non profit-making services, as in any other organization. Peter Drucker, the management writer, is on record as remarking that in certain respects non profit-making organizations are 'on the cutting edge … (for example) … the business of tomorrow will have to learn from the nonprofits how one manages people' (Ernstthal, 1989). In addition, the need for those in non profit-making organizations to think about their purposes and how to measure their results is more pressing than for others. In later chapters we will be looking at how some of these issues can be resolved.

CONCLUSION

Although there are many different ways of defining quality, it has been generally recognized in the literature of quality management that those definitions which emphasize a link between the customer, the customer's purpose and the product or service being received are the most helpful. Quality management then becomes a way of delivering products and services which, over time, are closer and closer to the customer's needs. While services, and non profit-making services in particular, cannot adopt techniques from industry uncritically, they are not as different as is sometimes supposed. Total quality management, as an overarching discipline, can help services as much as other organizations to face the challenge of change and to grow in relevance to their customers, thus securing their own future.

2

THE QUALITY GURUS

The quality management movement can be traced back many years, and emerged formally as a part of the management of mass-production techniques in manufacturing industry. It soon became clear that if a product was to be mass produced successfully then there had to be control over the correctness of the end product. If the product was supposed to be 2-inch bolts with a no. 6 thread which were later to be used with nuts of the same specification produced on a parallel production line, it was not much use if no. 8 thread bolts were produced, nor was it acceptable if only 50 per cent were correct. So inspection and testing were introduced, and in the aftermath of the First World War a number of professional associations were established. An example was the Technical Inspection Association (later the Institution of Engineering Inspection), founded in Britain in 1919. A key publication from this time, which built quality concepts on the then fashionable management theories of Frederick Taylor, was W. A. Shewhart's *Economic Control of Quality Of Manufactured Products* (1931). Shewhart was based at Bell Laboratories in the USA and his work took basic statistical techniques and turned them into a rigorous and exact discipline for monitoring the quality of products.

Such techniques, it was quickly realized, could only work if the specification of the product was sufficiently exact. You cannot determine whether something has been produced within acceptable tolerances unless what is acceptable has first been defined. From such considerations a definition of quality emerged:

> Quality is conformance to requirements.

As we will see, this definition is not incompatible with the ISO definition, introduced in Chapter 1, that 'quality is fitness for purpose', provided that in both cases it is the customer who is being addressed: it is the customer's requirements that are paramount, and the customer's purposes for which the product or service must be fit.

The real impetus to quality management, and the force which enabled it to escape from a preoccupation with inspection and testing on industrial production lines, came with the work of a number of key figures, generally known as the 'quality gurus', in the years after the Second World War. Curiously, the first of these individuals, and perhaps the most important, carried out his key work not in the victorious countries of the Western alliance but in defeated and impoverished Japan. Japanese products were generally regarded in the US and Britain as something of a joke: if a child's toy said 'Made in Japan' on it you could guarantee it would break within a week, even supposing it survived being removed from its packaging. In the US buyers avoided Japanese cars because, famously, they were not powerful enough to get up the hills of San Francisco. How things were to change! One catalyst for that change was an American called W. Edwards Deming, and it his work that we will describe first.

DEMING

Deming's early work was very much based on that of Shewhart but developed this approach much further and introduced the idea of Statistical Process Control (SPC). Deming argued that the real problem lay in variability, that is, that the typical manufactured product was not being manufactured consistently within the specification. He identified two types of variability. *Special variability* is caused by a particular operative or machine. For example, if a machine starts to malfunction then the products it turns out may be subject to special variability. Or, again, if a badly trained (or just incompetent) worker is allowed on the production line, the products they produce may be subject to a similar kind of variability. On the other hand, *common variability* applies to the whole operation. For example, the specification used in the manufacturing process may be incorrect and this will obviously affect all the products which are made. Common variability is the direct responsibility of management.

Deming introduced the use of statistical process control charts (also called SPC charts or control charts) to enable variability to be measured and its causes identified. They involve the taking of regular measurements at various stages of the manufacturing process and then the interpretation of the results to enable the causes of variability to be identified and corrected. These techniques continue in widespread use throughout the world. SPC in itself is described in Chapter 7.

Deming went much further than statistical techniques, however, and developed what is known as the PDCA cycle: Plan, Do, Check, Act (see Figure 2.1). The PDCA cycle is still widely used but at the time it was introduced it placed a novel emphasis on *management's* responsibility for quality. In order to produce a quality product it was necessary for management to take a systematic approach to planning, to put in place appropriate manufacturing methods and processes, to ensure that the products and hence the processes were properly checked and, as and when problems were identified, to take action to put things right, leading back into the planning process itself. Note that all four elements need to be included in the cycle: problems arise when management chooses to neglect one of the elements – for example it is surprising how often problems are identified yet no one does anything about them.

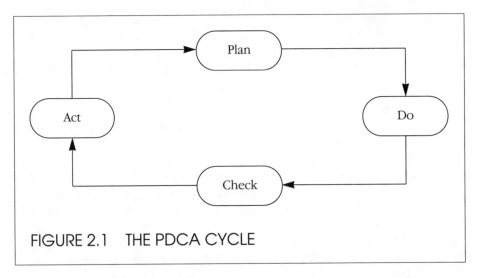

FIGURE 2.1   THE PDCA CYCLE

Deming's ideas were systematically adopted by Japanese companies and are credited with much of the improvement which proved revolutionary in Japan's development as an industrial nation. Suddenly, Western competitors found that Japanese products were better designed, better produced and more reliable than their own. They started to ask the question, why?

Deming turned his attention to American companies in the 1960s and 1970s but met with far less success. He identified one of the reasons as resistance to his ideas from both management and workers and an attitude which saw processes, and particularly technology, as the issue rather than human factors. After a long period Deming identified what he believed to be the 'seven deadly diseases' which were stifling American competitiveness and quality.

1.   Lack of purpose and lack of constancy of purpose.
2.   Overemphasis on short-term profit.
3.   A lack of effective ways to review and reward individuals' performance.
4.   Lack of long-term commitment to the company by management.
5.   Over-reliance on quantitative data by management and unwillingness to consider hidden and intangible factors.
6.   Excessive medical costs.
7.   Excessive warranty costs.

While these issues related especially to American industry (in particular the last two) it is instructive to consider them in relation to both US and European service sectors, including libraries and information services. We could ask ourselves : Are such services clear about their purposes? Are they characterized by constancy of purpose? Do they balance the long and short term? Are key individuals appropriately rewarded? Do staff give long-term commitment? Do they adequately consider non-quantifiable data in their decision making? Clearly some of the issues are more apposite to LIS than others, yet even to pose the questions gives an indication of the kinds of issues that library and information science professionals should be addressing as they begin to implement quality management.

Arising from his work and his identification of the seven deadly diseases, Deming put forward 14 key points which he believed needed to be addressed if US industry was to reassert its worldwide competitiveness:

1. Constancy of purpose, directed towards improvement of products and services with the aim of maintaining competitiveness, staying in business and creating employment.
2. Acceptance of the new post-war economic order with a need to become and remain competitive in the world economy and recover a leadership role emphasizing change as a future, as well as present, requirement.
3. Stop depending on inspection in the pursuit of quality: build quality into the product or service from the outset.
4. Stop awarding business on the basis of price alone: instead look at the total cost and seek to minimize that. Develop long-term relationships with a limited number of suppliers based on loyalty and trust.
5. Constantly improve the system of production and service, so improving quality and reducing costs.
6. Introduce on-the-job training.
7. Replace supervision by leadership: help and enable people and equipment to do a better job. Include within this concern the leadership/supervision of managers.
8. Drive out fear, so that everyone works effectively in a secure environment for the good of the company.
9. Break down interdepartmental barriers within the organization so that everyone works as a team and tries to foresee and forestall problems which may occur at any stage, even far down the production process.
10. Stop using slogans, targets and exhortations directed at the workforce. The real problems lie with the system and are beyond the power of the workforce to correct. Slogans and targets create adversarial relationships which harm overall productivity.
11. Substitute leadership for work quotas on the shopfloor. Eliminate management by objectives and by numerical goals: leadership replaces all these.
12. Remove barriers that prevent people, from the shopfloor to senior management, taking a pride in their workmanship.
13. Introduce a vigorous programme of education and training, with the emphasis on self-improvement.
14. Get everyone in the company involved in the process of transformation towards the quality company.

It is notable that Deming saw much of the responsibility for quality improvement resting with managers. Quality failures were not the result of recalcitrant workers and inefficient staff, but had to be addressed through leadership and purposeful change. A number of books by Deming are available (for example Deming, 1986) while a useful overview of his work has been provided by Walton (1991).

JURAN

Joseph Juran also worked in Japan and achieved distinction through his work there. Juran was less concerned with the detailed techniques of quality control and much more centred on the idea of management responsibility. He emphasized that quality issues need to be addressed through management action in the same way as strategic issues, financial issues or any other concerns. He suggested the use of a cyclical process of quality management (see Figure 2.2), linking quality planning, quality control and quality improvement in what he termed the 'quality trilogy'.

Juran saw a key issue within this triumvirate of quality management actions as the issue of training, beginning with the managers themselves. If managers could be persuaded to take quality planning, quality control and quality improvement seriously then middle management, supervisors and operational staff would also begin to think in the same way. Juran developed these ideas to show how each of the three elements could be realized by taking key actions. So, quality planning requires the manager to:

O   identify customers and their needs;
O   set quality goals;
O   develop quality plans to enable those goals to be achieved;
O   create ways to measure quality;
O   allocate or acquire the resources needed to implement the plans;
O   ensure the actions needed to implement the plans are taken.

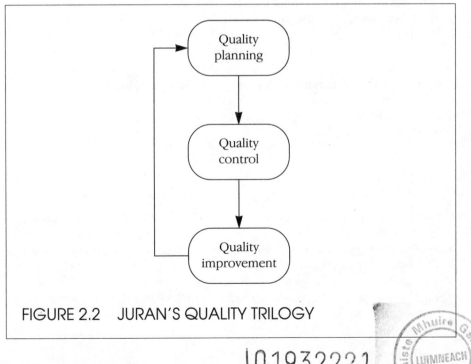

FIGURE 2.2   JURAN'S QUALITY TRILOGY

Quality control requires:

○   the development of meaningful quality measures;
○   evaluation of actions taken;
○   comparison of actual performance with quality goals;
○   action to correct any failure to achieve goals.

Quality improvement implies:

○   reducing wastage;
○   improving employee satisfaction;
○   improving profitability;
○   ensuring greater customer satisfaction.

Juran did not assume that the quality planning/quality control/quality improvement process would just happen of its own accord, but looked in detail at how managers could bring about change. He emphasized the need for training in particular and also tried to move away from the use of 'management-speak', with its empty slogans and buzz-words, to focus attention on the real issues, suggesting that instead of 90 per cent exhortation plus 10 per cent substance the reverse should be the case. In particular, Juran recognized both internal and external customers as having needs, an issue of immense importance in librarianship and information science as in other service-based organizations. He produced a 'Quality planning road map', the first step of which was to identify who the customers are.

All too often it is assumed that quality management is concerned only with the external customers – the end-users, as we now call them. But it is clear that unless we have equal concern for our internal customers the service as a whole will suffer. If the acquisitions staff have no concern for the library's subject specialists, or the IT specialists for the circulation desk staff, then we have a recipe for chaos and the library will rapidly sink into that well-known trait of poor services, where staff from one section blame each other for everything that goes wrong, and the commonest complaint among staff is 'no one ever tells me anything'. Juran's ideas and experience have been brought together in a number of his books and he remains a highly influential figure in quality management (see, for example, Juran, 1989, 1992; Juran and Gryna, 1993).

CROSBY

A third major American thinker in the field, Philip J. Crosby, offers a somewhat different approach from that of Deming and Juran, and moves towards a more holistic view of quality management. He too emphasizes management respon-sibility, but balances the contribution of both management and workers to the resolving of quality issues. Although Crosby's presentations (in person and through highly successful videos, including a BBC production) are not to every-one's taste, he can provide a highly motivational approach and his ideas are of lasting importance.

Crosby offers five 'absolutes' of quality management:

1.   Quality is conformance to requirements.
2.   There is no such thing as a quality problem.
3.   It is always less expensive to get it 'right first time'.
4.   The cost of quality is the only relevant performance measure.
5.   Zero defects is the only relevant performance standard.

These ideas need some elaboration. The first has been covered already but the second, the idea that 'there is no such thing as a quality problem', may seem a little surprising when first encountered. Crosby means that so-called quality problems are always created by bad management, and can be rectified by management. They do not exist by themselves. Attend to the management issue and the so-called 'quality problem' will be resolved.

Crosby talks and writes a great deal about the final two absolutes, which form the basis of what is probably his best-known book, *Quality is Free* (Crosby, 1979). By this phrase Crosby meant that if quality is improved, then the total costs of the operation will fall to such an extent that the savings will more than pay for the cost of introducing quality management. The need to pursue zero defects is also emphasized again and again in Crosby's work. In one of his video presentations he tells the story of an address he gave to US automobile manufacturers, in which he declared that their aim should be to produce vehicles with no defects (the 'zero defects' principle). He pointed out to them the cost in warranty claims, time, reputation and so on. They came back with the view that, while they accepted the theory of what he was saying, the best they could hope to achieve was three defects per vehicle. Crosby suggested that they should form an industry committee to decide which three defects should be incorporated. To his horror, they took him seriously and started to debate who should be on the committee.

It is informative to consider this anecdote alongside a recent advertising campaign in the UK for Lexus cars which was based squarely on '100 per cent customer satisfaction' and the promise to deliver it, based on a reputation for doing exactly that. The twin themes behind 100 per cent customer satisfaction were technological excellence, producing for example an almost silent car, and above all reliability. Yet again, the Japanese manufacturers have illustrated that the goal of zero defects is the only goal worth pursuing, and that when achieved, or even approached, it provides a marketing edge over their competitors.

As we will note later, zero defects is far from the performance standard achieved by most libraries and information services. Rather than accepting this as inevitable it is helpful to try to examine the systematic ways in which this defect problem can be managed. Crosby's standard offers a goal which, while it may rarely, if ever, be achieved, provides a key benchmark for producers and services to aim at. Another useful insight is to view zero defects alongside a process of negotiating agreement with customers on the requirements to be met, then ensuring that those requirements, and not others, are the ones that are met. As an example, McDonald's has in effect agreed with its customers to deliver beef-burgers etc. without defect, when requested. But this does not extend to meals which are not on its admittedly limited menu – it makes no attempt to satisfy a customer requirement for Beef Wellington.

The idea of the 'cost of quality' runs through much of Crosby's work, and he uses this concept to demonstrate that failure to introduce quality management is to ignore the true costs of an organization, and that quality failure, or non-zero defect situations, add very significantly to organizations' operating costs. It has been calculated that defects cost UK industry between £10,000 million and £20,000 million per annum (Price, 1990). While service industries' defects may be less easy to measure than those in manufacturing, there can be little doubt that they are just as significant. A Department of Trade and Industry publication (Mortiboys and Oakland, 1991) states that 'it costs the average service organisation up to 40% of budget (in) failing to satisfy customers' needs and expectations, or failing to do so right first time'. In just the same way, public sector service defects may be well hidden, but they are nevertheless real.

FEIGENBAUM

Armand V. Feigenbaum emphasized that quality management could only be pursued successfully if it was recognized that responsibility for quality extended to every individual in the organization and to every aspect of its operations. He is generally recognized as the founding father of total quality management (described in Chapter 7). Although his background in manufacturing - he was responsible for quality control at the US General Electric Company – led him to use manufacturing concepts in his early writings, his ideas are equally applicable to services. He emphasized that quality in manufacturing was not enough if it was accompanied by inadequate design, inefficient distribution, poor marketing and inadequate on-site support. He further developed the concept of the cost of quality and showed how total quality management could reduce overall costs by very significant amounts.

In many ways Feigenbaum's approach suggests that quality management is really just management writ large: it involves everyone in the organization and every process. Every member of staff needs to have a clear understanding of the organization's objectives and goals and how their role fits into that overall picture. Everyone needs to have a customer-oriented approach to their work and to be committed to meeting the customers' requirements, so that quality management becomes part of the organizational culture, a habit that is taken for granted as the approach that everyone will take.

The cost of quality is not an abstract issue for Feigenbaum but at the very centre of quality management. His key writings on the subject (e.g. Feigenbaum, 1983) show how quality costs can be divided into three categories, appraisal, prevention and failure, each of which must be reduced to the minimum. So, for example, appraisal costs must be recognized, measured and reduced by introducing procedures and mechanisms which diminish the need for appraisal to the bare minimum and, equally, are as efficient as possible.

OTHER INFLUENCES

A number of other figures are also starting to feature prominently, especially in recent years, as views from outside the US become more significant. While Deming did much of his work in Japan, and without challenging the significance of that work, the American cultural influences on many of the gurus are often very obvious. There are, however, features of other experts' work which should not be ignored. The most recent thinking seeks to broaden out beyond the organization itself to consider organizational culture within national and international cultures and to encompass the views and interests of the whole range of an organization's stakeholders, from the end-user of a product or service to the interests of society as a whole.

We will consider these approaches later but a number of other gurus are worthy of consideration in this introductory chapter. Genuchi Taguchi, a Japanese expert, suggested that it was possible to go beyond the idea of 'conformance to require-ments' and look at quality in terms of the loss which a customer experiences by taking a product or service. Taguchi suggests that we could define quality as 'the loss that is imparted from the time a product is shipped'. For an industrial organization these losses would start with customer dissatisfaction and include warranty and repair costs, loss of reputation and ultimately loss of potential or actual market share. Taguchi sees losses as related to any deviation from the absolute product standard, rather than deviation from the customer specification. Rather than tight conformance to specification, which defines acceptable limits, Taguchi suggests that the key issue is to minimize variation from the specific target value, because the loss increases as a quadratic function, i.e. as the square of the variation from the target value. While this definition is of particular application to industrial products it also has relevance to services, because it suggests that concentration on service delivery which varies from the provider's agreed set standard could provide a useful way to address quality issues. For example, looking for the causes of longer-than-standard delivery times for inter-library loans and whether they can be identified and corrected may be more important than trying to improve the overall delivery time, because users generally are more concerned with knowing that they can rely on delivery within a stated period than in compressing that period as much as possible.

Another important figure, Pat Townsend, rose to fame through his work with the Paul Revere Insurance Company in the United States. He distinguished between quality in perception and quality in fact. The former consists of producing the right thing or service and can be equated with effectiveness: the product is what the customer wants. Quality in fact is related to efficiency and consists of producing services or products correctly, according to the specification. (A similar distinction has been made in librarianship by Richard Orr and is discussed in Chapter 11.) Townsend also brought out the importance of expectation and showed how failures can occur because of a mismatch between expectations and outcomes. This is a very important issue for all services, including libraries and information services, and we will consider it in more detail in later chapters. Townsend's work is described in a key book, co-authored with J. E. Gebhardt, called *Commit to Quality* (Townsend and Gebhardt, 1986).

Finally, in this section it is worth considering the work of a highly influential management writer, Tom Peters, although he is not usually described as one of the quality gurus. Peters co-authored with Robert Waterman the best-seller *In Search of Excellence*. Published in 1982 it had, and continues to have, a remarkable impact on the practice of management. This is not the place for an extended treatment of the management literature, nor even of Peters's work, but it is useful to note the similarities between his approach and that of the quality gurus. *In Search of Excellence* was based on a detailed analysis of large American companies which were identified as 'excellent': companies which had achieved innovation over protracted periods and had a history of solid growth and profitability. It identified eight characteristics or principles which were common to the companies investigated (Peters and Waterman, 1982):

1. 'A bias for action': avoid lengthy discussion and debate, endless memoranda and committee meetings; instead, *do* something. Sometimes it almost seemed as if the motto was 'do anything as long as you don't sit around talking about it'.
2. Remain close to your customers. Find out what the customer wants and likes and concentrate on providing that.
3. Create smaller units. Encourage the formation of smaller groups or companies and give them autonomy to pursue their own inventiveness.
4. Productivity comes through people. Everyone in the organization needs to be aware that the company's success depends on them. This works the other way too: everyone should be aware that they too can share in the company's success.
5. 'Hands on, value driven.' Senior executives must stay close to the company's essential business and not operate in a divorced environment where they become out of touch with what is going on on the 'shopfloor', or with the feelings and reactions of the company's customers.
6. 'Stick to the knitting.' Companies should concentrate on their core business, doing what they are good at, rather than diversifying into a range of activities which bear little relationship to the core. Identifying what business you are in and sticking to it are key issues.
7. Keep staff structures simple and lean. Do away with complex hierarchies in favour of flatter structures with few layers. Keep the number of executives to a minimum.
8. Simultaneously promote looseness and tightness. There needs to be tolerance for staff yet dedication to the core values of the company.

A later volume, *A Passion for Excellence* (Peters and Austin, 1985) extended the analysis beyond the large, American corporate sector to look at smaller firms, including some from outside the US and some public sector services. The lessons were similar, although the eight principles were simplified. In later writings, such as the 1992 *Liberation Management*, Peters has moved towards more radical views on organizational change and organizational structures, although these are beyond the scope of the present volume (Peters, 1992). A useful summary of these ideas and their possible implications for libraries and information services has been provided in a recent paper by Barter (1994).

SUMMARY

Deming, Juran, Crosby and Feigenbaum are recognized as the most influential of the quality gurus, but it would be a mistake to think of them as each offering his own unique view of quality management. Rather they present variations on a theme, different perspectives on what is essentially the same message. The emphases can be summarized as:

O   Deming: statistical process control and the PDCA cycle, together with organization-wide involvement.
O   Juran: leadership and management responsibility.
O   Crosby: the five absolutes and company-wide participation.
O   Feigenbaum: organization-wide quality and TQM.

The major quality gurus come from a Japanese or North American cultural background, and there are dangers in accepting their views too readily. Indeed, there has been something of a reaction against them in recent years because of the difficulty of disentangling cultural influences from universal principles. We have already noted that for a number of reasons Deming found his ideas less acceptable in his native United States than in Japan, where they were developed and implemented with great success. These are important issues to consider, and the following principles should be applied:

1.   No one quality guru or quality system has all the answers. The quality system needs to be designed afresh for each organization, using the insights, principles and techniques which have proved effective elsewhere blended into an approach that is appropriate to the new circumstances.
2.   Just as change is taking place in all organizations and their business environment, so the quality system itself will need to change and develop over time. No quality system can be implemented and then simply left in place for all time.
3.   There are no quick fixes. There are plenty of 'How to' books on quality on the market which purport to offer the definitive methodology for introducing quality management. *Caveat emptor!*
4.   The Japanese do not have all the answers! There is much of great value to be learned from what they have done, but cultural differences are very important. The 'factory tour' approach, which assumes that what works in one culture and environment can be picked up and transplanted elsewhere, is false.

So, in summary, the quality gurus show that there are a limited number of key principles which, taken together, provide a useful starting-point for the introduction of quality management. These can be summarized as:

1.   The need for top management commitment and support.
2.   The need for long-term commitment.
3.   A fundamental reorientation towards meeting customer needs.
4.   Careful planning and the introduction of appropriate processes and procedures, including the use of quality management tools.
5.   Training and education.
6.   The involvement of everyone in the organization.
7.   Recognition of the cost of failures, the cost of quality.

These concepts will reappear as we consider quality from other angles and particularly in the later discussion of total quality management in Chapter 7.

3

THE INTERNATIONAL QUALITY ASSURANCE STANDARD ISO 9000

The International Organization for Standardization (ISO) ISO 9000 series is a series of standards concerned with quality assurance: their predecessor is better known in the UK as British Standard BS 5750. ISO 9001, 9002 and 9003 set out the essential requirements of quality management systems for varying types of organizations according to the types of product or service that they produce. A quality management system aims to provide a means of quality assurance, not a form of quality control (the differences were discussed in Chapter 1). A common misconception is that ISO is a quality control system as it refers to 'process control', 'inspection' and 'testing'. This view misses the fundamental point of the standard, which is to provide a model for managing the organization, be it a factory manufacturing widgets or an academic library, in such a way that quality is built in from the planning stage to delivery to the customer. The goal of the system is to demonstrate the organization's commitment to quality and to meeting the expectations and needs of both internal and external customers.

The use of standards in quality management can be traced back to long before the terms were coined. One of the earliest examples is to be found in the building of the pyramids of Ancient Egypt, where the development of the cubit provided a means of ensuring that materials met the precise requirements of the builders. Quality assurance principles are also to be found in the operation of the medieval craft guilds. The guilds regulated the standards of workmanship of its membership, enabling customers to have confidence that purchased goods would be of a standard quality and at a fixed price. Through the apprenticeship system, the level of training was controlled and any apprentice who could not work to the required standard was liable to have his apprenticeship terminated. Likewise guild members who produced shoddy goods or deviated from the prices set by the guild could be disciplined or even expelled.

The importance of supplies to the finished product was championed by Samuel Pepys of *Pepys Diary* fame. During the time that he was Secretary to King Charles II's Navy he exposed the corrupt system whereby inferior supplies were purchased at vastly inflated prices and introduced in its place a system of purchasing to defined and documented standards.

During and following the Industrial Revolution the management of quality shifted its emphasis to inspection and control. The use of unskilled workers and mass production relied on final inspection for maintaining the quality of manufactured goods. Production for a mass market meant that quantity rather than quality was the norm in many assembly lines, with increased productivity rather than increased customer satisfaction being the primary measure of company success. There was in this time little attempt to work to agreed standards, with sometimes absurd results. For example, in 1900 the lack of agreement in the rolling steel industry meant that there were no fewer than 75 varieties of tram rail with differing specifications available. Discussions between the industry and their customers eventually reduced this number to just five.

The need for standardization and the importance of being able to rely on the quality of input, production and finished goods was crucial to military production during the Second World War. In Britain and the USA standards of supplies, production and product were set by the military. This practice continued in the years following the war. The USA produced a standard MIL-Q-9859 to improve practices associated with military products. This evolved into a series of Allied Quality Assurance Publications (AQAPs) which were intended for use by North American and other NATO countries. The importance of quality of products for the emerging space technology programme was realized by NASA, which issued a series of documents laying down quality standards for the use of its contractors.

In 1969 the British Ministry of Defence modified the AQAPs to produce its own series of Defence Standards, the DEF 05-20 series, for use in the United Kingdom. Standardization began to spread beyond military production into areas where safety or high investment were primary concerns, with the Central Electricity Generating Board (CEGB) documenting quality assurance standards for nuclear power plants. By the 1970s other large industries were beginning to follow suit. An increasing number began to set up their own quality assurance programmes, documenting internal practice and imposing their own standards on suppliers. The result was a proliferation of different systems all with largely the same objectives. Suppliers of materials and components found the imposition of multiple standards burdensome as they became subject to several assessments by a variety of standards according to each manufacturer's criteria. Quality assurance, building in standards and controlling the quality of inputs, rather than quality control and reliance of inspecting out of faults, rose to the fore. Reflecting this, the British Standards Institution published its first standard relating to quality management, *BS 4891: A Guide to Quality Assurance*.

Becoming aware of the developing interest in quality systems and standards, the British Government set up the Warner Committee to investigate whether it would be practicable to develop a universally applicable standard, along the lines of the Defence Standards. The result of the 1977 Warner Report was the first BS 5750, which appeared in 1979. It was a new approach for much of industry, with a focus on prevention, on getting things right the first time rather than retrospective inspection to screen out faults. Its impact was limited at first, although by 1987 some 2,000 companies were accredited. However, the general consensus was that it was not broad enough in scope for general use and needed significant overhaul to be more acceptable to organizations. There was also international interest in the establishment of quality standards, with a number of countries producing their own standards.

By the 1980s the International Standards Organization was seeking to produce a common standard for quality assurance, working with individual countries and the European Committee for Standardization. The result was the publication in 1987 of ISO 9000, which was based on the initial issue of BS 5750. This series of documents was identical to the European Standard EN 2900: 1987 and was issued in Britain as BS5750: 1987, with the variation that the British Standard used a slightly different title, describing the standard as a 'specification' rather than the international versions which used the term 'model'. The standards were adopted worldwide, although they were not widely taken up in the USA which continued to use its own quality assurance standards, despite the early work of the United States in pioneering the use of internationally acceptable standards.

Quality management is not a static field; but rather it is dynamic, continuing to evolve in response to changes. By the mid 1990s ISO 9000 was used by a whole range of organizations but was open to criticism, misunderstanding and misinterpretation which suggested that it was time for the scope and wording of the standard to be reviewed. Service industries have found the standard particularly difficult to interpret, despite the publication of Part 8 of the British Standard which was intended as a guide for services. It is also a requirement of the ISO that all international standards be reviewed at five-yearly intervals and a revision of ISO 9000 was due in 1992. This coincided with the preparation of the British Standards Institution's strategy for quality standards in the 1990s, which was published in 1993 as *Vision 2000*. This document looked at the development of trends in the field of quality management and attempted to take a longer-term outlook.

The result was a recommendation for a two-stage revision of the standard to correct inconsistencies and errors in use, improve the wording of many of the clauses so that it could be more easily applied, especially in service industries, and take account of the move towards the principles of TQM. The first step was taken in July 1994 with the issue of BS EN ISO 9000: 1994, with input from industry, quality organizations, small businesses and government This standard covers relatively minor revisions although the terminology is somewhat clearer and the need for customer satisfaction, previously not specifically mentioned, is emphasized. The second revision is due in 1998 and is expected to be more extensive and concentrate on the TQM aspects.

THE PROVISIONS OF ISO 9000

The detailed requirements of the ISO 9000 series are described in the published standards themselves and in many published texts. For the library and information service field there is an excellent short guide by Debbie Ellis and Bob Norton of the UK

Institute of Management (Ellis and Norton, 1993) which covers, *inter alia*, the interpretation of the often rather difficult terminology used in the standards. Rather than repeat their work here, we describe the requirements of the standards in summary form below and refer readers to that work for further details.

As we have already noted, the essence of ISO 9000 is a statement of what the organization is doing to achieve quality, documented procedures which show how those actions are carried out consistently and how action is taken to amend the procedures when something goes wrong, and evidence of record keeping to enable compliance to the standard to be demonstrated. There will usually be three sets of documentation:

1.   a quality manual, containing the organization's quality policy and objectives, together with statements of who is responsible for what within the quality system, including organization charts, and a description of the quality system itself. This is usually quite a short document, but crucially it demonstrates in writing management's commitment to the quality system. It also indicates the scope of the application: it is perfectly possible to seek certification to the standard for only one or more parts of the organization's activities.

2.   a procedure manual, containing descriptions of all the procedures used by the organization. Very often the procedures are described by means of flow charts, showing how work progresses through the organization.

3.   Work Instructions, which are very detailed *aides mémoire* used by staff in carrying out specific tasks, for example how to log in to a specific database.

It is essential that there is a proper system for control of all this documentation, to prevent what would otherwise be the all-too-common situation of people working from different versions of procedures and work instructions. For this reason, a specified number of copies of the manuals is maintained, with an individual responsible for updating each. Superseded copies of procedures have to be returned for destruction.

Organizations implementing ISO 9000 will normally designate a member of staff as the quality manager or quality co-ordinator – the latter title has the advantage that it does not imply that one person is alone responsible for quality! This would, in most libraries and information services, be a part-time role undertaken alongside other duties. Other members of staff would be involved as 'internal auditors'. Their role is to go through a procedure with the member(s) of staff responsible for using it and check that the way in which they actually work is in accordance with what is written in the procedure itself. Wherever possible, the procedure will have been written by those staff and checked by a manager. Equally, the operational staff should be encouraged to change the procedure whenever they find a better way of doing things. In this way, rather than being a straitjacket, ISO 9000 becomes a tool to enable all staff to develop their working methods to meet customer requirements, but in a controlled and consistent fashion.

The quality system as a whole is subject to external assessment by one of the certification bodies which have been set up for this purpose. Some work only in a particular industry (e.g. Electricity Association Quality Assurance Ltd, Ceramic Industry Certification Scheme Ltd) while others can certify compliance in any industry (e.g. BSI Quality Assurance, SGS Yarsley Quality Assured Firms Ltd). The second type would be approached for certification in the library and information service field. Once approved, the organization receives a certificate and has the right to use the ISO 9000 symbol on its stationery, etc. Subsequent to a successful approval visit there are regular external audits and any problems identified have to be addressed and corrected if certification is to be retained.

THE APPLICATION OF ISO 9000

There are very many organizations, from virtually every field, which have successfully introduced ISO 9000 and the 'accredited firm' symbol has become a familiar sight in the UK and elsewhere. Although a large proportion of these applications are from the industrial sector, there is a growing body of evidence that the standard can be successfully, and beneficially, applied to a wide range of services. Barnard (1994) discussed the experience of implementing ISO 9000 at Macmillan Distribution Ltd, part of the Macmillan publishing group, and remarked, 'it is a paradox that one of the greatest anxieties about quality systems is the expected cost of implementing them, while in practice one of the major benefits is cost reduction'. He suggested, based on this practical experience, that the introduction of the quality system produced benefits in at least ten areas:

1.   Bringing managers and staff closer together in pursuit of a common goal.
2.   Less frustration caused by misunderstanding of how systems operate.
3.   Identification of deficiencies in systems and their resolution.
4.   Development of new contacts with customers as staff work to ensure compliance with systems defined in the quality system at every stage.
5.   Public relations benefits from 'showing we want to do better'.
6.   Improvements in liaison between departments in the company.
7.   Staff have increased pride in the company's performance.
8.   Pursuit of quality has strengthened awareness of the company's own style.
9.   A strategy has been developed to which everyone in the company can subscribe, and which forms the basis for further development.
10.   Cost savings and productivity gains.

The application of ISO 9000 to libraries and information services is covered in Chapter 8.

CONCLUSION

Despite the manufacturing and military origins of the standard, there is ample evidence that ISO 9000 can be applied to service industries, including the library and information services sector. A system such as ISO 9000 can be one of the main elements of a sustained and comprehensive approach to quality management and provides a systematic way to meet organizational objectives. The standard sets out a number of requirements for an organization's management system and documented procedures to show how objectives are to be achieved. The purpose of a documented system is to show how something is done, by whom and when, and it also provides evidence that practice is being followed and agreed service standards are being achieved. Internal audits and external assessment provide independent confirmation that the system is working as intended. However, the constant monitoring is not the same as end-of-line inspection, but a method of controlling what is happening and preventing problems before they happen. The results of audits and the corrective action needed as a result of errors must be brought to a management review of the system. The requirement for regular reviews provides a quality loop which enables the system to provide a way of improving service (Figure 3.1).

It is important to realize that ISO 9000 is not by itself a 'quick-fix' solution to improving quality but a tool which can be used for quality management. It has been heavily criticized as being expensive, bureaucratic and no guarantee of the quality of the resulting service or product. It must be admitted that the amount of documentation required needs handling carefully if one is not to disappear under the sheer volume of paper which could be generated. Record keeping is one of the main elements of the standard and should be viewed as being more than the keeping of statistical accounts. It is rather a very public demonstration of the effectiveness of the quality management procedures. Documented procedures provide a very good way of opening up the organization not only to outside customers, but also internally, breaking down barriers between departments. Most organizations which are serious about quality, having implemented ISO 9000, will want to move on to use other quality management tools in the search for total quality. As they do so, they will want to revisit the fundamentals of quality itself, including their understanding of customers and their requirements. It is therefore to the customer that we turn next.

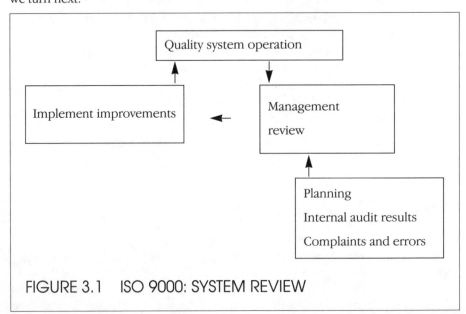

FIGURE 3.1   ISO 9000: SYSTEM REVIEW

4

THE CUSTOMER PERSPECTIVE

As we noted in Chapter 1, libraries have traditionally spoken of 'readers' or 'users' rather than customers, deliberately trying to capture a rather different kind of relationship from that typical of the industrial or commercial concern. Use of libraries has been seen as a co-operative enterprise with very definite obligations and responsibilities being placed on those who avail themselves of the 'privilege'. Traditionally, too, libraries have tended to restrict membership rather than market it, and often detailed definitions of who may or may not join the library feature prominently in the library regulations. However, while resistance to use of the term 'customer' continues in many quarters of the profession, there has in recent years been a shift towards a view of the library user much more akin to that of the private-sector customer. Part of the reason for this shift lies in the perception that services must be designed and delivered, not from a purely 'professional' or expert view, but to meet user needs, which are increasingly focused on concepts of access to information rather than storage of texts. There has thus been a shift in libraries and information services towards a view that would be familiar in many other environments. The centrality of the customer in the concerns of quality management has already been stressed. In this chapter some of the reasons behind this stress will be examined and their application to services in particular explored.

Customers cannot be assumed to be a heterogeneous group, of course, and for this reason it is usual for organizations to try to segment customers with common characteristics into groups so as to target goods and services to meet their particular and different needs. Segmentation is of course a well-known marketing tool. Indeed, the relationship between marketing and quality management is quite close in a number of respects, and this is one example. Organizations have realized that meeting customer requirements, whether it is done from a marketing or from a quality management perspective, is aided by the ability to target specific products or services to specific groups, or even to individuals. It is noteworthy, for example, that some Japanese car manufacturers have started to offer individually specified cars to customers. At the showroom the customer selects from a wide range of options, and that information is then fed back to the factory and the assembly line and the car produced to the individual's requirements. Apparently, this approach is unlikely to be introduced into the UK quickly since British motorists are used to immediate delivery of their cars and do not like to wait a few weeks for an individually specified model.

Nevertheless, while it may be impossible to address every person's needs individually in every sector, it is dangerous to assume that a single solution can be offered which will meet the needs of every customer (the 'any colour you like as long as it's black' approach). So, while it is useful for the academic library to describe its users *en masse* as 'students and academic staff' or for a public library to define the residential qualification needed for membership, it is only when we start to identify the different customers as individuals or groups that the quality of a product or service can be assessed. It is all too easy to assume that students form an amorphous group, for example, without focusing on the different needs that they have: part-time and full-time; straight from sixth form or mature; young or old; disabled; studying science or technology or art or business or literature; the permutations are numerous. Each group has its own needs and brings its own preconceptions to the use of a library or information service.

One other general point needs to be made concerning the customer base. While it is obvious that not every potential customer becomes an actual user, it is useful to try to identify and address the market as a whole, the larger group of potential *and* actual customers, when designing products and services. This is not the place for an extensive treatment of marketing, but it is notable that libraries have long been aware that their services are used by only a proportion of those who are eligible to make use of them. For example, some university students seem able to pursue their studies and achieve excellent results in their examinations without setting foot in a library. Equally, a significant proportion of the resident population of most areas does not use the public library system. There may be good reasons for this, but relatively little is known of why non-use occurs. Public services which operate under very considerable pressure from existing customers would not always see this issue as a priority, but a quality management perspective would suggest that unless a view is taken of the total potential market there is a danger that the service could be failing to achieve its overall objectives and mission. One way to approach these questions is through an analysis of stakeholder perspectives, which is described in the next section. Without this insight, some groups with disproportionate influence, or a history of use of the service, could dominate service receipt and hence attract an unfair share of the available resources.

STAKEHOLDERS

While those who use or are potential users of a library are the most obvious candidates for the term 'customer', considerable attention has focused in other sectors on the wide variety of groups and individuals who have an interest in the organization from other perspectives: the stakeholders. Stakeholders represent interests from the most individual to the global. Thus the British Standards definition of TQM remarks in a footnote: 'The objectives of an organization ... should always be compatible with the requirements of society' and 'an organization operates within the community and may directly serve it; this may require a broad conception of the term customer'. So, to take the academic library as an example, stakeholders might include:

O   students;
O   academic staff;
O   university support staff;
O   library managers;
O   library support staff;
O   university managers;
O   the government;
O   society: internationally, nationally, regionally and locally;
O   international research communities;
O   posterity.

Quality management approaches have not always recognized the importance of the stakeholder perspective, partly because it is assumed that a successful ('quality') company will generate high profits which will be enough in themselves to satisfy the major stakeholders, the shareholders and other investors. It may be that the reluctance of some public-sector bodies to accept quality management is in part due to a recognition, conscious or not, that the customer definition needs to be broadened. It is useful, therefore, to consider in each case whether the term 'customer' should be taken to include the various stakeholders. Indeed, Cameron suggested that one of the most critical activities of organizations is the establishment and maintenance of a coalition of external and internal individuals and groups – also called constituencies – which are supportive of the success of the organization (Cameron (1978, 1981)). Childers and Van House (1989b) have brought this work into the field of librarianship.

It is important to recognize that it is the organization's survival, including its ability to continue to supply goods and services perceived to be of value, which ultimately interests members of the coalition. It is wrong, however, to assume that all constituencies share the same interests. What is more, these different interests will almost certainly lead the stakeholders to have different views of quality itself. To take higher education as an example, quality, to the student, may be focused on the process of education – the lectures and lecturers, the support services, and so on – while employers might focus much more on the outputs of institutions and the skills which they bring with them into the world of work. Burrows and Harvey (1992) and Harvey and Green (1993) discuss this issue at some length. So balancing the needs of different stakeholders is much more than simply finding a way of reconciling different perspectives. Rather, it impinges on the very basis on which quality management is built: meeting customer requirements and producing goods and services which are fit for their purposes.

IDENTIFYING CUSTOMERS

Mention has already been made of the importance of considering both internal and external customers if quality services are to be delivered to the end-user. Internal customers are also stakeholders. Some effort must be made therefore both to identify and categorize the wide range of customers who are involved in any organization before their requirements are assessed. A useful way to do this is to consider the outputs that each member of staff produces and then to identify who they are passed to, or who has an interest in them. The process of producing an output should add value to a product. In some areas this is obvious: a new book is passed to a library assistant who adds value by labelling it and then passes it to the shelves where a user can consult it. Some outputs, especially in libraries, may generate only long-term interest, which is why one of the stakeholders of major libraries is posterity. It is also possible that some outputs may be found to have no customers, as would be the case were a library to add to stock books which are not of interest to any current reader nor of any likely interest to future users. More generally, as well as identifying all the customers of the organization, this is a valuable way to identify activities which have outlived their usefulness.

Services generally find it easier to identify their external customers than product-based industries because of the direct interaction which takes place when the service is delivered. One area which may make external customer identification less easy for libraries and information services in the future is the development of electronic delivery of services. For example, already many British university libraries' catalogues are accessible over the Internet, yet it is impossible to know who is using them and for what purpose.

It can also be helpful, in identifying internal customers, to work backwards through the organization identifying who produces the inputs that each later customer requires. For example, in a restaurant, the external customer requires the services of a receptionist, possibly a cloakroom attendant, a waiter, a wine waiter, an interior designer, and so on. For the waiter to serve the external customer he in turn needs to become the customer of the chef, who in his or her turn is the customer of a supplier of fresh produce. One of the advantages of this approach is that it helps clarify where management intervention is needed, as opposed to where it is actually input. As with other customers, it is necessary for there to be an explicit or implicit agreement on the requirements which are to be met in the internal customer–supplier, or quality, chain.

Although more will be said of this later, one of the characteristics of good customer–supplier relationships is the opportunity afforded for feedback. As we have seen, an older model of organizations saw producers or suppliers deciding for the customer what he or she needed, delivering it and showing a lack of interest in the customer's reaction. For example, someone goes into hospital, a doctor decides what kind of operation they need, they have the prescribed treatment and when the doctor has decided they are sufficiently recovered they are sent home. The patient may not have been consulted about the experience in any meaningful way or asked whether it could have been improved, although the fact that repeat custom is neither party's aim could have something to do with it! In libraries, it is not so long since the professional judgement of the librarian on what users ought to read was the prime factor in selecting acquisitions. Thankfully those days have gone, but it is still not uncommon to find feedback failure between internal customers, and to find failure to allow feedback from the end-user or final customer to influence the early steps in a process. Again, quality management is of help, partly because it reminds us that quality can only be defined by the customer since it is the customer's purposes we are trying to meet, but also because formal quality management systems build customer feedback into each stage of the chain.

Very often, especially when using services rather than buying products, customers are unsure of how their needs can best be met or even whether they should be a customer at all. They may perceive a need for information, for example, but be unable to formulate it precisely, have little idea of where the information is to be found and lack the ability to evaluate different sources. This would be recognized in other sectors as a classic opportunity for strong supplier–customer relationships to be built up, affording openings for added-value service. For example, in a commercial setting the customer might be encouraged to identify his or her lack of skills and to purchase training packages to enable those skills to be developed. In academic institutions, new students are usually offered some kind of information skills tuition, whether through a simple introduction to the library or more intensive, and sometimes credit-rated, courses. As a result not only is the library able to 'sell' another 'product', but also the customer becomes a more effective and hopefully more satisfied and longer-term user.

CUSTOMER SATISFACTION: INTRODUCTION

More will be said later about how customer satisfaction can be measured in Chapter 7, but for the moment we need simply note that for all quality management systems customer satisfaction is the central concern. It is not, however, the simple concept that it may at first appear.

EXPECTATION

Every potential customer will have some image of a service even before it is offered or encountered. Non-users of public libraries are generally aware that such services exist, even if they have never crossed the threshold of a particular library, and they may have used similar services elsewhere. Their image may be accurate or inaccurate, just as it may be positive or negative. If one day they decide to use the local library service, that image will form part of the baggage that they bring with them and will help to determine their expectations of what the service will have to offer them.

The potential customer may also hear about the service through advertisements, casual conversations or in many other ways. Each of these influences will affect the image that is held. When the service is approached, its immediate impact – such as whether it is forbidding or welcoming, clean or dirty, open or closed – will enable them to redefine the image still more. Regular users of the service may have a more realistic set of expectations than newcomers – or their expectations may be a reflection of what the service provider has been willing to offer in the past. However that may be, it remains true that one of the most powerful influences on customer expectations is previous experience of using a service.

In libraries and information services, customer expectations may be difficult to assess, partly because there is little direct interaction of more than a routine nature between library staff and customers. It is important therefore that steps are planned and taken to try to improve the library staff's level of understanding. It is all too easy to make assumptions based on professional judgement which turn out to be inaccurate. There is plenty of evidence from other sectors that managers frequently misunderstand customer expectations (see, for example, Zeithaml *et al.*, 1990).

Expectations are not static, of course, otherwise the advertising industry would have found it much harder to make a living. Just as many unplanned events can affect expectations so, too, service providers can take actions to promote a more positive image and so improve the expectations that customers and potential customers have of the service.

There is a variety of techniques which can be used to gauge customer expectations. Analysis of customer suggestions provides a simple device, especially if they are in a free format rather than replies to specific questions, as does a record of questions asked at enquiry and reception desks. Benchmarking (see Chapter 7) may help, enabling customer expectations of similar services to be examined. The involvement of customers in focus groups or user panels, again provided there is sufficient freedom and support for customers to express their real concerns, is another powerful tool. Finally, specific studies can be undertaken, for example by interviewing in depth a random sample of potential and actual customers.

PERCEPTION

Perceptions and expectations are closely linked, but while the latter are formed before the service is delivered, the former are created during that delivery process. They are not, of course, scientific evaluations of particular situations but rather impressions formed from personal experience. For example, the user forced to wait in a queue of 40 people for a book to be issued may perceive that it takes an unacceptably long time for an individual user to be served, regardless of the fact that the queue is moving quickly and it takes only a very few minutes for someone joining the end of the queue to reach the issue point.

Initial impressions are extremely important in setting customer perceptions, as we all know. A customer who pays to see a film will form a perception of the cinema from the moment he or she buys a ticket, tries to find the right screen, sits down and finds the seat comfortable or uncomfortable, and so on – and those perceptions will affect enjoyment of the film and, even more, whether the customer will pay a repeat visit. Drive your car into a garage for a service or repair, and if you are faced with an untidy jumble of spare parts, rusted exhausts and worn-out tyres then doubts will start to seep into your mind about the competence of the staff and the quality of work they will do. Enter a library and notice the untidily piled trolleys full of unshelved books and immediately doubts about the service on offer are formed.

One of the problems for services like libraries and information services, where multiple interactions take place (a point considered in Chapter 1), is that it takes only a single unfortunate incident for the customer's perception of the whole service to plummet. Provide an excellent online catalogue, a helpful enquiry desk, an efficient signing system, immediate issue of books and a free carrier-bag, but allow the customer to overhear a manager (clearly one not versed in quality management) tear a strip off a junior member of staff in public, and the whole perception can suddenly become entirely negative.

There are various ways in which services can try to improve customer perception. One is by striving for a service-wide image of consistency and efficiency: a house style for notices and leaflets, a dress code to identify staff and project a positive message, customer involvement through membership schemes (such as the frequent flyer programmes beloved of airlines) and so on. But such schemes can backfire if not handled with great care. The hotel receptionist who asks every arriving guest 'How can I help you?' in exactly the same tone and with exactly the same expression merely gives the impression that customers are being processed on a production line, and that perception sticks throughout the stay. British Airways identified the importance of spontaneity during its customer surveys some time ago and now seeks to be refreshingly different each time a customer uses the service. On a recent shuttle flight full of regular customers the captain welcomed passengers aboard, expressed the hope that everyone was comfortable and added 'If this is anyone's first flight, then please sit back and relax. It is my first flight too' (there was a long pause before he resumed) 'today'. The laughter throughout the cabin not only relaxed any tension but also gave an impression of spontaneity and humour which said to each passenger: 'Their airline treats us as human beings, not as seat fodder'. Of course, such spontaneity always carries a risk, but without risk taking no organization can survive or prosper.

Customers are quick to spot hypocrisy and are not as easily fooled as some companies like to think. Genuine efforts to involve them and treat them as valued parts of the enterprise will be rewarded by improved perception of the organizations and the products and services it provides.

DEMAND

There is considerable evidence that libraries operate in a situation where satisfaction and demand are closely linked, and a measure of satisfaction which fails to recognize this could be deeply flawed. Good service generates greater use, sometimes from what seems to be a limitless pool of latent demand. The converse can also be observed!

Even a library which offered a very poor service would probably retain some customers. They may be persistent, or easily satisfied, or use only very limited parts of the service (such as the warmth of the library on a cold day!) or as noted above they may have very low expectations of the service on offer. As a result, if asked the simple question 'Are you satisfied with the service you have received?' they might well answer positively and the library might gain a high rating on a simple scale of satisfaction levels. Conversely, the rating may even go down if the service is improved. More customers might be attracted, and they might be more critical, want even higher levels of service and be more knowledgeable about the range of services that was possible. So a 'better' service could, on this simple measure of satisfaction, be judged 'worse'. In fact there is some evidence (Buckland, 1975) that for academic libraries satisfaction level is adaptive and will tend towards a fixed point or at least fluctuate within a small range. It could be that good services attract more demand, become overstretched and cause satisfaction to drop back to below the previous level, thereby reducing demand so that the average remaining customer gets a better service, and so on.

Explicit demand for library and information services is thus also very different from need. Some needs remain unstated, for whatever reason, and the service manager may be unaware of them. It is important, therefore, that the manager tries to go beyond expressed demand to uncover the underlying needs which can then be the subject of refined or new services. If this is not done there is a danger that a poor service could be perpetuated – until its funding is withdrawn.

WRONGLY SATISFIED?

Libraries can be peculiarly susceptible to being misled by simple measures of customer satisfaction. An example is in reference work. If the enquirer receives an answer to a question he or she may be recorded as a 'satisfied customer', and the percentage of 'satisfied enquiries' recorded as a measure of the library's quality. Unfortunately there is ample evidence that an alarmingly high proportion of enquirers leave with a wrong or incomplete answer. For example, Head and Marcella (1993), in a study of reference services in Scottish public libraries, found that 'almost all (reference searches) were incomplete in one way or another, indicating either a lack of awareness of the full range of sources or an inability to relate those resources to the query which had been posed'. An earlier report by Williams (1987), in addition to reviewing studies which had included unobtrusive testing of reference services, found that 'telephone callers received the correct answer in less than two out of three cases (64%)'. Not knowing the answer to be wrong, they continue on their way as satisfied customers. The library can hardly claim to be achieving a quality service, however.

THE SATISFACTION GOAL

If there is one lesson that runs through all the work of the quality management gurus it is that 100 per cent customer satisfaction is the only goal worth having. It is also worth remembering that the goal of total customer satisfaction applies as much to internal as to external customers. While everyone recognizes that it is almost inevitable that occasionally a customer may not be entirely satisfied, striving for 99 per cent satisfaction is akin to aiming for 1 per cent dissatisfaction. Put in those terms, the 100 per cent customer satisfaction goal – the exact equivalent of Crosby's zero defects – makes sense.

CUSTOMER SATISFACTION: THE BASIC ATTRIBUTES

A number of writers have defined the key attributes of quality services in an attempt to understand what it is that leads not merely to customer satisfaction but to customer delight: the process of providing products and services which not only meet but exceed the customer's expectations. In this section we describe briefly some of these approaches.

GARVIN'S EIGHT DIMENSIONS OF QUALITY

Garvin (1987, 1988) identified eight attributes or dimensions which characterize a quality product or service for the customer. These are:

1.   **Performance.** These are the primary operating attributes of the product or service. For a car, for example, they would include acceleration, top speed, miles per gallon, size, comfort. For a library they would include availability of books from stock, access to databases, access to subject experts, somewhere to sit and work, and so on.

2.   **Features.** These are the secondary operating attributes, which add to a product or service in the customer's eyes but are not essential to it. For a car they might include a free sun-roof or alloy wheels; for a library they might range from free use of a stapler through to provision of a lift for the able-bodied as well as the disabled. It is not always easy to distinguish performance characteristics from features, especially as what is essential to one customer may be an optional extra to another. Nevertheless, there is a valid distinction to be made.

3.   **Reliability.** Customers place high value on being able to rely on a product or service. For products this usually means that they perform as expected (or better). For example a key issue for a car buyer is the probability of avoiding breakdowns or even minor malfunctions, so reliability is often at the top of the list of issues when car league tables are compiled. For libraries, a major issue is usually availability of advertised services. For example, is a working photocopier available or are the 'Out of order' notices in use again?

4.   **Conformance.** This was one of the key contributions of Taguchi (see Chapter 2). The question is whether the product or service meets the agreed standard. This may be a national or international standard or locally determined service standards. The standards themselves, however they are devised, must of course relate to customer requirements. It is interesting that service standards for libraries are now starting to emerge. They are considered further in Chapter 10.

5.   **Durability.** The normal definition of durability is 'the amount of use the product will provide before it deteriorates to the point where replacement or discard is preferable to repair'. This is applicable to libraries if we bear in mind that the answer may be 'infinity' for those items which are literally irreparable. For most customers, however, the library issues will centre on the question of the rate of obsolescence of information and hence on how

up to date the information provided is. It may be appropriate under this heading, therefore, to consider the age of the library's bookstock or the frequency of update of a CD-ROM database.

6.   **Serviceability.** When things go wrong, how easy will it be to put them right? How quickly can they be repaired? How much inconvenience will be caused to the customer and how much cost? This last will include not just the cost of the repair itself, but the inconvenience and consequential losses the customer faces. In general, libraries have not had to give a great deal of attention to these issues in the past but they could be of major importance if, for example, an online information service was being provided on a commercial basis. With the increase in use of IT-based systems libraries can be vulnerable to catastrophic failures. The 'service-ability' issues also occur, for example, in interlibrary loan services if the wrong item is supplied, no matter whose 'fault' it may be. The heading of 'serviceability' also includes such factors as whether the customer is treated with courtesy when things go wrong.

7.   **Aesthetics.** While this is a highly subjective area, it can be of prime importance to a customer. Is the service area clean and well designed? Is it welcoming? Does it appear user friendly or, as someone put the alternative, 'user lethal'? Everyone has come across libraries which look old, worn, gloomy and generally uncared for. Equally we all know libraries which are bright, well designed, welcoming and fresh. There are customers who prefer the former of course and others who would rather have a dog-eared and annotated text than a book fresh from the publisher. Nevertheless, all customers judge a library as much by its aesthetics as by its services.

8.   **Perceived quality.** This is one of the most interesting of attributes because it recognizes that all customers make their judgements on incomplete information. They do not carry out detailed surveys of 'fill rates' or examine the library's performance in answering reference enquiries over a six-month period. Most users do not read the library's mission statement or service standards – or even the 'welcome' leaflet. However, they will quickly come to a judgement about the library based on their preconceptions as users and on the reputation of the library among their colleagues and acquaintances.

It is interesting that Garvin's approach has been adapted to the question of 'information quality' by Marchand (1990), who sees in the approach a methodology for assessing the quality of information products as well as information services.

DETERMINANTS OF SERVICE QUALITY: ZEITHAML, PARASURAMAN AND BERRY

One of the most influential analyses of the customer's view of the quality of services was carried out by three American researchers, Zeithaml, Parasuraman and Berry (1990); see also Berry, Zeithaml and Parasuraman, 1990). They were motivated by the observation that the US economy had become highly dependent on services (they quoted figures which showed that only 11 per cent of American workers were still employed in factories or agriculture by 1987), yet the quality of service being delivered by all these service sector workers was too often 'indifferent, careless and incompetent'.

Zeithaml, Parasuraman and Berry worked with three focus groups in each of four sectors using market-research based methodologies to establish the criteria used by customers in assessing the quality of services. The sectors chosen for the study were retail banking, credit cards, securities brokerage and product repair and maintenance. They noted that customers find it more difficult to assess the quality of services than the quality of products and chose their methodology to enable the members of their focus groups to discuss in depth their expectations and experiences.

After analysing the data from the focus groups, Zeithaml, Parasuraman and Berry identified ten dimensions of service quality which appeared to be common across all of the services examined. These dimensions were as follows:

1.   *Tangibles.* Is the service an attractive place to visit? Are the staff appropriately dressed? Do they use modern, up to date equipment?
2.   *Reliability.* Is my telephone call returned when they said it would be? Are errors made on my bank statement? Does the washing machine work (first time) when it's been repaired?
3.   *Responsiveness.* When a problem occurs, is it quickly put right? Do they arrange to repair the washing machine at a time to suit *me*?
4.   *Competence.* Do front-line staff give the impression of knowing what they are doing? Similarly, does a repairer appear to know how to diagnose a fault and carry out a repair with confidence?
5.   *Courtesy.* Are staff pleasant, even when asked difficult (or what may appear to be 'silly') questions? Does the repairer wipe his or her shoes rather than trample mud all over my hall carpet? Do staff manage not to appear busy even when they are?
6.   *Credibility.* Does the service enjoy a good reputation – do people speak well of it? Are charges consistent with the level of service provided? Do I get a credible and worthwhile guarantee with a repair, such that I can have confidence that any problems will be put right quickly and without further expense?
7.   *Security.* Is it safe to use the service? For example, is my credit card safe from unauthorized use? Do I have confidence that the repair was properly carried out to an acceptable standard?
8.   *Access.* If I have a problem, can I get access to a senior member of staff to help me sort out the cause? Do they answer the telephone when I ring? Is it easy to find the repair company's premises?
9.   *Communication.* Is the service explained clearly and the options outlined comprehensively? Do they avoid using unnecessary jargon? Do they listen to me? If something unexpected occurs and the repair company cannot keep the appointment that they've made, do they contact me in good time to rearrange it?
10.   *Understanding the customer.* If I am a regular customer, does someone on the staff recognize me? Do they try to understand my individual needs?

Do they try to arrange the repair visit to meet my convenience rather than their own?

Building on these ten dimensions of service quality, Zeithaml, Parasuraman and Berry were able to define service quality in terms of the difference between customers' expectations of the service and their perceptions of the service actually delivered and to suggest key factors which influence expectations, including 'word-of-mouth communications, personal needs, past experience and external communications'.

Zeithaml, Parasuraman and Berry went on to analyse the ten determinants in detail and to provide a set of five key issues which are sometimes known as the 'Rater' set from the internal letters of each heading.

1.   *R*eliability
2.   *A*ssurance
3.   *T*angibles
4.   *E*mpathy
5.   *R*esponsiveness.

The Rater dimensions are defined in the following way:

○   **Reliability** is the 'ability to perform the promised service dependably and accurately'.

○   **Assurance** is 'knowledge and courtesy of employees and their ability to convey trust and confidence'.

○   **Tangibles** are the 'appearance of physical facilities, equipment, personnel and communication materials'.

○   **Empathy** is the 'caring, individualized attention the firm provides its customers'.

○   **Responsiveness** is 'willingness to help customers and provide prompt service'.

The Rater set was the basis of a methodology developed by Zeithaml, Parasuraman and Berry for application to the service sector in general. While it is beyond the scope of this book to describe the methodology in detail (the best source for further information is again Zeithaml *et al.*, 1990), their SERVQUAL instrument for measuring customers' expectations and perceptions has enormous scope for application in the library and information services sector. To ask what reliability, assurance, tangibles, empathy and responsiveness would mean to the service offered to the library user would be to invite a rather different view of the library from that given in most annual reports! Interestingly the SERVQUAL methodology has been used recently in the information sector within the European Commission funded EQUIP project, described in Chapter 8.

CUSTOMER SATISFACTION: AN EXAMPLE

A practical example of how the basic issues of customer satisfaction might work in practice is given by a 1992 advertising campaign by SAS International Hotels under the title 'If it's wrong, we'll put it right', with a banner heading, 'No excuse for not being perfect'. The customer is given a guarantee that if anything is wrong with the room and not put right in one hour, another will be provided or, if none is available, then the bill will be waived. Of particular interest is the list of 20 service aspects that are specifically guaranteed. These are clearly taken from an analysis of what the customers will expect to find in a quality hotel:

1. We guarantee that wake-up calls are made as requested.
2. We guarantee that the toilets will not make noises.
3. We guarantee that drains will not be blocked.
4. We guarantee that taps will not drip.
5. We guarantee that shower curtains will be effective.
6. We guarantee that water outlets will not fail to flow.
7. We guarantee that the telephone will be working properly.
8. We guarantee that the TV will have good sound quality and that the picture will be free from interference on all channels.
9. We guarantee that radio channels will be clear and without interference and that one channel will offer classical music only.
10. We guarantee that the trouser press will be in order.
11. We guarantee that, if the room has a mini-bar, it will be well-stocked.
12. We guarantee that all lamps will function correctly and that the free-standing lamp will operate in all positions.
13. We guarantee that all plugs and electric sockets will be working and that all plugs will be in their sockets.
14. We guarantee that all the furniture will be in good condition.
15. We guarantee that, in Royal Club rooms, the electronic safe will function correctly.
16. We guarantee that the hairdryer will work correctly.
17. We guarantee that the air-conditioning will function correctly.
18. We guarantee that office help will be available during normal hours if reserved in advance.
19. We guarantee that you will have access to copier, telex and telefax services.
20. We guarantee that all messages received will get through to you without delay.

Some of the issues covered by the SAS guarantee appear at first glance almost trivial until you try sleeping in a hotel room where the toilet cistern drips persistently all night long! It is interesting to see how a practical service guarantee maps on to the Rater approach: reliability, tangibles and responsiveness can all be found in the guarantee itself. The publicity helps to give an impression of responsiveness ('If it's wrong we'll put it right') while if the attitude expressed in the written guarantee translates into practice – which of course is an unknown until one tries the hotels – then one could expect empathy.

CONCLUSION

Tenner and DeToro (1992) suggest combining the Garvin, Zeithaml, Parasuraman and Berry and a number of other approaches to provide a compendium of quality characteristics under the simple formulation of faster, better, cheaper. They suggest that the key issue is to consider quality as having two components: *what* is provided to the customer and *how* the product/service is delivered: 'deliverables' and 'interactions'. Deliverables describe what is provided. Interactions describe 'characteristics of staff and equipment that impact on *how* customers experience the service process while it is performed'. It could be argued that libraries and information services have usually concentrated on the former and neglected the latter. Tenner and DeToro's approach is, however, particularly important for services such as libraries, because as we have seen very often the customer will be interacting directly with the service provider. Where product quality might be measured in terms of size, number, colour, packaging and so on, service quality is judged on friendliness, courtesy, lack of queuing, and reputation.

An interesting way to view the interactions between customer expectation, perceptions and experiences is to use an approach, sometimes known as a Kano map, which uses the concepts of 'basic', 'performance' and 'surprise' quality. Basic quality is concerned with all those aspects of the service which are taken for granted and would never be expected to feature in a formal or informal statement of service standards. So if you climb aboard a long-distance passenger train you expect it to be equipped with seats, if you receive a bank statement you expect it to be added up correctly, and if you go into a library in England and ask to see volume 3 of the *Encyclopedia Britannica* you expect to be offered the English language version.

Performance quality, on the other hand, consists of those aspects of the service which are in a sense negotiated between the customer and the supplier. So you might legitimately ask for a performance standard for train reliability or frequency of bank statements or library stock holding policy, and you might equally legitimately expect some measure of the service's actual performance against that standard to be available.

Surprise quality is at the opposite end of the spectrum from basic quality. In this case the issues do not feature because they are above what a normal customer would realistically expect. So, you do not expect that a stewardess will offer you a refreshing hot towel on the train (or at least not on British Rail), nor that the bank will enclose a get well card with your statement, or that the library will not only offer to print out the encyclopedia entry you need from its CD-ROM system but also give it to you in a binder free of charge. Often it is the small touches which generate surprise quality and which have the greatest effect.

The point of differentiating quality in these ways is that basic quality only has power to produce customer dissatisfaction. If you get it right no one notices; if you get it wrong customers are outraged. Performance quality can produce either satisfaction or dissatisfaction, depending on how well you meet customer requirements. Surprise quality cannot produce dissatisfaction, since it is totally unexpected, but it can produce very satisfied customers. Indeed, surprise quality may be the means by which, in a competitive market, you can differentiate one service from another – hence the vases of fresh flowers in first class carriages on long-distance inter-city trains, which presumably would not be feasible in an aircraft. However, there are dangers in trying to embark on surprise quality before basic quality has been set on a firm foundation, since all the good work of the higher levels of quality management can so easily be undone by failure at the basic level. The vase of flowers does not impress when it is placed on a filthy table.

5

THE QUALITY AWARDS

❖

It is instructive, while considering how quality might best be defined, to look in some detail at the major awards which are presented in Japan, the United States and Europe to organizations which can demonstrate quality. Major companies compete fiercely for these awards, which are regarded as highly prestigious and clearly offer a marketing edge to the winners. Each of the major awards has a set of detailed criteria against which a 'quality company' will be judged, and these criteria can be regarded as the equivalent of the clauses of a quality standard like ISO 9000. Companies often use the award criteria when devising their own quality systems, not just to place themselves in a good position to gain the award itself, but also because of the rigour with which they have been devised and the success which award winners have been able to demonstrate in the marketplace. In this section we will look at the three major awards: the Deming Prize, the Malcolm Baldridge National Quality Award and the European Quality Award.

THE DEMING PRIZE

The Deming Prize was established by the Union of Japanese Scientists and Engineers in 1950 – another piece of evidence of the early entry of Japanese industry into the quality field under W. Edwards Deming's influence. It was specifically designed to reward progress in the development and use of statistical process control. Each year two awards are made, one being a prize for organizations which have been able to demonstrate improved performance through the application of statistical process control (subdivided into an award for large and one for small organizations), the second for research into the theory or application of these techniques, that is for advancing the use of the approach. To be eligible for a Deming Prize a company must be approved by consultants (or 'counsellors') of the Union, who may be involved with the company for a period of years before an application is made.

The criteria or 'evaluation checkpoints' for the Deming Prize for organizations are divided into ten categories, as indicated below:

1. **Policy**
   - Corporate policy in relation to the business in general and product quality.
   - Communication of policy throughout the organization.
   - Long-term and short-term planning and the relationships between them.
   - Methods used to establish policy.
   - Use of statistical methods.
   - Monitoring of policy achievement.

2. **Management**
   - Clarity of boundaries of responsibility of managers.
   - Contact and communication between departments, and the appropriateness of functional boundaries.
   - Use of staff.
   - Monitoring and auditing of quality control processes.
   - Quality circle activities.

3. **Education**
   - Planned activities and achievements against those plans.
   - Awareness in the company of quality issues, especially quality control.
   - Training in statistical concepts and methods.
   - Use of educational resources from outside the organisation.
   - Quality circle activities (note that this arises under more than one heading).
   - The number of proposals for improvement made by staff.

4. **Information gathering**
   - Information gathering from outside the organization.
   - Speed of internal communications.
   - Communication of information between departments.
   - Statistical analysis of information.

5. **Analysis**
   - Selection of major problem areas.
   - Application and use of statistics.
   - Analysis of processes and quality.
   - Methods of analysis used.
   - Specialized techniques used.
   - Application of the results of analysis.

6. **Standardization**
   - Systems employed to achieve standardization.
   - Adherence to established standards.
   - Application of statistics.
   - Application of standards.

○ Stabilization of standards.
○ Revision of standards.
○ Content of standards.

7.   Control
○ System for cost and quality control of products.
○ Application of statistical methods for control.
○ Achievement of control.
○ Proposals for improvement submitted.
○ Quality circle activities (again).
○ Use of control conditions.

8.   Quality assurance
○ Methods for new product development.
○ Improvements made in control processes.
○ Inspection methods.
○ Monitoring and auditing of the quality assurance system.
○ Evaluation of product quality.
○ Analysis of product reliability.
○ Product safety.
○ Control of equipment ordering, procurement and servicing.
○ Application of statistical methods.

9.   Results
○ Projection of results.
○ Results which are not quantifiable.
○ Achievement of results against projections.
○ Quantitative results for product quality, profit, safety, costs and the general working environment.

10.   Future planning
○ Understanding of current position.
○ Measures for solving problem areas.
○ Long-term planning.

It will be seen that the Deming Prize criteria are firmly based on Deming's ideas and in particular on the application of quality control and statistical process control. Although many of the categories may seem somewhat remote from the concerns of libraries and information services, there is plenty of scope for application of the underlying concepts in that field. For example, under 'Information gathering', libraries and information services need to acquire information on their environment – the parent body, legislation, information products, professional developments, and so on – while the need to disseminate information internally with speed and efficiency, and to communicate between departments, is universal.

One area which seems to be missing from the Deming Prize criteria is that of the organization's customers: there is nothing explicit about customer satisfaction, nor a concern with meeting customer needs. This is a slightly unfair analysis, of course, since concern for the customer is implicit in such criteria as 'Quantitative results for product quality' and presumably safety is at least partly a concern for customers. Nevertheless, the contrast with the Malcolm Baldridge Award is striking: we will examine that next.

THE MALCOLM BALDRIDGE NATIONAL QUALITY AWARD

Malcolm Baldridge was a US Commerce Department Secretary who took a particular interest in quality matters and encouraged a number of initiatives: the award was set up in his honour by the US Congress in 1987. For this award there are seven categories, each with a quantitative weighting. The criteria and weightings are reviewed each year. In 1991, to take a recent example, the categories were as follows (with points out of 1,000 in brackets):

1.   **Leadership (100)**
     - Senior executive leadership (40).
     - Quality values (15).
     - Management for quality (25).
     - Public responsibility (20).

2.   **Information and Analysis (70)**
     - Scope and management of quality data and information (20).
     - Competitive comparisons and benchmarks (30).
     - Analysis of quality data and information (20).

3.   **Strategic Quality Planning (60)**
     - Strategic quality planning process (35).
     - Quality goals and plans (25).

4.   **Human Resources Utilization (150)**
     - Human resource management (20).
     - Employee involvement (40).
     - Quality education and training (40).
     - Employee recognition and performance measurement (25).
     - Employee well-being and morale (25).

5.   **Quality Assurance of Products and Services (140)**
     - Design and introduction of quality products and services (35).
     - Process quality control (20).
     - Continuous improvement of processes (20).
     - Quality assessment (15).
     - Documentation (10).
     - Business process and support service quality (20).
     - Supplier quality (20).

6.   **Quality Results (180)**
     - Product and service quality results (90).
     - Business process, operational, and support service quality results (50).
     - Supplier quality results (40).

7.   **Customer Satisfaction (300)**
  - Determining customer requirements and expectations (30).
  - Customer relationship management (50).
  - Customer service standards (20).
  - Commitment to customers (15).
  - Complaint resolution for quality improvement (25).
  - Determining customer satisfaction (20).
  - Customer satisfaction results (70).
  - Customer satisfaction comparison (70).

In an interesting article C. W. Reimann, the award director, distilled from the above criteria eight key factors which the award team are looking for when they examine an application (Main, 1990). They are:

1.   a plan to keep improving all operations continuously;
2.   a system for measuring those improvements accurately;
3.   a strategic plan based on benchmarks that compare a company's performance with the world's best;
4.   a close partnership with suppliers and customers that feeds information back into operations;
5.   a deep understanding of customers so that their wants can be translated into products and services;
6.   a long-lasting relationship with customers, going beyond the delivery of the product to include sales, service and ease of maintenance;
7.   a focus on preventing mistakes rather than merely correcting them;
8.   a commitment to improving the quality that runs from the top to the bottom of the organization.

THE EUROPEAN QUALITY AWARD

The European Foundation for Quality Management (EFQM), which was founded as recently as 1988, awards the European equivalent of the Deming and Baldridge prizes, the European Quality Award for companies. EFQM also offers a number of other prizes or awards, such as the Research Thesis Awards for the best doctoral thesis and the best masters thesis and the Media Award for the best journal article or broadcast programme on TQM.

The criteria for the European Quality Award are as follows:

1.   **Customer satisfaction** (20 per cent). Based on the views of the external customers of the organization on its products and services.
2.   **People** (18 per cent). An assessment of staff's views on the organization and the management of those staff in accordance with the principles of TQM.
3.   **Business results** (15 per cent). A comparison of the organization's achievements compared with its planned targets.

4.   **Processes** (14 per cent). The management of the internal processes of the organization.

5.   **Leadership** (10 per cent). The way all managers in the organization act in the move towards TQM.

6.   **Resources** (9 per cent). The use, management and preservation of the financial, technological and (interestingly) information resources of the organization.

7.   **Policy and strategy** (8 per cent). An analysis of the existence of vision, values and direction, and the way these are pursued.

8.   **Impact on society** (6 per cent). Recognition of the external environment of the organization, assessed by taking the views of the community in which it operates, including its impact on the global environment and related issues.

9.   **People management** (9 per cent). The ways in which people working in the organization are managed and empowered.

Figure 5.1 shows the assessment criteria diagrammatically. It is important to note that the criteria are split into two groups, enablers and results, both of which contribute 50 per cent to the total assessment. The idea is that 'processes' are the means by which the organization manages its total resources in order to produce results. However, these resources are most crucially defined to include all the 'people' aspects of the management process: leadership, management of staff and development of policy. Interestingly, the weighting given to leadership (10 per cent) exceeds that given to what would normally be thought of as 'resource management'.

One way of interpreting this structure is to read it from right to left. Start with Business results, which contribute 15 per cent to the final assessment. Business results can only be achieved by achieving People (i.e. staff) satisfaction, Customer

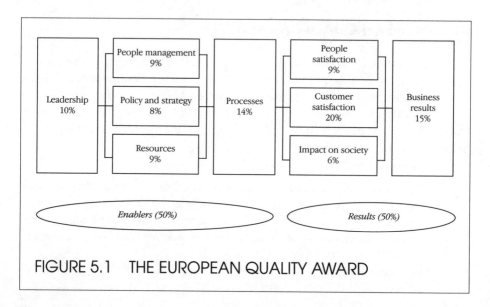

FIGURE 5.1   THE EUROPEAN QUALITY AWARD

satisfaction and a positive Impact on society. These three in turn are dependent on the internal processes of the organization, which produce the service or product which the customers receive. Processes themselves are dependent on People management, Policy and strategy and Resources. These three are themselves dependent on Leadership. The model enables the total contribution of each of these linked activities and concepts to be assessed. The first European Quality Award was won by Rank Xerox Ltd in October 1992.

CONCLUSION

The three major quality awards have a great deal in common, which is hardly surprising since they are all aimed at encouraging companies to implement quality management to the highest standards and to reward achievements in the field. Differences are mainly of emphasis, although there is significance in the various stresses within the award criteria which probably relate as much to cultural effects as to any other factor.

It has been suggested, for example, that while the Deming Prize takes 'management of quality' as its overall approach, the Baldridge Award concentrates on the 'quality of management' and the European Quality Award on the 'quality of corporate citizenship' (Nakhai and Neves, 1994). It is undeniable that the Deming Prize in particular is concerned principally with the use of statistical process control while the other two place much greater emphasis on customer satisfaction, company results, planning and outcomes. In some ways, the history of TQM can be seen in the awards. The tight focus of Deming on company-wide quality improvements through rigorous application of tried and tested techniques broadened into the Baldridge Award's concern with customer satisfaction and benchmarking (to which it has given a major boost) and led to the European Quality Award's concern with the broader environment in which the organization operates, including social issues. This is an emphasis that is redolent of the writings of many modern management gurus such as Peter Drucker who in *The New Realities*, wrote of the need for organizations to 'build into their own vision, their own behaviour, and their own values concern and responsibility for the common good' (Drucker, 1989). There is something to be learned from each award, and all have greatly encouraged the acceptance among both large and small firms of quality management as a discipline to be taken seriously and applied rigorously.

Having said that, we must also mention one of the criticisms of the awards, namely, that too many companies are chasing the award rather than quality itself. A small industry has grown up in the United States advising companies on how to prepare for and get the Baldridge Award. In addition, there has been criticism of Motorola for requiring all its suppliers to apply for a Baldridge Award (Main, 1990). A further complaint is that the awards represent 'creeping bureaucracy' (David Snediker, quoted in Main, 1990.). In Britain, a recent addition to the range of available awards has been the introduction of the Charter Mark scheme for public services. As this scheme is part of the Citizen's Charter initiative we will consider it in the next chapter.

6

THE CITIZEN'S CHARTER: A GOVERNMENT APPROACH TO QUALITY MANAGEMENT

❖

Since 1979 the UK Government has taken a number of steps to change the way in which both central and local government services are managed and delivered. There are numerous documents which record these changes but the most significant, certainly for libraries and information services, is probably *The Citizen's Charter*. Prior to its launch there had been a number of studies and reports on ways in which services could be made both more efficient and more responsive to both central government and their customers (see, for example, a 1988 report by the Efficiency Unit entitled 'Improving management in government' and the Audit Commission's various reports from this period, e.g. 'Managing services effectively', 1989).

The Prime Minister launched *The Citizen's Charter* itself in July 1991 as a ten-year programme designed 'to raise the standard of public services and make them more responsive to the needs and wishes of their users'. The identification of the term 'user' with 'citizen' is interesting, since the latter term is usually understood to imply a position which embraces both rights and responsibilities, while the former has a more unidirectional connotation. However that may be, the use of citizen's charters has spread to a number of other countries, and was an influence in the United States Government's 1993 'Reinventing Government' initiative.

It is undeniable that the UK *Citizen's Charter*, and the Conservative Government's policy which it embodies, is highly political in content and that a different government might well have taken a rather different view. It has, however, been a crucial policy which is of considerable interest in the context of quality management for three reasons. In terms of quality, it also draws on a wider vein of concern, for example that contained in the Labour Party's *Quality Street* publication (see the account by Wills, 1991).

The Citizen's Charter (1991) embodies the political framework which has swept the world since the fall of communism. It shifts public sector service providers away from a centralized (whether national government, local authority or 'professional' centred) planning basis towards a market model in which the user of the service decides what is 'bought' and therefore what services will be provided. This user-centredness of economic systems has given quality management itself a major boost in recent years.

The approach is, at least ostensibly, customer centred. There are concerns, of course, that the shift may be more apparent than real and there is evidence that charter approaches may be yet another way of enfranchising the vocal middle classes at the expense of less articulate sections of the population. Nevertheless, at least on the surface, the customer is placed at the centre of service delivery in the *Citizen's Charter*.

Finally, the principle is established in the charter that there should be explicit standards of service and that a key requirement is to achieve those standards consistently at minimum cost. This is, of course, an explicit statement that the issue is about quality, about the determination of customer needs, agreement in the level of service to be provided and monitoring of actual service provision.

The July 1991 *Citizen's Charter* was quickly followed, in November of the same year, by a consultation paper entitled 'Competing for Quality: Competition in the Provision of Local Services' issued jointly by the Department of the Environment, the Scottish Office and the Welsh Office. In this case the quality issue is explicit even in the title. The body of the paper made clear the Government's view that value for money could best be achieved through competition for the delivery of local services.

It should not be assumed from this that *The Citizen's Charter* is solely concerned with raising the quality of public services. High on the agenda for government has been the contracting out of services to the private sector, which may or may not have an implication for the quality of service a customer receives. Other measures, such as the intention to introduce greater openness in government at both local and national level, are no doubt to be welcomed, but again are not central to the achievement of quality. In many ways, the political issues surrounding *The Citizen's Charter* have clouded the debate on improving the quality of public services, which is a pity since public libraries in the UK were already addressing the key issues before the Government's initiative took shape.

It is sometimes difficult to disentangle the political elements of *The Citizen's Charter* from its quality implications. For example, underlying the charter, as the 1994 report made clear, is an analysis of whether a task needs to be done and if so whether the Government needs to be responsible for it. It is assumed that only if the answer to both questions is positive – that is, that the task *is* needed and *has* to be carried out by Government – should Government continue to exercise that responsibility. But some political viewpoints would argue that Government can legitimately take responsibility even if others *could* do so, and that the quality management implied in the charter is merely being pressed into a false position of support for a partisan stance.

It also has to be said that the very partial legislative force behind *The Citizen's Charter* leads to some odd emphases. For example, three years on, is it satisfactory that all that can be said on the issue of services for the disabled is that 'many services are making special efforts to take account of the views and needs of customers with special needs, for example people with disabilities' (*The Citizen's*

Charter: Second Report, 1994)? Equally, citizens who see the London Fire Brigade placing a large advertisement in the *Evening Standard* to tell them that 597 people were rescued at fires, and 1,630 elsewhere, between 1 April 1993 and 31 March 1994 may legitimately ask whether better value for money would be obtained by concentrating either on quality improvement or at least on more meaningful performance data.

THE PROVISIONS OF *THE CITIZEN'S CHARTER*

There are a series of different provisions embedded in *The Citizen's Charter*, of which the following are the most important:

1. The setting of standards of service and the monitoring of their achievement. Charters have been published by a wide range of public bodies, including a Patient's Charter for the National Health Service, a Charter for Further Education and one for Higher Education (it has been noted that neither of these was entitled 'A Student's Charter'!), a British Rail Passenger's Charter and a Benefits Agency Charter. Local authorities have published their own Charters, including Charters for Public Libraries. The Standards of Service incorporated in Charters are discussed below. The Audit Commission and Scottish Accounts Commission have statutory responsibility for advising on and requiring the publication of performance standards.

2. A commitment to openness, illustrated by a statutory requirement on public services to publish information about their activities and performance. Parents have a right to information on their children's progress (but, of course, they nearly always received it anyway, so this is hardly revolutionary). Some of the information published under these provisions has been highly tendentious, for example the league tables of schools' examination performance which measure crude outputs but not added value. Some information on central government has been published, but these provisions fall far short of a Freedom of Information Act.

3. Systems for dealing with customer complaints have been introduced or overhauled, and some provisions for compensation introduced for when things go wrong. In some areas there has been the introduction of a measure of independence in the determination of complaints, as with the Revenue Adjudicator in tax matters.

4. Performance-related pay has been introduced throughout the Civil Service and in many other public services.

5. Compulsory Competitive Tendering has been extended to a wide variety of government agencies and to many more local authority activities. Competitive tendering for public library services has been introduced: this is considered further in Chapter 13. The stimulus for this activity was summarized in the following paragraph:

    Local authorities have historically seen the direct provision of services to the community as one of their major tasks. However, we believe that now is the time for a new approach. The real task for local authorities lies in setting priorities, determining the standards of service which their citizens should enjoy, and finding the best possible way to meet them … We are convinced that the widest possible application of competition will benefit the local taxpayer and consumer of services alike (*The Citizen's Charter*, 1991).

6.   A Charter Mark scheme, which introduces a quality award for public services in the UK. This is described below.

THE CITIZEN'S CHARTER AND STANDARDS OF SERVICE

The Citizen's Charter has led to the production of a series of charters covering public services in Britain. While many have been treated with some cynicism, at least initially, they do form an attempt to specify, often for the first time, just what customers have a right to expect and what recompense they are entitled to when things go wrong. To take an example, the British Rail *Passenger's Charter* opens with the declaration:

> We want to give you
> – a safe, punctual and reliable train service,
> – clean stations and clean trains,
> – friendly and efficient service,
> – clear and up-to-date information,
> – a fair and satisfactory response when things go wrong.
>
> (British Railways Board, 1992)

As part of this commitment, information is now published on the reliability and punctuality of all passenger train services. Furthermore, there are provisions for giving discounts on season tickets if, over the previous 12 months, trains have on average been more than three percentage points below target for punctuality or more than one point below target for reliability. There are a number of other provisions for recompensing passengers, although some seem churlish in the extreme. For example, refunding the reservation fee when the company fails to reserve you a seat seems more akin to justice than recompense!

A second example of the use of standards of service within a Charter comes from the National Health Service (NHS). *The Patient's Charter* (Department of Health and Central Office of Information, 1993), as well as listing individuals' rights (e.g. 'to receive a full and prompt reply to any complaint you make about NHS services') sets out the standards which Family Health Service Authorities are expected to meet. These include:

> Where you are not registered with a family doctor, (to) find you one within two working days.

> To help you change doctors easily and quickly, and send you details of how to change and a list of doctors within two working days.

> To transfer your medical records quickly when you change doctor. This means within two working days for urgent requests and six weeks for routine requests.

Perhaps the greatest problem with these charters, and again British Rail's is typical, is that unless customers can see that they lead to real improvements in service they rapidly become disillusioned with the process and dismissive of the concept. What passengers want are meaningful responses to complaints and trains that run on time, not standard letters containing empty rhetoric or endless information about failures to adhere to the timetable. So the final paragraph of *The Passenger's Charter* has to be turned from mission to reality:

> We run the rail service for you the passenger
>
> We know you want us to do better: we know we can do better – and we will
>
> Care for our passengers is our prime concern: we intend to prove it. (British Railways Board, 1992)

THE CHARTER MARK SCHEME

The explicit objective of the Charter Mark scheme is 'to recognize and reward excellence in the delivery of public services'. Applications are judged by a panel consisting mainly of executives from large private sector companies, chaired (for the 1994 scheme) by Sir James Blyth, Chief Executive of the Boots Company plc. The first awards were made in 1992, when 36 public service organizations received the Charter Mark, while in 1993 the number had grown to 93. A number of libraries and other organizations in the library and information service field have received Charter Marks, including the London Borough of Bromley's Library Service and Kent County Arts & Library Service in 1992, and the Patent Office and the London Borough of Croydon's Library Service in 1993.

Organizations are judged against nine explicit criteria for the Charter Mark (*The Citizen's Charter: Charter Mark Scheme 1994: Guide for Applicants*, 1994). These are:

1. **Standards.** The organization must set performance standards and publicize them 'in a form which the citizen understands', monitor actual performance against those standards and publish that information. The assessment is particularly concerned to ensure that the standards being used are appropriate to customer service and are not just management information under another name. It is also expected that the standards will be challenging to the organization and cannot be met without real effort and innovation.
2. **Information and openness.** Information must be provided to individual customers to enable them to use the services available, and the information must be in clear English as well as in ethnic minority languages, in braille, etc. as appropriate. The information should include the cost of running the services and the names of managers who are responsible for them. There should be evidence that customer awareness of the information is assessed as well as customer satisfaction with it.
3. **Choice and consultation.** There should be evidence of 'regular, systematic customer consultation' as well as evidence of how the outcomes of that consultation process are fed back into decision making. In addition, organizations should show how they offer choice to customers.

4. **Courtesy and helpfulness.** Under this criterion the judging panel is looking for 'evidence that the organization puts the treatment of its customers first', including evidence 'that customers feel they are receiving a courteous and helpful service'. The criteria under this heading are quite prescriptive: for example, staff must always wear name badges and must give their names when answering the telephone or in correspondence.

5. **Putting things right.** Here the existence of an effective and easy-to-use complaints system is checked, including the availability of independent review wherever possible. The evidence submitted must show not only that the complaints system exists but that customers know about it. It must also be shown that information from the complaints received is being fed back into the planning and decision-making processes.

6. **Value for money.** The issue here is the progressive improvement in the value for money offered by the service, corroborated by some form of external assessment. The submission must include evidence of sound financial management, forward planning and performance monitoring.

7. **Customer satisfaction.** This is the first of three criteria which did not appear in the original proposals in *The Citizen's Charter* but have been added for the purpose of the Charter Mark scheme. The issue being examined is whether organizations can demonstrate that customers are satisfied with the service they are receiving, together with evidence of annual improvements in the level of satisfaction being achieved. Where customer satisfaction is low, there needs to be evidence of the steps being taken to improve it.

8. **Measurable improvements in the quality of service over the last two or more years.** The evidence under this criterion includes the ability to demonstrate that improvements have taken place in the key areas identified as being of concern to customers, and that any improvements are part of an ongoing planned programme of action, not one-off or 'windfall' gains. The customers should also have been made aware of improvements.

9. **To have in hand, or plan to introduce, at least one innovative enhancement to services without any extra cost to the taxpayer or consumer.** The idea behind this criterion is to encourage and stimulate innovation and new ways of thinking about and delivering services. There is a particular emphasis on services to the individual customer and on empowering the customer. An interesting requirement is that 'organizations have in place the systems to enable them to analyse the trade-off between quality, cost and other aspects of performance, and to set appropriate targets' especially as this seems to reveal a confusion between quality and grade (as discussed in Chapter 1).

The comments of those who have succeeded in being awarded a Charter Mark are interesting, since they reveal a range of motivations for making a submission, many of which are common to the other Quality Awards (see Chapter 5). For example, the Sports Division of Ipswich Borough Council remarked:

> Over the past two years we had concentrated on re-structuring and on compulsory competitive tendering. With many of these changes under way, it was time to look externally at our services, to re-focus on the most important element in our existence – the customer. The Charter Mark scheme seemed to be the ideal catalyst to focus on customer services, and so it proved to be (*The Citizen's Charter: Charter Mark Scheme 1994: Guide for Applicants*, 1994).

Other winners have stressed the benefits in public relations and improved morale that winning a Charter Mark has produced.

CONCLUSION

Much of the content of *The Citizen's Charter* has addressed quality issues quite explicitly and for public services it has therefore provided an impetus to at least re-examine how quality is being managed. It is unfortunate that political rhetoric has sometimes masked the very positive messages which the charter movement has to convey. Comparison of the Charter Mark scheme with the major international quality awards shows many common points. The Deming Prize's emphasis on quality assurance, the Baldridge Award's concentration on customer satisfaction and the European Quality Award's inclusion of measurement of achievements all find an echo in the Charter Mark criteria.

At the same time it is doubtful if *The Citizen's Charter* in itself is an adequate commitment to quality. There is little in it to help managers discover *how* to deliver quality: processes still need to be managed. Staff need to be brought into the mainstream of the initiative, both as the deliverers of quality internally and externally, and as major stakeholders in the enterprise. Furthermore, the view of the 'customer' is too limited. The immediate end-user of the library service is not the only stakeholder, and ways to bring a broader perspective into service planning and prioritization are much needed. To close a small branch library or a rural bus service on the grounds that it will not dissatisfy many current users is, as most people would recognize, an inadequate approach to public service management. Yet it could happen if *The Citizen's Charter*'s insistence on ever-increasing levels of current-user satisfaction is followed slavishly. Questions still need to be answered, also, about the impact of the resource base on public services. At what stage does a succession of cutbacks in inputs lead to an inevitable decline in outputs that customers still need and want?

7

TOTAL QUALITY MANAGEMENT

The term 'total quality management' or TQM has been appropriated by so many different vested interests that it has become difficult to identify precisely what it means. There is a British Standard BS 7850 which offers the following definition:

> Total Quality Management (TQM): Management philosophy and company practices that aim to harness the human and material resources of an organization in the most effective way to achieve the objectives of the organization.

Tenner and DeToro (1992) offer an alternative, redefining quality in the following terms:

> A basic business strategy that provides goods and services that completely satisfy both internal and external customers by meeting their explicit and implicit expectations. ... This strategy utilizes the talent of all employees, to the benefit of the organization in particular and society in general, and provides a positive financial return to the shareholders.

They then suggest that TQM is based on:

O   one objective: continuous improvement;
O   three principles: customer focus, process improvement and total involvement; and
O   six supporting elements: leadership, education and training, a supportive structure, communications, reward and recognition and measurement.

An alternative way of looking at TQM is suggested by Professor John S. Oakland of the European Centre for Total Quality Management at the University of Bradford, UK (Oakland, 1989). Quality itself follows the classic 'fitness for purpose' and 'meeting customer requirements' definitions, but Oakland places stress on 'quality chains' – the supplier–customer relationships which are at the core of both internal and external customer relationships (see Chapter 1). Continuous improvement is again a key objective. TQM is based first on management commitment and then on three key components: a documented quality management system, statistical process control and teamwork. Oakland describes 13 steps to TQM:

1.   Understanding quality;
2.   Commitment to quality;
3.   Policy on quality;
4.   Organization for quality;
5.   Measurement of the costs of quality;
6.   Planning for quality;
7.   Design for quality;
8.   System for quality;
9.   Capability for quality;
10.   Control of quality;
11.   Teamwork for quality;
12.   Training for quality;
13.   Implementation of TQM.

Lascelles and Dale (1993) emphasize that TQM requires a strategic decision at the highest level in the organization to apply quality concepts to all operations and all departments. Nine key features are identified:

1.   *Total ownership*. Everybody in the organization accepts ownership and responsibility for quality.
2.   *Quality improvement as a way of life*. The organization takes steps to develop a pervasive philosophy of quality improvement.
3.   *Partnership with suppliers and customers* enables quality improvement to extend beyond the boundaries of the organization.
4.   *Internal customers are acknowledged* and given special attention, recognizing that when internal customers are being satisfied then there will be positive effects on external customer satisfaction too.
5.   *Key performance indicators are identified* to enable the organization to measure its performance, assess improvements, monitor customer satisfaction and benchmark against the best in the field.
6.   *Employee participation is stressed* and changes are made to ensure that everyone's skills are fully utilized.
7.   *Teamwork is given high priority*, especially the use of teams to solve quality problems.
8.   *Internal barriers between sections and departments are removed* throughout the organization.
9.   *Simplification and standardization of processes and procedures* are constant aims.

The same authors stress that TQM is 'a journey and not a destination' and that the underlying theme must be one of continuous improvement. Total quality improvement (TQI) operates within a culture which recognizes that problems and opportunities exist and recognizes the responsibility of the organization as a whole to resolve problems and exploit opportunities.

In the remainder of this chapter we look in more detail at the component mechanisms and concepts of TQM as they might be applied to the library and information service field, drawing on the above models and others.

THE STARTING-POINT FOR TQM

TQM is a systematic and holistic approach to the management of organizations and there are dangers in taking too analytical an approach to it. Like all the best systems its whole is greater than the sum of its parts. Neither is it a goal in itself: any manager who thinks that their organization can 'achieve' TQM is seriously deluded. Commitment to TQM must be long term and organisation wide. It will show benefits, but only after months and years of sustained effort. It will be expensive to implement, but will prove economic as savings from turning failures into quality materialize; it will put the organization in the firing-line, because only 100 per cent customer satisfaction will do. TQM is not for the faint-hearted.

The key concepts must always be a focus on the customer and continuous improvement and these must inform and influence every other component of TQM, as Figure 7.1 illustrates. Much has already been said on this in earlier chapters and indeed 'customer focus' could be used as a description of the quality management movement itself. But TQM seeks to go beyond merely meeting expressed customer wants and needs to try to address needs and wants that customers did

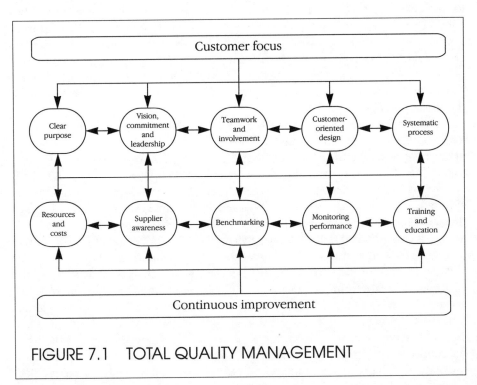

FIGURE 7.1   TOTAL QUALITY MANAGEMENT

not even know that they had by continually innovating and improving the service being offered. 'Delighting the customer' is a watchword in TQM.

However, before reaching the 'delight' phase all organizations need to focus on simply satisfying the requirements of their internal and external customers. TQM is, of course, no different from the general quality management literature in this regard. A 1994 advertising campaign at Heathrow Airport used the slogan 'We will not be satisfied with the standard of service you receive until you are' and that could be taken as a catch-phrase for all quality improvement programmes. It is all too easy to think that there is a customer focus when in fact the approach is one of 'experts' making assumptions about what customers want and need and then providing services based on those assumptions. This is a particular danger for any sector which has a strong professional ethos – medicine, law, architecture and librarianship would all be examples – and steps need to be taken to counter this tendency by taking deliberate actions to introduce a customer perspective, and to retain it. One of the problems for services in the public sector is that they are very often monopoly or near-monopoly suppliers. Students in a university rarely have any real alternative to using their own university's library. Bookshops are not a realistic alternative to the public library for many citizens; industrial information services may have a monopoly position within companies. Not only does this pose a problem for management, it may make customers uncertain about the level of service they should expect. Lack of competition presents problems for both management and customers, but this should act as an impetus for greater concern for the customer base rather than the opposite. Central to this endeavour will be efforts to improve and use the channels of communication between the organization and its customers: passive complaints and suggestion schemes will not be enough, and the organization seeking to implement TQM will place great emphasis on active communication. At a practical level this will manifest itself in customer care programmes but it will impinge on all activities from strategic management to the smallest detail.

An interesting and relevant parallel to the issue of achieving a customer perspective in libraries and information services lies in the current debate about health care in most Western countries. It is clear that a fully comprehensive health care system cannot be afforded in even the richest societies. People are living longer and needing more care; expensive treatments have been developed but cannot be afforded; diseases which were once regarded as incurable can now be fought with drugs or surgery. In brief, potential demand far exceeds supply, exactly as it does for most libraries and information services. Some form of rationing of public services is inevitable; the question is how this can be achieved.

At one extreme there are those who would simply suggest that we ask the customer what the priorities should be, and in democratic societies there is no acceptable alternative in the long run to the broad nature of services being determined by popular vote. But there are dangers in supposing that the detailed design of services, and service priorities, can be determined solely by holding a referendum of potential and actual service users. In a well-publicized experiment the State of Oregon used a voting system to try to decide which 'treatment pairs' (i.e. a condition and treatment – one condition might have more than one treatment and thus more than one treatment pair) to fund in its health services. Although the scheme produced useful information, and probably helped to give the whole issue of affordable health care choices a greater public profile, it also produced some odd results. For example, cosmetic breast surgery came out ahead of treatment for a fractured femur. The results were therefore adjusted by reference to professional judgement. Such a process may have been desirable in any case since public knowledge of different medical procedures may have been inadequate to enable informed judgements to be made.

A related problem can be found in the education system where the direct users of the service may not have the knowledge base on which to make judgements. Education is concerned with learning and it is generally accepted that, no matter how student centred learning becomes, some guidance is needed. Pupils are not best placed to be the sole determinants of the curriculum and students may not be the most effective selectors of teaching methods.

Yet these complexities do not rule out a customer-centred focus. Two issues need to be examined:

1.   A consideration of stakeholder approaches will enable a proper balance to be maintained between the needs of the direct users and those of others with an interest in the service. This balance will need to be reflected in agreed service standards.

2.   The way in which services are delivered will still need to take full account of the end-user. Libraries and information services have recognized this in their espousal of customer care training programmes, many of which are offered by professional associations, private sector trainers, and internally within larger organizations (see, for example, Trott, 1992). Undoubtedly there is still a long way to go. Nick Ross commented from personal experience on the delivery of hospital services:

> When my father was dying of cancer, he went from one hospital to another, ending up at the Royal Marsden in Sutton. It was a transformation – an utterly different scene ... I could take you to hospitals where the standard of care may be good clinically, but emotionally it is appalling. When my father died you could not have bought better service. I was a patient, too – my father was dying, therefore I was cared for. When the tea came round, I was offered tea. I was part of the family, part of the enterprise. One of the changes we need to make and can make at relatively little cost is to have a customer care campaign of the sort that BA (British Airways) has had and of the sort that has transformed BT (British Telecom), and progressively the banks, and so many other commercial institutions (Howell *et al.* 1994).

With such words of warning in mind, it is possible to provide an overview of the essentials of TQM by drawing on the wide variety of studies that have been carried out in this area, some of which have been described earlier. Bearing in mind that in this volume we are addressing a service industry, and a mainly public sector one at that, the following themes are key components to be addressed if TQM is to be introduced into libraries and information services.

CLEAR PURPOSE

A characteristic of quality organizations is that they are very clear about what they are trying to achieve – they have found an unambiguous answer to the key question, 'What business are we in?' (Peters and Waterman, 1982), and so do not spend time and resources trying to be all things to all people. One of the reasons that organizations, particularly those in the public service, can fail to provide quality products and services lies in a failure to define adequately their fundamental values and purposes and to articulate their vision in practice. Not only is this important for guiding current service or product delivery, it also affects at a fundamental level the strategic development of the organization. The balance between broad philosophical statements of too great a generality to be of any practical use, and narrowly focused formulations which are purely descriptive of current conditions is not easy to achieve. A common approach to defining purpose is the development and use of a mission statement, a method which is described in some detail below.

Interest in the development and use of mission statements has grown rapidly among UK libraries and information services in the last decade, with encouragement from parent bodies. For example, the Polytechnics and Colleges Funding Council (PCFC) issued a memorandum to institutions in early 1989 which contained the advice: 'Institutional Plans ... should describe succinctly the nature and position of the institution within the context of higher education ... (and) should include a statement of the purpose of the institution, its mission and its aims and objectives' (Polytechnics & Colleges Funding Council, 1989). In librarianship, a lead was given by the Library & Information Services Council (LISC) which included a model public library mission statement in a publication on public library objectives (Office of Arts and Libraries, 1991) – see Chapter 9. The Audit Commission, in the context of *The Citizen's Charter*, has also drawn attention to the need for public library mission statements. The British Library included a declaration of purpose, which might easily have been termed a mission statement, in its first Strategic Plan (British Library, 1989).

Perhaps the most useful description of the development of 'mission' as a concept in strategic management is given by Campbell (1990). In summary, he differentiates between two approaches to mission. The first, characterized as the strategy school of thought, is distinguished by the need to answer two basic questions: 'What business are we in?' and 'What business should we be in?' The classic paper was published by Levitt in 1960. He made the observation that most companies define the 'business they are in' too narrowly. British Rail should be regarded as being in transportation rather than railways; BP is in the energy rather than the oil business; librarians are in the information or culture rather than the library or book business – as, to be fair, we increasingly recognize. The importance of this broader vision is that it focuses effort on the fundamental purpose of the organization rather than on the means which it currently employs to achieve that purpose. It also helps to give the organization a focus on its market, on the needs of the people it serves, rather than on current strategies for providing for those needs. To give an historical example, in the last century a company with a transportation mission would have diversified out of canals into railways; a company which saw its purpose as providing canal transport would quickly have gone out of business when the railways arrived. More recently much of the Swiss watch industry suffered because of its slowness to recognize that it was in the business of selling well-designed and highly accurate watches rather than precision-engineered time-pieces. For our own sector, the mission statement which answers the question, 'What is this library or information service for?' is equally crucial, but the answer will obviously be different for different types of service. A national library will answer the question differently from an academic library, and the answer will in turn be different from that given by a public library or an industrial information service.

The second way of thinking about mission is characterized by Campbell (1990) as the 'cultural glue' approach. It is explicitly value laden and addresses ethical issues. So, for IBM mission is defined in terms of 'respect for the individual, dedication to service and quest for superiority in all things' (Watson, 1963). It is more a matter of how than what. It aims to give all employees, and hopefully all customers, a common set of values and behavioural standards. It incorporates ethical considerations and can lead to an almost religious fervour among its more devoted adherents. We have all become familiar with the practice of some Japanese companies of holding corporate keep fit sessions for all employees, and this is but one example of an attempt to enable employees to share the same corporate culture. Having only one canteen or restaurant for all employees may be a way of demonstrating a shared value that 'all people are of equal importance in this company'. Such values may then be articulated in the mission statement.

Some observers include statements of strategy within the mission statement. However, a more general pattern in a statement of mission is first to define the purpose and values and then the strategies in the form of strategic aims. Thus the danger of confusing ends and means is avoided.

At a simplistic level, the mission statement can be seen as no more than a statement of an organization's current activities: it is 'what we do'. It is the basic statement of where the organization is going and what it is seeking to become, but it is also more than that, for it sets the tone of the enterprise: it is value laden, because it says how the organization will act. Colin Marshall, Deputy Chairman and Chief Executive of British Airways, put it this way: 'A corporate mission is much more than good intentions and fine ideas. It represents the framework for the entire business, the values which drive the company and the belief that the company has in itself and what it can achieve' (Campbell, 1990).

A mission statement differs from a statement of aims or objectives because it is developed to express the nature of the organization and the place it seeks to occupy in its external environment. Mission has social and personal dimensions and cannot be achieved impersonally. Neither can it be imposed on an organization by one particular vested interest or stakeholder. Furthermore, mission is dynamic and the mission statement will seek to draw on the organization's developing understanding of its role, its opportunities and those aspects of its environment which in some sense threaten it. What is more, the mission statement is a cohesive force, since it deliberately avoids partisan approaches and requires, some would say demands, the assent of all those involved. This reinforces the concept of the mission statement as representative of the interests of the 'coalition', that is, all those individuals and groups who have a legitimate interest in the organization. As was noted in Chapter 4, an academic library's coalition, to take one example, might include its users, its staff, alumni, institutional managers, funding bodies and even the national interest in the shape of a relevant government department. Finally, the mission statement is action oriented. It provides the basis on which all those involved can take action, certain that they will be pulling together in the same direction.

This sounds very praiseworthy, but it can mask a very real danger. There is a tendency for mission statements to become 'motherhood' statements – generalized descriptions of goodness with which no one could possibly disagree. Lancaster (1977) noted that one library had come up with the resounding statement that its purpose was 'to assist people to become better members of their families and communities by promoting rational, democratic attitudes and values'. He commented: 'Social, spiritual and economic "objectives" of this type sound impressive, but they have very little meaning and utility except, perhaps, to persuade librarians of their value to society or, perhaps, to convince society of the value of libraries'. In other words, they cannot be translated into purposive action, still less can success or failure in attaining them be judged. The recognition of this fact is becoming increasingly evident in the literature:

> It is no longer sufficient merely to say we support the curriculum. We must decide and articulate what that time-honoured phrase really means. We must be able to express ... why (the library) is unique ... and how that uniqueness allows us to contribute to the intellectual life (of the university). A mission statement does just this' (Mosley, 1988).

Dubberly (1983), in the context of American public libraries, put it this way:

> The organization moves forward, full steam ahead, but those involved aren't really sure of where they are going. The books are ordered. The bills are paid. Buildings are even remodelled. All the daily objectives are completed. But is the organization carrying out its purpose? Are we accomplishing what really needs to be accomplished? You never will really know unless you have a mission or purpose statement for your library ... It tells you why you want to accomplish the goals for which you have objectives.

There is one danger of mission statements (or other statements of purpose for that matter) as a starting point for TQM and that is that the organization may start to define quality purely as the achievement of the corporate mission. In other words a service is fit for purpose if it aligns with the corporate mission, rather than if it is fit for the customer's purposes. Equally, customers' requirements may be perceived as legitimate only if they fit in with the organizational mission. There is a particular danger for public service organizations in this, because they are rarely able to respond to every demand placed on them. In seeking to focus their efforts so as to achieve quality by 'doing what they do well' they may exclude legitimate demands which fall outside the organization's own sense of purpose and mission. For this reason, mission needs to be revisited constantly and compared with the real needs of all customers, and users need to be recognized as the major stakeholders that they are.

VISION, COMMITMENT AND LEADERSHIP

Charles Handy, in his recent book *The empty raincoat: making sense of the future*, writes of visiting Malaysia and learning of that country's '2020 Vision Plan', a vision of how Malaysia will develop in the next 30 years (Handy, 1994). Based on a high level of economic growth, the Plan sets out how resources will be directed to education, care of the elderly, the handicapped and so on. Coming from the West, Handy admits to having expected to find some cynicism among the business community. He writes, 'instead I found excitement ... the headlines of the Plan were even pinned up in the taxis'. The Plan had provided a vision which citizens from every stratum of society could believe in and respond to.

It is not easy to generate such vision in any organization, let alone any country. The task is one of leadership, of senior managers having the courage to bring together the hopes, aspirations and desires of employees and customers to create and promulgate a new idea of how things could be. We could ask of public libraries, of academic libraries, of any kind of library: where is the vision of the future? What will this service be like in ten, 20, 30 years' time? What could it be doing that is new and exciting and relevant to its customers needs? Has that vision been spelled out? Do the staff believe in it?

Writer after writer on management in general, not only on quality management, have stressed the primacy of this aspect of senior managers' roles. Hayes (1993) wrote of library management, 'the primary responsibility of top management must be to have a vision of the library's role'. An interesting nuance of his comments is the inclusion of a professional vision on a national scale. In an age of networking, when library resources may most profitably be regarded as a shared resource, leadership of one single library and vision for its development may not be enough. National and international initiatives to enable users to access the wealth of information resources across the globe are dependent on that broader vision which in its turn depends on the individual contributions of professional librarians and information scientists, among others.

For this reason, we need to recognize that the world in which we operate is changing ever more rapidly, and to develop visions and scenarios to help us cope with, and indeed anticipate, those changes. One technique is called scenario planning and it has been used to great effect by the Royal Dutch Shell Group for many years. In *The Art of the Long View*, Peter Schwarz describes how Shell set up groups of senior staff, with input from external experts, to ask the all-important 'what if?' questions. Shell's senior managers were then asked to respond to these imagined scenarios and to say how they would act in the given circumstances. Of course, many of the ideas never came to anything, but some did: Shell had strategies in place to cope with the oil crisis of the early to mid 1970s and with the collapse of the Soviet Union (Schwarz, 1991).

Peters and Austin (1985) remark that the best leaders recognize that in a changing world there must be constant vision, and that vision is articulated through an almost passionate concern for values. Leaders should 'speak constantly of vision, of values, of integrity; they (should) harbour the most soaring, lofty and abstract notions', but simultaneously they need to 'pay obsessive attention to detail. No item is too small to pursue if it serves to make the vision a little bit clearer'. Crosby (1986) emphasizes the personal responsibility of leaders when he says 'the leader has to create the integrity of the operation by personal example'. Leadership is thus simultaneously concerned with the highest ideals and the tiniest details – and it operates in a climate of continuous change. The well-led organization will see change as an opportunity.

One final issue under this heading relates to what is known as the management of change. This is a complex business but one that increasingly is central to management itself. In the context of quality management, change is both internally generated and externally imposed. Quality management itself is concerned with change, with doing things better, more accurately, more consistently, more appropriately (see the discussion of the Japanese *kaizen* concept in Chapter 2). But it is also concerned with introducing change as a response to the external environment, both in response to the development of customers' requirements (and the requirements of new customers) and in exploiting opportunities presented by the environment, for example to reduce the cost of inputs. Change, then, is at the centre of quality management.

In recent years the management of change has received considerable attention from practitioners and researchers. A useful practical guide by Curzon (1989), designed for librarians, suggests that a sequence of steps can be used to plan, implement and evaluate change:

1. *Conceptualizing*: developing awareness and envisioning the change.
2. *Preparing*: getting the organization ready for change, for example by listening to staff, but being committed to the change.
3. *Organizing the planning group*: selecting staff to participate and building them into a team.
4. *Planning*: examining options, deciding on goals and objectives and then developing a plan.
5. *Deciding*: evaluating the options, deliberating and then making a decision.
6. *Managing the individual*: discussing the change and dealing with reactions to it, then monitoring its implementation.
7. *Controlling resistance*: identifying resistance, analysing its source and counteracting it.
8. *Implementing*: formal introduction of the change at the right time and then following it through.
9. *Evaluating*: re-examining the goals, identifying problems and making adjustments.

In many ways this scheme is oversimplified of course. In practice there are a number of changes taking place simultaneously and the process will not always follow through a series of identifiable, discrete steps in a neat and tidy fashion. Nevertheless it recognizes that change does not – or should not – merely happen, and that it has to be managed.

Issues which need to be considered in the management of change include the political and social context, resource availability and management style. Above all, however, change is dependent on people, on encouraging, persuading and enabling individuals to pursue purposeful change and improve the quality of their own outputs, whether as part of the internal quality chain or as direct products and services to end-users.

It is all too easy, especially in public services used to continuity in a secure environment, to treat external change as a threat rather than an opportunity, or to abrogate the responsibility of turning opportunity into reality. Yet libraries and information services operate in an environment of massive opportunity. Information technology and networking making information resources so much more widely available than in the past; learning through life; creating new educational roles for open learning and its support; expanded leisure time; creating new opportunities for exploiting cultural heritage; the list goes on. Do libraries have the vision that will enable them to exploit these opportunities? Have they done the scenario planning, looked at the alternatives and developed the strategies to take them into the future? And is the leadership in place to enable the vision to be turned into reality?

F. W. Lancaster, introducing a collection of essays under the title 'Libraries and the Future', observes that as we enter the twenty-first century 'significant changes will occur in the way in which sources of information, inspiration, and entertainment will be made available and these changes will have a major impact on the library and the library profession'. But he adds, ominously, that 'the most alarming thing that emerges from these essays is the fact that some of our most respected and senior librarians seem to feel that the library profession lacks the leadership needed to turn these changes to its advantage' (Lancaster, 1993b).

TEAMWORK AND INVOLVEMENT

Quite apart from any impetus gained from the adoption of quality concepts, organizations have moved in recent decades from hierarchical towards flatter structures which encourage participative management. Leadership is no longer exercised solely through direction, but involves enabling, supporting and facilitating staff at all levels to maximize their contributions to the organization. Teamwork enables problems to be tackled by more than one person at a time, and allows a mix of skills and abilities to be brought to bear. It can help to break down sectional and departmental barriers (although new barriers, between teams, must not be allowed to develop) and so overcome some of the quality problems which occur at the interfaces within the quality chain.

The essence of successful teams is that each of the members considers they are as a partner with other team members in achieving solutions to problems and appropriate outcomes to projects. The way in which teams work is important. The term 'synergy' is rather overworked these days, but the idea behind it is that of the parts of the body working together in harmony, although whether this is really the origin of the word seems to be in some dispute. Nevertheless, the ideas of harmonious co-operation and of the ability to achieve results which no individual team member could achieve are central to successful teamwork.

Bank (1992) uses the example of the 1989 New Zealand All Blacks rugby team to explore how teamwork can produce results. Under their captain, David Kirk, they put together a remarkable string of successes, even by their own high standards. Kirk, interviewed by Young (1991), identified five key points for successful teams:

1.   Team members need to be valued as individuals.
2.   Individuals need to feel integrated within a team.
3.   Captains must be fair to all individuals and treat them equally.
4.   The team must be confident.
5.   Individuals must enjoy themselves.

Of course, it is arguable to what extent the factors which make a sports team successful can be transplanted into a commercial organization or public service. But teamwork does seem to produce results, and there is plentiful evidence that teams generate much more job satisfaction than authoritarian and hierarchical structures.

Teamwork has, of course, been in evidence in libraries and information services for many years. Public libraries have adopted team-based structures, while academic libraries have used subject-based teams. David Minkoff, of Datastream International, has described the use of 'Self Managing Teams' in his organization:

> Everyone has ideas to improve the effectiveness of their job. They know more about their job than anyone else and are eager to share their thoughts and partici-pate in solutions if given a chance. Self Managing Teams give them this chance by including everybody from the most junior up to but excluding, manager level ... The teams meet regularly and during these meetings anyone can put forward ideas relating to quality or productivity improvements and, if the managers do not veto these ideas, they are implemented as quickly as possible (Minkoff, 1993).

Of course the manager's attitude to such teams is all important, for there is nothing worse than encouraging a team of people to come up with a series of ideas and then squashing them flat. Minkoff acknowledges this and advocates and encour-ages a 'let's give it a go' rather than a 'let's talk about it' approach. There is a strong argument for managers to allow virtually any suggestions to be implemented when teams are first set up so as to give encouragement to team members to continue to generate new ideas. More than that, it can be valuable to let, or even encourage, teams to make mistakes since that is the way in which both teams and individuals learn and grow. Minkoff refers to this as 'blameless error'. Allow people to try out new ideas, to take risks, to try the long shot, but ensure that they do so in a supportive atmosphere that is able to put any resulting problems right without seeking to blame someone for the error. To achieve this requires a high level of trust between team members and managers, and a truly open way of operating that enables people to admit that errors have been made and discuss both why things went wrong and what needs to be done to put them right. Some recent reports have suggested that the encouragement of risk taking has taken a backward step with the widespread adoption of downsizing and outsourcing, and through culture change programmes which are designed more to promote conformity than diver-sity (Nicholson-Lord, 1994). The well-known tendency of organizations to recruit people who reflect their existing values adds to the problem.

Successful teams also place a high value on individual development ('Training and learning', pp. 85–88, deals with this in greater detail). A team-based approach can produce an environment in which the *team* identifies where its weaknesses lie, what sort of skills it needs to develop, and then goes on to identify the appropriate team member or members to undertake training to fill that skills gap. The balance of abilities and competencies within a team can thus be developed to enable the team as a whole to function more effectively. Of course, some training will be appropriate for all team members, as for example in problem-solving techniques which will be needed if any problem is to be tackled successfully. Communication skills provide another example, since communication within the team and with others outside the team will be all important.

One particular type of team which features heavily in the quality management literature is the quality circle. Quality circles were very popular some years ago but have lost popularity, probably because the idea grew that they provided all the answers to quality problems: introduce quality circles and quality will take care of itself! Like all quick fixes, any immediate gains were quickly lost as the realization dawned that a much more comprehensive approach would be needed, and that far from a quick fix quality improvement represents the long haul. Indeed, it can be argued that unless quality circles, or quality improvement teams to use another common label, are embedded in the structure of the organization so that they become a way of life, they are unlikely to be effective. In other words, quality circles are really a manifestation of teamwork itself.

That is not to say that the work team and the quality circle need or even should be contiguous. There are advantages in drawing together a team of people from a variety of departments and sections, with a variety of skills and expertise, to work on a particular problem. As with any type of team, providing time and resources for training is extremely important and the roles individuals will play need to be defined. Quality circles and other teams need leadership and need to be 'facilitated'. Furthermore, there must be a clear way in which the ideas and solutions generated can be acted on. A quality circle must have a route to management, and must have the assurance that its ideas are being taken seriously, and acted on. If action is not possible, there must be a clear explanation of why not. Sometimes it may be possible to provide a quality circle with its own small budget to enable it to take action: this can help motivate the team by ensuring that the message that they are expected to make a significant contribution to the organization is unmistakable. Above all, quality circles need to be given the time, free from the pressure of everyday tasks, to be effective.

CUSTOMER-ORIENTED DESIGN

Plummer (1990) argues that the whole of the quality management approach can be summed up in the two steps 'Right design; Right execution'. The design of a product or service must incorporate the customers' requirements at the earliest stages, since an incorrect design cannot, by definition, provide quality. Furthermore, the cost of reworking (see 'Resources and costs', pp. 103–106) adds enormously to the cost of quality.

In the industrial sector there are of course well-known and nationally or internationally agreed standards for many aspects of design. Obvious examples include the exact dimensions of electrical plugs and sockets, the gauge of railway tracks and the sizes of floppy disks. In addition there are a wide variety of sources of information available to the designer of products; for example, trade associations, parts catalogues and customer or supplier specifications. Large companies will typically develop their own handbooks to guide internal design teams. To add to all this there are legislative requirements, for example from the Health and Safety at Work Act, 1974, the Sale of Goods Act, 1979 and the Consumer Protection Act, 1987.

For services the situation is less determined by external constraints, although there are standards and legislative issues which will need to be considered: copyright provisions affecting libraries and information services are an obvious example. Nevertheless, services tend to have greater freedom to design what they offer to their customers. The starting-point can unequivocally be the customers' needs. In some circumstances these will be the needs of existing customers of the service, especially where it is being redesigned. In others, market research will be needed to provide the information on which design can be based.

As we have already seen the delivery of services usually takes place at the point of contact between the service provider and the customer. This means that design has to consider not just *what* is to be delivered but *how* it is to be delivered. The insights of Garvin and others (see Chapter 4) will therefore be important in the service design process. Those criteria for achieving customer satisfaction need to be considered at this early stage, therefore, and they may well provide the means by which a service can differentiate itself from its rivals. The airlines, for example, are continually revising what at first appear to be secondary aspects of the service offered: the in-flight menu, the contours of the seats, the uniforms of the stewards and stewardesses. Since the basic transportation aspect of the business is more or less fixed (provided the airline gets it right) it is these aspects on which design may need to concentrate.

Teboul (1991) suggests that it is helpful to consider five principles when designing services:

1.   There is a trade-off between providing a highly standardized service at relatively low cost and introducing flexibility by increasing the number of staff involved in service delivery with subtle differences to the services offered. In some circumstances there may therefore be merit in subdividing the service delivery to meet the preferences of different customer groups, introducing basic and premium levels of service. Again, the airlines offer a good example of this through different classes of travel. This reflects the discussion of grade in Chapter 1, but note that quality service still has to be delivered at all levels.

2.   Recognizing that customers of services experience a series of 'moments of truth' (Chapter 1), it is important to maintain coherence of the total customer experience: a house style at the very least. It can be confusing for customers to find services being delivered differently by the same provider, even in simple things like the layout of forms – is the space for the customer's signature always in the same position? At a basic level, publicity or other printed material needs to use a common style, but more fundamentally the processes themselves need to be similar.

3.   Behind the delivery interface there will be a variety of support services as, for example, where a library operates an acquisitions function supporting its book provision. Without denying the importance of these support functions, it is worth bearing in mind that reducing them to a minimum and increasing the size of the interface will have the most direct effect on the customers. However, reducing support functions too far will have a detrimental effect on quality and customer perception. Design needs to strive for a proper balance.

4.   Because customers have varied demands, and because they vary those demands dynamically, it is desirable to introduce an element of flexibility in delivery. Services should be designed so that staff are free to respond to problems and to go out of their way to put things right when they go wrong. By freeing staff to take individualized actions in response to unexpected situations, any initial poor customer perception can be turned into satisfaction, even delight. So, if the railway company finds that through its own fault a customer has missed the last train home, providing a taxi on the staff's own initiative does not just make up for annoyance and frustration felt by the customer but also leaves an impression of care and concern. Of course the limits to such intervention have to be set in advance, and this itself is part of the design process.

5.   When services are being designed, it is important to consider their total cost and to examine the value that will be provided for that cost. For example, customers would be pleased if there were never a queue for service, but providing enough staff to achieve that would be prohibitively expensive, simply because of the pattern of demand. (Queuing theory enables us to model these effects mathematically.) The issue is therefore to provide an acceptable level of service at reasonable cost. Very often value analysis, coupled with a consideration of the service quality attributes discussed in Chapter 4, can encourage innovative design by finding new ways to deliver service so as to meet customer requirements through innovation rather than by assigning more resources.

SYSTEMATIC PROCESSES

Processes are the means by which organizations turn inputs into outputs and are thus central to any activity which they may undertake. The output of a process is a product, using that term to denote not just physical objects but information, services, paperwork, data, etc. The question of whether a particular process is necessary or is properly designed is an essential aspect of quality management, but so too is the issue of how the process operates.

A large part of management literature and practice is concerned with the improvement of processes. Taken in isolation this can be dangerous, since there is no point in improving a process which is inappropriate in itself or producing a product which is not what the customers want. Yet process improvement is a vital component of the total quality management approach because processes are so central to what the organization does, what it delivers to the customer and how change is handled.

We have already discussed the fact that many quality problems arise because of non-conformance to set standards, a lack of consistency in delivering the expected and promised product or service again and again. Crosby's insistence on getting it right first time is but one example of the emphasis placed on delivering what the customer wants in a systematic and error-free manner. To do this, the organization needs well-designed and consistent processes. A discipline called process management has developed to try to achieve exactly that, and 'business process re-engineering' is something of a growth industry at present. In this section we provide a much abbreviated description of the issues which need to be resolved if processes are to be managed successfully.

The key to improving performance, to getting more things right first time, is not taking corrective action after a product or service has been delivered and found faulty but correcting the process itself. So, if a new car develops a fault in its steering, the manufacturer needs to find out how the fault happened (i.e. how the process allowed it to occur) so that the process can be improved, rather than simply repairing the fault. Bear in mind also the internal customers of the organization. We are not talking purely of processes which affect the end-user directly, but of every process which takes place internally, within the organization.

It is not always easy, in a complex organization, to identify the individual processes which together contribute to total performance and customer satisfaction. One approach, based on a suggestion by Brache and Rummler (1988), is to go systematically through six key questions so as to identify the processes that have the most impact. It is important to approach this from the customer perspective, because the temptation is to analyse and concentrate on processes within sectional boundaries. For example, in a library the customer is not interested in the process whereby a book they order is acquired, processed and made available for loan, only in its eventual availability. The librarian, on the other hand, may be tempted to concentrate on the acquisitions process as it operates within the acquisitions section.

Brache and Rimmler's six questions are:

1. From the customer's viewpoint, which products and services are the most important?
2. How are these products and services produced? In other words, what are the processes?
3. How is customer demand recognized and turned into a product or service? What makes the organization take action?
4. Which processes are most visible to the customers?
5. Which processes have the greatest effect on performance standards, assuming those standards have been related to customer requirements?
6. Which processes do we believe (either because data shows it or just through the application of common sense) have the greatest potential for improvement?

One useful way to think about the management of processes is to use another six-fold approach, advocated by Pall (1987):

1. **Establish ownership.** Determine who in the organization is responsible for designing, operating and improving the process.

2.   **Undertake systematic planning.** Take a structured, systematic approach to the definition and documentation of the process, including all its sub-components and their interrelationships.

3.   **Establish control.** Ensure that every output is predictable and consistent and accords with customers' requirements.

4.   **Perform measurement.** Compare what is actually being produced with the customer requirement. Agree and implement criteria for accuracy, precision and frequency of data collection.

5.   **Introduce improvements.** Identify improvements and embed them permanently in the process itself.

6.   **Pursue the optimal solution.** Examine the efficiency of the process and make permanent changes to improve it.

Clearly, quality system approaches such as ISO 9000 (see Chapter 3) provide a means to identify and manage processes in a systematic way and as such they can provide a major contribution to TQM. The 20 clauses of ISO 9000 help organizations to ensure that processes are identified and documented and that feedback mechanisms are in place to ensure that the processes are changed whenever a non-conformance occurs. The discipline of external audit also helps to ensure that this is seen as a continuous process. However, it is all too easy to treat ISO 9000 as the ultimate goal in itself instead of as a step on the way to continuous improvement and total quality management. Central as process management is, it is not the whole story.

TRAINING AND LEARNING

It has frequently been observed of organizations, especially of those in the service sector, that staff are their most valuable resource. Staff are also probably their greatest single cost. A university, for example, may spend something of the order of 70 per cent of its total budget on staffing. In addition, as we enter the so-called Information Age, staff have become the repository of a second, frequently uncosted and undervalued resource, namely information and skills. From the perspective of any management system, it makes sense to ensure that this scarce and valuable resource is used to maximum effect. Total quality management places great stress on this issue, since it is recognized that the success of the whole organization, particularly its ability to meet the needs of its customers, is dependent on everyone taking responsibility for quality and having the skills to deliver the needed 'products' to their internal and external customers.

One development of considerable interest for TQM, although it arose independently, is the concept of the 'learning company'. The idea behind this concept is that organizations need to go beyond the training of individuals to encompass the whole company as a learning entity. In other words, the organization itself should be capable of learning, of adapting and changing in response to internal and external stimuli, through facilitating the learning of individuals, teams, sections, departments, and ultimately the whole enterprise. Of course organizations themselves cannot think or feel, so what is being suggested is the organization of individual learning in a systematic way that enables the total contribution to be brought to bear on the company's activities in a planned yet dynamic fashion. The learning company concept encompasses the wide view of customers that we described in Chapter 4; that is, all the stakeholders who have an interest in it and its activities.

The term 'learning company' is of relatively recent origin, but the ideas behind it have been around for a long time. Lippitt (1969) wrote of 'organization renewal', and Schon (1971) talked of 'learning systems', while Argyris and Schon (1978) wrote of 'organizational learning'. The concept was described by Peters and Waterman (1982) and more extensively by Garratt (1989), and has been applied in a number of sectors. For example, Attwood and Beer (1988) applied it to the National Health Service. Pedler *et al.* (1988, 1991) have written extensively on the subject and suggest that a learning company has eleven characteristics:

1. **A learning approach to strategy**, so that the process of formulating policies and strategies is itself structured as a learning process.

2. **Participative policy making**, which enables the views and interests of all the stakeholders to be brought into the equation and encourages participation from across the whole organization.

3. **'Informating'**, which means using information throughout the organization to help members understand what is happening, and not for punishment or reward. Information and information technology are thus the 'oil' which enables the organization to move forward its understanding and hence its actions.

4. **Formative accounting and control**, to enable people to learn from financial reports and to adjust their decision making and actions through this learning process. Accountants and financial officers see their role as consultants offering advice rather than 'scorekeepers and bean-counters'.

5. **Internal exchange**, which is a restatement of the quality management principle of internal customers, but emphasizing the need for co-operative relationships between sections.

6. **Reward flexibility**, which encourages openness in reward systems and involvement of staff throughout the organization in the determination of such systems, while the need for different rewards to reflect the different contributions that people make is recognized.

7. **Enabling structures**, for example through seeing appraisal schemes as opportunities for identifying learning and development needs rather than as a mechanism for reward or punishment. Structures and procedures are needed, but they should be reviewed regularly and changed whenever necessary.

8. **Boundary workers as environmental scanners,** so that all staff, but especially those with jobs at the interface between the company and the outside world, see part of their work as bringing information and intelligence back into the organization.

9. **Inter-company learning** could include meetings with competitors as well as with suppliers and customers, to learn and to share ideas, information and developments. Techniques such as benchmarking are used as part of this process.

10.   **A learning climate**, in which mistakes are seen as learning opportunities, and time is set aside to examine and discuss current practice, so as to engage in that other essential of TQM – continuous improvement.

11.   **Self-development opportunities for all**, including the external stake-holders. Everyone is given opportunities, and provided with resources, to undertake self-development.

Although we have described the learning company concept here for convenience, it will be seen that it intersects with TQM at many other points. Hammond and Wille (1994) suggest that the implementation of TQM is in fact identical to the establishment of a learning organization. This perspective reinforces the view that TQM is a holistic approach, where each component interacts with every other, so that just as the customer focus must be all-pervasive, so too learning must be part of the life-blood of every corner of the organization. However, there is a danger in assuming that training is the answer to every problem. Tenner and DeToro (1992) list five frequently used training initiatives that very often do not produce better quality, and the reason is clear enough. The root causes of problems often go way beyond any deficiencies in skills or knowledge on the part of front-line workers: to give but one example, setting up quality teams but at the same time encouraging inter-departmental rivalry is unlikely to produce many positive results no matter how much team-building training goes on. Management must address root causes if training is to be effective.

Strategies for promoting learning and self-development within organizations have been a matter of concern, quite apart from quality management perspectives, for some considerable time. Britain has recognized that it has fallen behind many other countries in the field of vocational training both within and outside companies, and the Confederation of British Industry (1989) published an influential report on the subject, with the Government subsequently introducing a variety of initiatives to try to address the problem. Other countries have recognized similar concerns. The European Union's Social Chapter, from which Britain has opted out, has a requirement that every worker should have access to vocational training throughout his or her working life.

One initiative which is engendering considerable interest is the 'Investors in People' scheme, which is run by Training and Enterprise Councils (TECs) through-out England and Wales and by Local Enterprise Councils in Scotland. Organizations which are deemed to meet the criteria are entitled to use the title 'Investor in People'. The criteria are:

1.   A public commitment from senior management to develop all employees to achieve business objectives.

2.   Regular reviews of the training and development needs of all employees.

3.   Action to train and develop individuals on recruitment and throughout their employment.

4.   Evaluation of investment in training and development to assess achievement and improve future effectiveness.

Companies which apply for the Investors in People standard are assessed by an external expert on behalf of the TEC and must undergo reassessment periodically.

The Government's aim is for half of all companies employing over 250 people to have achieved the standard by 1996. Pluse (1994) has written on its application to libraries.

MONITORING PERFORMANCE

In this chapter we will look in detail at ways in which quality can be measured: techniques such as these form an essential part of performance measurement and of total quality management. In Chapter 12 we will look at performance measurement in libraries and information services, since this is an area where the sector has very considerable experience. The purpose of this section is to provide some background to the subject.

To take practical steps forward in the implementation of quality management it is obviously necessary to be able to measure and assess the level of quality being delivered. The performance of an organization and of its constituent departments and sections needs to be measured to enable it to be managed systematically, both to identify where problems are occurring and to find opportunities for improvement. As we have seen, the data which is needed will be both quantitative and qualitative, since it must inform management of both the number of items or services being delivered and their attributes.

One of the dangers of performance measurement is that it is easy to concentrate on those aspects which are most easily measured rather than on those which are of most importance. One useful counter to this tendency is to derive, from the mission statement, a small number of critical success factors, carefully chosen to accord with customer requirements, which can serve as a means of assessing overall performance and how that performance is changing over time. As we will see in Chapter 13, libraries and information services have had a tendency to 'measure the measurable' in the past, with a vast amount of information collected on numerical counts of expenditure and book issues and very little on the friendliness of staff or the attractiveness and cleanliness of the premises. This is a question we return to in Chapter 13 when considering recent work on measuring the performance of libraries.

Clearly, a balance is needed. Quantitative data is important, especially in identifying trends over time and drawing attention to areas where management intervention is needed to resolve problems. Quality management demands an holistic approach, however, and it is achieving the proper balance between quantitative and qualitative measures which provides the greatest challenge to managers.

Since quality consists of meeting customer requirements it is fairly obvious that unless the extent to which the goods or services being produced actually meet those requirements can be measured it will be impossible to know whether quality is being improved, and still more difficult to make changes which will lead to systematic improvements. In general, it is useful to split performance measurement into three types, following the systems model (see Chapter 11):

1.   **Process measures**, which provide information on the internal processes of the organization, both those which deliver to internal customers and those which produce outputs for external customers.

2.   **Output measures**, which are concerned with the number and character-
     istics of the goods or services which the organization produces for external
     and internal customers.
3.   **Outcome measures**, of which the principle one is customer satisfaction,
     which provide information on the impact of the product or service on the
     customer. Both outcome and output measures need to be compared with
     measures of customer requirements.

The principle use of process measures is to control the processes which are used
to produce outputs. To achieve this it is necessary to measure the characteristics of
raw materials and other inputs received from suppliers as well as the behaviour
of the process itself. The principle users of these measures should be the people
who are responsible for the processes at each stage. In other words, what is
measured is those characteristics, and only those characteristics, needed to enable
control to be exercised and predetermined standards to be achieved.

Output measures are used to compare the characteristics of every product or
service delivered to the customer with the customer's requirements. Note that this
presupposes that those requirements are known, i.e. that a series of target values
has been established against which the comparison can be made. Outcome
measures are concerned with the impact the product or service has on the
customer and the extent to which that impact meets the requirements which the
customer had.

Data collection

There are a number of useful texts available to guide librarians and information
scientists in the collection of data to support managerial activity (e.g. Simpson,
1990; Lancaster, 1993a; Slater, 1990; Swisher and McClure, 1984) as well as many
general works in the field of statistical methods. It is beyond the scope of this book
to describe data collection techniques in detail. However, some general rules may
be helpful:

1.   It is important to determine the precise objective of the data collection
     exercise *before* the process is designed and implemented. A great deal of
     time can be wasted in collecting data which are either irrelevant to the key
     questions being asked or for which no precise question has been posed.
2.   The data collected must relate to the problem or process being examined
     and not simply be the data which it is easiest to collect. For example,
     librarians interested in library use should not simply collect data on the
     number of books issued. This is the issue of *validity*, and demands that
     attention be paid to whether the data really relate to the problem in hand.
3.   The methodology should be selected to be appropriate to the data
     collection exercise. The texts mentioned above, and the manuals
     described in Chapter 12, contain introductions to methodologies which
     those new to this work will find useful.
4.   Samples should be chosen carefully and in such a way that any possible
     bias is minimized. The population being examined needs to be specified
     and then a suitable sample determined. The sample is chosen to provide

results which provide an acceptable level of accuracy and reliability, but in as economical a fashion as possible. For example, one would not wish to interview every potential user of a library to determine what perceptions of the service are held. Equally, too small a sample, or one representative of only certain groups of users (such as the active users), could provide unrepresentative results which would be open to misinterpretation. Note that real data are almost never 100 per cent reliable: the real issue is whether the data are sufficiently reliable and accurate for the purpose. Again, texts on this subject should be consulted for guidance.

5.   The results of the data collection exercise should be analysed and presented in an easily understood form, e.g. as a histogram or pie-chart rather than as a bare table of figures. Again, the presentation chosen should be appropriate to the purpose and also to the people who will use it. Most PC-based software packages, such as Lotus 1-2-3 or Microsoft Excel, contain excellent presentation facilities.

6.   The history of the data collection exercise should also be recorded. The '5W1H' rule is a useful reminder. Record:

- O   what data was collected;
- O   why it was collected;
- O   when it was collected;
- O   who collected it;
- O   where it was collected;
- O   how it was collected.

This is particularly important if the data collection is likely to be repeated at intervals so as to build up a picture of changes over time.

Statistical process control

The term statistical process control (SPC) is used to describe a group of statistical techniques which can be applied to processes in order to monitor variability and so provide information on which to base quality improvement activities. Although it has its origins in manufacturing industry (see Chapter 2 and especially the work of Deming) SPC can be applied to any process, including those in services. For example, it has been used to help understand and control variability in queue lengths and in the time taken to answer telephone calls. The key concepts behind SPC are 'special' and 'common' variability (again, see Chapter 2) and the aim is to eliminate special variability, i.e. that variability which arises from specific events, such as a malfunctioning machine, and reduce to a minimum common variability, i.e. variability which is inherent in the process. The latter is said to represent 85 per cent of the causes of variability (see, for example, Edge, 1990) and is the clear responsibility of management.

Many SPC techniques will be known to library and information service professionals since they include the use of histograms and scatter diagrams, for example, but others are associated particularly with SPC and may not be so familiar, including Pareto analysis, capability analysis and control charts. In this section we describe some of these tools, although the field is complex and interested readers should consult standard textbooks of the field for further, more detailed information (e.g. Lock and Smith, 1990; Ozeki and Asaka, 1990).

Pareto analysis. Vilfredo Pareto was a nineteenth-century engineer and economist who examined the distribution of income and wealth in his native Italy. Because of his engineering background he had had an excellent training in mathematics, and was particularly interested in describing his findings in statistical terms. He discovered that 20 per cent of the population owned a very high proportion – over 80 per cent – of the wealth. He then showed how this distribution could be expressed as a cumulative curve which became known as Pareto's law.

Much later the importance of this law became apparent when statisticians looked at the value of the inventories held by large manufacturers. Again it appeared that about 80 per cent of the total inventory value was represented by only 20 per cent of inventory items. Conversely, the remaining 80 per cent of items represented only 20 per cent of the value. Gradually a number of other examples occurred in a wide variety of organizations and systems. Eighty per cent of a shop's business takes place in 20% of its opening times. 80% of problems in schools are caused by 20 per cent of the pupils. Eighty per cent of demand for books in a bookshop is concentrated on 20 per cent of the titles. The Pareto law or principle can be depicted graphically by plotting the activity along the horizontal axis and the cumulative percentage of occurrences along the vertical axis. Figure 7.2 shows a histogram and resulting cumulative distribution relating to the causes of vehicle breakdowns, illustrating how Pareto analysis can help to identify where action might best be concentrated. For a very wide range of phenomena, around 80 per cent of the occurrences will be generated by only about 20 per cent of the activities

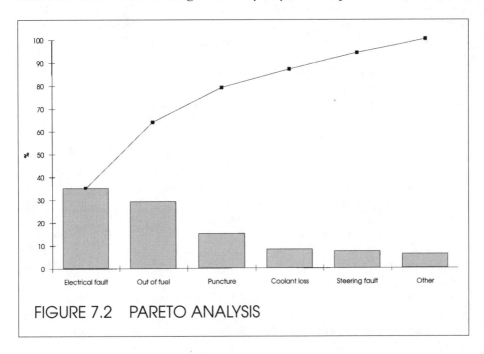

FIGURE 7.2   PARETO ANALYSIS

or events. The percentages are not exact, but they are remarkably stable within a small range.

For libraries and information services the applications and implications of the Pareto principle are considerable. Eighty per cent of users will arrive in 20 per cent of opening hours. Eighty per cent of demand will be concentrated on 20 per cent of the stock. As in other fields, attempts to reduce the unused parts of the opening hours or stock do not appear to result in significantly different distribution. Academic libraries' short loan collections, for example, despite being selected to contain only items in very heavy demand, seem to obey the Pareto principle.

More generally, the Pareto principle has been widely applied in quality management through the recognition that a small proportion of defects will generate a high proportion of the quality losses. Clearly, if effort is concentrated on the key 20 per cent, more may be achieved than if efforts are spread across all problems.

The graphical Pareto diagram can be used to perform an analysis of the quality problems which are being encountered. Histograms of problem areas can be drawn to identify where effort might most profitably be concentrated. Take, for example, reasons for library users being unable to find the books they need, which range from the items being out on loan and not in stock, through inability of users to find them, to mis-shelving, and so on. As an illustration from the library and information service field, Figure 7.3 shows how a graphical representation of this data can be used to identify the key areas for attention.

Control charts. Control charts are a powerful tool for identifying when and where problems due to special variability are occurring and thereby enabling action to be concentrated where it will be most valuable. One advantage of this approach is that it avoids the need for complex statistical calculations and can be applied quickly by middle managers to track the processes for which they are responsible, provided they have some fairly basic understanding of statistical concepts such as averages, range, variation, the normal distribution and standard deviations.

Figure 7.4 shows the simplest form of control chart with the upper control limit and lower control limit marked, as well as the expected mean. As each sample is taken and marked on the chart, it is immediately obvious if any point on the control chart is outside the control limits. (These are the maximum and minimum values permitted by the specification.) Care also needs to be taken to check over time that the process is not departing from the expected mean despite being within the control limits, for example by being always marginally below the centre line. Equally, the control chart can reveal a trend whereby the mean is shifting over time, and this can give advance warning of an impending problem. In a manufacturing example, it might show that a machine setting was drifting away from its acceptable tolerances. Finally, control charts sometimes reveal that data points have a wave form, that is, that the results rise and fall regularly over time. This could, for example, demonstrate the length of a queue varying during the day, or from month to month.

It is often useful to stratify the data used in control charts so as to remove known dissimilarities and reveal hidden variability. For example, a manufacturer who receives supposedly identical raw materials from two different sources may want to

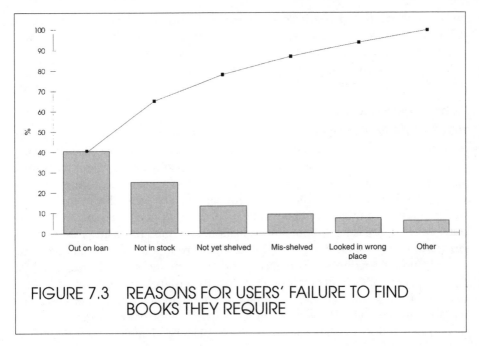

FIGURE 7.3   REASONS FOR USERS' FAILURE TO FIND
BOOKS THEY REQUIRE

stratify production data by material source so as to identify whether variability might be due to problems with the materials supplied. Supermarkets commonly stratify data on check-out throughput so as to identify problems with individual check-outs or operators, while libraries might want to stratify data by branch, or by type of user.

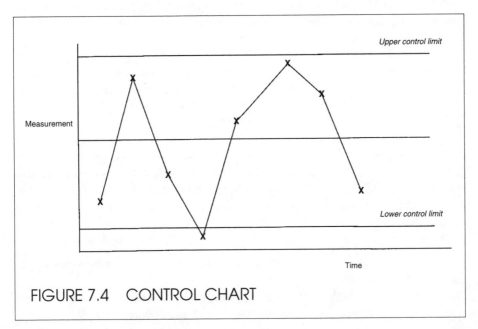

FIGURE 7.4   CONTROL CHART

Although control charts have not been widely reported as being in use in libraries, there are some known examples, for instance in the management of the acquisition of books, where a control chart can reveal whether unexpected variations in delivery and processing times are occurring. Again, stratification may be appropriate, for example to exclude donated material which has very low priority.

Problem-solving techniques

Brainstorming. Among various techniques for solving problems and generating new ideas, brainstorming is perhaps one of the best known. Because of TQM's emphasis on teamwork it has been used in many quality management initiatives, and can be helpful not only in generating ideas but as a team-building exercise. Its essence lies in bringing together a group of participants, preferably from different backgrounds, in a non-threatening atmosphere. Everyone is then encouraged to put forward their ideas, without any evaluation, and outrageous ideas are particularly encouraged. All ideas are recorded by the facilitator, again without comment or evaluation. Everyone is encouraged to build on the ideas already suggested by the group. Only at the end of this process does the group start to evaluate the ideas that have been thrown up. Again, though, this evaluation has to be non-threatening, and this is usually achieved by getting all participants to list the ideas they find most useful. In this way innovatory approaches can be identified. Later the group will concentrate on two or three possibilities which look promising and carry out more formal development and evaluation of these.

Fishbone diagrams. The fishbone diagram, also known as the cause and effect (C&E) diagram or the Ishikawa diagram after Kaoru Ishikawa who invented it, is used to help to separate causes from effects. For quality management this is important, since a great deal of wasted effort can be expended on trying to correct effects without addressing the underlying causes.

Figure 7.5 is a partially completed fishbone diagram which could be used to isolate the causes of low library use. The problem which has been identified is written on the right-hand side of the diagram. Categories of contributing causes are given at the end of each branch, and the causes themselves are written on sub-branches.

There are no hard-and-fast rules on categorizing causes and the analysis will depend on the circumstances. Where it is not clear how to categorize, it can be helpful to adopt a standard set of headings, such as '5Ps: People, Place, Price, Promotion, Product' or 5Ms: Methods, Machinery, Material, Maintenance, Manpower (sic)'. Usually these headings can be retitled quickly to suit the particular organization's interests and emphases once a start has been made on drawing the diagram.

There are some key rules to observe when using the fishbone diagram:

1.   It is essential to ensure that the problem is satisfactorily defined and is not itself a cause.
2.   Causes should be analysed as far back down the chain as possible: the aim is to identify root causes of problems, not intermediate causes.

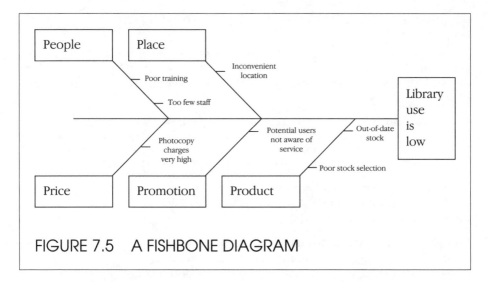

FIGURE 7.5   A FISHBONE DIAGRAM

3.   The temptation to list symptoms and problems rather than causes must be resisted.

4.   The diagram may become too large if there are very many possible causes. In such cases it may be necessary to concentrate on what appear to be key issues.

Fishbone diagrams are particularly useful for group work and can be used alongside brainstorming to provide structure to problem analysis in teams. Another method which is sometimes used is to display the partially completed diagram in the workplace and invite all staff to add causes and emphases as they occur to them.

Measuring customer satisfaction

The whole of quality management is based on the concept of satisfying customers' requirements, remembering that our definition of 'customer' is a broad one, encompassing all stakeholders, and that requirements are those which we have negotiated to meet rather than every possible need and want. It is obvious, therefore, that the measurement of customer satisfaction must be central to all attempts to implement and use quality management systems. It is particularly important that the measurement of customer satisfaction should be an active, rather than a passive, process. In other words, the organization must make efforts to investigate the satisfaction and dissatisfaction of its customers and potential customers and not simply rely on the input received from the customers as a matter of course. For example, the Ford Motor Company in America discovered that for every customer who made a complaint about a car they had bought there would be an average of six others who had experienced similar problems but who had not bothered to complain. Worse still, each of those seven dissatisfied customers would tell six other people about the problem they had experienced. As a result, for every problem brought to the company's attention, no less than 42 dissatisfied customers or potential customers would have been created. This has become known as Factor 42. All companies can ask themselves, 'How many dissatisfied customers and lost would-be customers does this complaint represent?' – 'What is our Factor X?'

The problem of customers who do not complain can be compounded where one group of stakeholders is perceived as being more powerful than another. Green (1990), in an interesting analysis of the concept of library user need, remarks of university libraries:

> A situation in which well-organised and articulate faculty members ventilate their own demands at frequent intervals, while the less confident voices of scattered undergraduates are heard only rarely, is all too likely to lead to attention and resources being devoted to the former at the expense of the latter.

Techniques for measuring customer satisfaction can be grouped under three headings: complaints and suggestions; routine feedback; and proactive research, each of which is described below.

Complaints and suggestions. While bearing in mind the criticisms above, complaints and suggestion schemes can form a useful *part* of any organization's strategy for assessing customer satisfaction. Complaints may be received through a formal complaints mechanism, although most companies would prefer to label such systems as suggestion schemes, and these may apply to both internal and external customers (usually through separate schemes). In addition, complaints may be received informally, for example at service points, and mechanisms should be put in place to record these (interestingly, this is one of the requirements of ISO 9000). Complaints may also be received in writing, at many different levels of the organization. It is important that *all* complaints are considered together and that the temptation to analyse only those received through formal channels should be resisted. Many customers are unwilling to submit a complaint in writing, partly because they may not want to risk being identified and partly because they may feel that the complaint is too trivial to commit to paper. However, as we have seen, many apparently trivial issues are the very matters which can turn satisfaction into dissatisfaction or, more positively, turn satisfaction into delight.

Internal suggestion schemes have proved extremely successful in many industrial companies. Cusumano (1985) reported on the operation of Toyota's employee suggestion scheme and found that during the 1950s and 1960s the company received an average of one suggestion per person per annum. Then in the 1970s the company linked its suggestion scheme to the newly-introduced quality circles, and found that the number of suggestions rose dramatically to over 30 per person per annum by the mid 1980s. Even more interesting was the observation that the percentage of those suggestions which were adopted by Toyota actually increased during this period. Tenner and DeToro (1992) suggest that four issues need to be addressed if an employee suggestion scheme is to be successful. Employees need to be 'aligned' with the company's objectives, so that suggestions are relevant to attaining those objectives; suggestions need to be implemented with the minimum of analysis and debate, since acceptance of a suggestion is a strong motivator to encourage yet more helpful suggestions; there needs to be some kind of linked reward system; and the performance of the suggestion scheme needs to be monitored and publicized.

Routine feedback. Within a service there are frequent opportunities for gaining feedback on customer satisfaction from the routine encounters which take place between staff and customers. Complaints are dealt with above, but a richer understanding can be gained by implementing ways of 'active listening' to customers by staff, and active listening to staff by managers. Obvious areas where this process can be put into effect include help-lines for purchasers of software or users of online services, reception desks in offices, enquiry and service desks in libraries and comments made to sales staff. Like all other aspects of quality management, staff need to be trained to undertake this work, and mechanisms are needed to ensure that the feedback received can be fed into the management system and used to effect planning and action.

Proactive research. All organizations need to go beyond the first two stages and undertake planned, systematic activities to gain a fuller understanding of customer satisfaction. Usually this will involve asking the customers and potential customers about their perceptions, expectations and experiences. We have already noted some methodologies which can be used to achieve this, including questionnaires, telephone surveys, focus groups and more specialized methodologies such as Zeithaml *et al.*'s (1990) SERVQUAL system. Two other methodologies, based on modelling or replicating users' experiences, may also be mentioned here.

The 'walk-through audit' (Rowley, 1994) is a technique of potential application to libraries and information services which seeks to replicate the experience of customers in using a service. The idea is to try to identify a typical visit and all that it entails, and then for the manager or someone else to go through that experience stage by stage noting the ease or difficulty each step presents. So a visit to a library to borrow a book might start with finding somewhere to park the car, negotiating the entrance with a toddler, trying to find the location of books on the subject in question, looking for a photocopier, trying to get change to use the photocopier, queuing up to borrow a book, and so on. For each activity a checklist, or 'design frame', of standard questions can be used.

A related technique is known as 'mystery shopping', although it could equally well be adapted as a mystery library user technique. The mystery shopper is employed, often through a specialist independent company, to pretend to be using the facilities being surveyed, acting in exactly the same way as a person genuinely going shopping, or whatever. For example, the technique is used by some brewers to check on the customer experience in their pubs. The issues covered include the cleanliness and appropriateness of the pub itself but also include assessment of a typical customer's experience of being served. One particularly interesting facet is the measurement of how long it takes to be served at the bar, with a sub-measurement of how long it takes for the staff to make eye contact with the customer. This last measure is based on the observation that customer satisfaction is strongly linked to having one's presence acknowledged (perhaps, but not necessarily, with a brief 'I'll be with you in ten seconds, sir') rather than to the absolute length of time that one has to wait. An equivalent finding could be applied to libraries, information centres and other services. Both these techniques, of course, can be applied successfully only if the model being followed closely maps real customer experiences and is not simply based on the imaginings, or professional judgement, of service deliverers.

It is not always recognized that measurement itself is but a part of management. Measuring processes, outputs and outcomes is all very interesting but unless it leads to purposive action it is wasted. It is surprising how often statistics are collected by organizations but never used – this is yet another example of unnecessary costs being incurred in producing products and services. Again, then, performance measurement must be seen as merely a part of the whole total quality effort.

BENCHMARKING: 'TO BE THE BEST'

One of the ways in which companies which have achieved a certain threshold of quality management seek to improve is by looking around them, both at their competitors and at companies in other sectors with whom they feel they may have some affinity, and examining in detail what it is that makes those companies good. Benchmarking, as this process of comparison is called, is really no more than the systematic sharing of good practice – and good ideas – with the ultimate aim of becoming the department, team or organization against which everyone else wants to benchmark.

Benchmarking provides a means of comparison between processes or activities and is usually used for comparing an organization's own standards and capabilities with those of rivals in the same field of business. It can be internal and carried out between similar departments, sections or divisions in order to identify the most efficient way of working and to improve standards throughout the organization. Alternatively internal benchmarking can be carried out over time to find out if service is declining, staying the same or improving. Benchmarking against the competition may be thought to have little in common with the library world, but library and information services are increasingly facing competition from rivals. Other libraries, bookshops, video stores and other leisure outlets, for example, can all be seen as competing for the library user's custom. Best practice benchmarking is another option, whereby the leaders set the standard, whatever their particular business: so libraries might examine Marks & Spencer, for example, regardless of the differences between the organizations' businesses.

Why benchmark?

Benchmarking measures an organization's operations, products and services against those of competitors in a ruthless fashion. It is a means by which targets, priorities and operations can be established that will lead to improvement or to competitive advantage. This does not necessarily mean that the organization is providing a poor service, just that the service could be better. The benchmarking concept requires every part of a company to benchmark itself externally against the best competitor companies or internally within divisions of the same company, with the aims of meeting organizational goals and increasing customer satisfaction. Benchmarking encourages the organization to look outwards, at other divisions and at other companies, and to focus on the user as customer. Although benchmarking is often used as a competitive tool, it is thus the customer who benefits.

A typology of benchmarking

A useful text on this subject (Camp, 1989) suggests that there are four different types of benchmarking:

1. **Internal benchmarking.** Often used within large organizations such as multinationals to compare the performance of one division or department against others. One of the advantages of internal benchmarking is that many of the variables, such as the way in which results are reported, can be controlled.

2. **Competitive benchmarking.** One of the most common forms of benchmarking, where a company seeks out information on its successful direct competitors' activities in order to identify how quality is being achieved. Not surprisingly, it can be difficult to obtain this information in a commercial environment. In a public service setting, such as that within which many libraries and information services operate, information may be shared much more readily.

3. **Functional benchmarking.** Here, a deliberate decision is made to target companies in dissimilar fields to see how a particular function is carried out elsewhere. So one company might identify financial control as an area for attention and seek to overtake its immediate competitors by importing ideas from a totally different sector. At least one academic library has tried 'just-in-time' techniques for book purchasing, borrowing the techniques from industry.

4. **Generic benchmarking.** In this case the idea is to go beyond particular functions and to identify the ways in which other companies, which may or may not be in a totally different industry, carry out their business. Generic benchmarking requires a broad vision, but it might, for example, be used to identify how the concept of 'flat' management structures can be applied in practice. Undoubtedly it is the most difficult form of benchmarking to accomplish successfully.

Benchmarking practice

The practice of benchmarking, although relatively new, is now well established. One methodology that has been widely adopted is known as the 'benchmarking wheel' and consists of five stages (see Figure 7.6).

1. **Plan.** The first step is to select an activity that would benefit the organization by improvement – keeping the user in mind. Priorities are set according to user priorities, not by what the organization thinks should be improved. Managers need to ensure that the activity selected will fit in with the overall service standard since it is of little use improving one minor aspect of the service if this would have a detrimental effect on other areas which would be of more importance to the user. At this stage it is useful to define why the activity chosen is important, in terms of improved service or its impact on the service.

    The planning stage should include an analysis of the activity so that as much as possible is known about it and about how it performs in relation

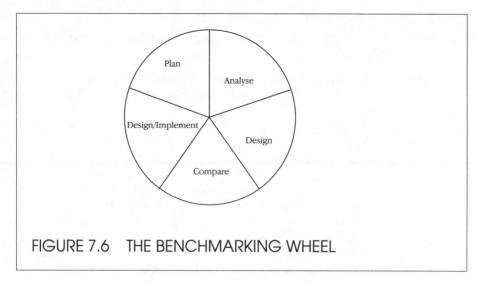

FIGURE 7.6   THE BENCHMARKING WHEEL

to other activities and there is clarity about what is needed to improve customer satisfaction. The scope and boundaries of the benchmarking activity can then be set to ensure that ensuing activity is sharply focused.

2.   **Analyse the process.** Next it is necessary to select what can be measured, i.e. the performance indicators which are to be used. A flow chart of the process should be prepared, providing a breakdown of each major activity into its components.

During this step a team, and a team leader with the skills and knowledge required, will be selected. It is far better to train and empower the organization's own staff, provided those with the necessary background can be found, rather than impose senior staff or people from outside.

The team can then break down the factors which influence the activity using Ishikawa or fishbone diagrams (see above) and then identify how supporting operations affect the overall activity using key performance indicators. It is important to cut out minor routines so that only the most important activities are addressed. It is all too easy to become bogged down in minor details or overwhelmed with a mass of information of marginal value.

3.   **Design the study and gather information.** In the third stage the team identifies organizations or departments as the benchmarking targets; these can be leaders, rivals or partners who are also aiming to improve practice. The benchmarking candidates need to be shortlisted to no more than three or four organizations, otherwise again the task will become too extensive. As part of the design the team should prepare questions to be asked in the three key areas: general organizational issues; process-related issues; and quantitative indicators. In addition, it is wise to gather as much background information as possible about each of the organizations to be benchmarked so that time is not wasted on unnecessary preliminaries, and to enable the questions to be refined.

4. **Compare performance.** For each of the organizations chosen the team compares targets with achievements of the organization and asks how its own organization compares. Flowcharts and fishbone diagrams of the topic as viewed by each of the organizations being studied are prepared, with particular attention to identifying the inputs that they use. Comparison of the sets of flowcharts and fishbone diagrams enables the team to identify the most important factors.

   Finally, the team can use the information gleaned from these analyses to compare the performance of each organization and to identify how their own organization is performing in comparison with the others. The gaps between its performance and that of the other organizations can now be determined.

5. **Design and implement improved activity.** The team, having analysed the data and identified the differences between the organizations, can now decide what is required to close the gaps by more effective operation (not by expecting staff simply to work harder!). The aim now must be to identify actions which will enable the organisation to perform better than the others - to become the benchmark leaders.

The final task for the benchmarking team is to prepare an improvement plan and submit it to management for approval. It is important that management then takes action.

The benchmarking wheel can then start to turn again, since benchmarking needs to be seen as a continuous activity. It is never possible to rest on laurels gained through earlier quality improvement actions, because both the world and the competition will have moved on. So the process of planning the next benchmarking exercise can begin.

SUPPLIER AWARENESS

No organization exists in a vacuum; all have external customers and suppliers and all operate in a social and cultural environment. Although quality management rightly emphasizes the key issue of meeting customer requirements, service industries in particular tend to be highly dependent in the quality of the goods and services which they themselves acquire. Libraries and information services are particularly vulnerable to this problem, since they rarely create information resources themselves but instead rely almost exclusively on information supplied in one form or another by others. The quality of information in books and journals, and even more so that in electronic media, is very difficult to control. Yet customer perceptions of the services as a whole may be greatly affected by any inaccuracies or other failures in the information supplied.

Libraries also suffer from having limited control over their suppliers. While *en masse* they may form the major market for a particular book or journal, acting individually they have very little influence over what is published and only limited ability to affect its quality through selective purchasing. Unlike major manufacturers in the electronics, automobile or furniture industries, who may be able to control their suppliers by threat of withdrawing orders and possibly forcing them into receivership, few individual libraries have the power to force suppliers to change their products.

Of course, there is some influence which can be brought to bear. By and large libraries purchase books and journals through agents rather than direct from publishers, and there is certainly competition between agents for library supply contracts. Furthermore, while the existence of retail price maintenance may have removed price competition, supplier assessment may still focus on quality issues such as speed of supply, accuracy and added value.

Going beyond competitive issues, the emphasis within a TQM culture is increasingly placed less on encouraging competition between suppliers and much more on the development of positive partnerships with suppliers. The belief behind this shift is that confrontational relationships with suppliers will destroy the basis on which quality can be developed in exactly the same way that confrontation between staff and departments inside the organization does. The satisfaction of the final customer is in the interest of both the organization and its suppliers, and a partnership offers the way to move quality forward.

The 1994 *Management Today* Best Small Company Award illustrates the benefits of co-operative relationships between organizations and their suppliers. Kitchen Range, based in Peterborough, supplies doughnuts and fruit pies to McDonald's restaurants throughout Europe, in other words to a fast-food company known for its obsessive attention to standardization. Yet the two companies work together without even a formal contract. 'Close liaison and mutual dependence, plus occasional "suggestions" from McDonald's are what keep the relationship going' (Wheatley and New, 1994).

In industry similar changes are becoming commonplace. Ford of Europe, for example, has moved from 'supplier quality assurance' to 'supplier quality assistance' and encourages its suppliers to participate in Ford's own quality improvement teams. There is evidence (for example, Masson, 1986) that companies which take this partnership approach with their suppliers experience measurable benefits, including fewer non-conforming supplied products, more reliable delivery times, shorter lead times and faster attention to changes in specification and design.

The co-operative approach is finding expression in the library and information service sector through the activities of the Centre for Information Quality Management (CIQM), an agency set up by the UK Library Association and UK Online User Group (UKOLUG) to enable users to report any problems they encounter when using commercially produced databases. These comments are forwarded to the publisher, supplier or host as appropriate and the centre then acts as a communications channel for any response (Armstrong, 1994a). The issue of service providers' possible liability for quality failures in such products has been addressed in a guidance note by the Library Association, which includes the warning:

> Information workers should be aware of the possibility that they could be held responsible in the event of inaccurate or incomplete information being provided from an online or CD-ROM database. At worst this could even lead to action for damages. It is instructive to note that most suppliers of CD-ROMs and online hosts have taken the precaution of including liability exclusion clauses in their

contracts, thus making it appear difficult to take action against them. (Library Association, 1994)

It has been reported that 'many of the problems reported to the CIQM team stem from a basic gap between user expectations and the real-world database as experienced at the workstation' (Armstrong, 1994b). From a quality management perspective this is an interesting finding, because it confirms that the basic problems are occurring at the customer interface through a failure to match products with customer requirements. It is of course debatable as to where the problem really lies. Does the customer have unrealistic expectations, as for example when his equipment is unsuited to use a complex database yet he presses ahead anyway? Was another customer misled when she read the product description and decided to purchase the database? Does the system do what it claims to do, and are those claims expressed in language which is incomprehensible to the typical customer? Armstrong reports that one suggestion is that we should move to 'labelling databases in much the same way that food or drugs are labelled ... the label would be attached to the publicity material rather than to the product itself and the factual elements would have to go beyond listing the database contents to include qualitative information'. In this way there would be a clear 'agreement' on what the customer could reasonably expect and efforts could be concentrated on ensuring that these expectations were met.

Minkoff (1993) reports on an approach taken by Datastream to the problem of erroneous data being found on the database: 'Customers of Datastream have got a "Data Guarantee". Any customer who spots an error on our database will get £10 for every fault found. If they find 100 at a time they get £1000. We pay out even if it is our supplier's fault because we think we should have spotted it. We are adding value to data coming in. No matter how good the suppliers think they are, our quality activity starts where theirs leaves off.'

RESOURCES AND COSTS

It would be specious to argue that levels of resourcing have no effect on the service which can be offered. Particularly in publicly funded services with elastic demand, such as most libraries and information services, the resource inputs will considerably affect the ability of the service to deliver the range of products which customers would ideally like. As we have noted, where there is no direct price charged to the users, as for example with students and an academic library, or where the price being paid is hidden among a broader charge, as with local taxpayers using public libraries, the market mechanism is weak and it is difficult for customers to know what they can legitimately expect to be provided. A clear definition of the service to be offered, agreed with the various stakeholders, therefore becomes essential. In some circumstances it may be appropriate to introduce charging or purchasing mechanisms to create a market. Some academic libraries are now funded by 'contributions' from the academic departments they serve, related to the service being offered.

However, if we accept that the resource base itself will affect the type and extent of services offered, there still remains the issue of reducing the cost of quality so as to ensure that all available resources are being targeted on the delivery of quality services to the external customer or end-user. These costs can best be thought of as leakage of resources away from service delivery, rather like the leakage from a mains service pipe reducing the water available at the tap in your house. The cost of quality can be characterized as:

○ **The cost of prevention.** Consists of the processes and actions taken to prevent mistakes and failures happening. A simple example would be a piece of software which demands the operator confirms an action before it is allowed to go ahead. No matter how desirable such a step might be, and no matter how small its actual cost, it does nothing more than prevent mistakes being made and does not of itself contribute to the end product or service. Note that this is not an argument for removing such routines, merely a recognition that some things which we do quite legitimately entail non-productive costs. Equally, a considerable amount of staff train-ing will be concerned with preventing error, and as such comes under the heading of a cost of quality. Preventative action is an important part of quality management, since one of the ground rules of TQM is that action is taken to improve processes rather than fire-fighting causes of errors and failures. But again, important as preventative management is, it does not directly add value to the end product.

○ **The cost of assessment, audit and appraisal.** Involves costs incurred in checking to ensure that quality standards are being met. Systems are put in place to inspect products, to check on conformance to the specification, to audit compliance, to survey customer satisfaction, and so on. Again, none of these add directly to the value of the service itself, essential as they may be to the achievement of quality. Clearly, like all quality costs, they need to be kept to a minimum. There is a lesson here for UK higher education which, by late 1994, was operating at least five separate systems of quality appraisal – all, incidentally, involving input from university library staff. Subject assessment by the Higher Education Funding Councils, insti-tutional process audit by the Higher Education Quality Council, research assessment by the Higher Education Funding Councils again, an external examiner system attached to every individual course of study, on top of lengthy internal university quality assurance processes, all backed up by endless poorly targeted surveys and league tables, whose relevance to customer service is tenuous at best, were all in place. This kind of approach to quality, and neglect of the costs of quality, would long ago have driven any commercial organization out of business.

○ **The cost of internal failure.** Consists of all those actions which take place within the organization before delivery to the customer which result in wasted work. In an industrial organization, for example, this would include the cost of scrapping components which failed to meet specification, the cost of reworking where that is possible, the cost of changes in specification or design which are introduced during the process. There is the infamous example, reported in 1988, of the nuclear-powered submarine being built at

Vickers Shipbuilding at Barrow-in-Furness in Cumbria which had a section of its hull welded into place upside-down (quoted in Bank, 1992). In libraries and information services, costs of internal failure would include the cost of reworking incorrect or incomplete catalogue records and the cost of reshelving books put back out of sequence (although the latter will also have an external failure cost, see below).

○ **The cost of external failure.** These tend to receive most attention because they consist of the costs incurred when the external customer is dissatisfied with a product or service. Again, manufacturing industry has shown most awareness of these costs. For example, car manufacturers have become aware of the cost of shipping defective products which then result in extensive warranty claims. In a library or information service these costs are not always obvious, partly because we do not accept warranty claims! In this there is much in common between services: we expect a car, or a hairdryer or a toaster to come complete with a written guarantee, and we expect to make use of that guarantee if things go wrong. Indeed, there is the concept of 'merchantable quality' should a warranty be non-existent or so worded as to disadvantage the customer. Yet we rarely expect a public service to provide a similar guarantee. This is starting to change, however, for example through the *Citizen's Charter* (see Chapter 6) so that under certain, very tightly defined, circumstances passengers can get a partial refund if British Rail's trains frequently run late. However, it is worth asking whether one reason that libraries do not recognize external quality costs is simply that we do not define precisely enough what the customer can expect in such a way that failure can be measured.

○ **The cost of exceeding customer requirements.** These occur when the product or service goes beyond what the customer needs or wants. There was the telecommunications company which put all its efforts into ensuring that subscribers' time was minimized (i.e. the time taken to get a dialling tone, the time taken to connect a call when a number was dialled, and so on) and then discovered that customers were not really concerned with that issue, provided performance was within reasonable limits, but were much more concerned with getting a clear line without interference. So the cost of reducing performance measures related to time to an absolute minimum was a waste, especially as those costs could have been directed to the issue that really concerned customers and which might give the company a competitive advantage through delivering quality – defined again as meeting the customers' requirements.

○ **The cost of lost opportunities.** Consists of failure to attract new customers or to deliver new products and services to existing customers or the loss of the customer base to competitors through quality failures. A classic example of this comes from the 'fast fit' car repair trade. Customers discover that they need a new exhaust for their car at short notice and typically ring round garages in the neighbourhood to find a supplier. Price will be a factor, but very often the key issue will be availability. The company which can quote a price, is equipped to do the job, has a good reputation, but does not have the right part available instantly from stock will probably lose the business. This is a quality cost (failure to meet customer requirements) and is categorized as a lost opportunity. Again, in libraries and information services these costs are not usually identified. Many publicly funded services are almost overwhelmed by customers anyway, so in the short term the lost opportunities do not seem particularly relevant. But this is a slippery slope which has led many an organization into oblivion. If, for example, public libraries were to lose customers who borrow nothing but videos, and it transpires that video and electronic multimedia books take over a high proportion of what was public library business, will failure to cultivate this customer base be seen in years to come as a lost opportunity? Equally, if academic libraries decide that their business is books, and let someone else worry about delivering online services, will their business decline as customers' requirements are met elsewhere?

There are standard techniques available for assessing the costs of activities in organizations which are as applicable in a TQM environment as in any other. Publications relevant to the information and library field include Roberts (1985) and Office of Arts & Libraries (1987), although they do not refer directly to the costs of quality. Texts on TQM (see, for example, Bank, 1992, and Tenner and DeToro, 1992) cover quality costs more explicitly.

TQM IN PRACTICE

There are many examples to be found of successful applications of TQM and of partial applications which have used, with benefit, techniques derived from the overall approach. Oakland and Porter (1994) provide some useful case studies of TQM implementations in a variety of industries, including:

○ the former NFC (National Freight Carriers), now known as Lynx, where action was taken to change the corporate culture to ensure that the right parcels were being delivered to the right address at the right time – cheerful service was not enough;

○ the Life Administration Home Service Division of the Prudential Assurance Company, including actions taken to measure customer satisfaction – of both internal and external customers;

○ the Esso Research Centre: the problem of TQM implementation in a research and development environment, where many of the measures are 'soft';

○ the Management Centre of the University of Bradford, where Oakland and Porter are based, which itself introduced TQM. A quality council, process quality teams and quality action teams were formed to work on the implementation, and all staff took part in a series of workshops designed not only to increase understanding of TQM but also to build more effective teams and 'to have fun'.

Among accounts of TQM in the service sector, Flood (1993) reports on an exercise carried out with the North Yorkshire Police Force while Bank (1992) provides insights into the implementation process in the Royal Mail. Morgan and Murgatroyd (1994) include a considerable number of examples of the use made by public sector services of quality management in their work.

CONCLUSION

Although in this chapter we have looked at a wide variety of approaches and tools which go towards a TQM approach, it is worth restating the fundamental fact that TQM itself is an holistic approach which begins and ends with an obsessive attention to customer requirements. Although some of the techniques used are taken from other management approaches – and it would be surprising were that not the case – they are used purely to enable the organization to promote quality throughout all its operations and activities. Definitions of TQM may vary, and all organizations will need to pick techniques and tools to meet their particular requirements, but the culture of continuous improvement and customer focus will be common to all.

PART II

LIBRARIES, INFORMATION SERVICES AND QUALITY

❖

8

LIBRARIES AND QUALITY: RECENT RESEARCH AND APPLICATIONS

❖

There is now a very considerable literature in the library and information service sector which at least uses the term quality, even if it is not always used in the same way. The majority of published papers in the field are descriptive; that is, they give a case study or other account of one or more aspects of quality management applied to a particular library or information service. However, there is also a growing body of research activity which is seeking to investigate how quality management concepts can be applied systematically to the sector. In the UK the British Library Research & Development Department is supporting research in the field, while the European Commission's Libraries Programme has selected for funding a number of projects which will examine the potential for and development of information technology based tools to assist library managers to use performance measurement and quality management, including support for ISO 9000 implementation. In this chapter we will examine some of the recent work in these areas within the library and information service field. Work on library effectiveness is covered in Chapter 11, while performance measurement, an area which has received particular attention within the field, is considered in Chapter 12.

INTRODUCTORY AND DESCRIPTIVE WORK

The 1992 Total Quality Management conference at the Library Technology Fair at the University of Hertfordshire (Total Quality Management, 1993) is a good starting point for examination of the library and information service quality management literature. It resulted in a useful collection of papers, including contributions from some of the leading figures in the application of quality management to the field (e.g. Brockman, 1993; Dawson, 1993). Martin (1993a) spoke about TQM and academic libraries (and incidentally has also published a guide in the *Library & Information Briefings* series (Martin, 1993b)). Brockman (1993), who has very much pioneered quality management at the Ministry of Defence and who has more

111

recently taken on the role of Coordinator of the Total Quality Management Information Network within the Ministry, gave a thoughtful contribution about quality management in the government library sector.

Whitehall (1992) provided an award-winning overview of quality literature in libraries and information services. The Circle of State Librarians' publication on *Developing Quality in Libraries: culture and measurement for information services* repays study (Foreman, 1992). The Library Association published its 'Quality Guidelines' in March of 1993 (Library Association, 1993a). Among accounts of implementations of TQM in public libraries, that by Curtis *et al.* (1993) stands out as a very practical approach in a highly political setting where considerations about the various stakeholders and the external environment loomed large. From an American corporate library perspective, an interesting account by Ertel (1993) stressed the TQM focus on continuous improvement and the essential of surveying customer needs on an ongoing basis. Sirkin (1993) explored some of the issues related to customer service in relation to libraries, including the question of expectations. A survey of TQM attitudes and activities among mainly commercial information-based organizations in Europe has also recently been published (Lester, 1994). The Quality Forum, based at Berkshire County Library, has provided an opportunity for exchange of experience on quality management between public libraries, while some libraries have created their own version of the Quality Forum to provide an expert sounding-board for the development of quality management: Kent County Arts & Libraries is one example. There has also been discussion in the professional press on 'Investors in People' (Pluse, 1994).

The literature also contains useful material on the application of specific quality management techniques to libraries and information services. BS 5750 (ISO 9000) is very helpfully explained in an Aslib Guide by Debbie Ellis and Bob Norton of the Institute of Management (Ellis and Norton, 1993) while Wedlake (1993) gives a briefer account of the main requirements. The implementation of BS 5750/ISO 9000 at the University of Central Lancashire Library is described in papers by Brophy (1993a) and Brophy *et al.* (1993), and there are case studies in the private sector from, for example, Dawson of Taylor Woodrow (1993). An account of implementation at Macmillan Distribution Ltd was described in Chapter 3, while a recent (1994) issue of the Library Association Record contained enthusiastic comments from school, college, university and public librarians. In the Scandinavian countries there is a wide-ranging study which is providing guidelines for ISO 9000 implementation in libraries, described below in more detail under 'Research and development studies' (see also Johanssen, 1992, 1993). As has already been noted, customer care programmes are very widely used in libraries and information services of all types. Further information on this aspect of quality management was provided in the study by Porter (1993) reported below (p. 115).

Library staff resistance to TQM is a factor highlighted in a paper by Butcher (1993) in relation to her experience at Oregon State University Library. In part, Butcher reports, staff were reacting against the TQM vocabulary, including terms such as customer, because in their view quality management as they understood it was suited to business and industry but not to academia. Butcher acknowledges the validity of some of this criticism if TQM is introduced with crude ideas of what these terms mean in the particular context, and suggests that, as we have already observed in Chapter 4, a service and in particular a public service needs a more sophisticated and complex understanding of the customer–supplier relationships. Other concerns were the style used to introduce TQM to library staff by the team brought into the university – members of which team seemed more concerned with gaining converts than actual TQM training. Again, this is an instructive observation. Because there was a university management enthusiasm for TQM, consultants were keen to sign up their first department and so prove their worth. A third issue raised by library staff was that TQM was no more than the latest in a long line of management fads and that much of what was being recommended, such as problem-solving teams, was taking place anyway.

These objections are not only a common experience but also have to be acknowledged as having a basic validity, especially where there is a sense of TQM being imposed by senior institutional or library management. One of the challenges of leadership is to encourage enthusiasm for quality management without alienating those who are not only at the sharp end of service delivery, but very often overworked into the bargain.

At Oregon State University the decision was made by the eight Library Division heads to pilot TQM in two areas. One team would be set up to work on the reshelving process in the library while the other would look at how government publications were handled from the acquisition stage until they became available to users on the library shelves. It has to be said that in many ways, although obviously a practical way to get started, the concept of a partial implementation appears to run against most common statements of TQM philosophy, since the need for an holistic approach, and one in which everyone is involved, is usually regarded as essential. On the other hand, any method which gets the library from interest (or disinterest!) to action has to be applauded. One outcome of this approach was the finding by the government publications team that customers were not in fact very concerned about identifying individual government publications but much more concerned about the difficulties of finding their way to the government publications unit in the library! The focus, following this clear signal of customers' true requirements, was to turn attention to the signs in the library. A general lesson learned from this and other experiences was that small incremental changes are the road to continuous improvement. The lesson from Peters and Austin (1985), as noted in Chapter 2, is well learned: 'pay obsessive attention to detail'.

In the same volume of papers on TQM (see Jurow and Barnard, 1993) a more theoretical approach, based on work done by the US Association of Research Libraries' Office of Management Services and discussed by a group of library directors at a meeting in Texas in January 1992, is described (Barnard, 1993). The model suggests a ten-stage process for implementing TQM in libraries, as outlined below. The ten stages are grouped into four phases.

○   **Phase 1: Exploration and decision making.** In the first phase library managers need to gather together information about quality management, including examining the literature (with particular reference to works concerned with the application of TQM to the sector, in the case described to education and research, or more generally to non profit-making organizations), attending conferences and training events, and contacting and visiting congruent organizations already involved in TQM. Once this information and understanding has been gained the library can move on to the second step in this phase, making the decision to implement TQM and, crucially, gaining top management commitment to it.

O   **Phase 2: Organising for quality.** The initial step in the second phase is to undertake a series of planning tasks which will provide the groundwork on which TQM implementation can be built. It is suggested that many of the tasks associated with this phase will be reasonably familiar to librarians who have been engaged in strategic planning. For example, the initial step will be to carry out an assessment of the library to determine whether its predominant culture is already sympathetic to the introduction of quality management. Alongside this environmental assessment there will be a process of seeking deeper understanding of both internal and external customers, in part by training staff to understand the issues behind customer expectations and customer satisfaction, and some of the techniques which can be used to achieve improvements. Finally, a vision needs to be articulated, supported by guidelines and actions which will enable the organization to move forward from what it is to what it wants to be.

O   **Phase 3: Start-up.** In order to move from the preparatory phases to action there are a series of steps which are needed to provide the base information for quality management application. In essence the library's managers need to identify first of all what are the needs and the expectations of their customers; second, to identify and then measure the critical processes which are being used by the library; third, to set up pilot project teams to tackle those critical processes which have been targeted for improvement and, fourth, they need to provide appropriate training to members of the teams to enable them to function. It is interesting to note that the training recommended for all members of the teams includes interactive skills, consensus decision making and problem solving processes.

O   **Phase 4: Planning.** The integration of the results of the project teams' considerations into library processes is seen as part of the final phase, which also includes a strategic planning and departmental planning activity. Within this phase also there is an emphasis on spreading the expertise of the initial project teams to all members of staff and involving them in teams and problem-solving activities. It is further suggested, in line with TQM practice, that a rewards and recognition programme should be implemented, although no suggestions are made as to how this might be achieved.

In addition to Barnard's description of the ARL model, Loney (1993) provides a description of the model which emphasizes the training implications that it involves and especially the idea that training should be seen as integral to the organization's operations, an aspect that we discussed in Chapter 7.

RESEARCH AND DEVELOPMENT STUDIES INTO QUALITY MANAGEMENT IN LIBRARIANSHIP AND INFORMATION SCIENCE

It is worth noting that the British Library Research & Development Department's (BLRDD) Research Plan 1993–98 has identified quality as a high priority area. The following paragraphs describe briefly some of the work which has been and is being funded by the department.

SURVEY OF CURRENT PRACTICE

Porter (1993) undertook this study for the British Library Research & Development Department in 1992. BLRDD had been aware for some time that quality management was an important area and that it merited attention, and commissioned this work as a ground-clearing exercise to examine quality management applications in academic and public libraries. A somewhat similar exercise is currently being carried out by Webb (1994) in the special libraries area, again with BLRDD support.

The study involved a literature review, produced a glossary of terms and through its survey work established an initial database of contacts. The survey of librarians in the two sectors asked whether they were involved in particular quality initiatives and, if so, why. There were obviously some terminological problems, particularly in the interpretation of terms such as continuous quality improvement (CQI) and customer care, an intriguing aspect being the number of librarians claiming not to be involved in customer care! Presumably fewer problems of definition were encountered when respondents were asked whether they were implementing BS 5750. The results of this survey are depicted in Figure 8.1 and show that a significant proportion of respondents were involved in one or more aspects of quality management.

The interpretation of these results does need to be treated with some care, but the general trend was clear and confirmed that this was an area where further work would be valuable. On that basis the need to provide supportive research and development was recognized.

MAPPING OF QUALITY ASSURANCE CONCEPTS

The Centre for Research in Library and Information Management at the University of Central Lancashire began a research study in June 1994 designed to provide a mapping of quality management concepts on to librarianship and information work. The aims of this work are:

(a)   To provide a conceptual framework for the adoption of quality management by library and information services.

(b)   To interpret the major quality management approaches being adopted by libraries and information services in generic terms, so as to facilitate the selection of appropriate quality management systems and techniques, and their implementation by libraries.

(c)   To explore the relationship between quality management and library performance measurement. (University of Central Lancashire, 1993)

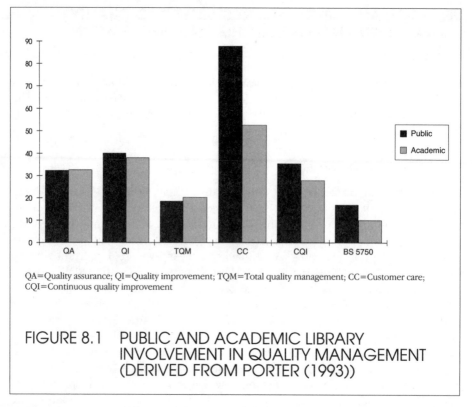

QA=Quality assurance; QI=Quality improvement; TQM=Total quality management; CC=Customer care; CQI=Continuous quality improvement

FIGURE 8.1   PUBLIC AND ACADEMIC LIBRARY
INVOLVEMENT IN QUALITY MANAGEMENT
(DERIVED FROM PORTER (1993))

Although at the time of writing the study is only half-way through its 15-month duration, the initial analysis of quality management systems has provided a focus on a number of key concepts and has been used to inform the development of this book, particularly the structure of Chapter 7. Key issues are:

O   **Customer requirements,** with a particular emphasis on the need to identify the gaps which occur between service providers' views of the quality of the service and those of the actual customers;

O   **Prevention of error,** with an emphasis on identifying, in a systematic manner, potential problems before customers are affected.

O   **Corrective action,** with emphases both on correcting the immediate problem so that the individual customer is satisfied, but more importantly correcting the underlying cause so that the problem does not recur.

O   **Standards,** which enable a consistent level of service to be provided. Many studies have shown that quality failures frequently occur because consistency is not maintained in relation to standards.

O   **Performance indicators,** linked to standards, but appropriate to the organization. Derivation of performance indicators from institutional goals is generally regarded as more appropriate than adopting those set by an external body. This issue has considerable importance for much of the work on performance measurement described in Chapter 12.

O   **Responsibility,** the idea that everyone in the organization must under-
         stand and practice quality.

These concepts are of course familiar from the quality management literature and
the interrelationship between them is important. At the time of writing this work
is ongoing.

QUALITY INITIATIVES IN PUBLIC LIBRARIES

This project, being undertaken jointly by the University of Sheffield and the
University of Loughborough, began in September 1994, again with BLRDD funding,
and is examining in detail the use of quality management systems and techniques
in public libraries, using a mainly case study approach and comparing the findings
with applications in commercial organizations. The aim is to look at organizational,
customer and policy issues and there are links with the public libraries' Quality
Forum, based at Berkshire County Libraries. The study is examining librarians'
motivation for becoming involved in quality management, the role of Charters and
Standards of Service (which have of course been particularly prominent in public
libraries because of the Government's Citizen's Charter initiative – see Chapters 6
and 13) and the effects of implementation. An evaluative literature review was
published by the team at the end of 1994 (Milner *et al.*, 1994).

BENCHMARKING

A study, again based at the Department of Information & Library Studies at
Loughborough University, is examining best practice benchmarking and its use in
the library and information service sector. The study will be looking at different
models of benchmarking, why managers choose to use benchmarking and the
suitability of different models to different types of library. The intention is to develop
two demonstrator projects, focusing on the academic and special library sectors.

INFORMATION MANAGEMENT AND QUALITY MANAGEMENT

Reference has already been made to the work of John Brockman of the UK Ministry
of Defence. Building on this earlier activity, Brockman, with Alan Gilchrist, an
independent consultant and Director of the European Consortium of Information
Consultants (GAVEL), is exploring the role of information and information
networks in facilitating corporate business improvement, including the use of such
networks to share best practice and ideas for quality improvement. Both Brockman
and Gilchrist are also involved in the benchmarking study described above.

ISO 9000 IMPLEMENTATION IN LIBRARIES AND INFORMATION SERVICES

A study led by the Royal School of Librarianship in Copenhagen began in January
1993 under the auspices of the Nordic Council for Scientific Information and
Research Libraries (NORDINFO) to investigate the development of formal quality
assurance systems in libraries. The aim is to prepare guidelines to the ISO 9000

standard for different sectors in the library field. Practical implementations at Norsk Hydro in Oslo and at the Jutland Telephone Company in Åarhus, Denmark have been used to develop and test the guidelines. In addition the work involves theoretical and practical studies on the application of TQM to libraries. The team is co-operating with a number of European organizations in the library and information service field, including the European Association of Information Services (EUSIDIC), GAVEL and the European Online User Group (EUROLUG). Background information on the work in Copenhagen is given in a paper by Johanssen (1992) while progress reports have appeared at intervals since then (Clausen, 1994a, 1994b). The guidelines are to be translated from Danish into an English language version (Gilchrist, 1994).

DATABASE QUALITY

In addition to the work of the Centre for Information Quality Management (CIQM) referred to above, a recent study looked at the quality of bibliographic records by examining use of the BLCMP database and checking how frequently records needed to be edited by member libraries before being added to their in-house catalogue databases (Chapman, 1993). This is an interesting example of a study which aimed to find one of the costs of quality described in Chapter 7, specifically the internal failure costs associated with having to rework a product bought in from a supplier. The issue is somewhat complicated by the fact that a reworked, externally supplied bibliographic record may be cheaper than the internally produced equivalent, but the potential savings from not having to edit records are still real. A European Commission funded study of database quality known as EQUIP (European Quality in Information Programme), using a methodology based on that developed by Zeithaml *et al.* (1990) (see Chapter 4) has recently reported and more work can be expected in this area (see Swindells, 1994, reported in Gilchrist, 1994).

QUALITY MANAGEMENT AND INFORMATION TECHNOLOGY

There has been some interest in examining how information technology might be used to support quality management for libraries and information services. A great deal of management information either is or could be produced automatically from library computer systems, and the question arises as to whether information technology based quality management support tools could be developed. There are a number of possible approaches to this, and of course a number of challenges. Clearly it will be necessary to go beyond the mere collection of statistics. Possibilities range from holding quality procedures manuals in electronic form, via the use of IT to track non-conformance and error correction, and on to the use of decision support and other modelling software. This last approach has been the focus of research at De Montfort University, Leicester, where an IT-based decision support system has been developed and operationally tested through the application of the *Keys to Success* manual (see Chapter 12). The data is partly internally generated and partly fed into the system from external sources, such as the academic library statistics discussed in Chapter 10. The team has also looked at the place of expert systems and executive information systems as a development of library decision support systems (Bloor, 1991; Adams *et al.*, 1993).

The main research activity in the area of quality management and IT at present is being funded by the European Commission under the Libraries Programme. De Montfort University is undertaking a ground-clearing study on performance measurement, and four projects to develop IT-based systems are expected to start in early 1995. These include the EQLIPSE project, led by the University of Central Lancashire, involving ten partners from seven European countries: the University of Central Lancashire (UK), Dynix Library Systems (Ireland), Dublin City University (Ireland), the National Microelectronics Applications Centre Ltd (Ireland), Universitäts und Landesbibliothek Münster (Germany), Copenhagen Business School Library (Denmark), Biblioteca Nazionale Centrale Vittorio Emanuele II (Italy), Stockholm University Library (Sweden), Stadtbüchereien Düsseldorf (Germany), and the University of the Aegean (Greece).

EQLIPSE is designed to fulfil the following objectives:

(i)   To research the state-of-the-art of appropriate quality management and performance measurement systems and their actual and potential application to libraries, based on recent studies in the field, the participants' own experience and further investigations of the key issues.

(ii)   To specify an EQLIPSE methodology which would conform to the relevant international standards, including both ISO 9000 and the impending ISO/TC46/SC8 standard on performance indicators for libraries, which would incorporate our research findings, provide detailed guidance on data collection, system management and other relevant features, be compatible with emerging IT trends and products, and provide an open functional specification that can be incorporated into mainstream library IT systems.

(iii)   To provide a prototype EQLIPSE system with appropriate quality management and performance measurement tools which can be integrated into a mainstream open, client-server based library IT system.

(iv)   To field trial the prototype system at two operational libraries so as to provide detailed testing and experience of its operability and validity.

(v)   From this prototype to develop a standard open EQLIPSE system and to test its implementation in six libraries chosen to provide a wide variety of types (academic, public, national), levels of IT, library environment and types of library systems. On this basis to deliver an implementable system specification and implementation manual which would enable the system itself to be adopted widely across the European Union.

(vi)   To produce a final report which, *inter alia*, would record the key issues raised in the Project, relate these to ongoing standards development (in both the technical and performance measurement areas) and provide recommendations for further actions in this area. (University of Central Lancashire *et al.*, 1994)

CONCLUSION

That there is considerable activity in the application of quality management to libraries and information services is not in doubt. The shift, from an interest in quality, which has been evident for many years, to active use of systematic methods of managing quality, is significant. It is also evident that research and development activity, which is seeking to understand how quality management techniques and philosophies can be applied, is on the increase. This is a healthy situation which augurs well for the future of customer-centred services in the field.

9

DEFINING PURPOSE:
THE MISSION OF THE LIBRARY

❖

The discussion in this chapter focuses on the use of the mission statement as a tool for defining library purpose and thereby providing a starting-point for quality management. However, it would be wrong to argue that only through a mission statement can purpose be defined. Some of the most stimulating discussions concerning the role of the library have come from very different traditions, yet have provided an influential input which has helped librarians and information scientists better define the business they are in. Among these voices those representing community librarianship have been prominent. In the context of quality management, these contributions are important because they focus on the needs of the library's users and potential users. John Dolan has written, for example:

> Image is not enough. For the community library in the inner city, image does not come first. What counts is the potential of the library to move with the people reflecting along the way their interests and concerns and giving resources and time to activities of consequence. In Manchester the effect of change both in the library and through the local librarian has been to change the role of the library. That process is still underway; it always continues and is never complete. (Dolan, 1989)

In a later paper in the same volume, Barugh (1989) quotes Bundy (1972) as questioning the whole professional ethos of the typical librarian. Note again the exhortation to develop services which meet the real needs of the customers the library should be serving:

> The daily struggle merely to survive in the streets of the communities that libraries purport to serve is not seen as requiring any serious response from this institution. The inhumane liberalism in which the profession has indulged for too long allows the institution to maintain the importance of service to all comers equally and thus to treat as equally compelling a request from a suburban housewife wanting to plan flower decorations for a dinner party, and the plight of a hungry child. The reality is that the deprived make next to no use of libraries and libraries do next to nothing to reach them. When this basic hypocrisy is exposed, librarians fly to their own defence. They point out that they are not social workers or lawyers; they are not against helping the poor, but they cannot cross the boundaries of their professional territory. And so like the other professionals, they allow people with needs

121

to fall into chasms which lie between the boundaries of the various professions because human problems do not define themselves neatly among these circum-scribed lines.

The purpose of this quotation is not to advance an argument as to whether Bundy is right or wrong, or to assess whether libraries have changed in the 20 years since that piece was written, but to illustrate the need to debate and agree on fundamen-tal purpose before any real advances can be made in delivering quality services. Just what is a library for? Whom is it meant to serve?

One way to begin to give answers to these questions substance is, as we have seen, to develop a mission statement. These have been quite common in libraries and information services in recent years and in the remainder of this chapter we will examine how they have been developed and the issues which they address.

THE PROCESS OF DEVELOPING A MISSION STATEMENT

A variety of approaches to the development of mission statements can be found in the professional literature. In some libraries the approach has been top-down, with a centrally drafted statement being circulated for comment. One library's approach was described as 'this (mission statement) was put together ... by a group of senior staff' (Brophy, 1991a), but there are dangers in such an approach. The author of a survey of polytechnic (i.e. institutional) mission statements came to the conclusion that 'it is as if senior management are the polytechnic. So what gets defined here is management's role within the institution, not the institution's role within higher education' (Earwaker, 1991). A study by Hardesty *et al.* (1988) showed that 'the library director plays a key role in the development of a mission statement' in American college libraries. Sometimes, however, the approach is bottom-up, although in this case there is a danger that the employees might dictate its terms at the expense of customers, who are unlikely to have as much opportunity to contribute. At the extreme, employees are asked to write their own personal mission statements: 'What is it that motivates me to come to work?'; 'What am I seeking to achieve?'; 'What values do I bring with me?'. This process itself is a valuable exercise, especially if the climate in which it is carried out is supportive and non-threatening and has been tried, with some success, in the library field (Bristol Polytechnic Library, 1987). However, its major problem lies in the difficulty in aggregating the individual mission statements in a meaningful way. A small group, working closely together, may be able to do so, although there is always the danger that assertive individuals will dominate the process and others will be out of sympathy with the end result. Furthermore, even if a final mission statement can be agreed, there is no guarantee that it will be in accord with institutional goals. All this goes to reinforce the fact that 'one of the more challenging components of the planning process is the development of the Mission Statement' (Leisner, 1986).

There is a very strong argument that much of the value of the mission statement lies in the process by which it is articulated. While it would be going too far to suggest that the end product – the mission statement itself – is irrelevant, it is in the process of thinking about mission, of debating alternatives, of bringing hidden values to the surface and of ensuring that all stakeholders are involved that so much of the value of the approach lies. If we commit ourselves to a serious and open debate on the purposes and values of our libraries then we empower all those who become involved: staff, users, managers, funders. We also commit ourselves, by the very act of embarking on the process, to listening and taking seriously each contribution to the debate.

This might be taken to be a recipe for management by democracy, but in fact it simply points up the need for managers to exercise true leadership: to avoid dictatorial approaches, even under the guise of participation, and instead to concentrate on the development of a vision of the future and strategies to achieve that vision to which all stakeholders can contribute. Management's role then focuses on providing the right environment in which the mission can be pursued by all: providing the space for individuals and groups to contribute in their own way; using the mission as a consistent guide to resource allocation; continually stressing purposes over means; facilitating communication between individuals and groups; stressing enthusiasm and enjoyment as legitimate values within the organization so as to promote personal job satisfaction; and so on.

MISSION STATEMENTS IN LIBRARIANSHIP AND INFORMATION SCIENCE

Published mission statements need to be approached with some care because of the range of processes by which they have been generated. They may reflect a partisan view (however 'rightly'), are undoubtedly written for a political purpose and, for the observer, have local significances which are not readily apparent. Such are the pressures of modern higher education that some statements may even have been produced under duress.

Most of the library mission statements which have been published in an accessible form are from North American libraries. There is, for example, an interesting collection published by the Association of College & Research Libraries (Hardesty *et al.*, 1985), a so-called 'flyer and kit' (a sort of do-it-yourself working paper collection) from the Association of Research Libraries' Office of University Library Management Studies, Systems and Procedures Exchange Center (Association of Research Libraries, 1979) and most notably the model mission statement produced by the Association of College and Research Libraries (ACRL Undergraduate Librarians Discussion Group and ULS Steering Committee, 1987).

A study by Brophy (1991b) included the analysis of 30 academic library mission statements and identification of the extent to which there is commonality of purposes and values between libraries in the sample. The most frequently cited purpose of the academic library identified in these library mission statements was 'to serve the needs of the users' or 'to provide services to the library's users'. Most libraries went on to define both the services (typically in terms of access to information, the second most frequently cited purpose) and the users (typically students and academic staff), although a few seem to feel that 'providing services to users' is an adequate definition of purpose. One or two statements even followed this track into pure tautology: 'to provide library services to users' hardly tells anyone anything about a library's values and purposes!

However, the general concentration on users and on services may be seen as confirmation that the majority of librarians are keen to embrace user-centred and service concepts at the highest level, reflecting the predominance of this view in the literature in recent years and lending weight to the view that quality management can provide relevant methodologies for managing libraries and information services. Access to information was more frequently mentioned in this sample than the provision of collections, a finding which would seem to lend weight to the view that 'access' as a philosophy is now well established and that the idea that libraries are in the information business is also commonplace.

For some reason, services to external clients were mentioned in this survey almost as often as support for learning and research. Given the limited success that academic libraries have had in this area, was this an example of a political point being made, ensuring that our funders know how seriously we take their exhortations to develop links with industry? It is equally interesting that the provision of a suitable study environment and the teaching of information skills both rated relatively low in this scale of popularity, as did the preservation of our heritage. Again, however, one should not make too much of this since it could be argued that all of these would be subsumed under a general reference to 'services'.

Statements about values as opposed to purposes are quite rare. One library included the statement that it should 'be friendly', while no less than four made a commitment to be a centre of excellence. However, even these statements were made within a context which stressed the purpose of the library and it would therefore appear that the majority of librarians do use mission statements as statements of purposes rather than of values.

Some mission statements lean towards the means of achieving the mission rather than the mission itself. For example, four libraries stated that part of their mission was 'to generate income'. This could, of course, be the case, although one cannot help thinking that institutions might have found better ways to achieve such a purpose. A similar point can be made in relation to co-operation with other libraries: is this not a means of achieving something rather than a purpose in its own right?

Perhaps the most striking feature of these mission statements was their similarity. Librarians do appear to be in general agreement on the mission of the academic library. It is a service, directed towards the support of the learning and research of users (predominantly members of the parent institution) through the provision of information resources. However, beyond this general agreement, mission statements do reveal differences. Some emphasize collection building, others access, yet others the teaching of information skills, while the preservation of our heritage of recorded knowledge is not forgotten.

A comment by Henty (1989) is important, albeit set in the context of objectives rather than mission. 'All libraries should be responsible for evaluating their own services, but this should be in terms of whether they meet the objectives set for them by their parent body, not in terms of whether they meet externally set and possibly incompatible objectives imposed from outside'. This issue, the reconciliation of conflicting demands placed on the library by different stakeholders, will be further considered in Chapter 11.

Although many examples of mission statements from all sectors of the library and information science profession can be cited, it is interesting to examine two statements which were developed at the national level. One was intended to define the scope and purpose of professional concerns. It is not explicitly a mission statement but does have obvious parallels. The second example was a model mission statement for the public library sector. The motivation behind the first lay in the frequently asked question, in an Information Age when many different professional groupings seek to lay claim to parts of the fastest growing industry the world has seen, as to the role librarians and information scientists can and should play. Computer scientists, economists, software engineers, networking specialists, publishers and many others are undertaking tasks the equivalents of which our profession might have considered its own in the past. So, what business are we all in? The Institute of Information Scientists sought to answer this question in the mid-1980s when it decided to revise its 'Criteria for Information Science' (Institute of Information Scientists, 1988). The criteria are used both to enable the institute to consider whether the work of potential members maps sufficiently closely on to information science for membership to be awarded to applicants, and also serves as the basis on which recognition of higher education courses can be based. The criteria are reproduced in Appendix I.

As will be seen, the institute defines a core area of information science which includes the characteristics, providers and users of information, information sources, information storage and retrieval, the analysis of information, the dissemination of information and the theory of information science. It is particularly interesting from a quality management perspective that in the first area there is explicit mention of 'finding and analysing user needs' as a core activity, and that the importance of the 'information chain', which of course has an affinity with the quality chain, is also highlighted. It is perhaps disappointing that in the second section, on information management, quality is not mentioned, although no doubt any future revision would want to bring this subject into the definition. The third section, on information technology, suggests that IT was seen as an enabling rather than a core concern when the criteria were formulated.

The second document is concerned with the development of a model mission statement for public libraries and was developed through discussions in the Library and Information Services Council (LISC) which set up a working party to prepare a manual on setting objectives for public libraries. Within this process the group developed a 'National Mission Statement for Public Libraries' (Office of Arts and Libraries, 1991), which is reproduced in Appendix II. It was emphasized that every public library service needed its own mission statement, and it was expected that the model would be adapted to reflect local needs and local political aspirations. The importance of ownership of the statement by stakeholders, specifically by library staff and elected members of local authorities, was a particular concern of the working party.

The importance of these two documents, and others like them, lies in their attempt to indicate those areas with which professionals should be most concerned and which should be given priority. As such they provide a step towards a quality management approach, which may be applied profitably to the broader responsibilities and activities of professionals as a whole and not only to the services which they manage.

CONCLUSION

The mission statement or other statement of purpose is clearly of importance in the management of libraries and information services, and in broader professional concerns. It provides a definition of purposes and values at a fundamental level and can thus help the library or information service to embark on quality management. Most librarians also recognize that mission statements provide a useful public relations opportunity, not least in discussions with institutional management, since there is not always a clear understanding among such groups of the role and purposes of information-based departments, nor of their wide-ranging service function. As yet, however, there is a lack of evidence as to the linkage between mission statements and management. There is little point in spending a great deal of time developing a mission statement if it is not put to use. Quality management provides a framework which might help move a service forward from mission to purposive action.

10

COMPARING LIBRARY AND INFORMATION SERVICES: STATISTICS, STANDARDS AND GUIDELINES

One of the principal ways in which libraries and information services have sought to manage the quality of the services they provide is through monitoring statistical measures, through the adoption of standards – usually for the sector in which they operate – and through the use of nationally agreed guidelines. While formal benchmarking – detailed examination of and comparison with the best in the sector, as described in Chapter 7 – has been limited, libraries have used a number of cross-sectoral approaches to provide an indication of how good a service is being provided. At the most basic level, these approaches have involved the collection of input and output counts, but there has also been a considerable development towards meaningful performance indicators through calculating means, ratios, etc. from the bare statistics. Systematic performance measurement will be considered in Chapter 11, while in this chapter we will examine some examples of the use of national, or industry-wide, statistics, standards and guidelines.

It is notable that the professional associations – the Library Association and the Institute of Information Scientists in the UK, the American Library Association and the Association of College & Research Libraries in the USA would be examples – have provided the fora within which standards and guidelines have been agreed. This reflects the origins of most such documents as the product of debate and agreement within professional circles, and raises an immediate issue in the context of a discussion of quality management as to the extent to which customer and stakeholder inputs have been introduced. Be that as it may, guidelines and standards have provided a major element of the profession's attempt to provide quality services, and they deserve examination.

LIBRARY STATISTICS

Basic statistics on library operations, and especially on raw inputs such as financial grants and books acquired and on outputs including book issues and opening hours, have been collected for many years. Concentrating purely on the UK, in the academic library sector the Standing Conference of National and University Libraries (SCONUL), in co-operation with the University Grants Committee (later Universities Funding Council) and the Council of Polytechnic Librarians (COPOL) have collected statistical and other information on their members' library activities for over a decade. Public library statistics have been collected and published by the Chartered Institute of Public Finance and Accountancy (CIPFA) for many years. Government library statistics have been gathered by the Committee of Departmental Libraries since 1987. Data on other libraries and information services are less easy to obtain (see Sumsion, 1993b), but a number of related bodies publish data which are useful to managers of libraries and information services, for example the Blackwell's periodicals price indexes published annually in the *Library Association Record*. The pre-eminent body in the library statistics field in the UK, however, is the Library and Information Statistics Unit (LISU) at the Department of Information and Library Studies of Loughborough University of Technology.

LISU produces a series of regular publications, including the *Average Prices of British Academic Books* and *Average Prices of USA Academic Books* (both twice a year), together with *UK Public Library Materials Fund and Budget Survey*, published annually. Work has also been done on collecting statistics on special libraries in the UK (Sumsion, 1993b). The most important publication is *LISU Annual Library Statistics*, featuring trend analysis of UK academic and public libraries and including calculated performance indicators and cross-sectoral trends. It provides data on total book issues, stock, expenditure, etc. for both public and academic libraries. A filofax format summary of the various published statistics is also available from LISU.

The published statistics can be used by individual managers for comparison purposes and as a rather crude form of benchmarking. Some quite sophisticated analyses are possible by grouping libraries and calculating averages in relation to chosen criteria. For example, Adams *et al.* (1993) took the average number of issues per annum per full-time equivalent student in the old polytechnics and compared the results with the maximum loan period and maximum number of items students were allowed to borrow. This showed a positive correlation between total loans per student and maximum number allowed on loan, and a negative correlation between total loans and loan period. This reflects work carried out by Buckland *et al.* (1970) nearly a quarter of a century earlier which suggested that the manipulation of loan periods and quotas provided a powerful management tool for influencing total loans.

STANDARDS AND GUIDELINES

The library and information science professions have developed many sets of standards, usually through their professional bodies, over the years. Two examples are given here although many others could have been cited.

The IFLA *Standards for University Libraries*, published in 1986, was an internationally agreed document prepared by a committee of librarians, which stated as its purpose 'to provide a means by which the quality of the library serving a university can be assessed, to offer guidance for improvements in the library, and to suggest a framework within which various countries or regions could develop their own statements of standards' (Lynch, 1986). The IFLA standards were grouped under ten headings, as follows:

1. **Purpose.** The need for every university library to have a clear definition of purpose, within the context of the purpose of the parent institution.
2. **Organization and administration.** A requirement that the organization and structure of the library be 'well defined and understood' and that the place of the library within the parent institution be defined. There should be a library committee.
3. **Services.** The need to relate the services on offer to the purpose of the library, the provision of reference and information services, maintenance of records of items 'in conformity with recognized standards of cataloguing and classification', and availability of 'most' items for consultation. 'Circulation procedures should be effective and efficient'.
4. **Collections.** To be of adequate size and scope, including all reading required of students. Collection development policies should be defined, and the collections should be reviewed regularly. Interlibrary lending should be developed.
5. **Staff.** The need for 'a sufficient number and variety of personnel', including appropriately qualified staff. Terms and conditions of employment of librarians should be the same as or 'consonant with' those of university teachers.
6. **Facilities.** The size, quality and attractiveness of buildings and their layout.
7. **Budget and finance.** The library 'should be provided with sufficient funding to enable it to develop appropriate collections, recruit and retain suitable staff, provide appropriate services, accomplish necessary operations, and satisfy user needs'.
8. **Technology.** The library 'should make use of electronic data processing and telecommunication systems'.
9. **Preservation and conservation.** The need for both a policy for preservation and conservation and a programme for carrying out the policy.
10. **Co-operation.** Reference to resource sharing, union catalogues, collection development and co-operative activity in preservation and conservation of materials.

A more recent example of a *Standards* document is the Standards for Performance and Resourcing for Scottish Further Education Colleges (Scottish Library & Information Council and Scottish Library Association, 1993). This document, as well as recommending minimum levels of provision, for example for the ratio of library materials to full-time equivalent student numbers, specifically refers to how quality can be improved and how its achievement might be measured. The suggestion is made that

> quality is most likely to be achieved by a library which exhibits three characteristics:
> a)   It possesses a rationale and aims to underpin its activities and policies.
> b)   It addresses the expectations of the parent college and its senior managers and:
>   i)   is service oriented; investigates and responds to clients' needs and helps them to exploit library collections and information resources; generally, adopts principles of good customer care;
>   ii) maintains effective links with the academic and managerial processes of the parent college;
>   iii) understands and responds to changes in education, approaches to learning and the policies of the parent college.
> c)   It passes the scrutiny of peers and reflects the professional consensus as to a library's proper activities (as expressed, for example, in this and similar documents). Where this consensus is not met, the college librarian should know how and why the library differs, and be able to justify the variance.

The first two of these paragraphs contain many of the elements of quality management within them: a statement of purpose or mission and associated aims; emphasis on stakeholder perspectives and on the customer; active involvement of customers; continuous change. The final paragraph is somewhat different, although in its stress on justifying differences it recognizes the need for services to be locally determined to meet local needs. Peer assessment, provided it reflects customer needs, can of course be a powerful tool in assuring quality, and contains elements of benchmarking within it, especially when used to spread good practice and not merely as a check that minimum standards are being reached.

The report recommends the use of a core set of 16 performance indicators, although each college is urged to develop additional indicators to meet local needs. The indicators recommended are divided into quantitative (both input and output) and qualitative sets, as follows:

O   **Quantitative indicators:** Numbers of clients; Size of stock; Proportion of stock added/replaced annually; Funding; Staff numbers; Accommodation; Items issued; Other items supplied; Enquiries handled; Opening hours; Number of visits; Study hours provided.

O   **Qualitative indicators:** Variety of stock; Staff qualifications and experience; Range of information support services; Satisfaction rates.

In addition, there is a very useful 'quality audit questionnaire' which can be used by external validators who are asked to assess the library provision.

The use of nationally set standards of service has declined in recent years in both the UK and the USA, largely as a result of the refocusing of management on autonomous units rather than on national 'norms'. To take public libraries as one example, the national government has shifted the emphasis of funding away from earmarking for specific services to general grant support, while leaving responsibility for providing the service in local hands. Whatever one might think of the politics of this change, it undoubtedly leads to different priorities for and levels of public library service in different areas. A second example would be academic libraries, which used to operate within some quite explicit national norms: the 1967 Parry Report, for example, set a target for the old British universities of 6 per cent of total university income to be spent on their libraries. In the then polytechnic sector, the Department of Education & Science used to guide decision making on new buildings by reference to a standard which stated, among other things, that there should be one seat for every seven full-time equivalent students.

Such standards were, of course, more often observed in the breach than in reality, and they were dropped fairly rapidly once their financial implications were fully realized. It is also interesting to note that most of the standards which were promulgated referred to input measures, such as the amount to be spent on the library, the number of books per head of population, the number of students per seat. There were no national standards for the outcomes of providing library services.

The shift away from explicit standards for libraries and information services towards more general guidelines is characterized by the development of documents which offer advice in the context of a particular activity or service rather than proscribing how or with what level of resource it should be offered.

NATIONAL COMPARISONS AND BENCHMARKING

As noted above, comparisons between libraries on a national basis, and to some extent regionally, can be made at a basic level by examination of the published statistics. Considerable efforts have been made by those responsible for these compilations to ensure that they are as comparable as possible, and where there are difficulties to flag up the difficulties. For example, the use of the resident population as the base for per capita calculations of public library performance indicators creates some anomalies for library authorities with large commuting populations (see Sumsion, 1993a). The limitations of these comparisons are fairly obvious, but they do at least provide a basis for managers to identify areas where their services appear to differ markedly from the norm and to take further action to investigate the reasons.

Another methodology for comparison of services which enjoyed popularity for some years was developed by the Research Libraries Group in the USA, and promulgated under the title 'Conspectus' (Association of Research Libraries, Office of Management Studies, 1989: Gwinn and Mosher, 1983). The aim of this methodology was to use an assessment of the local library collection in each subject area against a national norm to rate the area on a scale of zero to five, as follows:

0 – Out of scope (i.e. not collected)
1 – Minimal
2 – Basic information
3 – Instructional support (essentially student level)
4 – Research
5 – Comprehensive

The Library of Congress classification scheme was broken down into 7 000 areas for this exercise. It has proved of value to major research libraries, but for most libraries it fails to link the needs of the local customers to the collections being held. There is also a query as to its relevance in an age when access to information is so widely regarded as the more important part of academic libraries' mission than development of collections. For those interested in this area Lancaster (1993a) has detailed a number of other studies in the area of collection assessment against national or other subject bibliographies and related methodologies.

CONCLUSION

The library and information service profession in the UK, as in the USA, has developed quite sophisticated data collection schemes which provide detailed statistics on both inputs and outputs. Alongside these quantitative data there have been many examples of guidelines developed to assist librarians and those responsible for providing resources with a basic set of standards from which to work. Although the trend in recent years has been to recognize the importance of locally determined standards, these have to be set in a wider framework, not least because other interests are involved.

11

EFFECTIVENESS IN LIBRARY AND INFORMATION SERVICES

❖

Libraries and information services, and those researching in the field, have a long track record in the assessment of effectiveness, with contributions from many distinguished practitioners and researchers. Effectiveness has been a key concept, as we shall see, and has provided an important building-block on which advances in library quality management can be based. Effectiveness is, of course, concerned with the effect a library has on its users. The question is how that effect can be measured, and then how it can be made more positive than it currently is. One can go right back to the beginnings of libraries themselves and find the number of volumes in stock being cited as a measure of the value and usefulness of a library collection to users and potential users. The possession of particular titles, especially if they were unique to the library, would also indicate the importance of the collection. On the basis of these indicators scholars would travel from monastery to monastery, using not only the volumes for which a collection was famed but expecting to discover there yet more treasures, making the assumption that one famous volume would itself attract others – and that often proved to be the case.

In our own century the same has been true. The world's most famous collections, such as the British Library, the Bodleian, the Library of Congress and the Bibliothèque Nationale, have attracted scholars from across the world not only to consult a particular rare item, but also to explore the hidden treasures which those collections are known or thought to contain. For much of this century, and still in the popular imagination, the value or worth of a library has been very much bound up with, at one end of the scale its particular treasures, and at the other its sheer size, the grand total of volumes it contains, and the dramatically high numbers of miles of shelving needed to store all those possessions.

Yet it cannot be entirely accidental that interest in library effectiveness, as more than a simple measurement of size or possession of rarities, has increased with the recognition that the value of a library, particularly when it is viewed as more than a collection of books, is dependent on a wider variety of factors than size or rarity, and that many libraries and information services have been created to meet needs which cannot be described in such terms. What is more, we have now entered an era in which some of those responsible for funding question the very existence of libraries and ask whether their services could not be supplied in another way. Our profession has been fortunate that, in the past, the accepted folk wisdom has usually regarded a library as a good thing. Yet folk wisdom is no substitute for evidence and the politicians and senior managers who control library funding increasingly demand that the goodness or worth of the library be demonstrated. As Robert Munn wrote nearly three decades ago in his classic paper *The Bottomless Pit*:

> even the most 'library-minded' administrator's ... long-held article of faith that the Library is a Good Thing and somehow self-justifying is questioned. The young men are contemptuous of articles of faith. Even the fact that the prestige universities tend to have the largest libraries leaves them unmoved. They point out that this is simply the result of wealth, and that the prestige universities also have the best student psychiatric services. (Munn, 1989; originally published 1968)

It is perhaps worth recalling that Munn's 'young men' (and no doubt young women) will by now have risen to positions of power and influence; some, no doubt, are university vice-chancellors or government ministers. Even if we escaped rigorous examination in the past, we will not do so in the future.

It would be a wild exaggeration, of course, to claim that libraries and information services were not audited and assessed in the past, although it has to be said that there has been little evidence of a fundamental appraisal of the effectiveness of their services until recently. The major motivation now seems to come from the twin threats of financial stringency on the one hand and electronic networks, providing direct end-user access to what used to be the sole province of library and information services, on the other. Blaise Cronin has demanded, 'Why do we take university libraries for granted? Are we getting the service to which we are entitled? ... Do we really need university libraries of the kind we have today?' (Cronin, 1988). So the fundamental questions remain to be answered. What do information services and libraries contribute to the fulfilment of their parent bodies' missions and goals? How do we know whether any particular library is 'good', whatever that may mean? It is these questions which have led, over the past few decades, to an ever-increasing interest in library effectiveness and which are now leading to a similar interest in quality management.

Modern approaches to library and information service effectiveness have a number of origins both inside and outside librarianship and information science. Those specific to the profession include:

○ The work of S.C. Bradford, one-time librarian of the Science Museum in London, who surveyed the scientific journal literature and established Bradford's Law, which describes graphically or mathematically the distribution of citations of journal articles and shows how a relatively small proportion of the world's journal titles generates a high proportion of useful material (Bradford, 1948). Hence, why should any but the few nationally and internationally famous libraries subscribe to more than a carefully selected minority of titles in any subject? More than that, could not an effective library be developed which explicitly linked its selection policies to its own users' predicted core requirements? Bradford's initial work was continued in a series of studies by B. C. Brookes, working at University College London (e.g. Brookes, 1970), and by others.

○ The work of A. W. McClellan in public libraries – principally at Tottenham Public Library in London in the late 1950s and early 1960s – and the development of systematic ways of assigning shelf space dependent on demand (McClellan, 1962).

○ A classic paper by Verner W. Clapp and Robert T. Jordan which appeared in 1965 with the suggestion of basing evaluation of library collections on quantitative factors linked to a range of criteria instead of the then-current tendency to prescribe adequacy by collection size (Clapp and Jordan, 1965). Fussler and Simon (1969) were influential in demonstrating how actual library use could be measured reliably.

○ An influential monograph entitled *Library Effectiveness: a systems approach* by Philip Morse published in 1968, which treated the problem through the use of mathematical modelling (Morse, 1968). Work by F. F. Leimkuhler was in the same tradition (see, for example, Leimkuhler, 1966; Leimkuhler and Cooper, 1971).

○ The work of Richard Orr who drew attention to the need to distinguish between the two questions: 'How good is this library?' and 'How much good does this library do?' (Orr *et al.*, 1973). It is somewhat confusing that he tagged the first as being a question about quality, while the second was called a question about value. Unfortunately, this creates a separation of interests between users and funders: Orr suggested that the criteria for answering the 'How good is this library?' question should be the capacity of the service for meeting user needs (Buckland, 1988 prefers to call this 'capability'), while the question 'How much good does this library do?' should be answered by reference to 'the beneficial effects accruing from its use as viewed by those who sustain the costs'. This differentiation between different meanings of 'goodness' has been useful and influential. However, under the influence of quality management approaches which seek to link what Orr called 'quality' and 'value' through measuring the responsiveness of the service to all internal and external customer (i.e. stakeholder) requirements, it may be timely to rethink this analysis. From a quality management perspective 'How good is this library?' and 'How much good does this library do?' are not in fact separable. 'How good?' is only answerable in terms of the customers, again using that term in its broadest sense, and the extent to which their requirements are being met. They are also the only ones who can judge value. The division between outputs and outcomes remains real, but it is not acceptable to label as 'good' any process or output which does not help to meet customer requirements: a library which is 'good' also 'does good'. Conversely, if it does not 'do good' then it is meaningless to call it 'good'. Efficiency of process is, in itself, irrelevant.

○ Pioneering work by Hawgood and Morley at Durham University which tried to establish how the value of an academic library could be measured. The PEBUL (Project for Evaluating the Benefits from University Libraries) study, for example, used a reverse linear programming approach to try to infer the value of services from the priorities that librarians had accorded to them (University of Durham Computer Unit, 1969).

○   Work by Buckland, Hindle and others at Lancaster University in the late 1960s and early 1970s (see, for example, Mackenzie and Stuart, 1969) and subsequent work by Buckland at the University of California at Los Angeles and elsewhere. He refers in a 1988 publication to the volume of studies which have sought 'the grail of library goodness' (Buckland, 1988).

LIBRARY EFFECTIVENESS

Following Orr's work, the term 'effectiveness' came to cover some of the key issues of library management and because so much work has been done in this area it is worth spending some time in examining it. In particular it is useful to look at some of the implicit concepts of effectiveness which have been used as librarians and others have tried to devise organizational models which would ensure that effectiveness could be achieved. The following analysis is a brief summary.

It is first of all necessary to reiterate that effectiveness is concerned with the *effect* the organization has on its environment. A highly inefficient organization may be extremely effective, although presumably not as effective as it could be. The concern of studies of effectiveness is also with effects (not always quantifiable) which are in essence external to the organization itself, i.e. effects on external customers. It has been put in this way: 'organizational effectiveness is an *external* standard of how well an organization is meeting the demands of various groups and organizations that are concerned with its activities' (Pfeffer & Salancik, 1978). It follows that the assessment of effectiveness must be undertaken by viewing the organization from the point of view of those who receive its services, goods or other outputs. The connection with quality management is clear.

The most useful approaches to effectiveness are explicit about the different stakeholders and their interests. It is helpful to look at the different approaches to effectiveness which have been taken in the past from this standpoint. Note that we do not consider the basic commercial definition in which effectiveness is equated with profitable since this does not apply to the majority of libraries and information services. It is, however, an important consideration for many organizations which provide services to the sector, and may loom larger if contracted-out services become more common.

EFFECTIVENESS BY PRESCRIPTION OF INPUTS

Perhaps the most basic, though least satisfactory, approach to effectiveness occurs where there is an accepted level of resourcing with which the organization has to conform to be labelled 'effective'. In some fields this is laid down by statute while in others, such as librarianship or information science, it tends to be agreed by interested groups in the form of more or less structured standards. A particular characteristic is that these standards are designed for a group of similar organizations, rather than for one individual organization. An example from our field would be the Parry Report (1967) which seemed to suggest that library effectiveness was dependent on libraries receiving 6 per cent of the total university budget:

> The annual cost ... of library provision in a university of medium size would amount to about six per cent of the budget of such a university. Circumstances vary, and it would be undesirable and impracticable to impose standards centrally, but we believe that this represents a standard below which British university libraries should not be allowed to fall.

It is notable that the recent Follett Report (Joint Funding Councils' Libraries Review Group, 1993) coming after a gap of over 25 years, took the view that resource levels were a matter for local decision. 'All decisions involving financial priorities are to be taken locally, and no guidance is offered on the levels of service, stock or staffing which are likely to be needed' (Peasgood, 1994).

Another example of the approach to effectiveness by prescribing inputs, from the public library field, would be the 1962 *Standards for Public Library Services in England and Wales* which specified the number of volumes that should be added to stock each year per 1 000 population. Again, this is a judgement based purely on a count of inputs.

Effectiveness in these circumstances may be seen as the extent to which the library meets the set standards. These approaches have not had a great deal of impact on UK libraries and information services, where of course they have rarely had any legal standing, in part because the constituency which generally promotes them (primarily groupings of interested professionals or their allies) has limited influence on the library's resourcing and survival. On the other hand, there are certainly some instances, for example in the college library sector, where a prescription of inputs has had an effect. In some countries also, for example in Eastern Europe and the former Soviet Union, discussions still continue on the use of this approach, but in general it is no longer encountered with any frequency. Pleas to higher authority, such as funding bodies, to earmark library funding are an attempt to acquire this influence through surrogates, and have not been without some success in the past. It has to be said that they are highly unlikely to be successful in the future. The other, obvious, problem is that even if standards for inputs are met or exceeded there is no guarantee whatsoever that the customers will receive even a satisfactory service, never mind an excellent one.

EFFECTIVENESS BY INTERNAL PROCESSES

A common approach to effectiveness in both industry and services is to seek to optimize internal processes without regard to the effects on customers, and to claim that an operation is effective when all that has been achieved is efficiency. The older schools of management, such as F. W. Taylor's 'Scientific Management', encouraged the belief that if processes could be managed in such a way that all resource inputs, including people's time, were minimized, then success would be all but guaranteed. This confusion between efficiency and effectiveness can still be found in many organizations, and is a major barrier to quality management. All too often it is assumed that the customers' needs are being met, particularly where an industry enjoys a monopoly or near-monopoly in the market. It is not that process improvement is unimportant: indeed, as we showed in Chapter 7, it is one of the core requirements of TQM. But process improvement without relevance to the customers is a waste of both time and resources.

EFFECTIVENESS BY DIRECTION OR CONTRACT FULFILMENT

Although still unusual at the organizational level in the library field, this model exerts an influence of at least a minor nature in most organizations. It assumes that there will be a detailed definition of exactly what the organization is meant to do, and that effectiveness will be measured as the extent to which the organization actually meets these requirements. In contrast to the standards or inputs approach, the direction is individual to a particular organization. The approach has been most common with tasks which have little intellectual input, for example office cleaning or computer data entry, and is becoming more widespread with the development of contracted-out services. A volume of work is required, with a set degree of acceptable accuracy, in order to meet this external requirement. The importance of the approach to libraries and information services lies in two areas: its use within sub-units of the library or information service and the increasing use of individually negotiated contracts by funding bodies which include standards which have to be met. Internally, it may well be appropriate, for example, for someone to be employed solely to reshelve books. The person is performing effectively if the number reshelved each hour meets the target and there is an acceptable percentage of accuracy in the reshelving. Note particularly the strong correlation between power, expressed through resourcing, survival, or the award of contracts, and the ability to direct. The constituency may, if it feels the task is not being carried out effectively, withdraw its support with potentially disastrous consequences for those doing the work.

EFFECTIVENESS: THE PROFESSIONAL APPROACH

There is a tradition, particularly in services which are dominated by professions, to judge effectiveness as being a matter of acting in accordance with professional standards and agreements. There is some validity in this approach, where the standards can be demonstrated to be in accordance with the best interests of the customers. The *Standards for Performance and Resourcing* for Scottish Further Education Colleges (Scottish Library & Information Council and Scottish Library Association, 1993), described in the previous chapter, provides one example from the library and information sector. To give another example, from a different field, it is generally in the interests of patients that medical practitioners act in accordance with their Hippocratic oath, although the debate over euthanasia suggests that it might not always be the case. In academic institutions, peer review has an important place in virtually all quality assurance activities (see, for example, the contributions in Green, 1990). The professional review process is at its strongest when it incorporates the views and experiences of users and takes place in a non-confrontational setting which aims to explore and share good practice. Arthur and Lloyd report on a case study of the involvement of external librarians within such a peer review operated at Dundee Institute of Technology. They report, 'the process so far has shown clear benefits in producing a re-evaluation of what we ... mean by quality and where our priorities lie'.

However, the professional approach can have a number of disadvantages. Often it sets only minimum standards, but it may go to the opposite extreme and set impossible aspirational standards where professions are seeking to make political capital or demonstrate how essential they are, or simply putting the genuinely held beliefs of people committed to their profession and seeking to ensure it is able to give a satisfactory level of service. Second, there is a lack of evidence that all professionals have taken the views of customers into account when setting standards, witness the level of legislative backing that customers often need if they are to assert their rights. Again, the impression is often given that the standards are set for the benefit of the profession itself. For example, recent criticisms of the Solicitors' Complaints Bureau certainly centre on this view.

Libraries have of course moved away from the purely internal 'professional' approach in recent years, although Buckland (1988) refers to a case study by Levy *et al.* (1974) which 'implied that the librarians in a public library allowed their professional values to subvert the use of resources away from the best interests of the users (in the authors' opinion)'. The professional approach does have its dangers and there have been numerous 'professional guidelines' which give high priority to academic status for librarians working in universities, for example, without evidence of the difference this will make to the users. Despite this, a well-organized process of professional review can be an important tool in quality management.

EFFECTIVENESS BY TRADITION

Another common approach to assessing effectiveness is to appeal to historical precedent or tradition. Evidence that a university is acquiring fewer books per full-time equivalent student than in the past is sometimes commented on by library users as illustrating the library's deficiencies. An article in *The Times Higher* in November 1994, for example, uses data collected by the Publishers' Association to call for 'proper funding' for university libraries on the basis that 'all the ... universities spent less in total real terms (in 1992–93) than in the late 1970s' (Targett, 1994). Moore (1992) has pointed out that this approach lacks realism at a time when public expenditure is being cut back and wholesale privatization of public sector services is on the political agenda. The marginal rate of return for increased expenditure may not be very high, and in any case comparisons with previous funding levels now cut little ice. Without further evidence that users require more books (rather, say, than more periodicals or access to databases), that the books acquired in the past were the ones the users wanted, and so on, it does not in fact tell us anything about the effect of the library – only about resource inputs and possibly about potential demand.

EFFECTIVENESS: THE SYSTEMS APPROACH

By far the majority of studies of library effectiveness have taken the systems approach: its essence lies in its view of the library as an organization, within an external environment, which consumes resources (inputs), uses those resources within its own internal operations (processes), and produces products for a population of users (outputs). Usually the systems model will be extended to include some consideration of the effects the use of the products have on the users (outcomes): see Figure 11.1. In order to gauge effectiveness, it is necessary to be explicit about each of these stages, and about the measurable goals which tell the organization which of many possible products should be produced and the balance between competing demands. 'Effectiveness is measured by goal achievement' (Childers and Van House, 1989a).

The systems approach provides a very powerful model for the consideration of effectiveness, not only in the library field. Its key assumption is that goals can be determined and that performance in meeting those goals can be measured. As well as its strength in providing guidance for organizational effort or goal achievement herein also lies its weakness. Most studies which follow this approach end up by measuring what is easily measurable, or what they claim to be measurable. So issue statistics predominate over hours spent studying, number of books over friendliness, and so on. What the service does predominates over how it does it. The systems approach can also easily degenerate into a consideration of the library as a closed system in which the external environment and the end-users are all but forgotten. It is also rather easy to oversimplify the systems approach and neglect the sheer variety of customer needs which the average library or information service is seeking to address: in the systems view, it can be that a book issue is a book issue is a book issue ...

To counteract any tendency to ignore the environment in which the library or other organization operates, a variation on the systems model known as the 'open systems' approach has been developed. This goes out of its way to emphasize the interrelationship between the organization and its environment. 'To survive,

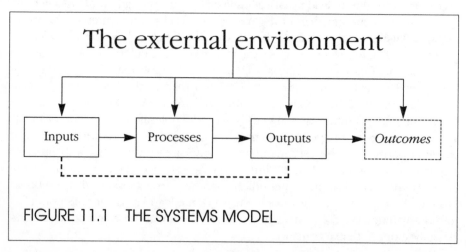

FIGURE 11.1   THE SYSTEMS MODEL

the organization must acquire resources, which are controlled by various external groups. Therefore the effective organization is one that responds to the demands of its environment according to its dependence upon the various components of the environment for resources' (Childers and Van House, 1989a; see also Pfeffer and Salancik, 1978). Again, while this approach has much to offer, it poses a peculiar problem in the many library and information service environments where the users are not, by and large, resource providers. In most settings, the customers pay for goods they receive; in academic institutions and public libraries, as we have seen, this is not the case, and care must be taken not to make assumptions that providing the funders with the service they demand will satisfy the actual users and the other stakeholders. Buckland (1988) has written extensively on these issues, particularly on the 'double feedback loop', by which different stakeholders influence the service. On the other hand, librarians and information scientists have not been particularly aware that effectiveness may be seen as a matter of meeting resource providers' expectations. It is surprising that there have been few studies of library effectiveness in these, admittedly rather nakedly political, terms.

The systems approach is most powerful, then, when goals are determined in relation to the desires of all the stakeholders. It must therefore be tied very closely to the views of those constituencies on what the organization should be doing. What do students want? What do academic staff want? What does institutional management want? What is the responsibility to society? What can each group be persuaded to want, or to support (e.g. academic staff may be persuaded to support services for their students where there is no direct benefit to them)? It is interesting that posing the questions in this way takes us back to the fundamental question of purpose, but purpose viewed from the perspective of the organization's environment – its coalition of stakeholders (see below). Once those purposes and the related goals are established, the systems approach provides mechanisms for understanding the interrelationships between inputs, processes, outputs and outcomes, and therefore goal achievement. This illustrates that the systems approach and quality management are closely related and by no means in conflict.

THE ORGANIC APPROACH TO EFFECTIVENESS

A somewhat different approach sees the organization as an entity in its own right which interacts with its environment but is essentially independent of it in terms of immediate goals. The model is that of a living organism; effectiveness is gauged by survival, by growth, by good health and well-being, by being concerned about itself as well as its 'users'. Empirical observation and some research demonstrates that most organizations do in fact pursue survival (as opposed to dynamic change in response to customer demands) as their primary objective. Pratt and Silverman, in the context of the then polytechnics, noted that the response to the radically new planning climate forced on institutions by the National Advisory Body in the late 1980s was that 'few of our institutions sought to make radical reappraisals of their objectives and functions ... (there was) a tendency to preserve academic profiles despite reductions in resources' (Pratt and Silverman, 1988). Sir Christopher Ball commented that 'academic democracy ... tends all too often to resist change, inhibit responsiveness and prevent decision' (Ball, 1990). Zweizig (1987) quotes a song from the film *Nashville* which runs 'We must be doin' something right / to last two hundred years' and comments 'That's the survival or growth syndrome. If you've lasted this long, you must be effective'. For academic or national libraries we might interpret this scenario as a view that the effective library is the one which survives, amassing collections as it has always done in the past: a powerful view in a country which has inherited Bodley's and Palazzo's heritage.

THE COALITION APPROACH TO EFFECTIVENESS

If we accept that effectiveness is in essence a matter of the effects of the organization on those in its environment then a coalition approach, developed from the systems model outlined above, provides useful insights. This approach seeks:

1.   to identify all the significant constituencies or stakeholders which make up the library's environment;
2.   to determine what each of those constituencies is seeking to achieve from its membership of the coalition, and how its aims are changing;
3.   to interpret those aims in terms of the library's overall mission and objectives;
4.   to suggest ways of assessing the degree of success of the library in meeting such aims.

A possible coalition for an academic library was outlined in Chapter 4. Childers and Van House (1989a, 1989b) suggest that for a public library in the United States the coalition (or, as they term it, the 'multiple constituencies') might consist of the following groups:

○   library managers;
○   library service staff;
○   trustees of the library;
○   users (chosen randomly as they come through the door);
○   friends of the library;
○   local officials from the library's funding body;
○   community leaders.

They used this coalition for a survey which asked respondents to rank 61 listed possible indicators of library effectiveness in order of importance to them: there was also space for respondents to add their own preferred indicators if they so wished. Interestingly, all 61 indicators were chosen as of at least some relevance by respondents.

The coalition approach offers the following advantages:

○   The central question of purpose, from which goals can be derived, is related to all who are in the organization's coalition.
○   It forces the organization to monitor its environment continuously and to see goals as dynamic.

O   Because the environment is subject to continual change so too is the organization: it is 'keyed in' to its environment.

O   Policies and strategies take account of the totality of the coalition.

O   Monitoring of effectiveness is related to the effect that the organization has on its constituencies.

What ties this together is the development and acceptance of a statement of purpose or mission statement together with associated objectives and goals to which the coalition gives its active support. Maintenance of the coalition can be seen as one of the manager's most important roles.

Faerman (1993) suggests that one way to bring together differing approaches to organizational effectiveness of potential relevance to libraries is the 'Competing values framework'. Based on work by Quinn and Rohrbaugh (1981, 1983) this approach acknowledges the competing and contradictory perspectives of stake-holders, enabling different models to be mapped on to the framework. So, for example, the framework acknowledges the contribution of the human relations model of organizations with its emphasis on the value of human resources, impor-tance of morale, etc.; the open system model encompassing adaptability, resource acquisition and the needs for external support; and the internal process model with the emphasis on control and internal communication. The same approach can be applied to managerial leadership in order to balance the competing values and rules which that demands. Faerman ends by suggesting that 'library administrators (and other managerial leaders) must become more comfortable with the concept of paradox. Conceptual opposites are not always opposites in reality. Good strate-gies can become bad strategies if followed to an extreme.' This brings us back to some of the concepts Tom Peters, Charles Handy and others have been exploring in recent works like *Thriving on Chaos* (Peters, 1992) and *The Empty Raincoat* (Handy, 1994). Library and information service effectiveness, and through it the achievement of quality services, may depend on recognizing the paradoxes and responding to them rather than pursuing a single strategy to its logical end.

CONCLUSION

Studies of library and information service effectiveness, particularly those based on the systems model and its variants, have provided a solid basis on which future advances in quality management in the sector can be built. Effectiveness and quality are closely linked, and further development of some of the studies outlined in this chapter, particularly with regard to the interests of all stakeholders, would provide advances not only in our understanding of the mechanics of library and information services' operations but also in our ability to respond to the needs of our customers. The combination of prior work on library effectiveness with quality management thus provides a major opportunity to make advances in service provision.

12

SYSTEMATIC PERFORMANCE MEASUREMENT FOR LIBRARIES AND INFORMATION SERVICES

❖

The measurement of library and information service performance has been an important area of activity for researchers and practitioners alike for many years. The discussion of library effectiveness in the previous chapter has drawn attention to some of this work. In this chapter we will examine some of the most influential recent work in greater depth. Performance measurement itself has been defined for librarians in a paper by Cronin (1982) as 'the process of systematically assessing effectiveness against a predetermined norm, standard or expressed goal', and thus consideration of it leads on naturally from the discussion in the previous chapter.

The terms 'performance measures' and 'performance indicators' can be distinguished, although many commentators have failed to do so consistently, as MacDougall (1992) has pointed out. Performance measures describe something directly in quantitative terms, such as the number of items lent by a library to a particular class of users. Performance indicators, while expressed quantitatively, infer from quantitative data something about the performance, or relative performance, of the organization or an aspect of its operations. So the number of refereed journal articles published by a scientist or scholar might be *measured* but then taken as an *indicator* of the quality of his or her research. To add to the confusion, it is possible to say that performance 'indicators (are) for measuring ... performance' (The Audit Commission, quoted in Sumsion, 1993a). So, issues per capita is a performance *indicator* to the UK Audit Commission but an output (performance) *measure* to the American Library Association (Van House *et al.*, 1987). These ambiguities are reflected in the discussion of some of the manuals and other publications described in more detail below. Maguire and Willard (1990) remark that not only does this confusion exist, but that many writers also confuse measures with the criteria on which they are based. However, 'perhaps (the) confusion does not matter so long as all parties know that confusion exists'.

Studies of library performance measurement are so extensive that it is impossible to review them comprehensively here. Goodall (1988) provided an excellent historical review while Lancaster and Baker (1991) published an evaluative account from an American perspective. An overview of techniques for evaluating libraries, now in its second edition, has appeared separately (Lancaster, 1993a). Key works in the field include De Prospo *et al.*'s (1973) work in the public library sector and Kantor's academic libraries' performance measurement volume (Kantor, 1984). Later contributions are considered in detail below. Henty (1989) compared the use of performance indicators in Australian, British and American libraries and commented on the British approach that it 'lacks indicators of quality. There has been no attempt to examine, for example, whether reference questions are answered correctly, or whether new materials being purchased relate to the teaching/research profiles of the institutions'. There has certainly been a shift from purely measuring input to a combination of measures of both input and output although most observers would seem to agree with Henty's comments (see, for example, a recent paper by Morgan, 1993). The practical difficulty of implementing performance measurement, especially where the aim is to measure qualitative factors, has been commented on by many observers, especially those involved in practice (see, for example, Abbott, 1990).

VAN HOUSE, WEIL AND McCLURE'S *MEASURING ACADEMIC LIBRARY PERFORMANCE*

One of the most influential recent publications in the field of library performance measurement was produced in the USA in 1990. *Measuring academic library performance: a practical approach* by Nancy A. Van House *et al.* was based on work carried out for the US Association of College & Research Libraries' Ad Hoc Committee on Performance Measures and published by the American Library Association. It is described as a 'practical manual' and answers four clear goals:

1.   To provide instruments which could 'measure the impact, efficiency and effectiveness of library operations';
2.   To enable library output to be quantified or explained in meaningful ways to university administrators;
3.   To provide instruments or measures 'which could be used by heads of units to demonstrate performance levels and resource needs to library administrators'.
4.   To enable 'data useful for library planning' to be gathered.

The committee also aimed to provide measures which were 'replicable in all types of academic and research libraries ... decision-related ... easy and inexpensive to apply and use ... user-oriented, and linked to library goals and objectives'.

The manual takes the general systems model of organizations, which was described above, and focuses on the measurement of outputs. This is an important emphasis because much measurement of library operations has concentrated on inputs (such as number of books acquired) or processes (such as the number catalogued) rather than on what is delivered. The manual identifies 15 measures, as follows:

1. General user satisfaction, defined as success in using the library during the visit when the survey is administered, user assessment of ease of the use of the library and overall satisfaction with the library during that visit.
2. Number of items issued, from statistics collected by circulation systems and any other sources.
3. Number of items used in the library but not issued, measured by counting the number of books needing to be reshelved (users are asked not to reshelve their own books during the survey period).
4. Total materials use: the sum of 2 and 3.
5. Materials availability: the percentage of user searches for specific materials which are successful.
6. Requested materials delay: the time users have to wait for materials which they want but which are not immediately available: either not on the shelf or not owned. This could, depending on the library, include the reservation service, interlibrary loans, retrieval from store or a document delivery service.
7. Attendance: the number of visits made to the library.
8. Remote users: any kind of use where the user does not come to the library, including document delivery services, access to the catalogue or databases and telephone, fax or e-mail requests.
9. Total uses: the sum of 7 and 8.
10. Facilities use rate: the proportion of time that a 'facility' (for example user seating, workstations, photocopiers, seminar rooms) is in use.
11. Service point use: the average number of users served at a staffed service point.
12. Building use: the average number of people in the library building.
13. Reference transactions: defined as 'an information contact that involves the knowledge, use, recommendations, interpretation or instruction of one or more information sources by a member of the library staff'.
14. Reference satisfaction: users' evaluation of the outcome of a reference request, using a survey with five key questions concerning relevance, the amount of information, how complete the response was, the helpfulness of staff and overall satisfaction rating.
15. Online search satisfaction: users' own evaluation of mediated online searches. The methodology suggested included seven questions, grouped under four headings: users' satisfaction with the performance of library staff in understanding the request; selecting databases and formulating a query; users' satisfaction with the product of the search, including relevance and currency; users' satisfaction with the time taken to provide an answer; and an overall assessment to the online search itself.

Clearly much of this methodology moves us forward from the collection of input and process statistics towards the assessment of quality. The surveys concerning user satisfaction are particularly interesting, and the inclusion of questions into such issues as relevance and completeness of information provided is directly related to the dimensions of quality identified in other fields.

The manual is helpful in two other regards. It contains extremely detailed methodologies, including sample survey forms and detailed instructions in determining sample sizes and analysing results. It also contains suggestions on strategies to adopt if the measures reveal situations which cause concern. For example, if materials availability appears to be a problem the authors advise using a methodology suggested by Kantor (1984) to follow up user failure at the shelf to determine the causes: was the book mis-shelved, just returned by another user but not yet shelved, out on loan, missing or perhaps not even owned by the library? Did the user go to the wrong shelf, or even search the wrong floor of the library, and so on?

The manual has been used widely in North America and to a lesser extent in the rest of the world. One example of its implementation in Europe is given in Lidman and Törngren (1993), where its use at Stockholm University Library is reported. The methodology has also been very influential in a number of groups concerned with library performance measurement, including the IFLA (International Federation of Library Associations and Institutions) and ISO (International Standards Organization) work described below.

OUTPUT MEASURES FOR PUBLIC LIBRARIES

In 1987 the American Library Association issued a revised version of Zweizig and Rodger's 1982 *Output Measures for Public Libraries* prepared by a team led by Charles McClure of Syracuse University, which included Zweizig, Nancy Van House of the University of California at Berkeley, Amy Owen of Utah State Library and Mary Jo Lynch of the ALA's Office for Research (Van House *et al.*, 1987). All are distinguished librarians with considerable experience in the field. The volume suggested the use of five sets of measures, including:

O   **Library use measures,** such as library visits per capita of the population served by the library and the percentage of that population registered as library users.

O   **Materials use measures,** including the average number of items circulated per capita of the population served, in-library materials use on the same basis and the 'turnover rate' or average number of circulations per volume owned.

O   **Materials access measures,** which are concerned with determining how successful users are in finding the materials they want. These measures include the 'title fill rate', which is the proportion of specific titles sought by users which were found during a visit, the 'subject and author fill rate' which is an equivalent measure for searches under subject or author, 'browsers' fill rate' which measures the proportion of users who were browsing and found something of interest, and a document delivery measure which measures the average time taken to supply an item (by reservation, recall, interlibrary loan, and so on) which was not immediately available when the user wanted it.

O   **Reference services,** incorporating a measure of the number of reference transactions per capita of the population and a 'reference completion rate' measure, defined as the proportion of reference transactions successfully completed (in the judgement of the librarian) on the same day as the request is made.

In addition to these five categories there are a number of suggestions of possible additional measures. For example, a library might want to measure the amount of 'programming' (tuition, lectures, etc.) which it provided and it is suggested that this might be achieved through calculating the total number of people attending such events and dividing that figure by the total population served.

The *Output Measures for Public Libraries* manual provides a very practical approach to performance measurement. It includes, for example, blank survey forms as well as detailed advice on how data should be collected and presented. It states that the person responsible for using the manual does not require a knowledge of statistics, although clearly some appreciation of the significance of choosing appropriate sampling periods, for example, is necessary.

KEYS TO SUCCESS: PERFORMANCE INDICATORS FOR PUBLIC LIBRARIES

The *Keys to Success* manual for public libraries (Office of Arts and Libraries, 1990) emerged from a British Library funded study which sought to provide a standardized approach to performance measurement for British public libraries. It was produced by an American team, King Research, assisted by an advisory group of British librarians and received government endorsement. For a number of reasons it has not been as successful as its American counterparts. In part, it was unfortunately timed (appearing after much delay) since the British Government launched *The Citizen's Charter*, with a somewhat different approach, shortly afterwards (see Chapter 13). The Audit Commission in England and Wales and Scottish Accounts Commission in Scotland were given statutory responsibility for defining performance standards for public authorities, including their public libraries, and took a different approach to that taken by the King Research team. In addition, some professional opinion felt that the recommended approach was over-elaborate and time-consuming to administer. Finally, the recommendations lacked prescription in some areas, for example: 'Book reading can be defined as a single incidence of reading ... or the sum of occasions of reading during a loan ... period. For reading of public library materials, the latter definition is suggested (although if two people read the book perhaps two readings should be counted)'. The American manuals tend to be far more prescriptive. Finally, there is curiously little reference to earlier work, apart from mention of the CIPFA (Chartered Institute of Public Finance and Accountancy) statistics, to which all public libraries have to contribute data, and passing references to the American *Output Measures for Public Libraries* document, described above. Despite these criticisms, as a documented approach to the subject of performance measurement, and one which drew on wide-ranging practical expertise, *Keys to Success* has considerable value and is therefore described in outline below.

Keys to Success recommended 21 performance *measures* and 16 performance *indicators* (for once the distinction was made clearly) which would provide a comprehensive picture of the performance of a public library. The performance measures (PM 1 to PM 21 below) were grouped into four categories:

1.   **Service input cost measures:**
   ○ PM 1 – Amount of resources applied to each service (financial, staff, facilities and premises, equipment and systems, stock, other);
   ○ PM 2 – Amount of funding applied to each service (i.e. the conversion of 'amount of resources' into monetary terms);
   ○ PM 3 – Attributes of the service which affect the cost and/or the quantity and/or quality of outputs. An example given was that the cost of equipment may vary depending on its reliability.

2.   **Service output measures:**
   ○ PM 4 – Quantities of outputs for each service (e.g. number of items issued, number of photocopies made);
   ○ PM 5 – Quality of output. Quality was defined as 'grade or goodness' (*sic*). Quality, in this definition, was to be 'measured' on a scale of 1 to 5 and could be related to factors such as relevance of online search outputs and the accuracy of cataloguing;
   ○ PM 6 – Timeliness of output, defined as the time between a request being made and the material to satisfy that request being received by the user. It was also suggested that for services such as inter-library loans, the time difference between when users wanted an item and when it was made available to them should also be measured;
   ○ PM 7 – Availability of service, measured by the number of hours the service is available. In some cases it may be appropriate to multiply this by the number of staff providing the service;
   ○ PM 8 – Accessibility of the service, which may involve measuring the physical distance a user has to travel, or the time it takes to get to the library. It may also be necessary to measure the accessibility of stock and equipment (e.g. an OPAC may be inaccessible because of heavy use, while stock may be inaccessible because it is kept on closed access). Physical accessibility for people with disabilities should also be measured.

3.   **Service effectiveness measures:**
   ○ PM 9 – Amount of use, measured by counting various factors such as number of loans, number of visits, requests for reference services, use of photocopiers, and so on;
   ○ PM 10 – Users' perceptions of attributes. The idea would be to ask users to rate general service performance, for example, on a scale of 1 (very bad) to 5 (very good), or an attribute of a service from 1 (not at all relevant) to 5 (extremely relevant). There is, however, a misunderstanding of the importance of users' perceptions in this section

where it is suggested that if hard information is available, such as a response time, then perception does not need to be measured. In fact, of course, and to use a common example, users forced to stand in a queue will almost always overestimate the time they have to wait: their perception is different from reality. A quality management perspective would argue that it is the perception and not the reality that is important;

○ PM 11 – User-expressed satisfaction, again recorded on a 1 to 5 numeric scale. There is a recommendation that satisfaction should be measured in relation to specific user needs, e.g. reference response time;

○ PM 12 – User-indicated importance, which provides a useful balance to measures of satisfaction, since users may be highly satisfied with a service which they regard as unimportant or highly dissatisfied with a service they regard as extremely important. Again a 1 to 5 rating scale can be used;

○ PM 13 – Purpose of use, which is an attempt to categorize users' purposes, for example into personal use, educational use, work-related use, and so on;

○ PM 14 – Consequences of use: 'all the purposes of use have some implications for the quality of life, the economy and other higher order effects'. True, but no suggestions are made as to how these effects can be measured and the section, acknowledging the difficulty, simply states that 'at least statements of consequences can be made'.

4.   Service domain measures:

○ PM 15 – Total population size, segmented into groups;

○ PM 16 – Total population attributes, being ways of categorizing the total population, for example by place of residence (recognizing the effect of users who work in the local authority area but do not reside in it), age, gender, occupation, and so on. The distinction between those eligible to use the library and those who actually do so is made here;

○ PM 17 – User population size, for example measured by counting registered borrowers, visitors to the library and users of specific services;

○ PM 18 – User population attributes, a way of segmenting the user population in the same manner as the total population;

○ PM 19 – Size of geographic area, measured in hectares;

○ PM 20 – Geographic area attributes, such as population density, availability of public transport. This measure was also to include the existence of physical barriers such as rivers and hills!

○ PM 21 – Information needs, a rather loosely defined concept (in terms of measurement) with the suggestion that categorization by type of information needed or type of material needed would be appropriate. Needs could be observed and the method chosen to satisfy them, such as 'from a library, a friend, a professional, (a) newspaper', recorded.

Having defined the 21 performance measures, *Keys to Success* went on to derive the 16 performance indicators (PI 1–16 below):

1.   **Operational performance indicators:**
- PI 1 – Productivity, regarded as the return on investment, and calculated by dividing the number of outputs by input costs. Reference enquiries dealt with per hour of staff time are given as an example;
- PI 2 – Cost per output, for example the cost per enquiry;
- PI 3 – Cost by attribute level, an indicator to be used complementarily with the previous one, to provide information on the relationship between the attributes (defined in the measures) and costs. An example given is that the average cost per output may be found to rise as relevance of response increases;
- PI 4 – Productivity by attribute levels, an example of which would be the productivity of cataloguing staff indicated by the number of items catalogued per hour of staff time.

2.   **Effectiveness indicators:**
- PI 5 – Turnover rate, being the relationship between the amount provided and the amount used. For example a library might measure average number of uses of stock, categorized by stock age. Various turnover rates are defined, and the definition varies from that given in *Output Measures for Public Libraries*;
- PI 6 – Amount of use by attribute level, which is intended to indicate how the defined attributes of output, such as timeliness, accessibility, and so on, influence the amount of use of a service;
- PI 7 — User satisfaction, divided into general user satisfaction and satisfaction with specific services or attributes of services;
- PI 8 – User satisfaction by attribute level, which is intended to indicate how user satisfaction varies with the attributes of output, which might also be described as user tolerance for different attribute levels;
- PI 9 – Amount of use by satisfaction level, an example being the amount of use of reference services divided by the level of user satisfaction with those services.

3.   **Cost-effectiveness indicators:**
- PI 10 – Cost per use, being the total input costs of a service divided by the amount of use. The authors note that this is often the same as PI 2: it is difficult to see when it would not be!
- PI 11 – Cost per user, being the input costs divided by the number of actual users of the service;
- PI 12 – Cost per capita, which is similar to PI 11 but relates costs to the population as a whole;
- PI 13 – Cost by satisfaction level, the idea here being to relate costs to the satisfaction level being achieved with the underlying assumption that higher satisfaction can be related to higher input cost.

4.   **Impact indicators:**
- PI 14 – Users as a proportion of the population, both overall and for individual services, such as service to the housebound;

○ PI 15 – Use per capita, again calculated for different services, such as reference enquiries and loans;
○ PI 16 – Needs fill rate, being the proportion of needs identified that are actually met. The use of various fill rates by *Output Measures for Public Libraries* is noted.

Keys to Success also provides some sample survey forms and guidance on how to design questionnaires, carry out surveys and calculate results. Inevitably in a publication of this kind these relatively short sections tend to be superficial. The problem faced by the authors was that if they did not use the entirely prescriptive approach of *Output Measures for Public Libraries* they would have to rely on library staff to design their own data collection instruments and could not assume that the necessary statistical and technical expertise would be available. However, it must be a matter of doubt as to whether a page and a half on questionnaire design, for example, would really prove adequate.

The possible application of *Keys to Success* to UK academic libraries was explored by Ford and MacDougall (1992), who concluded that the approach was not promising and that work on academic library performance measurement should follow a different path (see below).

Later work on performance indicators for British public libraries, which has been heavily influenced by *The Citizen's Charter*, is described in the next Chapter.

INTERNATIONAL FEDERATION OF LIBRARY ASSOCIATIONS/INTERNATIONAL STANDARDS ORGANIZATION

The International Federation of Library Associations and Institutions (IFLA) and a working party of the International Standards Organization (ISO) have been investigating the development of a standard set of performance indicators for libraries. The IFLA work was initiated by the Section for University and other General Research Libraries at the Sydney conference in 1988 and in its early stages considered five performance measures:

1.   relevance in collection development;
2.   degree of satisfaction of users;
3.   hours of opening;
4.   the average delay between ordering and availability on the shelves;
5.   the percentage of requested items actually obtained by users.

The work concentrated on academic libraries and some experimentation was carried out in libraries in Germany: a report on work at the Universitäts und Landesbibliothek Münster was published by Poll (1993) and a preliminary draft report is available (International Federation of Library Associations and Institutions, 1993).

The ISO work originated with a feasibility study led by Charles McClure of the University of Syracuse, USA, following a Danish proposal in 1991. Following that work, a working party, consisting of experts from the USA, UK, Denmark, France,

Germany, Ireland, Norway, Russia, South Africa and Sweden, met over a considerable time period. At the time of writing the draft standard is still under development and is to be considered at a meeting in Ottawa, Canada in May 1995. The draft relates library performance indicators to the ISO 9000 standard and draws on much of the key work in the field, including the IFLA work, *Measuring Academic Library Performance*, *Keys to Success* and *Output Measures for Public Libraries*. As is normal with international standards, there will be a period of consultation on the draft standard before it is confirmed.

UK ACADEMIC LIBRARIES' PERFORMANCE MEASUREMENT

The UK Standing Conference of National and University Libraries (SCONUL) and Council of Polytechnic Librarians (COPOL) – the two merged into a new body, also called SCONUL, in 1994 – have a long record of work on performance indicators for academic libraries. The origins of this work lie in the collection of statistics concerning inputs, processes and outputs by the libraries of higher education institutions which wished to compare themselves against their peers. At a time of growth, the statistics were frequently of use in demonstrating to management that further resources were needed, either to catch up with institutions which were better funded or to maintain or improve their position in the league tables over time (the 'professional approach' to effectiveness described in the previous chapter). In addition, the statistical compilations could be used in institutional 'quality assurance' inspections.

More recently the focus of this work has changed. The need for performance statistics remains, but there has been a broadening of focus to try to move explicitly the quality of provision in relation to the university's mission and performance. Background to this development can be found in a paper by Winkworth (1990).

A SCONUL document drawn up by Winkworth and Rear (1993) sets out a five-fold approach to assessment of the library of a higher education institution.

1.   **Integration.** To what extent is the library integrated into the university's teaching, learning and research activities? What evidence is there to support any integration claimed? How does communication between the library and the academic departments take place? Does this information feed into the planning and delivery of library services?

2.   **User satisfaction.** Are students, teachers and researchers satisfied with the library support they receive? What evidence is there for this? Particular areas identified include the supply of books and other materials, enquiry services, information skills tuition and study facilities.

3.   **Effectiveness.** Does the library have service delivery targets? Is it meeting them? It is suggested that targets should include time to process new acquisitions, interlibrary loan delivery times, queue lengths and the accuracy of answers to enquiries.

4.   **Efficiency.** The comparison between inputs and outputs. Examples of outputs should include the number of documents supplied, the number

of library visits and the number of study-place hours per week made available – although the last has been criticized as not being a true output measure since the real question is whether the study places are occupied. The efficiency calculation compares these outputs with total costs or with costs allocated to individual services where such data are available.

5.   **Economy.** A simple measure of the total library funding divided by student numbers compared to other institutions.

One of the most interesting aspects of these approaches is that they are intended to provide data for external quality assurance audit processes. In the UK there is currently a dual approach to quality audit of universities (see also Chapter 7, pp. 103–106). The Higher Education Quality Council (HEQC) pays a periodic visit to each university to examine its quality assurance procedures and mechanisms. In other words it is not concerned with a direct measure of the quality of each university's provision but with ensuring that the institution has in place suitable procedures to enable it to monitor quality itself and take action where necessary. The Higher Education Funding Councils (HEFCs), on the other hand, assess the quality of courses in individual subjects directly and examine such matters as drop-out statistics, student satisfaction and external expert assessment of courses. Following this dual approach, the SCONUL/COPOL library performance methodology suggests that in the case of the HEQC the emphasis should be on the integration of the library into the institution's affairs and on the accountability of the library for the services it delivers. With subject assessments by HEFC, the suggestion is that institutions should submit a general library profile covering integration, service standards and their achievements, efficiency and resourcing, and a separate report on user satisfaction supplemented by meetings between quality assessors and students. Since HEFCs are not the only bodies concerned with research it is further suggested that the Research Councils should be asked to satisfy themselves separately that library resources are sufficient to support research.

LIBRARY USER SATISFACTION

As the descriptions above indicate, there has been a continuing interest in measuring library user satisfaction for at least the last quarter-century. Both the *Keys to Success* and *Measuring Academic Library Performance* manuals contain sections on measuring satisfaction and they draw on a wide body of earlier work.

The most recent comprehensive survey of satisfaction with public library services was a study carried out for the Audit Commission by MORI between December 1991 and February 1992. The summary results are reproduced in a compilation published by the Library & Information Statistics Unit of the University of Loughborough (Sumsion, 1993a). In answer to the question, 'Overall, how satisfied or dissatisfied are you with the quality of your local library service?', 81 per cent of library users were either very or fairly satisfied while only 9 per cent were either fairly or very dissatisfied. Respondents were also asked for the criteria they use when judging satisfaction; it is interesting to compare the answers with the

Rater categories devised by Zeithaml *et al.* (1990) (see Chapter 4): Reliability, Assurance, Tangibles, Empathy, Responsiveness. For example, public library users rate 'an inviting atmosphere', 'helpful staff', 'comfortable seating' and 'attractive appearance' among their major criteria, exactly as the Rater methodology would predict. The MORI researchers posed the question in their final report, 'Should (the performance indicators used) include attitudinal factors (such as helpfulness of staff) which, though difficult to measure, are nevertheless considered very important by the public in gauging the performance of library services?' (ibid.).

Present work by the UK Standing Conference of National and University Libraries (SCONUL) has suggested a five-fold approach to library user satisfaction, based on work undertaken by Don Revill at Liverpool John Moores University. Five separate questionnaires are being piloted to establish:

1. General user satisfaction, including users' relative success in completing various activities, the number of items used while in the library, the time spent in the library and an assessment of ease of use as well as the level of satisfaction with the library service overall.
2. What is termed the 'quality of service', which is a measure of the users' perceptions of whether the service met their needs. This questionnaire is also designed to elicit information on use of alternative sources of materials.
3. Stock selection, including users' reasons for borrowing items, the type of use made (including photocopying) and the amount of 'document exposure'. This last is a means of assessing how much actual use of each item took place.
4. Availability of materials, including the proportion of searches for specific items which the user knew he or she needed that were successful.
5. Enquiries and reference services, measuring users' perceptions of these services.

Reference was made in Chapter 4 to work by Williams (1987) and Head and Marcella (1993) which indicated that libraries offer what appears to be a poor service in responding to customer reference enquiries. To these studies may be added similar work in the US (Paskoff, 1991; Hernon and McClure, 1986; Peat, Marwick, Mitchell and Co., 1975). Although, as noted before, some customers may be 'satisfied' by the wrong or partial answers they receive, it is a matter of concern that successive studies have identified a problem which must have a considerable impact on overall levels of satisfaction, yet as far as is known the solution has not been found. This would seem to be a fruitful area for further investigation.

CONCLUSION

Clearly approaches to library performance measurement have become much more sophisticated in recent years and the subject plays an important part in the management process in all types of library and information service. The monitoring of performance is important not only in the obvious sense of enabling the manager to know whether the service is improving or declining in terms of the chosen measures, but as a political weapon in acquiring resources and securing the library's place in the organization.

Three key issues need to be addressed in this area, however.

1.   It is too often assumed that all libraries, or at least all libraries of a particular type, should use the same set of indicators. This is convenient for funders who wish to compare one library with another, but rarely offers much insight into the quality of the library service. It is the principle behind the so-called 'league tables' published each year by *The Times* showing the expenditure per student on libraries by each UK university. The implication is that the higher up the league table, the better the library, ignoring the fact that expenditure is an input measure and that high levels of expenditure could indicate no more than inefficiency.

2.   All too often, performance measures are based on the philosophy of 'measuring the measurable'. The fondness of librarians for issue statistics over hard measures of in-library use illustrates this tendency.

3.   Performance measurement does not itself provide guidelines to management on what to do to improve the service: the example of reference service performance would seem to bear this out. The earlier discussion of quality management approaches in other sectors will have made it clear that very often knowing that things need to be improved is no more than the first step (albeit an important one) along the road to better services. Abbott (1990) remarked that 'it is the final implementation phase that can prove the most problematic ... measurement of quality may lead to beneficial organizational changes, but it cannot itself improve quality. This can only result from the actions arising from that measurement'. It is all too easy to think that because something has been measured it has been managed. Schlichter and Pemberton (1992) report on a study of 122 public libraries in California of which not only had 94 per cent not carried out an evaluation study in the last three years, but 78 per cent of those that had undertaken such work had not initiated any actions as a result.

13

CONTRACTING OUT AND CHARTERS FOR LIBRARIES

❖

The introduction of *The Citizen's Charter* has already been described in Chapter 6. As public services, public libraries were at the forefront of the implementation of the Charter, although its effect was also felt in other publicly funded library and information services, including those in government departments, universities and colleges. The purpose of this chapter is to review how libraries responded to the challenges for quality of service of the charter movement, including contracting out, and to draw some lessons for the future.

Libraries had of course already demonstrated interest and activity in this field before *The Citizen's Charter* was published, and they were quick to respond to the document itself. Clayton (1994) reports that he had collected examples of library user's charters from Berkshire, Cambridgeshire, Essex, Kent, Lewisham, Norfolk, Solihull and Wiltshire by early 1992. The Library Association published a discussion document within a year of the launch of *The Citizen's Charter* (Library Association, 1992a). This led to considerable debate and the publication of guidelines for public libraries (Library Association, 1992b). Following further debate a model charter for public libraries was published (Library Association, 1993a – see Appendix III), together with a statement of standards (Featherstone, 1994). Public libraries formed the Quality Forum to provide a vehicle for discussion, sharing of experience and information dissemination.

STANDARDS OF SERVICE AND PERFORMANCE INDICATORS

The Citizen's Charter itself, and the Local Government Act, 1992 which gave statutory powers to the Audit Commission and the Scottish Accounts Commission, referred to the need to measure standards of performance and to publicize the results. As a result, extensive discussions took place between representatives of the public libraries and of the audit authorities, with input from the Library Association, to try to reach a consensus on how service standards should be defined and measured and on the performance indicators to be used. A particular concern was to ensure consistency across different library authorities so as to enable comparisons to be made.

The debate itself is documented by Sumsion (1993a), who has drawn together not only the key discussion documents but also examples of performance indicators and user surveys from 11 library services (Berkshire, Bromley, Essex, Glasgow, Kirkcaldy, Manchester, Richmond-upon-Thames, Solihull, Surrey, West Sussex and Wiltshire).

For 1993–94, the following performance indicators were set by the audit authorities for all public library authorities in Great Britain:

1.   The number of *items issued* by the authority's libraries, subdivided into *books* and *other items*.
2.   The number of libraries which were *open*:

    O   45 hours per week or more;
    O   30–44 hours per week;
    O   10–29 hours per week;

    and mobile libraries.
3.   The number of *visits* by members of the public.
4.   The *amount spent per head of population* on books and other materials.
5.   The total *net expenditure per head of population*.

The indicators have been confirmed for subsequent use in 1994–95. In addition to these core indicators, the discussions led to agreement on a range of voluntary indicators which libraries could use if they wished and helped to clarify the basis on which information to support such indicators should be based. It is possible that the number of indicators which public libraries are required to calculate and publish will increase in the future, although there is concern that the process of measurement should not become so time-consuming that it defeats the objective.

The Library Association has taken a lead in trying to establish new standards for public libraries as part of the model charter for public libraries. Details were not available when this book was being written, although it is reported that 'good practice would be taken as the standard achieved by the top 25 per cent of respondents' to the questionnaire sent to public libraries by the study team (Anon. 1994).

COMPULSORY COMPETITIVE TENDERING FOR LIBRARY SERVICES

In the UK those responsible for public libraries, and some in the government sector, have been under pressure to consider contracting out of services to private sector competitors for a considerable period. Library services were specifically mentioned in *The Citizen's Charter* and a 1988 statement by the Minister for the Arts was quoted to provide the underlying thinking and rationale for the proposed changes: 'Library authorities will remain responsible for the nature and quality of any service they contract out. The only purpose of contracting out is to produce as good a service at less cost or a better service at the same price.' That statement had been made during the passage of the Local Government Act, 1988 which provided the legislative framework within which the contracting out processes would be operated, building on earlier provisions in the Local Government, Planning and Land Act, 1980.

In its response to the Government, the Library Association based its remarks on the minister's statement and confirmed its agreement with its avowed aim of improving services. It added, 'However, competition is only one element in promoting value for money: the establishment and promotion of good practice and effective management techniques, and further moves towards cooperation and, where appropriate, standardisation are other essential elements' (The Library Association, 1992a). The response had little to say about quality, and what was said was little more than a defence of existing standards of service: 'we reject the allegation ... that there is significant public criticism of the performance and efficiency of in-house workforces. This is simply not the case with public library services ... The library profession has shown itself adept and innovative in experimenting with new management structures and methods of service delivery' (ibid.). Such confidence did not extend to the idea of operating through contracting out of core functions: 'It is our view that no library authority could exercise this responsibility for stock management effectively by contracting it out, without adversely affecting the quality and nature of the service received by users'.

By this stage, of course, the argument had shifted from the ideal of customer-led public services to arguments about mechanisms for delivering those services. The real issue of improving quality became rather neglected and few of the contributions to the debate seemed to consider that issue at any length (see, for example, contributions to the 1991 International Library Technology Fair conference on contracting out (*Contracting out*, 1992)). It is worth noting, however, the ongoing debate on how customer-oriented public libraries really were: see the 1993 Comedia Report *Borrowed Time?*, for example (Greenhalgh *et al.*, 1993). A paper examining the issues from the private sector contractor's viewpoint seemed much more concerned with the effects on customers and the improvements in service that might be possible (Brice, 1992). These arguments, which are continuing, may be put in context if one accepts the views of Maurice Line, writing in F. W. Lancaster's collection of essays on *Libraries and the Future*, that 'the concept of all information as a public good will have all but disappeared by AD 2015. The private information sector will be very big by AD 2015 and will be carrying out some of the work traditionally carried out by libraries' (Line, 1993). He continued, 'Libraries by then will be operating in a much more commercial fashion'.

Much of the debate on contracting out has referred to it as an entirely new phenomenon. Yet is that the case? Moon (1993), quoted in Sumsion (1994), pointed out that:

> If we accept the definition of contracting out as being 'the process whereby Council invites tenders for the operation of a particular section of Council's activities, whereby Council is effectively leasing out that section of its operations', you will see that our regional library services are, in fact, a form of contracting out, although it has not been common practice to refer to them in this way.

One can go further and observe that, for the UK, the British Library's Document Supply Centre is effectively a contracting out of the responsibility of major libraries to stock comprehensive collections.

Since the initial discussions and reactions the Compulsory Competitive Tendering issue has moved on, albeit slowly. Again, concentrating on the associated quality issues, it was interesting to note a comment by the chief library adviser at the Department of National Heritage, in October 1993, to the effect that contracted out services could be subject to some kind of 'independent testing' as opposed to 'peer review' (Ashcroft, 1993, p. 29). In other words, the idea of professional judgement as the basis for evaluating quality was being rejected. By this time the Department had developed a strategy of pilot testing of contracting out and had selected a small number of sites for different parts of the library service to be tested against the market. Considerable stress was placed on how the service would be specified and how the performance of the successful contractor would be monitored. The five areas chosen for piloting were:

1.   A detailed client/contractor specification for the library service (Kent County Library).
2.   The use of business units to operate the whole library service on a contract basis, with market testing of one or more of them (London Borough of Brent Libraries).
3.   The franchising of services (Hertfordshire Libraries, Arts and Information Services).
4.   Contracting out cultural services (Hereford & Worcestershire Library).
5.   Whole service trusts (Dorset County Library).

The government was clearly disappointed that more 'volunteers' did not come forward to market test other aspects of library services.

The Brent experiment has progressed the furthest and generated the most interest and comment, both positive and negative (see, for example, Tyerman, 1993; Casale, 1994). One of the most interesting aspects of this experiment, however, is that it was based on a fundamental rethinking of the whole service delivery concept. So Tyerman noted:

> There had been a major restructuring of the library service in 1989 which was not functioning well. Responsibilities were confused and accountabilities ill-defined. Decision making was consistently passed up the hierarchy to senior managers; many key posts were unfilled because of budget freezes; there were dozens of *ad hoc* library closures; and there was a general perception in the minds of the public, Members (i.e. elected members of the council) and senior Council officers of poor performance. The last straw was a scandal that erupted over allegedly large scale stock losses. In response, a major review of the library service took place and culminated in 1991 in a second restructuring with the aims of providing a quality, value for money service and developing a customer orientated culture.

Among the changes introduced were:

O   service specifications detailing standards and levels of service;
O   customer service guarantees;
O   performance indicators;

O   a customer complaints system;
O   customer surveys;
O   quality awareness training for all staff.

From 400 expressions of interest received when the contract to run the first two libraries was advertised, four were selected to provide detailed tenders and eventually the in-house team won the contract. John Verstraete, who was a member of the successful team, was asked if the strategy had been to put in the lowest possible price and replied, 'No, we looked at a combination of quality and value for money. We saw restructuring and tendering as an opportunity to adjust and improve quality' (Casale, 1994). Of course, the jury is still out on whether quality improvements will be achieved, but Karen Tyerman regards the most significant change to date as 'a change in the culture of the organisation ... (and)... significant cost savings ... Projected over all six of the Brent libraries ... contracts would achieve savings of over one million pounds while at the same time improving the range and quality of service available' (ibid.).

The view from some of the other participants in the contracting out experiments appears to be rather different. Yinnon Ezra of Kent County is quoted as saying: 'Compulsory Competitive Tendering is old hat and it's time to move on to genuine partnerships (such as joint commercial relationships with publishers, the book supply trade, etc.) ... breaking up into a series of packages ... of integrated services is simply too expensive' ('Going to market ...', 1994). Hertfordshire appears to have rejected normal franchising arrangements, although Dorset is continuing to investigate running services through companies limited by guarantee and with charitable status.

Alongside these experiments the Department of National Heritage has commissioned a study from consultants KPMG Peat Marwick and Capital Planning Information, due to report in December 1994, into the feasibility and desirability of contracting out public library services. It remains to be seen whether one of the anticipated benefits, 'greater responsiveness to customers' needs', will be judged by the consultants to be a likely outcome of contracting out. The draft report of a separate review of public libraries, being carried out by Aslib (1994), took the view that public libraries should remain in the public sector although this could be through contracting out. The issues were still being considered at the time of writing.

CONCLUSION

While these are specific examples from the public library sector in the UK, and are specific to one type of library, they reflect a general trend in which outsourcing of services is becoming more common. Many organizations are concentrating on their core business and buying-in services of all kinds – transport, catering, information services, IT services, maintenance, and so on. Hayes (1993) cites a report which estimates that approximately 25 per cent of information activities have been outsourced by American businesses (Siegel and Griliches, 1991). The view of the external contractor is given by Lawes (1994), who writes of the experience of the British company TFPL in bidding for and operating contracts, and places this in the context of the wider shift towards contracting out of services and the implications of that trend for the library and information science professions. Among the key issues this raises is how the long-term strategic development of a library or information service can be secured when contracts for services typically run for no more than two or three years. One solution may be the 'shamrock' organization which retains at its centre the capacity for long-term planning but buys in professional and contract staff to undertake specific functions. It may be that public libraries will in years to come operate in a much-changed environment in which the local authority sets policy, strategy and the level of service while contracting the delivery of services to others. The effects of such a change on the quality of library services is a matter for debate until experience provides the answer, but the challenge is one that professionals in the field should be addressing urgently.

14

IMPLEMENTING QUALITY MANAGEMENT: FROM THEORY TO ACTION

The theory of quality management forms the backdrop, but the key issue for any library or information service manager lies in implementation and, ultimately, in the effect on service provision and customer satisfaction of actions taken to improve quality. Unless practical benefits can be demonstrated the exercise remains at best academic and at worst a costly drain on resources. The purpose of this chapter is to suggest some ways in which quality management can be implemented successfully, drawing on the techniques and approaches described in earlier chapters. Our approach is an amalgamation of issues drawn from the vast range of work in the field and it represents what we feel to be the most promising way forward for libraries and information services. Inevitably it is a personal view, and we offer no guarantee, nor even suggestion, that our approach will work in every situation. Adapt it to local circumstances, however, and results should start to be seen.

WHERE TO START?

TQM embraces such a wide number of concepts and techniques that it is not always easy to know where best to begin. Immediate advice may be along the lines of 'if you want to get there, I wouldn't start from here!' or 'it doesn't matter where you start, anywhere will do!'. Both are, in their own ways, true. But neither is very helpful.

It has to be said, however, that the starting point will depend on the particular organization and the culture within which it operates. For example, a public library in the UK will be under a legal obligation to implement the provisions of *The Citizen's Charter*, and having done so may wish to build quality initiatives on the basis formed by the charter's statutory requirements. So a natural development might be to undertake additional surveys of users' needs and preferences, to develop service standards and measures related to those findings and to implement actions designed to make the desired improvements. Or a decision might be taken that since the charter is already in place, perhaps other actions – such as benchmarking – are the place to start. An industrial information service, on the other hand, may wish to go for ISO 9000 implementation as a means of putting a quality management system in place which will have credibility both inside and outside the organization, perhaps drawing on the experience of other parts of the company.

All organizations will have taken some steps towards quality management, no matter what name has been used. There must have been some planning, some staff training, some – no matter how little – reference to customer needs. All organizations operate in environments which, equally, pay at least lip-service to quality management. Even the most cynical outsiders will recognize that quality itself is worth having, even when they do not like the methods suggested to achieve it. So there are many points at which an explicit quality management initiative can start.

THE FIRST ESSENTIAL: COMMITMENT

There is, however, one overriding requirement before any quality management should be undertaken: the full and long-term commitment of management to the process. For success any quality programme must be led from the top. Note 'led'; it will not work as it should if it is simply imposed from above – although from experience we would say that you cannot expect to change the culture overnight. Long-term commitment is particularly important, and the amount of time and effort needed should not be underestimated. Commitment needs to be communicated to all levels of staff, for without communication and feedback a quality initiative is doomed to failure. As an aid to communication Stebbing (1990) suggests that a first step should be an education and awareness campaign for all, including all levels of management.

A SECOND STEP: ARTICULATE THE VISION

Once committed, develop a vision of where the organization wants to go. Obviously you need to know where you are starting from, but just as important is to develop an idea of where you want to be in two, five, ten or even fifty years' time. It is that sense of vision which, when shared by all those involved, will provide the sense of purpose, confidence and sheer determination that will produce results. For the managers of libraries and information services, that will not be the easiest of tasks, because many pressures are conspiring to cloud the future. But the development of the vision does imply taking an optimistic view that the sector has something of value to offer to its customers in the longer term. Does our future lie in a role as the gateways to the electronic information universe, as distributed support centres of a universal commitment to life-long learning, as the custodians of humankind's recorded cultural inheritance, as the guarantors of freedom of information, or where? One of the manager's responsibilities is to try to put flesh on the bare bones of such ideas and then to persuade others to share in making the vision a reality.

THE THIRD REQUIREMENT: THE PARALLEL ORGANIZATION

Creating parallel organizations sounds as if it might be a dangerous business, and so it is. But quality management is so important to the health of the organization as a whole that it requires both the ability to cut across internal boundaries and the empowerment of individuals who can ensure that action is taken. Hand in hand with a move to flatten organizational structures and thus empower all employees, there is a need for teams to be created to sit down together to tackle real problems and come up with implementable solutions: then to have access to management to ensure that implementation takes place. It is inevitable that staff with the most enthusiasm for quality improvement will find themselves on these teams and indeed will be leading them. That, in itself, is no bad thing. However, it will set up tensions in the organization, and the leadership exercised by the teams will need to be undertaken with patience and tact. Opportunities must be created to allow all the different talents in the organization to be brought to bear, and a healthy dose of scepticism will do no harm as long as it is not allowed to prevent action. Indeed, a member of staff who will continuously demand to know what the impact of a proposed change will be on the customers – never mind the jargon being used – is invaluable. Only those who are not committed to improving the service that customers receive need be excluded.

MOVING TOWARDS ACTION: A QUALITY AUDIT

With managerial commitment, a clear vision, and a parallel organization in place, all that is needed before action can be taken is a clear agenda. To reach this point it is useful to carry out a quality audit, or 'gap analysis', mapping what is already in place (attitudes as well as systems) and so identifying where action might be targeted.

A quality audit might follow the following steps:

1.   What is the purpose of our organization and is its service/product clearly defined?

   O   Do we have a mission statement?
   O   Do we have priorities for action derived from that statement?
   O   Do we have critical success factors or have the key aspects of our service been identified in other ways?

2.   To what extent do we know, understand and quantify the needs, wants and preferences of our customers?

   O   Who are our customers?
   O   Are their needs similar or in conflict? If the latter, what are the areas of conflict?

    ○ What do they understand by 'quality'?
    ○ Can we draw a 'map' of internal customer–supplier relationships? (Could the organizational chart be used to produce it?)
    ○ What *are* our customers' requirements? How do we know?

3.   What is the cost of quality?

    ○ Can we identify areas where reworking takes place?
    ○ Do we dump the cost of quality on our customers?
    ○ Can we find concrete examples of quality costs?

4.   Is continuous improvement part of our culture?

    ○ What mechanisms are there for measuring whether the service we offer is improving?
    ○ How do customers feed their complaints and suggestions into our planning processes?
    ○ What evidence is there that customer complaints and suggestions lead to change?

5.   Are the processes we use appropriate and relevant?

    ○ Do we know who is responsible for each process?
    ○ Is each process documented and operated consistently?
    ○ Last time something went wrong, did we: (a) ignore it?, (b) put it right? or (c) put it right and change the process so it never happens again?

6.   Is current performance measured consistently?

    ○ Is there a consistent set of performance indicators which relates to customer needs?
    ○ Do we set targets? Do we know when we achieve them?
    ○ Have we agreed targets with the customers?
    ○ Do we measure both 'hard' (e.g. numbers of transactions) and 'soft' (e.g. friendliness) aspects of quality?
    ○ Is there evidence that action is taken on the basis of what we measure?

7.   Do we use appropriate tools to measure quality?

    ○ Are there tried and tested statistical techniques in use?
    ○ How are those measures used?
    ○ Do those who use the measures understand their significance?

8.   Are staff well trained?

    ○ Do we offer induction training to all new staff?
    ○ Do all staff understand what quality is?
    ○ How are staff training needs identified? Are they then acted on?

9.   How do we compare ourselves with others?

    ○ Do we use some form of benchmarking?
    ○ Is benchmarking used to gain ideas as well as to show how we rate against the 'competition'?

FROM PLANNING TO ACTION

The final step is to move forward from commitment, from vision, from action teams and from the action schedule into action itself. What should be done, by whom and when? Often this is the hardest step of all, because here we are asking people to change the way they have done things, possibly for a long period of time, and shift to a paradigm of continuous improvement, which implies continuous change. Barriers between departments and sections will have to be eroded, and the end-user, the customer, will have to be acknowledged as the most important person in the organization, all the time.

We began this book with a question, 'Why does quality matter?'. We hope that we have at least started to provide a response. But we recognize that the only real answer lies in the day-to-day experience of customers who come into contact with libraries and information services and hopefully go away satisfied. Actions which help more customers to be satisfied, and all customers to be more satisfied, have to be worthwhile. Anything else is, quite simply, a waste of time.

APPENDICES

❖

APPENDICES

APPENDIX I: CRITERIA FOR INFORMATION SCIENCE

❖

SECTION 1. CORE AREA: INFORMATION SCIENCE

The theory and practice of creating, acquiring, assessing and validating, organizing, storing, transmitting, retrieving and disseminating information.

1. **Information: its characteristics, providers and users.** Nature, properties and characteristics of knowledge and information flows. Generation, transfer and use of information. Elements in the information chain. The information industry and its history. Information needs and information seeking and user behaviour. Communications systems theory, design and evaluation. Human communication and communication in the organizational environment. User types. Finding and analysing user needs. Intellectual property and copyright. Roles of the public and private sectors.

2. **Information sources.** Sources of recorded information (e.g. textual material, computer files, online machine-readable databases and databanks, audio-visual and other records) and their information content. Individuals and organizations (local, national and international) which collect, extract and/or disseminate information (e.g. information brokers and consultants, expert individuals, libraries, information centres, documentation centres). Information sources in general and special subject fields. Major information services. Secondary sources of information (e.g. abstracts and indexes, publicly available computer files, library catalogues).

3. **Information storage and retrieval.** Media for information storage and choice and organization of those media for various information types (e.g. full text, abstracts, numeric and tabular data and audio-visual material, and combinations of these). The theory of classification and indexing of information content. Thesaurus construction. Search strategies for retrieving references, data, full text or combinations of these. The reference interview. Use of manual, automated and mixed systems (e.g. paper files, card

173

indexes, microform system, word processing, computerized systems). Use of human and technical networks for retrieval. Expert systems. Internal and external systems, services and networks. Input, indexing and output for successful retrieval. Evaluation of retrieval systems and secondary sources of information.

4. **Analysis of information.** The use of appropriate information sources for regular and systematic collection of information. The evaluation, interpretation and validation of that information, including the preparation of abstracts. The building of specialist files for storage and retrieval of evaluated information. Quantitative and qualitative analysis for the purpose of discovering novelty, trends, patterns, etc., and for the purpose of making hypotheses, trend projections, forecasts, etc. The preparation of state-of-the-art reports, reviews, overviews and scenarios.

5. **Dissemination of information.** Preparation of bibliographies and evaluated information reports. Effective presentation of information, including oral and written presentation skills. Proofreading, editing and presentation. Reprography and publishing, including desk-top publishing. Selective dissemination of information and other methods of current awareness.

6. **Theory of information science.** Theoretical studies of information: its nature, definition, content and significance. Development of theoretical models of information systems and processes. Research into information science.

SECTION 2. INFORMATION MANAGEMENT

The management of the total information resources of organizations:

1. **Planning.** Needs of organizations for information. Information requirements analysis. Impact of information on organizational performance. Organizational structures and operations. Information units within the organization. Integrating the information system with corporate strategy. Organization and methods. Techniques for work measurement. Operational research. Impact of computing and communications technologies.

2. **Communications.** Theories and models of communication and their applications to information systems. Communications audits. Information flow. Value added networks. Interpersonal communication. Intergroup communication. Voice communications. Data communications. Man–machine interaction.

3. **Management information and control systems.** The decision-making process and the role of management information. Data collection and analysis. Systems analysis, design and specification. Applications of computers, including office automation. Documentation management. Information provision for management control and business analysis. Application of system design to the organization of administrative units through data-flow analysis. Expert systems.

4. **Human resource management.** Job analysis, design and description. Job evaluation. Recruitment. Selection. Assessment. Training. Industrial relations. Staff management, motivation and interpersonal relations.

5. **Financial management.** Accounting. Cost analysis and control. Decision support. Programming, planning and budgeting, including the estimation of expenditure. Performance assessment – objectives, cost-effectiveness and cost-benefit analysis. Financial forecasting, policy making, planning.

6. **Promotion, economics and marketing.** Publicity and public relations. Production of newsletters, bulletins, etc. Economic factors. Marketing techniques and strategies, including market research.

7. **Political, ethical, social and legal factors.** Political climate. Role of government and government agencies. Ethical and legal factors including privacy, secrecy, freedom of information, health and safety, data protection, trans-border flow. Social factors.

SECTION 3. INFORMATION TECHNOLOGY

Technology which may be used in information science or information management.

1. **Computer systems: hardware and software.** Corporate and departmental computer hardware and personal workstations. Input and output devices. Storage devices and systems. Principles of operating systems and applications programs: software packages, especially for information storage and retrieval; programming. File design; record layout; file searching; file update. Database systems and database management. Feasibility studies; specifications; design; package appraisal; implementation; evaluation; documentation.

2. **Telecommunications.** Standards, protocols, interfaces. Types of equipment, e.g. modems; electronic and optical communication devices. Telecommunication networks (including local area networks, wide area networks).

3. **Information technology applications.** Information retrieval, videotex, teletext, computer typesetting, computer output microform (COM), speech synthesis and voice recognition, automation of library functions, office automation, compact disc technologies, video scanning and digitizing, satellite and cable TV, other methods of electronic publishing and document delivery, including telefacsimile. Machine translation.

4. **Environment.** Health and safety, ergonomics, data protection, copyright, piracy, encryption, etc.

SECTION 4. ANCILLARY SKILLS

The following are examples of important ancillary skills, but this section is not intended to be a comprehensive list.

1.   **Research procedures.** Research proposals. Investigation, data collection and sampling. Statistical significance analysis. Evaluation of results. Report writing.
2.   **Linguistics.** Natural and formal languages, linguistic classification. Semantics, syntactics, pragmatics. Relations of semantics and linguistics, psychology, logic and philosophy.
3.   **Foreign languages.** Use of foreign language information sources. Translating and abstracting from foreign languages.

APPENDIX II: MODEL MISSION STATEMENT FOR THE PUBLIC LIBRARY SERVICE

The public library is a major community facility whose purpose is to enable and encourage individuals or groups of individuals to gain unbiased access to information, knowledge and works of creative imagination which will:

O encourage their active participation in cultural, democratic and economic activities;

O enable them to participate in educational development through formal and informal programmes;

O assist them to make positive use of leisure time;

O promote reading and literacy as basic skills necessary for active involvement in these activities;

O encourage the use of information and an awareness of its value.

The local and community nature of the service requires special emphasis to be placed on the needs and aspirations of the local community and on the provision of services for particular groups within it.

Source: Office of Arts and Libraries (1991), *Setting objectives for public library services*, London: HMSO.

APPENDIX III: A CHARTER FOR PUBLIC LIBRARIES

❖

[published by the UK Library Association, 1993: the source of this document is hereby acknowledged]

1. Local Authorities in England, Scotland and Wales and the Education and Library Boards in Northern Ireland have a legal duty to give you a full and efficient library service.

2. Your local library service (insert name) has an important role in the community. We give everyone access to books, information and works of creative imagination which will:

    ○ encourage them to take part in cultural, democratic and economic activities;
    ○ educate them, either formally or informally;
    ○ help them make good use of their free time;
    ○ promote reading as a basic skill for life; and
    ○ make them aware of the value of information and encourage them to use it.

    We serve local communities. We meet the needs of particular groups within communities, while also giving access to wider resources through regional and national library networks.

3. **Charter statement**
    We will provide a high quality service. We will give value for money and will meet your needs.

    3.1 Elected councillors, the local community and library staff will work together to decide what these needs are. We will involve the community by:

        ○ speaking regularly to our users, local organizations and voluntary groups;

○   giving you a way to make suggestions and complaints; and

○   making regular surveys of people who use and do not use the library. We will publish the results of these as quickly as possible.

3.2   We will give special attention to those who need special facilities and services because of their education or ethnic origin or any disability.

4.   The Charter promise

4.1   We will publish a Statement of Standards covering all areas of our service. We will talk to our users before making any major changes to this Charter or its Statement of Standards. And we will let you know of any changes through all libraries and the local media.

4.2   We will produce an Annual Statement which will be available free of charge. This will show how close we have come to meeting our Charter commitments in the past year. It will also set out our targets for the coming year.

5.   Access

Each community will have a library service as described in the Statement of Standards.

5.1   We will publicise all our facilities and resources.

5.2   We will open at times to suit the local community. This will include weekends and some evenings.

5.3   If you cannot get to the library because you are old or sick, we will deliver services to you.

5.4   All libraries will have access for people with disabilities, including those with wheelchairs.

5.5   Signs inside and outside our buildings will be clear and in languages relevant to the community, with special provision for people with physical handicaps.

6.   Environment and facilities

6.1   All our buildings will be welcoming, clean, well-lit and well-maintained.

6.2   We will pay particular attention to the safety of our users and staff.

6.3   We will provide seats, study areas and also special facilities for children.

6.4   We will develop our buildings so that they can be used by the local community for other purposes as much as possible.

7.   Books and other stock

7.1   We will draw up a stock selection and management policy. This will include general guidelines and specific policies for different types of material.

7.2   The Statement of Standards says how much stock and what kinds of stock we will add to the library over the year.

7.3 All our stock will be clean and up to date. It will be presented in a clearly understandable order.

7.4 Our choice of stock will cover the educational, cultural, information and leisure interests of the local community.

7.5 The range and depth of our non-fiction materials will meet the needs of the local community.

7.6 We will buy enough copies of all the most important works of modern English fiction and poetry.

7.7 Our Chartered Librarians will choose the stock. They have the specialised knowledge which is needed to do this.

7.8 We will supply stock for people with sight and hearing difficulties according to need.

7.9 We will choose stock for ethnic minority communities with the help of people with relevant cultural and linguistic backgrounds.

7.10 We will collect and preserve stock relating to the local history of the area.

7.11 We will help you find stock by providing guides, catalogues and a readers' advisory service. There will also be a service for you to reserve stock which is not immediately available.

8. Information services

8.1 We will provide information services to encourage you to keep yourself informed and help you to exercise your democratic rights.

8.2 We will provide a community information service with a range of material on national and local services.

8.3 Larger libraries will provide information services for business and other specialised needs as well as for the general public.

8.4 All libraries will stock local newspapers. Larger ones will have national newspapers and magazines.

9. Staff

9.1 All our staff will be well trained, well informed and polite.

9.2 You will be able to speak to a Chartered Librarian when you need to.

9.3 You will never have to wait too long to be served.

9.4 The Statement of Standards sets out the number and type of staff, including specialists.

9.5 The Statement of Standards sets out a yearly training plan for all staff.

9.6 Our staff wear official badges and will give their names when they write or speak on the phone.

10. Encouraging people to use our services

10.1 We will introduce a programme to promote our services and to encourage everyone to use them.

10.2 We will organise activities for children to encourage them to use the library and to read regularly.

10.3   We will work with other organisations to promote literacy and reading.

11.   Monitoring our services.

We will keep a close check on all our services. We will make sure that they are effective, offer value for money and meet your needs.

BIBLIOGRAPHY

❖

Abbott, C. (1990), 'What does good look like?', *British Journal of Academic Librarianship*, 5, (2), 79–94.

Adams, R., Bloor, I., Collier, M., Meldrum, M. and Ward, S. (1983), *Decision support systems and performance assessment in academic libraries*, London: Bowker-Saur.

Anon. (1994), 'All change: is it for better or worse?', *Library Association Record*, 96, (11), 614–16.

Anon. (1994), 'Going to market doesn't blow Brent's house down', *Library Association Record*, 96, (11), 581–2.

Argyris, C. and Schon, D.A. (1978), *Organizational learning: a theory in action perspective*, New York: Addison-Wesley.

Armstrong, C. (1994a), 'The Centre for Information Quality Management (CIQM): a single phone number for all your woes!', *Library Technology News*, 12, April, 3–5.

Armstrong, C. (1994b), 'What you see is what you get: closing the gap between expectation and reality', *Information World Review*, December, 29.

Arthur, J. and Lloyd, I. (1992), 'Quality assessment of the academic library: a case study of Dundee Institute of Technology, *British Journal of Academic Librarianship*, 7, (3), 187–95.

Ashcroft, M. (ed.) (1993), *Piloting competitive tendering: proceedings of a seminar held in Stamford, Lincolnshire on 27th October 1993*, Stamford, Lincs: Capital Planning Information.

Aslib (1994), 'Department of National Heritage review of the public library service in England and Wales: draft report', London: Aslib.

Association of College and Research Libraries (ACRL), Undergraduate Librarians Discussion Group and ULS Steering Committee (1987), 'The mission of a university undergraduate library: model statement', *College & Research Libraries News*, 48, (9), 542–4.

Association of Research Libraries, Office of Management Studies (1989), *Qualitative collection analysis: the Conspectus methodology*, SPEC Kit 151, Washington, DC: Association of Research Libraries.

Association of Research Libraries, Office of University Library Management Studies, Systems and Procedures Exchange Center (1979), *Goals and objectives in ARL libraries*, SPEC Kit No. 58, Washington, DC: Association of Research Libraries.

Attwood, M. and Beer, N. (1988), 'Development of a learning organization', *Management Education and Development*, 19, (3), 201–14.

Audit Commission (1989), *Managing services effectively: performance review*, London: HMSO.

Ball, C. (1990), *More means different: widening access to higher education*, London: Royal Society of Arts.

Bank, J. (1992), *The essence of total quality management*, Hemel Hempstead: Prentice-Hall.

Barnard, S.B. (1993), 'Implementing total quality management: a model for research libraries', *Journal of Library Administration*, 18, (1/2), 57–70.

Barnard, M. (1994), 'Quality costs in distribution', *The Bookseller*, (4642), 28, 30.

Barter, R.F. Jr. (1994), 'In search of excellence in libraries: the management writings of Tom Peters and their implications for library and information services', *Library Management*, 15, (8), 4–15.

Barugh, J. (1989), 'The relationship between community librarianship and community information', in Astbury, R. (ed.), *Putting people first: some perspectives of community librarianship*, Newcastle-under-Lyme: AAL Publishing, 36–42.

Bell, J. (1994), 'In search of distinctiveness', *The Bookseller*, (4639), 18–19.

Berry, L.L., Zeithaml, V.A. and Parasuraman, P. (1990), 'Quality counts in service too', *Business Horizons*, 28, (3), 44–52.

Bloor, I. (1991), *Performance indicators and decision support systems for libraries*, British Library Research Paper 93, London: British Library.

Brache, A.P. and Rummler, G.A. (1988), 'The three levels of quality', *Quality Progress*, 21, (10), 46–51.

Bradford, S.C. (1948), *Documentation*, London: Crosby Lockwood.

Brice, J. (1992), 'In a Buyer's Market: contracting out information services', in *Contracting out: the information business: key issue 91*, Hatfield, University of Hertfordshire Press, 65–79.

Bristol Polytechnic Library (1987, unpublished), *LEAP: Library Evaluation and Assessment Project: Draft Report*.

British Library (1989), *Gateway to knowledge: the British Library strategic plan 1989–1994*, London: The British Library Board.

British Railways Board (1992), *The British Rail passenger's charter* London: British Railways Board.

British Standards Institution (1972), *BS 4891: a guide to quality assurance*, London: BSI.

British Standards Institution (1993), *Vision 2000: a strategy for international standards' implementation in the quality arena during the 1990s*, London: BSI.

Brockman, J. (1993), 'TQM and government departmental and agency library and information services', in *Total quality management: the information business: key issue 92*, Hatfield: University of Hertfordshire Press, 57–69.

Brookes, B.C. (1970), 'The growth, utility, and obsolescence of scientific periodical literature', *Journal of Documentation*, 26, (4), 283–94.

Brophy, P. (1991a), personal communication.

Brophy, P. (1991b), 'The mission of the academic library', *British Journal of Academic Librarianship*, 6, (3), 135–47.

Brophy, P. (1993a), 'Towards BS 5750 in a university library', in Ashcroft, M. and Barton, D. (ed.), *Quality Management: towards BS 5750: Proceedings of a seminar held in Stamford, Lincolnshire on 21st April 1993*, Stamford, Lincs: Capital Planning Information.

Brophy, P. (1993b), 'What's in a name?', *Library Management*, 94, (1108), 27–9.

Brophy, P., Coulling, K. and Melling, M. (1993), 'Quality management: a university approach', *Aslib Information*, 21, (6), 246–8.

Buckland, M.K. (1975), *Book availability and the library user*, New York: Pergamon.

Buckland, M.K. (1988), *Library services in theory and context*, 2nd ed., London: Pergamon.

Buckland, M.K., Hindle, A., Mackenzie, A.G. and Woodburn, I. (1970), *Systems analysis of a university library*, Lancaster: University of Lancaster Library.

Bundy, M.L. (1972), 'Urban information and public libraries', *Library Journal*, 97, (2), 161–91.

Burrows, A. and Harvey, L. (1992), 'Defining quality in higher education: the stake-holder approach', paper presented to the AETT Conference on Quality in Education, University of York, 6–8 April.

Butcher, K.S. (1993), 'Total quality management: the Oregon State University Library's experience', *Journal of Library Administration*, 18, (1/2), 45–56.

Cameron, K.S. (1981), 'Domains of organizational effectiveness in colleges and universities', *Academy of Management Journal*, 24, (1), 25–47.

Cameron, K. (1978), 'Measuring organizational effectiveness in institutions of higher education', *Administrative Science Quarterly*, 23, (4), 604–29.

Camp, R.C. (1989), *Benchmarking*, Milwaukee, WI: Quality Press.

Campbell, A. (1990), *A Sense of mission*, London: Hutchinson Business Books.

Carlzon, J. (1987), *Moments of truth*, Cambridge, MA: Ballinger Publishing.

Casale, M. (1994), 'How Brent won its own contract', *Library Manager*, 2, 10–11.

Chapman, A. (1993), *Quality of Bibliographic Records in a Shared Cataloguing Database: a case study using the BLCMP database*, British Library Research and Development Department Report 6120, London: British Library.

Childers, T. and Van House, N.A. (1989a), 'The grail of goodness: the effective public library', *Library Journal* 114, (16), 44–9.

Childers, T. and Van House, N.A. (1989b), 'Dimensions of public library effectiveness', *Library & Information Science Research*, 11, (3), 273–301.

Citizen's Charter (1991), Cm 1599, London: HMSO.

Citizen's Charter: Charter Mark Scheme 1994: Guide for Applicants, (1994), London: HMSO.

Citizen's Charter: Second Report: 1994 (1994), Cm 2540, London: HMSO.

Clapp, V.W. and Jordan, R.T. (1965), 'Quantitative criteria for adequacy of academic library collections', *College & Research Libraries*, 26, (5), 371–80.

Clausen, H. (1994a), 'The Nordic information quality project: a halfway report', *New Library World*, 95, (1114), 21–2.

Clausen, H. (1994b), 'Quality in the Nordic countries: ISO 9000, certification and all that', *Information World Review*, December, 51.

Clayton, C. (1994), 'LA support for needs of users', *Library Association Record*, 96, (6), 319, 321.

Confederation of British Industry (1989), *Towards a skills revolution*, London: Confederation of British Industry.

Cronin, B. (1982), 'Performance measures and information management', *Aslib Proceedings*, 34, (5), 227–36.

Cronin, B. (1988), 'The uncontested orthodoxy', *British Journal of Academic Librarianship*, 3, (1), 1–8.

Crosby, P.B. (1979), *Quality is Free*, New York: McGraw-Hill.

Crosby, P.B. (1986), *Running things: the art of making things happen*, New York: McGraw-Hill.

Curtis, M., Jennings, B., Wheeler, S. and White, L. (1993), 'Quality assurance in Kent', *Public Library Journal*, 8, (1) 1–4.

Curzon, S. (1989), *Managing change: a how-to-do-it manual for planning, implementing and evaluating change in libraries*, New York: Neal-Schuman.

Cusumano, M.A. (1985), *The Japanese auto industry: technology and management at Nissan and Toyota*, Cambridge, MA: Harvard University Press.

Dawson, A. (1993), 'Corporate libraries: the Taylor Woodrow experience', in *Total quality management: the information business: key issue 92*, Hatfield, Herts: University of Hertfordshire Press 82–88.

De Prospo, E.R., Altman, E. and Beasley, K. (1973), *Performance measures for public libraries*. Chicago, IL: American Library Association.

Deming, W.E. (1986), *Out of the crisis: quality, productivity and competitive position*, Cambridge, MA: MIT Press.

Department of Health and Central Office of Information (1993), *The Patient's Charter: and family doctor services* London: HMSO.

Dolan, J. (1989), 'Community librarianship in a Northern inner city', in Astbury, R. (ed.), *Putting people first: some perspectives of community librarianship*, Newcastle-under-Lyme: AAL Publishing, 8–16.

Drucker, P. (1989), *The new realities: in government and politics: in economics and business: in society and world view*, London: Harper & Row.

Dubberly, R.A. (1983), 'Why you must know your library's mission', *Public Libraries*, 22, (3), 89–90.

Earwaker, J. (1991), 'Boo to the barbarians', *The Times Higher Education Supplement*, 29 March, 14.

Edge, J. (1990), 'Common and special problems', in Lock, D. (ed.), *Gower Handbook of quality management*, Aldershot: Gower, 351–74.

Efficiency Unit (1988), *Improving management in government: the next steps*, London: HMSO.

Ellis, D. and Norton, B. (1993), *Implementing BS 5750 / ISO 9000 in libraries*, London: Aslib.

Ernstthal, H.L. (1989), 'Drucker talks nonprofit', *Association Management*, 41, November, 22–8.

Ertel, M. (1993), 'Quality management in the Apple Laboratory', paper presented at the open session on quality and quality management in libraries, IFLA conference, Barcelona, Spain, 22–27 August.

Faerman, S.R. (1993), 'Organizational change and leadership styles', *Journal of Library Administration*, 19, (3/4), 55–79.

Featherstone, T. (1994), 'Setting the standard', *Library Association Record*, 96, (2), 96.

Feigenbaum, A.V. (1956), 'Total quality control', *Harvard Business Review*, 34, (6), November, 93–101.

Feigenbaum, A.V. (1983), *Total quality control*, 3rd ed., New York: McGraw-Hill.

Flood, R. (1993), *Beyond TQM*, Chichester, West Sussex: John Wiley.

Ford, G. and MacDougall, A.F. (1992), *Performance assessment in academic libraries: final report on a feasibility study*, British Library RDD Report 6085, London: The British Library.

Foreman, L. (1992), *Developing quality in libraries: culture and measurement for information services*, London: HMSO for Circle of State Librarians.

Fussler, H.H. and Simon, J.L. (1969), *Patterns in the use of books in large research libraries*, Chicago, IL: University of Chicago Press.

Garratt, B. (1989), *The learning organization*, London: Fontana.

Garvin, D.A. (1983), 'Quality on the line', *Harvard Business Review*, September–October, 64–75.

Garvin, D.A. (1987), 'Competing on the eight dimensions of quality', *Harvard Business Review*, 101–09.

Garvin, D.A. (1988), *Managing quality*, New York: Free Press.

Gerstner, E. (1985), 'Do higher prices signal quality?', *Journal of Marketing Research*, 22, (5), 209–15.

Gilchrist, A. (1994), 'Beyond 5750', *Inform*, 170, December, 5–6.

Goodall, D.L. (1988), 'Performance measurement: an historical perspective', *Journal of Librarianship*, 20, (2), 128–44.

Green, A. (1990), 'What do we mean by user needs?', *British Journal of Academic Librarianship*, 5, (2), 65–78.

Greenhalgh, L., Landry, C. and Worpole, K. (1993), *Borrowed time? The future of public libraries in the United Kingdom*, Bournes Green: Comedia.

Gwinn, N.E. and Mosher, P.H. (1983), 'Coordinating collection development: The RLG Conspectus', *College and Research Libraries*, 44, (1), 128–40.

Hammond, V. and Wille, E. (1994), 'The learning organization', in Prior, J. (ed.), *Gower Handbook of Training and Development*, 2nd ed., Aldershot: Gower.

Handy, C. (1994), *The empty raincoat: making sense of the future*, London: Heinemann.

Hardesty, L. et al. (1988), 'Development of college library mission statements', *Journal of Library Administration*, 9, (3), 11–34.

Hardesty, L., Hastreiter, J. and Hendelson, D. (1985), *Mission statements for college libraries*, Clip Notes #5, Washington: American Library Association, Association of College & Research Libraries, College Libraries Section, College Library Information Packet Committee.

Harvey, L. and Green, D. (1993), 'Defining quality', *Assessment and Evaluation in Higher Education*, 18, (1), 9–34.

Hayes, R.M. (1993), *Strategic management for academic libraries: a handbook*, Westport, CT: Greenwood Press.

Head, M.C. and Marcella, R.A. (1993), 'Testing question: the quality of reference services in Scottish public libraries', *Library Review*, 42, (6).

Henty, M. (1989), 'Performance indicators in higher education libraries', *British Journal of Academic Librarianship*, 4, (3), 177–91.

Hernon, P. and McClure, C.R. (1986), 'Unobtrusive reference testing: the 55 percent rule', *Library Journal*, 111, (7), 37–41.

HMSO (1962), *Standards for public library service in England and Wales*, London: HMSO.

Howell, J., Maxwell, R. and Ross, N. (1994), 'Priorities for healthcare: who sets them?', *RSA Journal*, CXLII (5454), 35–49.

Imai, M. (1986), *Kaizen: the key to Japan's competitive success*, New York: Random House.

Institute of Information Scientists (1988), *Criteria for Courses in Information Science and for Corporate Membership of the Institute of Information Scientists*, London: Institute of Information Scientists.

International Federation of Library Associations and Institutions. Section of University Libraries and other General Research Libraries (1993), *Measuring Quality: International Guidelines for Performance Measurement in Academic Libraries*, preliminary draft, Münster, Germany: Universitäts und Landesbibliothek Münster (for IFLA).

Johanssen, C.G. (1992), 'The use of quality control principles and methods in library and information science practice', *Libri*, 4, (44), 283–95.

Johanssen, C.G. (1993), 'Can the ISO standards on quality management be useful to libraries, and how?', paper presented at the Open Session on Quality and Quality Management in Libraries, IFLA Conference, Barcelona, Spain, 22–27 August.

Joint Funding Councils' Libraries Review Group (1993), *Report*, chair: Sir Brian Follett, Bristol: Higher Education Funding Councils.

Juran, J.M. (1989), *Juran on leadership for quality: an executive handbook*, New York NY: Free Press.

Juran, J.M. (1992), *Juran on quality by design: the new steps for planning quality into goods and services*, New York: Free Press.

Juran, J.M. and Gryna, F.M. (1993), *Quality planning and analysis: from product development through use*, London: McGraw-Hill.

Jurow, S. and Barnard, S.B. (1993), 'Integrating total quality management in a library setting', *Journal of Library Administration*, 18, (1/2), whole issue.

Kantor, P.B. (1984), *Performance measures for public libraries*, Chicago, IL: American Library Association.

Lancaster, F.W. (1993b), 'Introduction: threat versus opportunity', in Lancaster, F.W. (ed.), *Libraries and the Future: essays on the library in the twenty-first century*, New York NY: Haworth Press, 1–4.

Lancaster, F.W. (1993a), *If you want to evaluate your library …* , 2nd ed., London: Library Association Publishing.

Lancaster, F.W. (1977), *The measurement and evaluation of library services*, Washington, DC: Information Resources Press.

Lancaster, F.W. and Baker, S.L. (1991), *The measurement and evaluation of library services*, 2nd ed., Arlington, VA: Information Resources Press.

Lascelles, D.M. and Dale, B.G. (1993), *The Road to quality*, Bedford: IFS Ltd.

Lawes, A. (1994), 'Contracting out', *New Library World*, 95, (1114), 8–12.

Leimkuhler, F.F. (1966), 'Systems analysis in university libraries', *College and Research Libraries*, 27, (1), 13–18.

Leimkuhler, F.F. and Cooper, M.D. (1971), 'Analytical models for library planning', *Journal of the American Society for Information Science*, November–December, 390–8.

Leisner, T. (1986), 'Mission statements and the marketing mix', *Public Libraries*, 25, (3), 86–7.

Lester, D.E. (1994), *The Impact of Quality Management on the Information Sector: a study of case histories*, Luxembourg: EUSIDIC.

Levitt, T. (1960), 'Marketing myopia', *Harvard Business Review*, July–August, 45–56.

Levy, F., Meltsner, A.J. and Wildavsky, A. (1974), *Urban Outcomes: Schools, Streets and Libraries*, Berkeley, CA: University of California Press.

Library and Information Statistics Unit, *Average Prices of British Academic Books*, Loughborough: LISU, Dept. of Information and Library Studies, Loughborough University, published twice yearly.

Library and Information Statistics Unit, *LISO Annual Library Statistics*, Loughborough: LISU, Dept. of Information and Library Studies, Loughborough University, published annually.

Library and Information Statistics Unit, *UK Public Library Materials Fund and Budget Survey*, Loughborough: LISU, Dept. of Information and Library Studies, Loughborough University, published annually.

Library Association (1992a), *Libraries and the Citizen's Charter: a Library Association discussion document*, London: Library Association.

Library Association (1992b), *The charter approach: Library Association guidelines for public libraries*, London: Library Association.

Library Association (1993a), *A Charter for public libraries*, London: Library Association.

Library Association (1993b), *LA/COFHE guidelines: managing after incorporation: quality matters*, London: Library Association.

Library Association (1994), *Information quality and liability*, London: Library Association.

Lidman, T. and Törngren, M. (1993), 'The quality audit at Stockholm University Library', paper presented at the open session on quality and quality management in libraries, IFLA Conference, Barcelona, Spain, 22–27 August.

Line, M.B. (1993), 'Libraries and information services in 25 years' time: a British perspective', in Lancaster, F.W. (ed.), *Libraries and the Future: essays on the library in the twenty-first century*, New York: Haworth P., 73–83.

Lippitt, G.L. (1969), *Organization renewal*, New York: Appleton-Century-Crofts.

Lock, D. and Smith, D.J. (eds.) (1990), *Handbook of quality management*, Aldershot: Gower.

Loney, T. (1993), 'TQM Training: the library service challenge', *Journal of Library Administration*, 18, (1/2), 85–95.

Lynch, B.P. (1986), *Standards for university libraries*, IFLA Professional Reports No. 10, The Hague: International Federation of Library Associations and Institutions, Section of University Libraries and other General Research Libraries.

MacDougall, A.F. (1992), 'Performance measures: today's confusion, tomorrow's solution?', *IFLA Journal*, 17, (4), 371–8.

Mackenzie, A.G. and Stuart, I.M. (eds) (1969), *Planning library services*, Lancaster: University of Lancaster Library.

Maguire, C. and Willard, P. (1990), 'Performance measures for libraries: statistical, organizational and cosmetic', *Australian Academic & Research Libraries*, 21, (4), 262–73.

Main, J. (1990), 'How to win the Baldridge Award', *Fortune*, April, 67–76.

Marchand, D. (1990), 'Managing information quality', in I. Wormell (ed.), *Information quality: definitions and dimensions*, London: Taylor Graham, 7–17.

Marshall, C. (1991), 'Culture change: no science but considerable art', Comino Lecture, 13 June 1990, *RSA Journal*, January, 895.

Martin, D., 'Academic libraries', (1993a), in *Total quality management: the information business: key issue 92*, Hatfield, Herts: University of Hertfordshire Press, 38–45.

Martin, D. (1993b), 'Total quality management', *Library & Information Briefings*, 45.

Masson, R.J. (1986), 'User–vendor relationships in the Scottish electronics industry', *International Journal of Quality and Reliability Management*, 3, (2), 51–5.

McClellan, A.W. (1962), *The logistics of public library bookstocks*, unpublished typescript. Later published by the Association of Assistant Librarians under the same title (1978), London: Association of Assistant Librarians (Library Association).

Milner, E., Kinnell, M. and Usherwood, B. (1994), 'Quality management: the public library debate', *Public Library Journal*, 9, (6), 151–7.

Minkoff, D. (1993), 'Quality: participation plus change', in *Total quality management: the information business: key issue 92*, Hatfield, Herts: University of Hertfordshire Press, 70–81.

Moon, V. (1993), 'Regionalisation and co-operation', unpublished paper, NZLIA Conference, Tauranga, New Zealand.

Moore, N. (1992), 'The ABC approach to consumer service: quality management in a service profession', in Foreman, L. *Developing quality in libraries: culture and measurement for information services*, London: HMSO for Circle of State Librarians, 7–12.

Morgan, C. and Murgatroyd, S. (1994), *Total quality management in the public sector*, Oxford: Oxford University Press.

Morgan, S. (1993), 'Performance assessment in higher education libraries', *Library Management*, 14, (5), 35–42.

Morse, P.M. (1968), *Library effectiveness: a systems approach*, Cambridge, MA: MIT Press.

Mortiboys, R. and Oakland, J. (1991), *Total quality management and effective leadership: a strategic overview*, London: Department of Trade and Industry.

Mosley, M.M. (1988), 'Mission statements for the community college LRC', *College and Research Libraries News*, 49, (10), 653–4.

Munn, R.F. (1989), 'The bottomless pit, or the academic library viewed from the administration building', *College & Research Libraries*, 50, (6), 635–7. (Reprinted from *College & Research Libraries*, January 1968.)

Nakhai, B. and Neves, J.S. (1994), 'The Deming, Baldridge and European Quality Awards', *Quality Progress*, April, 33–7.

Nicholson-Lord, D. (1994), 'Boring firms "are killing creativity" in the workplace', *The Independent*, 2537, 8.

Oakland, J.S. (1989), *Total quality management*, Oxford: Butterworth-Heinemann.

Oakland, J.S. and Porter, L. (1994), *Cases in total quality management*, Oxford: Butterworth-Heinemann.

Office of Arts and Libraries (1987), *A costing system for public libraries: a model developed by Cipfa Services Ltd (in conjunction with the Institute of Public Finance Ltd.)*, Library Information Series No. 17, London: HMSO.

Office of Arts and Libraries (1990), *Keys to success: performance indicators for public libraries*, Library Information Series No. 18, London: HMSO.

Office of Arts and Libraries (1991), *Setting objectives for public library services*, London: HMSO.

Orr, R.H. (1973), 'Measuring the goodness of library services: a general framework for considering quantitative measures', *Journal of Documentation*, 29, (3), 313–32.

Ozeki, K. and Asaka, T. (1990), *Handbook of quality tools: the Japanese approach*, Cambridge, MA: Productivity Press.

Pall, G.A. (1987), *Quality Process Management*, Englewood Cliffs, NJ: Prentice-Hall.

Paskoff, B.M. (1991), 'Accuracy of telephone reference service in health science libraries', *Bulletin of the Medical Library Association*, 79, (2), 182–8.

Peasgood, A. (1994), 'Follett and some prevailing winds', *British Journal of Academic Librarianship*, 9, (1/2), 39–47.

Peat, Marwick, Mitchell & Co. (1975), *California public library systems: a comprehensive review with guidelines for the next decade*, Los Angeles, CA: Peat, Marwick, Mitchell & Co.

Pedler, M., Burgoyne, J. and Boydell, T. (1988), *Learning Company Project Report*, Sheffield: Manpower Services Commission.

Pedler, M., Burgoyne, J. and Boydell, T. (1991), *The learning company: a strategy for sustainable development*, London: McGraw-Hill.

Peters, T. (1992), *Liberation management: necessary disorganization for the nanosecond nineties*, London: Macmillan.

Peters, T. and Austin, N. (1985), *A passion for excellence: the leadership difference*, New York NY: Random House.

Peters, T. and Waterman, R.J. (1982), *In search of excellence: lessons from America's best run companies*, New York: Warner Bros.

Pfeffer, J. and Salancik, G.R. (1978), *The external control of organizations,* New York: Harper & Row.

Pirsig, R.M. (1974), *Zen and the Art of Motorcycle Maintenance*, London: Bodley Head.

Plummer, R. (1990), 'Design objectives', in *Gower handbook of quality management*, Lock, D. (ed.), Aldershot: Gower, 103–16.

Pluse, J. (1994), 'People: your most valuable investment', *Library Association Record*, 96, (2), 93–5.

Poll, R. (1993), 'Quality and performance measurement: a German view', *British Journal of Academic Librarianship*, 8, (1), 35–47.

Polytechnics & Colleges Funding Council (1989), unpublished paper, 10 February.

Porter, L. (1993), *Quality initiatives in British library and information services*, British Library Research and Development Department Report 6105, London: British Library.

Pratt, J. and Silverman, S. (1988), *Responding to constraint: policy and management in higher education*, Milton Keynes: Society for Research into Higher Education and Open University Press.

Price, F. (1990), 'The quality concept and objectives', in *Gower Handbook of Quality Management*, Lock, D. (ed.), Aldershot: Gower, 3–11.

Quinn, R.E. and Rohrbaugh, J. (1981), 'A competing values framework to organizational effectiveness', *Public Productivity Review*, 5, 122–40.

Quinn, R.E. and Rohrbaugh, J. (1983), 'A spatial model of effectiveness criteria: towards a competing values approach to organizational analysis', *Management Science*, 29, 363–77.

Roberts, S.A. (1985), *Cost management for library and information services*, London: Butterworths.

Roome, N. (1994), 'Front line forum: library staff tell all', *CoFHE Bulletin*, 73, Winter, 4–5.

Rowley, J. (1994), 'Customer experience of libraries', *Library Review*, 43, (6), 7–17.

Sandelands, E. (ed.) (1994), 'Strategies for service quality', *Library Management*, 15, (5), (complete issue).

Schlichter, D.J. and Pemberton, J.M. (1992), 'The emperor's new clothes? problems of user survey as a planning tool in academic libraries', *College & Research Libraries*, May, 257–65.

Schon, D.A. (1971), *Beyond the stable state*, New York, NY: Random House.

Schwarz, P. (1991), *The art of the long view*, New York, NY: Doubleday.

Scottish Library & Information Council and Scottish Library Association (1993), *Libraries in Scottish Further Education Colleges: standards for performance and resourcing: the report of a working party*, Scottish Library & Information Council and Scottish Library Association.

Shaughnessy, T.W. (1987), 'The search for quality', *Journal of Library Administration*, 8, (1), 5–10.

Shewart, W.A. (1931), *Economic control of quality of manufactured products*, London: Macmillan.

Siegel, D. and Griliches, Z. (1991), *Purchased services, outsourcing, computers, and productivity in manufacturing*, Working Paper no. 3678, Cambridge, MA: National Bureau of Economic Research.

Simpson, I.S. (1990), *How to Interpret Statistical Data: a guide for librarians and information scientists*, London: The Library Association.

Sirkin, A.F. (1993), 'Customer service: another side of TQM', *Journal of Library Administration*, 18, (1/2), 71–83.

Slater, M. (ed.) (1990), *Research methods in library and information studies*, London: Library Association Publishing.

Stebbing, L. (1990), *Quality management in the service industry*, London: Ellis Horwood.

Sumsion, J.W. (1993a), *Practical performance indicators – 1992: documenting the Citizen's Charter consultation for UK public libraries with examples of PIs and surveys in use*, Occasional Paper No. 5, Loughborough: Library and Information Statistics Unit, Department of Information and Library Studies, Loughborough University of Technology.

Sumsion, J.W. (1993b), *Report on statistical pilot survey of UK special libraries*, Loughborough Library and Information Statistics Unit, Department of Information and Library Studies, Loughborough University of Technology.

Sumsion, J. (1994), 'Strategic research areas and possible research models for UK public libraries' *Library Review*, 43, (4), 7–26.

Swindells, N. (ed.) (1994), *Specifying and measuring the quality of information products and services: proceedings of a workshop held on June 8th 1994*, Birkenhead, Merseyside: Ferroday Ltd on behalf of the European Commission DGXIII.

Swisher, R. and McClure, C.R. (1984), *Research for decision making: methods for librarians*, Chicago, IL: American Library Association.

Tann, J. (1993), 'Dimensions of quality in library settings', in Ashcroft, M. and Barton, D. (eds.), *Quality management: towards BS 5750: Proceedings of a seminar held in Stamford, Lincolnshire on 21st April 1993*, Stamford, Lincs: Capital Planning Information, 23–31.

Targett, S. (1994), 'Libraries' book cash halved', *The Times Higher*, 1151, 4.

Teboul, J. (1991), *Managing quality dynamics*, Hemel Hempstead, Herts: Prentice-Hall.

Tenner, A.R. and DeToro, I.J. (1992), *Total quality management: three steps to continuous improvement*, Reading, MA: Addison-Wesley.

Total Quality Management: the information business: key issue 92, (1993), Hatfield, Herts: University of Hertfordshire Press.

Townsend, P.L. and Gebhardt, J.E. (1986), *Commit to quality*, London: Wiley.

Trott, F. (ed.) (1992), *Customer care in information services: proceedings of a seminar held on Wednesday 6 November 1991 at BT Laboratories, Ipswich*, London: The Library Association, Information Services Group.

Tyerman, K. (1993), 'The Brent Project: establishing business initiatives and market testing', in Ashcroft, M. (ed.), *Piloting Competitive Tendering: Proceedings of a seminar held in Stamford, Lincolnshire on 27th October 1993*, Stamford, Lincs: Capital Planning Information.

University Grants Committee (1967), *Report of the Committee on Libraries* (The Parry Report), London: HMSO.

University of Central Lancashire (1993, unpublished), 'Research proposal submitted to the British Library Research and Development Department'.

University of Durham Computer Unit (1969), *Project for evaluating the benefits from university libraries* (The PEBUL Project), Durham: University of Durham.

University of Hertfordshire Press (1992), *Contracting out: the information business: key issue 91*, Hatfield, Herts: University of Hertfordshire Press, 1992.

Van House, N.A., Weil, B.T. and McClure, C.R. (1987), *Output measures for public libraries: a manual of standardized procedures*, 2nd ed., London: American Library Association.

Van Nievelt, M.C.A. (1989), 'Quality, the superior index of performance', *Proceedings of the European Quality Management Forum*, Eindhoven, The Netherlands: European Foundation for Quality Management, 65–70.

Walton, M. (1991), *Deming management at work*, London: Mercury Books.

Watson, T.J. Jr. (1963), *A Business and its beliefs: the ideas that helped build IBM*, New York, NY: McGraw-Hill.

Webb, S. (1994), personal communication.

Wedlake, L.J. (1993), 'An introduction to quality assurance and a guide to the implementation of BS 5750', *Aslib Proceedings*, 45, (1), 23–30.

Wheatley, M. and New, C. (1994), 'The marks of excellence', *Management Today*, November, 96–104.

Whitehall, T. (1992), 'Quality in library and information services: a review', *Library Management*, 13, (5), 23–35.

Williams, R. (1987), 'An unobtrusive survey of academic library reference services', *Library and Information Research News*, 10, (37/38), 12–40.

Wills, J. (1991), 'Chartered streets', *Local Government Chronicle*, 17 May, 15–16.

Winkworth, I. (1990), 'Performance indicators for polytechnic libraries', *Library Review*, 39, (5), 23–41.

Winkworth, I. and Rear, J. (1993), 'Draft Proposals based on evidence to a sub-committee of the Higher Education Funding Council's Libraries review', London: Standing Conference of National and University Libraries and Council of Polytechnic Librarians (unpublished paper).

Young, R. (1992), 'The role of involvement in leadership and motivation of world-class sports team', unpublished MBA paper, Cranfield School of Management. Quoted in Bank, J. (1992), *The Essence of Total Quality Management*, Hemel Hempstead, Herts: Prentice-Hall.

Zeithaml, V.A., Parasuraman, A. and Berry, L.L. (1990), *Delivering quality service: balancing customer perceptions and expectations*, London: Collier-Macmillan.

Zweizig, D.L. (1987), 'So go figure: measuring library effectiveness', *Public Libraries*, Spring, 21–4.

Zweizig, D.L. and Rodger, E.J. (1982), *Output Measures for Public Libraries*, Chicago: ALA.

INDEX

High Resolution Radar

The Artech House Radar Library

Radar System Analysis by David K. Barton

Introduction to Electronic Warfare by D. Curtis Schleher

Electronic Intelligence: The Analysis of Radar Signals by Richard G. Wiley

Electronic Intelligence: The Interception of Radar Signals by Richard G. Wiley

Principles of Secure Communication Systems by Don J. Torrieri

Multiple-Target Tracking with Radar Applications by Samuel S. Blackman

Solid-State Radar Transmitters by Edward D. Ostroff et al.

Logarithmic Amplification by Richard Smith Hughes

Radar Propagation at Low Altitudes by M.L. Meeks

Radar Cross Section by Eugene F. Knott, John F. Shaeffer, and Michael T. Tuley

Radar Anti-Jamming Techniques by M.V. Maksimov et al.

Introduction to Synthetic Array and Imaging Radars by S.A. Hovanessian

Radar Detection and Tracking Systems by S.A. Hovanessian

Radar System Design and Analysis by S.A. Hovanessian

Radar Signal Processing by Bernard Lewis, Frank Kretschmer, and Wesley Shelton

Radar Calculations Using the TI-59 Programmable Calculator by William A. Skillman

Radar Calculations Using Personal Computers by William A. Skillman

Techniques of Radar Reflectivity Measurement, Nicholas C. Currie, ed.

Monopulse Principles and Techniques by Samuel M. Sherman

Receiving Systems Design by Stephen J. Erst

Designing Control Systems by Olis Rubin

Advanced Mathematics for Practicing Engineers by Kurt Arbenz and Alfred Wohlhauser

Radar Reflectivity of Land and Sea by Maurice W. Long

High Resolution Radar Imaging by Dean L. Mensa

Introduction to Monopulse by Donald R. Rhodes

Probability and Information Theory, with Applications to Radar by P.M. Woodward

Radar Detection by J.V. DiFranco and W.L. Rubin

Synthetic Aperture Radar, John J. Kovaly, ed.

Infrared-to-Millimeter Wavelength Detectors, Frank R. Arams, ed.

Significant Phased Array Papers, R.C. Hansen, ed.

Handbook of Radar Measurement by David K. Barton and Harold R. Ward

Statistical Theory of Extended Radar Targets by R.V. Ostrovityanov and F.A. Basalov

Radar Technology, Eli Brookner, ed.

MTI Radar, D. Curtis Schleher, ed.

High Resolution Radar

Donald R. Wehner

Artech House

Library of Congress Cataloging-in-Publication Data

Wehner, Donald R., 1931–
  High resolution radar.

  Includes bibliographies and index.
  1. Radar. 2. Synthetic aperture radar. I. Title.
Tk6580.W44 1987   621.3848   87-931
ISBN 0-89006-194-7

Copyright © 1987
ARTECH HOUSE, INC.
685 Canton Street
Norwood, MA 02062

International Standard Book Number: 0-89006-194-7
Library of Congress Catalog Card Number: 87-931

10 9 8 7 6 5 4 3 2

Contents

Preface

The famous British *chain-home* air-defense radar system became operational before the historic Battle of Britain in the summer of 1940. By that time, the United States had begun to field its own land-based and shipboard search radars. Before the end of World War II, the development of the magnetron oscillator brought microwave radar into widespread use. Numerous other major radar developments took place and radar systems for a whole host of military applications became operational by the end of the war. Radar thus became a key element of military operations on land, at sea, and in the air. Indeed, it is believed by some that the most decisive weapon of that war was not the atomic bomb, as commonly thought, but radar. After the war, developments came more slowly, but the role of radar became well established, for defense, and later for many civilian applications.

Now, after 50 years, radar is considered by some to be a mature art, a fairly well defined technology without room for dramatic new capability or application. This view is proving to be only partly valid. Wideband microwave technology and modern signal processing methods now make it possible to resolve physical features of ships, aircraft, space objects, and the earth's surface. This increased resolution capability has provided the means to extend the original radar concept of *ra*dio *d*etection *a*nd *r*anging to include capabilities for high resolution mapping, target recognition, and a growing list of nonmilitary remote-sensing tasks, unrelated to either detection or ranging. At the same time, high resolution techniques are being used to solve problems for carrying out traditional radar tasks of search, track, and weapon control in increasingly difficult surveillance environments.

The purpose of this book is to set forth in one volume the basic theory relating to design and analysis of radar systems that depend upon spatial resolution to accomplish the above-mentioned tasks. The first four chapters cover familiar radar topics such as the range equation, radar cross section, waveforms, data sampling, processing, and system design. For each topic, familiar relationships are redefined or restated, as required, to accommodate analysis in terms of time, space, and frequency resolution. In addition, some less familiar topics are included that relate to design and analysis of low distortion, high resolution radars. Later chapters discuss applications of the basic principles developed in the earlier chapters with respect to synthetic aperture radars, inverse synthetic aperture radars, and related radars. The last chapter covers application of high resolution techniques to problems associated with conventional search radar surveillance environments.

Subject matter covered in the book is closely related to work carried out by me, or under my direction, during the past 20 years, on high resolution radar systems at the Naval Ocean Systems Center (NOSC). The reader will notice occasional reference to NOSC or discussion of its work. Work at other government facilities and agencies is also cited, as well as that of some private companies. Also noted will be occasional reference to some concepts that are identified as yet to be demonstrated or still in the experimental phase. It is hoped that these items will provide some perspective as to the present status of high resolution radar and some appreciation for actual system design.

This book was developed from a set of course notes that I wrote for the purpose of teaching seminars on high resolution radar. The course notes formed the basis of seminars taught within the US Navy, at universities, and for private companies since about 1981. They are now also used for upper-level university courses on radar at Arizona State University and San Diego State University. Problems appearing at the end of each chapter were used as homework exercises for the university courses. Answers to even-numbered problems are included in the book.

I am indebted to Dr. Thomas E. Tice, professor at Arizona State University, for his many useful suggestions, assistance, and encouragement. Dr. Tice and I jointly taught most of the above-mentioned seminars. This and his use of the course notes in his upper-level radar course at Arizona State University have provided me with valuable feedback. I would also like to acknowledge the help given to me over many years by Robert G. Rock, scientist at the Naval Ocean Systems Center, in developing many of the concepts discussed in the book. Finally, mention should be made of the contribution by members of the Radar Branch at NOSC, who built experimental equipment, conducted analysis, carried out testing, and processed data associated with many of the topics covered in the book.

Chapter 1
Introduction

Many excellent books are now available for students and engineers interested in the design of modern search and track radar systems. Some of the key areas covered in depth are detection theory, clutter discrimination, target range and velocity tracking, signal processing, counter-countermeasures, and reflectivity. By comparison, books devoted to high resolution radar, synthetic aperture radar, and radar target imaging [1–6] are less numerous. These topics encompass some of the newer developments in radar for which the emphasis has shifted away from detection and tracking toward spatial resolution for target recognition, mapping, and imaging functions. This emphasis has focused increased attention on the processing of echo signals produced by wideband microwave illumination.

Synthetic aperture radar (SAR), first demonstrated in the early 1950s, is probably the most well known departure from conventional uses of radar for detection and tracking functions. Synthetic aperture mapping by airborne or spaceborne radar is achieved by coherent processing of reflectivity data collected from the earth's surface over relatively wide bandwidths at shifting viewing angles presented during surface illumination. The processing of the long echo data records associated with SAR bears only a distant relationship to coherent and noncoherent processing for detection and tracking. Although relatively low resolution, narrow bandwidth pulses were used for some of the early SAR demonstrations, later work to improve SAR resolution produced much of what is now a large technological base for transmitting, receiving, and processing signals at bandwidths corresponding to spatial resolutions as fine as one foot.

Inverse synthetic aperture radar (ISAR), a more recent variation of SAR, is a method for imaging objects, such as ships, aircraft, or spacecraft, from the wideband echo signals that are produced as the object rotates to present a changing viewing angle to the radar. Recent advances toward producing extremely high resolution ISAR imagery represent a further departure from conventional radar processing methods.

Interestingly, it appears that variations of radar techniques that were originally developed for mapping and imaging now appear to be able to solve heretofore difficult detection and tracking problems. Looking to the future of radar surveillance, it seems clear that the trend is toward exploitation of wider bandwidths, not only for high resolution mapping and imagery, but also for detection in increasingly difficult surveillance environments. For the nonmilitary user, high resolution reflectivity data, collected from earth and ocean surfaces illuminated by overhead platforms, is providing a wealth of information about the earth's resources. Typical users are scientists in the fields of geology, agriculture, and oceanography.

The emphasis in this book is placed on the operational application of high resolution radar as opposed to instrumentation-range applications. High resolution instrumentation radar for imaging real targets or scale models on outdoor and indoor ranges involves the same fundamental principles as operational radar, but presents a different problem. The target's viewing angle in an instrumentation system is under the control of the range operator. By contrast, for operational radars, target viewing angle is less directly controlled and may not even be known. For this reason, issues of image distortion, image plane determination, velocity correction, and sampling criteria are treated differently when a high resolution capability is designed for an operational radar. Probably of greater significance is the emphasis on bandwidth. It is possible, in principle, to obtain spatial resolution of targets at a single frequency by collecting reflectivity data over a wide range of controlled viewing angles. However, the range of target viewing angles seen by operational radars is limited by the available target dwell time. Spatial resolution, therefore, strongly depends on the radar bandwidth, which is a radar parameter entirely independent of target behavior and geometry. Bandwidth for operational radars is achieved at a high cost. Therefore, waveform selection to reduce cost and allow the same radar to perform both detection and recognition becomes an important issue.

Increased bandwidth, while not originally the major thrust in radar development, was known from the beginning to provide certain advantages. The use of short pulses containing energy spread over wide bandwidths was known to make it possible to separate targets* in range. Ability to operate in jamming environments was known to improve by rapidly changing the radar's transmitter and receiver frequency over large bandwidths. As radar technology has matured in many respects, radar bandwidth has become a major design parameter.

---

*The term *radar target* as used throughout this book refers to any object of interest to the radar operator.

Throughout the book, the term *radar bandwidth* will refer to the extent of the frequency band over which target reflectivity data are collected, regardless of radar waveform. *Short-pulse radars* and *pulse-compression radars* are wideband radars by virtue of the bandwidth associated with their transmitted pulses. Echo signals from these types of radars contain components of frequency spread over the transmitted pulse bandwidth. We will also discuss other types of radars that directly collect target reflectivity data over wide bandwidths in the frequency domain by sampling reflectivity *versus* transmitter frequency.

1.1 ADVANTAGES OF INCREASED RADAR BANDWIDTH

The fundamental advantage offered by wide radar bandwidth is increased information about the presence, location, and identity of targets, such as ships, aircraft, and the earth's surface features. Such increased information is produced by the additional, independent target reflectivity data that can be collected. For example, consider a narrowband pulsed radar designed for aircraft and ship surveillance, operating at a single polarization. Assume that aircraft or ships occupy only a small portion of the radar's antenna beamwidth and are unresolved in range so that each echo pulse is a measure of the reflectivity of the entire aircraft or ship at an instantaneous viewing angle. If the target's viewing angle were then changing due to either radar or target motion, the radar could be said to be able to collect target reflectivity data in one dimension: reflectivity *versus* viewing angle. The same radar operated over a wide frequency band, for example, by changing the transmitter frequency from pulse to pulse, collects target reflectivity data in two dimensions: reflectivity *versus* frequency and viewing angle. To the extent that the additional dimension provides additional independent samples of target reflectivity data, then there is increased information about the target's presence, location, and identity. With regard to echo sample independence, it is well known that microwave reflectivity of targets, such as ships, aircraft, or the earth's surface features, fluctuates rapidly with both viewing angle and frequency. Thus, data collected over a wide range of viewing angles or frequencies can be expected to contain a large number of independent samples of target reflectivity data.

Target recognition of ships, aircraft, and objects in space is probably the most well known type of information provided by high resolution radar data. These types of targets, viewed over a wide range of frequencies and viewing angles, provide independent samples of their reflectivity related to their physical characteristics. Echo amplitude and phase data collected *versus* frequency and viewing angle from such a target can be converted into reflectivity estimates *versus* one or more dimensions of target space. Such data, called the *radar target image,* provide information about a target's identity and other characteristics of interest. Similarly, aircraft- and satellite-borne radars generate images of the earth's surface (maps) that provide several types of earth surface information, which is vital to both military and nonmilitary users.

A quantitative relationship between the available independent target echo data and target information probably cannot be defined in any general sense. However, a quantitative assessment of the benefits of radar bandwidth can be obtained by relating the available content of independent reflectivity data to radar bandwidth and data collection time without regard to the contribution of such data to target information. Consider the echo signal produced by a short, single-frequency, transmitted pulse reflecting from an extended target illuminated by the radar's antenna beam at a fixed viewing angle. The echo signal can be thought of as a measure of the reflectivity of the target *versus* range delay. Temporal resolution of the echo signal, by way of proper receiver design, can approach that of the transmitted pulse duration (pulsewidth). In terms of transmitted pulse bandwidth β, the temporal resolution is about $1/\beta$. To sample such an echo pulse unambiguously, according to the Nyquist criteria, requires a sampling rate of at least 2β samples per second for a total of $2\beta\delta t$ samples from an echo pulse to be sampled over a range-delay extent δt. Sampling at the Nyquist rate of 2β will then produce $2\beta\delta t$ independent samples of target reflectivity, assuming that each resolved range-delay cell produces an independent sample of reflectivity. The total data content from the sampled echo signal, when quantized onto m resolvable bits in amplitude, is $2m\beta\delta t$ bits. The three quantities that determined the echo signal's data content were transmitted signal bandwidth, sampled range-delay extent, and quantization. For a given level of quantization and a given range-delay extent to be sampled, the data content of a single echo pulse is seen to be directly proportional to bandwidth.

1.2 DATA-COLLECTION APERTURE

The term *aperture* appears frequently throughout this book. It will first be encountered when discussing real, physical radar antennas in Chapter 2, where the term refers to the effective size of an antenna in terms of collecting incident signal power. Later, in Chapter 6, the term *synthetic aperture* will be used to refer to the ground-track length over which earth surface reflectivity data is collected, then processed, to obtain fine along-track resolution. Finally, in Chapter 7, the term *frequency-space aperture* will be used to refer to data collection over both frequency and viewing angle. Both *synthetic aperture mapping* and *inverse synthetic aperture imaging* can be explained in terms of processing reflectivity data collected over fine increments of frequency and viewing angle. At this point, radar imagery relates closely to x-ray, acoustic, and other types of tomography now used to produce body tissue imagery for medical diagnostics.

The part of the data-collection aperture that is produced by change of frequency can be generated in a few milliseconds (or during the target's range-delay extent if a short pulse is used). The part of the aperture that is produced by change in radar viewing angle, however, requires physical motion by the radar or target. Typically, a fraction of a second to several seconds are required to produce the needed segment of viewing angle for mapping and target imaging from a single radar. An optical aperture, such as that found on a camera, is produced by setting a fixed, circular light-collection area. Conversely, the radar frequency-space aperture is dynamically produced by frequency and viewing angle changes occurring in grossly differing time frames. Resolution along the line of sight to the target (*slant-range* resolution) is determined by the radar's bandwidth. Resolution transverse to the line of sight (*cross-range* resolution) is determined by wavelength and the viewing-angle segment over which reflectivity data are collected.

1.3 RANGE RESOLUTION

Perhaps the most well known characteristic of high resolution radar is its ability to resolve sources of reflection in the slant-range dimension. The fundamental relationship for the inherent range resolution associated with radar bandwidth is given by the expression:

$$\Delta r_s \approx \frac{c}{2\beta} \tag{1.1}$$

This expression and variations of it will occur repeatedly in this text for various applications of high resolution radar. A target's reflectivity *versus* frequency and its high-range-resolution range profile at any instant are related by the Fourier transform. Thus, in principle, measurement of a target's reflectivity *versus* frequency over a given bandwidth is equivalent to measuring its time-domain echo response to a short pulse or an equivalent waveform of the same bandwidth. Both frequency and time measurements and their associated processing will be discussed in this book.

1.4   NARROWBAND REPRESENTATION

The term *high-range-resolution* (HRR) *radar* implies the use of wideband signals. To obtain high range resolution, however, the signal bandwidth need only be wide in terms of absolute bandwidth in Hz. Fractional bandwidth, defined as a signal's bandwidth divided by its center (carrier) frequency, may actually be quite narrow for high resolution systems. For this reason, it is often possible to represent high-resolution-radar waveforms and signals by using narrowband approximations.

A real signal $s_r(t)$ can be defined to be a *narrowband signal* if its Fourier components $S_r(f)$ are primarily confined to a bandwidth β that is small compared to its center (carrier) frequency $\bar{f}$. A typical high resolution waveform that often meets this criterion is the *chirp pulse*. This is a radio frequency (RF) pulse consisting of a time-limited sine wave, which is phase modulated in such a way that linear frequency modulation results across the pulse duration. This waveform and the magnitude of its two-sided Fourier transform are illustrated in Fig. 1.1(a) and 1.1(b), respectively. (The spectrum $\Psi(f)$ in Fig. 1.1(b) will be discussed below.) We can see that the carrier is modulated in amplitude and phase at a slow rate, as compared to its sinousoidal variation, and the spectrum of the waveform is narrow relative to the center frequency $\bar{f}$.

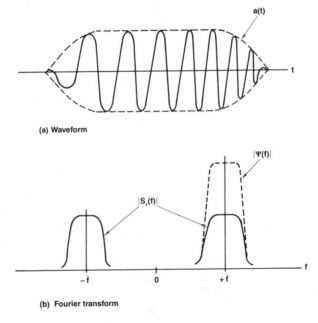

(a) Waveform

(b) Fourier transform

Fig. 1.1 Chirp-Pulse Waveform and its Fourier Transform

Any narrowband waveform can be represented by the expression:

$$s_r(t) = a(t) \cos [2\pi \bar{f} t + \theta(t)] \tag{1.2}$$

where $a(t)$ describes the amplitude modulation and $\theta(t)$ describes the phase modulation of a carrier signal at $\bar{f}$. As signal bandwidth increases, (1.2) remains valid, but $a(t)$ and $\theta(t)$ lose their significance for describing amplitude and phase modulation of a carrier.

A narrowband signal can also be expressed as the real part of a complex exponential function as follows:

$$s_r(t) = \text{Re}\{a(t)e^{j[2\pi \bar{f} t + \theta(t)]}\} \tag{1.3}$$

In this book, the term *complex representation* of a signal will refer to the exponential function itself. The complex representation of the narrowband waveform given by (1.2) and (1.3) is

$$s(t) = a(t)e^{j[2\pi \bar{f} t + \theta(t)]} \tag{1.4}$$

Equation (1.4) can also be written as

$$s(t) = a(t)e^{j\theta(t)}e^{j2\pi \bar{f} t}$$

where $a(t)\, e^{j\theta(t)}$ is referred to as the *complex envelope* of the waveform because it contains both the amplitude and phase modulation of the narrowband signal $s_r(t)$.

The terms *pre-envelope* and *analytic signal* are used to denote a more general complex representation, given by

$$\psi(t) = s_r(t) + j\hat{s}_r(t) \tag{1.5}$$

where $\hat{s}_r(t)$ is the Hilbert transform of $s_r(t)$, which is the real waveform. The analytic signal is not restricted to representation of narrowband signals, but the representation only applies to band-limited signals. From (1.5), the real waveform, can be expressed in terms of $\psi(t)$ as

$$s_r(t) = \text{Re}|\psi(t)|e^{j \text{ arg } \psi(t)} \tag{1.6}$$

where

$$\text{arg } \psi(t) = \tan^{-1} \frac{\hat{s}_r(t)}{s_r(t)}$$

The magnitude $|\psi(t)|$ of the analytic signal is the envelope of the real signal $s_r(t)$.

Components of the Fourier transform $\Psi(f)$ of $\psi(t)$ below zero frequency are of zero amplitude, and they are related to the Fourier transform $S_r(f)$ of $s_r(t)$ according to

$$\Psi(f) = \begin{cases} 0, & f < 0 \\ S_r(f), & f = 0 \\ 2S_r(f), & f > 0 \end{cases}$$

The transform of the analytic signal representation of the chirp waveform is illustrated in Fig. 1.1(b). For narrowband signals:

$$|\psi(t)| \approx a(t)$$

and

$$\arg \psi(t) \approx 2\pi \bar{f} t + \theta(t)$$

where $a(t)$ is the envelope (amplitude modulation) of the real waveform and $\theta(t)$ is the phase modulation.

DiFranco and Rubin [7] show that the rms difference between $|\psi(t)|$ of (1.6) for rectangular RF pulses of up to 50% fractional bandwidth and $a(t)$ for narrowband rectangular RF pulses differ by less than 20%. (Fractional bandwidth here is defined as the reciprocal of $T_1\bar{f}$, where T_1 is the RF pulsewidth.) Based on this result, the narrowband expression of (1.3) is justified for most high resolution waveforms discussed in this book, whether band-limited or not, because application is primarily to a radar signal fractional bandwidth of less than 20%.

The reader is advised to refer to DiFranco and Rubin [7], Cook and Bernfeld [8], and Rihaczek [9] for more complete discussions of complex waveform representation.

1.5   HIGH-RESOLUTION-RADAR BANDWIDTH

A radar used for over-the-horizon (OTH) surveillance may operate over more than two octaves of the high frequency (HF) band (3 MHz to 30 MHz)*, but resolution is so low that it would not be thought of as a high resolution radar. On the other hand, a synthetic aperture radar op-

---

*Reference to frequency bands will be consistent with radar bands assigned by the International Telecommunication Union (ITU).

erating with only 5% bandwidth somewhere in the X-band region (8.50 GHz to 10.68 GHz) could produce very high resolution maps. While some have proposed multioctave microwave radar systems for surveillance applications, the term *wide bandwidth,* when applied to operational radars in the present book, mostly refers to an operating frequency range of less than 1.0 GHz. Much wider bandwidth is employed for some instrumentation radar cross-section ranges.

Some general categories of radar bandwidth are pulse-to-pulse frequency-agile bandwidth, instantaneous bandwidth, frequency-modulation bandwidth, and tunable bandwidth. For our purposes, the term *wide bandwidth radar* will generally refer to operational radars for which the frequency can be varied rapidly (from 0.1 s to instantaneously) over bandwidths greater than 25 MHz. More fundamentally, we will be dealing with radars having sufficient bandwidth together with other characteristics that allow resolution of features on individual targets and the earth's surface.

1.6 TOPICS COVERED IN THE BOOK

Chapters 2, 3, and 4 review basic radar principles with emphasis on resolution in range and velocity. Chapter 5 introduces the concept of reflectivity measurements in the frequency domain using stepped-frequency waveforms. Synthetic aperture radar and inverse synthetic aperture radar are discussed in Chapters 6 and 7. The next two chapters discuss two experimental concepts: techniques for imaging using monopulse methods (Chapter 8) and imaging with noncoherent radar (Chapter 9). Finally, in Chapter 10, application of high resolution and wideband processing techniques is discussed for electronic counter-countermeasures, low-flyer detection, low probability of intercept radar, and reduced fluctuation loss.

PROBLEMS

1.1   What is the range delay to the moon at distance of 239,000 miles (384×10^6 m)?

1.2   A ship of 200 m in length is viewed bow-on with a radar. What is the range-delay extent seen by the radar?

1.3   What is the approximate sampling rate required for unambiguous sampling of echo signals produced from range-extended targets by a single-frequency pulse radar having 10 m resolution?

1.4   A low resolution radar illuminates a large, stationary target from a fixed range and viewing angle with 1000 pulses, all at the same frequency. (a) How many independent samples of reflectivity data are obtained from each echo pulse? (b) How many independent samples of reflectivity data could be obtained if either frequency or viewing angle were allowed to vary without limit between pulses?

1.5   (a) How many real samples per second are required for unambiguous sampling of the range-extended echo signal of a radar if the receiver were matched to the transmitted pulse duration of 2.0 μs? (b) What is the equivalent sample separation in target slant range?

1.6   Two point targets are separated by 3.0 m in slant range. (a) What radar bandwidth is required to resolve the two targets? (b) If the radar is a monotone pulse radar, what should the transmitted pulse duration be?

1.7   Which of the following signals could be accurately represented in complex form by (1.4): (a) a 10 μs video pulse (no RF carrier); (b) a 10 Hz to 20 kHz audio signal; or (c) a 2.0 ns RF echo pulse from a 10 GHz radar?

REFERENCES

1.   Rihaczek, A.W., *Principles of High-Resolution Radar,* New York: McGraw-Hill, 1969.

2.   Cutrona, L.J., "Synthetic Aperture Radar," in *Radar Handbook,* Chapter 23, M.I. Skolnik, ed., New York: McGraw-Hill, 1970.

3.   Harger, R.O., *Synthetic Aperture Radar Systems: Theory and Design,* New York: Academic Press, 1970.

4.   Kovaly, J.J., *Synthetic Aperture Radar,* Dedham, MA: Artech House, 1981.

5.   Mensa, D.L., *High Resolution Radar Imaging,* Dedham, MA: Artech House, 1981.

6.   Hovanessian, S.A., *Introduction to Synthetic Array and Imaging Radars,* Dedham, MA: Artech House, 1980.

7.   DiFranco, J.V., and Rubin, W.L., *Radar Detection,* Dedham, MA: Artech House, 1980, pp. 57–61.

8.   Cook, C.E., and Bernfeld, M., *Radar Signals,* New York: Academic Press, 1967, pp. 60–68.

9.   Rihaczek, A.W., *Principles of High-Resolution Radar,* New York: McGraw-Hill, 1969, pp. 15–27.

Chapter 2

Application of the Radar Range Equation to High Resolution Radar

The acronym, *radar* (*r*adio *d*etection *a*nd *r*anging), falls short of defining the scope of today's active electromagnetic surveillance. Radar now includes other important functions in addition to detection and ranging. Modern high resolution radars provide ground mapping, and, more recently, target recognition and imaging. A more precise definition might be "active electromagnetic surveillance." Nonetheless, the basic equation expressing the range at which a target can be detected remains fundamental to modern radar design. Even for imaging radar systems, where the purpose may be recognition rather than detection, variations of the radar range equation are employed to analyze imaging performance.

In its most basic form, the radar equation expresses target detection range in terms of radar parameters and target *radar cross section* (RCS). In this chapter, we will first derive the radar equation itself. Then, each parameter will be discussed from the viewpoint of high resolution applications. Finally, the radar equation will be applied to examples of four simple types of high resolution radar systems.

2.1 DERIVATION OF THE RADAR EQUATION

Figure 2.1 illustrates one method of deriving the expression for received radar-echo power. The radio frequency (RF) power in watts from the transmitter is P_t. The power density incident on a target at range R in meters for transmitting antenna gain G_t toward the target is given in watts per square meter by

$$s_I = \frac{P_t G_t}{4\pi R^2}$$

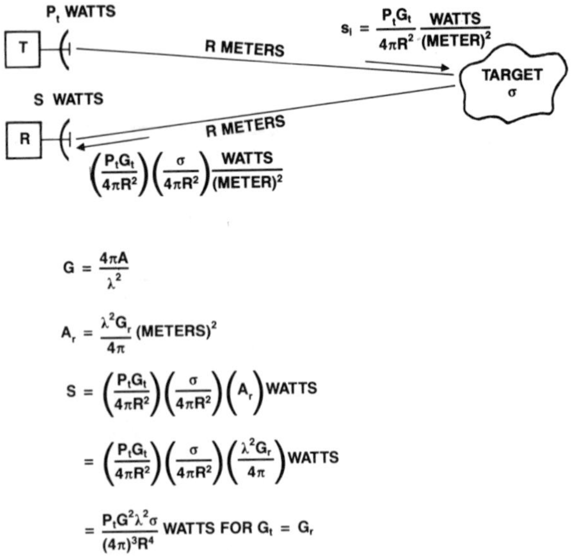

The figure contains the following labeled elements:

P_t WATTS

T

R METERS

$S_i = \dfrac{P_t G_t}{4\pi R^2} \dfrac{\text{WATTS}}{\text{(METER)}^2}$

TARGET
σ

S WATTS

R

R METERS

$\left(\dfrac{P_t G_t}{4\pi R^2}\right)\left(\dfrac{\sigma}{4\pi R^2}\right)\dfrac{\text{WATTS}}{\text{(METER)}^2}$

$$G = \frac{4\pi A}{\lambda^2}$$

$$A_r = \frac{\lambda^2 G_r}{4\pi} \;(\text{METERS})^2$$

$$S = \left(\frac{P_t G_t}{4\pi R^2}\right)\left(\frac{\sigma}{4\pi R^2}\right)\left(A_r\right) \text{WATTS}$$

$$= \left(\frac{P_t G_t}{4\pi R^2}\right)\left(\frac{\sigma}{4\pi R^2}\right)\left(\frac{\lambda^2 G_r}{4\pi}\right) \text{WATTS}$$

$$= \frac{P_t G^2 \lambda^2 \sigma}{(4\pi)^3 R^4} \text{WATTS FOR } G_t = G_r$$

Fig. 2.1 Key Elements of Radar Range Equation, Method A

The target scatters incident power in all directions, including back to the radar. The scattered power from a target of radar cross section σ in square meters is $P_t G_t \sigma/(4\pi R^2)$. (A definition of radar cross section will be given below.) The resulting echo power density at the radar becomes

$$s_e = \frac{P_t G_t \sigma}{4\pi R^2} \times \frac{1}{4\pi R^2} \; \text{W/m}^2$$

The received echo power in watts at the terminals of a receiver antenna of effective aperture A_r in square meters facing the target is

$$S = \frac{P_t G_t \sigma}{4\pi R^2} \times \frac{1}{4\pi R^2} \times A_r$$

Antenna effective aperture, defined for receiving, is the ratio of the received power out of the antenna terminals to the power density of the incident wave. From basic antenna theory, the gain of a lossless antenna is related to the antenna's effective aperture A by the expression:

$$G = \frac{4\pi}{\lambda^2} A$$

Effective aperture of antennas that are large in terms of wavelength can approach the physical aperture of the antenna for uniform, in-phase field illumination and low thermal loss. Received echo power in terms of receiving antenna gain G_r is

$$S = \frac{P_t G_t \sigma}{4\pi R^2} \times \frac{1}{4\pi R^2} \times \frac{\lambda^2 G_r}{4\pi} = \frac{P_t G_t G_r \lambda^2 \sigma}{(4\pi)^3 R^4} \tag{2.1}$$

For radar antenna gain $G = G_t = G_r$ (monostatic radar), the received echo signal power becomes

$$S = \frac{P_t G^2 \lambda^2 \sigma}{(4\pi)^3 R^4}$$

Various sources of system loss exist in practical radar systems. The symbol L ($L \leq 1$) as used here will designate total system loss. For total system loss, L:

$$S = \frac{P_t G^2 \lambda^2 \sigma L}{(4\pi)^3 R^4} \tag{2.2}$$

A second method of deriving S is shown in Fig. 2.2, which introduces the concept of radiation intensity U_s (power per unit solid angle) at the target range R directed back toward the radar.

Note that radar waveform parameters such as duty cycle and pulse-width (or pulse duration) do not enter the above equations for received echo power. When the terms *radar peak power* or *pulse power* are used, they refer to average power during each transmitted RF pulse. The received echo signal power S, then, refers to the RF pulse power of the echo signal. If the transmitted power is averaged over multiple pulses, (2.2) expresses the average received power.

The ability of the radar receiver to detect received echo signals depends on the radar receiving system sensitivity, denoted S_r. When S_r is below the available received power S, the target can be detected. Sensitivity is determined by the effective noise temperature, bandwidth of the receiving system, and the signal-to-noise power ratio at the receiving system input that is required to declare a detection at the receiving system output according to prescribed probabilities of detection and false alarm. When only thermal noise is considered, the noise power (to be discussed later in this chapter), referred to the receiving system input, is $kT_s\beta_n$. Thus, radar receiving system sensitivity in watts is given by

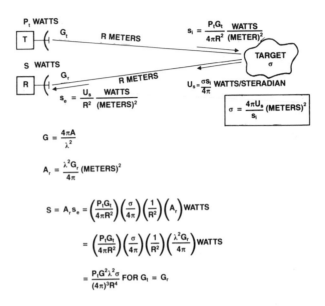

Fig. 2.2 Key Elements of Radar Range Equation, Method B

$$S_r = kT_s\beta_n(S/N)_{in}$$

where k is Boltzmann's constant (1.38×10^{-23} joules per kelvin [J/K]), T_s is the receiving system noise temperature in kelvins (K), β_n is the receiving system *noise bandwidth* (to be discussed later), and $(S/N)_{in}$ is the input signal-to-noise power ratio required for detection. The required input signal-to-noise ratio of a pulsed radar for given probabilities of detection and false alarm depend upon target echo fluctuation statistics, the number of pulses processed before making a detection decision, and the processing gain for each pulse.

The range equation, in terms of input signal-to-noise ratio, as written in a common form, then becomes

$$R = \left[\frac{P_t G^2\lambda^2\sigma L}{(4\pi)^3 kT_s\beta_n(S/N)_{in}}\right]^{1/4} \qquad (2.3)$$

The radar equation as expressed above for free space is an exact equation. There are no approximations in the equation itself. However, arriving at the values of the parameters for specific designs and analyses usually involves many approximations. Efforts over the years, however, have made it possible to analyze and predict radar performance accurately for most situations of interest. Range is in meters for P_t and $kT_s\beta_n$ in watts, λ in meters, and σ in square meters. The quantities G, L, and S/N are power ratios.

These parameters will now be discussed individually with a view toward high resolution radar applications.

2.2 TRANSMITTER POWER

Transmitter power P_t is the RF power in watts transmitted by the radar. It is common to refer to transmitter power P_t measured at the antenna terminals. This will be a slightly lower power than the output of the radar transmitter because of transmission line and *duplexer* losses. Most radar systems share a common transmitting-receiving antenna. A duplexer is then required to isolate the high power of the radar transmitter from the sensitive receiving system. Most radar systems operate by transmitting a continuous train of RF pulses having the same power. As stated above, the terms *peak power* and *pulse power* are commonly used to refer to the average power transmitted during the pulse. Average power then refers to the transmitted power averaged over many pulses. Later, the term *instantaneous peak power* will be used to refer to the instantaneous peak signal power out of a matched-filter receiving system. The instantaneous peak power of a steady-state sinusoidal signal is twice the average power of the signal.

Some radars transmit continuously, often through separate transmitting and receiving antennas. They are called *continuous-wave (CW) radars.* In the past, CW radars mostly operated at a single frequency, but wideband CW waveforms are now under development. The transmitting power of CW radars is usually quoted as the average power.

High resolution radar systems place special demands on transmitters. Transmitters are peak-power-limited. A few megawatts of pulse power is about the highest that is available from transmitters in the microwave radar bands. While this may seem to be a large amount of power, relatively small pulse energy is produced when the pulse duration is reduced to about 10 ns or less to obtain a corresponding range resolution of five feet or less. Thus, to obtain useful radar ranges, relatively longer pulses are coded in phase or frequency for pulse compression in the radar receiving system. This increases the demand for waveform fidelity in terms of phase and amplitude distortion over the transmitted bandwidth.

The transmitted power for phased-array radars would be the transmitter power at the terminals of each array element times the number of elements.

2.3   ANTENNA GAIN

The gain G of an antenna is the ratio of the transmitted radiation intensity in a specified direction relative to that from an isotropic radiator with the same input RF power (i.e., relative to that from a hypothetical radiator that radiates its input power evenly in all directions). The term *gain* is often used to refer to an antenna's directivity (multiplied by an aperture efficiency factor). Directivity is the ratio of maximum transmitted radiation intensity to average radiation intensity (defined for transmitting antenna).

Gain associated with an antenna's physical aperture will be realized only if incident power at all portions of the aperture (receiving antenna) is coherently integrated over the bandwidth of the radar signal.* For most wideband systems, this is achieved within a few dB with simple antennas, such as the parabolic reflector antennas fed by a single primary feed. The effective aperture obtained with wideband pulses may decrease, however, for large phase-steered array antennas, regardless of the bandwidth of individual components of the array. The phase gradient across the aperture used for the steering of phased arrays is inherently frequency-sensitive because of the phase *versus* frequency dependence on the physical spacing of array elements. True time-delay steering can avoid reduction in aperture efficiency for wideband waveforms, but it is often too lossy, complex, and costly for practical applications.

2.4   WAVELENGTH

The center wavelength of wideband radars considered in this book will generally range from about one meter downward. Above one meter, the fractional bandwidth required to achieve range resolution finer than a few meters becomes too high for practical radar designs. Even for wideband systems operating at wavelengths shorter than one meter, the instantaneous fractional bandwidth may vary enough that the effect of wavelength on received echo power may be of concern. It appears from the radar range equation of the form (2.2) that echo power increases with wavelength if all other parameters are held constant. Actually, the situation is more complicated than this. First, the target's RCS is a complex function of wavelength, as will be discussed below. Second, as wavelength decreases, the antenna gain of an ideal, constant-aperture antenna increases according to $G = 4\pi A/\lambda^2$. Hence, received power, from (2.2) in terms of antenna

---

*The property of *reciprocity* is assumed so that antenna gain, directivity, aperture size, and loss parameters are identical for both transmitting and receiving.

aperture A, becomes

$$S = \frac{P_t\left(\frac{4\pi A}{\lambda^2}\right)^2 \lambda^2 \sigma L}{(4\pi)^3 R^4} = \frac{P_t A^2 \sigma L}{4\pi\lambda^2 R^4}$$

Thus, for a fixed effective aperture, echo power actually decreases when wavelength increases.

Three antenna conditions can be encountered relative to wavelength:

1. constant aperture A (large antennas);
2. constant gain G (small antennas);
3. variable A and G (medium-sized antennas).

Only the first condition normally applies for operational high resolution radars. For most systems of interest, the fractional bandwidth and, thus, the fractional wavelength are less than 20%. The resulting echo power decrease due to the increase in wavelength, for constant aperture, is less than 2.0 dB. While this is significant, it does not normally become a key consideration for most wideband radar designs.

2.5 RADAR CROSS SECTION

2.5.1 Definition

The concept of radar cross section (RCS) refers to the effective echoing area of a target. Radar cross section will first be discussed in general terms before considering the implications for wideband systems. One way to look at the concept of RCS is to consider the radar as the center of an imaginary spherical surface containing the target, as shown in Fig. 2.3. The RCS of the target is then the area on the sphere's surface at the target position that isotropically reradiates all of its incident power at the same *radiation intensity* (power per unit solid angle) as the target reradiates toward the radar receiver.

Another view of RCS is based upon the scattering characteristics of a conducting sphere. A spherical conductor of large circumference relative to wavelength will reradiate back toward the radar with a radiation intensity which is equivalent to that resulting from isotropic reradiation of all the power intercepted by its cross-sectional area. (See Fig. 2.4) Therefore, radar cross section is often defined in terms of the equivalent cross-sectional area of a spherical conductor. A sphere with radius $a \gg \lambda$ will have a RCS equal to its physical cross-sectional area πa^2. This can be shown analytically and demonstrated experimentally. Thus, a target's RCS may be defined

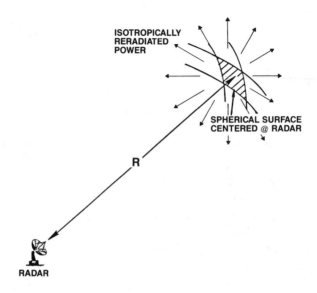

Fig. 2.3 Isotropic Reradiation of RF Power Incident upon a Spherical
Surface Segment of Area $= \sigma$

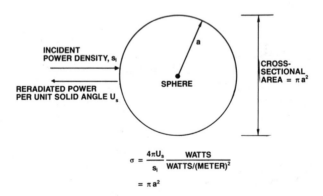

$$\sigma = \frac{4\pi U_s}{s_i} \quad \frac{\text{WATTS}}{\text{WATTS/(METER)}^2}$$

$$= \pi a^2$$

Fig. 2.4 RCS of Spherical Conductor

as the physical cross section of a perfectly conducting sphere in the same position as the target, which reradiates toward the radar at a radiation intensity equal to that of the target.

Some shorthand definitions of RCS are given below:

$$\sigma = \frac{(4\pi) \cdot (\text{power per unit solid angle scattered toward the receiver})}{\text{power density of the incident wave at the target}}$$

$$= \frac{\text{equivalent isotropically reradiated power}}{\text{incident power density}}$$

$$= \frac{4\pi U_s}{s_I}$$

The term *radar cross section*, to be precise, refers to a specified polarization component of scattered energy. Normally, a radar transmits at some specific polarization, such as horizontal or vertical, and receives at the same polarization. Radar cross section of a target for this condition respectively refers to the horizontally or vertically polarized component of energy scattered in the direction of the receiving antenna. The more general term, *scattering cross section*, refers to scattering at all polarizations. For complex targets, most of the scattered energy is usually at the incident polarization so that radar cross section and scattering cross section do not differ greatly.

When the radar transmitting and receiving antennas are colocated, cross section refers to scattering in the direction toward the source. This is called *monostatic cross section*. In a *bistatic radar*, where the source and receiver are separated, cross section refers to scattering in the direction of the receiver.

2.5.2 Sources of Backscatter

As we increase the resolution at which the target is observed, the concept of RCS changes significantly. With the advent of high-range-resolution radar, the fact was established that radar targets and clutter, observed at a given aspect to the radar, are made up of individual reflection points, also called *backscatter sources, scatterers,* "flare" spots, or "hot" spots of reflection on the target or clutter. Generally, it was found that backscatter sources on ships and aircraft remain roughly fixed in (target) location over aspect variations of up to about 30°. Backscatter sources for an aircraft are illustrated in Fig. 2.5. At a given aspect, each reflection point reflects energy at some amplitude and phase relative to that from other reflection points.

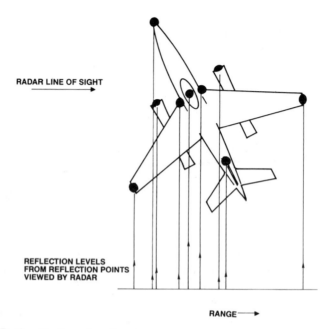

RADAR LINE OF SIGHT

REFLECTION LEVELS
FROM REFLECTION POINTS
VIEWED BY RADAR

RANGE

Fig. 2.5 Radar Backscatter Sources

It is thought that most major backscatter sources at any given target aspect are produced by specular reflection from relatively flat surfaces of the target presented normal to the radar and from corners. Other mechanisms are known to exist. *Creeping-wave* reflection occurs where the energy actually propagates along the surface of some part of the target to reappear directed toward the radar. Various resonance effects are also known to produce reflection.

Behavior of backscatter sources can be further understood by considering the physical sources of backscatter on real targets. Table 2.1 lists theoretical cross sections of some ideal geometric shapes, which could, at any target aspect, approximate certain portions of the target's physical features. Note that for a given physical cross-sectional area $\mathcal{A}$, a sphere produces the least RCS of any of the shapes and its RCS is independent of wavelength for $a \gg \lambda$. The RCS of all of the other shapes is seen to be wavelength-dependent, increasing as wavelength decreases. However, the likelihood is small that an ideal shape extends over more than a few wavelengths on an actual target. The last column of Table 2.1 lists cross sections of ideal shapes having dimensions of $a = 4\lambda$ to give some indication of RCS *versus* ideal shape representations of portions of real targets. Because the backscatter sources of a real target will remain respectively spherical, cylindrical, flat, dihedral, or trihedral over only a few wave-

Table 2.1   Radar Cross Section of Some Ideal Geometric Shapes

Geometric Shape	Dimension	Cross-Sectional Area[1] ($\mathcal{A}$)	Maximum Radar Cross Section[2] (σ)	$\dfrac{\sigma}{\mathcal{A}}$	$a = 4\lambda$
Sphere	radius a	πa^2	πa^2	1	1
Cylinder	$l \times$ radius a	$2la$	$\dfrac{2\pi a l^2}{\lambda}$	$\dfrac{\pi a}{\lambda}$	4π
	(thin wall, open ended)			(for $l = a$)	(for $l = a$)
Flat Plate	$a \times a$	a^2	$\dfrac{4\pi a^4}{\lambda^2}$	$\dfrac{4\pi a^2}{\lambda^2}$	64π
Dihedral Corner	a, a, a	$a^2\sqrt{2}$	$\dfrac{8\pi a^4}{\lambda^2}$	$\dfrac{8\pi a^2}{\sqrt{2}\lambda^2}$	$\dfrac{128\pi}{\sqrt{2}}$
Square Trihedral	$a, a, a,$	$\dfrac{3a^2}{2}$	$\dfrac{12\pi a^4}{\lambda^2}$	$\dfrac{8\pi a^2}{\lambda^2}$	128π

Notes:
[1]Seen at orientation for maximum RCS.
[2]Highly accurate only for $a \gg \lambda$.

lengths at microwave frequencies, the effective echoing area can be thought of as an aperture that is limited and tends to remain independent of frequency. This is illustrated in Fig. 2.6 for a hypothetical ship target. Directivity of limited-aperture backscatter sources of the target is low so that changes in reflectivity with aspect are small.

Phase of the reflection from individual scatterers of a target is determined by their range location relative to the radar. While reflection amplitude is relatively constant over small aspect changes, reflection phase of scatterers on ship and air targets changes rapidly at microwave frequencies. The rate of change of phase *versus* target aspect to the radar increases with radar frequency.

In summary, targets at microwave frequencies can be thought of as consisting of multiple reflectors, each of which has the following general characteristics:

1. reasonably constant reflection amplitude *versus* small aspect change;
2. rapidly changing reflection phase *versus* aspect;
3. weak relationship of effective echoing area to frequency.

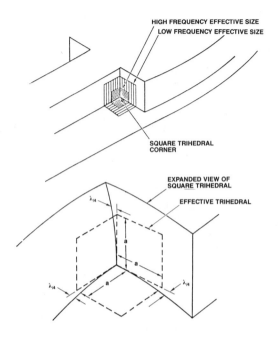

Fig. 2.6 Effective Trihedral Size on Hypothetical Ship Superstructure

2.5.3   RCS for Low Resolution Radar

Individual sources of backscattering are not resolved with low resolution radar. For example, a radar waveform of pulse duration T_1 is a narrow-bandwidth waveform for targets of length l, when $l \leq cT_1/2$, where c is the propagation velocity. The factor of one-half comes about because the range delay to any part of a target is the two-way propagation delay. For targets of less than 150 m range extent, for example, a pulse duration of 1.0 μs would be a narrow-bandwidth waveform according to this criterion. The effect can be visualized by considering reradiated energy from the far-range edge of the target arriving back to interfere with reradiation still occurring at the near-range edge. (Here, we assume a matched receiver, to be discussed later.) In the extreme case of a fixed frequency, continuous-wave radar ($T_1 = \infty$), scatterers appearing over the entire detection range of the radar produce interfering echo signals. Not even separate targets can then be resolved in range.

Thus, for narrow-bandwidth waveforms, backscattered energy from multiple scatterers within the target is superimposed to produce the echo signal. Amplitude and phase of the resulting signal are highly sensitive to small variations in the distances between scatterers. These distances will likely vary significantly in terms of wavelength, even for small target-aspect shifts or radar frequency shifts. The well known phenomenon of target fluctuation, observed on radar displays of envelope-detected echo signal *versus* range delay, illustrates the effect.

Radar cross section is a power ratio (power divided by power density). Therefore, phase does not appear in the definition of RCS. To retrieve the notion of phase, a target's echo transfer function relating backscattered to incident electric fields at a given frequency can be defined as

$$h = \frac{E_s}{E_I} = \sqrt{\sigma}\, e^{j\theta}$$

where the point of reflection is taken to be at radar range R to some point within the target. Then,

$$\sigma = |h|^2$$

Target dimensions are assumed small relative to radar range so that h is independent of R. Each scatterer of a target, observed at a given target aspect and radar frequency, will have an echo transfer function given by

$$h_k = \sqrt{\sigma_k}e^{j\phi_k} \tag{2.4}$$

where σ_k is the radar cross section of the kth scatterer alone. If the relative radar range from some point within the target at range R to each scatterer is d_k, the quantity ϕ_k in (2.4) is the two-way phase $4\pi d_k/\lambda$ of the kth scatterer. The narrowband RCS, in square meters, of a target composed of n scatterers becomes

$$\sigma = \left| \sum_{k=1}^{n} \sqrt{\sigma_k}e^{j(4\pi d_k/\lambda)} \right|^2$$

This phasor addition is illustrated in Fig. 2.7.

The important result of the effect shown in Fig. 2.7 is that the magnitude of the phasor sum of the echoes from individual backscattering centers will fluctuate rapidly in time, even for small aspect changes of the target. Slight changes of the radar frequency will also change the relative phase between backscattering centers and thereby produce changes in the narrowband echo magnitude. Target fluctuation affects detectability. For a required probability of detection greater than about 0.33, a higher threshold of signal-to-noise ratio must be set as a criterion for detection to maintain the same false-alarm probability as expected for a steady target.

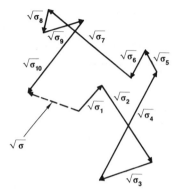

Fig. 2.7 Phasor Addition of Components of Narrowband Target Back-
    scatter

Below 0.33, the advantage is with a fluctuating target. The effect is illustrated in the well known target-detection curves developed by Swerling
[1]. An example is Fig. 2.8 obtained from Nathanson [2]. Figure 2.8 plots
calculated values of the required signal-to-noise ratio per pulse at the input

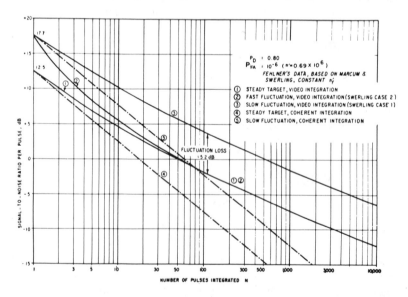

Fig. 2.8(a) Detectability Factor (*S/N*) *versus* Number of Pulses (P_D =
    0.8) (From Nathanson, F.E., *Radar Design Principles*, New
    York: McGraw-Hill, 1969, p. 82. Reprinted with permission.)

to a radar detection system *versus* number of pulses integrated to produce a probability of detection of 0.8 (Fig. 2.8(a)) and 0.5 (Fig. 2.8(b)) with a probability of false alarm of 10^{-6} in each case. Plots are shown for video and coherent integration of steady targets and of slowly and fast fluctuating targets. Video integration implies that input RF pulses are converted into video pulses in a *predetection* process before integration. Results are quite insensitive to the type of predetection used. For example, video integration of either square-law detected pulses or linear detected pulses would produce essentially the same results.

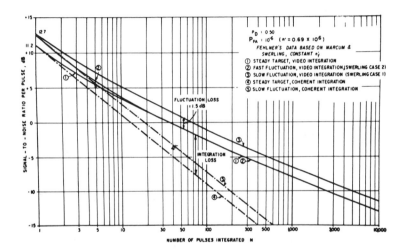

Fig. 2.8(b) Detectability Factor (*S/N*) *versus* Number of Pulses (P_D = 0.5) (From Nathanson, F.E., *Radar Design Principles,* New York: McGraw-Hill, 1969, p. 81. Reprinted with permission.)

Large variations in echo amplitude *versus* target aspect are noted for experimental RCS measurements of an aircraft shown at 450 MHz and 1100 MHz, respectively, in Fig. 2.9 and 2.10. Notice that the fluctuation rate is larger at the higher frequency. Narrowband RCS averaged over several degrees of azimuth aspect for large, complex targets does not vary in any systematic manner with frequency or polarization. Some experimental results for aircraft are shown in Table 2.2. Figure. 2.11 indicates RCS (averaged over 360° of aspect) *versus* ship length, based on experimental data at grazing angles from numerous ships.

Table 2.2   Aircraft Target Cross Section (Mean RCS in dBm^2)
(Averaged over 5° of Azimuth Aspect)

	Vertical Polarization			*Horizontal Polarization*		
	1300 MHz	2800 MHz	9225 MHz	1300 MHz	2800 MHz	9225 MHz
Small Aircraft (Version A)						
0°	7	12	11	8	11	10
45°	7	10	7	5	8	5
90°	20	22	19	18	22	18
135°	7	10	8	4	8	8
180°	10	14	17	12	10	14
Small Aircraft (version B)						
0°	5	7	7	8	6	4
45°	6	6	6	5	5	4
90°	22	23	22	21	21	21
135°	6	7	5	5	5	3
180°	7	6	9	4	9	8
Medium Aircraft						
0°	12	13	12	8	13	12
45°	10	11	8	8	9	8
90°	20	22	21	22	23	23
135°	8	8	7	6	7	7
180°	5	12	7	7	7	8
Large Aircraft						
0°	17	18	15	18	18	16
45°	16	19	16	15	16	16
90°	31	29	28	33	32	32
135°	15	15	14	12	12	13
180°	19	17	16	14	18	17

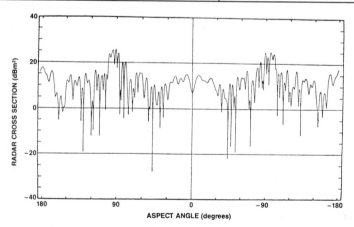

Fig. 2.9 RCS of Aircraft at 450 MHz, Zero-Degree Tilt Angle, Horizontal
Polarization.

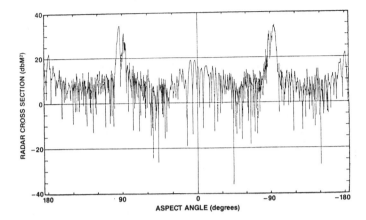

Fig. 2.10 RCS of Aircraft at 1100 MHz, Zero-Degree Tilt Angle, Horizontal Polarization.

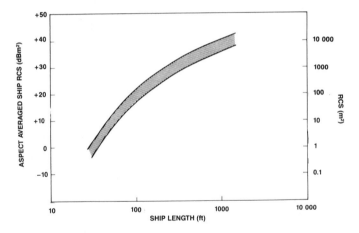

Fig. 2.11 RCS *versus* Ship Length.

2.5.4 RCS for High Resolution Radar

High resolution radar can resolve individual scatterers of a target. To the extent that scatterers of a target are resolved, their fluctuation is reduced. An easy way to visualize resolution of individual target-backscattering elements is to think of the resolution associated with a very short monotone pulsed radar. The range resolution with pulsewidth T_1 is about $\Delta r_s = cT_1/2$. For example, to resolve backscatter elements separated by 1.0 m in range, the pulsewidth T_1 must be less than or equal to

$$\frac{2\Delta r_s}{c} = \frac{(2)(1.0 \text{ m})}{3 \times 10^8 \text{m/s}} = 6.7 \text{ ns}$$

This requires a radar bandwidth of about $\beta = 1/T_1 = 150$ MHz.

So far, target resolution of backscatter elements has been discussed only in terms of range resolution. Radars, however, can be designed to measure and resolve in amplitude, range, bearing, and velocity (Doppler). Modern wideband radar techniques now make it possible to resolve scatterers on individual targets in slant range and cross range. The concept of target RCS changes accordingly. Likewise, detection criteria can also change.

According to Berkowitz [3] the average narrowband radar cross section $\bar{\sigma}$ of a target containing a distribution of a large number of equal backscattering elements can be approximated by

$$\bar{\sigma} = m\sigma_e \tag{2.5}$$

where m is the number of backscatter elements and σ_e is the RCS of each element.

Three types of element cross section σ_e can be defined:

(1)
$$(\sigma_e)_r = \frac{\bar{\sigma}}{m_r}$$

where $(\sigma_e)_r$ is the cross section for elements resolved in range only, m_r is the number of range elements resolved, and $\bar{\sigma}$ the average narrowband RCS of the target,

(2) $\quad (\sigma_e)_D = \dfrac{\bar{\sigma}}{m_D}$

where $(\sigma_e)_D$ is the element cross section for Doppler-only resolved elements and m_D is the number of Doppler elements resolved, and

(3) $\quad (\sigma_e)_{rD} = \dfrac{\bar{\sigma}}{m_{rD}}$

where $(\sigma_e)_{rD}$ is the element cross section for elements resolved in range and Doppler, and m_{rD} is the number of range-Doppler elements resolved. These relationships have been established experimentally in only a very approximate fashion, but they are helpful for predicting range performance of target imaging radars.

2.6 SYSTEM LOSS

System loss is a term that normally includes transmission line loss, propagation loss, receiving system loss, and signal processing loss before detection or display. High resolution radar systems can produce additional loss due to radar mismatch over the required wide bandwidth. Values calculated by Blake [4] of signal loss *versus* frequency for two-way transit through the atmosphere are plotted in Fig. 2.12. Except for extreme bandwidths or operation near atmospheric absorption peaks, we can see that propagation loss is essentially constant over radar bandwidth. Total radar system loss, not including propagation loss, typically ranges from -6 to -10 dB for a well designed wideband radar system. The symbol L in this text has values equal to or less than unity.

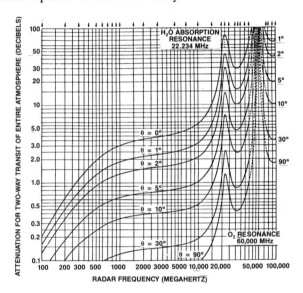

Fig. 2.12 Calculated Absorption Loss for Two-Way Transit of the Entire Troposphere at Various Elevation Angles (From Blake, L.V., *Radar Range-Performance Analysis,* Norwood, MA: Artech House, 1986, p. 219. Reprinted with permission.)

2.7 RANGE ATTENUATION

The radar equations (2.1) and (2.2) contain the term $1/R^4$. This means that for free-space conditions, received echo power decreases as the fourth power of range if all other parameters remain constant. The received echo power, for radars operating near the earth, is a much more complex function $g(R)$ of several propagation factors. Factors that affect $g(R)$ are earth curvature, atmospheric diffraction, atmospheric loss, multipath reflection, atmospheric ducting, and tropospheric scattering.

Free-space propagation of power P_t from a transmitter antenna of gain G_t to a receiver antenna of effective aperture A_r and gain G_r at range R produces received power, given by

$$S = \frac{P_t G_t}{4\pi R^2} A_r = P_t \frac{G_r G_t \lambda^2}{(4\pi)^2 R^2}$$

Free-space propagation attenuation between two isotropic antennas $(G_r = G_t = 1)$ is the ratio:

$$\frac{S}{P_t} = \left(\frac{\lambda}{4\pi R}\right)^2$$

The actual propagation attenuation for an isotropic transmitting and receiving antenna is defined to be

$$\frac{S}{P_t} = g(R)$$

Then, for free-space propagation, we have

$$g(R) = \left(\frac{\lambda}{4\pi R}\right)^2$$

The free-space radar equation of the form (2.2), where $G = G_r = G_t$, can therefore be rewritten as

$$S = P_t \frac{G^2 \lambda^2 \sigma}{(4\pi)^3 R^4} L = P_t G^2 \left(\frac{\lambda}{4\pi R}\right)^2 \left(\frac{\lambda}{4\pi R}\right)^2 \frac{4\pi}{\lambda^2} \sigma L$$

The echo power for non-free-space propagation is

$$P_r = P_t G^2 [g(R)]^2 \frac{4\pi}{\lambda^2} \sigma L$$

where $g(R)$ is the one-way propagation attenuation, defined above to be the ratio of received to transmitted power between two isotropic radiators separated by range R.

As an example of the use of the quantity $g(R)$, Fig. 2.13 is a calculation of one-way attenuation $g(R)$ and free-space attenuation for a radar operating against a low-flying target. The factor $g(R)$ is, in general, frequency-dependent. The contribution by multipath lobing effects, in particular, is highly frequency-dependent.

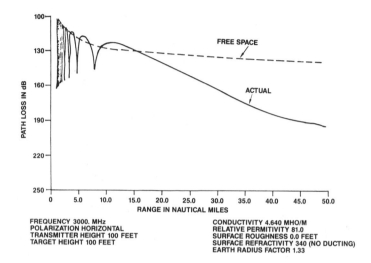

FREQUENCY 3000. MHz
POLARIZATION HORIZONTAL
TRANSMITTER HEIGHT 100 FEET
TARGET HEIGHT 100 FEET

CONDUCTIVITY 4.640 MHO/M
RELATIVE PERMITIVITY 81.0
SURFACE ROUGHNESS 0.0 FEET
SURFACE REFRACTIVITY 340 (NO DUCTING)
EARTH RADIUS FACTOR 1.33

Fig. 2.13 Propagation Path Attenuation for No Ducting Conditions (One-Way) (From the Integrated Refractive Effects Prediction System (IREPS] developed by H. Hitney *et al.* at the US Naval Ocean Systems Center [NOSC], San Diego, CA.)

Radio waves are slightly curved downward by the earth's atmosphere. The effect is a function of the refractive nature of the atmosphere at any particular time. A well known refractivity model often used to account for this effect is called the *CRPL* exponential reference atmosphere.* Range *versus* height plots of ray paths for this model are based on an index of refraction given by

$$1.0 + .000313\ e^{-.043859 h_2}$$

where h_2 is the target height in thousands of feet. Figure 2.14, from Blake [5], is an example of plots obtained by the model for earth-based radar (or radio) systems. An approximate expression for radar line-of-sight range

---

*Central Radio Propagation Laboratory of the National Oceanic and Atmospheric Administration (NOAA).

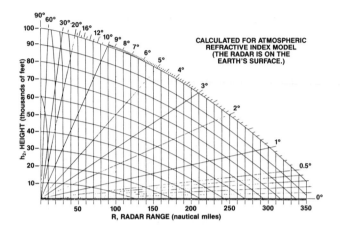

Fig. 2.14 Effect of Refraction on Radar Line of Sight (From Blake, L.
V., "Radio Ray (Radar) Range-Height-Angle Charts," *Microwave Journal*, Oct. 1968, pp. 49–53. Reprinted with permission.)

for antenna height h_1 and a target height h_2 is [6]:

$$R = \sqrt{2h_1} + \sqrt{2h_2}$$

where h_1 and h_2 are expressed in feet and R is in statute miles. The radar
horizon is determined by setting $h_2 = 0$.

2.8   RECEIVING SYSTEM SENSITIVITY

Received echo signals compete with receiving system noise, jamming
signals, and unwanted signals such as sea, land, and rain clutter. Receiving
system sensitivity is typically defined to be the product of receiving system
noise power N referred to the input of the receiving system times the
minimum power ratio $(S/N)_{in}$ of signal to noise required at the receiver
input for detection. The expression can be written as

$$S_r = N \left(\frac{S}{N} \right)_{in} \tag{2.6}$$

Noise power is expressed in terms of *noise temperature,* which relates
to the thermal noise power $kT\beta_n$ available to a load matched to a resistor
at temperature T in kelvins (K). The term k is Boltzmann's constant in

joules per kelvin (J/K) and β_n is the noise bandwidth over which the thermal noise power is measured. Noise power at the input to a radar system is similarly expressed as

$$N = kT_s\beta_n$$

where T_s is the receiving system noise temperature that accounts for all sources of radar system noise, including environmental noise seen by the radar antenna. Receiver sensitivity from (2.6) in terms of system noise temperature becomes

$$S_r = kT_s\beta_n\left(\frac{S}{N}\right)_{in} \tag{2.7}$$

Equation (2.7) for radar systems is sometimes written in terms of a *noise factor* (also called *noise figure*) defined as $F = T_s/T_0$. Sensitivity in terms of noise factor defined this way becomes

$$S_r = kFT_0\beta_n\left(\frac{S}{N}\right)_{in} \tag{2.8}$$

The noise temperature T_0 is the standard noise temperature 290 K. The more common noise factor related to effective noise temperature will be defined below.

It is assumed that noise power, when defined in terms of noise temperature, is uniformly distributed (white) over the entire RF spectrum. Noise bandwidth to be used for calculation of noise power is obtained from the receiving system bandpass characteristics. Usually, it is the intermediate frequency (IF) portion of the radar receiver that sets the receiving system bandpass characteristics. In any case, the noise bandwidth in (2.7) and (2.8) is given by

$$\beta_n = \frac{1}{|H(\bar{f})|^2}\int_{-\infty}^{\infty}|H(f)|^2 df \tag{2.9}$$

where $H(f)$ is the receiving system transfer function (frequency response characteristic) and $|H(\bar{f})|^2$ is the receiving system power gain at the center frequency $\bar{f}$. Noise bandwidth is approximately equal to the bandwidth measured, for example, at the half-power points of the receiving system. However, as (2.9) indicates, noise bandwidth is determined by the normalized power gain *versus* frequency of the receiving system. If we think of this in another way, a receiving system that has a noise bandwidth β_n, defined by (2.9), will produce a level of noise power at its output which is equal to that from a receiving system with a rectangular bandpass characteristic of bandwidth β_n.

2.8.1 Preamplifier Noise Specification

A manufacturer is likely to quote the noise performance of a low-noise preamplifier receiver in terms of an *effective noise temperature T_e,* or a related noise factor F_n. Effective noise temperature is the temperature that accounts for added noise produced by the receiver. Noise factor F_n of a receiver at a given frequency is defined as

$$F_n = \frac{\text{signal-to-noise in at } T_0 = 290 \text{ K}}{\text{signal-to-noise out}}$$

$$= \frac{S}{kT_0\beta_n} \div \frac{GS}{G(kT_0\beta_n + kT_e\beta_n)}$$

$$= \frac{T_e}{T_0} + 1$$

where S is the input signal power and G is the gain of the receiver, which is assumed to be linear. Effective noise temperature is therefore related to this definition of noise factor by the expression:

$$T_e = T_0(F_n - 1)$$

Often, the preamplifier has sufficient gain so that following portions of the radar receiving system do not contribute significant additional noise. Then, radar system noise power is the antenna noise power $kT_a\beta_n$ plus the effective noise power of the preamplifier $kT_e\beta_n$. In terms of radar system noise temperature, the relationship is given by

$$T_s = T_a + T_e$$

For example, assume that a manufacturer specifies a high-gain, low-noise preamplifier to have a noise factor $F_n(\text{dB})$ of 6 dB. Effective noise temperature is then $290(4 - 1) = 870$ K. If the radar antenna temperature for expected search directions is 150 K, the radar system noise temperature is

$$T_s = 150 + 870$$
$$= 1020 \text{ K}$$

Assume an input signal-to-noise requirement for detection that is set to be 15 dB at the input to the detector and a receiving system noise bandwidth of 1.0 MHz. Then, the sensitivity is

$$S_r = (k) (1020)(1.0 \times 10^6)(32)$$
$$= 4.5 \times 10^{-13} \text{ W } (-123 \text{ dBW})$$

The radar system noise factor F is $T_s/T_0 = 1020/290 = 3.52$ (5.5 dB).

Radar system noise factor F defines a radar receiving system sensitivity that varies as the antenna is directed toward regions of different absolute temperature. The noise factor F_n above conforms with the noise factor defined by the IEEE [7], familiar to many disciplines other than radar. F_n defines receiver low-noise performance *versus* frequency independently of other system parameters.

2.9 MATCHED-FILTER SIGNAL-TO-NOISE RATIO

The peak signal-to-noise ratio at the output of a radar receiver is maximized if the radar receiving system is *matched* to the received signal. The concept and precise definition of a matched filter are discussed in Chapters 3 and 4. A fundamental principle of radar, first discussed by North [8] and further developed by Turin [9], states that regardless of radar waveform, the peak signal to (average) noise power ratio of the output response of a matched-filter receiver is equal to twice the received signal energy E divided by the noise power per Hz. The expression in terms of the ratio of the peak instantaneous signal power to (average) noise power is

$$\left(\frac{\hat{S}}{N}\right)_{\text{out}} = \frac{2E}{N_0} \tag{2.10}$$

where N_0 is defined for a single-sided spectrum. (Noise power per Hz in terms of a two-sided spectrum with positive and negative frequencies is $N_0/2$.)

On the basis of (2.10), received pulses of average power S over a pulse duration T_1 will produce a peak signal-to-noise ratio at the output of a matched-filter receiver, which is

$$\left(\frac{\hat{S}}{N}\right)_{\text{out}} = \frac{2ST_1}{N/\beta_n}$$

where N is the available noise power within the matched-filter receiver bandwidth β_n. The input signal-to-noise ratio in terms of peak output signal-to-noise ratio becomes

$$\left(\frac{S}{N}\right)_{\text{in}} = \frac{1}{2T_1\beta_n}\left(\frac{\hat{S}}{N}\right)_{\text{out}} \tag{2.11}$$

Peak signal $\hat{S}$ here refers to the peak of the instantaneous signal power seen during the matched-filter output response to an input pulse. Detection curves, such as those given in Fig. 2.8 relating the required minimum signal-to-noise ratio for detection to the probabilities of detection and false alarm, are usually plotted in terms of average signal-to-noise ratio S/N at the peak of the receiver output response envelope at some intermediate frequency. When the waveform frequency components are confined to a band that is small compared to the IF center (midband) frequency, the instantaneous peak power at any point along the response envelope is approximately twice the average power at the same point. Throughout this book, S/N will refer to *average* signal-to-noise ratio at the peak of the *output* response envelope of the receiving system (before any pulse-to-pulse video integration). The signal-to-noise ratio at the input to a matched-filter receiver, from (2.11) in terms of S/N, therefore, becomes

$$\left(\frac{S}{N}\right)_{\text{in}} = \frac{1}{T_1\beta_n}\left(\frac{S}{N}\right) \tag{2.12}$$

Receiving system sensitivity from (2.7) for a required output signal-to-noise ratio S/N, then, is

$$S_r = kT_s\frac{1}{T_1}\left(\frac{S}{N}\right) \tag{2.13}$$

The radar equation (2.3), using (2.12), can then be rewritten as

$$R = \left[\frac{P_tG^2\lambda^2\sigma LT_1}{(4\pi)^3kT_s(S/N)}\right]^{1/4} \tag{2.14}$$

This form of the equation is independent of radar bandwidth. Although the above discussion referred to reception of an individual pulse, the concept of matched filtering is far more general. For example, if multiple pulses are coherently summed without loss during time T, (2.13) and (2.14) apply with $T_1 = T$ and P_t equal to the average power over the time interval T.

A filter matched to the transmitted pulse is also matched to a target echo signal when the target range extent is small compared to radar range resolution. Conversely, a filter matched to the echo signal at any instant from a highly resolved range-extended target generally differs from a filter matched to the transmitted pulse. Despite the mismatch, we almost always attempt to match the receiving system to the transmitted waveform, rather than the target echo.

2.9.1 Time-bandwidth Product

The quantity $T_1\beta_n$ in (2.12) is called the *time-bandwidth product* of a waveform. The time-bandwidth product of a single pulse can be made greater than unity by some form of phase or frequency coding. Pulse compression processing in a matched-filter receiver reduces the response width and increases the signal-to-noise ratio at the peak of the output envelope. The factor by which the signal-to-noise ratio at the output of a signal processor is increased over that at the input is defined as the *signal processing gain*. The processing gain for each pulse of a pulse-compression radar approaches $T_1\beta_n$ when the magnitude $|H(f)|$ of the receiving system transfer function approaches the shape of the waveform spectrum (i.e., approaches the matched condition).

Receiving system sensitivity, noise, and signal-to-noise relationships for matched filters are treated more completely in the literature [10, 11, 12].

2.10 RADAR RESOLUTION AND BANDWIDTH

2.10.1 Range Resolution

Range resolution of a radar can be defined in terms of its ability to resolve point targets that are separated in range to the radar. Resolution in the range domain corresponds to resolution in the time (range-delay) domain. A radar able to resolve echo pulses separated by a time interval

Δt can resolve point targets separated by $c\Delta t/2$ of radial range to the target (slant-range) in free space. The factor of two comes about because of the two-way travel of energy to and from each point target.

Consider the (sin $\beta\pi t)/\pi t$-shaped video pulse shown in Fig. 2.15(a). This pulse has a width of $1/\beta$ at the -4 dB points. Its Fourier transform is the rectangular spectrum shown in Fig. 2.15(b). Next, consider the ability to resolve two of these pulses in the time domain. Both pulses are assumed to be stationary. Resolution will be defined as the delay difference between two equal pulses that results in a -4 dB crossover point, as shown in Fig. 2.15(c). Resolution associated with the (sin $\beta\pi t)/\pi t$ video pulse, according to this definition, is $1/\beta$. Thus, the expression $\Delta t = 1/\beta$ for time-domain resolution is an exact expression when applied to video pulses having a rectangular spectrum of bandwidth β, assuming that a -4 dB crossover is considered adequate for resolution of two equal pulses. We can see from Fig. 2.15(a, c) that, according to this definition, resolution is also equal to the pulsewidth at the -4 dB points.

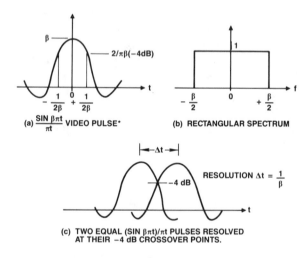

(a) $\dfrac{\text{SIN } \beta\pi t}{\pi t}$ VIDEO PULSE*

(b) RECTANGULAR SPECTRUM

(c) TWO EQUAL (SIN $\beta\pi t)/\pi t$ PULSES RESOLVED AT THEIR -4 dB CROSSOVER POINTS.

*t = 0 CORRESPONDS TO ROUND-TRIP ECHO DELAY

Fig. 2.15 Resolution Associated with Pulses Having a Rectangular Spectrum

Radar pulses are not usually the video pulses shown in Fig. 2.15. Instead, pulses of RF power are transmitted and received. Carrier frequency of practical systems is normally much higher than any frequency components of the pulse envelope. Resolution, however, is related to the envelope, rather than the RF carrier, of the received echo pulses. The pulse envelope is recovered in the radar receiving system by using detection or baseband mixing techniques followed by low-pass filtering to remove the carrier. The video pulse and its spectrum in Fig. 2.15, therefore, can be thought of as the envelope response to a fixed-point target following low-pass filtering.

2.10.2 Doppler Resolution

Radar resolution can also refer to the ability of a radar to resolve target radial velocity. In fact, target imaging will be explained later in terms of range-velocity resolution of multiple-scatterer targets that present a Doppler gradient to the radar as the viewing angle changes. The Doppler frequency f_D produced by a single-point scatterer at radial velocity v_t is

$$f_D = \frac{2v_t}{\lambda} = \frac{2fv_t}{c}$$

for $f \gg f_D$, where f is the radar frequency, λ is the wavelength, and c is the propagation velocity.

Doppler resolution of a radar is fundamentally related to coherent-integration time of the echo signal. Coherent integration can be achieved in several ways. A simple bandpass filter tuned to a Doppler-shifted signal will coherently integrate the signal over an integration time that is approximately equal to the reciprocal of the filter bandwidth. Today, it is common to carry out Doppler filtering of sampled echo data by using the *discrete Fourier transform* (DFT) method. Use of the DFT to obtain high resolution in both range and velocity from the same wideband echo data will be discussed in subsequent chapters.

The relationship $\Delta t \approx 1/\beta$ for range-delay resolution has an exact analogy in the Doppler domain. Let time and frequency be interchanged for the Fourier transformed pairs of Fig. 2.15, as given in Fig. 2.16, to represent envelopes, of a Doppler-shifted signal of duration T and its spectrum for $f \gg f_D$ and $f_D \gg 1/T$, respectively. The Doppler frequency spectrum associated with the constant level, Doppler-shifted signal of duration T has a bandwidth $1/T$ at the $2/\pi$ (-4 dB) points. A resolution of $\Delta f_D = 1/T$, therefore, is achieved by coherently integrating a constant level echo signal during time T. The perfect integrator is a filter having the ideal bandpass characteristic of Fig. 2.16(b). Doppler filtering in practical systems is carried out at or near baseband.

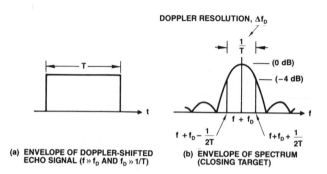

(a) ENVELOPE OF DOPPLER-SHIFTED   (b) ENVELOPE OF SPECTRUM
    ECHO SIGNAL (f » f$_D$ AND f$_D$ » 1/T)   (CLOSING TARGET)

Fig. 2.16 Resolution of Constant-Level Doppler-Shifted Signal of Duration T

2.10.3 Range-Doppler Resolution

The rectangular representation for the envelopes of the pulse spectrum in Fig. 2.15 and the Doppler shifted signal in Fig. 2.16 allow us to define range-delay and Doppler resolution precisely in terms of bandwidth and signal duration, respectively. The resulting equations:

$$\Delta t = \frac{1}{\beta} \text{ (fixed range delay)} \tag{2.15a}$$

and

$$\Delta f_D = \frac{1}{T} \text{ (constant Doppler)} \tag{2.15b}$$

for resolution at the -4 dB points are exactly true only for the idealized rectangular representations of signal spectrum and signal time envelope, respectively. This idealized situation is seldom encountered in practice. However, the above expressions for resolution can be assumed to be approximately correct for any well matched, moderately weighted radar system. It is common to refer to resolution at the -3 dB width instead of the -4 dB width of the response function. For a given signal bandwidth the range-delay resolution, measured at the -3 dB points, would appear to be slightly better than that measured at the -4 dB points. Likewise, Doppler frequency resolution associated with a given signal duration would also appear to be slightly improved when measured at the -3 dB points of the Doppler frequency response.

The above discussion of resolution has been based on a monotone pulse for range resolution and a continuous Doppler return for velocity resolution, but the relationships of range resolution to radar bandwidth and velocity resolution to signal integration time will be found to be fundamental in the following chapters, regardless of waveform and processing. *Super-resolution* processing concepts can significantly improve the radar resolution predicted by the simple expressions given above. Super resolution is achieved by trading off signal-to-noise performance or by introducing ambiguities, which require *a priori* information to resolve.

Principles of radar resolution are discussed in substantial depth by Rihaczek [13].

2.11 RADAR DETECTION RANGE FOR HIGH-RESOLUTION RADARS

Radar *detection range* of a high resolution radar system can be determined from (2.14), which assumes that the receiving system is matched to the signal waveform of duration T_1. Neither radar resolution nor waveform bandwidth appear in this form of the radar equation. It is, however, assumed that the target of cross-section σ to be detected has a range-delay extent which is small relative to radar resolution, so the echo signal power to be detected is that produced by the entire target.

Transmitter power P_t of a pulsed radar in (2.14) is the average power transmitted during pulse duration T_1 of the transmitted waveform. Transmitter power P_t for a pulsed Doppler radar, when the signal is to be integrated over multiple pulses, is given by

$$P_t = (\text{pulse power}) \cdot \frac{T_1}{T_2}$$

For a continuous-wave (CW) radar, P_t is the average power of the sinusoid.

Although written in terms of pulsewidth T_1, (2.14) expresses detection range in terms of signal duration, which may extend over multiple pulses or some *integration time, T,* to which the receiving system is matched.

Table 2.3 illustrates the use of (2.14) for calculation of radar detection range of four hypothetical high resolution radars operating at 10 GHz. The first two radars provide high resolution in the range-delay domain. The second two produce high resolution in the Doppler-frequency domain. Parameters were chosen to approximate the operation of the radars in a search mode with a target dwell time of 0.1 s. Signal-to-noise ratio required for detection is based on a required probability of detection of 0.8 and a

Table 2.3 Free-Space Detection Range Calculations for Four Types of High Resolution Radars

Parameter	Symbol	Short-Pulse (200 pulses integrated)	Pulse-Compression (200 pulses integrated)	Pulsed Doppler ($T = 0.1$ s)	CW ($T = 0.1$ s)
Pulse (or CW) Power	—	$.5 \times 10^6$ W	$.5 \times 10^6$ W	5000 W	1000 W
Pulsewidth { actual	—	20 ns	1.0 μs	1.0 μs	—
compressed	—	20 ns	20 ns	1.0 μs	—
PRI	T_2	500 μs	500 μs	5.0 μs	—
Average Power	—	20 W	1000 W	1000 W	1000 W
Waveform Bandwidth	β	50×10^6 Hz	50×10^6 Hz	10^6 Hz	0
Signal Duration	T_1	20 ns	1.0 μs	0.1 s	0.1 s
Transmitted Power[1]	P_t	$.5 \times 10^6$ W	$.5 \times 10^6$ W	1000 W	1000 W
Target RCS	σ	1.0 m²			
Boltzmann's Constant	k	1.38×10^{-23} J/K			
Wavelength	λ	.03 m			
Antenna Gain	G	2000 (33 dB)			
System Noise Temperature	T_s	500 K			
Loss	L	0.1(-10 dB)			

Table 2.3 (cont'd)

Parameter	Symbol	Short-Pulse (200 pulses integrated)	Pulse-Compression (200 pulses integrated)	Pulsed Doppler ($T = 0.1$ s)	CW ($T = 0.1$ s)
Probability of Detection	P_D	0.8			
Probability of False Alarm	P_{FA}	10^{-6}			
Required S/N (Fig. 2.8(a), Case 1)	S/N	1.6(2.0 dB) ($n = 200$)	1.6(2.0 dB) ($n = 200$)	59(17.7 dB) ($n = 1$)	59(17.7 dB) ($n = 1$)
Detection Range (from Eq. (2.14))	R	20.1 km (10.9 nmi)	54 km (29 nmi)	82 km (44 nmi)	82 km (44 nmi)
Resolution $\begin{cases} \Delta t = 1/\beta \\ \Delta f_D = 1/T \end{cases}$		$\Delta t = 20$ ns —	$\Delta t = 20$ ns —	— $\Delta f_D = 10$ Hz	— $\Delta f_D = 10$ Hz

[1] Average power during signal duration.

probability of false alarm of 10^{-6}, using the Swerling case 1 detection curves of Fig. 2.8(a). Video integration of the 200 pulses received during the 0.1 s dwell time is assumed for the short-pulse and pulse-compression radars. Lossless coherent integration is assumed over the 0.1 s dwell time for the pulsed Doppler and CW radars. Signal-to-noise ratio required for detection for these two radars is then based on $n = 1$, as though a single 0.1 s pulse were presented for detection.

PROBLEMS

2.1   Exposure of personnel to microwave radiation is to be limited to 5 mW per cm^2 of average power density. What is the minimum distance that must be maintained from a search radar of 2.5% duty cycle and 2.0 MW pulse power if the maximum antenna gain seen in the direction of personnel is 10 dB above isotropic?

2.2   We wish to develop an active radar target simulator to be used on deployable buoys on the ocean surface. The simulator repeats incident radar pulses omnidirectionally in azimuth to simulate ship targets for deception purposes. Assume that the simulator is to simulate echoes from ship targets of $\sigma = 10^5 m^2$ as seen by hostile airborne surveillance radars at 100 nmi (185.2 km). The radars operate at 10^6 W of pulse power with an antenna gain of 35 dB. What is the required transmitted pulse power to the simulator antenna of 7 dB gain? Assume free-space conditions.

2.3   A radar achieves a 100 nmi single-pulse detection range against air targets using monotone pulses of 20 μs duration. The radar is converted to a pulse-compression radar using 100 μs pulses with a pulse-compression ratio of 100. Other parameters remain the same. What is the single-pulse detection range of the pulse-compression version?

2.4   A radar uses a parabolic reflector antenna with a diameter of 3.0 m. Frequency is 3000 MHz. Half-power beamwidth in degrees is given approximately by 58 λ/D. (a) Calculate the half-power beamwidth. (b) Calculate the cross-range distance in meters between half-power points at a slant range of 10 nmi (18.52 km).

2.5   A ground-based search radar operates at 3.0 GHz with 1.0 MW pulse power. Total radar loss is -6 dB. Pulse duration is 10 μs. Pulse repetition rate is 400 pulses per second. The antenna rotates at 15 rpm in azimuth. Antenna gain at the target elevation is 34 dB. System noise factor is 3 dB. The receiver is matched to the transmitted pulse. (a) What is the input signal-to-noise ratio per pulse produced by a 1.0 m² target at a range of 200 km? (b) How many echo pulses occur per beam dwell? (c) What is the output signal-to-noise ratio produced by a nonfluctuating, nonmoving target of $\sigma = 1.0 \text{ m}^2$, following coherent integration during the target dwell? Assume a rectangular beamwidth in azimuth of 1.0°.

2.6   Show that the directivity of an idealized (rectangular beam shape) narrowbeam antenna with a two-dimensional beamwidth of θ_1 degrees by θ_2 degrees is given by

$$G = \frac{41253}{\theta_1 \theta_2}$$

2.7   The input signal-to-noise ratio of an X-band radar produced by a fixed sphere of 1.0 m diameter is 15 dB. A second sphere with a 2.0 m diameter is introduced well within the radar's beamwidth, but slightly displaced in range delay from the first sphere. What range of signal-to-noise values are possible? Neglect shadowing effects. Assume that total range delay greatly exceeds the range displacement between spheres and that pulsewidth is greater than the range displacement.

2.8   What is the radar range against a 1.0 m² target for a detection probability of 0.8 with a false alarm rate of 10^{-6} using the search radar of Prob. 2.5? Use Swerling case 1 statistics and assume video integration of multiple pulses occurs on each scan.

2.9   A 2-D search radar scans in azimuth at 7 1/2 rpm. Azimuth beamwidth is 5.0° and antenna gain is 30 dB. Peak power is 250 kW. Wavelength is 1.0 m. Receiving system effective noise temperature is 300 K. Antenna noise temperatures is 200 K. Pulse duration is 10 µs, system loss is −6 dB, and the PRF is 250. (a) What is the single-pulse detection range in free space against a 1.0 m² Swerling case 1 target for $P_D = 0.5$, $P_{FA} = 10^{-6}$? (b) How many echo pulses occur during the beam dwell? (c) What is the single-scan detection range if multiple pulses per beam are video-detected, summed, then presented for detection?

2.10   How many pulses must be integrated (video integration) to increase free-space detection range by a factor of two over that for single-pulse detection range, assuming a Swerling case 1 target and $P_D = 0.8$ and $P_{FA} = 10^{-6}$?

2.11   What is the signal-to-noise improvement if n equal echo pulses from the same target can be coherently added?

2.12   A radar transmitted signal is expressed $Ae^{j2\pi ft}$ at the antenna terminals. What is the expression at the antenna terminals for the received signal of amplitude B, produced by a point target at range R?

2.13   Echoes are received from a target illuminated by 0.1 μs pulses. What is the approximate average RCS seen at each resolved range cell from a target of 1500 m^2 average RCS, extending 150 m in slant range?

2.14   Compute the minimum detectable signal power, based on an input signal-to-noise threshold of 15 dB for (a) a narrowband radar, $\beta = 10$ Hz; and (b) a wideband radar, $\beta = 100$ MHz. Assume a radar system noise temperature of 500 K for each radar.

2.15   What is the single-pulse detection range of a surface-based 35 GHz radar operating against a spaceborne target of $\sigma = 10$ m^2 that is at an elevation angle of 2.0° to the radar? Assume the following parameters and use Fig. 2.12:

  $P_t = 1.0$ MW for 100 μs pulses;
  $G = 45$ dB antenna gain;
  $L = 0.25$ (-6 dB) (radar system loss, not including atmospheric absorption loss);
  $T_s = 1500$ K;
  $S/N = 10$.

2.16   Propagation attention $g(R)$ is to be determined under specific propagation conditions for a ground-based radar by measuring intercepted power *versus* range at various altitudes. This is to be carried out with a calibrated airborne receiver flying at specified range-height profiles. Show that in terms of the ratio of intercepted to transmitted power:

$$g(R) = \frac{1}{G_r G_I} \left(\frac{P_I}{P_t} \right)$$

where G_r and G_I are the radar and airborne receiver antenna gains, respectively.

2.17   A ground-based search radar detects an air target at 200 nmi. The target, at a height of 50,000 feet, is handed over to a weapon-control tracking radar. (a) At what angle from the horizon will the antenna of the tracking radar be pointed if standard atmospheric conditions exist? (b) Compare the pointing angle to that for a free-space, flat-earth assumption.

2.18   A highway police radar operating at 10 GHz observes a Doppler shift of 1500 Hz when the radar is pointed at a moving car. What is the radial speed of the car toward the radar in miles per hour?

2.19   What is the approximate velocity resolution that can be provided by a 1.0 GHz air-search radar of 5° beamwidth that scans at 15 rpm in azimuth? Assume coherent integration over the beam dwell time.

2.20   What is the radar range resolution provided by a monotone pulse if it has a spectrum that can be approximated by a rectangular spectrum of 250 KHz width?

2.21   What is the single-pulse detection range of the short-pulse radar from Table 2.3?

REFERENCES

1. Swerling, P., "Probability of Detection for Fluctuating Targets," *IRE Trans.,* Vol. II-6, April 1960, pp. 269–308.
2. Nathanson, F.E., *Radar Design Principles,* New York: McGraw-Hill, 1969, pp. 81–82.
3. Berkowitz, R.S., *Modern Radar,* New York: John Wiley and Sons, 1965, p. 567.
4. Blake, L.V., *Radar Range-Performance Analysis,* Norwood, MA: Artech House, 1986, p. 219.
5. Blake, L.V., "Radio Ray (Radar) Range-Height-Angle Charts," *Microwave Journal,* Oct. 1968, pp. 49–53.
6. Skolnik, M.I., ed., *Radar Handbook,* New York: McGraw-Hill, 1970, p. 29-10.
7. Jay, F., ed., *IEEE Standard Dictionary of Electrical and Electronic Terms,* Third Edition, New York: IEEE, 1984, pp. 574–575.
8. North, D.O., "An Analysis of the Factors which Determine Signal/ Noise Discrimination in Pulse-Carrier Systems," *Proc. IEEE,* Vol. 51, No. 7, July 1963, pp. 1016–1027. (From RCA Labs. Tech. Dept. No. PTR-6C, June 25, 1943).

9. Turin, G.L., "An Introduction to Matched Filters," *IRE Trans. Information Theory,* Vol. IT-6, June 1960, pp. 311–329.
10. Barton, D.K., *Radar System Analysis,* Dedham, MA: Artech House, 1979.
11. DiFranco, J.V., and W.L. Rubin, *Radar Detection,* Dedham, MA: Artech House, 1980.
12. Skolnik, M.I., ed., *Radar Handbook,* New York: McGraw-Hill, 1970.
13. Rihaczek, A.W., *Principles of High-Resolution Radar,* New York: McGraw-Hill, 1969.

Chapter 3
High Resolution Radar Design

3.1 INTRODUCTION

High resolution radar, as discussed in this book, has been made possible by numerous modern developments, such as wide-bandwidth microwave components, high-speed digital processing, and digitally controlled frequency sources.

The theory and fundamental design principles for application of high resolution radar to target imaging, target detection, and electronic counter-countermeasures had been in place, for the most part, awaiting the availability of the technology. This chapter will introduce some basic design considerations for high resolution radar and describe some key radar components.

3.2 INSTANTANEOUS FREQUENCY AND DELAY

Time-dependence of the signal frequency and frequency-dependence of the signal delay are of interest when designing or analyzing high resolution radar systems. Two distinct categories of interest can be delineated: *system design* and *system distortion analysis*.

Design of wideband high-resolution radar systems often involves the deliberate introduction of a signal frequency variation with time and a signal delay variation with frequency. For example, by design, the frequency of a transmitted chirp-pulse waveform of a pulse-compression radar varies linearly with position in time along the pulse. Also, by design, signal delay through a pulse-compression filter varies linearly with frequency. Both the waveform and the filter are said to be dispersive.

System distortion analysis involves a determination of the deviation from designed time variations of signal frequency (interpulse or intrapulse) and the deviation from designed delay *versus* frequency characteristics of the radar system. Portions of a wideband radar are often carefully designed to produce some desired dispersion characteristic, while an attempt is made to avoid dispersion throughout the rest of the radar. Examples of unwanted signal frequency variation are (1) random fluctuations due to *phase noise* and (2) deviation from a *linear FM chirp*. Examples of unwanted delay variation *versus* frequency are (1) dispersion in waveguide transmission lines and (2) dispersion in otherwise nondispersive transmission lines caused by multiple mismatches along the line. Other examples of unwanted frequency and delay variations are to be found in subsequent chapters of this book. First, we will introduce the notions of *instantaneous frequency* and *instantaneous delay*.

3.2.1 Instantaneous Frequency

The term, instantaneous frequency, refers to the *time-dependent frequency* of a signal. The complex expression for a narrowband signal (small fractional bandwidth) can be written as

$$s(t) = a(t)e^{j\psi(t)}$$

where $a(t)$ is an amplitude modulation envelope and $\psi(t)$ is signal phase $2\pi \bar{f} t + \theta(t)$ at time t for carrier frequency $\bar{f}$ and phase modulation function $\theta(t)$. The instantaneous frequency of the signal is its rate of phase change given by

$$f = \frac{1}{2\pi} \frac{d[\psi(t)]}{dt} \tag{3.1}$$

The amplitude modulation term $a(t)$ for small fractional bandwidth does not affect instantaneous frequency.

To illustrate the concept of instantaneous frequency, consider the echo from an accelerating target seen by a single-frequency pulsed Doppler radar. Doppler frequency is given by $2v\bar{f}/c$, where v is the target's radial velocity toward the radar, c is propagation velocity, and $\bar{f}$ is the transmitted carrier frequency. Velocity v is assumed to be small relative to c. Instantaneous phase advance of the echo signal from a target at time t is given by

$$\psi(t) = \frac{4\pi\bar{f}}{c} \left(R - vt - a\frac{t^2}{2} \right)$$

where R is the target range at time $t = 0$, v is the velocity toward the radar at $t = 0$, and a is the acceleration toward the radar. The complex form of the echo signal observed with the radar transmitting at frequency $\bar{f}$ is given by

$$s(t) = a(t) \exp j\left[2\pi\bar{f}t - \frac{4\pi\bar{f}}{c}\left(R - vt - a\frac{t^2}{2} \right) \right]$$

In a typical arrangement, $a(t)$ is a term that defines the envelope of a train of fixed-frequency transmitted pulses. The instantaneous frequency of the echo signal, from (3.1), at time t, is

$$f = \left(1 + \frac{2v}{c} + \frac{2at}{c} \right)\bar{f}$$

The result for typical values of pulse duration, wavelength, and target velocity is a series of echo pulses for which the carrier frequency increases linearly with time history during target acceleration.

In the above example, the frequency of the echo pulses from the accelerating target varied linearly from pulse to pulse with time history because of the quadratic phase term, while the transmitted signal frequency remained constant. Variation of frequency within each pulse produced by the target acceleration would be very slight for typical pulsed Doppler radar parameters. For pulse-compression radar, the transmitted chirp pulse itself contains a quadratic phase term by design. Therefore, a linear change of frequency (called *linear frequency modulation,* or linear FM) exists on each echo pulse, even when the target itself is stationary.

A pulse-compression type of SAR exhibits both interpulse and intrapulse linear frequency change. Interpulse (pulse-to-pulse) frequency change in a side-looking SAR is produced by a stationary ground target during beam illumination as the radar accelerates, traveling a straight-line path, first toward the target, then away from it. In addition, each echo pulse contains the designed linear FM, which, for typical systems, greatly exceeds the slight FM within the pulse caused by target acceleration.

3.2.2 Phase Delay and Group Delay

Delay characteristics of a network can be defined in terms of insertion phase through the network *versus* signal frequency. An input signal of phase $2\pi ft + \psi_i$ exits the network with a phase of $2\pi f[t - \tau_p(f)] + \psi_i$, where $\tau_p(f)$ is the frequency-dependent *phase delay* through the network and ψ_i is the input phase. The frequency-dependent insertion phase is the output phase minus input phase, written as

$$\varphi(f) = -2\pi f \tau_p(f)$$

Phase delay through the network, for phase in radians, therefore, is

$$\tau_p(f) = -\frac{\varphi(f)}{2\pi f} \tag{3.2}$$

Of more interest for many wideband radar design issues is *group delay*. Group delay, also called envelope delay and instantaneous delay, is the delay of energy through the network, associated with a narrow frequency band of signals. An example of group delay is the delay of a RF pulse through a dispersive network. If the spectrum of the pulse contains a relatively wide band of frequencies, then delay of the lower frequency components of the pulse spectrum will be different than delay of the higher frequency components, causing the output pulse envelope to have a different shape than that of the input pulse. Delay of the pulse will thus be difficult to define. However, a pulse having a spectrum that contains a relatively narrow band of frequencies may not distort badly so that we can define delay of the pulse envelope through the network (group delay).

The notion of group delay can be more precisely defined by reference to insertion delay of a contiguous, amplitude modulated RF carrier. See Fig. 3.1. Sinusoidal amplitude modulation, illustrated in Fig. 3.1(b), is associated with the superposition of two monotone signals of constant amplitude, separated in frequency by the amplitude modulation frequency. If the two equal signal components are separated in frequency by $\pm df$ from a center frequency $\bar{f}$, then the voltage into the dispersive network of Fig. 3.1(a) is given by

$$s_i(t) = \sin 2\pi(\bar{f} - df)t + \sin 2\pi(\bar{f} + df)t$$

By use of a trigonometric identity, we can write

$$s_i(t) = 2 \cos 2\pi(df t) \sin 2\pi(\bar{f} t)$$

This form shows that the input voltage of the group of two signals appears as a carrier at frequency $\bar{f}$, amplitude modulated at a low frequency rate df.

At the output of the network, assuming the monotonic increase of insertion phase *versus* frequency of Fig. 3.1(c), the signal becomes

$$s_o(t) = \sin\left[2\pi(\bar{f} - df)t + (\phi - d\phi)\right]$$
$$+ \sin\left[2\pi(\bar{f} + df)t + (\phi + d\phi)\right]$$
$$= 2\cos\left(2\pi dft + d\phi\right)\sin\left(2\pi\bar{f}t + \phi\right)$$

where ϕ is the insertion phase at the carrier frequency $\bar{f}$, $\phi - d\phi$ is the insertion phase at frequency $\bar{f} - df$, and $\phi + d\phi$ is the insertion phase at $\bar{f} + df$.

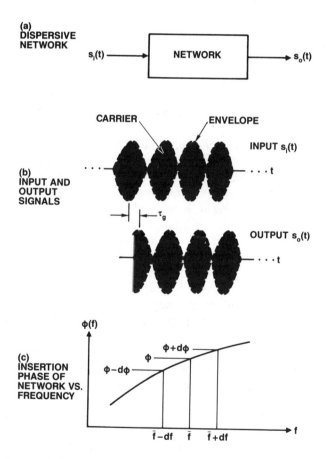

Fig. 3.1 Group Delay

The group delay $\tau_g(f)$ is the delay of the modulation envelope. In other words, group delay is the phase delay associated with the insertion phase at frequency df. Insertion phase of $d\phi$ at df is related to group delay (phase delay of the envelope through the network) by

$$d\phi(f) = -2\pi df \tau_g(f)$$

Group delay is, therefore,

$$\tau_g(f) = -\frac{1}{2\pi}\frac{d\phi(f)}{df} \tag{3.3}$$

Note from (3.2) and (3.3) that phase delay and group delay are equal only when the carrier phase is linearly related to frequency (i.e., for no dispersion).

3.3 DISTORTION IN WIDEBAND SYSTEMS AND COMPONENTS

The performance of wideband radar systems is degraded by *signal distortion* occurring anywhere in the system, including the propagation path. Signal distortion occurs through any transmission system for which, over the signal bandwidth, amplitude response is not flat and the signal delay is not constant. The result is reduced signal-to-noise ratio, reduced resolution, and increased time sidelobes. For noncoherent integration of narrow-bandwidth pulses, as in conventional frequency-agile radar systems, distortion does not usually become a significant factor affecting system performance. As signal bandwidth increases to obtain high range resolution, the transfer function of the entire radar system must be considered in order to evaluate system performance. In this section, we will derive analytical expressions for signal distortion. Application will be made for some key radar components.

Consider the response of a linear network with a transfer function $H(\omega)$ and impulse response $h(t)$ when the input signal to the network is $s_i(t)$. The frequency response is given by

$$S_o(\omega) = H(\omega)S_i(\omega)$$

and the time-domain response is given by

$$s_o(t) = h(t) * s_i(t)$$

where the asterisk denotes convolution, $S_o(\omega)$ is the spectrum of the signal, and $\omega = 2\pi f$.

The steady-state transfer function of a linear network is expressed in complex form as

$$H(\omega) = A(\omega)e^{j\phi(\omega)} \tag{3.4}$$

For an ideal linear network, $A(\omega)$ is a constant, independent of frequency, and $\phi(\omega)$ increases linearly with frequency to produce constant delay *versus* frequency. A short pulse is passed undistorted through an ideal linear network. The effect on signal fidelity of amplitude and phase deviation from the ideal is often studied by using the technique of paired echoes developed by MacColl of Bell Telephone Laboratories in 1931 [1] and amplified by Wheeler of Bell Telephone Laboratories in 1939 [2]. The concept states that a small sinusoidal variation of either phase or amplitude with frequency in a linear system produces a pair of echoes at the output in the time domain, one lagging and one leading the major response to the input signal.

Figure 3.2(a) illustrates a band-limited RF input pulse. This pulse would pass undistorted through a network that remains ideal over all frequencies contained in the input pulse. Figure 3.2(b) shows the phase and amplitude of a transfer function of a nonideal network exhibiting sinusoidal ripple across the signal bandwidth. Figure 3.2(c) shows the resulting distorted response, containing paired echoes of the major response to the input pulse.

Any actual system produces some distortion. Radar signal distortion is produced by amplitude and phase ripple associated with the radar's transfer function as seen from the transmitter to the processed echo response. The transfer function is the product of individual transfer functions of components in the signal transmission-line path, including transmitter, transmission line, duplexer, antenna, propagation media, receiver components, signal processing, and display.

For a nonideal, but linear, system, the amplitude and phase of the transfer function can be described as a Fourier series expansion about the frequency band of interest. The amplitude and phase components of the transfer function expressed in (3.4) then become

$$A(\omega) = a_o + \sum_i a_i \cos(ic\omega)$$

$$\phi(\omega) = b_o\omega + \sum_i b_i \sin(ic\omega) \tag{3.5}$$

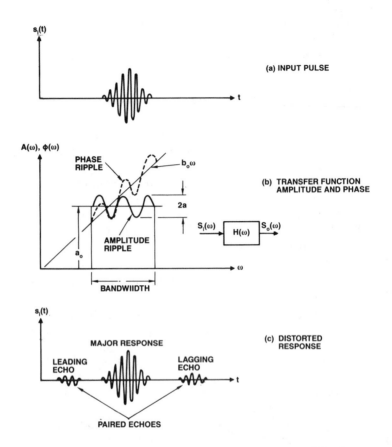

Fig. 3.2 Paired Echoes Produced by Amplitude and Phase Ripple

where the two summation terms represent the amplitude and phase variation from ideal behavior, and a_o, a_i, b_o, b_i, and c are constants. The two expressions for (3.5) are general. By proper selection of the constants, we can describe the transfer amplitude and phase of any passive network (or active device operating in a linear region). If only one sinusoidal term of the Fourier series is considered, the expressions reduce to

$$A(\omega) = a_o + a_1 \cos c\omega$$

$$\phi(\omega) = b_o\omega + b_1 \sin c\omega \qquad\qquad (3.6)$$

The paired echo analysis by MacColl uses this form to solve for an output signal $s_o(t)$ produced by an input signal $s_i(t)$. The result is expressed as

$$s_o(t) = a_o J_o(b_1) s_i(t + b_o)$$

$$+ J_1(b_1) \left[\left(a_o + \frac{a_1}{b_1} \right) s_i(t + b_o + c) \right.$$

$$\left. - \left(a_o - \frac{a_1}{b_1} \right) s_i(t + b_o - c) \right]$$

$$+ J_2(b_1) \left[\left(a_o + \frac{2a_1}{b_1} \right) s_i(t + b_o + 2c) \right.$$

$$\left. + \left(a_o - \frac{2a_1}{b_1} \right) s_i(t + b_o - 2c) \right]$$

$$+ J_3(b_1) \left[\left(a_o + \frac{3a_1}{b_1} \right) s_i(t + b_o + 3c) \right.$$

$$\left. - \left(a_o - \frac{3a_1}{b_1} \right) s_i(t + b_o - 3c) \right]$$

$$+$$

$$\vdots$$

$$(3.7)$$

where $J_o(b_1)$, $J_1(b_1)$, $J_2(b_1)$, *et cetera*, are Bessel functions of the first kind.

For small distortion, a_1 and b_1 are small. When b_1 is less than about 0.5 radians:

$$J_o(b_1) \approx 1$$

$$J_1(b_1) \approx \frac{b_1}{2}$$

and

$$J_i(b_1) \approx 0 \text{ for } i > 1$$

For these approximations, (3.7) becomes

$$s_o(t) = a_o \left[s_i(t + b_o) \right.$$

$$+ \frac{1}{2}\left(\frac{a_1}{a_0} + b_1\right) s_i(t + b_o + c)$$

$$+ \left. \frac{1}{2}\left(\frac{a_1}{a_o} - b_1\right) s_i(t + b_o - c)\right] \qquad (3.8)$$

The relative amplitude of the paired echoes is $a_1/(2a_o)$ for zero phase ripple, and $b_1/2$ for zero amplitude ripple. Echoes are displaced in time from the main response by $\pm c$. Figure 3.3(a, b), obtained from (3.8), indicates the phase and amplitude ripple that can be tolerated in a system to obtain a given peak-to-sidelobe level of distortion. The expression (3.8) indicates that a single sinusoidal variation of the transfer function in either phase or amplitude produces a single pair of echoes, one on each side of the main response. The echoes are reduced replicas of the main response, which itself is not distorted.

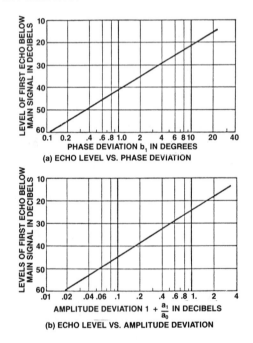

Fig. 3.3 Echo Levels *versus* Phase and Amplitude Deviation (From Klauder, J.R., *et al.*, "The Theory and Design of Chirp Radars," *Bell System Technical J.*, Vol. 39, No. 4, 1960, p. 781. Reprinted with permission.)

Although the effect of system amplitude and phase ripple is described above in terms of paired echoes, these pairs may not be readily apparent in a real system. A single, small sinusoidal variation of either the phase or amplitude term in (3.6) for the system transfer function of (3.4) produces a single echo pair of time sidelobes. The transfer function of a real system exhibits the more complex behavior described by the Fourier series expansion terms in (3.5) for which many echo pairs would result.

There is considerable variation among filtering methods to equalize the amplitude and phase ripple across the radar's bandwidth. Short-pulse and pulse-compression radar systems use various types of equalization filters realized in hardware. Stepped-frequency imaging radars, to be discussed later, may carry out phase and amplitude correction as part of digital signal processing. Equalization filters, in principle, can be designed by synthesizing an auxiliary transfer function, which produces flat amplitude and linear phase transfer characteristics when connected to the network to be equalized. This can be done in two separate steps: *amplitude equalization* and *phase equalization*.

Figure 3.4 illustrates an equalization filter design to equalize distortion in the time domain. Consider the transmission of a single short pulse.

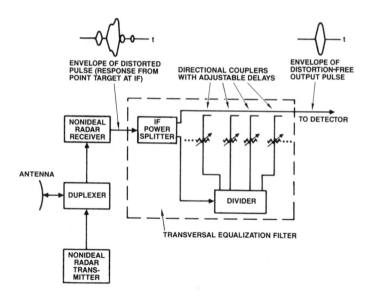

Fig. 3.4 Transversal Equalization Filter

The distorted response at some convenient IF is split into two transmission lines, one line going directly to the detector and the other line going to a divider. The divider further splits the signal into multiple lines, one for each time sidelobe to be cancelled. Each time sidelobe on the direct line to the detector is cancelled by adjusting the amplitude and delay positions of one of the lines to present a reduced main-lobe response, which cancels the selected sidelobe. The transversal equalizer allows the *"tweeking up"* of a system for best performance.

3.4 LONG-LINE EFFECT

Distortion in wideband radar systems can be produced by multiple reflections along transmission-line paths. A single mismatch in a nondispersive transmission line, while reducing the amount of transmitted signal, does not distort wideband signals. When two or more mismatches occur anywhere along the transmission path from the transmitter to receiver output, the interference caused by superposition of the two or more resulting waves traveling in the same direction can produce a nonlinear phase variation with frequency. The *long-line effect* was evaluated by Reed [3] by computing the phase *versus* frequency behavior of the voltage transfer function of the transmission line. This is the ratio of the voltage response of the mismatched line to the voltage response when the line is matched to the source. The analysis here follows Reed's approach.

From transmission-line theory, the voltage and current at the input of the lossless transmission line of Fig. 3.5 can be expressed in terms of receiving-end conditions as follows:

$$V_1 = V_2 \cos \beta l - jI_2Z_0 \sin \beta l$$

and

$$I_1 = jV_2 \frac{\sin \beta l}{Z_0} - I_2 \cos \beta l$$

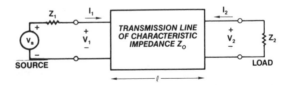

Fig. 3.5 Transmission Line Connected to Source and Load

for line length l and phase constant* β. (Time variation of phase is omitted from all terms for convenience.) This pair of equations can be written in the form of *ABCD* matrix equations:

$$V_1 = AV_2 - BI_2 \tag{3.9}$$
$$I_1 = CV_2 - DI_2$$

where

$$\begin{bmatrix} A & B \\ \\ C & D \end{bmatrix} = \begin{bmatrix} \cos \beta l & jZ_0 \sin \beta l \\ \\ j\dfrac{\sin \beta l}{Z_0} & \cos \beta l \end{bmatrix}$$

The transmission-line equation (3.9) must satisfy the following source and load conditions:

$$V_1 = V_s - Z_1I_1 \tag{3.10a}$$

and

$$V_2 = -Z_2I_2 \tag{3.10b}$$

The voltage transfer function of the transmission line is the ratio of the output voltage V_2, across a load Z_2, to the voltage $V_s/2$ produced across a load Z_1, matched to the source. (Source and load impedances Z_1 and Z_2 are generally mismatched to the transmission-line impedance Z_0.) The transfer function is found by eliminating I_1, I_2, and V_1 from (3.9) and (3.10). The result is

$$G_T = \frac{2V_2}{V_s} = \frac{2}{A + \dfrac{B}{Z_2} + Z_1C + \dfrac{Z_1}{Z_2}D}$$

By substituting the *ABCD* parameters, the expression for the transfer function becomes

---

*To conform with common convention, the symbol β will be used here to represent *phase constant*. Elsewhere in this book, β will represent *bandwidth*.

$$G_T = \frac{\left(\dfrac{2}{1 + Z_1/Z_2}\right)}{\cos \beta l + jF_T \sin \beta l} \tag{3.11}$$

where

$$F_T = \frac{Z_0^2 + Z_1 Z_2}{Z_0(Z_1 + Z_2)} \tag{3.12}$$

A complex load impedence to a transmission line can be converted to a pure resistance by moving it along the transmission line to its maximum impedance point. Likewise, a complex source impedance can be converted to a pure resistance by adding an appropriate line length to the source. The pure resistance point of a line (maximum impedance point) is the *voltage standing-wave ratio* (VSWR) of the line times its characteristic impedance. Therefore, the factor F_T of (3.12) can be expressed in terms of the equivalent pure resistance source and load impedances Z_1 and Z_2. Normalized values Z_1/Z_0 and Z_2/Z_0 are then the VSWRs at the source and load, respectively.

When both the source and load impedences are matched to Z_0 so that $Z_0 = Z_1 = Z_2$, (3.11) reduces to the matched condition:

$$(G_T)_m = \frac{1}{\cos \beta l + j \sin \beta l} = e^{-j\beta l} \tag{3.13}$$

The insertion phase angle from (3.13) is βl, where

$$\beta l = \frac{2\pi}{\lambda} l = \frac{2\pi f}{c} l$$

The phase angle βl is seen to vary linearly with frequency for the matched condition.

For the mismatched condition, the insertion phase from (3.11) becomes

$$\phi = \tan^{-1}(F_T \tan \beta l)$$

If either $Z_1 = Z_0$ or $Z_2 = Z_0$, the factor F_T of (3.12) becomes unity so that the phase angle becomes equal to βl. Thus, a single mismatch at either the source or load end of the line does not produce a nonlinear insertion phase *versus* frequency response.

Insertion phase ϕ for mismatched source and load conditions is equal to the insertion phase βl for the matched condition only if βl is any integer multiple of $\pi/2$. Insertion phase *versus* frequency for the mismatched condition varies about the linear phase response of the matched condition as shown in Fig. 3.6.

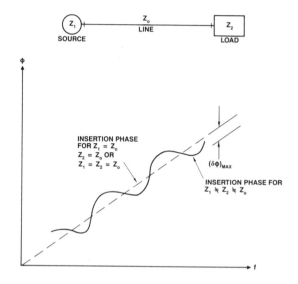

Fig. 3.6 Long-Line Insertion Phase *versus* Frequency (From Reed, J., "Long-Line Effect in Pulse-Compression Radar," *Microwave Journal*, Sept. 1961, p. 99. Reprinted with permission.)

The difference between matched and mismatched insertion phase is

$$\delta\phi = \phi - \beta l = \tan^{-1}(F_T \tan \beta l) - \beta l \qquad (3.14)$$

The maximum phase deviation $(\delta\phi)_{max}$ from the linear insertion phase βl is obtained by differentiating $\delta\phi$ of (3.14) with respect to frequency and setting the result to zero, assuming that Z_1, Z_2, and Z_0 are real and independent of frequency, and that βl is directly proportional to frequency. The result can be expressed as

$$\tan[(\delta\phi)_{max}] = \frac{F_T - 1}{\sqrt{4F_T}} \qquad (3.15)$$

If we write (3.12) in terms of normalized resistances, this results in the expression:

$$F_T = \frac{r_1 r_2 + 1}{r_1 + r_2} \tag{3.16}$$

where

$$r_1 = \frac{Z_1}{Z_0}$$

and

$$r_2 = \frac{Z_2}{Z_0}$$

The quantities r_1 and r_2 are the input and output VSWRs, respectively. Curves of constant phase deviation $(\delta\phi)_{max}$ are plotted in Fig. 3.7 *versus* r_1 and r_2 by using (3.16) with (3.15).

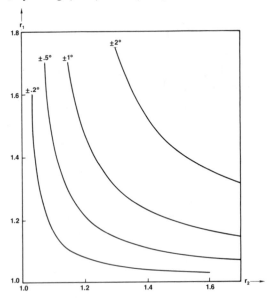

Fig. 3.7 Loci of Maximum Phase Deviation in Terms of Input and Output VSWR (From Reed, J., "Long-Line Effect in Pulse-Compression Radar," *Microwave Journal,* Sept. 1961, p. 100. Reprinted with permission.)

3.5   THE MATCHED FILTER AND AMBIGUITY FUNCTION

3.5.1   Matched Filter

The concept of a *matched filter* is a very general notion, common to many aspects of radar signal analysis. A filter matched to a given input signal is an optimum filter for signal reception when the received signal is corrupted by additive white Gaussian noise. The filter is optimum in several senses. These include maximizing the output signal-to-noise ratio, and maximizing the accuracy of parameter estimation (for parameters such as delay, Doppler frequency, and signal amplitude). A matched filter to an input signal $s_i(t)$ with spectrum $S_i(f)$ is defined in terms of the matched-filter transfer function $H(f)$ and the corresponding impulse response function $h(t)$ as follows:

$$H(f) = GS_i^*(f)e^{-j2\pi f\tau} \tag{3.17a}$$

and

$$h(t) = Gs_i^*(\tau - t) \tag{3.17b}$$

where G is gain (or loss) of the filter, τ is a fixed delay through the filter, and $H(f)$ is the Fourier transform of $h(t)$. The asterisk refers to the conjugate form. The basic relationships stated in (3.17), assuming unity gain and fixed time delay of zero through the filter, are

$$H(f) = S_i^*(f) \tag{3.18a}$$

and

$$h(t) = s_i^*(-t) \tag{3.18b}$$

Complex quantities are implied throughout. The transfer function of a filter matched to any signal, except for a linear phase *versus* frequency slope, is proportional to the conjugate of the spectrum of the signal. The matched-filter impulse response, except for a fixed delay, is proportional to the conjugate of the time inversion of the signal.

Matched filters are not normally designed to match an input signal. Instead, the match is made to the transmitted waveform, which remains constant, regardless of the target. It is possible to design filters matched to very wideband waveforms. A well known type of matched filter for high resolution radar is the pulse-compression filter.

3.5.2 Ambiguity Function

Like the concept of matched filtering, the concept of an *ambiguity function* is also a very general notion, common to many aspects of radar signal analysis. A radar waveform's ambiguity function is probably the most complete statement of the waveform's inherent performance. It reveals the range-Doppler position of ambiguous responses, and defines the range and Doppler resolution.

The ambiguity function $\chi(\tau, f_D)$ of a waveform $s_1(t)$ can be defined as the *cross-correlation* of a Doppler-shifted version $s_1(t) \exp (j2\pi f_D t)$ of the waveform with the unshifted waveform. From the definition of cross-correlation, we can write

$$\chi(\tau, f_D) = \int_{-\infty}^{\infty} [s_1(t)e^{j2\pi f_D t}] [s_1^*(t - \tau)] dt$$

Rearranging the terms in the integral produces the following common form of the ambiguity function:

$$\chi(\tau, f_D) = \int_{-\infty}^{\infty} s_1(t)s_1^*(t - \tau)e^{j2\pi f_D t} dt \qquad (3.19)$$

It is common to refer to the absolute value of $\chi(\tau, f_D)$ as the ambiguity surface of the waveform. The shape of the ambiguity surface is entirely dependent upon waveform parameters. A normalized expression is obtained by requiring that

$$\int_{-\infty}^{\infty} |s_1(t)|^2 dt = 1$$

With this normalization, the magnitude of the ambiguity function has a value at (0, 0) of unity. Examples of ambiguity surfaces generated by (3.19) are shown in Figs. 3.8 and 3.9. Level contours are illustrated for two idealized waveforms: Gaussian-envelope monotone pulse (Fig. 3.8) and Gaussian-envelope linear frequency modulated (chirp) pulse (Fig. 3.9).

3.5.3 Matched-Filter Response Function

Closely related to the notion of the ambiguity function is the *matched-filter response function* of a signal or waveform. The filter's output signal spectrum, produced by an input signal $s_i(t)$, is

$$S_o(f) = H(f)S_i(f)$$

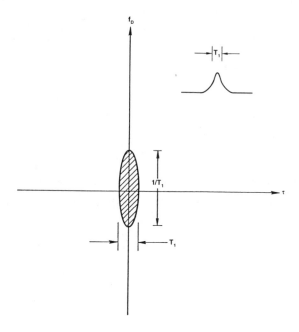

Fig. 3.8 Level Contour of Ambiguity Function of a Gaussian-Envelope Monotone Pulse

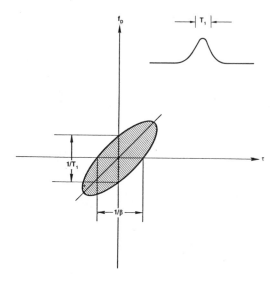

Fig. 3.9 Level Contour of Ambiguity Function of a Gaussian-Envelope Chirp Pulse

where $H(f)$ is the filter's transfer function and $S_i(f)$ is the input signal spectrum. The temporal response of the filter to the signal $s_i(t)$ is

$$
\begin{aligned}
s_o(t) &= h(t) * s_i(t) \\
&= \int_{-\infty}^{\infty} h(t - \tau) s_i(\tau) \, d\tau
\end{aligned}
$$
(3.20)

where the asterisk indicates convolution.

The convolved response $s_o(t)$ can be thought of as the signal produced at the output of the matched filter shown in Fig. 3.10 when the signal described by $s_i(t)$ passes through the filter. When the input signal is Doppler-shifted, the convolved response, using (3.20), becomes

$$
s_o(t, f_D) = \int_{-\infty}^{\infty} h(t - \tau) s_i(\tau) e^{j2\pi f_D \tau} d\tau
$$

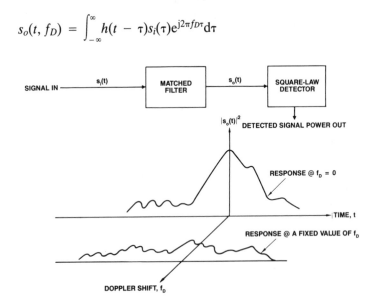

Fig. 3.10 Matched-Filter Response Function

From (3.18b) for $h(t)$ matched to $s_i(t)$:

$$
h(t - \tau) = s_i^*[-(t - \tau)] = s_i^*(\tau - t)
$$

Then,

$$
s_o(t, f_D) = \int_{-\infty}^{\infty} s_i^*(\tau - t) s_i(\tau) e^{j2\pi f_D \tau} d\tau
$$

By rearranging terms, we have

$$s_o(t, f_D) = \int_{-\infty}^{\infty} s_i(\tau)s_i^*(\tau - t)e^{j2\pi f_D\tau}d\tau \tag{3.21}$$

Similarity to the ambiguity function, expressed by (3.19), is obvious when the input signal $s_i(t)$ is taken to be the transmitted waveform $s_1(t)$. The matched-filter response function of a waveform and its ambiguity function are terms that are sometimes used interchangeably.

The input signal $s_i(t)$ to the matched filter of a high resolution radar is likely to be the extended echo signal produced by the superposition of the echo responses from multiple scatterers of the target.

3.6 WIDEBAND MIXING AND DETECTION

Mixers and detectors of many forms appear in numerous components of RF equipment, including radar systems. Mixers are used for frequency translation of RF input signals. In the typical case for radar, echo signals at frequencies occupying the input bandwidth of the radar's microwave receiver are translated to some lower IF. Detectors are used to convert RF pulses into video pulses by removing the RF signal, leaving only a pulse envelope. The term *video detection* should not be confused with the term *target detection*, which is a decision process. Target detection decisions may be based on the magnitude of individual or summed video-detected pulses, sometimes called *predetected pulses.*

Since World War II, mixers and detectors have been designed using *semiconductor diodes*, originally called *crystals*, operating in the nonlinear region of their current *versus* voltage curves. Much of their behavior for various applications in radar, including wideband radar, can be understood in terms of the nonlinear response of a diode to an applied voltage. Diode current *versus* voltage is illustrated in Fig. 3.11.

The output voltage of a diode is the voltage across the load Z_0, which is assumed to be small relative to the diode impedance. In the forward conducting region, diode current I produced by an applied voltage V can be described by the series:

$$I = a + bV + cV^2 + dV^3 + \cdots \tag{3.22}$$

where a, b, c, and d are constants.

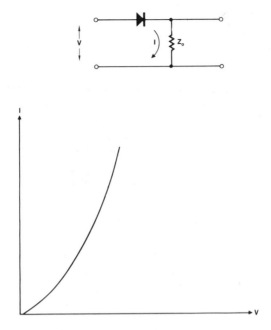

Fig. 3.11 Mixer Diode Current *versus* Voltage

3.6.1 Mixers

The voltage V applied to a mixer diode is the sum of the voltages of two or more input RF signals to be mixed. The first term of (3.22) is the direct current (dc) offset. This term contains no RF signals. The second term, because it is linear, contains only signals at the same frequencies as those of the input signal components of the applied voltage V. Higher-order terms in (3.22) produce *mixer products*. The mixer products contain the desired translated signal frequencies. The squared term is of interest for mixing.

Typically, a *fixed-frequency local oscillator* (LO) *signal* is mixed with a relatively lower-level echo signal to produce a difference frequency output called the *IF signal*. A receiver that uses a mixer in this manner to translate a frequency band of signals to a convenient IF band is called a *superheterodyne (superhet) receiver*. Today's technology makes it possible to translate signals with octaves of bandwidth at microwave frequencies.

Mixer performance is often analyzed by assuming that the diode is biased to operate in a current *versus* voltage region represented by the third term of (3.22). (Bias is not actually needed to obtain desired performance in many cases.) The diode is then said to be operating in its *square-law region.* Higher-order terms produce mixer products containing generally unwanted signals that are filtered out. The first two terms, if present, are not of interest because they do not produce mixer products.

In the square-law region, for two input signal voltages V_1 and V_2, the diode current represented by the third term is

$$I = c(V_1 + V_2)^2 = c(V_1^2 + 2V_1V_2 + V_2^2) \tag{3.23}$$

Only the product term of (3.23) is normally of interest in mixer applications. The other two terms contain second-harmonic frequencies of the two input signals, respectively, which can be filtered out.

Consider two input signals expressed as

$$V_1 = B \cos (2\pi f_1 t + \psi_1) \tag{3.24a}$$

and

$$V_2 = B' \cos (2\pi f_2 t + \psi_2) \tag{3.24b}$$

where ψ_1 and ψ_2 are the relative phases of V_1 and V_2, respectively. The product term of the square-law response into an impedance Z_0, produced by the current given by (3.23), is

$$s(t) = IZ_0 = 2cV_1V_2Z_0$$

with V_1 and V_2 from (3.24a) and (3.24b), the product term becomes

$$s(t) = 2cBB'Z_0[\cos (2\pi f_1 t + \psi_1)] \cdot [\cos (2\pi f_2 t + \psi_2)]$$

By use of the trigonometry identity for the product of two cosine functions, and after dropping the constants $2c$ and Z_0,

$$\begin{aligned} s(t) = {} & BB' \cos [2\pi(f_1 - f_2)t + \psi_1 - \psi_2] \\ & + BB' \cos [2\pi(f_1 + f_2)t + \psi_1 + \psi_2] \end{aligned} \tag{3.25}$$

Two input signals produce a mixer product, which is seen to contain frequencies equal to the sum and difference of the two input signal frequencies. Most often, the mixer output illustrated in Fig. 3.12(a) is filtered as shown in Fig. 3.12(b) such that only the difference frequency signal appears

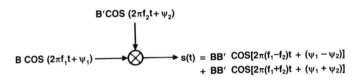

(a) MIXER SQUARE-LAW PRODUCTS OF TWO SINUSOIDAL INPUT SIGNALS.

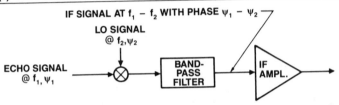

(b) SUPERHET MIXER.

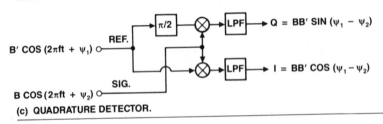

(c) QUADRATURE DETECTOR.

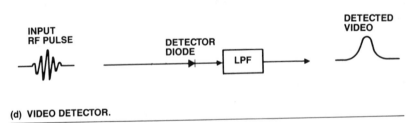

(d) VIDEO DETECTOR.

Fig. 3.12 Mixing and Detection

at the output of the filter. Signals produced by other product terms of
(3.22) are also filtered out.

In the standard superheterodyne configuration, one of the mixer
inputs is the local oscillator signal and the other is the echo signal. The
output IF signal $s(t)$ is seen in (3.25) to be proportional to the amplitudes
B and B' of the two input signals, respectively. Therefore, for a constant-
amplitude LO signal, the IF signal is linearly related to the input RF echo
signal amplitude.

3.6.2   Quadrature Detection

Quadrature detection is used in various types of coherent radar systems to recover echo signal phase relative to the transmitted carrier. For high resolution radar, echo signal amplitude and phase data are collected at frequencies extending over a wide bandwidth. Typically, echo amplitude and phase relative to the transmitted phase are required for each pulse of a set of narrowband pulses spread over a wide band of discrete frequencies. To meet this requirement, the echo signal is mixed with a LO signal that is frequency-shifted from pulse to pulse in synchronism with the transmitted signal. For other high resolution applications, such as a short-pulse radar, the amplitude and phase *versus* range delay along an extended wideband echo pulse is required relative to the fixed-frequency carrier of the transmitted pulse. Here, a stable oscillator provides (1) the RF input from which short pulses are generated and (2) the reference LO to the quadrature detector. Practical systems operate with the stable LO and echo signal at some convenient IF that is lower than the transmitted signal.

Quadrature detection can be thought of as a mixing operation that translates the echo signal to *baseband* to recover echo amplitude and phase in the form of quadrature components of the echo signal. A quadrature detector is illustrated in Fig. 3.12(c).

For *quadrature mixing,* also called *synchronous detection,* both the reference LO signal and the echo signal carrier are at the same frequency, except for Doppler shift. The output of the lower mixer in Fig. 3.12(c), following low-pass filtering, is then represented by the first term of (3.25) with $f_1 = f_2$, in effect,

$$s(t) = BB' \cos (\psi_1 - \psi_2)$$

This is a video signal, hence the term quadrature or synchronous *detection.* This signal is called the *in-phase* (*I*) output of the mixer. A second mixer with the reference signal delayed by $\pi/2$ rad of phase produces a *quadrature* (*Q*) output. The *I* and *Q* output pair is called the *baseband signal.* A Doppler-shifted echo signal will produce a baseband signal at the Doppler frequency. In pulsed Doppler radar, the transmitted signal is amplitude modulated into discrete pulses at some *pulse repetition interval* (PRI). Doppler shift then appears as a pulse-to-pulse phase shift.

Figure 3.13(a, b) illustrates synchronous detection directly to baseband. Practical systems are likely to operate as shown in Fig. 3.13(c), so that filtering and amplification can be done more conveniently at lower frequencies.

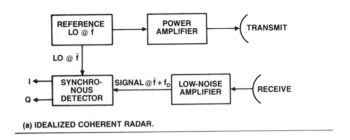

(a) IDEALIZED COHERENT RADAR.

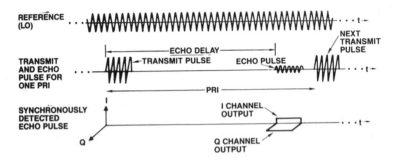

(b) WAVEFORMS FOR SYNCHRONOUS DETECTION.

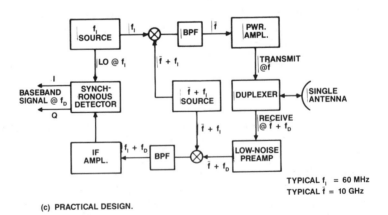

TYPICAL f_i = 60 MHz
TYPICAL $\bar{f}$ = 10 GHz

(c) PRACTICAL DESIGN.

Fig. 3.13 Synchronous Detection

3.6.3 Square-Law and Linear Detection

Detectors using microwave diodes operating in their square-law region are used in high resolution radars, as well as in radars in general, for envelope detection of echo pulses at RF or IF. Square-law characteristics are approximated for low signal levels. Detector video output current in the square-law region is proportional to input RF power. Flat response over octaves of bandwidth is possible. Linear detectors operate in the linear current *versus* voltage region of the diode by using high signal levels biased so that only positive swings conduct. The output envelope of an ideal linear detector, following low-pass filtering, is represented by the second term of (3.22). Detector video output current in the linear region is proportional to RF voltage. Operation of a video detector is illustrated in Fig. 3.12(d).

3.7 SELECTION OF LOCAL-OSCILLATOR FREQUENCY

The *local oscillator frequency* of a superheterodyne receiver for a wideband-radar must be carefully selected so as to avoid responses to signals in the preselector bandwidth that are not related to the echo signal. These responses, called *spurious responses,* become more of a problem as percentage bandwidth increases. Selection of a LO frequency can be made on the basis of calculations for *forbidden zones* of the LO frequency that result in spurious responses in the IF passband. These spurious responses occur at frequencies equal to the differences in frequency between harmonics m and n of the unwanted signal and LO frequencies, respectively. Once the forbidden zones are located for the radar center frequency and bandwidth, it is possible to select an optimum LO frequency that at least avoids the low-order spurious responses. In turn, this determines the center of the IF passband.

Assume that the LO frequency f_{LO} is chosen so that an echo signal at frequency f appears at an intermediate frequency $f_I = |f - f_{LO}|$. Spurious responses then occur for the following two cases [4]:

Case I: $f - f_{LO} = nf_{LO} - mf'$
Case II: $f - f_{LO} = mf' - nf_{LO}$

where m and n are harmonic numbers starting with zero, and f' is the frequency of an unwanted signal within the preselector passband that results in a spurious output within the receiver's IF bandwidth.

Forbidden LO frequencies for case I occur at

$$f_{LO} = \frac{f + mf'}{n + 1}$$

The minimum LO frequency for the harmonic set (m, n) that will result in a spurious output is seen to occur when f and f' are minimum (i.e., both are at the low end of the preselector passband). The maximum LO frequency for spurious response will occur when f and f' are maximum (i.e., both are at the high end of the passband). Therefore, for a receiver with a preselector band covering a frequency range of f_e to $f_e + \beta$, forbidden LO frequencies produced by the case I conditions will lie between the values:

$$f_{LO} \text{ (min)} = \frac{f_e + mf_e}{n + 1} = \frac{m + 1}{n + 1} f_e$$

and

$$f_{LO}(\text{max}) = \frac{f_e + \beta + m(f_e + \beta)}{n + 1} = \frac{m + 1}{n + 1} f_e + \frac{m + 1}{n + 1} \beta$$

for the harmonic set (m, n) of the signal and LO frequencies, respectively. Forbidden LO frequencies for case II occur at

$$f_{LO} = \frac{mf' - f}{n - 1}$$

The minimum LO frequency that will result in a spurious output will occur for f' at the minimum preselector frequency f_e and the desired signal frequency f at $f_e + \beta$. The maximum LO frequency for spurious response will occur for f' at the maximum preselector frequency $f_e + \beta$ and the desired signal frequency f at f_e. Thus, forbidden LO frequencies produced by the case II condition lie between the values:

$$f_{LO}(\text{min}) = \frac{mf_e - (f_e + \beta)}{n - 1} = \frac{(m - 1)f_e}{n - 1} - \frac{\beta}{n - 1}$$

and

$$f_{LO}(\text{max}) = \frac{m(f_e + \beta) - f_e}{n - 1} = \frac{(m - 1)f_e}{n - 1} + \frac{m\beta}{n - 1}$$

No harmonics of undesired low-level signals exist above $m = 1$, but particular care must be taken to avoid (m, n) harmonics of $(0, 1)$, $(0, 2)$, $(0, 3)$, and $(0, 4)$. The *zeroth* harmonic (a dc component) of signal frequency may be present, regardless of signal level. Figure 3.14 indicates forbidden LO frequency choices for an experimental high-range-resolution radar with 600 MHz bandwidth and a center frequency of 3.2 GHz. For

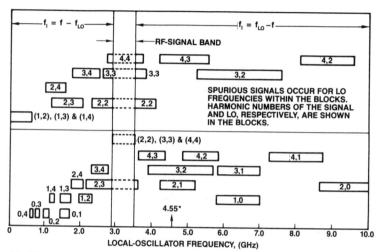

Fig. 3.14 Forbidden LO Frequencies between zero and 10 GHz for a 2.9 to 3.5 GHz Radar (through the Fourth Harmonic (m, n) of Signal and LO, Respectively)

this radar, it was decided to use a LO frequency of $f_{LO} = 4.55$ GHz. This resulted in an IF band of 1.05 GHz to 1.65 GHz. The only possible spurious signals from this choice of LO frequency up to the fourth harmonics result from (m, n) values of $(2, 1)$, $(3, 2)$, and $(4, 3)$. Spurious response, according to Lepoff [4], drops off at 10 dB per harmonic order. Unavoidable spurious responses can be suppressed by using balanced mixers.

3.8 DATA SAMPLING

3.8.1 Time-Domain Sampling

Wideband radar signals are often sampled, then converted to digital quantities, before data processing for target detection or imaging. The type of sampling required depends upon the type of waveform selected and its bandwidth. The simplest type of waveform is probably a short pulse. To sample echo signals produced by a short-pulse radar without introducing ambiguity requires that the sampling rate meet the Nyquist criteria. Nyquist's sampling theorem states that if a signal has no frequency components above some frequency f, then the signal is completely determined by sample values of the signal separated by in time $1/(2f)$, extending over the signal duration. Normally, it is not feasible to sample the RF form of a radar echo signal at this rate. To reduce the required sampling rate, the signal is usually mixed down to an IF carrier or to baseband (zero IF carrier).

A target echo signal produced by a single, short transmitted pulse is illustrated in Fig. 3.15(a). Its spectrum is illustrated in Fig. 3.15(b). Assume that pulse spectral components outside the bandwidth β can be neglected. Maximum frequency components of the down-converted baseband version of the echo signal are then reduced to $\beta/2$, as shown in Fig. 3.15(c). When converted to baseband, the echo signal is composed of I and Q components, each having a spectrum as shown in Fig. 3.15(c). Low-pass filtering of either the I or Q outputs need pass no frequencies higher than $\beta/2$. Sample spacing in time, therefore, must be equal to or less than $1/\beta$ s for each output for a total of 2β samples per second. One sampled I and Q pair of real samples taken simultaneously is called a *complex sample*. Except for an unknown phase, the echo signal can be unambiguously determined by β complex samples per second. This corresponds to a spacing equal to or less than $1/\beta$, which is the temporal resolution associated with the pulse. Baseband samples of the echo signal of Fig. 3.15(a) are indicated in Fig. 3.15(d).

Even at baseband, the required sampling rate for high resolution radar is high. For example, to achieve 1.0 m resolution, the echo signal bandwidth from (1.1) is

$$\beta \approx \frac{c}{2\Delta r_s}$$

$$= \frac{3 \times 10^8}{2 \times 1}$$

$$= 150 \text{ MHz}$$

To achieve unambiguous sampling for this resolution requires a sampling rate of 150×10^6 complex samples per second. Sampling and digitizing at this rate are difficult from a technological standpoint. To complicate the problem further is the reduction in dynamic range, which occurs when sampled data at high sampling rates is converted into digital quantities. Dynamic range is reduced because the sampling time aperture available to quantize the sampled data into fine quantization levels is decreased to accommodate high sampling rates. Thus, sampling rate and quantization are traded off. Figure 3.16 approximately represents a line of constant difficulty for the current state of this technology. Two *analog-*

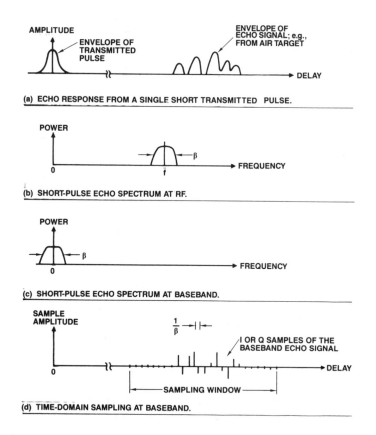

Fig. 3.15 Echo Signal, Signal Spectrum, and Sampling

to-digital (A/D) *converters* are required, one to digitize the *I*-channel samples and one to digitize the *Q*-channel samples. Each converter is required to convert β real samples per second if the signal bandwidth is β.

3.8.2 Frequency-Domain Sampling

The limitation of wideband radar signal processing that is associated with time-domain sampling can be circumvented for some applications by sampling in the frequency domain. Frequency-domain sampling can be carried out by transmitting narrowband pulses, which are coded in frequency from pulse to pulse. For example, each pulse of a sequence (called *burst*) of pulses could be transmitted at a carrier frequency that is shifted by a constant amount from that of the previous pulse. Echo signals from

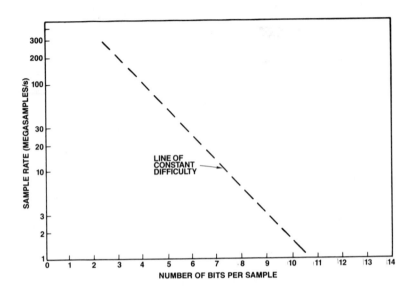

Fig. 3.16 Line of Constant Difficulty of Technology for High-Speed Sampling and A/D Conversion

such a pulse sequence form *discrete* frequency-domain samples of the target's reflectivity. While the pulses of the sequence are spread over a wide bandwidth β, sampling can be carried out on each narrowband echo pulse at baseband. Typically, one I and Q pair is collected from each received pulse, as illustrated in Fig. 3.17. Thus, the dynamic range of the A/D converter can be large, for example, 12 to 14 bits. Sampled data collected in discrete steps over a total bandwidth β can be processed to form target range profiles with a range resolution equivalent to that obtained by transmitting a pulse of duration 1/β.

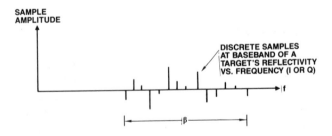

Fig. 3.17 Frequency-Domain Sampling

To determine the required frequency spacing for unambiguous sampling in the frequency domain, we must consider Nyquist's theorem for sampling in the frequency domain. This theorem states that the spectrum of a signal is exactly determined by samples of the spectrum separated by $1/(2\delta t)$Hz, when the signal is zero everywhere, except during some delay interval δt. The delay interval δt, associated with a highly resolved target that produces reflection over a range extent l is $2l/c$. Thus, for unambiguous sampling of a target's reflectivity in the frequency domain, real frequency samples are required to be taken at intervals of

$$\Delta f \leqslant \frac{1}{2\delta t} = \frac{c}{4l}$$

Complex samples may be taken at $\Delta f = c/(2l)$.

As an example, the frequency steps required for unambiguous frequency-domain sampling of a 300 m target must be spaced by a maximum of

$$\Delta f = \frac{c}{2l}$$

$$= \frac{3 \times 10^8}{2 \times 300}$$

$$= 0.5 \text{ MHz}$$

If range resolution is to be 1.0 m, 300 frequency samples are required for a total bandwidth of 300×0.5 MHz $= 150$ MHz, the same as that required to obtain 1.0 m resolution when using a short pulse.

3.9 SPECTRAL PURITY

Generation of high resolution images for smaller targets such as aircraft, due to reasons stated above, may require collection of target echo data in the frequency domain at discrete frequencies as described above. Discrete-frequency-coded transmitted waveforms can be obtained by means of *frequency multiplication* of signals from frequency synthesizers or other frequency sources. *Spectral purity* of the resulting transmitted signal affects image quality. To predict the spectral purity of a radar's transmitted signal, the spectral purity of the frequency source must first be known. Hence we must evaluate the effect of multiplication to the transmitting frequency. Of interest for pulse-to-pulse discrete-frequency-coded waveforms is the standard deviation (σ) of frequency, which is the root mean square (rms) value of the random pulse-to-pulse frequency deviation from the mean of the code frequency for each pulse. The terms *rms deviation* and *standard deviation* will be used interchangeably when discussing spectral purity in terms of the deviation from a desired code frequency.

A spectrally pure signal source produces a single, constant-frequency signal. The phase of the signal advances linearly with time, and no amplitude modulation exists. Spectral purity is usually discussed in terms of either sideband noise power or deviation from a constant frequency.

Noise sidebands and frequency deviation of stable frequency sources are primarily produced by phase modulation. Amplitude modulation (AM) noise sidebands are generally negligible by comparison. Phase noise power for frequency sources, while much higher than the AM noise, is typically orders of magnitude below the carrier.

To evaluate the effect of phase noise and frequency deviation on radar system performance, including performance of wideband radar systems, requires interpretation of spectral purity specifications for devices such as frequency synthesizers and transmitters. The basic component of interest is often the stable oscillator that serves as the frequency source. Two common types of specifications are (1) single-sideband-to-carrier noise power ratio per Hz *versus* offset frequency, and (2) standard deviation of frequency fluctuation occurring over a specified averaging time. The first performance parameter has been widely used for evaluation of narrowband Doppler radar performance. Of interest for some high resolution imaging systems is the second performance parameter, which is usually defined in terms of the *Allan variance* [5].

The Allan variance is an expression for frequency variance in terms of repeated samples of frequency deviation, averaged over a time interval τ. The true variance (infinite number of samples) of a random variable x is expressed in terms of the expected values of x^2 and x according to the relationship [6]:

$$\sigma^2 = E(x^2) - E^2(x)$$

A sampled estimate of variance called *sample variance*, defined for n sample values x_i of x, is expressed as

$$(\sigma)_s^2 = \frac{1}{n} \left[\sum_{i=0}^{n-1} x_i^2 - \frac{1}{n} \left(\sum_{i=0}^{n-1} x_i \right)^2 \right] \qquad (3.26)$$

The expected value of the variance, based on the sampled estimate, can be shown [7] to be related to the true variance according to the expression:

$$E[(\sigma)_s^2] = \frac{n-1}{n}\sigma^2$$

Thus, the estimate of variance from (3.26) can be said to be biased by the factor $(n-1)/n$ from the true variance. True variance in terms of sample variance is, then,

$$\sigma^2 = \frac{n}{n-1}E[(\sigma)_s^2]$$

$$= \frac{1}{n-1}\left[\sum_{i=0}^{n-1}x_i^2 - \frac{1}{n}\left(\sum_{i=0}^{n-1}x_i\right)^2\right]$$

Allan defines average frequency deviation during the interval from t to $t + \tau$ as

$$\bar{f}(t, \tau) = \frac{\phi(t + \tau) - \phi(t)}{2\pi\tau} \tag{3.27}$$

where $\phi(t)$ is the instantaneous phase-angle deviation (rad) measured at time t. The Allan variance, based on n samples of $\bar{f}(t, \tau)$, where $t = iT$, $i = 0, 1, 2, \ldots, n - 1$, and $T \geq \tau$ is expressed as

$$\sigma^2(n, T, \tau) = \frac{1}{n-1}\left\{\sum_{i=0}^{n-1}[\bar{f}(iT, \tau)]^2 \right.$$

$$\left. - \frac{1}{n}\left[\sum_{i=0}^{n-1}\bar{f}(iT, \tau)\right]^2\right\} \tag{3.28}$$

If $n = 2$, (3.28) becomes

$$\sigma^2(2, T, \tau) = (1/2)[\bar{f}(0, \tau) - \bar{f}(T, \tau)]^2 \tag{3.29}$$

This definition represents one estimate of frequency variance during time interval τ, based on two samples $\bar{f}(0, \tau)$ and $\bar{f}(T, \tau)$ of the frequency deviation, separated by the sample spacing T.

The measurements indicated in (3.29) are conveniently made by connecting the output of the two identical sources to be measured to a mixer followed by a low-pass filter. A precision digital counter is used to measure the time τ required for some set number of periods of the low-pass filter's output voltage. Average phase drift $\phi(t + \tau) - \phi(t)$ is then determined, which, from (3.27), determines $\bar{f}(0, \tau)$ at $t = 0$ and $\bar{f}(T, \tau)$ at $t = T$. If the two signal sources have the same phase noise statistics, the Allan variance for either source is the measured variance divided by $\sqrt{2}$. The Allan variance can be dependent to some extent on the time T between samples of length τ. Multiple measurements of $\sigma^2(2, T, \tau)$ are usually taken to be averaged.

As a rule, the Allan variance of a source is quoted in terms of a variance of the fractional frequency deviation, expressed as

$$\sigma_y^2 = \frac{\sigma^2(2, T, \tau)}{\bar{f}^2}$$

where $\bar{f}$ is the long-term average frequency of the source.

The standard deviation of a radar's transmitter frequency can be estimated by multiplying σ_y of the frequency source by the transmitter's center frequency. This assumes that the only source of frequency fluctuation is the frequency source itself. Frequency multipliers or other transmitter components may further degrade spectral purity to some extent. Further degradation occurs due to phase pushing and pulling, which is to be discussed below.

The standard deviation of fractional frequency *versus* averaging time quoted for one type of modern frequency synthesizer is given in Table 3.1. The value of T is not provided, but results are not expected to depend significantly on time between samples.

Table 3.1   Fractional Frequency Deviation of a Typical Synthesizer

τ	σ_y
10^{-3} s	1.5×10^{-10}
10^{-2} s	1.5×10^{-11}
10^{-1} s	5×10^{-12}
1 s	5×10^{-12}
10 s	5×10^{-12}
100 s	1×10^{-11}
24 h	5×10^{-10}

Consider, as an example, a high-range-resolution radar using a stepped-frequency waveform, operating at a center frequency of 3.2 GHz. Assume that to achieve a range of 10,000 nmi ($2R/c$ = 0.12 s) without significant range-profile distortion for this waveform requires that frequency deviation of the frequency steps from that for a uniform step size must be less than 1.0 Hz during the range-delay interval. From Table 3.1, the fractional frequency deviation is about 5×10^{-12} during the interval of 0.12 s. The corresponding expected rms deviation at center frequency $\bar{f}$ during the echo delay is

$$\begin{aligned}
\sigma &= \bar{f}\sigma_y \\
&= 3.2 \times 10^9 \times 5 \times 10^{-12} \\
&= 0.016 \text{ Hz}
\end{aligned}$$

which easily meets the 1.0 Hz frequency stability requirement for imaging out to 10,000 nmi.

3.10 FREQUENCY SYNTHESIZERS

Modern frequency synthesizers allow switching to precise, stable frequencies for diverse applications. For the radar designer, frequency synthesizers make it possible to design radars that rapidly tune over a wide band of discrete frequencies. This capability to provide discrete-frequency-coded waveforms is important to many applications of wideband radar. Two basic classes of frequency synthesizers are the *direct* and *indirect* types. For wideband radar applications, the direct synthesizer is of greater interest because it is able to switch from frequency to frequency in a short time as compared with typical radar pulse repetition intervals (PRIs). Indirect synthesizer outputs are generated from tunable oscillators that are phase locked in frequency increments related to a stable reference. The phase locking process typically requires from 0.5 to 5 ms to establish lock for each new frequency. The direct synthesizer, by comparison, can typically change frequencies in less than 10 μs. Output frequencies produced with the direct method are synthesized from a basic reference signal by selecting combinations of frequency addition, subtraction, multiplication, and division using mixers, multipliers, and dividers.

Actually, the direct synthesizer was developed earlier. R.R. Stone of the US Naval Research Laboratory (NRL) developed it in 1949 [8]. Hewlett-Packard (HP) built the 5100-series of direct synthesizers as part of their line of general-purpose test equipment in the early 1960s [9]. The first ISAR images of ships and aircraft were generated in 1975 from radar data collected at the Naval Ocean Systems Center in San Diego by using a stepped-frequency waveform obtained from a HP 5100B/5110B frequency synthesizer.

It is worthy of note that the indirect synthesizer was developed after the direct synthesizer in order to reduce spurious response and phase noise, which were problems with the early direct synthesizers. The indirect synthesizer developed later was also less costly than the early *add-and-divide* type of synthesizer developed by Stone of NRL. More recently, R.J. Papaieck developed a *binary-coded-decimal* (BCD) type of direct synthesizer [10], which combines most of the advantages of direct and indirect synthesizers. Both the add-and-divide and BCD direct synthesizer designs require a set of *comb* frequencies. Output frequencies for the add-and-divide design are synthesized from selections from ten comb frequencies, using divide-by-ten *decade* units. Output frequencies for the BCD design are synthesized from selections of two comb frequencies. Basic operation of the Stone and Papaieck types of direct synthesizers is illustrated in Figs. 3.18 and 3.19. These are greatly simplified design examples, both producing only 1000 frequency combinations. Each example provides synthesized output frequencies of 20.000 to 20.999 MHz in 1000 Hz steps.

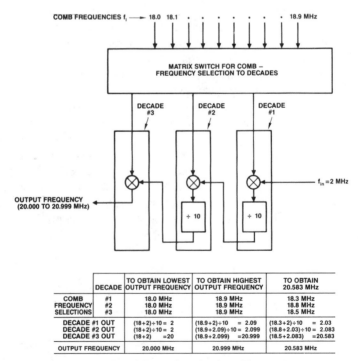

		TO OBTAIN LOWEST OUTPUT FREQUENCY	TO OBTAIN HIGHEST OUTPUT FREQUENCY	TO OBTAIN 20.583 MHz
	DECADE			
COMB FREQUENCY SELECTIONS	#1	18.0 MHz	18.9 MHz	18.3 MHz
	#2	18.0 MHz	18.9 MHz	18.8 MHz
	#3	18.0 MHz	18.9 MHz	18.5 MHz
DECADE #1 OUT		(18+2)÷10 = 2	(18.9+2)÷10 = 2.09	(18.3+2)÷10 = 2.03
DECADE #2 OUT		(18+2)÷10 = 2	(18.9+2.09)÷10 = 2.099	(18.8+2.03)÷10 = 2.083
DECADE #3 OUT		(18+2) = 20	(18.9+2.099) = 20.999	(18.5+2.083) = 20.583
OUTPUT FREQUENCY		20.000 MHz	20.999 MHz	20.583 MHz

Fig. 3.18 Add-and-Divide Direct Synthesizer Example

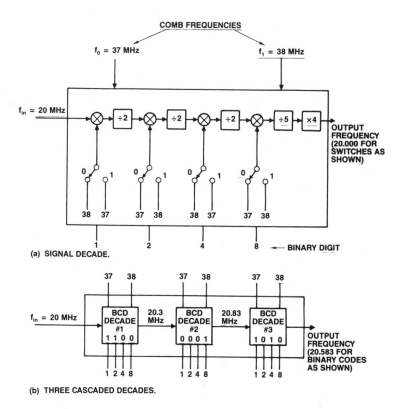

Fig. 3.19 BCD Direct Synthesizer Example

3.10.1 Add-and-Divide Design (Stone)

Examples of comb frequency settings for three output frequencies are shown in Fig. 3.18 for the add-and-divide type: lowest frequency, highest frequency, and an arbitrarily selected frequency of 20.583 MHz. Three decades are used to produce the 1000 possible frequency selections. A set of 10 comb frequencies for this example are spaced by the frequency increment $\Delta f = 0.1$ MHz. This is the increment of the lowest-order decade (decade #1). A value for the input frequency f_{in} was selected to result in the desired output base frequency of 20 MHz. Assume that by suitable filtering only *sum* frequencies are allowed out of the mixers. The lowest frequency, 20.000 MHz, then will occur for $f_{in} = 2.0$ MHz when the bloc of $n = 10$ comb frequencies are selected according to the expression:

$$f_i = f_0 + i\Delta f, \quad i = 0\text{--}9$$
$$= 18.0, 18.1, \cdots, 18.9 \text{ MHz}$$

These selections are consistent with Stone's formula [8]:

$$\frac{f_0 + f_{in}}{n} = f_{in}$$

Other comb and input frequency combinations can be found to produce the same output frequencies. Actual designs are based on practical considerations such as ability to filter spurious responses. Filters for this purpose are not shown in Fig. 3.18, nor are other frequency filters, which pass only the sum frequency outputs of the mixers. Additional decimal places for increments of output frequency selection are possible by adding more decades in the series.

3.10.2 Binary-Coded-Decimal Design (Papaieck)

The BCD synthesizer of Fig. 3.19 uses three BCD decades to synthesize the same 1000 frequencies between 20.000 and 20.999 MHz, as shown for the add-and-divide example in Fig. 3.18. This is done with the BCD design by using only two comb frequencies, selected according to the formulas:

$$f_0 = 1.8 f_{in} + 10\Delta f$$

and

$$f_1 = f_0 + 10\Delta f$$

where f_{in} is both the input frequency and the lowest output frequency, and Δf is the single decade frequency-step size. The two comb frequencies for our simplified design example are $f_0 = 37$ MHz and $f_1 = 38$ MHz with $\Delta f = 0.1$ MHz. The BCD settings that result in the lowest output frequency of 20.0 MHz for a single decade are indicated in the upper diagram of Fig. 3.19. The settings correspond to the binary number 0000. This and other frequencies can be checked by following through the single decade with the switches set according to four-digit binary numbers associated with the output frequency to be selected. Filters following each of the mixers allow only *difference* frequency outputs. The filters themselves are not shown. Binary settings for an output frequency of 20.5 MHz for the single BCD decade, for example, are 1010 in the 1, 2, 4, and 8 binary digits, respectively (left to right in Fig. 3.19(a)). This corresponds to the binary number 0101, which is 5 in decimal form (i.e., 5 of the 0.1 MHz increments above the lowest output frequency, 20.000 MHz). The highest output frequency for decimal stepping of a single decade is 20.9 MHz for binary settings 1001, the binary number equivalent to the decimal number 9. (A single BCD decade could actually produce 16 frequency increments, 20.0 to 21.5 MHz, if it were not to be used in the decimal system.) Other frequency settings are possible by setting in the corresponding binary number.

Multiple decades in series add further decimal places of output frequency selection increments. Suppose an output frequency of 20.583 MHz were desired, as was the case for the add-and-divide synthesizer in the first example. The cascaded BCD decade binary settings in Fig. 3.19(b) are seen from left to right to be 1100, 0001, and 1010, respectively, corresponding to binary numbers 0011, 1000, and 0101, respectively. In decimal form, these are the numbers 3, 8, and 5, which result in the 0.583 MHz added to 20.000 MHz.

3.10.3 Summary

We can see that either of the above simple synthesizer design examples can be extended to cover any desired range of output frequencies spaced by any desired increment. For example, a frequency range of 10.000 to 10.999 MHz could be obtained by mixing with a stable 10 MHz signal, or by changing the comb frequencies in the above examples. Another decimal place could be obtained by adding another decade. Furthermore, the entire frequency selection process can be digitally controlled or programmed to produce any desired sequence of frequencies. Many other strategies are possible besides the two approaches given above.

3.11 TRANSMISSION LINES FOR WIDEBAND RADAR

Radar systems usually use either coaxial transmission line or waveguides to conduct transmitter power to the antenna and echo signals to the receiver. Coaxial lines operating with *transverse electric and magnetic (TEM)* fields are nondispersive (constant delay, independent of frequency), except for mismatches along the line, as discussed above. However, as the loss increases for longer lines, the loss variation with frequency results in increased amplitude distortion for wideband systems. Unless the loss is equalized, the fidelity of wideband signals will degrade. Low-loss coaxial runs of up to about 100 feet, well matched at each end, allow radar bandwidths of 25% or more at frequencies up to the top end of S band

(2.30 to 3.70 GHz).*

High power radars operating above S band nearly always require waveguides for transmission over more than a few feet. This is because of reduced peak-power-handling capability of the smaller diameter coaxial lines that are required at higher microwave frequencies to avoid losses associated with propagation at unwanted higher-order modes. Waveguides also have the advantage of low loss and good impedance matching over wide bandwidths. Unfortunately, for wideband radar applications, waveguides are frequency-dispersive. Dispersion occurs because waveguides propagate in the dispersive *transverse-electric* (TE) and *transverse-magnetic* (TM) modes, instead of the nondispersive TEM mode. Of most interest for radar is the rectangular waveguide propagating in its lowest order mode, TE_{10}. The propagation constant of rectangular waveguides operating below cut-off frequency in the TE_{10} mode is expressed as

$$\gamma_p = j\frac{2\pi f}{v} \sqrt{1 - \left(\frac{f_c}{f}\right)^2} \text{ rad/m} \tag{3.30}$$

assuming a lossless waveguide, where f is the frequency of propagation, f_c is waveguide cut-off frequency, and v is propagation velocity of the medium inside the guide.

Distortion produced by transmission through waveguides can be evaluated in terms of waveguide insertion phase characteristics. As an example, insertion phase *versus* frequency will be calculated for the WR-284 S-band waveguide. The cut-off frequency of this guide, when propagating in the TE_{10} mode, is 2.078 GHz. Phase linearity will be examined over a 400 MHz bandwidth from 3.05 to 3.45 GHz. Table 3.2 lists values of the *propagation constant* from (3.30), *linear phase* (with slope equal to the difference in WR-284 phase constants at the two band edges divided by the bandwidth), and *deviation* from linear phase *versus* frequency. The band-edge phase deviation is seen to be 6.8°/m when the phase reference is zero at the band center.

Phase deviation from a linear best fit is one-half this amount, ±3.4°/m at the band edges. For a 30 m WR-284 waveguide run, the effective phase deviation will be about 100°. The paired-echo theory discussed above for this deviation would predict extreme distortion of a short RF pulse containing frequencies from 3.05 to 3.45 GHz. Only two meters of waveguide would retain ±6.8° band-edge deviation. From Fig. 3.3, this amount of phase deviation would result in time-sidelobe levels of −25 dB if no other sources of distortion existed in the radar. Distortion predicted by paired-echo analysis is pessimistic because phase deviation in waveguide trans-

---

*The actual ITU assignments are 2.30 to 2.50 GHz and 2.70 to 3.70 GHz.

Table 3.2   Frequency Dispersion in WR-284 Waveguide

Frequency (GHz)	Propagation Constant (°/m)	Linear Phase (°/m)	Phase Deviations from Linear (°/m)
3.05	2679.1	2685.9	−6.8
3.15	2840.8	2842.3	−1.5
3.25	2998.7	2998.7	0.0
3.35	3153.2	3155.1	−1.9
3.45	3304.8	3311.6	−6.8

mission lines from linear phase mostly consists of what is called *quadratic-phase error,* which will be discussed later in relation to pulse-compression systems. As much as $\pi/4$ rad of quadratic phase error (measured at the band edges) can be tolerated by unweighted signals before significant distortion occurs. Weighted signals are even more tolerant because weighting reduces the effect of phase deviation at the band edges where the deviation is highest.

Some methods for reduction of waveguide-produced distortion are selection of *smaller waveguide size* to operate farther from cut-off frequency, use of *waveguide equalization filters,* and *FM slope adjustment* (on chirp-pulse compression radars).

3.12   WIDEBAND MICROWAVE POWER TUBES

Of importance to most moderate to high power radar designs is the transmitter *tube.* Fortunately, for wideband radar developers, power tubes are available over a wide range of microwave frequencies. Radars tend to be divided into two categories, based on transmitter type: *coherent* radars and *noncoherent* radars. Coherent radars transmit signals by power amplification of an input RF drive signal. In other words, phase coherence is maintained through the transmitter. Coded waveforms are generated at low power, and LO signals for the receiver can be coherently related to the transmitted signal. Noncoherent radars transmit signals from power oscillators (usually *magnetrons*). Frequency depends on the power oscillator characteristics as well as the applied voltage and current. Waveforms for noncoherent radars are normally limited to either monotone pulse or monotone CW. General characteristics of types of power tubes available for operation in the microwave radar bands will be discussed briefly.

Klystron power amplifiers are inherently narrowband devices, but stagger-tuned, linear-beam klystrons may have up to 10% bandwidth. The klystron was invented in 1939 by W.W. Hanson, R.H. Varian, and S.F. Varian. The *traveling wave tube* (TWT) is a linear-beam tube, some types of which can operate over very wide bandwidths. The TWT was invented in 1940 by R. Kompfner [11]. This amplifier is characterized by continuous interaction of an electron beam with a helix or coupled cavity. Octave bandwidths are possible with helix TWTs, but at relatively low power. About 10% to 30% bandwidth is possible at higher power with coupled-cavity TWTs.

The magnetron power oscillator was the device that made microwave airborne radar possible during World War II, and it is now so closely associated with radar that common microwave ovens, because they use magnetron output power to heat food, are sometimes called *radar ovens*. The magnetron was invented in 1921 by A.W. Hull, but the device was not used for radar until 1939 when J.T. Randal and H.A.H. Boot of the UK invented the resonant-cavity traveling wave magnetron, which worked at frequencies within S band (2.30 to 3.70 GHz). Raytheon Company in the US developed the means for high-volume production of magnetrons at low cost. This made it possible for the US and the UK to field thousands of microwave radars for surface and airborne platforms during World War II. Pulse magnetrons can generate pulses as short as 50 ns, equivalent to a range resolution of about 25 feet. Frequency-agile coaxial magnetrons can now produce pulse-to-pulse frequency-agile bandwidths of up to 400 MHz at frequencies within X band (8.5 to 10.68 GHz).

Fig. 3.20(a) shows a cut-away view of a tunable coaxial magnetron. Slow tuning is done by adjustment of the tuning piston. A frequency-agile magnetron operates by driving the piston with a motor through a bellows, as shown in Fig. 3.20(b). Typical tuning rates are 70 Hz for a 60 MHz tuning range. (One cycle of tuning takes the frequency from one end of the tuning range to the other and back.) Maximum tuning rates are lower at wider tuning ranges. In some designs, a servo motor provides servo control of the magnetron's frequency. Other frequency-agile techniques exist. While they do not possess signals of particularly wide instantaneous bandwidths, frequency-agile magnetrons can provide a radar with the advantage of improved detection and electronic counter-countermeasures performance. The potential for target imaging with frequency-agile magnetrons will be discussed in Chapter 9.

The *crossed-field amplifier* (CFA) can produce microwave power levels that are high enough for long-range air search. It is similar in some ways to a magnetron, but the CFA is an amplifier, not an oscillator. Characteristically, CFAs are relatively low-gain devices, but they operate at high efficiency and 10% or more bandwidth is possible. *Amplitron* amplifiers are backward-wave CFAs with the capability of a slightly wider bandwidth than the forward-wave CFA.

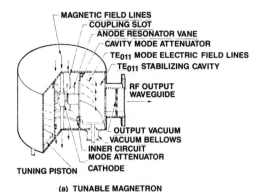

(a) TUNABLE MAGNETRON

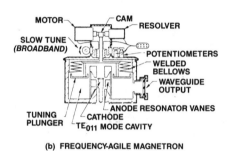

(b) FREQUENCY-AGILE MAGNETRON

Fig. 3.20 Tuneable and Frequency-Agile Magnetrons (From *The Frequency Agile Magnetron Story,* by John R. Martin of Varian Associates, pp. 9–10.)

Amplitude and phase distortion occur in wideband signals transmitted through high power transmitter tubes. In most cases, because power amplifier tubes are driven into saturation, the amplitude tends to be flat across the pulsewidth. It is, therefore, the phase ripple during the pulse or from pulse to pulse that is of most concern. Phase ripple produced by the ripple of the current or voltage applied to the tube is listed for various tubes in Table 3.3, obtained from Cook and Bernfeld [12].

3.13 WIDEBAND SOLID-STATE MICROWAVE AMPLIFIERS

Development of low-noise, *solid-state* amplifiers has made it possible to design wideband, low-distortion receivers for high resolution radars. When solid-state components emerged in the 1960s, they not only provided low-noise characteristics, small size, and low power requirements, but their flat response and low phase distortion simplified wideband radar design.

Table 3.3 Transmitter Phase Ripple

Tube Type	Phase Ripple (rad)
Klystron	$1/2 \dfrac{\delta V}{V} \phi$
TWT	$1/3 \dfrac{\delta V}{V} \phi$
CFA	$1/25 \dfrac{\delta V}{V} \phi$
Triode	$50\left(\dfrac{\delta I}{I}\right)$
Tetrode	$(1{-}50)\left(\dfrac{\delta I}{I}\right)$
Amplitron	$40\left(\dfrac{\delta I}{I}\right)$

$\dfrac{\delta V}{V}$ is the fractional voltage ripple;

$\dfrac{\delta I}{I}$ is the fractional current ripple;

ϕ is the electric length of the tube in radians (insertion phase).

Source: Cook, C.E., and M. Bernfeld, *Radar Signals,* New York: Academic Press, 1967, p. 395.

High power, solid-state devices for use as transmitters have since been developed and found application in the lower microwave bands (1 GHz and below).

3.14 WIDEBAND ANTENNAS

Simple microwave antennas, such as waveguide horns, slots, and dipoles, provide adequate instantaneous bandwidth with sufficiently low phase and amplitude ripple for most high resolution radar applications. When fed by these antennas, parabolic reflectors or lenses and various fixed array antennas also can be designed to possess adequate instantaneous bandwidth. The problem comes with *phase-steered array antennas.* Here, a phase slope across the aperture is electronically set to steer the beam. Unfortunately, because it depends upon fixed spacing of the physical elements, the phase slope changes with radar frequency. Thus, for a given steering command, a phase-steered array radiating a wideband waveform does not radiate power in a single direction. Likewise, received power does not arrive from a single direction. The antenna, therefore, suffers reduced directivity. The use of wideband components in the array does not help. The problem becomes severe when the phased-array aperture has dimensions involving many wavelengths. A reduction of directivity would become evident for a planar array as the beam is steered off from the zero-phase slope at broadside. If not solved, the problem renders large phase-array radars useless for HRR or target imaging. One possible solution, as yet untested, is to operate the radar with pulse-to-pulse, frequency-stepped waveforms. These waveforms may allow time between pulses to adjust the phase shifters at each pulse to keep the antenna on target as the frequency is shifted. Another potential solution involves delay steering of phase-steered subarrays. A third solution may lie in the use of focal-plane arrays, where fixed beams are selected by activating the needed elements in a focal plane, instead of steering a single beam by adjusting all elements in the more conventional aperture-plane array. This is not to say that phased-array radars are now limited to narrow-bandwidth operation. Existing phase-steered systems can operate at over 10% bandwidth or several hundred MHz for search and tracking functions, but instantaneous bandwidth remains quite narrow, which may limit application for high resolution radar.

PROBLEMS

3.1 What is the instantaneous frequency within the envelope $a(t)$ of a chirp pulse defined as $s(t) = a(t) \exp[j2\pi(\bar{f}t + Kt^2/2)]$?

3.2 What is the insertion phase and the group delay at 3.0 GHz through a 20 m, air-filled, TEM-mode transmission line?

3.3 Derive the expressions for the in-band phase delay and group delay through a pulse-compression filter that has a transfer function given by $H(f) = A(f) \exp[j\pi(f - \bar{f})^2/K]$.

3.4 A 300 m/s target observed with a 10 GHz Doppler radar begins accelerating at 5 m/s^2 toward the radar at some time $t = 0$. (a) What is the instantaneous frequency of the echo signal at $t = 0$ and $t = 10$ s? (b) What is the instantaneous Doppler frequency shift in each case?

3.5   The total transfer function of a 1.0 GHz short-pulse radar receiver
measured from receiving antenna terminals to display input has
the following steady-state amplitude and phase characteristics over
its pulse spectrum:

$$A(\omega) = 1 + .02 \cos (8 \times 10^{-8}\omega)$$
$$\phi(\omega) = -10^{-8}\omega - .02 \sin (8 \times 10^{-8}\omega)$$

What are the paired echo amplitudes and delay positions relative
to the main response to a 10 ns echo pulse from a point target?

3.6   What is the delay position of the main response seen at the short-
pulse radar display of Prob. 3.5 relative to the antenna terminals,
based on (3.3) (expressed in angular frequency ω) and (3.8)?

3.7   Show that the value c in (3.6) with respect to the number of cycles
of ripple across bandwidth β of the transfer function $A(\omega)e^{j\phi(\omega)}$ is
given by

$$c = \text{(number of cycles of ripple)}/\beta$$

3.8   A short-pulse radar receiver with a 1.0 GHz center frequency has
linear phase response, but 20 cycles of amplitude ripple appear in
the receiver transfer function over its 10% bandwidth. The amplitude of the ripple is 20% of the average amplitude response.
What are the amplitudes and positions of the resulting paired
echoes relative to the main response?

3.9   Compute the maximum allowable amplitude ripple in a network
that has zero phase ripple and the maximum allowable phase ripple
in a network that has zero amplitude ripple if the sidelobes of the
output response for each network are to be at least 46 dB below
the peak. Check the results with Fig. 3.3.

3.10   A short-pulse radar receiver is to use the transversal equalization
filter shown in Fig. 3.4 to reduce time sidelobes introduced by
phase and amplitude ripple in the radar system. (a) How many
divider outputs are required to cancel five prominent time sidelobes? (b) If the input peak-to-sidelobe level for the highest sidelobe is 15 dB, what is the output peak-to-sidelobe level,
assuming that the filter itself is distortion free?

3.11   A radar transmitter is connected to an antenna by a long transmission line. The input VSWR to the line varies from 1.0 to 1.4,
and the output VSWR varies from 1.0 to 1.6 over the radar fre-

quency band. What is the maximum possible phase deviation from linear? Assume zero loss.

3.12 What is the maximum possible phase deviation from linear phase *versus* frequency produced by a long transmission line? Given are the following VSWR conditions:

(a) input VSWR = 1.0, output VSWR = 2.0;
(b) input VSWR = 2.0, output VSWR = 1.0;
(c) input and output VSWR = 2.0.

Assume zero loss.

3.13 Show that the expression for time response of the pulse that has a spectrum given by $S(f) = \text{rect}\,(f/\beta)$ (where $\text{rect}\,(f/\beta) = 1$ for $|f/\beta| \leq 1/2$ and zero elsewhere) is

$$s(t) = (\sin \pi\beta t)/(\pi t)$$

3.14 Show that the time response of a RF pulse that has the spectrum $S(f) = \text{rect}\,[(f - \bar{f})/\beta]$ is given by

$$s(t) = e^{j2\pi\bar{f}t}\frac{\sin \pi\beta t}{\pi t}$$

Assume that $\text{rect}\,[(f - \bar{f})/\beta] = 1$ for $|f - \bar{f}|/\beta \leq 1/2$ and zero elsewhere.

3.15 Show that the expression $H(f) = \text{rect}\,(f/\beta)$, ($\text{rect}\,(f/\beta)$, defined as in Prob. 3.13) is the transfer function of a filter matched to a video pulse expressed as

$$s(t) = \frac{\sin \pi\beta t}{\pi t}$$

3.16 A rectangular pulse at a carrier frequency $\bar{f}$ is expressed as

$$s(t) = \text{rect}\,(t)e^{j2\pi\bar{f}t}$$

where $\text{rect}\,(t) = 1$ for $|t| \leq 1/2$ and zero elsewhere. Show that the normalized impulse response function of a filter matched to this pulse is given by $h(t) = s(t)$.

3.17 (a) Write the integral expression $\chi(\tau, 0)$ for the ambiguity function of a rectangular pulse for $f_D = 0$. Let the rectangular pulse be represented by rect (t) = 1 for $|t| \leqslant 1/2$ and zero elsewhere. (b) Plot the graph of $\chi(\tau, 0)$.

3.18   A square-law detector is to be designed for envelope detection of microwave pulses of 10 ns duration at the half-power points. What are the approximate band-edge frequencies of the output filter that is matched to the detected video pulse?

3.19   Two sinusoidal signals of voltages x_1 and x_2 and frequencies f_1 and f_2, respectively, are applied to a mixer operating in the square-law region. By using (3.23), show that the output spectrum contains the sum and difference frequencies of x_1 and x_2, and their second harmonics. Assume that $x_1 = A \cos 2\pi f_1 t$ and $x_2 = B \cos 2\pi f_2 t$.

3.20   Show that the cubic and fourth-power terms of the current response to applied voltage $\cos 2\pi f_1 t$ to a mixer produce the first and third harmonics, and the *zero*th (dc), second, and fourth harmonics, respectively, of the input signal.

3.21   A radar illuminates a 1.0 m^2 target. The echo signal at an IF is at 0.3 V rms. The first target is replaced by a second target at the same range and the IF signal goes up to 1.2 V rms. Assume an ideal mixer and a linear receiver. What is the RCS of the second target?

3.22   A high-range-resolution radar uses a wideband square-law detector to detect target-range profiles. The profiles, when amplified and displayed linearly on a wideband oscilloscope, show two major peaks at 2.2 and 1.1 V, respectively. What is the ratio of RCS at the corresponding two resolved target locations? Assume that the receiver is operating in its linear range, except for square-law detection.

3.23   The radar system of Fig. 3.13(a) illuminates a fixed target at range R. (a) In terms of R, what is the phase, relative to the reference signal, of the signal represented by the I and Q outputs of the synchronous detector? (b) Express the individual I and Q outputs for output signal magnitude A. Assume that the normalized reference signal is $\exp(j2\pi \bar{f} t)$ and ignore all delay, except for two-way propagation delay $2R/c$.

3.24   Assume that an ideal (square-law) mixer is to translate to an IF those signals appearing within a 500 MHz frequency band, centered at 3.20 GHz. The LO frequency is at 4.55 GHz. What are the band edges of an ideal (rectangular response) bandpass filter of bandwidth 500 MHz at the IF output that provide spurious-free signal translation to an IF centered at 1.35 GHz?

3.25 A short-pulse radar is to obtain 4.0 m range resolution. (a) What is the required sampling rate, in terms of complex sample pairs per second, to sample the baseband range profiles? (b) What is the required sampling rate, in terms of real samples per second, if the echo signals are square-law detected before sampling?

3.26 Range-profile data are sampled at baseband at 100 megasamples per second. What is the maximum dynamic range in dB that the sampled data can retain, based on Fig. 3.16, in terms of relative signal along the range profile?

3.27 A ship model 5.0 m in length sits on a turntable in an anechoic chamber. Frequency-domain reflectivity measurements are to be made at small increments in angle as the model is rotated through 360° relative to the radar. What is the maximum frequency-step size and minimum number of steps required to be able to obtain 0.1 m range resolution unambiguously at all rotation positions.

3.28 What is the standard deviation of frequency during an averaging time of 1.0 s of an ideal 5.4 GHz transmitter driven from a 100 MHz frequency source multiplied up to the radar frequency? Assume that Table 3.1 is applicable for the frequency source.

3.29 (a) What are the 10 comb frequency settings that must be made available to each decade of an add-and-divide synthesizer design that generates outputs of 10.0000 to 10.9999 MHz from a 1.0 MHz input? (b) How many decades are required?

3.30 What are the binary digit settings in the order 8 4 2 1 that will produce an output signal of 20.8 MHz from the synthesizer of Fig. 3.19(a)?

3.31 Use the definition of group delay, (3.3), and the expression (3.30), to show that the group delay per unit length of a rectangular waveguide operating below cut-off in the TE_{10} mode is given by

$$\tau_g/l = \frac{1}{v} \frac{1}{\sqrt{1 - \left(\frac{f_c}{f}\right)^2}}$$

where f_c is the cut-off frequency and v is the velocity of propagation in the medium inside the guide.

3.32   What is the delay dispersion through 30 m of the waveguide of
             Table 3.2 over the 400 MHz frequency range?

REFERENCES

1.   MacColl, L.A., unpublished manuscript, cited by C.R. Burrows in
     "Discussion of Paired-echo Distortion Analysis," *Proc. IRE (Correspondence)*, Vol. 27, June 1939, p. 384.
2.   Wheeler, H.A., "The Interpretation of Amplitude and Phase Distortion in Terms of Paired Echoes," *Proc. IRE,* Vol. 27, June 1939,
     pp. 359–384.
3.   Reed, J., "Long-Line Effect in Pulse-Compression Radar," *Microwave Journal,* Sept. 1961, pp. 99–100.
4.   Lepoff, J.H., "Spurious Responses in Superheterodyne Receivers,"
     Microwave Journal, June 1962, pp. 95–98.
5.   Allan, D.W., "Statistics of Atomic Frequency Standards," *Proc.
     IEEE,* Vol. 54, No. 2, Feb. 1966, pp. 221–230.
6.   Papoulis, A., *Probability, Random Variables, and Stochastic Processes,* New York: McGraw-Hill, 1965, p. 144.
7.   Papoulis, A., *Probability, Random Variables, and Stochastic Processes,* New York: McGraw-Hill, 1965, p. 246.
8.   Stone, R.R., Jr., and H.F. Hastings, "A Novel Approach to Frequency Synthesis," *Frequency,* Sept. 1963, pp. 24–27.
9.   "HP Direct-Type Frequency Synthesizers, Theory, Performance and
     Use," Hewlett Packard Application Note 96, Jan. 1969.
10. Papaieck, R.J., and R.P. Coe, "New Technique Yields Superior
     Frequency Synthesis at Lower Cost," *Electronic Design News,* Oct.
     20, 1975, pp. 73–79.
11. Gilmour, A.S., Jr., *Microwave Tubes,* Dedham, MA: Artech House,
     1986.
12. Cook, C.E. and M. Bernfeld, *Radar Signals,* New York: Academic
     Press, 1967, p. 395.

Chapter 4
High-Range-Resolution Waveforms
and Processing

4.1 INTRODUCTION

The genesis of wideband radar came about at the end of World War II when the peak power limitations of microwave transmitting tubes were beginning to manifest themselves. There appeared to be a growing gap between the requirements of long-range detection and high resolution. In order to achieve the high resolution, shorter pulses were employed with the result that less energy was being transmitted per pulse. The need for unambiguous range measurement prevented raising the pulse repetition rate so that increasing the peak power seemed to be the only available option. However, the dilemma began to be resolved when it was realized that range resolution need not be limited by pulse length. If the frequency of the carrier, which usually had been constant, were instead varied over some frequency bandwidth, this bandwidth would determine range resolution, according to (1.1) of Chapter 1, written as

$$\Delta r_s \cong \frac{c}{2\beta} \tag{1.1}$$

where Δr_s is the range resolution, β is the frequency excursion (bandwidth), and c is the propagation velocity. In principle, the range resolution can be made arbitrarily small by transmitting a signal of large enough bandwidth. The pulse length can then be stretched as much as necessary to radiate the energy required to detect distant and small targets without losing resolution. Consequently, microwave power tubes can be operated at the relatively high duty factors at which they tend to be most efficient. This is even more true of the solid-state power sources that are now beginning to supplant thermionic tubes. Also, high operating voltages, which had previously been a source of unreliability and even danger in the operation of tubes, could now be kept within manageable bounds. One of the pioneers of the new type of radar, apparently imagining himself to be able to hear both a typical short pulse as well as the new frequency modulated one, wrote a Bell Laboratories memorandum entitled: "Not with a Bang, but with a Chirp!" (B.M. Oliver, Bell Laboratories, 1951). This was the first use of the term *chirp* to describe linear frequency modulation of pulses for pulse compression [1].

To this day, chirp radars remain an important class of high resolution radar. However, more recently, wideband processing to achieve high range resolution is carried out by using a variety of waveforms in addition to linear frequency modulation within each transmitted pulse, as is done in chirp radar. Some waveforms to be described in this chapter are (1) *direct short pulse*, (2) *digital phase coding*, (3) *discrete frequency coding*, and (4) *stretch*. Resolution on the order of inches has been achieved.

Waveform selection for any radar design is closely tied to transmitter type. The simplest type of radar transmitter is probably the magnetron oscillator. Magnetron radars are called noncoherent radars because the transmitted signal is determined only by the oscillation characteristics of the magnetron. By contrast, coherent radar systems using power amplifiers, such as a traveling wave tube or a klystron, generate the transmitted signal by power amplification of an input RF waveform. We shall see in this and subsequent chapters that methods exist to collect wideband reflectivity data from targets using many categories of waveforms. Given below are some common radar types, categorized according to transmitter and listed with likely waveforms to achieve HRR:

- Fixed-frequency magnetron—Direct short pulse;
- Dithered magnetron—Frequency-agile magnetron imaging (described in Chapter 9);
- Wideband, CW power amplifier—Discrete frequency coding and digital phase coding;
- Low PRF, wide-instantaneous-bandwidth power amplifier—Chirp and stretch [2];
- High PRF, wideband power amplifier—Discrete pulse-to-pulse frequency coding.

Table 4.1 lists six waveforms for providing HRR capability. The first four are briefly discussed further. Then, the concept of chirp-pulse compression will be discussed in more detail. Synthetic range-profile generation from pulse-to-pulse, discrete frequency-coded waveforms is discussed in Chapter 5.

Table 4.1   HRR Radar Waveforms

Common Name of Waveform	Concept	Usage Example
Direct Short Pulse	Transmission and reception of very narrow pulses	RCS diagnostics and missile range safety
Binary Phase Coding	Binary phase coding and decoding of individual pulses or CW signals	Missile proximity-fuze systems
Discrete Frequency Coding (Contiguous)	Superposition of harmonically related stepped-frequency waveform segments	May be applicable to airborne intercept (AI) radars, missile guidance, and synthetic aperture radar (SAR)
Stretch [2]	Time-bandwidth exchange	Long-range imaging and SAR mapping
Chirp	Linear FM coding of transmitted pulse, compression of received echo pulse	Small-target detection and target recognition
Discrete Frequency Coding (Pulse-to-Pulse)	Conversion of frequency-domain reflectivity data into *synthetic* range profiles	Target recognition

4.2   SHORT-PULSE WAVEFORMS

High range resolution using short pulses is possible with both coherent and noncoherent radars. In coherent systems, very short RF pulses
have been generated by using even shorter video or RF pulses to drive
ringing filters. The filter bandwidth is designed to correspond to that of
the desired RF pulse length, which then approximates the true impulse
response of the filter. (See Fig. 4.1.) Resolution of three inches has been
achieved for RCS diagnostics. Magnetron transmitters in noncoherent radars can be turned on and off rapidly enough to generate pulses as narrow
as 50 ns, which corresponds to about 25-foot resolution.

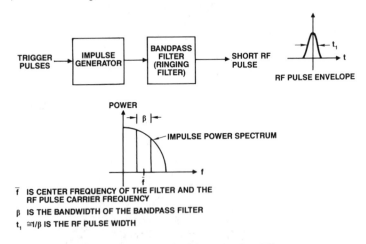

Fig. 4.1 Generation of Short Pulses with a Ringing Filter

Short-pulse HRR radar can be used for experimental purposes at
short range. One application is to locate backscatter sources of surface
and air vehicles or models of vehicles. An example of a search-radar
application of short-pulse waveforms is the AN/FPS-114 system developed
at the Naval Ocean Systems Center (NOSC) in San Diego. In the AN/
FPS-114, a fixed-frequency magnetron generates 110 ns pulses to provide
adequate resolution for location of individual small craft at sea from van-
tage points along suitable coastal sites for the purpose of missile test-range
safety.

4.3   BINARY PHASE CODING

Phase-coded waveforms consist of various digitally controlled phase
modulations on the transmitted carrier signal. Usually, the modulation

used is *phase-reversal modulation* (also called *binary phase coding*), wherein the phase of the carrier is switched between $\pm 180°$ according to a stored digital code. The resulting echo signal is compressed by correlation with a stored reference of the code or by matched-filter processing. Both individual pulses and continuous-wave signals can be phase coded. The range-delay resolution of these waveforms is equal to the reciprocal of the bit rate. Range resolution down to less than a foot has been demonstrated to be possible, but problems with Doppler ambiguity and dynamic range seem to have prevented widespread use of binary phase codes for wideband applications. Figure 4.2 illustrates a common phase-reversal modulation-demodulation technique for generating binary phase-coded waveforms from digital codes and converting the resulting echo signals into digital signals for matched filtering. Figure 4.3(a) shows a simple three-bit binary code and the resulting phase-reversal modulated RF pulse. Figure 4.3(b) illustrates the digital response to a single point target seen in one quadrature channel out of a digital filter matched to the three-bit transmitted waveform. Figure 4.3(c) illustrates the required processing of both quadrature outputs to produce compressed responses that are independent of the unknown phase delay of the target.

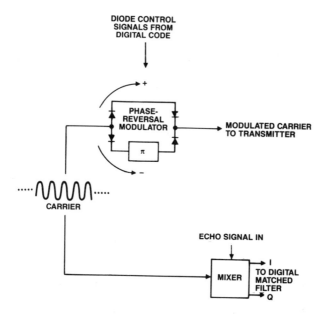

Fig. 4.2 Phase-Reversal Modulation and Demodulation

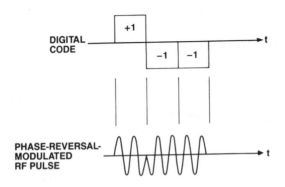

(a) 3-bit code and waveform

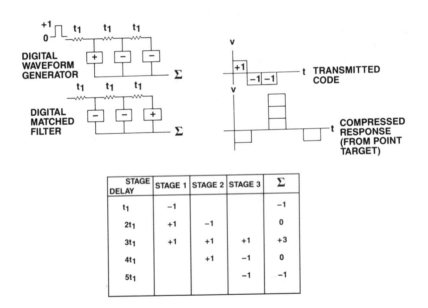

STAGE DELAY	STAGE 1	STAGE 2	STAGE 3	Σ
t_1	−1			−1
$2t_1$	+1	−1		0
$3t_1$	+1	+1	+1	+3
$4t_1$		+1	−1	0
$5t_1$			−1	−1

(b) Digital matched filtering

Fig. 4.3 Digital Matched-Filter Processing Illustrated for a Three-Bit Binary Code

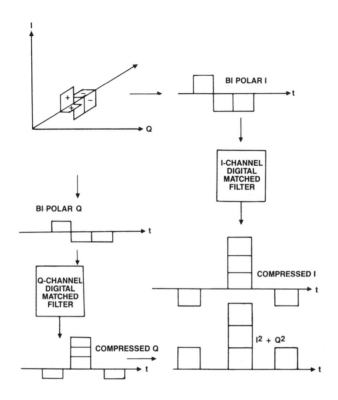

(c) Quadrature processing

Figure 4.3 illustrates processing of an input signal from a single point target. An input signal, in general, is the range-extended echo signal produced by reflections from the multitude of scatterers illuminated by the radar antenna beam. The echo signal from a single point target is a delayed replica of the transmitted waveform reduced in size. The range-extended signal will generally contain many overlapped replicas of the waveform.

The output response to an echo signal $s_i(t)$ produced by a transmitted binary phase-coded waveform can be determined by carrying out the discrete version of the convolution process:

$$s_o(t) = h(t) * s_i(t)$$

where $h(t)$ is the matched-filter impulse response and the asterisk denotes convolution. A single period of a contiguous sequence or a single coded pulse at carrier frequency $\bar{f}$, code length n, and bit length t_1, can be defined in complex form by the expression:

$$s_1(t) = \sum_{i=0}^{n-1} \text{rect } (t)e^{j(2\pi\bar{f}t + \psi_i)}$$

where

$$\text{rect } (t) = 1, \, it_1 \leqslant t \leqslant (i + 1)t_1$$
$$= 0, \text{ elsewhere}$$

and where $\psi_i = 0$ or π, according to the code sequence. Practical digital codes may be many bits in length. The *Barker Code* sequences [3] are called optimum codes because, for zero-Doppler shift, the peak-to-sidelobe ratio following matched filtering is $\pm n$ for all code lengths, where n is the number of bits in the coded waveform. Nine Barker sequences have been developed with code lengths of up to 13 bits.

The filter matched to a binary coded pulse is a network with an impulse response that is the time-inverse sequence of the coded pulse. Continuous phase-coded waveforms may consist of a contiguous sequence of identically coded segments. Such a waveform is called a periodic phase-coded waveform. The filter matched to the continuous type of waveform is normally designed so that its impulse response is the time-inverse sequence of one coded segment of the waveform. An eight-bit, phase-coded, pulse waveform is illustrated in Fig. 4.4 along with its matched filter and the output response to the echo signal from a single point target. We can see that the compressed pulsewidth t_1 for this ideal representation is equal to the bit duration. The matched filtering of Fig. 4.4 occurs at the carrier RF by contrast with that for Fig. 4.3, where matched filtering is a digital process.

The process of discrete convolution of the signal from a single point target is illustrated in Fig. 4.5 in terms of the binary bits associated with the phase-reversal modulation of the binary phase-coded pulse of Fig. 4.4. We can observe that the folding aspect of convolution, as seen from Fig. 4.3(b), comes about because the first bit of the code arrives first. This is also illustrated in Fig. 4.5, where we can see that the bit stream moves across the matched filter "first-bit-first." For simplicity, Fig. 4.5 illustrates only one quadrature component of the convolution so that $h(t) = s_1(-t)$, which is the time reversal of $s_1(t)$. The set of $s_o(t)$ values in the lower part

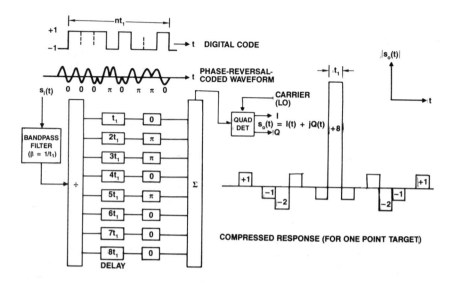

Fig. 4.4 Eight-Bit Phase-Coded Waveform and Its Matched Filter (Response to a Single Point Target Is Illustrated)

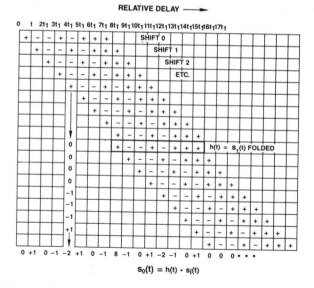

Fig. 4.5 Discrete Convolution of a Signal from a Single Point Target with the Binary-Coded Waveform of Fig. 4.4 (for One Quadrature Channel)

of Fig. 4.5 are the convolved values at each time displacement through the matched filter. For illustration, we show the individual products at shift 4, which are summed to produce the convolved value $s_o(4t_1) = -2$. The pulse-compression ratio of a binary phase-coded pulse is simply the code length n.

4.4 CONTINUOUS DISCRETE FREQUENCY CODING

Discrete frequency coding to improve resolution is a concept that was known early in the evolution of radar. A recent development uses the CW transmission illustrated in Fig. 4.6(a), whereby the frequency is shifted from one time segment to another in a periodic manner. In this way, the problem of *transmit-to-receive leakage,* associated with single-frequency CW radars, is reduced. The received signal at any instant is likely to be composed mostly of echoes at frequencies offset from the transmitted frequency. Further, because the waveform is coded in frequency, it is possible to measure the target range delay associated with a given frequency segment in a manner similar to that used for pulsed radar. Waveform segments are synthesized from a common stable oscillator and thereby coherently related. *Multiple-frequency echo responses* are processed to produce HRR by using coherent multiplexing. This is accomplished by first applying appropriate delays to each frequency segment to align the segments in time. Coherent addition of the n aligned responses then produces a HRR response. Actual processing is likely to be carried out following down-conversion to a convenient IF. The symbols f_0 to f_{n-1} will represent the waveform before up-conversion to the transmitted frequencies. This type of waveform possesses some aspects of pulse compression, but it is also related to *synthetic HRR* to be discussed in Chapter 5.

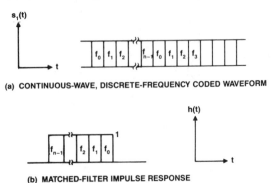

(a) CONTINUOUS-WAVE, DISCRETE-FREQUENCY CODED WAVEFORM

(b) MATCHED-FILTER IMPULSE RESPONSE

Fig. 4.6 Continuous-Wave, Periodic, Discrete Frequency-Coded Waveform and the Impulse Response of Its Matched Filter

A stepped-frequency version can be defined in terms of a contiguous, repeating sequence of waveform segments, each of time duration T_1 stepped Δf in frequency in n steps over some repetitive period nT_1. A single period of n frequency steps for a contiguous periodic waveform can be described in complex form by the expression:

$$s_1(t) = \sum_{i=0}^{n-1} \text{rect } (t)e^{j2\pi(f_0+i\Delta f)t}$$

where

$$\text{rect } (t) = 1, iT_1 \leq t \leq (i + 1)T_1$$
$$= 0, \text{ otherwise}$$

The filter matched to this waveform will have an impulse response $h(t)$ that is the time-reverse order of the conjugate of one period of the waveform. The impulse response, shown in Fig. 4.6(b), can be expressed in terms of the nonrepeating function:

$$h(t) = s_1^*(-t)$$
$$= \sum_{i=0}^{n-1} \text{rect } (-t)e^{j2\pi(f_0+i\Delta f)t}$$

where

$$\text{rect } (-t) = 1, iT_1 \leq t \leq (i + 1)T_1$$
$$= 0, \text{ otherwise}$$

Figure 4.7 illustrates a four-frequency periodic waveform with its matched filter. The duration of the response to a point target will be shown to be less than that of each frequency segment. This is in contrast to that for the binary phase-coded pulse, where the compressed pulse duration is equal to the bit size t_1.

The action of the matched filter illustrated in Fig. 4.7 can be explained by assuming that the individual bandpass filter responses to an in-band segment are zero beyond $\pm T_1$ from the peak response. The delay lines in Fig. 4.7 produce alignment of these responses so that signals at all n frequencies appear in the summation network one time for each nT_1 s period, and remain for $2T_1$ s. It is convenient to match step size Δf to frequency segment duration T_1 by setting Δf equal to $1/T_1$. As we shall see below, this criteria ensures that the matched-filter response approaches

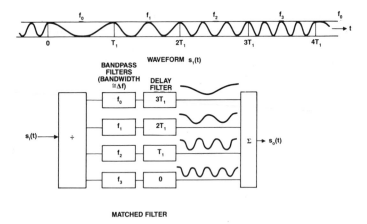

Fig. 4.7 Four-Frequency Periodic Waveform and Its Matched Filter

zero beyond the unambiguous range window associated with the waveform.

Figure 4.8(a) illustrates the convolution of a contiguous, periodic, stepped frequency-coded waveform with its matched filter. (This corresponds to the response, normalized to unity, to a fixed point target at zero range.) Only discrete shifts are indicated in the figure. A response occurs when the signal is shifted in time to positions where its set of discrete frequencies overlap in time with the corresponding set of delayed response functions of the bandpass filter. The overlap for each frequency is assumed to last for $2T_1$ s and occurs every nT_1 s, as discussed above. The matched-filter response during the overlap time is the coherent summation of the aligned signals of the n frequency steps.

Response in complex form to a point target is expressed as

$$s_o(t) = a(t) \sum_{i=0}^{n-1} e^{j2\pi(f_0 + i\Delta f)t}$$

where $a(t)$ is the envelope of the output responses of the n bandpass filters, which peak at $t = 0, nT_1, 2nT_1, \ldots$, (referred to the output of the delay lines) and are zero for beyond $\pm T_1$ from the peaks. Taking the constant frequency f_0 term outside the summation, we have

$$s_o(t) = a(t)e^{j2\pi f_0 t} \sum_{i=0}^{n-1} e^{j2\pi(i\Delta ft)}$$

RELATIVE DELAY →

0	T_1	$2T_1$	$3T_1$	$4T_1$	$5T_1$	$6T_1$	$7T_1$	$8T_1$	$9T_1$	$10T_1$		
•	f_3	f_2	f_1	f_0	f_3	f_2	f_1	f_0	•	SHIFT 0		
	•	f_3	f_2	f_1	f_0	f_3	f_2	f_1	•	SHIFT 1		
		•	f_3	f_2	f_1	f_0	f_3	f_2	•	SHIFT 2		
			•	f_3	f_2	f_1	f_0	f_3	•	ETC		
			•	f_3	f_2	f_1	f_0	•				
				f_3	f_2	f_1	f_0	$h(t) = s_1(t)$ folded				
			•	f_0	f_3	f_2	f_1	f_0	•			
			•	f_1	f_0	f_3	f_2	f_1	f_0	•		
			•	f_2	f_1	f_0	f_3	f_2	f_1	f_0	•	
			•	f_3	f_2	f_1	f_0	f_3	f_2	f_1	f_0	•
			•	f_0	f_3	f_2	f_1	f_0	f_3	f_2	f_1	f_0

(a) Convolution process

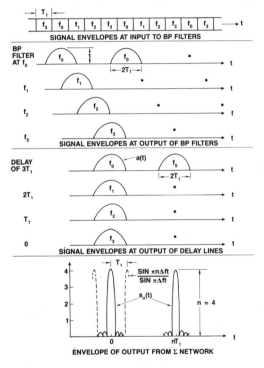

(b) Signals associated with the convolution process

Fig. 4.8 Convolution of a Signal from a Single Point Target with the Discrete Frequency-Coded Periodic Waveform of Fig. 4.7

The remaining summation term is the expression for a Fourier series, except that the summation is over a finite number n of frequencies. An identity used to analyze the response of linear antenna arrays [4] is given by

$$\sum_{p=0}^{\beta-1} e^{+j\alpha p} = \frac{\sin \dfrac{\beta\alpha}{2}}{\sin \dfrac{\alpha}{2}} \, e^{j[(\beta-1)/2]\alpha}$$

By using this identity with

$$\beta = n$$
$$p = i$$

and

$$\alpha = 2\pi\Delta ft$$

we obtain

$$s_o(t) = a(t)e^{j2\pi f_0 t} \frac{\sin \dfrac{2\pi n\Delta ft}{2}}{\sin \dfrac{2\pi\Delta ft}{2}} \, e^{j2\pi[(n-1)\Delta ft/2]}$$

after rearranging terms

$$s_o(t) = a(t)e^{j2\pi[f_0+(n-1)\Delta f/2]t} \frac{\sin \pi n\Delta ft}{\sin \pi\Delta ft}$$

The quantity $f_0 + (n-1)\Delta f/2$ is the average frequency, which is the carrier frequency. The expression for the matched-filter response to the point target can be rewritten as

$$s_o(t) = a(t) \frac{\sin \pi n\Delta ft}{\sin \pi\Delta ft} e^{j2\pi\bar{f}t}$$

where $\bar{f}$ is the carrier frequency.

The $\sin \pi n\Delta ft/(\sin \pi\Delta ft)$ term for $T_1 = 1/\Delta f$ has a peak response of magnitude n at $t = 0$, $\pm T_1$, $\pm 2T_1$, $\pm 3T_1$, ... Polarity is positive at $t = 0$, and depends upon the value of n at the other peak magnitude positions. Resolution at the -4 dB points is equal to the reciprocal of the waveform bandwidth $n\Delta f$. The bandpass filter response term $a(t)$ is assumed to be zero at $|t| \geqslant T_1$, referred to the delay-line output. Peaks in $s_0(t)$ occur at intervals of nT_1, where n is the number of frequency segments in one period of the periodic sequence. Signals associated with the convolution process for a point-target input signal are illustrated in Fig. 4.8(b). The matched-filter response for periodic, discrete frequency-coded waveforms can be characterized as follows:

1. Peak response to an input signal from a fixed point target is n times the input signal voltage level.
2. Responses occur at delay intervals of nT_1, where n is the number of frequency segments of length T_1 s.
3. An unambiguous range-delay window of nT_1 s is obtained for $T_1 = 1/\Delta f$.
4. Delay resolution is $1/(n\Delta f)$ at the -4 dB points.

All of the above characteristics would also be seen in a series of discrete Fourier transforms, produced from sampled data obtained at each frequency within each period of the same periodic waveform. The discrete Fourier transform (DFT) method for stepped-frequency pulse waveforms is called *synthetic processing*.

An advantage of the continuous, discrete frequency-coded waveform is its inherent unambiguous response in Doppler and the independent ambiguity control in range. Because individual frequency segments are generated from a single stable source (e.g., by way of a frequency synthesizer), the echo signal can be down-converted to a single CW signal, which is then unambiguous in Doppler. Range ambiguities can be independently controlled, at least conceptually, by adjusting the period length. A more recent variant of this waveform, now under development, is a pseudoperiodic version in which the frequency code is changed from period to period. In this variant, no range ambiguities appear at all, and a true *thumbtack ambiguity response* exists. The practical advantages of this approach are being investigated for target imaging and detection.

4.5 STRETCH

An important class of waveforms used for modern high resolution mapping and target imaging falls under a category called *stretch* waveforms. The stretch concept provides HRR by transmitting a linear FM pulse, then down-converting the echo signal with a frequency-modulated LO signal of identical or slightly different FM slope. The resulting echo spectrum corresponds to a range profile. The original concept, developed by Caputi

[2], involved a narrow bandwidth pulse-compression filter to compress the residual FM pulse after mixing with a LO signal of slightly different FM slope. Other implementations for long-range target imaging and synthetic aperture radar use pulses with identical linear FM on transmit and LO with no additional pulse compression. One method of using the stretch waveform to obtain a HRR signature of a target is illustrated in Fig. 4.9. The stretch process is a type of chirp-pulse compression, the original (and still most common) form of which is discussed below.

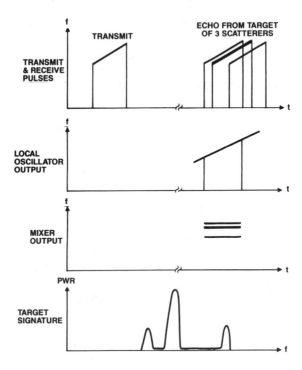

Fig. 4.9 Stretch Waveform and Processing

4.6 CHIRP-PULSE COMPRESSION

The term *pulse-compression radar* refers to the transmission of relatively long coded pulses and the processing of resulting echo signals into high resolution responses in a pulse-compression receiver. The transmitted energy can be either phase coded or frequency coded as discussed above, and coding can be generated by either digital or analog techniques. For HRR applications, only the analog frequency coding called *chirp* radar (including stretch) has been used to any significant extent. The more general term, pulse-compression radar, is therefore often used to refer to the chirp type of pulse-compression radar. The chirp waveform will now be analyzed in more detail because many of the general characteristics of pulse compression may be observed in this simple waveform. The chirp radar concept is described in detail by Klauder *et al.* [1], and the discussion here is based mostly on Klauder's classic analysis. Some of the figures and plotted curves, as indicated, have been obtained from that reference.

A chirp transmitted waveform is illustrated in Fig. 4.10. Figure 4.11 illustrates the action of the pulse-compression network to compress an input chirp pulse. Delay *versus* frequency behavior of a pulse-compression network is shown in Fig. 4.12(a), and the resulting response envelope from an unweighted chirped pulse is shown in Fig. 4.12(b).

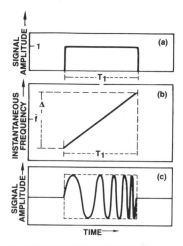

(a) TRANSMITTER PULSE ENVELOPE
(b) TRANSMITTED PULSE FREQUENCY
   VS. PULSE DURATION
(c) TRANSMITTED PULSE RF WAVEFORM

Fig. 4.10 Chirp-Radar Transmitted Signal (From Klauder, J.R., *et al.*, "The Theory and Design of Chirp Radars," *Bell System Technical J.*, Vol. XXXIX, No. 4, July 1960, p. 750. Reprinted with permission.)

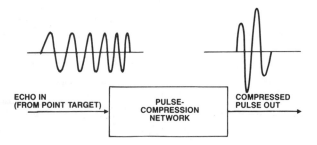

Fig. 4.11 Pulse-Compression Network and Response to a Chirped Input Pulse

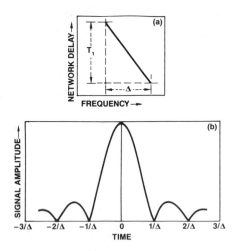

Fig. 4.12 Chirp Pulse-Compression Network Characteristic and Compressed Pulse (From Klauder, J.R., *et al.*, "The Theory and Design of Chirp Radars," *Bell System Technical J.,* Vol. XXXIX, No. 4, July 1960, p. 751. Reprinted with permission.)

Analytically, the transmitted signal from a chirp radar with frequency *versus* delay slope K over pulse duration T_1 can be expressed in complex form as

$$s_1(t) = \text{rect}\left(\frac{t}{T_1}\right) e^{j2\pi(\bar{f}t + Kt^2/2)} \tag{4.1}$$

where $\bar{f}$ is the carrier frequency, and

$$\text{rect}\left(\frac{t}{T_1}\right) = 1, \quad \text{if } \left|\frac{t}{T_1}\right| < 1/2$$

$$= 0, \quad \text{if } \left|\frac{t}{T_1}\right| > 1/2$$

The phase of $s_1(t)$, from (4.1), is

$$\psi(t) = 2\pi(\bar{f}t + Kt^2/2) \tag{4.2}$$

Phase of the chirp waveform varies quadratically with either time advance or delay from the pulse center. The frequency *versus* time behavior of the chirp signal is its *instantaneous frequency*. From (4.2), using (3.1) of Chapter 3, instantaneous frequency becomes

$$f = \frac{1}{2\pi}\frac{d\psi}{dt} = \bar{f} + Kt \tag{4.3}$$

During the pulse duration T_1, the instantaneous frequency given by (4.3) changes from $\bar{f} - KT_1/2$ to $\bar{f} + KT_1/2$. This *frequency sweep*, after Klauder, is symbolized by Δ, and a quantity called *dispersion factor* is symbolized by D, where

$$D = T_1\Delta \tag{4.4}$$

Dispersion factor D is also called the *time-bandwidth product* of the waveform. (It should be noted that an uncoded pulse of duration T_1, although $\Delta = 0$, has a time-bandwidth product of about unity by virtue of its bandwidth $\beta \approx 1/T_1$.)

4.6.1 Analysis Based on Phase Equalization

The pulse-compression network is a phase equalizer that equalizes the quadratic phase response of the chirp pulse. The transfer function of a phase equalization network, with delay *versus* frequency slope P, is written as

$$H(f) = e^{j\pi P(f-\bar{f})^2} \tag{4.5}$$

The amplitude characteristic of the equalization network's transfer function will be assumed to be unity. (The effect of frequency weighting to reduce sidelobes will be discussed later.) Instantaneous insertion delay (group delay) is obtained by differentiating the phase of (4.5) with respect to frequency. By using (3.3) of Chapter 3, we can write for f in Hz:

$$\tau_g(f) = -\frac{1}{2\pi}\frac{d}{df}[\pi P(f - \bar{f})^2] = -P(f - \bar{f}) \text{ s} \qquad (4.6)$$

Note from (4.6) that insertion delay is zero when $f = \bar{f}$. The total transfer function of an actual radar system will result in additional fixed and dispersive delay through transmission lines and other components. Fixed delay produces linear insertion phase *versus* frequency and does not affect the shape of the pulse-compression filter's output pulse. Additional undesired dispersive delay will be assumed, for now, to be small.

Refer to Fig. 4.10(b), where the frequency *versus* delay slope of the transmitted chirp pulse is $K = \Delta/T_1$. By referring to Fig. 4.12(a), we can see that the delay *versus* frequency slope of the pulse-compression network is $P = T_1/\Delta$. If $P = K^{-1}$ over band Δ, we have a pulse-compression filter. Only this case is treated, which relates to the concept of a matched filter in terms of phase response. An expression will now be developed for the compressed echo pulse from a point target when the delay equalization filter's delay *versus* frequency slope matches the time-inverse of the frequency *versus* delay slope of transmitted chirp pulse.

The complex spectrum $S_i(f)$ of the input echo signal $s_i(t)$ is defined as

$$S_i(f) = FT[s_i(t)]$$

where the symbol *FT* refers to the Fourier transform. The spectrum of the output signal from the pulse-compression network is given by

$$S_o(f) = H(f)S_i(f)$$

where $H(f)$ is the network transfer function. Fourier analysis allows the output response $s_o(t)$ to be defined as

$$s_o(t) = h(t) * s_i(t)$$

where $h(t)$ is the network impulse response. For the normalized response to a single point target $s_i(t) = s_1(t)$. The point-target response can therefore be written as

$$s_o(t) = h(t) * s_1(t) \qquad (4.7)$$

The asterisk in (4.7), as before, denotes convolution, defined for the two functions $h(t)$ and $s_1(t)$ of the variable t as

$$h(t) * s_1(t) = \int_{-\infty}^{\infty} h(t - \tau) s_1(\tau)d\tau = \int_{-\infty}^{\infty} s_1(\tau) h(t - \tau)d\tau \qquad (4.8)$$

The impulse response $h(t)$ is the inverse Fourier transform of the network's transfer function $H(f)$. Therefore, the impulse response associated with $H(f)$, expressed in (4.5) for $P = K^{-1}$, is written

$$h(t) = \int_{-\infty}^{\infty} H(f)e^{j2\pi ft}df$$

$$= \int_{-\infty}^{\infty} e^{j2\pi[ft+(f-\bar{f})^2/2K]}df$$

This integral can be evaluated by converting to a form given by

$$h(t) = \int_{-\infty}^{\infty} e^{j(af^2+2bf+c)}df$$

$$= \int_{-\infty}^{0} \cos(af^2 + 2bf + c)df + j\int_{0}^{\infty} \sin(af^2 + 2bf + c)df$$

which can be found in the table of integrals by Gradshteyn and Ryzhik [5]. The integral, according to Klauder, is evaluated in Campbell and Foster [6]. The result by either method is expressed as

$$h(t) = \sqrt{\frac{j\Delta}{T_1}} e^{j2\pi(\bar{f}t - Kt^2/2)} \qquad (4.9)$$

The complex output from (4.1), (4.7), (4.8), and (4.9), therefore, is

$$s_o(t) = \int_{-\infty}^{\infty} s_1(\tau)h(t - \tau)d\tau$$

$$= \sqrt{\frac{j\Delta}{T_1}} \int_{-T_1/2}^{+T_1/2} e^{j2\pi[\bar{f}\tau + K\tau^2/2 + (t-\tau)\bar{f} - K(t-\tau)^2/2]}d\tau$$

After rearrangement of terms, we have

$$s_o(t) = \sqrt{\frac{j\Delta}{T_1}} e^{j2\pi(\bar{f}t - Kt^2/2)} \int_{-T_1/2}^{+T_1/2} e^{j2\pi Kt\tau}d\tau$$

The integral term can be integrated as follows:

$$\int_{-T_1/2}^{+T_1/2} e^{j2\pi Kt\tau} \, d\tau = \int_{-T_1/2}^{+T_1/2} (\cos 2\pi Kt\tau + j \sin 2\pi Kt\tau) d\tau$$

$$= \frac{1}{2\pi Kt} \int_{-T_1/2}^{+T_1/2} (\cos 2\pi Kt\tau) \, 2\pi Kt d\tau + j0$$

$$= \frac{\sin \pi KtT_1}{\pi Kt}$$

Because $\Delta = KT_1$ and recalling from (4.4) that time-bandwidth product D is $T_1\Delta$, the output of the matched filter becomes

$$s_o(t) = \sqrt{D} \, j \, \frac{\sin (\pi\Delta)t}{(\pi\Delta)t} \, e^{j2\pi(\bar{f}t - Kt^2/2)} \qquad (4.10)$$

The response envelope is

$$\sqrt{D} \left| \frac{\sin (\pi\Delta)t}{(\pi\Delta)t} \right|$$

This is the familiar $(\sin x)/x$ expression with $x = (\pi\Delta)t$. The normalized power at the half-power points of the envelope is

$$\left| \frac{\sin (\pi\Delta)t}{(\pi\Delta)t} \right|^2 = \frac{1}{2}$$

which is satisfied by $(\pi\Delta)t = 1.39$. The time interval on each side of the peak response, then, is

$$\tau \Big|_{-3 \text{ dB}} = \pm \frac{1.39}{\pi\Delta} = \pm \frac{0.443}{\Delta}$$

so that the half-power compressed pulse duration is

$$t_1 = 2\tau \Big|_{-3 \text{ dB}}$$

$$= \frac{0.886}{\Delta} \text{ s}$$

Pulse duration at the -4 dB points is $t_1 = 1/\Delta$.

We will show later that frequency weighting reduces the $(\sin x)/x$ sidelobes, illustrated in Fig. 4.12(b), and slightly increases the compressed pulse duration. The increase in pulse duration occurs because of the ef-

fective reduction in bandwidth produced by weighting.
  Significant conclusions are given below.

1. The amplitude of the compressed pulse is increased over that of the input pulse by $\sqrt{D}$ and the new pulse duration is about $1/\Delta$. The corresponding radar range resolution for swept bandwidth Δ is $c/2\Delta$.
2. Frequency modulation exists in the compressed pulse, but in the reverse sense from that of the transmitted pulse. (Compare the instantaneous frequency of the output $s_o(t)$ from (4.10) with that of the input $s_1(t)$ from (4.1).)
3. The $(\sin x)/x$ output, which is unweighted, results in peak sidelobes of 13 dB below the main response.
4. The input and output pulse envelopes, although they are both time functions, are related in form by a Fourier transform.

  We can show analytically that signal-to-noise ratio is maximum for a pulse-compression network for which $K = \Delta/T_1 = 1/P$. The transmitted chirp pulse can be generated either passively or actively, as will be discussed below.

4.6.2 Effect of Rectangular Pulse Shape

  The above analysis of pulse compression in terms of a phase-equalization filter relates to matched filtering. However, as discussed in Chapter 3, an actual matched filter is defined as a network for which the impulse response $h(t)$ and transfer function $H(f)$ are related to the waveform time and frequency functions $s_1(t)$ and $S_1(f)$, respectively, as follows:

$$H(f) = S_1^*(f)$$
$$h(t) = s_1^*(-t)$$

The equalization filter defined by (4.5) and (4.9) does not fully meet these criteria because the effect of the rectangular pulse shape was not taken into consideration. The spectrum $S_1(f)$ of the finite-length chirp signal $s_1(t)$, given by (4.1), is a complicated function involving complex Fresnel integrals. The spectrum derived by Klauder *et al.* is expressed as

$$S_1(f) = \sqrt{\frac{T_1}{2\Delta}}\, e^{-j\pi(f-\bar{f})^2/K}\, [C(z_2) + jS(z_2) - C(z_1) - jS(z_1)]$$

where $C(z)$ and $S(z)$ are the Fresnel sine and cosine integrals. The arguments z_2 and z_1 are defined as

$$z_2 = -2(f - \bar{f})\sqrt{\frac{T_1}{2\Delta}} + \sqrt{\frac{T_1\Delta}{2}}$$

$$z_1 = -2(f - \bar{f})\sqrt{\frac{T_1}{2\Delta}} - \sqrt{\frac{T_1\Delta}{2}}$$

The transfer function of the phase-equalization network, defined in (4.5) for $P = K^{-1}$, can be seen to meet the criteria $H(f) = S_1^*(f)$ insofar as its phase response is concerned, but its amplitude does not contain the complex Fresnel integral functions associated with the rectangular pulse shape.

A normalized form of the absolute value of the spectrum $S_1(f)$ is

$$\sqrt{\frac{\Delta}{T_1}} |S_1(f)| = \frac{1}{\sqrt{2}} \{[C(z_2) - C(z_1)]^2 + [S(z_2) - S(z_1)]^2\}^{1/2}$$

It can be shown that $|S_1(f)|$ is a function only of the factor D and $(f - \bar{f})/\Delta$. The calculated spectra for three values of D are shown in Figs. 4.13, 4.14, and 4.15 from Klauder et al. [1]. Rectangular bandpass characteristics are shown comparatively for each value of D.

We can easily show from the definition of a matched filter that, in terms of magnitude, a matched-filter transfer function and the normalized input spectrum to which it is matched are identical. Figures 4.13, 4.14, and 4.15 show that a rectangular passband is approached for large values of D. For smaller values of D, the mismatch to an idealized chirp pulse will result in reduced signal-to-noise ratio. Figure 4.16, obtained from Klauder, illustrates this. We can see, however, that the degradation of signal-to-noise ratio is small, even for low dispersion. Thus, approximation of a rectangular transfer function (sharp cut-off filter of width Δ) is normally attempted in the design of pulse-compression filters for systems where the chirp signal is a linearly swept, constant-level pulse. Complicated transfer functions with amplitude characteristics, such as those shown in Figs. 4.13, 4.14, and 4.15, are not normally needed. Amplitude weighting of the frequency response, to be discussed below, is often superimposed on the rectangular response, usually by means of a separate weighting filter to reduce time sidelobes.

The mismatch between an ideal rectangular chirp signal and a phase-equalization network that is band-limited by a rectangular filter transfer function can also be viewed intuitively. The spectrum of the ideal chirp

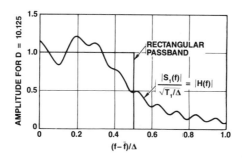

Fig. 4.13 Spectral Amplitude of a Rectangular Chirp Signal and Magnitude of the Transfer Function of Its Matched Filter for $D = 10.125$ Compared to a Rectangular Bandpass Characteristic, the Shape is Symmetric about the Point $(f - 2\bar{f})/\Delta = 0$ (From Klauder, J.R., *et al.*, "The Theory and Design of Chirp Radars," *Bell System Technical J.*, Vol. XXXIX, No. 4, July 1960, p. 756. (Rectangular passband added and symbols modified.) Reprinted with permission.)

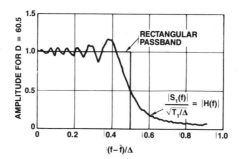

Fig. 4.14 Spectral Amplitude of a Rectangular Chirp Signal and Magnitude of the Transfer Function of Its Matched Filter for $D = 60.5$ Compared to a Rectangular Bandpass Characteristic (From Klauder, J.R., *et al.*, "The Theory and Design of Chirp Radars," *Bell System Technical J.*, Vol. XXXIX, No. 4, July 1960, p. 757. (Rectangular passband added and symbols modified.) Reprinted with permission.)

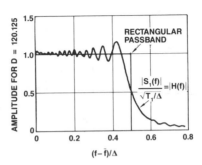

Fig. 4.15 Spectral Amplitude of a Rectangular Chirp Signal and Magnitude of the Transfer Function of Its Matched Filter for $D = 120.125$ Compared to a Rectangular Bandpass Characteristic (From Klauder, J.R., *et al.*, "The Theory and Design of Chirp Radars," *Bell System Technical J.*, Vol. XXXIX, No. 4, July 1960, p. 757. (Rectangular passband added and symbols modified.) Reprinted with permission.)

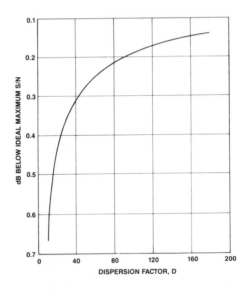

Fig. 4.16 Degradation in *S/N* from Ideal Maximum When the Rectangular Chirp Signal Passes through a Delay Equalizer and a Sharp Cut-Off Filter of Width Δ; the Degradation Decreases Rapidly as the Dispersion Factor D Increases (From Klauder, J.R., *et al.*, "The Theory and Design of Chirp Radars," *Bell System Technical J.*, Vol. XXXIX, No. 4, July 1960, p. 772. Reprinted with permission.)

signal defined by (4.1) contains both the unlimited spectrum of frequency components produced by the assumed rect (t/T_1) envelope and the desired frequency components of the linear FM spectrum. For a chirp signal of large time-bandwidth product, the desired spectrum of the linear FM dominates.

The chirp signal of (4.1) can be generated by driving a voltage-controlled oscillator with a time-varying drive voltage that results in the desired linear frequency ramp. This method is sometimes called *active chirp generation*. A chirp signal can also be generated by driving a linearly dispersive filter with a very short video or RF pulse. This method is called *passive chirp generation*. The required pulse-compression filter for passive chirp generation can be an identical filter, but arranged in the receiver system in such a manner, to be described below, as to provide the inverse of the delay *versus* frequency function of the filter when used as the chirp generator. For this situation, exact matched filtering is achieved, regardless of how small is the dispersion D.

4.6.3   Weighting

The idealized transfer function of a phase-equalization filter, expressed by (4.5), for a chirp bandwidth Δ, was shown to produce a compressed pulse having a half-power width of $t_1 = .886/\Delta$. The signal-to-noise ratio is maximum when the pulse is processed with a matched filter. A rectangular bandpass characteristic, while limiting receiver noise, was shown to result in a slight mismatch, even when band edges are set at the edges of the chirp FM. An actual radar system is band-limited according to the transfer function of the entire radar system, including propagation effects that vary with frequency. Normally, we attempt to provide flat frequency response over the entire chirp bandwidth. Weighting filters are designed to modify the flat response to provide desired trade-offs between signal-to-noise ratio, time sidelobes, and resolution performance. An example of the amplitude response of a (raised cosine) weighting filter is illustrated in Fig. 4.17. Signal-to-noise degradation is shown in Fig. 4.18, where the bandpass response is that of the Gaussian-taper filter. It is assumed that no other band-limiting is applied. Reduction in signal-to-noise ratio, as compared with that for a lossless matched filter without weighting, approaches infinity for zero loss at the band edges and increases very slowly for increased weighting. Weighting can greatly reduce time sidelobes of the compressed pulse with a penalty of only slight degradation in resolution and signal-to-noise performance. We can see this for Gaussian weighting from Fig. 4.19, and for Gaussian and three other types of weighting from Fig. 4.20.

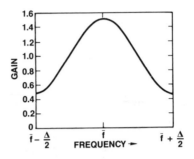

Fig. 4.17 Weighting Filter Amplitude Response (Raised Cosine) (From Klauder, J.R., *et al.,* "The Theory and Design of Chirp Radars," *Bell System Technical J.,* Vol. XXXIX, No. 4, July 1960, p. 782. Reprinted with permission.)

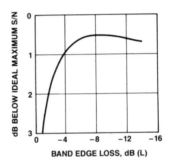

Fig. 4.18 Degradation in *S/N* from Ideal Maximum When the Rectangular Chirp Signal Passes through a Delay Equalizer and a Smooth, Gaussian-taper Filter, which Introduces a Loss of $L(L \leq 1.0)$ at the Band Edges (From Klauder, J.R., *et al.,* "The Theory and Design of Chirp Radars," *Bell System Technical J.,* Vol. XXXIX, No. 4, July 1960, p. 775. Reprinted with permission.)

4.6.4 Hardware Implementation

The above analysis for chirp-pulse compression is quite general and implementations differ greatly. Relatively narrowband pulse-compression radars normally use delay lines made of very thin strips of aluminum or steel to produce frequency-dispersed pulses. Dispersion occurs at so-called *acoustic wavelengths.* Longitudinal acoustic waves, propagated from one end of a properly designed strip, disperse nearly linearly over about a 10% bandwidth at, typically, 5–45 MHz. Such lines can be used for pulse

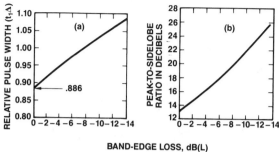

Fig. 4.19 (a) Increase in Half-Power Pulsewidth *versus* L ($L \le 1.0$), Where L is the Gaussian Filter Band-Edge Loss; (b) the Relative Amplitude between the Maximum of the First Adjacent Sidelobe and the Central Maximum of the Output Signal Following Shaping by a Gaussian Filter (From Klauder, J.R., *et al.*, "The Theory and Design of Chirp Radars," *Bell System Technical J.*, Vol. XXXIX, No. 4, July 1960, p. 776. Reprinted with permission.)

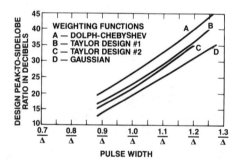

Fig. 4.20 Pulse Widening due to Weighting (From Klauder, J.R., *et al.*, "The Theory and Design of Chirp Radars," *Bell System Technical J.*, Vol. XXXIX, No. 4, July 1960, p. 784. Reprinted with permission.)

compression by translating the radar echo signal to an IF signal, then transducing to acoustic vibrations at one end of the line. The compressed output signal is transduced back to a signal voltage at the other end of the line for display or threshold comparison in a detection circuit. Bandwidths for these types of devices are limited to less than about 20 MHz, hardly in the category of HRR radar as discussed in this book. Transmitted signals have been actively generated to match the pulse-compression line and passively generated by driving a dispersive line with a very short video pulse to match the pulse-compression line. A number of relatively narrowband devices have also been developed to use nondispersive acoustic media. In this case, the dispersion is achieved by arrangement of electric-to-acoustic signal transducer lines on the surface of the medium.

Early work with HRR radar was carried out by taking advantage of the frequency-dispersive characteristics of waveguides, both to generate wideband FM chirp pulses and to compress the received echo signals. A disadvantage is the requirement for long lengths of heavy and bulky waveguide. To produce differential delay over chirp-pulse durations greater than about 0.05 µs requires impractically long lengths of guide. Smaller dispersive devices have been developed for HRR systems since the earlier use of waveguides. One such device is the *folded tape meander line* (FTML) [7]. In this device, a conducting tape is folded back and forth onto itself with dielectric spacers between the folds. The entire line is immersed in dielectric. Ground planes are placed above and below the line. The number of folds, their length, and spacing of the folds and ground-plane combine to determine the desired dispersive delay characteristic. An example, shown in Fig. 4.21, was used in an early US Navy experimental radar [8] to compress 0.3 µs pulses to 2.0 ns. This FTML required an amplitude-equalization filter. A combined equalization and weighting filter, shown in Fig. 4.22, was one type that was used [9]. Performance is shown in Fig. 4.23.

Fig. 4.21 Folded-Tape Meander-Line Type of Phase Equalization Filter

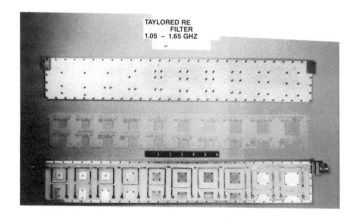

Fig. 4.22 Amplitude Weighting and Equalization Filter (From Wehner, D.R., "Tailored Response Microwave Filter," *IEEE Trans. Microwave Theory and Techniques,* Vol. MTT-17, No. 2, Feb. 1969, p. 116. Reprinted with permission.)

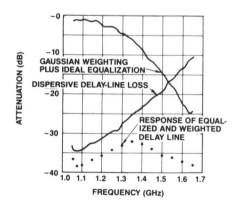

Fig. 4.23 Amplitude Equalization and Weighting Filter Performance (From Wehner, D.R., "Tailored Response Microwave Filter," *IEEE Trans. Microwave Theory and Techniques,* Vol. MTT-17, No. 2, Feb. 1969, p. 116. Reprinted with permission.)

More recently, various types of *surface acoustic wave* devices (Fig. 4.24) and *bulk acoustic wave* devices have been developed, which are capable of time-bandwidth products of more than 5000 and bandwidths greater than 1000 MHz. These are usually very small devices, which can be easily duplicated once they have been designed. The use of FTML devices and waveguides for phase equalization has now become outmoded due to these later developments.

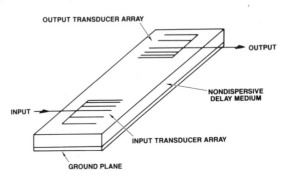

Fig. 4.24 Surface Acoustic Wave (SAW) Dispersive Delay Line

The transmitted chirp pulse can be generated passively or actively, as indicated in Fig. 4.25(a) and 4.25(b), respectively. The choice of technique depends upon several criteria. Passive generation is reliable and the pulse-expansion filter can be identical to the pulse-compression filter if the expansion is done at an IF and then mixed upward to the transmitted RF. Hence, the identical filter will perform pulse compression in the receiver at the opposite IF sideband. Passive generation of the transmitted pulse, however, is not always easy to achieve for HRR because losses are high and circuits may be too delicate for an impulse of sufficient power to achieve a reasonable output signal-to-noise ratio. The passive method also lacks the advantage of the active chirp method, which permits adjustment of the chirp slope to correct for quadratic phase distortion (to be discussed below) in waveguides or from other components. Active generation, on the other hand, requires a highly linear delay *versus* frequency slope that may be difficult to achieve for large time-bandwidth products.

A passive pulse-expansion filter impulse must be generated with either a video or RF pulse containing broadband energy spread over the bandwidth of the desired chirp signal. A video pulse and its spectrum are illustrated in Fig. 4.26. Of interest is the flatness of the video pulse spectrum across the bandwidth Δ centered at $\bar{f}$, the chirp-pulse center frequency.

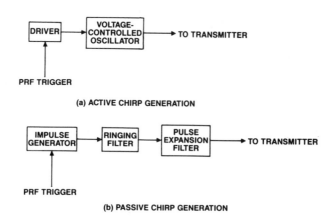

Fig. 4.25 Passive and Active Chirp Generation

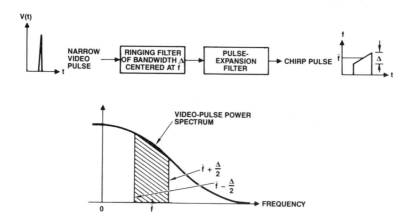

Fig. 4.26 Video Pulse and Video Pulse Spectrum for Passive Chirp Generation

Variations in power over the bandwidth Δ of the video-pulse spectrum for a linear system translate to variation in power over the chirp-pulse delay extent. The required flatness can be estimated on the basis of paired-echo theory. For example, signal variation across Δ must be less than $\pm.5$ dB, based on Fig. 3.3(b) of Chapter 3, to ensure that time sidelobes introduced by the spectral power slope are less than 30 dB below the peak response. Actual degradation would be less for a frequency-weighted system because of the reduced effect of a deviation from flatness at the band edges.

A ringing filter is often used to provide a better match between the video pulse and the pulse-expansion filter. More useful RF power is thereby available from the filter than can be acquired directly from the video pulse for a given pulse power level. Typically, the expansion filter is limited in its peak input voltage, but must be driven as hard as possible short of voltage breakdown in order to obtain an adequate signal-to-noise ratio output. The ringing filter provides a 6 dB advantage in this regard over the direct impulse because its RF drive power for the same peak voltage is 6 dB higher than the unipolar video-pulse drive power.

4.6.5 Quadratic Phase Distortion

The phase and amplitude ripple seen in a pulse-compression radar will produce distortion of the compressed signal in the form of paired echoes, as discussed in Chapter 3. Another source of distortion that is unique to chirp waveforms is called *quadratic phase distortion,* which is produced by any quadratic phase *versus* delay deviation from that associated with the matched chirp slope. The distortion can be produced by either slope error in the generated chirp signal or dispersive components (other than the phase equalizer), including RF transmission lines in the radar system. Figure 4.27 illustrates deviation from linear phase *versus* frequency produced by unwanted dispersion in the radar system.

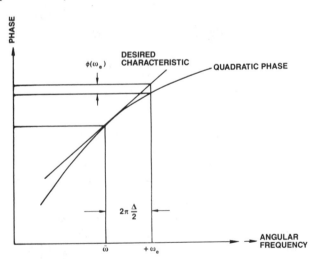

Fig. 4.27 Quadratic Phase (Shown as Phase Deviation from Center Frequency to the High End of the Band over which Pulse Compression is to be Carried Out)

The ideal transfer function for phase equalization of a chirp waveform, given in (4.5), can be written in terms of chirp pulse length T_1 and dispersion factor D as

$$H(f) = \exp j\frac{\pi T_1^2}{D}(f - \bar{f})^2$$

This transfer function has the *desired* quadratic phase characteristic, which, expressed in angular frequency, becomes

$$\phi(\omega) = \frac{T_1^2}{4\pi D}(\omega - \bar{\omega})^2$$

where ω is the instantaneous angular frequency and $\bar{\omega}$ is the center angular frequency. The desired instantaneous chirp delay, written in terms of angular frequency, becomes

$$\tau_g(\omega) = -\frac{d\phi}{d\omega} = -\frac{T_1^2}{2\pi D}(\omega - \bar{\omega}) \tag{4.11}$$

which is another form of (4.6). Similar expressions for *undesired* quadratic phase and equivalent delay error are

$$\phi(\omega) = \frac{1}{2}T_0^2(\omega - \bar{\omega})^2 \tag{4.12}$$

and

$$\tau_d(\omega) = -\frac{d\phi}{d\omega} = -T_0^2(\omega - \bar{\omega}) \tag{4.13}$$

where T_0^2 is a constant. We can see that the delay error expressed in (4.13) is of the same form as (4.11) for delay associated with a chirp matched filter. Angular frequency ω in rad/s instead of frequency f in Hz will be used henceforth in connection with unwanted quadratic phase error so as to distinguish from the desired phase and delay *versus* frequency characteristics of the chirp signal.

With no weighting, the main response and sidelobe structure of a compressed pulse are degraded with quadratic phase error as low as $\phi = \pi/8$ rad. On heavily weighted pulses, values of $\phi = \pi$ can be tolerated with less than ~1.5 dB loss in peak response and less than 38 dB sidelobes [1].

Chirp waveforms are often used with waveguide radar systems. The waveguide, if its group delay is assumed to vary linearly with frequency over the band of interest, produces quadratic phase error that can be corrected by adjusting the transmitted FM slope. Quadratic phase error, evaluated at the band edges $\pm f_e$ of the chirp pulse, from (4.12), becomes

$$\phi(\omega_e) = \pi^2 \frac{T_0^2(\Delta)^2}{2} \text{ rad}$$

where

$$\Delta = 2\left|(f_e - \bar{f})\right| = \frac{1}{\pi}\left|(\omega_e - \bar{\omega})\right|$$

The constant T_0^2 in terms of band-edge phase error then becomes

$$T_0^2 = \frac{2}{\pi^2\Delta^2}\,\phi(\omega_e)$$

The magnitude of the resulting delay error at either band edge $\pm\omega_e$, from (4.13), is

$$
\begin{aligned}
\left|\tau_d(\omega_e)\right| &= T_0^2\left|(\omega_e - \bar{\omega})\right| \\
&= T_0^2\pi\Delta
\end{aligned}
$$

By substituting for T_0^2, we have

$$\left|\tau_d(\omega_e)\right| = \frac{2\phi(\omega_e)}{\pi\Delta}$$

Total chirp delay error over the entire band Δ (in Hz) is

$$2\left|\tau_d(\omega_e)\right| = \frac{4\phi(\omega_e)}{\pi\Delta}$$

Figure 4.28 from Cook and Bernfeld [10] shows calculated curves for pulse widening and amplitude degradation as a function of mismatched time-bandwidth factor $2|\tau_d(\omega_e)|\Delta$ for compressed pulses weighted for -36 dB sidelobes.

For the 30 m length of WR-284 waveguide referred to in Chapter 3, the phase deviation is $(6.8°/\text{m}) \times (30\text{ m}) \approx 200°$. If a pulse-compression filter is originally matched to a 400 MHz chirp pulse, the chirp delay error introduced by this length of waveguide is

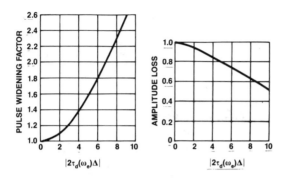

Fig. 4.28 Pulse Widening and Amplitude Loss of Mismatched Chirp Pulse with Weighting (From Cook, C.E., and M. Bernfeld, *Radar Signals*, New York: Academic Press, 1967, p. 159. Reprinted with permission.)

$$2|\tau_d(\omega_e)| = \frac{4 \cdot 200 \cdot \dfrac{2\pi}{360}}{\pi \cdot 400 \cdot 10^6}$$

$$= .011 \ \mu s$$

Quadratic distortion produced by the 30 m of waveguide length could be equalized by decreasing the chirp-pulse duration by $2|\tau_d(\omega_e)| = .011 \ \mu s$ with the same chirp bandwidth, as indicated in Fig. 4.29. The reader will recall that, because the instantaneous delay of the waveguide approximates a linear delay *versus* frequency function, the waveguide can be used for passive generation of HRR chirp waveforms, but impractical lengths of waveguide are needed to obtain significant energy transmitted per pulse.

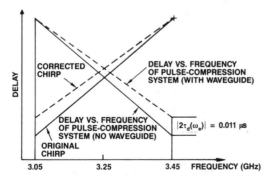

Fig. 4.29 Waveguide Quadratic Distortion Correction by FM Slope Adjustment (for Slope Error Produced by 30 m of WR-284 Waveguide)

4.7 DIGITAL PULSE COMPRESSION

The chirp-pulse compression process can also be carried out digitally on echo data sampled at baseband. Pulse compression was described above in terms of the mathematical process of convolution. Likewise, digital pulse compression is also a convolutional process. A digitized version of the echo pulse at baseband is convolved with a digitized reference function that corresponds to the matched filter's impulse response function. Digital convolution, however, employs a discrete Fourier transform process equivalent to convolution. The process is sometimes called *fast convolution.* Although more complex, it is faster than direct convolution because of efficiencies obtained by using *fast Fourier transform* (FFT) algorithms. The DFT equivalent to convolution can be described in terms of the convolution theorem, which relates the convolution expression and its Fourier transform. This is a very important relationship for many areas of engineering and scientific analysis. It states that the Fourier transform of the convolution of one function with another is the product of the Fourier transform of the first function multiplied by the Fourier transform of the second function. The convolution theorem, in terms of an input echo signal $s_i(t)$ and the impulse response $h(t)$ of the matched filter, is expressed as

$$FT[s_i(t) * h(t)] = S_i(f) H(f)$$

Thus, convolution in the time domain can be carried out by multiplication in the frequency domain. The quantity $S_i(f)$ is the spectrum of the echo signal from one transmitted pulse. The transfer function $H(f)$ is the Fourier transform of the impulse response of the matched filter.

Following each transmitted pulse, the echo signal in each quadrature channel out of a quadrature mixer is sampled at or above the Nyquist rate, which is Δ complex samples per second for chirp bandwidth Δ. Sampling is carried out over some desired range window corresponding to the target-range extent to be processed. Each sample is converted into digital quantities by using analog-to-digital techniques. The result is a digitized complex-range profile, one profile from each transmitted pulse. This is the input range data. The discrete version of the matched filter's transfer function (also called *reference function*) can be stored directly as a series of digitized complex pairs. This transfer function will remain constant for a particular chirp waveform.

Pulse compression, regardless of the method, convolves the received echo signal, after appropriate down-conversion, with a matched-filter reference function. For analog pulse compression, the convolution process is accomplished by simply passing the echo signal through a physical matched filter and an appropriate weighting filter. For digital pulse compression, the convolution process could be carried out by convolving each digitized range profile with a digitized matched-filter impulse response as a reference function. If fast convolution is used, the digitized range data are convolved as shown in Fig. 4.30 by first transforming to the frequency domain, then vector multiplying with the discrete version of the transfer function $H(f)$, and, finally, transforming back to the time-domain, which gives the compressed range data.

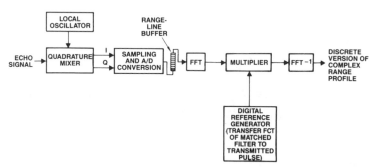

Fig. 4.30 Digital Pulse Compression

Use of the convolution theorem for digital pulse compression is based upon using the DFT as an approximation to the continuous Fourier transform. The DFT process transforms n discrete values spaced by Δt in the time domain into n discrete values spaced by $\Delta f = 1/(n\Delta t)$ in the frequency domain. In shorthand notation, the convolution response becomes

$$DFT[s_i(l\Delta t) * h(l\Delta t)] = S_i(i\Delta f) \cdot H(i\Delta f)$$

Both functions $s_i(l\Delta t)$ and $h(l\Delta t)$ are periodic with the same period $n\Delta t$ s. Because the DFT process is periodic, discrete versions of the input echo signal and impulse response function are required to be generated such that the resulting periodic response is a replica of the desired aperiodic result.

Consider first the analog process illustrated in Fig. 4.31 for the pulse compression of the input signal produced by two point targets, which appear within an assumed radar-range extent as shown. The rectangular waveforms of Fig. 4.31 represent envelopes of the transmitted and echo signals. An analog chirp waveform is represented in Fig. 4.31(a). The input signal is represented in Fig. 4.31(b) along with the radar's matched-filter impulse response. Figure 4.31(c) represents the compressed signal pro-

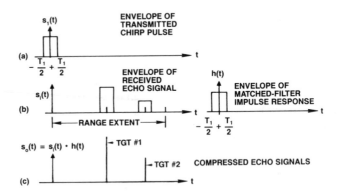

Fig. 4.31 Analog Pulse Compression (Example for Two Targets)

duced by convolving the input signal with the matched-filter impulse response. Convolution for analog signals is carried out by passing the input signal through a matched filter realized in hardware—for example, a surface acoustic wave (SAW) device.

Now, consider the digital pulse-compression process illustrated in Fig. 4.32. The transmitted chirp signal $s_1(t)$ of Fig. 4.32(a) and the received baseband signal $s_i(t)$ and matched-filter impulse response $h(t)$ of Fig. 4.32(b) are respectively identical to those of Fig. 4.31(a) and 4.31(b). Figure 4.32(c) illustrates discrete versions of both the received signal and matched-filter responses. A common period length n must be set sufficiently large that the convolutional result of one period does not overlap that of the succeeding period. This is achieved by applying the following rule to the discrete versions of both $s_i(t)$ and $h(t)$:

$$n \geq \frac{T_1 + \dfrac{2(R_2 - R_1)}{c}}{\Delta t} - 1 \qquad (4.14)$$

Zeros are added to the echo data samples and to the $T_1/\Delta t$ samples of the impulse response function, as shown in Fig. 4.32(c), to produce the common period of length n. At this point, the two resulting data sets of Fig. 4.32(c) could be convolved to produce the compressed signal. However, use of the convolution theorem carried out by the FFT algorithm for the DFT, although not shown, is implied. The DFTs of $s_i(i\Delta t)$ and $h(i\Delta t)$ can be defined, respectively, as follows:

$$S_i(i\Delta f) = \sum_{l=0}^{n-1} s_i(l\Delta t) \exp\left(-j\frac{2\pi}{n}il\right), \quad 0 \leq i \leq n - 1 \qquad (4.15)$$

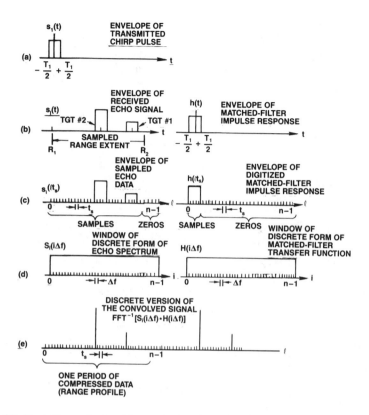

Fig. 4.32 Fast Convolution Example for Two Targets

and

$$H(i\Delta f) = \sum_{l=0}^{n-1} h(l\Delta t) \exp\left(-j\frac{2\pi}{n}il\right), \quad 0 \le i \le n-1 \qquad (4.16)$$

where

$$\Delta f = \frac{1}{n\Delta t}$$

The FFT algorithm calculates (4.15) and (4.16) for values of

$$n = 2^\gamma \qquad (4.17)$$

where γ is an integer. Equation (4.17) imposes a second requirement on the selection of n when the convolution theorem is to be applied with the FFT algorithm to generate the compressed signal. The first requirement, (4.14), applies whether or not the FFT type of DFT is used. A third requirement in the selection of n is that the sampling rate f_s equal or exceed the Nyquist sampling rate, which is related to the chirp bandwidth Δ. The Nyquist requirement is expressed as

$$f_s \geq 2\Delta \tag{4.18}$$

This last criterion can be met by taking complex samples at baseband, spaced by $1/\Delta$.

Application of (4.15) and (4.16) by using the FFT algorithm produces the discrete versions of the echo spectrum $S_i(i\Delta f)$ and matched-filter transfer function $H(i\Delta f)$, illustrated in Fig. 4.32(d). Next, these quantities are vector multiplied to form the frequency spectrum of the pulse-compressed output. The final step is to perform the inverse (frequency-to-time) fast Fourier transform (FFT^{-1}) of the output frequency spectrum to obtain the output range-delay response. Of interest is the response made up of the first n discrete values $l = 0$ through $n - 1$. This result, illustrated in Fig. 4.32(e), replicates that of Fig. 4.31(c) for analog pulse compression when the criteria expressed in (4.14), (4.17), and (4.18) are met. Table 4.2 lists minimum acceptable values of period length n *versus* both sampling interval and length of signal plus chirp pulse.

Convolution and correlation by using the FFT are described in more detail by O.E. Bringham [11].

Table 4.2 Minimum Acceptable Period Lengths for Discrete Convolution (Assuming Complex Sampling)

Chirp Pulse Length plus Sampled Range-Delay Extent, $T_1 + \dfrac{2(R_2 - R_1)}{c}$	*Minimum Acceptable Period Length n versus Sampling Interval,* Δt						
	1	2	5	10	20	50	Δt (ns)$\rightarrow$
10 ns	16	4	2				
20 ns	32	16	4	2			
50 ns	64	32	16	4	2		
100 ns	128	64	32	16	4	2	
200 ns	256	128	64	32	16	4	
500 ns	512	256	128	64	32	16	
1 μs	1024	512	256	128	64	32	

4.8 DISTORTION PRODUCED BY TARGET RADIAL MOTION

Up to this point, our analysis of methods for obtaining HRR performance from radar systems has assumed a stationary target. Doppler shift produced by target radial velocity, however, reduces peak response and degrades resolution. The nature of this distortion is probably best studied from the behavior of the ambiguity function. Two ideal waveforms will be considered: the *short monotone pulse* and *linear FM (chirp) pulse.* Expressions for the rectangular envelopes of the two waveforms are

$$s_1(t) = \sqrt{\frac{1}{T_1}} \ \text{rect} \left(\frac{t}{T_1} \right) \tag{4.19}$$

for the monotone pulse, and

$$s_1(t) = \sqrt{\frac{1}{T_1}} \ \text{rect} \left(\frac{t}{T_1} \right) \exp \ (j2\pi K t^2/2) \tag{4.20}$$

for the chirp pulse. The term rect (t/T_1) is defined as for (4.1). The waveforms are normalized according to the expression:

$$\int_{-\infty}^{\infty} |s_1(t)|^2 dt = 1$$

This has the result that the ambiguity surface has unit height at the origin. The ambiguity functions for the rectangular monotone and rectangular chirp pulses are determined from (3.19) together with (4.19) and (4.20). Results are expressed as follows:

$$|\chi(\tau, f_D)| = \left| \left(1 - \frac{|\tau|}{T_1} \right) \frac{\sin \ [\pi f_D T_1 (1 - |\tau|/T_1)]}{\pi f_D T_1 (1 - |\tau|/T_1)} \right|, \quad |\tau| < T_1$$
$$= 0, \qquad\qquad\qquad\qquad\qquad\qquad\qquad\qquad |\tau| > T_1 \tag{4.21}$$

for the monotone pulse, and

$$|\chi(\tau, f_D)| = \left| \left(1 - \frac{|\tau|}{T_1} \right) \frac{\sin \ [\pi (K\tau + f_D)(T_1 - |\tau|)]}{\pi (K\tau + f_D)(T_1 - |\tau|)} \right|, \quad |\tau| < T_1$$
$$= 0, \qquad\qquad\qquad\qquad\qquad\qquad\qquad\qquad\qquad |\tau| > T_1 \tag{4.22}$$

for the chirp pulse, where τ is the delay relative to the origin and f_D is the

Doppler shift produced by the moving target. Critical features of the ambiguity functions, (4.21) and (4.22), can be discussed with reference to Figs. 4.33 and 4.34. In each case, the ambiguity surface extends from $-T_1$ to $+T_1$ in range delay and $-\infty$ to $+\infty$ in Doppler. Doppler frequency response at zero delay points have $(\sin x)/x$ profiles for both the FM and monotone pulses. Also, the responses for both monotone and FM pulses are maximum at matched delay and Doppler shift points $\tau = 0$ and $f_D =$

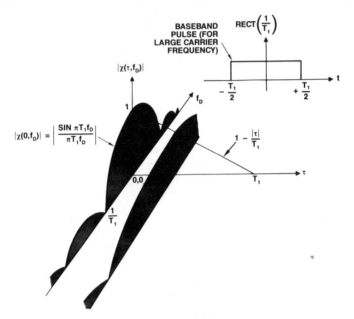

Fig. 4.33 Ambiguity Function for Rectangular Monotone Pulse

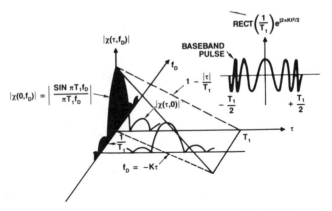

Fig. 4.34 Ambiguity Function for Rectangular Chirp Pulse

0, respectively. Range-delay resolution is optimum at $f_D = 0$ and the response broadens as $|f_D|$ increases.

A distinctive feature of the FM-pulse ambiguity function is its range-Doppler coupling characteristic. A Doppler shift produces a range-delay shift in the response. Profiles parallel to the Doppler axis for FM pulses maximize above the line $f_D = -K\tau$ through the origin of the f_D, τ coordinates. Profiles for the monotone pulses, by comparison, are maximized above the $f_D = 0$ axis.

It is clear from Figs. 4.33 and 4.34 that, for either monotone or FM pulses, the pulse duration T_1 determines tolerance to Doppler shift. Response to a target observed with a monotone pulse degrades with target radial velocity. Resolution is reduced and sidelobes increase. The peak of the zero-Doppler response occurring at a given range delay is seen to go to zero at $f_D = 1/T_1$, and at that Doppler frequency the range-delay response bears no resemblance to the matched response at zero Doppler. By contrast, the chirp waveform is *Doppler-invariant*. Location of the peak shifts with Doppler frequency, but the response remains relatively unaffected well beyond $f_D = 1/T_1$.

4.9 DISPLAY, RECORDING, AND PREPROCESSING OF HRR ECHOES

For simple viewing of a target's HRR profile, the RF echo pulses can be envelope-detected and then displayed on a wideband oscilloscope activated by a range-delay trigger pulse. The detector and oscilloscope's phase and amplitude characteristics then become part of the total system transfer function. Distortion, in terms of decreased resolution and time sidelobes, occurs in the manner discussed for RF components in Chapter 3. However, wideband video detectors and oscilloscopes are available today with sufficiently flat amplitude response and low phase ripple to view target range profiles obtained with greater than 500 MHz bandwidth.

Display can be achieved by connecting the wideband video output to the y-axis of a wideband oscilloscope. The horizontal sweep is set to move across the x-axis during the time interval associated with the range window to be observed. The result is an *A-scope display* of the target's range-profile signature. A range-delay trigger pulse starts the range window. The horizontal sweep time sets the extent of the range window delay. Range-delay jitter must be about an order of magnitude better than the range resolution; otherwise, blur will appear on the A-scope display.

Jitter-free range-delay trigger pulses to track moving targets can be generated by the circuit shown in Fig. 4.35. A stable oscillator, followed by shaping and divider circuits, generates the radar's PRF. A *voltage-*

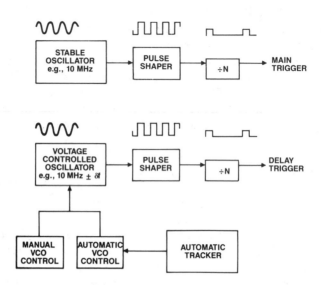

Fig. 4.35 Range Tracker for HRR Radar

controlled oscillator (VCO), in the form of a second stable oscillator, is adjusted in frequency slightly above and below the first oscillator to generate a variable delay trigger. The delay is continuously set to track the target as it moves in range delay. Manual range tracking is carried out by setting the VCO voltage drive so that a delay starts the oscilloscope sweep just ahead of the arrival of the target's range-profile echo. An earlier version of a range tracker used a motor-driven phase shifter, as shown in Fig. 4.36, to generate the delay trigger from a single fixed oscillator.

High-range-resolution target range profiles, as viewed on an oscilloscope, have had some limited value. Early work in the 1960s at the Naval Ocean Systems Center (NOSC), San Diego, demonstrated that air and ship targets were largely made up of individual backscatter sources. Targets were found to be easily tracked through severe land clutter by manually tracking the target's range profile as it "moved through" a clutter background producing much higher return. It was also apparent that the range-profile *signatures* were unique to target type within a limited range of target aspect angles. Sea clutter showed up as individual scatterers (called *spikes*), which appeared and disappeared with lifetimes on the order of three to five seconds.

Recording of HRR target or clutter signatures was originally done at NOSC by photographing the A-scope display. It was soon found necessary to develop a digital recording capability in order to obtain suitable data for analysis to determine *target recognition* potential. Later, *clutter analysis* was also carried out by using digitized data.

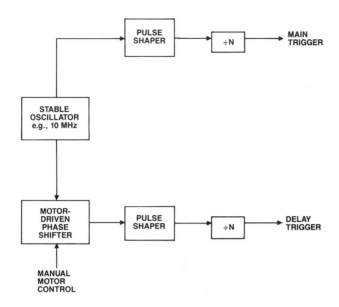

Fig. 4.36 Range Tracker for HRR Radar Using a Motor-Driven Phase
Shifter

The digitizing of short-pulse or pulse-compression data requires
samples of the detected envelope of the range profile at range intervals
separated by an amount equal to or less than the compressed pulse duration. For a 500 MHz pulse-compression radar, for example, the compressed pulse duration will be about two nanoseconds. This corresponds
to a sampling rate of 500×10^6 samples per second. As of this writing,
sampling and A/D conversion at these rates are still in the development
phase. Usually, dynamic range is limited to less than six binary bits when
sampling above about 200×10^6 samples per second.

An early method used at NOSC to circumvent this problem employed
a *serial sampling system* closely related to the design of wideband sampling
oscilloscopes. The concept is to sample the target signature at the radar's
PRF while advancing the sample position of each pulse. In this way, the
entire signature is sampled during n radar pulses, where n is the number
of samples that comprise the desired range window. The technique provides sampling of wide dynamic range for those target signature features
that do not vary significantly during n radar pulses. Range tracking was
carried out as described above.

As data are sampled in this way they can be converted to digital
values over a wide dynamic range with a relatively low speed A/D converter. This serial sampling method was used to collect aircraft and ship

signature data from a ground site at NOSC. The technique was used to collect the first dynamic HRR signature measurements of ships and aircraft targets in motion. A block diagram of the sampling system is shown in Fig. 4.37. Also shown in the figure is a second sampling mode that is able to collect samples from a selected modulating portion of the range-profile video signature. In both modes, only one sample of the signature is obtained for each radar pulse. The serial sampling technique, therefore, "throws away" signal energy, which, if sampled, could provide a higher output signal-to-noise ratio.

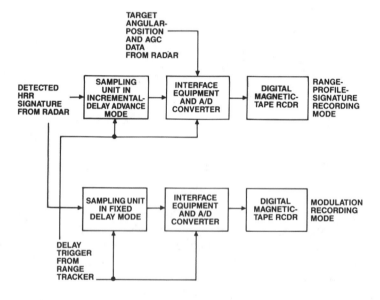

Fig. 4.37 Target Signature and Modulation Recording (Serial Sampling)

The problems of sampling, digitizing, and processing HRR signatures obtained in the time domain remain formidable for resolution less than about five feet. For this reason, frequency-domain sampling techniques have been developed, such as for stretch and synthetic range-profile generation, which provide increased resolution over that possible with present technology for direct sampling of the compressed pulses.

Examples of HRR signatures are shown in Figs. 4.38, 4.39, and 4.40. Figures 4.38 and 4.39 were obtained by photographing range profiles appearing on a wideband CRT. Figure 4.40 was obtained by using the range-profile recording system of Fig. 4.37.

Fig. 4.38 HRR Signature of T-28 at S Band (1.0 ft Resolution, Nose Aspect)

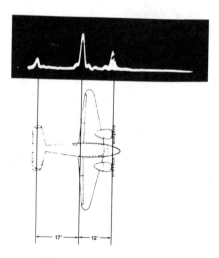

Fig. 4.39 HRR Signature of C-45 Aircraft at S Band (1.0 ft Resolution, Tail Aspect)

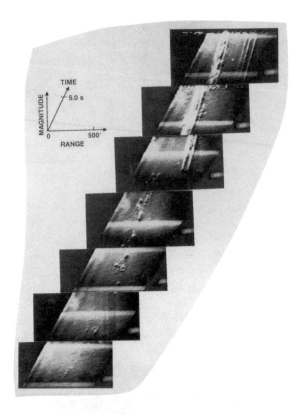

Fig. 4.40 HRR Signatures of Diving Diesel Submarine Collected at S Band
Using the Range-Profile Recording System of Fig. 4.37

PROBLEMS

4.1   Show that $H(f) = e^{-\pi f^2}$ is the correct expression for the transfer function of the matched filter to a Gaussian-shaped video waveform expressed as

$$s_1(t) = e^{-\pi t^2}$$

4.2   A filter that has a rectangular bandpass filter characteristic of bandwidth β and center frequency $\bar{f}$ is driven by an ideal impulse. Use the Fourier shift theorem to show that the complex expression for the normalized output signal is given by

$$s_o(t) = e^{j2\pi \bar{f} t} \frac{\sin \pi \beta t}{\beta \pi t}$$

Assume $\bar{f} \gg \beta$.

4.3 What are the peak sidelobe levels in dB of the envelope of the output pulse of Prob. 4.2?

4.4 Determine the half-power temporal resolution of the envelope of the monotone Gaussian pulse expressed by

$$s(t) = e^{-\pi t^2} e^{j2\pi \bar{f} t}$$

Assume resolution $\gg 1/\bar{f}$.

4.5 A Gaussian-shaped waveform is represented by

$$s_1(t) = \frac{1}{\sigma \sqrt{2\pi}} e^{-t^2/(2\sigma^2)} e^{j2\pi \bar{f} t}$$

(a) What is the duration of the pulse envelope in terms of σ at the half-peak points? (b) What is the range resolution associated with this RF pulse at the half-peak points for $\sigma = 2.0$ ns? Assume resolution $\gg 1/\bar{f}$.

4.6 (a) What is the achievable compression ratio of a 5.0 μs, 32 bit binary phase-coded pulse waveform? (b) What is the range resolution? (c) What is the waveform bandwidth?

4.7 (a) Write the complex expression for the baseband form of the waveform illustrated in Fig. 4.4. (b) Write the expression for its matched filter.

4.8 Using a block diagram like Fig. 4.5, show that the binary phase-coded Barker code $+ + + - +$ has a peak response of $+5$ and peak-to-sidelobe ratio of $+14$ dB.

4.9 Show that as the number of frequency steps n in a contiguous, discrete frequency-coded waveform approaches infinity, the envelope of the matched-filtered response near the peak approaches that of a compressed chirp pulse of the same bandwidth. Assume both waveforms are matched-filtered but unweighted and that the frequency-segment length T_1 is equal to the reciprocal of the frequency-step size.

4.10 Show that the pulse-compression ratio of an n-element discrete frequency-coded pulse following matched-filter processing is approximately n^2 for large n when the frequency-segment length T_1 is equal to the reciprocal of the frequency-step size.

4.11 A radar is to be designed for five-foot (1.524 m) range resolution. What are the required clock rates to generate the discrete delay segments of (a) a phase-coded waveform, and (b) a 32-element, contiguous, stepped frequency-coded waveform, where segment duration equals the reciprocal of frequency-step size? (Either coded pulses or periodic waveforms may be assumed.)

4.12 We want to use a periodic stepped frequency-coded waveform for unambiguous resolution of isolated targets of up to 300 m in length with 10 m resolution. Assume uniformly stepped frequencies in each period with step size set equal to the reciprocal of frequency-step duration. (a) What is the total bandwidth required? (b) What is the frequency-step size if frequency-step duration is matched to target length? (c) What is the waveform period in number of steps? (d) What is the waveform period in seconds?

4.13 A radar transmits 100 μs pulses, each with a linear FM of 250 MHz over the pulse duration. Compression is to be accomplished using stretch processing by first mixing the echo signal with a reference having an identical FM slope. What is the time-bandwidth product of the signal before and after mixing? Assume a point target.

4.14 A stretch waveform is used to obtain signatures of space objects from earth-based radar stations. The waveform consists of 100 μs chirp pulses with 500 MHz bandwidth. Echo signals are processed as in Prob. 4.13 by mixing with a LO that is a replica of the reference to the transmitted signal. What is the total bandwidth seen at IF when a 30 m target is to be observed?

4.15 A monotone-pulse radar has a pulse duration of 5.0 μs. (a) What is its approximate slant-range resolution? (b) If the radar were redesigned so that the same pulse envelope is frequency modulated with linear FM over 100 MHz, what is the new range resolution? (c) What is the time-bandwidth product in each case?

4.16 What is the approximate frequency-modulation bandwidth across a single compressed chirp pulse of dispersion $D = 100$ and pulse duration 2.0 ns.

4.17 A pulse-compression radar transmits a rectangular chirp pulse with 500 MHz bandwidth. What is the approximate slant-range resolution after Dolph-Chebyschev frequency weighting that results in 30 dB sidelobes?

4.18 With reference to the MacColl paired-echo analysis, compute the amplitude deviation in a pulse-compression radar system if the sidelobes of the output response are to be at least 46 dB below the peak. Assume no phase distortion. Amplitude deviation is defined here as $(1 + a_1/a_0)$, expressed in dB. Calculate from the equations, then compare with Fig. 3.3(b) of Chapter 3.

4.19 A pulse-compression filter for a radar has a time-bandwidth product of 80. Two methods of chirp generation are being considered: (1) active generation with a VCO that produces a rectangular-envelope chirp, and (2) passive generation by an impulse of a dispersive filter of the same time-bandwidth product. Assuming equal losses and no weighting in each method, use Fig. 4.16 to compare the optimum signal-to-noise ratio performance.

4.20 A 2.0 μs chirp pulse with chirp slope $K = 5 \times 10^{13}$ Hz/s undergoes pulse compression in a phase equalizer exhibiting a delay *versus* frequency slope of $P = 0.2 \times 10^{-13}$ s/Hz, followed by a Gaussian weighting filter of 100 MHz bandwidth at the -8 dB points. No other band-limiting is involved. (a) What is the chirp-pulse FM bandwidth? (b) What is the degradation in signal-to-noise ratio from that of an ideal filter matched to the chirp pulse? (c) What is the compressed pulse duration at the half-power points? (d) What are the peak-to-sidelobe levels? Use Figs. 4.18 and 4.19.

4.21 The pulse-compression receiver of a chirp-pulse radar is matched to a transmitted 10 μs linear FM pulse of 200 MHz bandwidth centered at 3.25 GHz. The only source of distortion is 60 m of WR-284 waveguide. (a) What is the approximate band-edge phase deviation from the best linear fit, based on Table 3.2 of Chapter 3? (b) What is the equivalent chirp-delay error? (c) What is the fractional pulse widening and amplitude loss based on Fig. 4.28? (d) What new pulse length of the same bandwidth is required to equalize the quadratic error produced by the waveguide?

4.22 Show that if $\phi(\omega_e) = \pi$ is the maximum tolerable phase deviation at the band edges of a chirp pulse, then the fractional time-delay mismatch requirements for active chirp generation can be expressed as

$$\frac{|T_1 - T_1'|}{|T_1|} = \frac{4}{T_1\Delta}$$

where $|T_1 - T_1'|$ is the allowable delay mismatch over the chirp bandwidth Δ of pulse length T_1.

4.23 What is the maximum tolerable fractional-delay mismatch, based on the criterion of Prob. 4.22 for the active chirp generation of a 20 μs pulse with 200:1 compression ratio.

4.24 A chirp pulse is to be generated by an impulse to 100 m of WR-284 waveguide. The output of the waveguide is filtered by a 400 MHz rectangular filter, band centered at 3.25 GHz. From Table 3.2 of Chapter 3 and the discussion of quadratic phase distortion, what is the time-bandwidth product of the chirp pulse?

4.25 Gaussian weighting following ideal, unweighted equalization is used to reduce time sidelobes as seen by a 250 MHz chirp-pulse compression radar. Rectangular chirp pulses are transmitted. (a) What is the half-power compressed pulsewidth before weighting? (b) What is the half-power pulsewidth following Gaussian weighting to reduce peak sidelobes to 25 dB below the main response? (c) Assuming that no other band-limiting occurs, what is the S/N loss following weighting? Use Figs. 4.18 and 4.19.

4.26 What length of WR-159 air-filled waveguide ($f_c = 3.711 \times 10^9$ Hz) is required for chirp-pulse compression to produce 0.05 μs pulses of 500 MHz chirp bandwidth at 5.3 GHz center frequency? Compute delay based on the expression for the waveguide propagation constant given in Prob. 3.31 of Chapter 3.

4.27 Digital pulse compression of echo data produced by a 1.5 μs transmitted chirp waveform is to be carried out over a sampled range extent of 5.0 nmi (9260 m). The range-delay sample spacing is 10 ns. Assume that fast convolution is to be used to convolve each sampled block of range data with a digitized reference of the transmitted pulse. (a) What minimum common period length is required in terms of the number of complex samples? (b) How many zeros will be added to the time-domain samples of the signal data?

4.28 A 9.5 GHz pulse-compression radar transmits 10 μs chirp pulses. Resolution is 150 m. A target approaches the radar at a radial velocity of 300 m/s. What is the apparent range shift produced by the target's Doppler shift?

4.29   Detected HRR target range profiles are to be recorded digitally by using the serial sampling method described in Fig. 4.37 (range-profile-signature recording mode). What is the maximum allowable incremental-delay advance required for unambiguous sampling of the range profile data collected by using a chirp-pulse radar of 500 MHz bandwidth?

REFERENCES

1. Klauder, J.R., *et al.*, "The Theory and Design of Chirp Radars," *The Bell System Technical J.,* Vol. XXXIX, No. 4, July 1960, pp. 745–808.
2. Caputi, W.J., "Stretch: A Time-Transformation Technique," *IEEE Trans. Aerospace and Electronic Systems,* Vol. AES-7, No. 2, March 1971, pp. 269–278.
3. Cook, C.E., and M. Bernfeld, *Radar Signals,* New York: Academic Press, 1967, p. 245.
4. Kraus, J.D., *Antennas,* New York: McGraw-Hill, 1950, pp. 76–77.
5. Gradshteyn, I.S., and I.M. Ryzhik, *Tables of Integrals, Series and Products,* Fourth Edition (Translated from the Russian), 1965, New York: Academic Press, p. 397.
6. Campbell, G.A., and R.M. Foster, *Fourier Integrals for Practical Applications,* New York: D. Van Nostrand Company, 1942.
7. Cook, C.E., and M. Bernfeld, *Radar Signals,* New York: Academic Press, 1967, pp. 476–483.
8. Maynard, J.H., and B.F. Summers, "An Experimental High-Resolution Radar for Target-Signature Measurements," *Supplement to IEEE Trans. Aerospace and Electronic Systems,* Vol. AES-3, No. 6, Nov. 1967, pp. 249–256.
9. Wehner, D.R., "Tailored Response Microwave Filter," *IEEE Trans. Microwave Theory and Techniques,* Vol. MTT-17, No. 2, Feb. 1969, pp. 115–116.
10. Cook, C.E., and M. Bernfeld, *Radar Signals,* New York: Academic Press, 1967, p. 159.
11. Bringham, E.O., *The Fast Fourier Transform,* Englewood Cliffs, NJ: Prentice-Hall, 1974, Sec. 13.

Chapter 5
Synthetic High-Range-Resolution Radar

5.1 FREQUENCY-DOMAIN TARGET SIGNATURES

Any signal can be described as either a function of *time* or a function of *frequency*. The echo signal from a range-extended target illuminated by a short RF pulse usually is observed in the time domain. Its amplitude and phase *versus* frequency is the echo signal spectrum, which is a frequency-domain description of the signal. Because descriptions of a signal as functions of time and frequency are equivalent, the signal spectrum can be obtained from its time-domain response and *vice versa*. Thus, measurements of a target's echo signal in the time and frequency domains provide equivalent data for determining target reflectivity.

Consider first a radar that transmits short monotone pulses. The target's reflectivity profile in range delay can be defined as its echo signal amplitude and phase *versus* delay measured with respect to the carrier signal of the transmitted pulse. For pulse-compression radars, the output of the matched filter is approximately the same as the echo produced by a short RF pulse of the same bandwidth and transmitted at the same wavelength as the chirp pulse. In either case, a time-domain measurement of reflectivity produced by a single transmitted pulse is generated nearly instantaneously.

A continuous series of short RF pulses transmitted at a fixed pulse repetition frequency can be defined as a Fourier series of steady-state frequency components with a frequency spacing equal to the radar's PRF. Rather than transmitting the continuous train of short pulses, assume that all of the equivalent steady-state frequency components were transmitted. Then, the Fourier series of the received echoes at each frequency from a steady-state target would appear in the time domain as a periodic set of identical range profiles of period equal to the radar's PRI. The profiles would be identical to those produced by the train of short pulses, assuming identical radar and target geometry parameters. Reflectivity equivalent to that measured from the train of short pulses could be obtained from measurements of the amplitude and phase of the received Fourier series frequency components relative to the respective transmitted component. This set of frequency-domain measurements of reflectivity is the spectrum of the time-domain echo pulse train.

In practice, what we want is the HRR reflectivity profile of a target, not the periodic echo response. Therefore, frequency spacing can be the reciprocal of the target's range-delay extent, instead of the reciprocal of the radar's PRI. Also, the time duration of each transmitted frequency component need only be sufficient to produce an approximation to the steady-state echo response. This is achieved for a pulse duration that is somewhat greater than the target range-delay extent. As we will see in this chapter, if a series of RF pulses were transmitted stepped in frequency from pulse to pulse over a bandwidth β, the set of echo amplitude and phase measurements made relative to each transmitted pulse can be transformed by using the DFT into the range-profile equivalent of echo amplitude and phase measurements obtained relative to a short RF pulse of bandwidth β.

Thus far, the term *reflectivity* has been used to refer to the amplitude and phase of the echo response at a given viewing angle for a given set of radar parameters. Reflectivity in terms of radar cross section *versus* range delay could be measured by an ideal radar by using square-law detection of the echo signal power S, from (2.2) in Chapter 2. Absolute RCS of the target, in principle, could then be determined by solving for σ in terms of S and the other radar parameters of (2.2). Square-law detection responses from a short-pulse radar, in this way, could be converted to target-range profiles of target RCS *versus* range delay. An uncalibrated, but otherwise ideal, radar using square-law detection would generate profiles for which the signal is proportional to absolute RCS.

An envelope-detected range profile is illustrated in Fig. 5.1(a). Actual range-profile signatures from real targets appeared in Figs. 4.38, 4.39, and 4.40 of Chapter 4. Early work to assess the target classification potential of these signatures was carried out by using sampled data as illustrated in Fig. 5.1(b). To avoid the requirement for realignment to reference signatures, it was found to be convenient to operate with frequency-domain signatures composed of the magnitudes of the DFT of the sampled range profiles, which were invariant to alignment in the time domain. A DFT signature is illustrated in Fig. 5.1(c). Later, it was found that equivalent data could be obtained, while avoiding HRR processing altogether, by collecting the echo power over the same bandwidth used to obtain the

HRR profile, but by transmitting narrowband pulses stepped in frequency from pulse to pulse. These data were called *multiple frequency signature* (MFS) data.

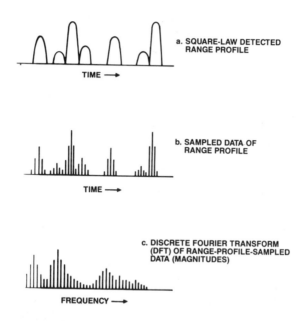

Fig. 5.1 Frequency Spectrum from Samples of Envelope-Detected HRR Profiles

Although found to be useful for target recognition, MFS data could not be transformed into range profiles because phase information was lost in the video detection process. To obtain a discrete frequency signature that is the frequency-domain equivalent of a time-domain signature requires retention of echo amplitude and phase at each frequency. When this is done, the process is sometimes called *synthetic range-profile processing* because the target's range profile is not actually measured directly. In this chapter, a technique will be described for obtaining target range-profile signatures synthetically by processing echoes resulting from narrowband transmitted pulses stepped in frequency.

Synthetic processing avoids certain practical design problems associated with obtaining HRR capability with pulse-compression waveforms. Development of wideband pulse-compression radar made it possible to resolve target scatterers for various purposes including target recognition, target imaging, and detection of small objects on the sea surface. Unfortunately, HRR pulse-compression waveforms impose severe bandwidth requirements on radar designs, which are unnecessary for other surveillance functions. The entire radar system transfer function, from transmitter through receiver, for pulse-compression processing, must possess the bandwidth associated with a desired resolution. This is often neither desirable nor required for normal search and track functions, and entails additional cost and complexity. Synthetic HRR, by contrast, is a capability that can be achieved with many types of existing and planned search and tracking radars, possibly including magnetron radars, to carry out target recognition, target imaging, and other functions requiring HRR in addition to normal search and track functions.

A form of synthetic range-profile generation will now be discussed that is applicable to coherent radar systems using stepped-frequency waveforms. An early version of this technique is described by Ruttenberg [1] for use with magnetron radars operating in a coherent-on-receive mode.

5.2   CONCEPT OF SYNTHETIC RANGE-PROFILE GENERATION

The process for generating a synthetic range profile of a target in the radar beam can be summarized as follows:

1. Transmit a series of *bursts* of narrowband pulses, where each burst consists of n pulses stepped (shifted) in frequency from pulse to pulse by a fixed frequency step size Δf.
2. Set a range-delayed sampling gate to collect I and Q samples of the target's baseband echo response for each transmitted pulse.
3. Store the quadrature components of each of the n echo signals from each transmitted pulse burst. Each stored echo burst of data approaches the equivalent of the instantaneous discrete spectral signature of the target if burst times are short relative to target aspect change.
4. Apply frequency weighting to each burst of data and corrections for target velocity, phase and amplitude ripple, and quadrature sampling bias and imbalance errors.
5. Take an inverse discrete Fourier transform (DFT^{-1}) of the resulting set of n complex frequency components of each echo burst to obtain an n-element synthetic range-profile signature of the target from each burst. Repeat the process, if needed, for N bursts to obtain N slant-range profiles, one range profile for each burst.

The stepped-frequency waveform removes the requirements for both wide instantaneous bandwidth and high sampling rates by sampling near-steady-state reflectivity *versus* frequency of the illuminated target. A functional block diagram of a stepped-frequency radar is shown in Fig. 5.2. A series of N stepped-frequency transmitted bursts is illustrated in Fig. 5.3. The transmitted and reference waveforms are shown in Fig. 5.4. Envelopes of RF signals are illustrated. Narrowband pulses are assumed.

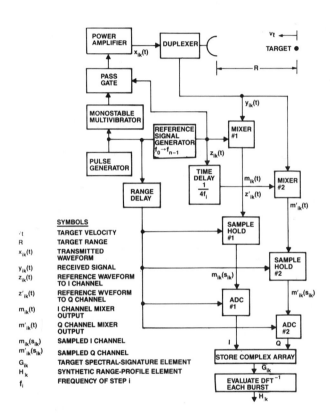

Fig. 5.2 Stepped-Frequency Radar System

The process can be described analytically by considering a single point target with radial motion relative to the radar. A train of stepped-frequency transmissions with resulting echoes from a moving target are shown in Fig. 5.5. A single point target is assumed at range R when time is zero. For the analysis to follow, the burst number k in Figs. 5.2 and 5.3 will be dropped because only one burst is analyzed. The transmitted waveform is $x_i(t)$. The received waveform is $y_i(t)$. Echo delay $\tau(t)$ is a function of time.

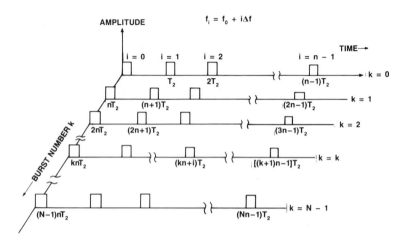

Fig. 5.3 Representation of N Bursts of n Frequency-Stepped Pulses

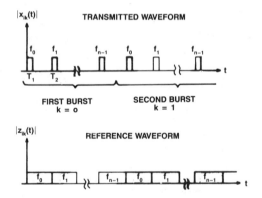

Fig. 5.4 Stepped-Frequency Transmitted Waveform and Reference Waveform

A stepped-frequency transmitted waveform of amplitude B_i at frequency step i is expressed as

$$x_i(t) = B_i \cos(2\pi f_i t + \theta_i), \quad iT_2 \leq t \leq iT_2 + T_1$$
$$= 0, \qquad\qquad\qquad \text{otherwise}$$

where θ_i is the relative phase at frequency step i. The received signal is,
then,

$$y_i(t) = B_i' \cos \{2\pi f_i[t - \tau(t)] + \theta_i\}, \quad iT_2 + \tau(t) \leq t \leq iT_2 + T_1 + \tau(t)$$
$$= 0, \qquad\qquad\qquad\qquad\qquad \text{otherwise}$$

where B_i' is the echo amplitude at frequency step i, and

$$\tau(t) = \frac{R - v_t t}{c/2} \qquad\qquad (5.1)$$

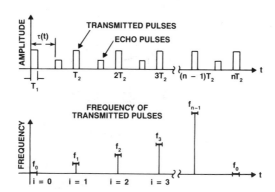

Fig. 5.5 Stepped-Frequency Waveforms and Echo Pulses

for radial velocity v_t of the target toward the radar. Each transmitted pulse is obtained from a reference signal expressed as

$$z_i(t) = B \cos (2\pi f_i t + \theta_i), \quad iT_2 \leq t \leq iT_2 + T_2$$

where B will be assumed to be constant. The resulting baseband mixer product output (from a single mixer) is

$$m_i(t) = A_i \cos [-2\pi f_i \tau(t)], \quad iT_2 + \tau(t) \leq t \leq iT_2 + T_1 + \tau(t)$$
$$= 0, \qquad\qquad\qquad\qquad\qquad \text{otherwise}$$

where A_i is the amplitude of the mixer output at frequency step i. The phase of the mixer output is

$$\psi_i(t) = -2\pi f_i \tau(t)$$

From (5.1),

$$\psi_i(t) = -2\pi f_i \left(\frac{2R}{c} - \frac{2v_i t}{c} \right)$$

This is the total echo phase advance seen from transmission to reception for each pulse.

The mixer output $m_i(t)$ is sampled at time $t = S_i$, where S_i is constantly advanced to produce a sample at the center of each echo pulse. This is accomplished by setting the sampling time according to the expression:

$$S_i = iT_2 + \frac{T_1}{2} + \frac{2R}{c}$$

Phase of the sampled mixer output then becomes

$$\psi_i = -2\pi f_i \left[\frac{2R}{c} - \frac{2v_i}{c} \left(iT_2 + \frac{T_1}{2} + \frac{2R}{c} \right) \right] \qquad (5.2)$$

The sampled output from one mixer is

$$m_i = A_i \cos \psi_i$$

For quadrature mixing, the sampled mixer output is

$$G_i = A_i[\cos \psi_i + j \sin \psi_i]$$

Written in complex form, the sampled output becomes

$$G_i = A_i e^{+j\psi_i} \qquad (5.3)$$

Change in sampling delay S_i over the interval $iT_2 + 2R/c$ to $iT_2 + T_1 + 2R/c$ (i.e., over the pulse duration), for most frequencies and target velocities of interest, does not significantly alter the sampled outputs G_i, except for the effect of the transmitted pulse-envelope shape. The sampled quadrature mixer output signals G_i for each transmitted burst are samples of target reflectivity in the frequency domain. The n complex samples in each burst are transformed by inverse Fourier transform to a series of range-delay reflectivity estimates H_l. This series of complex quantities is also referred to as the target's complex range profile. The inverse discrete Fourier transform (DFT^{-1}) is expressed as

$$H_l = \frac{1}{n} \sum_{i=0}^{n-1} G_i e^{+j(2\pi/n)li}, \ 0 \leqslant l \leqslant n - 1 \qquad (5.4)$$

where n is the number of transmitted pulses per burst. From (5.4), with (5.3),

$$H_l = \frac{1}{n} \sum_{i=0}^{n-1} A_i \exp{(j\psi_i)} \exp{j\frac{2\pi}{n}li}$$

The normalized synthetic response, assuming $A_i \approx 1$ for all i, is

$$H_l = \frac{1}{n} \sum_{i=0}^{n-1} \exp{j\left(\frac{2\pi}{n}li + \psi_i\right)} \qquad (5.5)$$

Equation (5.5) at range R and zero target velocity with ψ_i from (5.2) becomes

$$H_l = \frac{1}{n} \sum_{i=0}^{n-1} \exp{j\left(\frac{2\pi li}{n} - 2\pi f_i \frac{2R}{c}\right)}$$

For frequency step size Δf, $f_i = f_0 + i\Delta f$ so that

$$H_l = \frac{1}{n}\left[\exp{-j\left(2\pi f_0 \frac{2R}{c}\right)}\right] \sum_{i=0}^{n-1} \exp{j\left[\frac{2\pi i}{n}\left(\frac{-2nR\Delta f}{c} + l\right)\right]}$$

The above expression can be simplified by using the following identity,* which has been used for phased array antenna analysis [2]:

$$\sum_{p=0}^{\beta-1} e^{+j\alpha p} = \frac{\sin{\frac{\beta\alpha}{2}}}{\sin{\frac{\alpha}{2}}} e^{j(\beta-1)\alpha/2} \qquad (5.6)$$

For

$$\beta = n$$
$$p = i$$

---

*Symbols α and β as used here represent variables associated with this identity only, and do not refer to bandwidth as is the case elsewhere in this text.

and

$$\alpha = \frac{2\pi y}{n}$$

with

$$y = \frac{-2nR\Delta f}{c} + l$$

We obtain

$$H_l = \frac{1}{n}\left[\exp\left(-j2\pi f_0 \frac{2R}{c}\right)\right] \frac{\sin \pi y}{\sin \frac{\pi y}{n}} \exp\left(j\frac{n-1}{2}\frac{2\pi y}{n}\right)$$

The magnitude of the synthetic range profile then becomes

$$|H_l| = \left|\frac{\sin \pi y}{n \sin \frac{\pi y}{n}}\right| \qquad (5.7)$$

We can show that the envelope of the synthetic range profile described by (5.7) for $2R/c = t$ is identical to that for the matched-filter response of the periodic discrete frequency-coded waveform described in Chapter 4. In both cases, a stepped-frequency waveform was assumed, each with n frequency steps of Δf Hz per burst (called *period* in Chapter 4).

Discrete values $|H_l|$ of a synthetic range-profile envelope produced by a point target are illustrated in Fig. 5.6 along with the corresponding profile envelope. Responses to a point target will maximize at $y = 0, \pm n, \pm 2n, \pm 3n, \ldots$ The range index nearest each of these peak responses will be referred to as $l = l_0$. Range positions corresponding to range index l_0 are given by

$$R = \frac{cl_0}{2n\Delta f}, \frac{c(l_0 \mp n)}{2n\Delta f}, \frac{c(l_0 \mp 2n)}{2n\Delta f}, \ldots$$

An unambiguous range length of $c/2\Delta f$ is evident.

Range positions $l = 0$ to $n - 1$ within the profile envelope are determined by the choice of frequency-steps. Range resolution can be defined as the range increment between any two adjacent discrete range positions. A set of n frequency steps produces n equally spaced range increments within the unambiguous range length $c/2\Delta f$, so that

$$\Delta r_s = \frac{c}{2n\Delta f} \tag{5.8}$$

It can be shown that for large n the resolution defined as the range distance between the $2/\pi$ points of the synthetic range profile (envelope) given by (5.7) approaches the *sampling resolution* given by (5.8). This is equivalent to the delay resolution measured between the $2/\pi(-4$ dB) points of the $(\sin \beta\pi t)/\pi t$ shaped envelope of a single *real* pulse having a rectangular spectrum of bandwidth $\beta = n\Delta f$.

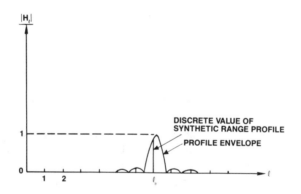

Fig. 5.6 Synthetic Range Profile for a Single Fixed-Point Target (Normalized Response)

Equation (5.8) can be seen to conform to (1.1) of Chapter 1, which expresses the fundamental dependence of radar range resolution on radar bandwidth. The stepped-frequency bandwidth is $n\Delta f$. A hypothetical set of stepped-frequency echo signals at baseband produced by a multiple-scatterer target and the resulting complex range profile are illustrated in Fig. 5.7.

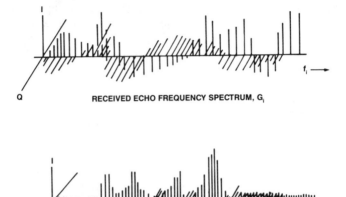

Fig. 5.7 Hypothetical Discrete Echo Spectrum and Resulting Range Profile

5.3 RANGE-EXTENDED TARGETS

The range profile described by (5.7) is that of a point target. In other words, complex samples G_i were assumed to be obtained from pulses arriving at the radar receiver with the amplitude and phase of an echo signal from a point target. Amplitude and phase of echo pulses in the more general case are those of the coherent sum of echoes from multiple scatterers. The angular extent over which scatterers are coherently summed is determined by the radar antenna beamwidth. The range extent over which scatterers are coherently summed is determined by the receiving system bandwidth as seen up to the point where I and Q samples are taken. It is convenient to assume that receiving system bandwidth is matched to the transmitted pulse duration T_1. Then, the range extent over which scatterers contribute to the amplitude and phase of an echo pulse is approximately $cT_1/2$. Design considerations for two types of extended targets will now be discussed: (1) a single, extended, but isolated, target, such as an aircraft or a ship seen in a clutter-free environment; and (2) an extended target in the presence of clutter or other scatterers.

To obtain the undistorted range profile of an isolated target, the complex sample of reflectivity collected at each frequency step must approximate that obtained from a steady-state signal. Stated differently, echo signals arriving from each of the multiple scatterers of the target must be summed in the receiver before sampling with nearly equal weighting across the target's range (and azimuth) extent. This condition is met for a much narrower receiver bandwidth than the reciprocal of the target range-delay extent, assuming that the cross-range extent of the target is immersed in the radar antenna beamwidth. When receiver bandwidth is matched to transmitter pulse duration T_1, distortion-free range profiles are approximated for T_1 that is much greater than the range-delay extent of the target.

The requirement that pulse duration exceed target range-delay extent in order to obtain distortion-free synthetic processing must be compromised to prevent ambiguous synthetic responses to targets that are not isolated in range delay. Received echo pulses produced by the coherent sum of echoes from individual scatterers extending outside a range-delay interval $1/\Delta f$ will produce ambiguous range profiles. In terms of transmitted pulse duration T_1, scatterers which extend over a pulse interval $T_1 \gg 1/\Delta f$ will produce responses that are folded into the unambiguous range extent $c/2\Delta f$. Ambiguity is avoided by setting $T_1 = 1/\Delta f$. This matched condition falls short of meeting the requirement that T_1 be much greater than the range-delay extent of the target. The compromise, however, is required to obtain an unambiguous range profile of a target in the presence of clutter and to conduct frequency-domain SAR mapping by using stepped-frequency waveforms (an as yet untested concept to be discussed in Chapter 6).

5.4 EFFECT OF TARGET VELOCITY

Relationships given in (5.7) and (5.8) were obtained by assuming a target at a fixed range. The effect of target velocity can be examined by considering a point target at range R with velocity v_t toward the radar. The synthetic range profile of the moving target can then be expressed from (5.5), with ψ_i from (5.2), as

$$H_l = \frac{1}{n} \sum_{i=0}^{n-1} \exp j\left\{ \frac{2\pi}{n} li - 2\pi f_i \left[\frac{2R}{c} - \frac{2v_t}{c}\left(iT_2 + \frac{T_1}{2} + \frac{2R}{c} \right) \right] \right\}$$

$$= \frac{1}{n} \sum_{i=0}^{n-1} e^{j\psi_i}$$

where

$$\Psi_i = \frac{2\pi}{n} l i - 2\pi f_i \left[\frac{2R}{c} - \frac{2v_t}{c} \left(i T_2 + \frac{T_1}{2} + \frac{2R}{c} \right) \right]$$

In terms of quadrature components, we have

$$H_l = \frac{1}{n} \sum_{i=0}^{n-1} \cos \Psi_i + j \frac{1}{n} \sum_{i=0}^{n-1} \sin \Psi_i \tag{5.9}$$

The phase of H_l is

$$\Phi_l = \tan^{-1} \frac{\displaystyle\sum_{i=0}^{n-1} \sin \Psi_i}{\displaystyle\sum_{i=0}^{n-1} \cos \Psi_i}$$

The magnitude of H_l in (5.9) was evaluated for parameters associated with an experimental wideband US Navy radar at the Naval Ocean Systems Center. Results are shown in Fig. 5.8 for a 256-step burst, and in Fig. 5.9 we have results for a 25-step burst. The characteristic shift in peak response associated with moving targets observed with linear (up-chirp) FM coded waveforms is apparent in these results. For targets with positive velocity toward the radar, the shift is to an earlier time (i.e., less delay).

The effect of target velocity shown in Figs. 5.8 and 5.9 can also be predicted by referring to the ambiguity surface of an equivalent chirp pulse. In Fig. 4.34 of Chapter 4, the peak response at $\tau = 0$ out of the matched filter to a chirp pulse of duration T_1 becomes zero when Doppler frequency reaches $f_D = 1/T_1$. A point target at velocity v_t produces a Doppler frequency shift at a center RF frequency $\bar{f}$ of $2v_t \bar{f}/c$. The velocity that produces the first null response at the matched range-delay position for synthetic processing of an n step burst at a PRI of T_2 can therefore be expected to occur for

$$\frac{2v_t \bar{f}}{c} = \frac{1}{nT_2}$$

where nT_2 corresponds to chirp pulse duration T_1. For the parameters of Fig. 5.9, the first Doppler null response occurs for velocity:

$$v_t = \frac{c}{2\bar{f} n T_2}$$

$$= 10.4 \text{ m/s}$$

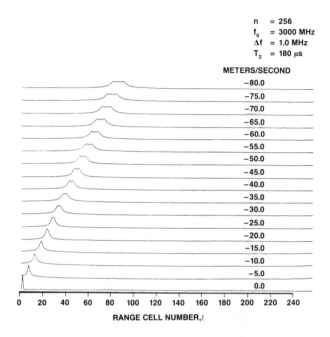

Fig. 5.8 Synthetic Range Profile of a Point Target for Various Velocities at the Same Range (256 Frequency Steps) (Courtesy of John A. Bouman, formerly of the Naval Weapons Center, China Lake, CA., now at ESL, Inc.)

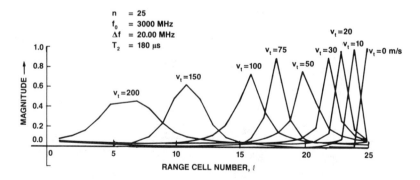

Fig. 5.9 Synthetic Range Profiles of a Point Target at Different Velocities (25 Frequency Steps)

In Fig. 5.9, we can see that the response of a statioinary target has nulled at a range position where a 10 m/s target produces a peak response. Serious distortion does not appear in Fig. 5.9 until a velocity of over 30 m/s is reached.

Examples of actual synthetic range profiles are shown in Figs. 5.10, 5.11, and 5.12. The significance of synthetic range-profile processing can be illustrated by considering Fig. 5.13. A stepped-frequency radar is shown observing a target using a pulse duration of 3.0 μs, equivalent to about 1500 feet in range delay. Radar resolution from (5.8) when 256 frequency steps of 1.0 MHz are used is about two feet. The target, although *immersed* in the resolution cell associated with the transmitted pulse, is resolved into individual scatterers by using the synthetic process.

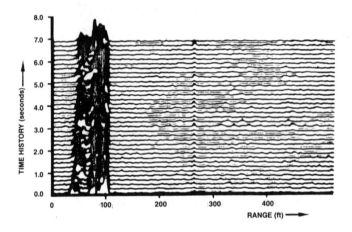

Fig. 5.10 Synthetic Range Profiles of Fishing Boat

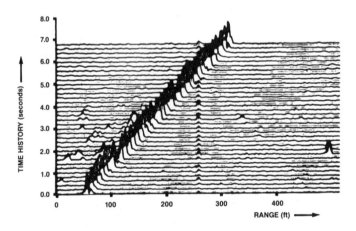

Fig. 5.11 Synthetic Range Profiles of Moving Small Craft

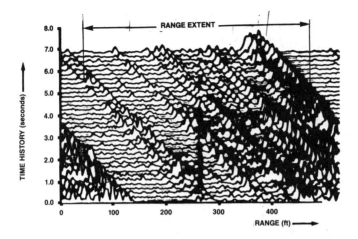

Fig. 5.12 Synthetic Range Profiles of Moving Ship

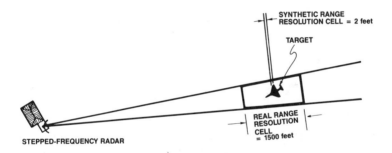

Fig. 5.13 Synthetic and Real Resolution Cells

5.5 RANGE-PROFILE DISTORTION PRODUCED BY FREQUENCY ERROR

The derivation of (5.7) for the synthetic range profile of a point target assumed precise Δf frequency steps. Any frequency deviation from $f_i = f_0 + i\Delta f$ results in distortion. Random frequency error in f_i produces random phase error, which reduces the peak value of the range profile of a point target and introduces noise elsewhere along the profile. In other words, the noticeable effects will be a reduction in the expected value of the response at the peaks of a target range profile and a random response at the nulls. Positions of peaks and nulls are not disturbed. The effect will now be examined for the point target case to assess distortion caused by random frequency error and to determine the relationship of this distortion to radar range.

To examine the effect for a point target, (5.3) with ψ_i from (5.2) for zero target velocity is rewritten

$$G_i = \exp j\left(-2\pi f_i \frac{2R}{c} - vx_i\right) \tag{5.10}$$

where vx_i is the random phase error produced by random frequency error x_i in the ith frequency step. A random error x_i in frequency step i produces a random phase error in G_i of $-2\pi(2R/c)x_i$. For ideal coherent transmitter systems, the only frequency error is that produced by the frequency synthesizer. Thus, v in (5.10) will be defined to be $v_s = 2\pi(2R/c)$.

Reduction in range-profile response produced by phase errors is derived by substituting (5.10) into (5.4) and solving for the peak response of the expected value $E[H_l(x_i)]$, which occurs at $y = 0, \pm n, \pm 2n, \pm 3n,$ . . . The result, derived at the end of this chapter, assuming a normal probability distribution of frequency error, is

Magnitude of Peak $E[H_l(x_i)] = C_f$ at positions of peak $|H_l|$

where

$$C_f = \exp\left(-\frac{v_s^2 \sigma_s^2}{2}\right)$$

The symbol C_f is the characteristic function of the random frequency variable x, and the symbol σ_s refers to the standard deviation of the frequency error of the frequency synthesizer. Acceptable values of standard deviation of frequency error σ_s will be calculated for $v\sigma = 1.0$ (-4.3 dB loss) to illustrate the effect on range performance.

Tolerances of synthesizer frequency error related to range delay for $v_s\sigma_s \leq 1.0$ are computed from

$$v_s\sigma_s = 2\pi \frac{2R}{c}\sigma_s \leq 1.0$$

for which

$$\sigma_s \leq \frac{1.0}{2\pi \dfrac{2R}{c}}$$

In terms of range in nmi, we have

$$\sigma_s \leq \frac{1.0}{2\pi \dfrac{2 \cdot 1852\ R(\text{nmi})}{3 \times 10^8\ (\text{m/s})}}$$

$$\leq \frac{12{,}891}{R(\text{nmi})}$$

Maximum tolerable frequency error for several values of radar range are listed in Table 5.1.

Table 5.1 Tolerable Frequency Deviation
versus Radar Range (-4.3 dB Loss)

R (nmi)	σ_s (Hz)
10	1289.0
100	129.0
1,000	13.0
10,000	1.3
100,000	0.13

The commercially available synthesizer of Table 3.1 of Chapter 3, when multiplied to 3.2 GHz, was shown to produce about 0.02 Hz rms frequency excursion for averaging time $2R/c = 0.12$ s, corresponding to ranges out to beyond 10,000 nmi. We may conclude that distortion due to synthesizer-produced phase noise does not present a problem at useful ranges.

A more complete analysis would need to consider pulse-to-pulse phase noise produced by *pushing* and *pulling* of the transmitter transfer phase by pulse-to-pulse variation of the pulse modulation (current and voltage) and output impedance, respectively.

5.6 RANGE TRACKING

Synthetic HRR techniques can be used to generate synthetic range profiles of moving targets such as ships or aircraft. Range tracking is required to sample the echo signal phase and amplitude from each transmitted pulse as the target moves either in or out in range from the radar. The sampling of mixer outputs $m_{ik}(t)$ and $m'_{ik}(t)$ of Fig. 5.2 produces a pair of I and Q samples of each echo pulse. Phase determined from each I and Q pair is nearly independent of the location of pulse sampling. Amplitude and, therefore, signal-to-noise ratio decrease for sampling at the pulse edges due to pulse shape as determined by the transmitter-receiver band-pass characteristic. Synthetic HRR tracking requirements are not as severe as those for real HRR. The delay trigger position for real HRR target tracking to prevent blurring on the A-scope display or degradation of the recorded data is required to move from pulse to pulse with precision, corresponding to range jitter that is far less than the range-delay resolution. By contrast, for synthetic HRR, incremental shifting of the sample position along the echo pulse does not significantly affect the I and Q samples, and has proved to be a convenient way to adjust the delay trigger for target tracking. Increments of range shift may be a convenient fraction of the echo pulse duration that is much greater than the synthetic delay resolution.

Figure 5.14 is a block diagram of a tracking system used for exper-imental ISAR imaging tests for the US Navy at the Naval Ocean Systems Center (NOSC). A basic clock is set to generate a frequency that when properly divided results in convenient range readout increments. The NOSC tracker uses a 8.09 MHz clock rate to drive *down counters* for both the main (transmitter) trigger and the delay trigger. The result is a main-trigger count interval of 123.6 ns, which corresponds to a .01 nmi range increment. The main-trigger counter, following each count down to zero, is reset to a count n_t, corresponding to the desired PRF. For example, a reset count of $n_t = 1500$ produces a PRF of 5.39 kHz, corresponding to an unambiguous range of .01 nmi $\times$ 1500 = 15 nmi. A main trigger is generated and the counter is reset back to 1500 each time the counter is counted down to zero from 1500.

The delay-trigger counter is clocked at the same rate as the main-trigger counter, but the reset count n_r is controlled either manually or automatically by means of an *up-down counter*. Assume that it is desired to move the delay trigger in range delay toward that of a target echo of interest. The count n_r set in the delay-trigger down counter is then set to some value less than 1500 that corresponds to the range delay of the target. Both the main-trigger counter and delay-trigger counter are driven by the same clock and are reset at the same instant. Thus, the range counter will count down to zero to generate a delay-trigger pulse to sample the target echo signal before the next main trigger occurs. The delay-trigger reset count for close-in targets will approach zero. For targets near the maximum unambiguous range of 15 nmi, the reset count will be near the 1500 count that is set in the main-trigger down counter. For moving targets the delay-trigger reset count changes continuously to maintain target track.

The delay-trigger reset count n_t is produced by the up-down counter in the middle part of Fig. 5.14. The count in this counter is adjusted up or down as needed for range tracking by manual or automatic control of the voltage-controlled oscillator (VCO). Gross rate is controlled by the VCO rate switch. Typically, the up-down counter is counted up or down at rates less than ±500 Hz for tracking of most targets of interest. Automatic range tracking is achieved by controlling the VCO from a conventional early-late gate range-tracking circuit. The *end-of-sequence* (EOS) burst input of Fig. 5.14 prevents the count of the up-down counter to the range counter from changing during a burst.

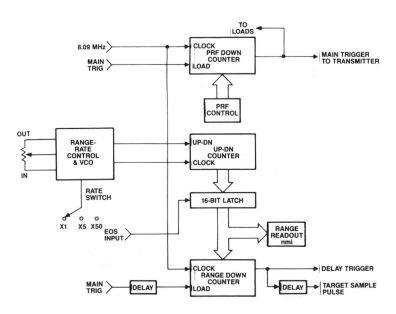

Fig. 5.14 Digital Range Tracker

5.7 LOSS PRODUCED BY RANDOM FREQUENCY ERROR

We will develop an expression for the expected value of the peak of the synthetic range-profile response for a single point target in terms of standard deviation σ of frequency and associated radar parameters. The synthetic range profile is generated by the IDFT of the complex samples from an n-element burst given by (5.3). The sampled output G_i from a point target at range R, obtained when the reference frequency f_i contains random frequency error x_i, is given by (5.10). Substitution for G_i from (5.10) into (5.4) yields

$$H_l(x_i) = \frac{1}{n} \sum_{i=0}^{n-1} e^{-j\left(2\pi f_0 \frac{2R}{c}\right)} e^{j\left[\frac{2\pi i}{n}\left(\frac{-2n\Delta f R}{c} + l\right)\right]} e^{-jvx_i}$$

Let

$$y = \frac{-2n\Delta f R}{c} + l$$

Then,

$$H_l(x_i) = e^{-j\left(2\pi f_0 \frac{2R}{c}\right)} \frac{1}{n} \sum_{i=0}^{n-1} e^{j\left(\frac{2\pi i}{n}\right)y} e^{-jvx_i} \qquad (5.11)$$

The expected value [3] of $H_l(x_i)$ is

$$E[H_l(x_i)] = \int_{-\infty}^{\infty} \int_{-\infty}^{\infty} \cdots \int_{-\infty}^{\infty} H_l(x_i)p(x_0, x_1, \ldots, x_{n-1})dx_0 dx_1 \ldots dx_{n-1}$$

where $p(x_0, x_1, \ldots, x_{n-1})$ is the joint probability density of random frequency error $x_0, x_1, \ldots, x_{n-1}$. Substitution of $H_l(x_i)$ from (5.11) gives

$$E[H_l(x_i)] = \int_{-\infty}^{\infty} \int_{-\infty}^{\infty} \cdots \int_{-\infty}^{\infty} \frac{1}{n} \sum_{i=0}^{n-1} e^{-j\left(2\pi f_0 \frac{2R}{c}\right)} e^{j\left(\frac{2\pi i}{n}\right)y} e^{-jvx_i}$$

$$\cdot p(x_0, x_1, \ldots, x_{n-1})dx_0 dx_1 \ldots dx_{n-1} \qquad (5.12)$$

For $p(x_i)]$ independent of $p(x_j)$ for all i and j except $i = j$, and exchanging summation and integration, then (5.12) becomes

$$E[H_l(x_i)] = \frac{1}{n} \sum_{i=0}^{n-1} \int_{-\infty}^{\infty} \int_{-\infty}^{\infty} \cdots \int_{-\infty}^{\infty} e^{-j\left(2\pi f_0 \frac{2R}{c}\right)} e^{j\left(\frac{2\pi i}{n}\right)y} e^{-jvx_i}$$

$$p(x_0)p(x_1) \ldots p(x_{n-1})dx_0 dx_1 \ldots dx_{n-1} \qquad (5.13)$$

where $p(x_i)$ is the probability density function of frequency error x_i. By carrying out the summation in (5.13) for $i = 0, 1, 2, \ldots, n - 1$, we have*

$$
\begin{aligned}
E[H_l(x_i)] = {} & \frac{1}{n} \int_{-\infty}^{\infty} e^{-j\left(2\pi f_0 \frac{2R}{c}\right)} e^{j\frac{2\pi \cdot 0}{n} y} e^{-j\nu x_0} p(x_0) \left[\int_{-\infty}^{\infty} p(x_1) dx_1 \right. \\
& \left. \cdot \int_{-\infty}^{\infty} p(x_2) dx_2 \ldots \int_{-\infty}^{\infty} p(x_{n-1}) dx_{n-1} \right] dx_0 \\
& + \frac{1}{n} \int_{-\infty}^{\infty} e^{-j\left(2\pi f_0 \frac{2R}{c}\right)} e^{j\frac{2\pi \cdot 1}{n} y} e^{-j\nu x_1} p(x_1) \left[\int_{-\infty}^{\infty} p(x_0) dx_0 \right. \\
& \left. \cdot \int_{-\infty}^{\infty} p(x_2) dx_2 \ldots \int_{-\infty}^{\infty} p(x_{n-1}) dx_{n-1} \right] dx_1 \\
& + \\
& \quad . \\
& \quad . \\
& \quad . \\
& + \frac{1}{n} \int_{-\infty}^{\infty} e^{-j\left(2\pi f_0 \frac{2R}{c}\right)} e^{j\frac{2\pi(n-1)}{n} y} e^{-j\nu x_{n-1}} p(x_{n-1}) \left[\int_{-\infty}^{\infty} p(x_0) dx_0 \right. \\
& \left. \cdot \int_{-\infty}^{\infty} p(x_1) dx_1 \ldots \int_{-\infty}^{\infty} p(x_{n-2}) dx_{n-2} \right] dx_{n-1}
\end{aligned}
$$

Because, for all i,

$$
\int_{-\infty}^{\infty} p(x_i) dx_i = 1
$$

Then,

$$
E[H_l(x_i)] = \frac{1}{n} \sum_{i=0}^{n-1} e^{-j\left(2\pi f_0 \frac{2R}{c}\right)} e^{j\frac{2\pi i}{n} y} \int_{-\infty}^{\infty} e^{-j\nu x_i} p(x_i) dx_i
$$

---

*The index $i = 0$ is indicated, but not multiplied out, in the hope of maintaining clarity.

A normal distribution with standard deviation σ and zero mean will be assumed, so that for all i,

$$p(x) = \frac{1}{\sigma\sqrt{2\pi}} e^{\left(-\frac{x^2}{2\sigma^2}\right)} dx$$

Then,

$$E[H_l(x_i)] = \frac{1}{n} \sum_{i=0}^{n-1} e^{-j\left(2\pi f_0 \frac{2R}{c}\right)} e^{j\frac{2\pi i}{n}y} \int_{-\infty}^{\infty} \frac{1}{\sigma\sqrt{2\pi}} e^{-j\nu x_i} e^{-\frac{x^2}{2\sigma^2}} dx$$

Terms not including the index i can be brought out of the summation, so that

$$E[H_l(x_i)] = e^{-j\left(2\pi f_0 \frac{2R}{c}\right)} \frac{1}{n} \sum_{i=0}^{n-1} e^{j\frac{2\pi i}{n}y} \int_{-\infty}^{\infty} \frac{1}{\sigma\sqrt{2\pi}} e^{-j\nu x} e^{-\frac{x^2}{2\sigma^2}} dx \qquad (5.14)$$

Equation (5.14) can be simplified by using the notion of a characteristic function. The characteristic function of the random variable x is the Fourier transform of its probability density function $p(x)$ (with the sign reversed). The integral term of (5.14), therefore, can be viewed as containing the characteristic function of the zero-mean normal probability density, from Papoulis [4], which is

$$C_f(t) = FT[p(x)], \text{ with } j = -j;$$

$$= \int_{-\infty}^{\infty} \frac{1}{\sigma\sqrt{2\pi}} e^{jtx} e^{-\frac{x^2}{2\sigma^2}} dx$$

where the symbol t is used here because the reversed-sign Fourier transform corresponds to the commonly used inverse transform from frequency

f to time t. The characteristic function for a zero-mean normal distribution with standard deviation σ of the random frequency variable x becomes [5]:

$$C_f(t) = e^{-\frac{\sigma^2 t^2}{2}}$$

Thus, for $t = -v$, the integral term in (5.14) becomes

$$C_f(-v) = \int_{-\infty}^{\infty} \frac{1}{\sigma\sqrt{2\pi}} e^{-jvx} e^{-\frac{x^2}{2\sigma^2}} dx = e^{-\frac{v^2\sigma^2}{2}}$$

Then, (5.14) becomes

$$E[H_l(x_i)] = e^{-j\left(2\pi f_0 \frac{2R}{c}\right)} \frac{1}{n} \sum_{i=0}^{n-1} e^{j\frac{2\pi i}{n}y} e^{-\frac{v^2\sigma^2}{2}}$$

$$= e^{-j\left(2\pi f_0 \frac{2R}{c}\right)} e^{-\frac{v^2\sigma^2}{2}} \frac{1}{n} \sum_{i=0}^{n-1} e^{j\frac{2\pi i}{n}y} \tag{5.15}$$

Application of the identity (5.6) to (5.15) yields

$$E[H_l(x_i)] = \frac{1}{n} e^{-j\left(2\pi f_0 \frac{2R}{c}\right)} e^{-\frac{v^2\sigma^2}{2}} e^{j\frac{n-1}{2}\frac{2\pi}{n}y} \frac{\sin \pi y}{\sin \frac{\pi y}{n}} \tag{5.16}$$

which is the expected value of the synthetic range profile H_l expressed as a function of the variance σ^2 of the frequency error.

The peak response of the expected value of the range profile occurs at $y = 0, \pm n, \pm 2n, \pm 3n, \ldots$ Peak responses can be seen to occur at the same positions as for the ideal response (5.7). The expected value given by (5.16) of the peak at $y = 0$ becomes

$$\text{Peak } E[H_l(x_i)] = e^{j\left(-2\pi f_0 \frac{2R}{c}\right)} e^{-\frac{v^2\sigma^2}{2}}$$

In terms of absolute value with $C_f = \exp(-v^2\sigma^2/2)$:

$$\text{Magnitude of Peak } E[H_l(x_i)] = C_f \qquad\qquad (5.17)$$

From (5.17), if the frequency variance about the desired frequency were zero ($\sigma^2 = 0$), the magnitude of the peak response of the expected value of the range profile would be unity. With random frequency error present, the peak value is reduced to $\exp(-v^2\sigma^2/2)$, where σ^2 is the variance (also called *dispersion*) of frequency, and v is the constant that relates phase error to frequency error. Note that the position in range of the peak of the expected value is a function of neither the random frequency error nor its variance. The magnitude of the peak response, however, is dependent on σ and, hence, on the random frequency error.

Nulls of the expected values of the range profile given by (5.16) occur at $y = \pm(1, 2, 3, \ldots n - 1)$. At these values of y, the expected minimum values become zero. Null positions, as well as peak-value positions, as we can see are unchanged by frequency error.

PROBLEMS

5.1   A radar is to be designed to generate synthetic range profiles of ship targets that are up to 300 m in length with 2.0 m resolution. (a) What is the minimum required number of pulses per burst and maximum frequency-step size? (b) What is the minimum pulse-width?

5.2   The definition of the discrete inverse Fourier transform, (5.4), normalizes the synthetic range response $|H_l|$ by $1/n$. (a) Show by using L'Hospital's rule that before normalization the peak value of $|H_l|$ of (5.7), derived on the basis of (5.4) for a point target, is equal to n. (b) Show that processing of a burst of n stepped-frequency echo pulses into a synthetic range profile results in a coherent processing gain of n. (c) What is the signal processing gain (improvement in S/N from input to output) in dB, assuming lossless coherent processing for each burst of 256 stepped frequencies processed into synthetic range profiles?

5.3 The detection range of the pulse-compression radar in Table 2.3 of Chapter 2 for video integration of 200 pulses was shown to be 54 km with respect to a 1.0 m^2 target. What would be the detection range for the same size target if one burst of $n = 200$ stepped-frequency pulses were processed into a synthetic range profile before detection as a single echo pulse? Assume the same processed resolution so that target fluctuation is unaffected and all other parameters, except required S/N and signal processing gain, remain the same.

5.4 To what accuracy must target velocity be corrected to maintain tolerable synthetic range-profile distortion for a radar operating at a center frequency of 5.4 GHz with a 2000-pps PRF by using a stepped-frequency waveform with 128 pulses per burst? Use the criterion that uncorrected velocity must be within one-half the velocity for which the response nulls (first null along $\tau = 0$ on the ambiguity surface).

5.5 A radar uses a frequency synthesizer to generate stepped-frequency waveforms for synthetic target-range profile generation. Measurements of the transmitted phase variation at each of several frequencies within the frequency band indicate a standard deviation (pulse-to-pulse) of 65° phase variation averaged across the frequency band. What will be the synthetic range-profile distortion at the maximum unambiguous range for a stationary target in terms of signal power loss?

5.6 What is the maximum allowable rms frequency deviation $\sigma(f_r)$ in Hz during the interpulse time on the 8.09 MHz reference oscillator in Fig. 5.14 to keep the sample gate within the $\delta t = \pm 0.1$ μs (rms) central region of the delayed echo pulses. Compute $\sigma(f_r)$ at maximum unambiguous range delay $T_2 = 1/\text{PRF}$.

5.7 Compare the results of Prob. 5.6 to the allowable rms error in Hz of the 10 MHz reference oscillator in Fig. 4.35 to maintain 0.1 ns rms delay error for the same PRF.

REFERENCES

1. Ruttenberg, K., and L. Chanzit, "High Range Resolution by Means of Pulse-to-Pulse Frequency Shifting," *IEEE EASCON Record*, 1968, pp. 47–51.

2. Kraus, J.D., *Antennas*, New York: McGraw-Hill, 1950, pp. 76–77.

3.   Papoulis, A., *Probability, Random Variables, and Stochastic Processes,* New York: McGraw-Hill, 1965, p. 239.
4.   Papoulis, A., *Probability, Random Variables, and Stochastic Processes,* New York: McGraw-Hill, 1965, p. 153.
5.   Papoulis, A., *Probability, Random Variables, and Stochastic Processes,* New York: McGraw-Hill, 1965, p. 159.

Chapter 6
Synthetic Aperture Radar

6.1 INTRODUCTION

Synthetic aperture radar (SAR) is an airborne (or spaceborne) radar mapping technique for generating high resolution maps of surface target areas and terrain. The first experimental demonstration of SAR mapping occurred in 1953 when a strip map of a section of Key West, FL was generated by frequency analysis of data collected at 3 cm wavelengths from a C-46 aircraft by a group from the University of Illinois [1]. Some useful SAR references are Kovaly [2], Cutrona [3], Harger [4], and Hovanessian [5]. Synthetic aperture radar is used to obtain fine resolution in both slant range and cross range. *Cross-range resolution* refers to resolution transverse to the radar's line of sight. The term *slant range* refers to the line-of-sight range to distinguish from cross range. Resolution in the slant range to the radar is often obtained by coding the transmitted pulse, typically FM chirp coding. Cross-range resolution is obtained by coherently integrating echo energy reflected from the ground as the aircraft or spacecraft carrying the radar travels above and alongside of the illuminated area to be mapped.

The term *synthetic aperture* refers to the distance that the radar travels during the time that reflectivity data are collected from a point to be resolved on the earth's surface, which remains illuminated by the real antenna beam. The length of the synthetic aperture of a side-looking SAR is the ground-track distance over which coherent integration occurs. *Synthetic length* depends on antenna beamwidth and varies with range delay. *Synthetic aperture length* shrinks in the side-looking case for echoes arriving from points closer to the radar, and increases for echoes arriving from points farther from the radar. The effect for ideal processing is to produce constant cross-range resolution *versus* range. Indeed, maximum possible cross-range resolution is approximately equal to one-half of the real aperture's cross-range dimension. Figure 6.1 illustrates a side-looking SAR configuration.

Echo energy collected from each range-resolved scatterer in the area to be mapped is made to arrive in phase at the output of the radar processor in order to realize the narrow beamwidth associated with the long, synthetically generated aperture. This is achieved by first correcting for all movement of the aircraft that deviates from straight-line motion. At this point, we have what is called *unfocused SAR*. Then, for *focused SAR*, the *quadratic phase error* is corrected. Quadratic phase error is produced by straight-line motion of the radar past each point of the mapped area.

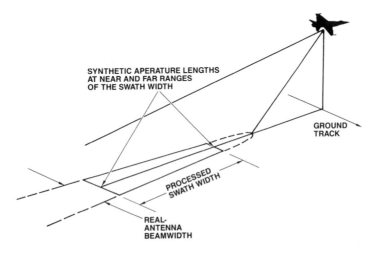

Fig. 6.1 Side-Looking SAR Radar

It is possible to achieve a second form of SAR, sometimes called *spotlight SAR*, illustrated in Fig. 6.2, in which the radar antenna tracks a particular target area of interest over some azimuth angle $\Delta\phi$. Here, the cross-range resolution is limited not by antenna size, as for side-looking SAR, but by target dwell time. Synthetic aperture length for small $\Delta\phi$ can be thought of as the tangential distance that the radar travels while moving through the angle $\Delta\phi$ to the target.

A third type of SAR is achieved by integrating echo energy as the antenna is scanned in azimuth. This is called *Doppler beam sharpening*. Here, for constant azimuthal scanning rate, relatively long integration time will occur at portions of the scanning angle near the direction of platform

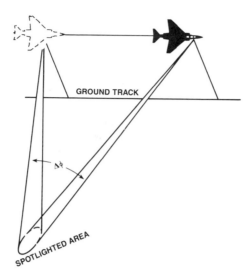

GROUND TRACK

Δφ

SPOTLIGHTED AREA

Fig. 6.2 Spotlight SAR

motion, as compared with near broadside portions of the scan. This tends to produce constant cross-path resolution and effectively sharpens the real antenna beam. Side-looking SAR and spotlight SAR shall be discussed in this chapter.

Inverse synthetic aperture radar (ISAR), to be discussed in detail in Chapter 7, can be explained in terms of SAR with reference to the spotlight form of SAR. After correcting for random deviation from straight-line motion and quadratic phase error, a spotlight SAR can be thought of as if the radar were flying a portion of a circle around the target area. It is clear that, although the radar moves about the target, the same data would be collected if the radar were stationary and the target area rotated, which is precisely what occurs in ISAR. The aspect motion of the target relative to the radar is used to generate a radar map of the target, which is called the *target image*.

Some fundamental characteristics of the side-looking SAR concept can be explained in terms of *equirange* and *equi-Doppler* lines on the earth's surface to be mapped by a moving radar platform above the earth. Consider the side-looking SAR illustrated with the coordinate system of Fig. 6.3. Equirange lines on the earth's surface are the intersections with the earth's surface of successive concentric spheres centered at the radar. Points on each of these spheres are equidistant from the radar. Equi-Doppler lines on the earth's surface are produced by intersections with the earth's surface of coaxial cones, which are concentric about the radar platform's flight

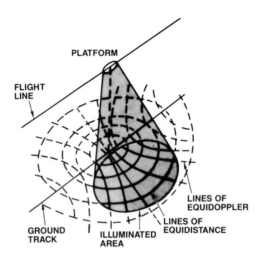

Fig. 6.3 SAR Range-Doppler Coordinates (From Fig. 1 of Elachi, C., *et al.*, "Spaceborne Synthetic-Aperture Imaging Radars: Applications, Techniques, and Technology," *Proc. IEEE,* Vol. 70, No. 10, Oct. 1982, p. 1175. Reprinted with permission.)

line as the axis and the radar position as the apex of the cones. Points on each of these cones appear at constant velocity relative to the radar. The zero-velocity cone is a plane perpendicular to the line of flight through the radar's position. The cones for maximum positive and negative velocity are straight lines on the flight axis extending ahead of and behind the radar, respectively. A flat-earth surface results in a coordinate system made up of the families of the concentric circles and hyperbolas shown in Fig. 6.3.

At any instant, the radar is able to view that portion of the range-Doppler coordinate system which is illuminated by the real antenna beam. The distribution of echo power from the illuminated area, as a function range delay and Doppler, is the SAR image for that area. Brightness of an image pixel is proportional to the echo power from the corresponding range-Doppler cell on the earth's surface. The mapping resolution is determined by the ability of the radar to measure differential range delay and differential Doppler. Ideally, resolution is independent of radar range, but the image will degrade as thermal or other noise sources begin to determine pixel brightness at low echo signal levels.

6.2 REAL-APERTURE RADAR MAPPING

Before we begin to develop SAR theory, let us first consider mapping with real aperture, side-looking radar as illustrated in Fig. 6.4. Here, the cross-range resolution is directly obtained as a result of the narrow antenna beam produced by a long, real antenna aperture operating at a relatively short wavelength.

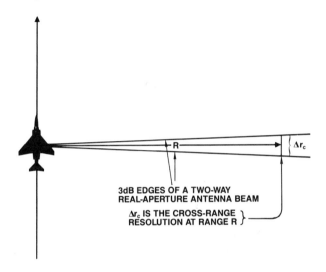

Fig. 6.4 Real Aperture Mapping Radar Operating in the Side-Looking Mode

Resolution of a radar is commonly defined in terms of the extent, at the half-power points, of the one-way or two-way power response to a point target measured in range delay, Doppler shift, or angle of the target to the radar. Cross-range resolution of a real aperture radar can likewise be defined as the cross-range extent measured between the half-power points of the one-way power response to a point scatterer, as illustrated in Fig. 6.5. The total transfer power response, however, actually involves the two-way power gain of the antenna. An idealized radar (Fig. 6.6) using a linear superheterodyne receiver will generate an IF signal power level to the display that is proportional to the echo signal power appearing at the antenna terminals. If we assume square-law detection, the detected IF signal voltage to the display will be proportional to echo signal power.

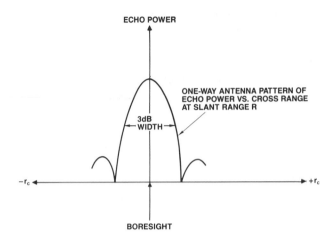

Fig. 6.5 Cross-Range Resolution Associated with a Real Aperture Antenna

The echo signal, given the above assumptions, is displayed as brightness by a linear display. Display brightness is then proportional to the echo signal power appearing at the output of the receiving antenna terminals. The real aperture antenna of the radar functions as a power transfer function that operates twice on the signal to be displayed: once to transmit and once to receive. In each case the power response function to a scatterer displaced in azimuth angle ϕ from boresight will be the antenna power gain function $|Z(\phi)/Z(0)|^2 = G(\phi)$, where $Z(\phi)$ is the signal response at angle ϕ from boresight and $G(\phi)$ is the antenna power gain at ϕ. Thus, from the standpoint of the idealized radar transfer function, it appears logical to define resolution in terms of the two-way half-power beamwidth of the antenna. This would make brightness proportional to $G^2(\phi)$, as indicated in Fig. 6.6. The transfer response of an actual, real beam-mapping radar, however, may produce resolution corresponding more closely to its one-way antenna pattern.

Cross-range resolution Δr_c of a real aperture radar according to the one-way definition is the cross-range distance at some range R, corresponding to the one-way half-power azimuth beamwidth $\phi_{3\text{ dB}}$ of the antenna power-gain pattern. Therefore, for small beamwidths,

$$\Delta r_c = R\phi_{3\text{ dB}} \tag{6.1}$$

The *power gain pattern* for a cross-range antenna length l will now be determined for an ideal, uniformly illuminated antenna to illustrate a general approach, which shall be used later for discussing synthetic apertures.

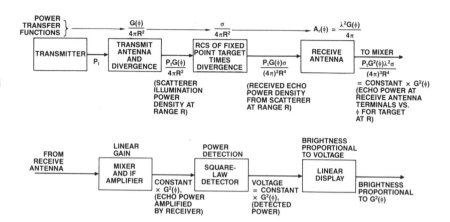

Fig. 6.6 Transfer Function of Idealized, Real Aperture Mapping Radar

Figure 6.7 illustrates a line antenna of length *l*. Assume that the antenna continuously integrates incident radiated energy as though there were an infinite number of array elements, spaced infinitesimally close to one another along the line. All radiation from the boresight direction to the line antenna, from a source located at infinite range, will arrive at the same phase, which is taken to be zero phase. For radiation arriving from off-boresight angles, the arrival phase at the antenna is a function of distance along the line antenna, as indicated in Fig. 6.7.

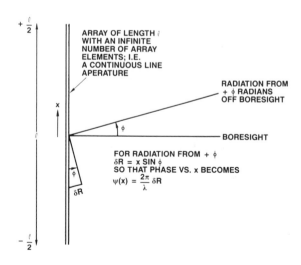

Fig. 6.7 Real Aperture Line Antenna

Consider the signal from a point target at angle $+\phi$ rad from boresight. The signal to one element of the line array will be taken to be a 1 V signal, which has a phase advance $\psi(x) = (2\pi/\lambda)x \sin \phi$. The integrated response written in complex form becomes

$$Z(\phi) = \int_{-l/2}^{+l/2} e^{j\psi(x)}dx$$

By expanding the exponential in terms of its quadrature components, we have

$$Z(\phi) = \int_{-l/2}^{+l/2} \cos [\psi(x)]dx + j \int_{-l/2}^{+l/2} \sin [\psi(x)]dx$$

The imaginary term, being odd, integrates to zero, leaving only the real component, which integrates to

$$Z(\phi) = \frac{\sin \left(\dfrac{\pi}{\lambda} l \sin \phi\right)}{\left(\dfrac{\pi}{\lambda} l \sin \phi\right)} l \tag{6.2}$$

If normalized to unity at $\phi = 0$, the one-way antenna power gain becomes

$$\left|\frac{Z(\phi)}{Z(0)}\right|^2 = \frac{\sin^2 \left(\dfrac{\pi}{\lambda} l \sin \phi\right)}{\left(\dfrac{\pi}{\lambda} l \sin \phi\right)^2}$$

At the half-power points, we have

$$\frac{\sin^2 \left(\dfrac{\pi}{\lambda} l \sin \phi\right)}{\left(\dfrac{\pi}{\lambda} l \sin \phi\right)^2} = \frac{1}{2}$$

which is a transcendental expression. The graphical solution for the argument is

$$\frac{\pi}{\lambda} l \sin \phi \approx \pm 1.39$$

At the half-power points of the response, we have

$$\sin \phi \mid_{3 \text{ dB}} \approx \pm 0.44 \frac{\lambda}{l}$$

For small beamwidth, the off-boresight angle corresponding to the half-power points is

$$\phi \mid_{3 \text{ dB}} = \pm 0.44 \frac{\lambda}{l}$$

Thus, the one-way half-power beamwidth is

$$\phi_{3 \text{ dB}} \approx 0.88 \frac{\lambda}{l} \tag{6.3}$$

The two-way half-power beamwidth is found by setting

$$\frac{\sin^4 \left(\frac{\pi}{\lambda} l \sin \phi \right)}{\left(\frac{\pi}{\lambda} l \sin \phi \right)^4} = \frac{1}{2}$$

The two-way beamwidth becomes $0.64 \, \lambda/l$. From (6.1) and (6.3), the one-way resolution Δr_c in cross range for a real aperture mapping radar operating in the side-looking mode becomes

$$\Delta r_c \text{ (one way)} \approx 0.88 \, R \frac{\lambda}{l} \tag{6.4a}$$

The two-way resolution is

$$\Delta r_c \text{ (two way)} \approx 0.64 \, R \frac{\lambda}{l} \tag{6.4b}$$

We can see that improved resolution occurs for short wavelengths and large apertures in the cross-range dimension. Also, the resolution is a direct function of range. The resolution Δr_c for actual antennas, where nonuniform weighting is used to reduce sidelobes, will be approximately $R\lambda/l$.

A side-looking, real aperture radar used by the US Coast Guard for environmental resource monitoring flys in the Falcon HU-25A aircraft shown in Fig. 6.8. This is AIREYE, an advanced ocean surveillance system developed by Aerojet. The radar is the Motorola *side-looking airborne radar* (SLAR) [6]. Imagery shown in Fig. 6.9 was recorded over Santa Barbara Channel near Santa Barbara, CA. The radar can detect oil seepage and spills, which would appear as darker streaks on the imagery. Oil spills appear as "holes" in the radar image because the oil dampens the surface-wave motion on the water, making it less reflective. Other ocean-wave phenomena can be detected as well as ice and icebergs.

Excellent mapping is possible by using real aperture radars. However, our discussion now turns to means of improving resolution by synthetically generating a very long aperture.

Fig. 6.8 AIREYE Ocean Surveillance Aircraft Carrying a Real Aperture Side-Looking Radar (Note the long, real aperture antenna hanging below the aircraft.) (From Sentz, J.D., Jr., and J.D. Wiley, "Radar's Growing Role in Ice, Pollution Surveillance," *Sea Technology*, Aug. 1985, p. 27. Reprinted with permission.)

6.3 SAR THEORY (UNFOCUSED APERTURE)

Figure 6.10 illustrates the geometry for generating a synthetic aperture. A synthetic aperture of length $\mathscr{L}$ is generated by an airborne or spaceborne side-looking radar as it flies along the indicated ground track from $-v_p T/2$ to $+v_p T/2$, where v_p is the platform's ground-track velocity

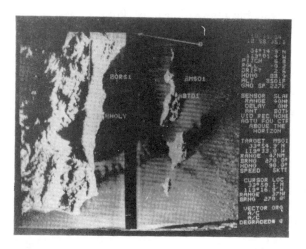

Fig. 6.9 Santa Barbara Channel as Seen with a Side-Looking Radar (From Sentz, J.D., Jr., and J.D. Wiley, "Radar's Growing Role in Ice, Pollution Surveillance," *Sea Technology*, Aug. 1985, p. 27. Reprinted with permissioin.)

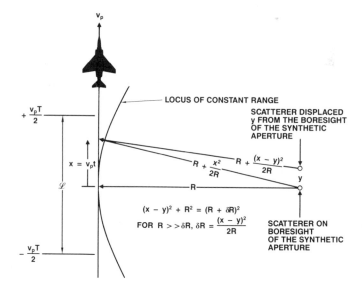

Fig. 6.10 Geometry for Generating a Synthetic Aperture

and T is the available integration time. Point targets are shown at both boresight and displacement y in cross range from the radar. Targets are illuminated for a time determined by radar range R, the aircraft velocity v_p, and the real aperture beamwidth. Time t is taken to be zero when the aircraft is at the minimum range R to the point target at $y = 0$. A range variation δR from R exists before and after $t = 0$.

Resolution of the synthetic aperture of Fig. 6.10 will now be determined by developing the resulting two-way power-gain response $|Z(y)/Z(0)|^2$, where $Z(y)$ is the response to a point target at cross-range distance y from boresight. Similarly to real aperture analysis, the resolution will be taken as the cross-range distance between the half-power points of the power gain response to a point target. The SAR response $Z(y)$ is the phasor sum of the echo signal, which is received from a point target at y and integrated over time $-T/2$ to $+T/2$. Echo signal phase at each position along x is the two-way phase relative to transmission phase, such as would be obtained by quadrature mixing with the radar's stable oscillator. (This is by contrast to the one-way phase of the signal at each element with real aperture integration as discussed above.)

The two-way phase advance of the echo signal from a point target at position $y = 0$ is

$$\psi_1(t) = -\frac{4\pi}{\lambda} \frac{v_p^2 t^2}{2R} \tag{6.5}$$

This is a quadratic phase term resulting from straight-line platform motion past the scene to be mapped. We will now examine what is referred to as *unfocused SAR*, which results when this term is not corrected and thus remains in the expression for power gain response of the synthetic aperture.

The two-way phase advance of the echo signal from a point target at position y is

$$\psi_2(t, y) = -\frac{\frac{4\pi}{\lambda}(x - y)^2}{2R} \tag{6.6}$$

where

$$x = v_p t$$

Note that $\psi_2(t, y)$ in (6.6) includes the $\psi_1(t)$ term. The normalized echo signal written in complex form is

$$e^{j\psi_2(t,y)} = \cos\psi_2(t, y) + j \sin\psi_2(t, y)$$
$$= \cos\left[-\psi_2(t)\right] - j \sin\left[-\psi_2(t)\right]$$

At first, it will be assumed that the PRF is high enough so that the echo signal can be treated as though it were a continuous signal. This continuous signal is then processed by integrating it over a time interval $-T/2$ to $+T/2$.

The summed response of the echo signal, assuming uniform illumination during integration time T, is expressed as a function of point target location y as

$$Z(y) = \int_{-T/2}^{+T/2} \exp\left[-\frac{j4\pi}{2R\lambda}(v_p t - y)^2\right] dt$$

By expanding the exponential in terms of its quadrature components, we have

$$Z(y) = \int_{-T/2}^{+T/2} \cos\left[\frac{2\pi}{R\lambda}(v_p t - y)^2\right] dt - j\int_{-T/2}^{+T/2} \sin\left[\frac{2\pi}{R\lambda}(v_p t - y)^2\right] dt$$

The power response is then given by

$$|Z(y)|^2 = \left\{\int_{-T/2}^{+T/2} \cos\left[\frac{2\pi}{R\lambda}(v_p t - y)^2\right] dt\right\}^2$$
$$+ \left\{\int_{-T/2}^{+T/2} \sin\left[\frac{2\pi}{R\lambda}(v_p t - y)^2\right] dt\right\}^2 \tag{6.7}$$

These integrals can be written in terms of the Fresnel sine and cosine integrals:

$$C(z) = \int_0^z \cos\left(\frac{\pi}{2}s^2\right) ds$$

and

$$S(z) = \int_0^z \sin\left(\frac{\pi}{2}s^2\right) ds \tag{6.8}$$

where s is a variable of integration.

Power gain response of an unfocused synthetic aperture, when normalized to peak gain at $y = 0$, can be expressed, in terms of the Fresnel integrals of (6.8), as

$$\frac{|Z(y)|^2}{|Z(0)|^2} = \frac{T^2\left(\dfrac{R\lambda}{4v_p^2T^2}\right)\{[C(\eta - \zeta) + C(\eta + \zeta)]^2 + [S(\eta - \zeta) + S(\eta + \zeta)]^2\}}{T^2\left(\dfrac{R\lambda}{4v_p^2T^2}\right)[4C^2(\eta) + 4S^2(\eta)]}$$

$$= \frac{[C(\eta - \zeta) + C(\eta + \zeta)]^2 + [S(\eta - \zeta) + S(\eta + \zeta)]^2}{4[C^2(\eta) + S^2(\eta)]} \qquad (6.9)$$

where

$$\eta = \frac{v_pT}{\sqrt{R\lambda}} \text{ and } \zeta = \frac{2y}{\sqrt{R\lambda}}$$

The power gain response, (6.9), is maximized at the peak of the response to a target at $y = 0$, when $C^2(\eta) + S^2(\eta)$ is maximum. Examination of the values of Fresnel integrals plotted in Fig. 6.11 for $C(z)$ and $S(z)$ indicates that the peak of the quantity $C^2(\eta) + S^2(\eta)$ occurs at $\eta \approx 1.2$.

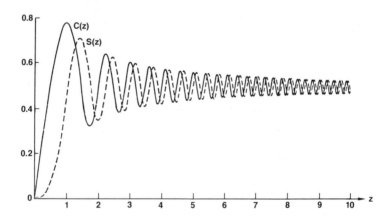

Fig. 6.11 Plots of the $C(z)$ and $S(z)$ Fresnel Integrals

Thus, the peak power response to a point target occurs for

$$\eta = 1.2 = \frac{v_p T}{\sqrt{R\lambda}}$$

The optimum unfocused aperture length corresponding to $\eta \approx 1.2$ is

$$\mathscr{L} = v_p T \approx 1.2 \sqrt{R\lambda}$$

Longer integration time does not contribute to the integrated response at $y = 0$ because of the uncorrected quadratic phase term $\psi_1(t)$ of (6.5), which is part of the total phase advance $\psi_2(t, y)$ associated with the two-way echo delay.

The half-power resolution corresponding to this length is found by solving for the value of ζ that satisfies $|Z(y)/Z(0)|^2 = 0.5$ at $\eta = 1.2$. The result is $\zeta \approx 0.5$, so that

$$\Delta r_c = 2|y| = \zeta \sqrt{R\lambda} \approx 0.5 \sqrt{R\lambda} \qquad (6.10)$$

We can see here that the resolution of an unfocused synthetic aperture degrades as the square root of range and wavelength.

We will show in the following discussion that the Fresnel terms disappear when the quadratic phase term $\psi_1(t)$ of (6.5) is cancelled, which is attempted in most SAR designs. However, the above analysis is sometimes used to assess the reduced resolution due to the presence of residual uncorrected quadratic phase.

6.4 SAR THEORY (FOCUSED APERTURE)

The quadratic phase term $\psi_1(t)$ of (6.5), produced by the straight-line platform motion, can be subtracted from the total phase advance $\psi_2(t)$ to generate what is called a *focused aperture*. Then, from (6.5) and (6.6), the corrected two-way phase term is

$$\psi_2(t, y) - \psi_1(t) = -\frac{\frac{4\pi}{\lambda}(x - y)^2}{2R} - \left(-\frac{\frac{4\pi}{\lambda}x^2}{2R} \right)$$

$$= -\frac{4\pi}{\lambda}\left(-\frac{xy}{R} + \frac{y^2}{2R} \right)$$

where $x = v_p t$.

The corrected response to a point target at a cross-range distance y from boresight then becomes

$$Z(y) = \int_{-T/2}^{+T/2} \exp\left[-\frac{j4\pi}{\lambda} \left(-\frac{v_p t y}{R} + \frac{y^2}{2R} \right) \right] dt$$

The absolute value of $Z(y)$ is

$$|Z(y)| = \left| \int_{-T/2}^{+T/2} \exp\left(j\frac{4\pi}{\lambda} \frac{v_p t y}{R} \right) dt \right|$$

The result, after carrying out the integration similarly to that for (6.2), is

$$|Z(y)| = \left| \frac{\sin\left(\dfrac{2\pi v_p T y}{R\lambda} \right)}{\dfrac{2\pi v_p T y}{R\lambda}} \right| T$$

The normalized radar response *versus* cross-range distance from boresight becomes

$$\frac{|Z(y)|^2}{|Z(0)|^2} = \frac{\sin^2\left(\dfrac{2\pi v_p T y}{R\lambda} \right)}{\left(\dfrac{2\pi v_p T y}{R\lambda} \right)^2}$$

This can also be considered as the two-way power gain response for the focused synthetic aperture antenna of length $\mathcal{L} = v_p T$.

The half-power points of the two-way pattern occur for

$$\frac{\sin^2\left(\dfrac{2\pi v_p T y}{R\lambda} \right)}{\left(\dfrac{2\pi v_p T y}{R\lambda} \right)^2} = \frac{1}{2}$$

for which

$$\frac{2\pi v_p T y}{R\lambda} = \pm 1.39$$

so that, for $v_p T = \mathcal{L}$, we have

$$y|_{3 \text{ dB}} = \pm .22 \frac{R\lambda}{\mathcal{L}}$$

Resolution measured at the half-power points is, therefore,

$$\Delta r_c = .44 \frac{R\lambda}{\mathcal{L}}$$

Cross-range resolution Δr_c is seen to be inversely proportional to the array length $\mathcal{L}$. It is half the one-way resolution associated with a real aperture of the same length, as we can see by comparison with (6.4a). This can be shown to occur because of two-way synthetic antenna phase advance *versus* one-way real antenna phase advance.

Cross-range resolution can be expressed in terms of the SAR's real aperture by assuming that the synthetic integration length is limited by the one-way beamwidth of the real antenna. For a small real aperture beam-width $\phi_{3 \text{ dB}}$, we can write

$$\mathcal{L} = R\phi_{3 \text{ dB}}$$

With $\phi_{3 \text{ dB}}$ from (6.3),

$$\mathcal{L} = 0.88R \frac{\lambda}{l}$$

where l is the real aperture length of the SAR antenna. Then,

$$\Delta r_c = \frac{0.44R\lambda}{0.88R\frac{\lambda}{l}} = \frac{l}{2} \tag{6.11}$$

For a side-looking SAR, we can see that resolution is limited by the real aperture size. A small real aperture along the cross-range dimension results in better SAR resolution by contrast with real aperture mapping, where large cross-range aperture produces better resolution.

In summary, it is possible to increase the cross-range resolution of surface-mapping radars over that of real aperture mapping radars by co-herently integrating target echo signals as the radar platform passes by the area to be mapped. Maximum possible resolution occurs for focused SAR when quadratic phase error and all other phase errors are corrected before integration. The SAR technique is essential for spaceborne radar mapping of the earth's surface, where useful resolution is not likely to be achieved with practical real apertures. The following equations were derived above for resolution associated with three types of apertures in increasing order of two-way resolution:

real aperture (6.4b):

$$\Delta r_c \approx 0.64 \; R \; \frac{\lambda}{l}$$

unfocused SAR (6.10):

$$\Delta r_c \approx 0.5 \; \sqrt{R\lambda}$$

focused SAR (6.11):

$$\Delta r_c \approx \frac{l}{2}$$

Resolution *versus* range for the above three types of apertures is plotted in Fig. 6.12 for a 3.0 m real aperture at $\lambda = 3.0$ m.

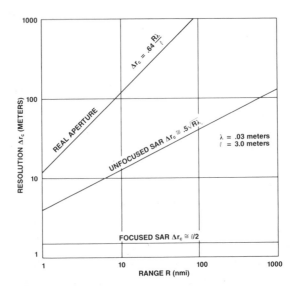

Fig. 6.12 Resolution *versus* Range for Three Generic Types of Mapping Radars at .03 m Wavelength

6.5 SAR THEORY FROM DOPPLER POINT OF VIEW

The focused-aperture SAR concept can also be explained from the point of view of differential Doppler signals produced by scatterers separated in cross range relative to the radar. This viewpoint leads more directly to the ISAR concept, which is to be discussed in Chapter 7.

Consider the airborne SAR of Fig. 6.13 at the instant that the aircraft is directly beamed on boresight to the center of two point targets, both at range R, which are located in cross range at $-y$ and $+y$, respectively, from the radar. The instantaneous velocity of the radar past the two targets, for small real beams, will produce an echo signal containing a pair of instantaneous Doppler offset frequencies $-(2\bar{f}/c)\omega y$ and $+(2\bar{f}/c)\omega y$ for a radar center frequency $\bar{f}$, where ω is the instantaneous angular velocity of the aircraft relative to the centroid of the two targets.

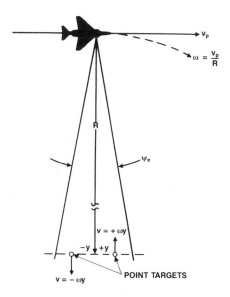

Fig. 6.13 Source of SAR Cross-Range Doppler

The Doppler frequency separation is

$$\delta f_D = \frac{4}{c}\,\omega y\bar{f}$$

For a Doppler frequency resolution Δf_D, the cross-range resolution becomes

$$\Delta r_c = 2|y|$$

$$= \frac{c}{2\omega \bar{f}} \Delta f_D$$

As discussed in Chapter 2, ideal processing of a uniform signal can achieve frequency resolution, measured at the -4 dB points, equal to the reciprocal of integration time T. Therefore, for integration over a uniform gain *versus* angle region of a real beam:

$$\Delta r_c = \frac{c}{2\omega T \bar{f}}$$

Cross-range resolution, written in terms of wavelength, becomes

$$\Delta r_c = \frac{1}{2} \frac{\lambda}{\omega T} \qquad (6.12)$$

For coherent integration over a beam segment ψ of constant gain:

$$\Delta r_c = \frac{1}{2} \frac{\lambda}{\psi}$$

For total beam integration during the beam dwell time of a real antenna with an equivalent rectangular beamwidth ψ_e, we can write $\omega T = \psi_e$. Resolution is often of interest for total beam integration of a uniformly weighted antenna. An equivalent rectangular beamwidth is often defined for uniformly weighted antennas by requiring equal values of the integrated two-way voltage response from the equivalent rectangular beam and a uniformly weighted antenna, each with the same peak response (e.g., normalized to 1.0). We will assume for the SAR case that the voltage is not affected by the slight range difference associated with straight-line motion of the radar platform past the pair of point targets.

The normalized one-way response $Z(\phi)$, expressed in (6.2) for a uniformly weighted real antenna, is $Z(\phi)/l$. Integration will be carried out between azimuth angles $\phi = -\pi/2$ to $+\pi/2$ from boresight. The response will actually lie mostly between the null positions. Integration of the response for a rectangular-beam antenna will be carried out between $\phi = -\psi_e/2$ to $+\psi_e/2$. By setting the integration of the rectangular antenna's two-way response equal to that for the uniformly weighted antenna, we have

$$\int_{-\psi_e/2}^{+\psi_e/2} (1)^2 d\phi = \int_{-\pi/2}^{+\pi/2} \left(\frac{Z(\phi)}{l}\right)^2 d\phi$$

Solving for ψ_e, with $Z(\phi)$ from (6.2), we have

$$\psi_e = \int_{-\pi/2}^{+\pi/2} \frac{\sin^2\left(\frac{\pi}{\lambda} l \sin \phi\right)}{\left(\frac{\pi}{\lambda} l \sin \phi\right)^2} d\phi$$

For most cases of interest, the beamwidth is so small that $\sin \phi \approx \phi$. Nearly all of the integrated response results from azimuth angles $\phi \ll \pi/2$. By assuming a narrow beamwidth for which the response is negligible beyond $\pm \pi/2$, the equivalent rectangular beamwidth becomes

$$\psi_e \approx \frac{\lambda}{\pi l} \int_{-\infty}^{+\infty} \frac{\sin^2 x}{x^2} dx = \frac{2\lambda}{\pi l} \int_{0}^{+\infty} \frac{\sin^2 x}{x^2} dx = \frac{\lambda}{l} \qquad (6.13)$$

where $x \approx (\pi/\lambda) l\phi$ and $dx \approx (\pi/\lambda) l \, d\phi$. For integration over a uniformly weighted narrowbeam antenna, the expression for cross-range resolution, given by (6.12) becomes

$$\Delta r_c = \frac{1}{2} \frac{\lambda}{\psi_e} = \frac{l}{2}$$

where $\omega T = \psi_e$. This is the same relation (6.11) that was developed for focused SAR from the viewpoint of antenna theory.

We may conclude that resolution provided by total beam integration for a uniformly weighted antenna is the same as that provided by integration over the antenna's equivalent rectangular beamwidth, which, when defined as above, is given in (6.13) as $\psi_e = \lambda/l$. An antenna's equivalent rectangular beamwidth will also be referred to as its effective beamwidth.

The expressions given above for cross-range SAR resolution were based on the response produced by coherent integration during the real beam dwell time of the reflected signals from point targets. Coherent integration of the signal received along the resulting synthetic aperture produced the fine cross-range resolution associated with a large aperture. From the Doppler viewpoint, coherent integration of the Doppler-shifted signal from each of the pair of point targets seen by the SAR produced fine Doppler resolution, which was shown to be related directly to cross-range resolution. In practice, the coherent integration process may take several forms. The most common approach (discussed later in this chapter) is to correlate the azimuthal signal data collected along known range *versus* azimuth trajectories to a suitable azimuthal reference to achieve azimuth compression.

6.6 CHIRP-PULSE COMPRESSION SAR

6.6.1 Resolution

Fine range resolution produced by conventional side-looking SAR, spotlight SAR, or Doppler beam sharpening is often obtained via some type of pulse-compression method, chirp-pulse compression being the most common. Later, we will discuss a frequency-agile SAR concept, wherein range resolution is achieved synthetically as described in Chapter 5. The resolution Δr_s in range for pulse-compression SAR is approximately $c/2\beta$, where β is the transmitted pulse bandwidth. For a chirp pulse, β is approximately the frequency range Δ over which frequency modulation exists. Cross-range resolution Δr_c for a perfectly focused SAR, from (6.12), is $\lambda/(2\omega T)$ with $\omega T = \psi$ rad, where ψ is the integration angle. The equivalent rectangular beamwidth ψ_e of a real antenna is substituted for ψ when integration is carried out over the entire real antenna beamwidth in azimuth. From (6.13), the equivalent rectangular beamwidth of a uniformly weighted real antenna is λ/l.

Therefore, for side-looking SAR, regardless of how slant-range resolution is achieved, the cross-range resolution produced by integration over small real beams is

$$\Delta r_c = \frac{1}{2}\frac{\lambda}{\psi_e} = \frac{l}{2} \qquad (6.14)$$

The cross-range resolution possible with spotlight SAR for integration over a small angle $\psi = \Delta\phi$ rad becomes

$$\Delta r_c = \frac{1}{2}\frac{\lambda}{\Delta\phi} \qquad (6.15)$$

For small integration angles ψ and $\Delta\phi$, a cross-range integration length of $R\psi$ exists for side-looking SAR and $R\Delta\phi$ for spotlight SAR, respectively, where $R\psi$ and $R\Delta\phi$ are the synthetic aperture lengths for each type of SAR.

6.6.2 Data Collection

Figure 6.14(a) illustrates the process of collecting SAR data obtained with a chirp-pulse compression radar. As the platform containing the radar travels above and alongside of the area to be mapped, chirp pulses are transmitted at some PRF, which is assumed here to be constant. Time between pulses is made sufficiently long to prevent ambiguous range responses, at least over the effective illuminated range extent wherein echo signals may appear above the noise. A slightly different patch of the earth's surface is illuminated by each transmitted pulse. Each time a pulse is transmitted, the echo signal is sampled at some range sample spacing, or continuously recorded, over some portion of the illuminated range extent, called *range swath*.

The collected data comprise a set of reflectivity measurements in two dimensions. The dimensions of the data format can be referred to in several ways: slant range *versus* cross range, range delay *versus* time history, fast time *versus* slow time, and range *versus* azimuth. A data record (Fig. 6.14(b)) will extend in slant range over the range swath and continuously in cross range along the flight path over which data are collected.

The data set does not resemble a map of the terrain before processing. Rather, echoes from individual point targets are dispersed in both range and azimuth, as illustrated by the data collection element in Fig. 6.14(b). Range and azimuth compression, to be described later, produce the desired maps.

It will be convenient to refer to a *rectangular* data-collection element illustrated in Fig. 6.14(c) for side-looking SAR. This element is sampled by approximately $\eta_s \times \eta_c$ samples. This is the area bounded in cross-range extent by two slant-range segments, each of length $cT_1/2$, which is the *slant-range integration length*. The slant-range extent is bounded by two cross-range arc segments, each of approximate length $R\psi$, which is the *cross-range integration length*. For side-looking SAR, $R\psi$ is the *synthetic aperture size*. When defined in this way, the data-collection element contains the two-dimensional dispersed response to a point target. The data-collection element approaches a true rectangle for small ψ when $R \gg cT_1/2$. A total of η_s complex echo samples are collected during range integration time T_1 for each of N transmitted pulses occurring within the azimuthal integration angle ψ. A total of $\eta_c = N$ samples is collected along the length $R\psi$ of each resulting range cell.

Data collected from the slant-range and cross-range space indicated in Fig. 6.14 are processed to achieve range and azimuth compression. Compression in range is from $cT_1/2$ to Δr_s, where Δr_s is the slant-range resolution. The compression in azimuth is from $R\psi$ to Δr_c, where Δr_c is the cross-range resolution.

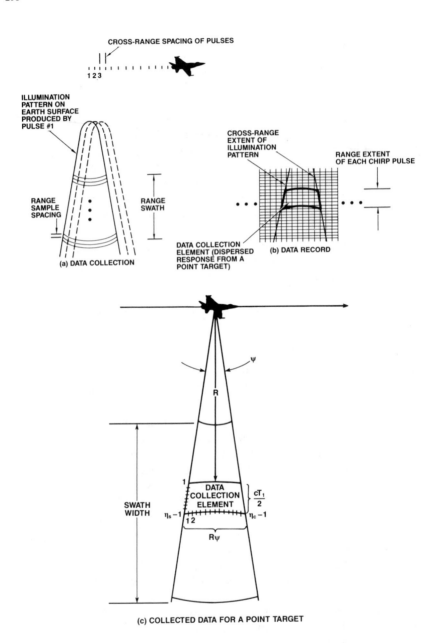

Fig. 6.14 SAR Data Collection

Echo signals produced from each linear FM pulse of bandwidth β to meet the Nyquist sampling criteria must be sampled by at least β complex samples per second. This corresponds to a complex sample spacing of $1/\beta$ in range delay and to a range resolution of $\Delta r_s = c/2\beta$. In other words, the range-delay echo signal produced by each chirp pulse is required to be sampled at a slant-range spacing equal to or less than the slant-range resolution Δr_s, produced by the transmitted chirp bandwidth.

Sampling requirements in cross-range are similar. At the nearest approach of a side-looking SAR in straight-line motion past a surface point target, the range rate and, therefore, the Doppler shift will vary linearly with time (history), passing through zero frequency at boresight. During the target dwell time for small real beamwidth, the Doppler shift therefore approximates linear FM. Azimuth compression, then, can be thought of as compression of the frequency modulated Doppler signal produced during the integration length $R\psi$. Therefore, the azimuth echo signal in each range cell is required to be sampled at a cross-range spacing equal to or less than the cross-range resolution Δr_c, produced by the Doppler FM seen across the real beamwidth during its dwell time at range R.

Unambiguous data sampling of the two-dimensional dispersed response occurs when

$$\eta_s \Delta r_s \geq \frac{cT_1}{2} \tag{6.16}$$

and

$$\eta_c \Delta r_c \geq R\psi \tag{6.17}$$

with one complex sample per resolution cell.

6.6.3 Slant-Range Sampling Criteria

The minimum number of required samples following each transmitted pulse, for unambiguous slant-range sampling of each integration length $cT_1/2$, is obtained from (6.16) as

$$\eta_s \geq \frac{cT_1}{2\Delta r_s} = T_1 \Delta$$

where Δ is the chirp-pulse bandwidth.

In practice, the design of pulse-compression radars that use data sampling techniques is often limited in resolution by the maximum available A/D conversion rates. For example, if the A/D conversion rate is 100 megabytes per second, this translates to about 1.5 m slant-range resolution for unambiguous sampling, according to (6.16), i.e.,

$$\Delta r_s = \frac{cT_1}{2\eta_s}$$

$$= \frac{c}{2} \frac{1}{(\eta_s/T_1)}$$

$$= \frac{3 \times 10^8}{2} \times \frac{1}{100 \times 10^6} = 1.5 \text{ m}$$

for $\eta_s/T_1 = 100 \times 10^6$ complex samples per second. Actual SAR systems of this resolution, to avoid sampling at these rates, tend to rely on analog means for recording echo data on film. This is followed by optical processing. *Frequency-agile SAR,* to be described later in this chapter, is a concept that avoids the requirement for high A/D converter rates to achieve high resolution. High-speed A/D conversion can also be avoided by means of stretch waveforms, mentioned in Chapter 4.

6.6.4 Cross-Range (Azimuth) Sampling Criteria and PRF

The minimum number of samples required for unambiguous azimuth sampling of the azimuthal integration length $R\psi$ at each range position is the processed integration length divided by the cross-range resolution associated with the integration length of the entire real beam. From (6.17) and (6.14), we obtain

$$\eta_c \geq \frac{R\psi}{\Delta r_c} = \frac{R\psi}{\dfrac{1}{2} \dfrac{\lambda}{\psi_e}} \text{ samples} \tag{6.18a}$$

Integration may be carried out over the entire real beam. An estimate of the minimum number of samples can then be made under the assumption that the effective integration beamwidth is given by the equivalent rectangular beamwidth ψ_e. For $\psi = \psi_e$, we have

$$\eta_c \geq \frac{2R\psi_e^2}{\lambda} \text{ samples} \tag{6.18b}$$

Equation (6.18a) applies when the integration is carried out over an angle $\psi \neq \psi_e$. Equation (6.18b) applies when resolution is achieved by coherent integration over the effective (equivalent rectangular) beamwidth of the real antenna so that $\Delta r_c = \lambda/2\psi_e$. Two situations in which integration angle and effective beamwidth differ are (1) when coherent integration is carried out over segments of the real beam to form multiple *looks* of reduced resolution for speckle reduction (a method described later), and (2) for spotlight SAR, where coherent integration is carried out over an angle $\Delta\phi$ that generally is not equal to the effective beamwidth ψ_e of the real antenna. The significance of this, in terms of required PRF, will be discussed below.

6.6.5 Pulse Repetition Frequency (PRF) Requirements

Radar PRF must meet the Nyquist criteria for sampling of the Doppler signal produced by the effective rotation, as seen by the radar, of the cross-range extent of the earth's surface from which echo signals may arrive. From Fig. 6.15, Doppler bandwidth produced by scatterers at range

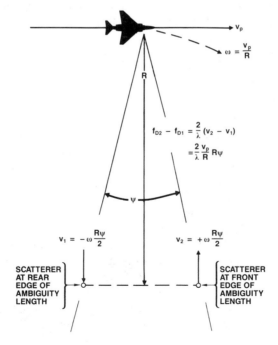

Fig. 6.15 Doppler Spread Associated with Cross-Range Ambiguity Length

R, extending over cross-range length $R\psi$, is

$$f_{D2} - f_{D1} = \frac{2}{\lambda} \frac{v_p}{R} R\psi$$

Cross-range length $R\psi$, expressed in terms of Doppler bandwidth, becomes

$$R\psi = \frac{R\lambda}{2v_p} (f_{D2} - f_{D1})$$

A cross-range ambiguity length $(R\psi)_{max}$ associated with the Nyquist PRF $1/T_2$, equal to $f_{D2} - f_{D1}$, can be defined as

$$(R\psi)_{max} = \frac{R\lambda}{2v_p T_2} \tag{6.19}$$

An illuminated cross-range extent greater than $(R\psi)_{max}$ will be undersampled. Required PRF, for reasons stated above, must be defined in terms of real antenna beamwidth. Nyquist sampling in a side-looking SAR mode requires that $(R\psi)_{max} \geqslant R\psi_e$, so that, from (6.19) and (6.13), we have

$$\frac{1}{T_2} \geqslant \frac{2v_p}{R\lambda} R\psi_e \approx \frac{2v_p}{l} \tag{6.20}$$

Multiple coherent looks taken across the real azimuth beamwidth produce the cross-range resolution given by (6.12), where $\psi = \omega T$ is the *single-look integration angle*. This reduced resolution from that available from the entire real beam is traded off for reduced speckle noise when multiple looks are added noncoherently. However, received Doppler spectrum is produced by rotation past the cross-range extent illuminated by the entire real beam. Adequate sampling of this band of Doppler frequencies requires the PRF given by (6.20).

Equation (6.20) can also be obtained from the viewpoint of grating lobes in the *synthetic aperture pattern*. From Fig. 6.16, the two-way phase difference between echo radiation from an on-boresight scatterer and an off-boresight scatterer, displaced ϕ radians from boresight, is $(4\pi/\lambda)v_p T_2$ sin ϕ for a PRI of T_2. When the phase difference is 2π, the signal from the off-boresight scatterer is coherently integrated, producing a spurious response referred to by antenna designers as a *grating lobe*.

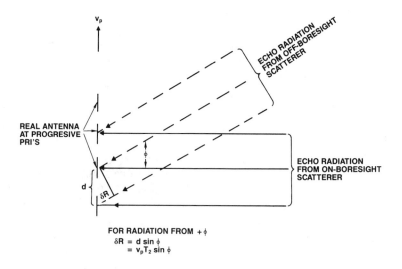

FOR RADIATION FROM $+\phi$
$\delta R = d \sin \phi$
$= v_p T_2 \sin \phi$

Fig. 6.16 SAR Grating-Lobe Geometry

Grating lobes occur for

$$2\pi = \frac{4\pi}{\lambda} v_p T_2 \sin \phi$$

or, solving for $\sin \phi$,

$$\sin \phi = \frac{\lambda}{2v_p} \frac{1}{T_2}$$

For grating-lobe angles ϕ that are large compared to real antenna beam-width, there will be negligible grating-lobe responses. This is the situation for most aircraft SAR applications in which speed is relatively slow.

A minimum PRF criterion can be established as the PRF that produces a grating lobe at the first null of the real beam pattern. A higher PRF will then produce grating lobes that fall outside the real main beam. The first null of a uniformly weighted antenna can be seen from (6.2) to occur for $\sin \phi = \lambda/l$, leading to the criterion that

$$\frac{1}{T_2} \geq \frac{2v_p}{l}$$

Note that this is identical to (6.20), which was determined by requiring that PRF be greater than the Nyquist sampling rate for complex sampling in cross range. It may be desirable to avoid grating-lobe responses more safely by setting the grating-lobe angle farther from the main beam, for example, at the second null. Then, the PRF criterion becomes

$$\frac{1}{T_2} \geq \frac{4v_p}{l}$$

There is no cross-track beam traveling past the target in an ideal spotlight SAR mode. An unambiguous cross-range length for small integration angle $\Delta\phi$, however, can still be defined by (6.19) through substitution of $v_p |\sin \phi|$ for the platform speed v_p, where ϕ is the squint angle of the real beam from straight ahead. The maximum unambiguous cross-range length $(R\psi)_{max}$, as for the side-looking SAR, must be greater than the illuminated cross-range length $R\psi$. Therefore, for spotlight SAR, the required PRF for unambiguous sampling is $(2v_p |\sin \phi|)/l$.

An additional consideration regarding PRF occurs when the combination of large illuminated range extent and high platform speed is involved, as in the case of spaceborne SAR. Data *foldover* in slant range is prevented by requiring a sufficiently low PRF so that echoes arriving from each pulse do not overlap those from the previous pulse. For illuminated range extent ΔR_l, the minimum PRI to avoid overlapping is $2\Delta R_l/c$. Maximum PRF is $c/(2\Delta R_l)$. At the same time, the PRF must be sufficiently high to avoid undersampling of the illuminated cross-range extent. Selection of the PRF to meet these conflicting criteria will be discussed later, using the SEASAT spaceborne SAR as a design example.

6.6.6 Square Resolution

In a spotlight SAR mode, it may be desirable to maintain *square* resolution, defined as $\Delta r = \Delta r_s = \Delta r_c$. Slant-range resolution is given by

$$\Delta r_s = \frac{c}{2\beta}$$

Cross-range resolution is

$$\Delta r_c = \frac{1}{2} \frac{\lambda}{\omega T}$$

For squint angle ϕ with $\omega = (v_p |\sin \phi|)/R$, we have

$$\Delta r_c = \frac{R\lambda}{2Tv_p |\sin \phi|}$$

The bandwidth that results in square resolution, based on the above expressions, becomes

$$\beta = \frac{cv_pT}{\lambda R} |\sin \phi| \qquad\qquad (6.21)$$

Theoretically, *square-resolution zooming* could be done dynamically by increasing chirp bandwidth, according to (6.21), to improve slant-range resolution as dwell time is increased to improve cross-range resolution and *vice versa.*

Square resolution for side-looking SAR, if desired, requires that the slant-range resolution $c/(2\beta)$ equal the cross-range resolution $\lambda/(2\psi)$ for integration over a rectangular beam segment ψ. Square resolution then requires that $\beta = c\psi/\lambda$. If integration of the entire beam is considered, $\psi = \psi_e \approx \lambda/l$, from (6.13), so that $\beta \approx c/l$. Variable resolution may be impractical, however, for pulse-compression radar designs. The stepped-frequency approach described below could provide this capability in future systems.

6.6.7 Design Tables and Block Diagrams

Table 6.1 lists the expressions derived above for chirp-pulse compression SAR. A generic block diagram is illustrated in Fig. 6.17. A stable master oscillator supplies a timing reference, radar center frequency $\bar{f}$, intermediate-frequency reference at f_I, and difference frequency $\bar{f} - f_I$, as shown. A motion sensor operates at the antenna. Such motion data can be converted into phase-correction signals to the transmitter or phase-correction data to be used in a motion-compensation computer. Additional processing that is commonly carried out, but not indicated in Fig. 6.17, may be for weighting, equalization, and correction for earth curvature, cell migration, and quadratic phase distortion. The processor itself may be *optical,* which carries out optical processing of data records on film, or a *digital* processor, which processes data collected in digital form. The trend is toward digital processing. Both approaches will be discussed further in this chapter.

Table 6.1 Summary of Chirp-Pulse Compression SAR Equations

Parameters	Symbol	Expression	
		Side-Looking	Spotlight
Slant-Range Resolution	Δr_s	$\dfrac{c}{2\beta}$	$\dfrac{c}{2\beta}$
Maximum Unambiguous Slant-Range Extent	ΔR_l	$\dfrac{cT_2}{2}$	$\dfrac{cT_2}{2}$
Slant-Range Integration Length	$\dfrac{cT_1}{2}$	$\dfrac{cT_1}{2}$	$\dfrac{cT_1}{2}$
Cross-Range Resolution[2]	Δr_c	$\dfrac{1}{2}\dfrac{\lambda}{\omega T} = \dfrac{1}{2}\dfrac{\lambda}{\psi}, \dfrac{l}{2}^{[1]}$	$\dfrac{1}{2}\dfrac{\lambda}{\omega T} = \dfrac{1}{2}\dfrac{\lambda}{\Delta\phi}$
Cross-Range Ambiguity Length[2]	$(R\psi)_{max}$	$\dfrac{R\lambda}{2v_pT_2}$	$\dfrac{R\lambda}{2T_2 v_p |\sin\phi|}$
Cross-Range Integration Length[2] (Synthetic Aperture)	$\mathcal{L} = R\psi$	$R\dfrac{\lambda}{l}^{[1]}$	$R\Delta\phi$
Minimum Number of Complex Samples per Slant-Range Integration Length	$(\eta_s)_{min}$	$T_1\beta$	$T_1\beta$
Minimum Number of Complex Samples[2] per Cross-Range Integration Length	$(\eta_c)_{min}$	$\dfrac{2R\psi\psi_e}{\lambda}, \dfrac{2R\psi_e^2}{\lambda}$	$\dfrac{2R\Delta\phi\psi_e}{\lambda}$
Unambiguous PRF[2]	$\dfrac{1}{T_2}$	$\geqslant \dfrac{2v_p\psi_e}{\lambda} \approx \dfrac{2v_p}{l}^{[1]}$	$\geqslant \dfrac{2\psi_e v_p|\sin\phi|}{\lambda} \approx \dfrac{2v_p|\sin\phi|}{l}$
Required Bandwidth[2] for $\Delta r_s = \Delta r_c$	β	$\dfrac{c\psi}{\lambda}, \dfrac{c}{l}^{[1]}$	$\dfrac{c\Delta\phi}{\lambda} = \dfrac{cTv_p|\sin\phi|}{\lambda R}$

[1] Applies when integration in the side-looking mode is carried out over the effective beamwidth available from a real antenna of length l.

[2] For small integration angle and small real beamwidth.

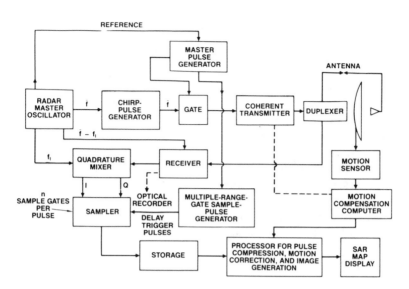

Fig. 6.17 Chirp-Pulse Compression SAR Block Diagram

6.7 STEPPED-FREQUENCY SYNTHETIC APERTURE RADAR

It is possible to generate SAR maps by using the stepped-frequency waveforms discussed in Chapter 5 to replace pulse compression as a means to obtain range resolution. Although as yet untested for SAR, stepped-frequency waveforms for ISAR (to be described in Chapter 7) have been under investigation for several years. Cross-range resolution can be obtained as in pulse-compression radars by coherently integrating range-resolved echo signals obtained during the real beam dwell time. Slant-range resolution with stepped-frequency waveforms, by contrast with that for pulse-compression radars, is obtained synthetically using a Fourier transform process.

Stepped-frequency SAR maps could be generated from data collected in the frequency *versus* viewing-angle domain by using two transforms: (1) an inverse discrete Fourier transform of the complex samples of reflectivity data obtained during each stepped-frequency burst to acquire the complex range profile for each burst, and (2) a discrete Fourier transform of samples of the Doppler time-history response in each synthetically generated range cell to obtain Doppler resolution. Stepped-frequency SAR, in principle, can perform high resolution mapping with frequency-agile, narrowband radars (including magnetron radars, using concepts to be discussed in

Chapter 9). In addition, zooming capability is possible by interrupting the side-looking mode to adjust the stepped-frequency bandwidth and target dwell time. Adjustment of bandwidth changes range resolution and adjustment of dwell time changes cross-range resolution. Dwell time is adjusted by angle-tracking of the area to be zoomed. Square resolution is possible by adjusting bandwidth in concert with dwell time.

The stepped-frequency SAR concept involves generating synthetic slant-range profiles in one or more narrowband (*coarse*) range cells at the changing viewing angles provided by SAR platform motion. Transmission of coherently related, pulse-to-pulse, frequency-stepped waveforms in a continuous series of bursts, with n pulses per burst, produces sets of n echo signals, which are the frequency-domain measurements of reflectivity data from each burst. The n complex values per burst, sampled at a given viewing angle in each coarse range-cell position, are transformed by using the inverse Fourier transform to yield the n-element synthetic range profile in that coarse range cell. Because viewing angle changes continuously with SAR platform motion, discrete viewing angles are obtained only approximately.

6.7.1 Resolution

Synthetic slant-range resolution produced by each burst of n pulses stepped in Δf frequency steps, from (5.8) of Chapter 5, is

$$\Delta r_s = \frac{c}{2}\frac{1}{n\Delta f} \tag{6.22}$$

Cross-range (azimuth) resolution is obtained as in the case of pulse-compression SAR by coherent processing over the integration angle ψ in each synthetic range cell. Cross-range resolution for both the side-looking and SAR modes is expressed in exactly the same way as for pulse-compression SAR.

6.7.2 Sampling

The sampling of stepped-frequency SAR data can be discussed from the viewpoint of the data-collection element in Fig. 6.14, which was used to describe sampling of pulse-compression SAR data. As for pulse-compression SAR, the data-collection element is bounded by two segments of slant-range integration length $cT_1/2$ and two segments of cross-range integration length $R\psi$. Unlike pulse-compression SAR, the dispersed response to a point target exists only in the azimuth dimension. Resolution in slant-range is obtained from the nondispersed responses sampled at each of the n frequency steps for each coarse range cell.

Unambiguous sampling of the data-collection element occurs for the conditions stated in (6.16) and (6.17). One burst of n echo pulses, sampled at a given range-delay position, produces a single range profile extending $cT_1/2$ in the range dimension (for $T_1 = 1/\Delta f$), and N bursts of n pulses sampled during integration angle ψ produce a data-collection element of cross-range extent $R\psi$. This is analogous to chirp-pulse compression SAR, where the dispersed response to a point target from each chirp pulse of length T_1 is a range profile of the same extent $cT_1/2$ in range, and the response to N pulses transmitted during integration angle ψ is a data-collection element of cross-range extent $R\psi$. Data for five narrowband range cells are illustrated for the side-looking mode in Fig. 6.18.

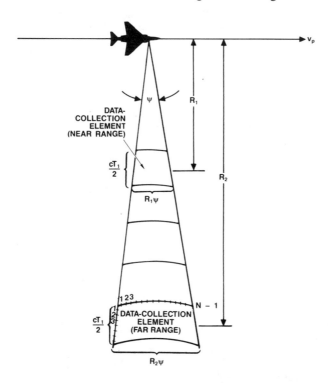

Fig. 6.18 Synthetic Range-Profile Data Produced by N Bursts of n Stepped-Frequency Pulses Transmitted during Integration Angle ψ and Sampled at Five Range Positions

6.7.3 Slant-Range Sampling Criteria

A *slant-range ambiguity length* is expressed in terms of step size Δf as

$$w_s = \frac{c}{2}\frac{1}{\Delta f} = \frac{c}{2}\frac{n}{(n\Delta f)}$$

Up to the point of sampling the in-phase and quadrature outputs of a quadrature detector, the ideal receiving system would be a matched filter to the transmitted pulse of duration T_1. Integration length is then $cT_1/2$. For $cT_1/2 > c/(2\Delta f)$, foldover would occur due to integration of scatterers outside the unambiguous range length. For $cT_1/2 < c/(2\Delta f)$, the echo signal would contain energy integrated from a range depth smaller than the n-element slant-range ambiguity length.

The matched condition for which the integration length equals the ambiguity length in slant range is

$$\frac{cT_1}{2} = \frac{c}{2}\frac{n}{(n\Delta f)}$$

If we solve for pulse duration corresponding to unambiguous step size, then we have

$$T_1 = \frac{1}{\Delta f} \tag{6.23}$$

The number of pulses per burst for this condition, from (6.23) and (6.22), becomes

$$n = \frac{cT_1}{2}\frac{1}{\Delta r_s} \tag{6.24}$$

6.7.4 Cross-Range (Azimuth) Sampling Criteria and PRF

The required number of samples in each resolved range cell per azimuthal integration length $R\psi$ is given by (6.18a). Azimuth sampling by using the stepped-frequency waveform occurs at the burst rate $1/(nT_2)$. One sample is collected in each synthetic range cell for each burst. As viewing angle rotates through ψ rad, each cell is sampled by η_c samples, one sample for each burst. The minimum number of samples required for unambiguous sampling during ψ rad, from (6.18a) with $\eta_c = N$ bursts, becomes

$$N \geq \frac{2R\psi_e\psi}{\lambda} \text{ bursts} \tag{6.25a}$$

where ψ_e is the effective beamwidth of the real beam. For integration over the entire effective beamwidth, we have

$$N \geq \frac{2R\psi_e^2}{\lambda} \text{ bursts} \tag{6.25b}$$

Each burst of n pulses corresponds to a single pulse of a pulse-compression waveform. The effective PRF of the stepped-frequency system is thereby reduced by n. Equation (6.19) for unambiguous cross-range length in terms of PRF when applied to stepped-frequency waveforms becomes

$$(R\psi)_{max} = \frac{R\lambda}{2v_p n T_2} \tag{6.26}$$

Equation (6.20) for required PRF becomes

$$\frac{1}{T_2} \geq n\frac{2v_p\psi_e}{\lambda} = n\frac{2v_p}{l} \tag{6.27}$$

6.7.5 Sampling over Multiple Coarse Range Cells

The foregoing analysis of stepped-frequency SAR considered the relationships between radar system parameters associated with one data-collection element in the side-looking mode, obtained from samples collected at some range R. If we assume that the receiver is matched to the transmitted pulsewidth T_1 and that $T_1 = 1/\Delta f$, the imaged slant-range extent is $cT_1/2$. For practical systems, multiple narrowband (coarse) range samples may be required to increase the imaged slant-range extent to multiples of $cT_1/2$. At other range sample positions, both the number of frequency steps per burst and the burst rate remain fixed, but the number N of bursts processed to compose each unambiguously sampled image frame of each sampled coarse range cell will increase with range, according to (6.25a) or (6.25b).

6.7.6 Spotlight Zooming

Stepped-frequency SAR in a spotlight mode is illustrated in Fig. 6.19. For spotlight zooming, the frequency synthesizer is programmed to produce the bandwidth β, determined from (6.21) for $\beta = n\Delta f$. While in the real-time side-looking mode, a target of interest is observed and the zooming capability is implemented to magnify the target. To accomplish this, the target of interest is tracked in range and azimuth, while bandwidth $n\Delta f$ is increased accordingly to produce slant-range resolution equal to the increased cross-range resolution in the coarse range cell being tracked.

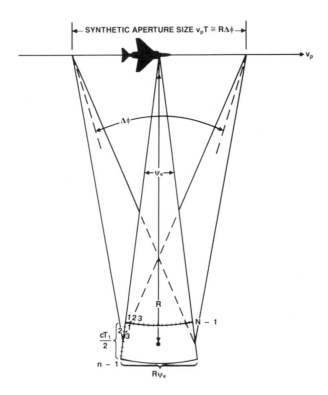

Fig. 6.19 Spotlighted Area Produced by N Bursts of n Pulses Sampled at Range Delay $2R/c$ over Integration Angle $\Delta\phi$ Centered at $\phi = 90°$

6.7.7 Design Tables, Waveforms, and Block Diagram

Table 6.2 lists expressions derived for stepped-frequency SAR. Expressions for slant-range resolution, slant-range and cross-range integration lengths, and number of samples per integration length for stepped-frequency SAR are identical to those for pulse-compression radar with $\beta = n\Delta f$. The unambiguous PRF using stepped-frequency waveforms for either side-looking or spotlight modes is higher than that for pulse-compression SAR by a factor of n, where n is the number of pulses per burst. Compare (6.27) and (6.20). Pulse-to-pulse frequency separation, however, may allow operation in the otherwise range-ambiguous region of PRF.

Waveforms for unambiguous and ambiguous range are illustrated in Figs. 6.20 and 6.21, respectively. In the side-looking mode of stepped-frequency SAR, each burst produces k sets of n complex echo samples, spread throughout the desired swath-delay interval. Figure 6.20 illustrates sampling when the PRF corresponds to the unambiguous range so that PRF $\leq c/(2\Delta R_l)$, where ΔR_l is the illuminated range extent over which significant echo power is received. Figure 6.21 illustrates sampling when PRF $\geq c/(2\Delta R_l)$. In Fig. 6.21, echo foldover is avoided by frequency separation between pulses. In this way, the PRF might be made sufficiently high to avoid synthetic aperture grating-lobe problems, discussed above. Receiver blanking would likely be required in this case.

Further study is needed to characterize degradation of system performance by relative motion of the target and radar platform during the burst time, and to develop appropriate motion-compensation algorithms. In addition, further study is needed in the areas of memory and computation speed requirements for mapping operations.

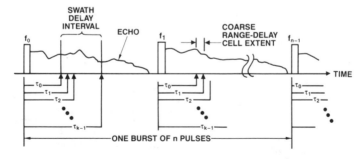

Fig. 6.20 Stepped-Frequency SAR Sampling (Unambiguous Range)

Table 6.2 Summary of Stepped-Frequency SAR Equations

Parameters	Symbol	Expression Side-Looking	Expression Spotlight
Slant-Range Resolution	Δr_s	$\dfrac{c}{2n\Delta f}$	$\dfrac{c}{2n\Delta f}$
Slant-Range Ambiguity Length	w_s	$\dfrac{c}{2\Delta f}$	$\dfrac{c}{2\Delta f}$
Slant-Range Integration Length	$\dfrac{cT_1}{2}$	$\dfrac{cT_1}{2}$	$\dfrac{cT_1}{2}$
Cross-Range Resolution[2]	Δr_c	$\dfrac{1}{2}\dfrac{\lambda}{\omega T} = \dfrac{1}{2}\dfrac{\lambda}{\psi}, \dfrac{l}{2}$[1]	$\dfrac{1}{2}\dfrac{\lambda}{\omega T} = \dfrac{1}{2}\dfrac{\lambda}{\Delta\phi}$
Cross-Range Ambiguity Length[2]	$(R\psi)_{max}$	$\dfrac{R\lambda}{2v_p r T_2}$	$\dfrac{R\lambda}{2nT_2 v_p\,|\sin\phi|}$
Cross-Range Integration Length[2] (Synthetic Aperture)	$\mathcal{L} = R\psi$	$R\dfrac{\lambda}{l}$[1]	$R\Delta\phi$
Pulses per Burst for Matched Condition (Eq. (6.24))	n	$\dfrac{cT_1}{2}\dfrac{1}{\Delta r_s} = T_1 \cdot (n\Delta f)$	$\dfrac{cT_1}{2}\dfrac{1}{\Delta r_s} = T_1 \cdot (n\Delta f)$
Minimum Number of Bursts per Cross-Range Integration Length[2]	N	$\dfrac{2R\psi\psi_e}{\lambda}, \dfrac{2R\psi_e^2}{\lambda}$[1]	$\dfrac{2R\Delta\phi\psi_e}{\lambda}$
Unambiguous PRF[2]	$\dfrac{1}{T_2}$	$\geq n\dfrac{2v_p\psi_e}{\lambda} \approx n\dfrac{2v_p}{l}$[1]	$\geq n\dfrac{2\psi_e v_p\,|\sin\phi|}{\lambda} \approx n\dfrac{2v_p\,|\sin\phi|}{l}$
Required Bandwidth[2] for $\Delta r_s = \Delta r_c$	$n\Delta f$	$\dfrac{c\psi}{\lambda} = \dfrac{c}{l}$	$\dfrac{c\Delta\phi}{\lambda} = \dfrac{cTv_p\,|\sin\phi|}{\lambda R}$

[1] Applies when integration in the side-looking mode is carried out over the effective illumination length available from a real antenna of length l.

[2] For small integration angle and small real beamwidth.

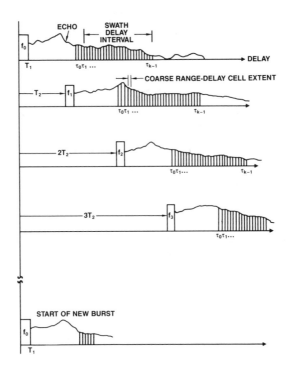

Fig. 6.21 Stepped-Frequency SAR Sampling (Ambiguous Range)

Figure 6.22 is a generic block diagram of a stepped-frequency system. Similarity to the block diagram Fig. 6.17 for pulse-compression SAR is apparent. The key difference is the means for achieving the fine resolution in slant-range. A controlled-frequency synthesizer is used in stepped-frequency SAR to generate the waveforms for synthetic range-profile processing, instead of a chirp generator and the pulse-compression scheme as for pulse-compression processing.

It may be possible to avoid platform motion compensation by using a variation of the technique to be described in Chapter 7 for ISAR data motion compensation with stepped-frequency waveforms. This is suggested by the dotted lines associated with motion compensation in Fig. 6.22.

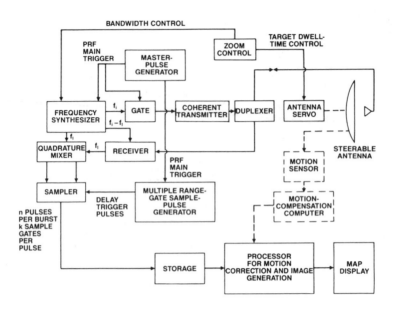

Fig. 6.22 Stepped-Frequency SAR Block Diagram

6.8 RANGE CURVATURE AND RANGE WALK

Range curvature refers to the curved response in range that occurs for side-looking SAR as the radar platform first approaches, then recedes from, each scatterer entering the real antenna beam. This change in range becomes more pronounced at long ranges and for long cross-range integration lengths. For airborne SAR, range is relatively small so that the curvature may produce much less than one range-cell shift as the beam travels across scatterers. Multiple range cells of curvature, however, may occur for spaceborne radars. In Fig. 6.10, the range-delay shift of a target *versus* time history can be seen as

$$\delta R = \frac{(v_p t - y)^2}{2R}$$

where y is the target displacement from boresight. The associated two-way phase advance, from (6.6), is the quadratic function:

$$\psi_2(t) = -\frac{4\pi}{\lambda} \frac{(v_p t - y)^2}{2R}$$

Both optical and digital processing of SAR data from spaceborne radars may require that the range curvature δR be removed before carrying out azimuth compression. Optical processing removes the curvature with conical lenses (or equivalent tilted cylindrical lenses). Digital processing to achieve azimuth compression of compressed range data requires algorithms that achieve integration of range-compressed data along known curved paths of range *versus* azimuth.

Correction of the quadratic phase response $\psi_2(t)$ produced by range curvature in SAR can be considered as a focusing procedure. As is the case in optics, SAR focusing is a two-dimensional process. The collected SAR data are focused in both slant range and cross range to form an image. Ordinary optical telescopes are normally focused simultaneously in the slant-range and cross-range dimensions by adjusting one focal length. SAR data focusing, by contrast, is usually carried out separately, first in the slant-range dimension (range compression), then in cross range (azimuth compression). Independent focusing in azimuth and range is adequate when range curvature results in range migration of less than one range cell. A two-dimensional focusing process is required when range curvature exceeds one range cell.

Range walk is produced when scatterers enter and leave the azimuthal integration extent at different slant ranges. This occurs with spaceborne SAR because of the earth's cross-track rotation beneath the satellite. Range curvature and range walk are illustrated together in Fig. 6.23. Range walk can be removed before azimuth focusing by corrections based on known orbit or flight-path parameters. Azimuth focusing can then be achieved within some range *focusing depth* to be defined below.

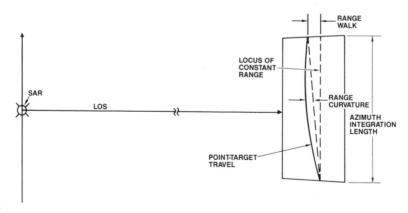

Fig. 6.23 Range Curvature and Range Walk as Seen by the Radar

Tracks of range walk and range curvature have the same shape for every scatterer within limited range excursions, as shown in Fig. 6.24. To achieve azimuth focusing, integration over the coherent integration angle ψ must be carried out along the range-delay path associated with range curvature and range walk for each two-dimensional resolution cell in the final image. Shortcut methods are possible when curvature is limited.

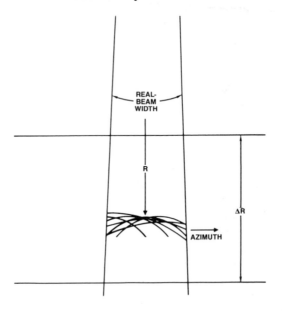

Fig. 6.24 Tracks of Individual Scatterers as Seen by the Radar, Showing Range Walk and Range Curvature (Curvature is Exaggerated)

The amount of range curvature and the focusing depth for a given SAR design can be determined by reference to Fig. 6.25. The slant range to a scatterer at the edge of the antenna beam is

$$R + \delta R = \sqrt{R^2 + \left(\frac{v_p T}{2}\right)^2} \qquad (6.28)$$

The integration time T used here will first refer to time of travel past a scatterer from leading edge to trailing edge of the effective angular extent ψ_e of the entire real beam. This may include multiple-look integration time if multiple sequential looks are noncoherently added for speckle reduction.

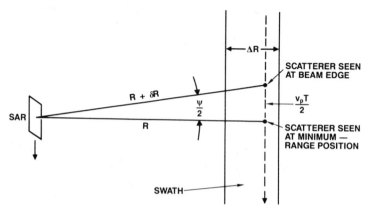

Fig. 6.25 Range Curvature Geometry

For angular extent ψ_e, we have

$$T = \frac{R\psi_e}{v_p}$$

With this substitution into (6.28), we obtain

$$R + \delta R = R\sqrt{1 + \left(\frac{\psi_e}{2}\right)^2}$$

The range shift, from the real-beam center to either edge, obtained by subtracting R from both sides, is

$$\delta R = R\left[1 + \left(\frac{\psi_e}{2}\right)^2\right]^{1/2} - R$$

By means of a binomial series expansion for small ψ_e, we obtain

$$\delta R = R\left[1 - \frac{1}{2}\left(\frac{\psi_e}{2}\right)^2 + \ldots\right] - R$$

$$\approx \frac{1}{8} R\psi_e^2 \tag{6.29}$$

From the real-beam center to either edge, the slant-range cell migration for cell size Δr_s is

$$M' \approx \frac{\delta R}{\Delta r_s}$$

$$\approx \frac{1}{8} \frac{R\psi_e^2}{\Delta r_s} \tag{6.30}$$

Coherent integration angle ψ is substituted for ψ_e when (6.29) and (6.30) are written for coherent integration of a single look over beam segment $\psi < \psi_e$.

Assume now that by some means the range-compressed azimuth response to a point target is obtained along the curved path associated with M' range cells of migration from some range R of nearest approach. Range walk is assumed to be insignificant or corrected. A filter matched to the curved azimuth response of the point target at this range will then be mismatched at all other ranges. At ranges greater than or less than R, the azimuth response exhibits quadratic phase deviation from the response at R. This is exactly analogous to quadratic phase distortion, discussed in Chapter 4 in terms of deviation from desired linear phase response of components for chirp-pulse systems. As will be discussed below, the SAR azimuth response to a point target, because of the curved range response, is also quadratic in phase. This results in a *chirped* Doppler echo signal, centered with zero frequency at boresight (for side-looking radars). A limit of $\phi(\omega_e) = \pi$ rad of phase deviation from the matched condition at the frequency band edges was suggested in Chapter 4 as a value of phase deviation that results in acceptable output pulse distortion and sidelobe levels in the weighted response from a pulse-compression filter. Some references assume $\pi/2$ rad.

A SAR range focusing depth $(\Delta R)_f$ can be established, based on a maximum quadratic phase error $\phi(\omega_e)$. Phase error can be expressed as the difference in two-way phase between the beam-edge range curvature calculated for minimum ranges $R + (\Delta R)_f/2$ and R. The focusing depth illustrated in Fig. 6.26 can then be defined in terms of acceptable quadratic phase error $\phi(\omega_e)$. The resulting expression in terms of cross-range resolution, given by (6.12) with $\omega T = \psi$, is

$$(\Delta R)_f = \frac{8(\Delta r_c)^2}{\lambda} \tag{6.31}$$

for $\phi(\omega_e) = \pi/2$.

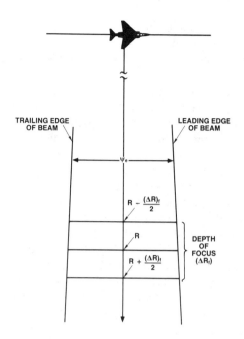

Fig. 6.26 Range Focusing Depth

Range curvature as discussed above applies to side-looking SAR. In a spotlight mode, the effect is better understood in terms of slant-range migration, which is to be discussed for ISAR.

6.9 SPECKLE NOISE

Quality of SAR imagery, because it is produced by coherent processing, is degraded by *speckle noise*. Speckle noise arises from random variations in earth surface roughness. The mechanism can be understood by considering a single SAR image picture element (called *pixel*) and its corresponding resolved, uneven patch of earth surface. Two-way distances traveled by energy reflected from various unresolved surface areas within the resolved uneven patch may differ by the equivalent of several wavelengths for most earth features at commonly used SAR frequencies. *Pixel intensity* is produced by detection of coherently added reflections from all surface areas of a resolved patch. An adjacent patch differing only in detailed roughness produces a different pixel intensity. The result is random and unordered pixel-to-pixel variation, unrelated to macroscopic features of the terrain being mapped. Variance of pixel intensity about some mean intensity is called speckle noise. It should be noted that speckle noise consists of spatial, not temporal, variation of pixel intensity.

Speckle noise has been referred to as *multiplicative noise,* by contrast to $kT_s\beta$ thermal noise, which is additive. The ratio of signal to thermal noise can be increased by increasing the radar transmitter power or reducing the receiving system noise temperature and losses. These methods leave signal to speckle noise unaffected. Signal to speckle noise, rather, is reduced by noncoherent integration of two or more independent coherent *looks* at the same part of the earth's surface. One way to achieve this is by noncoherently summing the superimposed processed SAR scenes viewed from different portions of the real beam. Four-look SEASAT imagery, to be discussed below, is carried out in this manner.

An analysis of speckle can be made on the basis of the probability density of pixel intensity as detected from quadrature components of processed coherent data from each look. Although often referred to as a *detector,* a quadratic detector is also a *mixer.* As with any mixer, operation in the square-law region produces a signal output amplitude that is linearly related to signal input amplitude. A random echo signal will produce bipolar I and Q outputs of random amplitude. The mean amplitude is assumed to be zero in each channel.

The process of generating image pixels from the processed quadrature outputs is also referred to as a *detection process.* Here, the process is square-law detection because pixel intensity is made to be proportional to the echo power from the corresponding resolved feature on the earth's surface. For a single look, the pixel intensity is

$$I(1) = x_1^2 + x_2^2$$

where x_1 and x_2 are the amplitudes of the I and Q outputs, respectively, from the quadrature mixer. We will assume that pixel amplitude components x_1 and x_2 have the zero-mean Gaussian density, given by

$$p(x) = \frac{1}{\sigma\sqrt{2\pi}}\, e^{-x^2/2\sigma^2}$$

where σ^2 is the variance of x.

Intensity produced by n_e multiple looks is given by

$$I(n_e) = x_1^2 + x_2^2 + \cdots + x_n^2$$

where $n = 2n_e$. If the random variables x_i are normal and independent with the same variance σ^2, the probability density of pixel intensity for single and multiple looks can be represented by the chi-squared density [7] given by*

$$p(y) = \frac{1}{2^{n/2}\sigma^n \Gamma\left(\frac{n}{2}\right)} y^{(n-2)/2} e^{-y/2\sigma^2}$$

where

$$y = x_1^2 + x_2^2 + \cdots + x_n^2$$

and

$$\Gamma(i + 1) = i! \quad \text{if } i = 1, 2, \ldots, n, \text{ where } 0! = 1$$

The symbol y in the chi-squared density corresponds to the intensity obtained by summing the squares of the amplitudes $x_1, x_2, \ldots, x_n$. Look-1 pixel intensity is $x_1^2 + x_2^2$. Look-2 intensity is $x_3^2 + x_4^2$. Look-3 intensity is $x_5^2 + x_6^2$, et cetera. The probability densities of pixel intensity for single-look and multiple-look processing can be respectively expressed as

$$p[I(1)] = \frac{1}{2\sigma^2} \exp\left[-I(1)/2\sigma^2\right] \tag{6.32}$$

for single-look processing ($n = 2$), and

$$p[I(n_e)] = \frac{1}{\Gamma(n_e)} \frac{1}{(2\sigma^2)^{n_e}} [I(n_e)]^{n_e - 1} \exp\left[-I(n_e)/2\sigma^2\right] \tag{6.33}$$

for multiple-look processing, where $I(1)$ and $I(n_e)$ are single-look and multiple-look pixel intensities, respectively, and $n_e = n/2$ is the number of looks. The variance of the random variable x_i is given by

$$\sigma^2 = E(x_i^2) - E^2(x_i)$$

where $E(x_i)$ refers to the expected value of x_i. Because we assumed zero-mean density for the I and Q amplitude components (balanced quadrature

---

*The symbol n here does not refer to the number of radar pulses as elsewhere in the text, but rather to the number of Gaussian-density random variables forming the chi-squared distributions.

processing), we have

$$E(x_i) = 0$$

so that

$$\sigma^2 = E(x_i^2)$$

Mean pixel intensity resulting from single-look processing is

$$\bar{I}(1) = E(x_1^2 + x_2^2)$$
$$= E(x_1^2) + E(x_2^2)$$

The expected values of x_1^2 and x_2^2 produced by identical I and Q processing are themselves identical, so that

$$\bar{I}(1) = 2\sigma^2$$

where σ is the standard deviation of the I and Q components of pixel intensity. By substituting $2\sigma^2 = \bar{I}(1)$ into (6.32) and (6.33), we obtain

$$p[I(1)] = \frac{1}{\bar{I}(1)} \exp\left[-I(1)/\bar{I}(1)\right]$$

and

$$p[I(n_e)] = \frac{1}{\Gamma(n_e)} \frac{1}{\bar{I}(1)} \left[\frac{I(n_e)}{\bar{I}(1)}\right]^{n_e-1} \exp\left[-I(n_e)/\bar{I}(1)\right]$$

The single-look and multiple-look densities (6.32) and (6.33) can be shown to have standard deviations respectively given by

$$\sigma[I(1)] = 2\sigma^2$$

and

$$\sigma[I(n_e)] = \sqrt{n_e}\,\bar{I}(1)$$

The signal-to-speckle-noise ratio for a single-look is the ratio of mean to standard deviation $\bar{I}(1)/\sigma[I(1)]$, which is unity. Pixel signal-to-speckle-noise ratio, following noncoherent integration of n_e looks, is the ratio of mean to standard deviation $\bar{I}(n_e)/\sigma[I(n_e)]$. Mean intensity $\bar{I}(n_e)$ for n_e looks is n_e times that of a single look. Therefore, the ratio of signal to speckle noise, following n_e looks, is

$$\frac{S}{N}(n_e) = \frac{n_e\bar{I}(1)}{\sqrt{n_e}\bar{I}(1)} = \sqrt{n_e}$$

Actual single-look and multiple-look speckle as seen with the SEASAT system, described below, are shown in Figs. 6.27 and 6.28.

Fig. 6.27 Four-Look SEASAT SAR Map of the Sonara Sand Dune Field in Baja California (Courtesy of Dr. D.N. Held of NASA Jet Propulsion Laboratory.)

Fig. 6.28 Speckle Pattern as Seen in a Single Look at the Area Outlined in Fig. 6.27 (Courtesy of Dr. D.N. Held of NASA Jet Propulsion Laboratory.)

6.10 DESIGN EXAMPLES

Performance will now be evaluated for two types of SAR designs to illustrate the use of the various expressions developed above. The first design to be evaluated will be a spaceborne SAR with the approximate parameters of the JPL SEASAT design [8] that was put into orbit in June 1978. SEASAT was in operation for a total of 105 days. During that time, about 50 hours of SAR data were collected for the National Aeronautics and Space Administration (NASA). The second SAR design to be evaluated will be a hypothetical airborne SAR. The performance of these two types of SAR systems will be evaluated on the basis of their basic radar design parameters, independently of the type of processing that may have been implemented. Processing architectures are to be discussed later in this chapter. Expressions from Tables 6.1 and 6.2 will be used to determine most performance parameters. We should bear in mind that parameters for an actual design would be derived iteratively by using similar expressions to achieve desired performance.

6.10.1 SEASAT

The actual SEASAT design operated at 1275 MHz. The antenna was a 10.7 m by 2.16 m array producing a 1.0° real beamwidth in azimuth and a 6° elevation beamwidth. This real beam shape illuminated an earth surface of about 15 km by 100 km in area. The SEASAT concept is shown in Fig. 6.29. Several PRFs were actually used, but a nominal value is given in the list of SEASAT parameters, Table 6.3. The transmitted pulse was a chirp pulse. Data was down-linked to three US stations (Fairbanks, Goldstone, and Merritt Island) and two foreign stations.

The ratio of pixel signal to thermal noise is determined by solving the radar equation for the nominal SEASAT parameters of Table 6.3. The signal-to-noise ratio for each look, produced by the n coherently integrated echo pulses per look, is

$$\frac{S}{N} = \frac{P_t G^2 \lambda^2 \sigma T_1 L n}{(4\pi)^3 R^4 k T_s} \tag{6.34}$$

Radar cross section σ of resolved surface features depends upon the terrain to be mapped. Values for average land-clutter return, $\gamma_m = \sigma°/\sin \theta_d$, for three types of terrain at $\theta_d = 15°$ to $70°$ incidence at 1.25 GHz was obtained from Nathanson [9, Table 7.13]. Values for the sea clutter reflection coefficient $\sigma°$ at sea states 0 and 3, both at $60°$ incidence, were obtained from the same reference [9, Table 7.8]. These clutter return values are listed

Table 6.3 SEASAT Design Parameters (Approximate)

Design Parameter	Symbol	Value
Center Frequency	$\bar{f}$	1275 MHz (λ = 0.235 m)
Bandwidth	β	19 MHz
Pulse Duration	T_1	34 μs
Peak Power	P_t	1000 W
PRF	$\dfrac{1}{T_2}$	1500 pps (nominal)*
Radar System Noise Temperature	T_s	650 K
Satellite Altitude	h_1	800 km
Antenna Gain	G	35 dB (3162)
Incident Angle	θ_d	67° (at beam center)
Antenna Beamwidth in Azimuth	$\phi_{3\ dB}$	1.0° (17.4 × 10^{-3} rad)
Platform Velocity (Ground Track)	v_p	6.6 km/s
System Loss	L	−3 dB (L = 0.5)
Number of Looks	n_e	4
Single-Look Coherent Integration Angle	ψ	0.30° (5.24 × 10^{-3} rad)
Range to Center of Swath	R	854 km
Pulses per Look	n	1024

*Actual SEASAT PRF selections were 1463, 1537, and 1645. A PRF of 1500, however, will be used for illustration.

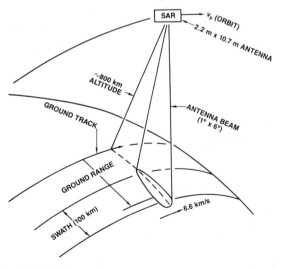

Fig. 6.29 SEASAT SAR System

here in Table 6.4. Also included are the conversions from terrain values of γ_m to σ values at $\theta_d = 67°$. Sea clutter return at the nominal incidence angle of $\theta_d = 67°$ for the SEASAT system is not expected to deviate significantly from that listed for 60°.

Average signal-to-noise ratio per pixel, from (6.34), for a single look, is

$$\frac{S}{N} = 1.02 \, \sigma \tag{6.35}$$

for SEASAT parameters listed in Table 6.3.

Table 6.4 Land and Sea Clutter Return

Terrain	dB(γ_m) (for $\theta_d = 15°$ to 70°)[1]	γ_m	$\sigma(\text{m}^2)$ for 25 m × 25 m Resolution Cell at $\theta_d = 67°$
Desert and Roads	−32	6.31×10^{-4}	0.36
Open Woods	−15	3.16×10^{-2}	18.2
Cities	−11	7.94×10^{-2}	45.7
Sea State	$\sigma° \left(\text{dB} \dfrac{\text{m}^2}{\text{m}^2} \right)$ at $\theta_d = 60°$[1,2]	$\sigma° \left(\dfrac{\text{m}^2}{\text{m}^2} \right)$ at $\theta_d = 60°$	$\sigma \, (\text{m}^2)$ at $\theta_d = 60°$
0	−32	6.31×10^{-4}	0.39
3	−20	1.0×10^{-2}	6.25

Note: $\gamma_m = \dfrac{\sigma°}{\sin \theta_d}$ = mean clutter return with $\sigma°$ in m^2 of RCS per m^2 of surface area resolved.[3]

   $\sigma = (25 \times 25)\sigma°$
      $= (25 \times 25)\gamma_m \sin \theta_d$

[1]Source: Nathanson, F.E., Radar Design Principles, New York: McGraw-Hill, 1969, pp. 238 and 273.
[2]Sea clutter returns listed for horizontal polarization.
[3]Incident power density is proportional to $\sin \theta_d$ so that the quantity $\gamma_m = \sigma°/\sin \theta_d$ tends to be constant over wide variations of (15° to 70°) incident angle.

Results obtained by using (6.35) for the three terrain conditions and sea state 3 with σ values from Fig. 6.4 are listed in Table 6.5. Other performance factors were calculated from expressions listed in Table 6.1 and expressions (6.30) and (6.31).

Table 6.5 SEASAT Performance Calculations

Performance Parameter	Expression	Value for SEASAT Design Parameters
Cross-Range Resolution (Four-Look)Processing	$\Delta r_c = \dfrac{1}{2}\dfrac{\lambda}{\psi}$	22.4 m*
Slant-Range Resolution	$\Delta r_s = \dfrac{1}{2}\dfrac{c}{\beta}$	7.89 m
Ground-Range Resolution	$\dfrac{\Delta r_s}{\sin 23°}$	20.2 m*
Maximum Unambiguous Illuminated Range Extent (along the Ground Assuming a Flat Earth)	$\dfrac{\Delta R_I}{\sin 23°} = \dfrac{cT_2}{2}\dfrac{1}{\sin 23°}$	256 km
Cross-Range Ambiguity Length (at Center of Swath)	$(R\psi)_{max} = \dfrac{R\lambda}{2v_p T_2}$	23 km
Single-Look Integration Length at Center of Swath	$\mathscr{L} = R\psi$	4.5 km
Single-Look Integration Time	$T = nT_2$	0.68 s
Average Pixel Signal-to-Noise Ratio (per Look)	$\dfrac{S}{N}\begin{cases}\text{desert}\\\text{woods}\\\text{cities}\\\text{sea (SS-3)}\end{cases}$	−4.4 dB +12.6 dB +16.7 dB +8.0 dB
Range Migration during Four Looks	$M' = \dfrac{1}{8}\dfrac{R(4\psi)^2}{\Delta r_s}$	6 cells
Range Focusing Depth per Look for $\phi(\omega_e) = \dfrac{\pi}{2}$	$(\Delta R)_f = \dfrac{8(\Delta r_c)^2}{\lambda}$	17 km

*The actual SEASAT resolution cell size after processing is reported to be 25 m × 25 m [8].

The signal-to-noise ratio required to recognize (detect) the presence of an earth feature can be estimated by assuming a fluctuation model for look-to-look signal power. On the basis of Swerling case 2 statistics (fast fluctuation look-to-look) for $P_D = 0.5$ and $P_{FA} = 10^{-6}$, a signal-to-noise ratio of about $+7$ dB is required after the noncoherent integration of four looks. Signal-to-noise ratio produced by actual earth surface features will vary above and below those predicted in Table 6.5.

Table 6.5 shows that at the center of its range swath the SEASAT design results in a resolution capability of about 25 m by 25 m on the earth's surface. The PRF is sufficiently high to provide a cross-range ambiguity length of 23 km. This is adequate for unambiguous sampling of the Doppler spread produced by the 18.7 km illuminated cross-range extent associated with the effective beamwidth of $\lambda/l = 0.022$ rad (1.25°) in azimuth. At the same time, the PRF is sufficiently low to provide a maximum unambiguous illuminated ground-range extent of 256 km, which is quite adequate to sample the ~100 km of illuminated ground extent associated with the 6° elevation beamwidth. Synthetic-aperture size is 4.5 km for each coherent look. Pixel signal-to-noise ratio is adequate to observe most terrain features, except desert and very low sea states. The SEASAT design, to achieve the needed signal-to-noise ratios with its modest transmitter power, was required to look down steeply with a 67° incidence angle in order to increase the backscatter coefficient and to shorten the range. Regarding range curvature, six cells of range migration at range center are produced in four looks. The resulting depth of focus is 17 km, based on $\lambda/4$ m residual variation across the real-beam response.

Additional issues concerning orbit position uncertainties and range walk are not considered in this example. A realistic analysis of space radar design would also involve precise determination of orbital mechanics.

6.10.2   Airborne SAR

The second example for which performance will be evaluated is hypothetical. It is an illustration of the stepped-frequency SAR concept described above. Let us assume an antenna of approximately 2.0 m in length by .35 m in height, which would provide about 35 dB gain with an effective azimuth beamwidth $\psi_e = \lambda/l$ of .015 rad (.86°). Only the side-looking mode is to be evaluated. If a target area of interest were discovered in the relatively low resolution side-looking mode, the radar operator could slew the antenna to zoom in on this area. At the same time, bandwidth would be adjusted upward to produce a slant-range resolution equal to the increased cross-range resolution resulting from the increased target dwell time that occurs as the antenna beam spotlights the target area of interest. Table 6.6 lists design parameters for the radar.

Table 6.6 Hypothetical Airborne SAR Parameters
(for 12 m by 12 m Resolution and 85 km Range)

Design Parameter	Symbol	Value
Center Frequency	$\bar{f}$	10 GHz
		(λ = .03 m)
Pulse Duration	T_1	2.5 μs
Peak Power	P_t	1000 W
Radar System Noise Temperature	T_s	1000 K
Aircraft Altitude	h_1	15 km
Incident Angle	θ_d	10° (at 85 km)
Antenna Gain	G	35 dB (3162)
Antenna Effective Beamwidth in Azimuth	ψ_e	0.86° (0.015 rad)
Platform Velocity	v_p	150 m/s
System Loss	L	−3 dB (L = 0.5)
Number of Looks	n_e	4
Required Single-Look Integration Angle	$\psi = \dfrac{\lambda}{2\Delta r_c}$	1.25 × 10^{-3} rad
Required Bandwidth	$n\Delta f = \dfrac{c}{2\Delta r_s}$	12.5 MHz
Frequency-Step Size	$\Delta f = \dfrac{1}{T_1}$	400 kHz
Number of Steps per Burst	$n = \dfrac{n\Delta f}{\Delta f}$	32 (nearest 2^n)
PRF	$\dfrac{1}{T_2} \geq n\dfrac{2v_p\psi_e}{\lambda}$	≥ 4800, select 5783*
Bursts per Azimuth Integration Length	$N \geq \dfrac{2R\psi\psi_e}{\lambda}$	≥ 106, select 128*
Number of Pulses per Look at Range R = 85 km	$nN = \dfrac{R\psi}{v_p}\dfrac{1}{T_2}$	4096

*Selected to make nN compute to exactly 4096 pulses per look at R = 85 km.

Pixel signal-to-noise ratio for the hypothetic airborne SAR design parameters of Table 6.6 are determined by using (6.34) with Nn substituted for n. The radar cross section σ, as for the SEASAT example, depends upon the terrain to be mapped. Clutter cross section from Nathanson [9, Tables 7.6 and 7.11], is tabulated here in Table 6.7. The signal-to-noise ratio for four noncoherently added looks at 85 km is

Table 6.7 Land and Sea Clutter Returns
(for $\theta_d = 10°$)

Terrain	$\sigma°\left(dB\ \frac{m^2}{m^2}\right)^{1,2}$	$\sigma°\left(\frac{m^2}{m^2}\right)$	$\sigma(m^2)$ for 12 m × 12 m Resolution Cell
Desert	−26	2.51×10^{-3}	0.36
Open Woods	−23	5.01×10^{-3}	0.72
Cities	−15	31.6×10^{-3}	4.55
Sea State	$\sigma°\left(dB\ \frac{m^2}{m^2}\right)$	$\sigma°\left(\frac{m^2}{m^2}\right)$	$\sigma(m^2)$
0	−49	1.25×10^{-5}	.0018
3	−32	6.31×10^{-4}	.091

[1]Source: Nathanson, F.E., *Radar Design Principles*, New York: McGraw-Hill, 1969, pp. 236 and 263.
[2]Median backscatter for vertical polarization.

$$\frac{S}{N} = \frac{P_t G^2 \lambda^2 \sigma T_1 L N n}{(4\pi)^3 R^4 k T_s}$$

$$= 32.2\ \sigma$$

Performance parameters are listed in Table 6.8.

The hypothetical stepped-frequency SAR system operates at much shorter ranges than the SEASAT design. Thus, range curvature is greatly reduced. Also, the shorter range permits greatly reduced sampling rates for the cross-range Doppler response. In the SEASAT design, the PRF of 1500 pulses per second was shown to provide 23 km of unambiguous cross-range sampling. This was adequate with some margin to sample the Doppler band of frequencies produced by the 18.7 km cross-range extent illuminated by the real antenna. The shorter range of the airborne SAR design allows the use of a stepped-frequency or frequency-agile waveform of 32 pulses per burst to generate range profiles. The resulting unambiguous cross-range length of 1536 m at the far range of the swath (85 km) is adequate for sampling the Doppler frequency spread produced by the azimuth extent $R\psi_e = 1275$ m at that range associated with the .015 rad effective beamwidth of the real antenna. The high PRF, however, results in an unambiguous range of only 26 km. To achieve the specified 85 km range would require sampling as shown in Fig. 6.21. Range migration, because it is of less than one cell, is not seen as an issue. The stepped-frequency design, because of multiple pulses required for each coarse range

Table 6.8 Hypothetical Airborne Radar Performance

Performance Parameter	Expression	Value
Cross-Range Resolution (per Look)	$\Delta r_c = \dfrac{1}{2}\dfrac{\lambda}{\psi}$	12 m
Slant-Range Resolution (~ Ground-Range Resolution)	$\Delta r_s = \dfrac{1}{2}\dfrac{c}{n\Delta f}$	12 m
Maximum Unambiguous Illuminated Range Extent	$\Delta R_I = \dfrac{cT_2}{2}$	26 km
Cross-Range Ambiguity Length	$(R\psi)_{max} = \dfrac{R\lambda}{2v_p n T_2}$	1536 m
Single-Look Integration Length at 85 km	$\mathcal{L} = R\psi$	107 m
Single-Look Integration Time	$T = nNT_2$	.71 s
Average Pixel Signal-to-Noise Ratio (per Look)	$\dfrac{S}{N}\begin{cases} \text{desert} \\ \text{woods} \\ \text{cities} \\ \text{sea (SS-3)} \end{cases}$	+11 dB +14 dB +22 dB +5 dB
Range Migration during Four Looks	$M' = \dfrac{1}{8}\dfrac{R(4\psi)^2}{\Delta r_s}$	0.02 cells
Range Focusing Depth per Look for $\phi(\omega_e) = \dfrac{\pi}{2}$	$(\Delta R)_f = \dfrac{8(\Delta r_c)^2}{\lambda}$	38 km

cell, tends to require high PRF as resolution increases, or when longer ranges are necessary. Implementation of the stepped-frequency CW waveform, discussed in Chapter 4, could provide another means to overcome the effects of range ambiguity.

6.11 SAR PROCESSING

Synthetic aperture radar processing began in the mid-1950s using optical techniques. Radar data recorded on film rolls onboard the SAR aircraft were processed into maps on optical benches on the ground by using special lenses and coherent light sources. Optical processing of this type is often considered to be the conventional method for SAR mapping and optical techniques are still employed when the application requires extreme resolution. The trend in SAR mapping, however, is now clearly toward digital processing. Although quite complex, SAR digital processing offers the advantages of accuracy and flexibility. Digital processing techniques have advanced dramatically since early SAR development, while conventional optical techniques have not experienced significant improvement.

6.11.1 Input Data

The following discussion of SAR processing methods will be restricted to conventional chirp-pulse SAR systems with antenna beams looking 90° from the direction of platform motion. Processing of stepped-frequency SAR data will not be discussed here, but will be treated in connection with ISAR in Chapter 7. After first defining the form of received signals from chirp pulses, we will discuss both optical and digital processing methods. Finally, methods for processing SEASAT digitized data will be discussed as an example.

The signal received from surface features by a chirp-pulse SAR is dispersed in both range delay and azimuth time-history. Range- and azimuth-compression of this two-dimensional signal produce a focused image (map) of the surface. The form of the signal will be defined under the assumptions of rectangular-shaped real antenna beams, rectangular chirp waveforms, and straight-line SAR platform motion.

The chirp waveform, as discussed in Chapter 4, was expressed in complex form as

$$s_1(t) = \text{rect}\left(\frac{t}{T_1}\right) e^{j2\pi(\bar{f}t + Kt^2/2)} \tag{4.1}$$

where $\bar{f}$ is the center frequency, T_1 is the uncompressed pulsewidth, K is the chirp rate, and

$$\text{rect}\left(\frac{t}{T_1}\right) = 1, \text{ if } \left|\frac{t}{T_1}\right| < \frac{1}{2}$$

$$= 0, \text{ if } \left|\frac{t}{T_1}\right| > \frac{1}{2}$$

for zero delay set to be at the center of the chirp pulse. A single point target in the real beam at range delay τ will produce a normalized response expressed as

$$s(t - \tau) = \text{rect}\left(\frac{t - \tau}{T_1}\right) e^{j2\pi[(t-\tau)\bar{f} + K(t-\tau)^2/2]} \tag{6.36}$$

for

$$\text{rect}\left(\frac{t - \tau}{T_1}\right) = 1, \text{ if } \left|\frac{t - \tau}{T_1}\right| < \frac{1}{2}$$

$$= 0, \text{ if } \left|\frac{t - \tau}{T_1}\right| > \frac{1}{2}$$

The response, after mixing with a continuous reference signal at $\bar{f}$, is at baseband and may be expressed as

$$s'(t - \tau) = \text{rect}\left(\frac{t - \tau}{T_1}\right) e^{-j2\pi[\bar{f}\tau - K(t-\tau)^2/2]} \tag{6.37}$$

Now, consider the geometry of Fig. 6.30 compared to that of Fig. 6.10. The range delay τ to a point target, displaced y in cross range from

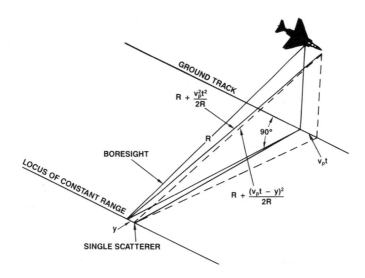

Fig. 6.30 SAR Range Delay to a Single Scatterer

boresight for minimum range distance R and a platform velocity v_p, is

$$\tau \approx \frac{2}{c} \left[R + \frac{(v_p t - y)^2}{2R} \right] \tag{6.38}$$

where $t = 0$ is at boresight and $R \gg v_p t$. Range delay expressed in (6.38) is the delay to the point target during the azimuthal integration time T, which is the duration of time that the real antenna beam illuminates the target. Delay will be assumed to remain constant during the chirp pulse. Substitution for range delay from (6.38) into the first term of the exponential of (6.37) will now be carried out to illustrate the two-dimensional quadratic phase response to each scatterer. Also required is a second amplitude term, which, assuming uniform illumination during integration time T, is defined by

$$\operatorname{rect}\left(\frac{t - T}{T}\right) = 1, \text{ if } \left|\frac{t - T}{T}\right| < \frac{1}{2}$$

$$= 0, \text{ if } \left|\frac{t - T}{T}\right| > \frac{1}{2}$$

where T is the time-history (azimuth) delay y/v_p. The baseband response to a single point target, with $\bar{f} = c/\lambda$, becomes

$$s'(t - \tau) = \operatorname{rect}\left(\frac{t - \tau}{T_1}\right) \operatorname{rect}\left(\frac{t - T}{T}\right)$$

$$\cdot \exp\left\{-j4\pi\left[\frac{(v_p t - y)^2}{2\lambda R} - K\frac{(t - \tau)^2}{4} + \frac{R}{\lambda}\right]\right\} \tag{6.39}$$

As we can see from (6.39), the phase of the baseband echo response to a point target is the sum of two quadratic phase functions and a constant range-delay phase. The frequency of the response for the complex representation varies above and below zero. Zero frequency corresponds to the target positioned at range-delay τ and azimuth position y.

The first exponential term of (6.39) contains a slowly varying quadratic phase function corresponding to the Doppler frequency change that occurs as the slant-range distance to the point target first decreases, then increases. A second point target, offset in cross-range from the first, would produce a phase response corresponding to an offset Doppler response. The second exponential term contains a rapidly varying quadratic phase function, corresponding to the chirp frequency deviation from the center frequency of the delayed pulse. A second point target, offset in slant-range from the first, would produce a phase response corresponding to an offset frequency deviation.

The two-dimensional signal from a single point target is illustrated in Fig. 6.31 for an azimuthal integration length that is sufficiently short to make range curvature appear negligible. (Curved responses are illustrated later.) The received echo signal from a point target will extend over the uncompressed pulse duration T_1 and will be centered in range delay at the target's range-delay position τ. The signal at the target's range delay will extend in azimuth over the integration time T, corresponding to the synthetic aperture size, and will be centered at the target's azimuth delay. It is assumed that the delay τ is essentially constant during each echo pulse, but varies according to (6.38) during the target's dwell time T. Symbols t_1 and t_2 in Fig. 6.31, sometimes called *fast time* and *slow time,* refer to range delay and time history, respectively. The third exponential term of (6.39) is a phase term dependent upon the closest approach in range of the radar platform to the point target, a term ideally made a constant by flying the platform in a straight line.

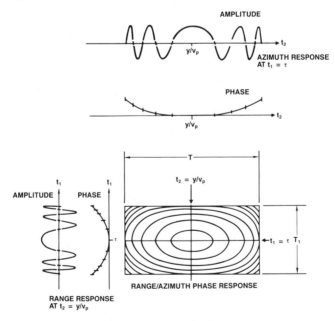

Fig. 6.31 Two-Dimensional Quadratic Phase Response to a Point Target Observed with a Side-Looking SAR Assuming Small Range Curvature

The response of a single point target in terms of data-collection space will extend over the integration lengths in range and azimuth. The area $cT_1/2 \times v_pT$ is the data-collection element (for small curvature) that contains the dispersed response to a point target.

6.11.2 Optical Processing

Conventional optical SAR processing is carried out on film rolls that contain the two-dimensional phase history of the response of target scatterers, which were produced as the SAR platform traveled alongside the range swath to be mapped. Both range and azimuth compression can be done optically. Film rolls are exposed on an *optical film scanner,* which is illustrated in Fig. 6.32. The input to the scanner is the coherent echo signal shifted down to bipolar video. Light intensity from a *cathode ray tube* (CRT) in the scanner is modulated by the bipolar video signal. This is the baseband echo signal produced by reflection from multiple scatterers on the illuminated earth surface. The film roll is exposed as it moves past the CRT in a direction perpendicular to the range sweep of the intensity modulated light spot. A bias voltage may be used to produce the desired film exposure.

After recording the SAR phase history, the film is brought to an optical bench, where it is focused to form the image. Data recording of the response from a single point target is illustrated in Fig. 6.33. An actual film recording would contain the phase histories of the numerous scatterers on the surface to be mapped. Individual scatterers' phase histories are likely to overlap one another, but will ideally focus to individual points.

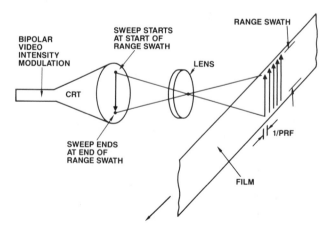

Fig. 6.32 SAR Optical Film Scanner

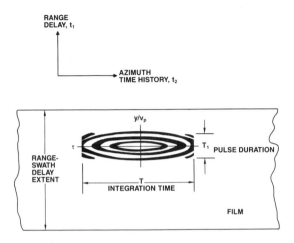

Fig. 6.33 Optical Film Record of Phase History of a Single Point Target (Side-Looking SAR with Insignificant Range Curvature)

Phase history on film is similar to the Fresnel zone plates used in optics. The quadratic nature of the phase response makes it possible to diffract coherent light passing through the film to produce focused images.

Phase history recorded on a SAR film roll focuses incident coherent light at different focal lengths in azimuth and elevation. The situation can be thought of as *astigmatism,* which can be optically corrected by the use of cylindrical lenses. Separate focal lengths occur because recorded phase is the sum of separate phase components in each dimension. From (6.39), the slant-range component of recorded phase of the echo from a point target is $4\pi K(t - \tau)^2/4$. This dimension of phase is recorded in the range dimension at a sweep velocity of v_r. Also from (6.39), the azimuth component of phase of the same point target is $-4\pi(v_p t - y)^2/(2\lambda R)$. This component of phase is recorded in the azimuth dimension at the film transport velocity of v_a. The resulting two-dimensional phase history in range and azimuth focuses collimated light passing through the film at different focal lengths in range and azimuth.

Focal length associated with SAR phase history recorded on film can be compared to other, more familiar optical focusing mechanisms. Figure 6.34 illustrates three equivalent focusing mechanisms (each shown for one dimension). Light in each mechanism propagates in a manner so as to encounter quadratically distributed delay in the cross-axis dimension labeled x. The quadratic phase function results from variation in time delay in Fig. 6.34(a, b). Figure 6.34(c) illustrates one dimension of quadratically distributed phase history recorded on SAR film. For each case, the one-way phase function for light at wavelength λ_l is

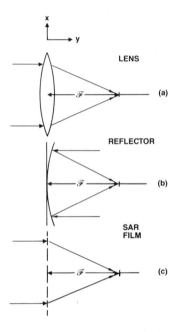

Fig. 6.34 Equivalent Focusing Mechanisms

$$\psi(x) = -\frac{2\pi}{\lambda_l}\frac{x^2}{2\mathcal{F}} \tag{6.40}$$

where $\mathcal{F}$ is the optical focal length. This result for the reflector in Fig. 6.34(b) is directly analogous to that found from Fig. 6.10 and the accompanying discussion regarding the quadratic phase response produced by the SAR platform moving past a point target on the earth's surface. With the proper optics, focusing results when collimated coherent light is passed through the zone plate formed by the film record of the quadratically distributed responses to individual scatterers.

For sweep velocity v_r and film transport velocity v_a, the x dimension of the recorded signal is $x_1 = v_r(t_1 - \tau)$ in range and $x_2 = v_a(t_2 - y/v_p)$ in azimuth. Therefore, $\psi(x)$ of (6.40), written in terms of t_1 and t_2, becomes

$$\psi(t_1) = -\frac{2\pi}{\lambda_l}\frac{v_r^2(t_1 - \tau)^2}{2\mathcal{F}_r} \tag{6.41a}$$

in the range dimension, and

$$\psi(t_2) = -\frac{2\pi}{\lambda_l} \frac{v_a^2\left(t_2 - \dfrac{y}{v_p}\right)^2}{2\mathscr{F}_a} \tag{6.41b}$$

in the azimuth dimension, where t_1 and t_2 refer to range delay and time history, respectively. Optical focal lengths $\mathscr{F}_r$ and $\mathscr{F}_a$ can be expressed in terms of radar parameters by setting the magnitude of the two optical phase components given in (6.41a) and (6.41b) equal to their corresponding RF phase components from (6.39) as follows:

$$\psi(t_1) = \frac{2\pi}{\lambda_l} \frac{v_r^2(t_1 - \tau)^2}{2\mathscr{F}_r} = 4\pi K \frac{(t_1 - \tau)^2}{4}$$

in range, and

$$\psi(t_2) = \frac{2\pi}{\lambda_l} \frac{v_a^2\left(t_2 - \dfrac{y}{v_p}\right)^2}{2\mathscr{F}_a} = \frac{4\pi}{\lambda} \frac{(v_p t_2 - y)^2}{2R} = \frac{2\pi}{\lambda} \frac{\left(t_2 - \dfrac{y}{v_p}\right)^2 v_p^2}{R}$$

in azimuth. By solving for the two focal lengths and recalling from Chapter 4 that chirp slope $K = \Delta/T_1$, we obtain

$$\mathscr{F}_r = \frac{v_r^2}{\lambda_l K} = \frac{v_r^2 T_1}{\lambda_l \Delta}$$

for the optical focal length in the range dimension, and

$$\mathscr{F}_a = \frac{v_a^2 \lambda R}{2\lambda_l v_p^2}$$

for the optical focal length in the azimuth dimension.

The two focal lengths are illustrated in Fig. 6.35. Azimuth focal length is normally longer than range focal length, and it varies linearly with range across the width of the film because of increased radius of range curvature of input data at increasing range.

SAR optical processing corrects for the astigmatism by using cylindrical lenses. In addition, conical or tilted cylindrical lenses correct for the linear variation of azimuth focal length with range. Figure 6.36 illustrates a simplified configuration. The data film on the left has a vertical range focal plane followed by the tilted azimuth focal plane. A cylindrical lens

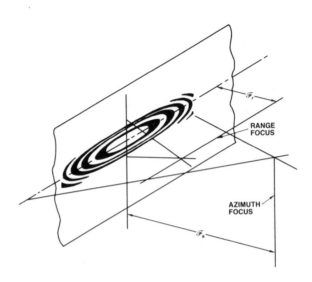

Fig. 6.35 Range and Azimuth Focal Lines of Point-Target Phase History (From Elachi, C., *et al.*, "Spaceborne Synthetic-Aperture Imaging Radars: Applications, Techniques and Technology," *Proc. IEEE,* Vol. 70, No. 10, Oct. 1982. Modification of Fig. 23, p. 1191. Reprinted with permission.)

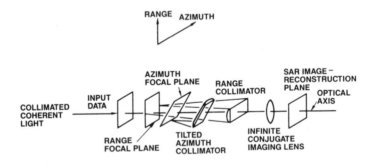

Fig. 6.36 Simple Optical SAR Processor (From Elachi, C., *et al.*, "Spaceborne Synthetic-Aperture Imaging Radars: Applications, Techniques and Technology," *Proc. IEEE,* Vol. 70, No. 10, Oct. 1982, p. 1191, Fig. 24. Reprinted with permission.)

is oriented so that its input focal plane coincides with the tilted azimuth focal plane of the data film to collimate rays in the azimuth dimension. A second cylindrical lens, further to the right, is placed so that its input focal plane coincides with the vertical range focal plane of the data film to collimate rays in the range dimension. With both dimensions collimated, targets will be focused at infinity to the right. A spherical lens focuses targets on the SAR image plane.

Actual optical processors are far more complicated in practice. Usually, the SAR image is made continuously. Both the SAR data film and output SAR image film are driven, and a slit in the range dimension produces continuous exposure of the SAR image. In addition to performing the above focusing, lenses are also designed to correct for range curvature and range walk.

6.11.3 Digital Processing

Generation of SAR images is a two-dimensional process, regardless of the employed processing technique. Optical SAR processors process the range-azimuth analog data simultaneously in time. Digital SAR processors often resort to a series of two one-dimensional processes to produce the two-dimensional result from digitized input data. The advantages of increased accuracy and flexibility in digital processing are obtained at the expense of considerable complexity. It is beyond the scope of this section to cover the field of SAR digital processing. Rather, a two-dimensional correlation method of processing that is applicable to chirp-pulse compression SAR will be discussed in an attempt to report some of the important issues. Two-dimensional correlation achieves *pulse compression in slant range* (range compression) and *azimuth compression in cross range* (azimuth compression).

The idealized response to a single point target viewed with a chirp radar was expressed in (6.39). This equation contains similar quadratic terms in both range-delay and time-history dimensions. Lenses are able to perform the two-dimensional compression in optical SAR processors. The lenses were shown to possess quadratic phase functions, which collimated the light through the data film, so that individual target responses could be focused into points on the image film. This process has also been described as *two-dimensional optical convolution* [3]. Digital processors for pulse-compression SAR, in an analogous process, may convolve the discrete two-dimensional data with a discrete two-dimensional, matched-filter impulse response function instead of lenses. The response function, in general, is made up of the impulse response $h(t_1)$ of the chirp signal for range compression and a similar function $h(t_2)$ for azimuth compression. As before, t_1 refers to range delay (fast time) and t_2 refers to time history (slow time).

Synthetic aperture radar processing, however, is often described in terms of *correlation*, rather than convolution. Instead of referring to the impulse response of the matched filter in range delay or in azimuth time history, the concept of *range and azimuth reference functions* is used. The equivalent reference functions in range and azimuth are the time inverses of the complex conjugates of the respective matched-filter impulse responses. Correlation of the range-delayed signal with a range reference is the equivalent of convolution of the same signal with the impulse response of the matched filter to the transmitted waveform. A similar equivalence holds in the azimuth dimension.

The reference function for range correlation is the *point-target response in range*. The reference function for azimuth correlation is the *point-target response in azimuth*. A two-dimensional reference function is the dispersed response in range and azimuth. Azimuth and range compression of two-dimensional signal data will now be described for the ideal case in which the two dimensions of the reference function can be defined independently. This idealization is valid for processing of a data block for which azimuth extent is sufficiently small that range curvature and range walk can be neglected, and wherein range extent is sufficiently small that a single azimuth reference produces azimuth focusing at all ranges in the block.

Figure 6.37 illustrates a block of digitized two-dimensional data that includes the idealized response from a single point target at delay τ and azimuth position y. Each resolved element contains a complex data sample. The response to two separate point targets is illustrated in Fig. 6.38(a).

Two-dimensional correlation with the two-dimensional reference produces an image block containing the two targets in focus as indicated in Fig. 6.38(c). Columns of range *data lines* are first correlated against the range reference. The correlated result for each range data line is a new set of range-compressed data lines. Range-correlated results are shown in Fig. 6.38(b). Rows of azimuth data lines are then correlated against the azimuth reference to obtain two-dimensional correlated results, shown in Fig. 6.38(c).

The two one-dimensional processes produce the required two-dimensional image of Fig. 6.38(c) without distortion because the same range reference was assumed valid for all range columns and the same azimuth reference was assumed valid for all azimuth rows.

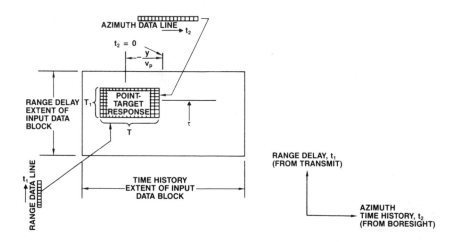

Fig. 6.37 SAR Data Block for Chirp Waveform Showing Response to a Point Target Centered at $t_1 = \tau$, $t_2 = -y/v_p$ (Small Range Curvature)

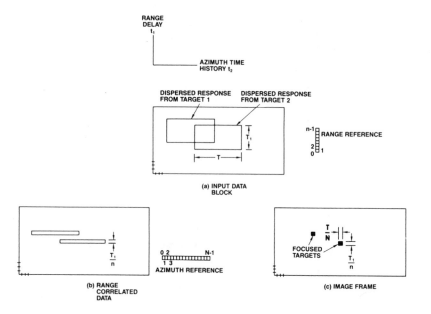

Fig. 6.38 Processing of SAR Input Data Containing Two Point Targets (Small Range Curvature)

6.11.4 Nonindependent References

Independent range and azimuth references were employed in Figs. 6.37 and 6.38. This was possible because of the stated assumption of sufficiently small range curvature, range swath, azimuth integration angle, and range walk. Consider the case in which range compression produces such closely spaced azimuth lines that azimuth responses are not contained along individual lines. This occurs when M' of (6.30) exceeds unity. Azimuth compression for each image pixel must then be carried out along curved paths in range.

The azimuth reference is also range-dependent. Figure 6.39 illustrates the response of a chirp-pulse SAR to two point targets at the same azimuth position, but separated in range at opposite edges of a SAR range swath. The response for both targets remains quadratic in both range and azimuth (as viewed along their curved range responses), but we can see that the azimuth reference at near range differs from that at far range. The curve is longer, but less pronounced, for the response to the target at far range.

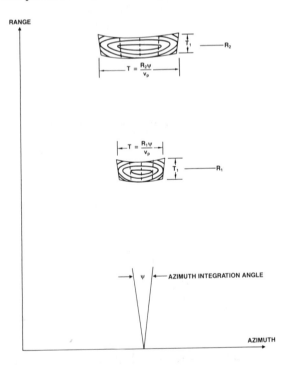

Fig. 6.39 Response to Two Point Targets at the Same Azimuth Position but Separated in Range (Chirp-Pulse Compression SAR)

Therefore, an azimuth reference for range R_1 matches to a larger FM Doppler slope than one for R_2. The range reference, because it is determined only by radar waveform, is independent of azimuth position.

Finally, range walk caused by cross-track earth motion beneath a satellite SAR, unless corrected, produces responses that walk through range cells.

Range-dependent range curvature and range walk result in responses from individual scatterers that travel through range cells and require a range-dependent reference. In principle, image formation is still possible by using two-dimensional processing from known geometry. For example, after range compression, the reflectivity of each two-dimensional resolution cell could be established by using azimuth compression of range-compressed data along the range *versus* azimuth path which a scatterer would travel in that two-dimensional resolution cell. This approach should be avoided in practical processors because of its extreme complexity. The SEASAT digital SAR processor, described below, is an example of one shortcut method for carrying out two-dimensional processing. Another method is *polar reformatting,* which is described for ISAR in Chapter 7.

6.11.5   Fast Correlation

We discussed convolution of sampled echo data produced by a chirp radar using FFT processing in Chapter 4. The method was called *fast convolution.* Fast convolution of discrete data was accomplished with a discrete version of the matched-filter impulse response to the chirp signal. The same process could have been described in terms of *fast correlation* with a reference function equal to the time inverse of the conjugate of the point-target response in range. Synthetic aperture radar data sets can be processed by using a two-dimensional fast correlation method. Such a method, because of the use of the FFT algorithm, is usually faster than direct correlation, just as fast convolution is faster than direct convolution. Fast convolution is based on the discrete form of the convolution theorem, which, for echo signal $s(t)$ convolved with impulse response $h(t)$, is expressed as

$$FT[s(t) * h(t)] = S(f) \cdot H(f) \tag{6.42}$$

where $H(f)$ is the Fourier transform of $h(t)$ and $S(f)$ is the Fourier transform of $s(t)$.

An equivalent expression can be written in terms of correlation. From the definitions of convolution and correlation, the following equivalence can be written:

$$FT[s(t) * h(t)] = FT[s(t) \otimes h^*(-t)]$$

where $\otimes$ denotes cross correlation. The matched-filter transfer function $H(f)$ for the transmitted waveform $s_1(t)$ is $S_1^*(f)$ and the time-inverse of the complex conjugate $h^*(-t)$ of the matched-filter impulse response $h(t)$ is $s_1(t)$, where $s_1(t)$ is the point-target response, which becomes the reference function. Equation (6.42) for the convolution theorem, therefore, can be rewritten as the correlation theorem, expressed as

$$FT[s(t) \otimes s_1(t)] = S(f) \cdot S_1^*(f)$$

where

$$S(f) = FT[s(t)]$$

and

$$S_1(f) = FT[s_1(t)]$$

Thus, the correlation of a signal with a reference function is obtained by multiplying their respective Fourier transforms, then using the inverse Fourier transform to translate back to the time domain.

Of interest for fast correlation is the discrete version of the correlation theorem, which is expressed in shorthand notation as

$$DFT[s(l\Delta t) \otimes s_1(l\Delta t)] = S(i\Delta f) \cdot S_1^*(i\Delta f), \text{ for } i, l = 0, 1, 2, \ldots, n - 1$$

where $s(l\Delta t)$ and $s_1(l\Delta t)$ are both periodic with the same period $(n - 1)\Delta t$ for sampling interval Δt and $S(i\Delta f)$ and $S_1^*(i\Delta f)$ are also periodic, but of period $(n - 1)\Delta f$. As stated in words, the discrete Fourier transform of the correlation of two periodic functions of period $(n - 1)\Delta t$ is equal to the product of the discrete Fourier transforms of the two periodic functions. Fast correlation is carried out by using the fast Fourier transform type of discrete Fourier transform.

Fast correlation of two-dimensional SAR data with independent range and azimuth references is illustrated in Fig. 6.40. Here, rows of range response data $s(t_1)$ are transformed into rows of frequency response $S(f_1)$. (Note that rows and columns are reversed from those of Fig. 6.38 to facilitate arrangement of the block diagram.) Rows of frequency response are then multiplied, element by element, by the frequency-domain form of the range reference to form rows of frequency-response products.

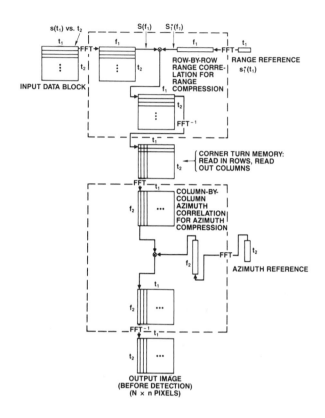

Fig. 6.40 Fast Correlation with One-Dimensional References

Row-by-row inverse Fourier transforms of these products produce cross-correlated responses in the range domain *versus* time history t_2. The data have now undergone range compression. Range-compressed rows are stored in a *corner turn memory,* from which cross-range (azimuth) data columns are read out column by column. Azimuth correlation is then carried out in exactly the same way as range correlation, except that it is done in the time-history dimension instead of the range-delay dimension. The final result is the *output image frame.* The above process is illustrated in terms of a processor block diagram in Fig. 6.41. The same process could also be described in terms of fast convolution.

Fast convolution or correlation by means of FFT processing of discrete data requires special care because of the aperiodic nature of the data and reference. This was discussed in Chapter 4 in connection with digital pulse compression of one-dimensional range data. We showed that it is possible to generate valid convolution of a finite length of sampled range

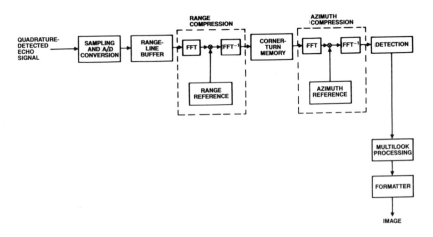

Fig. 6.41 Fast Correlation Processor for Chirp-Pulse Compression SAR

data by establishing a common periodic length for both the signal and impulse responses, which is sufficiently large so that the convolution result of one period does not overlap that of the succeeding period. We saw that this is possible by adding zeros to the discrete impulse response function so as to satisfy (4.14).

Digital SAR processing, however, may involve *subimage processing* from relatively large input data blocks. Correlation in the range or azimuth dimension using the FFT for the resulting long data lines can be more conveniently carried out by techniques referred to as *overlap-save* or *overlap-add* [10]. In each of these processes, the input data line is divided into subsections that are overlapped by the extent of the reference function. Subsections will then correspond to periodic lengths, which, when correlated with a reference function of the same period, produce a periodic response equivalent to direct aperiodic correlation without the FFT processing. The overlap-save technique saves the cross-correlation result for the part of the period that excludes the *end effect* at the front of each period. The end-effect result is invalid in that it does not represent the true aperiodic result. Except for the first section, the lost end-effect part of the cross-correlation result is restored when we make a composite reconstruction of the individual sections. The overlap-add process is similar, but data samples within the overlap portion of each data section are replaced with zeros. Composite reconstruction of the cross-correlation result of all sections then provides valid representation of the true aperiodic result with no invalid end effect.

Subimages can be generated by initially correlating the first section of each input range data line with the range reference. The azimuth section length is the number of correlated range data line sections chosen to be read into the corner turn memory. Azimuth data line sections read out of the corner turn memory are correlated with the azimuth reference. The result is one subimage. The next subimage in the range dimension is developed by repeating the process in the next section of range data lines. The next subimage in the azimuth dimension is developed by processing the series of range data line sections corresponding to the next azimuth section, and so forth. The process will now be described for SEASAT SAR data as an example.

6.11.6 SEASAT Processing Example

SEASAT data were collected during the 100 days of SEASAT's life by down-linking signals to tracking stations over an analog data line. Down-linked echo signals were digitized and recorded on a high-speed recorder. Data processing has since been carried out both optically and digitally. The type of digital process carried out by the Jet Propulsion Laboratory's (JPL) Interim Digital SAR Processor (IDP) on SEASAT data is discussed here to illustrate the principles discussed above. Details of the IDP processor have been described in reports by the JPL, Pasadena, CA, for NASA and in the open literature by Elachi *et al.* [8] and Wu [11].

A SEASAT range data line was obtained from each pulse of the radar extending over a range window of 288 μs. An analog-to-digital sampling rate of 45×10^6 real samples per second provides one complex sample for each 6.7 m of slant-range.* Slant-range resolution associated with the 19 MHz waveform bandwidth is 7.89 m. SEASAT azimuth (cross-range) resolution associated with its synthetic aperture length, based on its real aperture size of 10.7 m in azimuth, from (6.11), is about 5.35 m. The nominal SEASAT PRF of 1500 for the 6.6 km/s of beam travel over the ground produces one complex sample in each range cell for each 4.4 m of cross-range (azimuth) travel. Both range and azimuth sampling are thus shown to occur at a rate slightly higher than the Nyquist rate of one complex sample per resolution cell. The processor generates 100 km by 100 km SAR maps from about 15 s of time history of the 288 μs range data blocks. Four coherent looks are noncoherently integrated, which degrades the available resolution from the real beam by a factor of four.

---

*Input data of the actual processor were sampled at an offset frequency from baseband. Complex data will be assumed for this example.

Four-look processed resolution is nominally 25 m by 25 m. The processing
follows the general form illustrated in Figs. 6.40 and 6.41. The 100 km by
100 km coverage is made up of multiple subimages generated by range
and azimuth sectioning of the data using the overlap-save procedure in
each dimension. Section lengths are 2048 complex data samples in range
by 2048 complex data samples in azimuth, as indicated in Figs. 6.42(a)
and 6.44(a).

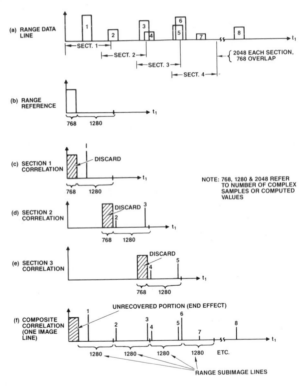

Fig. 6.42 SEASAT Range Correlation of Data Line Containing Dispersed
Response to Eight (Hypothetical) Point Targets

    The range reference function for range correlation is about 34 μs in
duration. It is represented by 768 discrete complex values, corresponding
approximately to SEASAT's 34 μs pulse duration multiplied by one-half
the sampling rate of 45×10^6 real samples per second. Data integration
for four coherent looks in azimuth extends slightly beyond the 1.0° half-
power points of the real beamwidth in azimuth. Antenna beam dwell time,
corresponding to the four 0.3° looks at the beam's center in elevation at
range center, is approximately

$$T = \frac{R(4\psi)}{v_p}$$

$$= \frac{(854 \times 10^3)(2\pi/360)(4)(0.3)}{6600}$$

$$= 2.71 \text{ s}$$

As with the range reference function, the azimuth reference function is represented by discrete complex values of the same time spacing as that of the data. Data spacing in azimuth is the reciprocal of the 1500 complex azimuth samples per second (one sample per pulse repetition interval) produced in each range cell, which is 4065 samples per line, generated during the 2.71 s of beam dwell time at beam center. Actually, 4096 complex values are used to represent four coherent-integration looks. At the 4.4 m sample spacing in azimuth, this covers an azimuth extent equal to the four-look cross-range integration length of about 18 km.

Image quality depends upon the accuracy with which the azimuth reference function represents the phase history of point targets in the real beam. Azimuth phase history can be represented by a quadratic function analogous to the quadratic function that represents the range reference. The azimuth reference function can be defined if the Doppler frequency at the azimuth center of illumination (Doppler centroid) and Doppler frequency slope (Hz/s) are known. This corresponds to the requirement that the instantaneous RF frequency be known at the center of the FM chirp pulse and RF frequency slope (Hz/s). Uncertainties in SAR platform attitude and Doppler echo spectrum produced by the earth's rotation below the satellite can require special preprocessing programs to generate the azimuth reference function. However, no such variations occur in the range reference because the FM chirp generator in the radar determines the reference independently of platform attitude and orbit considerations.

Clutter lock and *autofocusing* are methods used to estimate the Doppler centroid and Doppler frequency, respectively, based on the SAR data [8]. The clutter-lock method sets the Doppler centroid of the reference to that of the received spectral response from the illuminated surface area. Autofocusing sets the Doppler frequency slope to produce minimum azimuth blur in the processed image, as determined by spatial frequency analysis, or by adjusting for minimum registration error between looks.

Range correlation is performed first. The sectioned range data are illustrated in Fig. 6.42(a). The reference function in range is shown in Fig. 6.42(b). The range reference in the spectral domain can be separately generated in a preprocessing program. Fast correlation is performed on each of the 2048-element sections of the input data with the results as indicated in Fig. 6.42(c, d, e). The composite result for one range data line is shown in Fig. 6.42(f). The overlap-save process results in 2048 − 768 = 1280 complex values saved from each section. Range walk in the IDP is corrected to the first order by sliding the range lines as needed to align their starting samples. Finer correction is carried out by selecting from one of several range reference functions that vary by a fraction of a range cell in delay. This provides range-walk interpolation to within a fraction of a range cell.

Correlated range data is stored in a corner turn memory, then read out in the azimuth dimension. The data read out are transformed line by line (or column by column, as in Fig. 6.40) into azimuth spectral data. Range curvature in the IDP processor is compensated in the azimuth spectral domain by using a process that is efficient in terms of processor time, covering the known range curvature [11]. This process is illustrated in Fig. 6.43. The range curvature of a particular point target is shown plotted in the azimuth spectral data domain as range delay *versus* Doppler frequency. Because quadratic phase history is assumed, the range delay of a point target *versus* Doppler frequency, and its range delay *versus* azimuth time history are represented by the same curve, except for a constant factor.

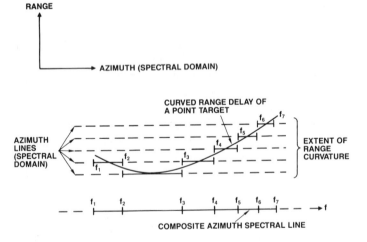

Fig. 6.43 Range Curvature Compensation in the Azimuth Spectral Domain (Based on Fig. 3 from Wu, C., *et al.,* "SEASAT Synthetic-Aperture Radar Data Reduction Using Parallel Programmable Array Processors," *IEEE Trans. Geoscience and Remote Sensing,* Vol. GE-20, No. 3, July 1982. Reprinted with permission.)

To correlate the near-range azimuth spectral line of data in Fig. 6.43, the spectral form of the azimuthal reference requires vector multiplication by the spectral data that appear along the curved path. The product comprises the composite spectral line in the lower part of the figure. Another composite spectral line is obtained from spectral data that appear along the same curve when it is shifted outward in range to the next azimuth spectral line. The process of shifting to the next azimuthal reference is repeated until all the curved data in the spectral domain have been converted into composite lines free of curvature. The piecewise-linear approximation of the curved delay provides advantages in terms of memory storage requirements and flexibility in reference updating [11].

The fast correlation process now proceeds with row-by-row multiplication of composite azimuth spectral lines by the spectral form of the reference function, as shown in Fig. 6.40. Azimuth correlation can then be thought of as being performed on curvature-free azimuth time-history data. Figure 6.44(a) illustrates a single range cell of composite azimuth data from which an image line is to be generated. Individual looks at a given point target occur at separate portions of the total Doppler spectral response to the target. The first look at the leading edge of the beam contains only positive Doppler shift because range decreases during the first look. The last look contains only negative Doppler shift because range increases. The spectrum of the reference functions to each look likewise occupies a separate portion of the spectrum of a hypothetical reference for the total beam response, as is illustrated in Fig. 6.44(b).

Fast correlation for each look uses the overlap-save process to correlate azimuth data sections of 2048 elements, each with their 1024-element, single-look reference function. The result is $2048 - 1024 = 1024$ azimuth values saved per subimage data line. Only 256 of the 1024 values ultimately must be saved, however. This can be understood by recalling that for the SEASAT velocity and PRF, the total synthetic-aperture length of 18 km is sampled with 4096 complex samples spaced 4.4 m apart. Pixels produced by one look will represent the equivalent of about 22 m in resolution. In other words, azimuth data is oversampled by about a factor of four for integration during each look. Azimuth data are originally sampled at or above the Nyquist rate for the total aperture because the actual phase history is that of the Doppler spectrum produced by the total aperture. Therefore, 2048 complex values per section are retained up to the point where the inverse FFT is performed in the azimuth compression process. The inverse FFT then must be performed on only 512 of the 2048 spectral values for unambiguous representation of the reduced single-look resolution. Of the 512 resulting time-domain values, only 256 are saved,

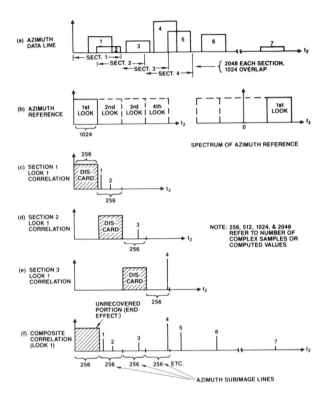

Fig. 6.44 SEASAT Azimuth Correlation of Data Line Containing Dispersed Response to Seven (Hypothetical) Point Targets

as indicated in Fig. 6.44(c, d, e), which are detected (converted to magnitude only) to form image pixels. Figure 6.44(f) indicates that saved azimuth subimage lines register side by side to form a contiguous azimuth image line as in the range domain.

A contiguous set of subimages of 1280 azimuth lines are generated with 256 pixels per line. The corresponding subimages from four looks are added noncoherently. Subimages are assembled to form an image of 5800 azimuth lines with 5144 pixels per line. This is called a SEASAT-A SAR frame and covers an area 100 km by 100 km with about 25 m by 25 m resolution. A four-look SEASAT image of the San Diego, CA, area, obtained from data collected during revolution 107, is shown in Fig. 6.45.

Fig. 6.45 SEASAT Image of San Diego Area

PROBLEMS

6.1 What is the approximate cross-range (azimuth) resolution at 50 km range for a 15 GHz radar with a 1.0 m diameter side-looking antenna operating in the following ground-mapping modes: (a) real aperture, (b) optimized unfocused SAR, and (c) focused SAR?

6.2 A real aperture radar in a low-altitude aircraft is desired to produce radar maps with 25 m by 25 m resolution at a range of 25 nmi (46.3 km). Aerodynamic considerations limit antenna length to 10 m. What are the required radar parameters of bandwidth and radar frequency? Assume the system transfer function of Fig. 6.6.

6.3 A real aperture mapping radar employs 0.25 μs pulses (no pulse compression). What is the matched-filter output signal-to-noise level against a 1.0 m^2 point target at 10 nmi (18.52 km)? Parameters are as follows: $P_t = 100$ kW, $G = 33$ dB, $\lambda = .03$ m, $L = -6$ dB, and $T_s = 500$ K.

6.4 (a) An unfocused synthetic aperture radar operating at $\lambda = 0.03$ m is in an aircraft traveling at 200 m/s. What is the data integration time that produces peak responses at a range of 40 km? (b) What is the corresponding cross-range (linear azimuth) resolution?

6.5 Show that the effective rectangular beamwidth ψ_e that produces the same integrated response as a uniformly weighted antenna is 1.14 times its one-way half-power beamwidth ϕ_3 dB.

6.6 Real beam antenna gain for narrowbeam lossless antennas can be defined to be

$$G = \frac{4\pi}{\phi_e \, \theta_e}$$

where ϕ_e and θ_e are the equivalent rectangular beamwidths (constant gain over widths ϕ_e and θ_e). Show from Prob. 6.5 that for uniformly illuminated apertures

$$G = \frac{4\pi}{\phi_3 \text{ dB} \; \theta_3 \text{ dB}} F_g^2$$

where $F_g = .88$. All beamwidths are in terms of radians.

6.7 A side-looking ($\phi = 90°$) airborne radar with a 1.0 m diameter antenna is to operate in a focused SAR mode to generate surface maps at low grazing angles. Echo signals can be detected out to a range extent of 100 nmi (185.2 km). (a) What is the maximum PRF required to avoid range ambiguity? (b) At this PRF, what is the maximum platform speed to avoid Doppler ambiguity?

6.8 A spotlight SAR ($\phi \approx 90°$) operates at a center frequency of 5.4 GHz. Platform speed is 780 kts (400 m/s). (a) What is the finest possible cross-range resolution for 10 s of spotlight time at 100 nmi (185.2 km)? (b) What is the required minimum PRF to avoid azimuth foldover for a real beamwidth of $\psi_e = 1.43°$ (.025 rad)? (c) What is the maximum illuminated slant-range extent at the minimum PRF before range-ambiguous responses occur?

6.9 What bandwidth will produce *square resolution* for a focused side-looking SAR ($\phi = 90°$) operating at a center wavelength of .03 m, assuming integration is carried out over the entire radar antenna beamwidth of 1.5° (.0262 rad)?

6.10 An airborne side-looking SAR flying at 300 kts (154 m/s) and operating at 9.4 GHz sees a railway train at 25 nmi (46.3 km). How far in cross-range does the train appear to be off the track if it is moving with a radial component of 5 kts (2.57 m/s) relative to the radar?

6.11   Use (6.14) to show that range curvature expressed in (6.30) can also be expressed independently of beam integration angle as

$$M' = \frac{R\lambda^2}{32\,\Delta r_s(\Delta r_c)^2}$$

6.12   Show that the general form of (6.31) for the range depth of focus based on $\phi(\omega_e)$ rad of allowable quadratic phase error at the azimuth Doppler band edges is

$$(\Delta R)_f = \frac{16\,(\Delta r_c)^2}{\pi\lambda}\,\phi(\omega_e)$$

6.13   Range curvature is corrected at some range R. Show by using (6.29) that the range extent over which there is less than one range cell of range migration is given by

$$(\Delta R)_M = \frac{8\Delta r_s}{\psi^2}$$

where ψ is the angle over which either single or multiple looks are to be taken.

6.14   (a) What is the cross-range resolution of the SEASAT design of Table 6.3 associated with data from four looks that are processed coherently as a single look for increased resolution? (b) What is the new range depth of focus? Assume uniform illumination over the four looks.

6.15   Use the expression in the text for the chi-squared density to show that the probability densities of pixel intensity for single-look and multiple-look processing are given by (6.32) and (6.33), respectively. Assume that the outputs of the I and Q channels have the zero-mean Gaussian probability density $p(x)$ given in the text.

6.16   What improvement factor (dB) in signal-to-speckle-noise ratio is achieved compared with that for one look in the SEASAT design by noncoherently adding four coherent looks based on zero-mean, Gaussian-distributed, quadrature inputs to the pixel intensity detector for each look?

6.17   (a) How many additional single looks are possible for the hypothetical radar of Table 6.6 within the effective beamwidth of the real beam? (b) What is the corresponding improvement in pixel signal-to-speckle-noise over that for four looks (assuming zero-mean Gaussian quadrature pairs are detected to produce pixel intensity values)? (c) What is the increased range migration from beam center to either beam edge at the far edge of the range swath (85 km) across the increased total multiple-look angle?

6.18   What is the minimum PRF that could be used in the SEASAT radar for unambiguous sampling of the Doppler bandwidth produced across the antenna's 3 dB beamwidth?

6.19   What is the range and azimuth size on data collection film of the dispersed response recorded from a point target during a single SEASAT look if CRT sweep velocity is 100 m/s and film transport velocity is .01 m/s? (b) What are the optical focal lengths in range and azimuth for optical processing with a source at 0.6 μm (0.6 × 10^{-6} m)? Assume a range of 854 km.

6.20   (a) How many sections of 2048 range data samples are required after overlap to carry out range processing of the total 288 μs range swath of SEASAT echo data produced by each 34 μs pulse? (b) What range extent of data in meters is discarded at the beginning of each range profile of echo data?

6.21   (a) How many sections of 2048 complex azimuth data samples are required after overlap to carry out 100 km of azimuth processing of SEASAT data? (b) What azimuth extent of data in meters is discarded at the beginning of each 100 km × 100 km of processed image data?

REFERENCES

1.   Sherwin, C.W., J.P. Ruina, and R.D. Rawcliffe, "Some Early Developments in Synthetic Aperture Radar Systems," *IRE Trans. Military Electronics,* Vol. MIL-6, No. 2, April 1962, pp. 111–115.
2.   Kovaly, J.J., *Synthetic Aperture Radar,* Dedham, MA: Artech House, 1976. (A collection of 33 reprints covering the development, theory, performance, effect of errors, motion compensation, processing, and application of SAR.)
3.   Cutrona, L.J., "Synthetic Aperture Radar," Ch. 23 of *Radar Handbook,* M.I. Skolnik, ed., New York: McGraw-Hill, 1970, pp. 23-1 to 23-25.

4. Harger, R.O., *Synthetic Aperture Radar Systems: Theory and Design,* New York: Academic Press, 1970.
5. Hovanessian, S.A., *Introduction to Synthetic Array and Imaging Radars,* Dedham, MA: Artech House, 1980.
6. Sentz, J.D., Jr., and J.D. Wiley, "Radar's Growing Role in Ice, Pollution Surveillance," *Sea Technology,* Aug. 1985, pp. 27–29.
7. Papoulis, A., *Probability, Random Variables and Stochastic Processes,* New York: McGraw-Hill, 1965, p. 250.
8. Elachi, C., *et al.,* "Spaceborne Synthetic-Aperture Imaging Radars: Applications, Techniques and Technology," *Proc. IEEE,* Vol. 70, No. 10, Oct. 1982, pp. 1174–1209.
9. Nathanson, F.E., *Radar Design Principles,* New York: McGraw-Hill, 1969, pp. 236, 238, 263, and 273.
10. Brigham, E.O., *The Fast Fourier Transform,* Englewood Cliffs, NJ: Prentice-Hall, 1974, Sec. 13-3.
11. Wu, C., "A Digital Fast Correlation Approach to Produce SEASAT SAR Imagery," *IEEE 1980 Int. Radar Conf. Record,* April 28–30, 1980, pp. 153–160.

Chapter 7
Inverse Synthetic Aperture Radar (ISAR)

7.1 COMPARISON OF SAR AND ISAR

Inverse synthetic aperture radar (ISAR) is a technique that can be used operationally to image targets such as ships, aircraft, and space objects. The technique also has application to instrumentation radar for evaluating radar cross section of targets and target models. Basic theory with respect to instrumentation-range measurements is covered in a book by Mensa [1] and in journal articles by Chen and Andrews [2] and Walker [3]. Imaging of aircraft targets is also discussed by Chen and Andrews [4]. Imaging of planets and space objects is discussed by Ausherman *et al.* [5]. Theory and design principles from the viewpoint of operational applications will be discussed in this chapter with the emphasis on ship and aircraft imaging.

The ISAR concept will be explained by starting with a review of the more familiar synthetic aperture radar (SAR) concept, described in Chapter 6. Synthetic aperture radar was discussed in terms of an airborne (or spaceborne) radar mapping technique for generating high resolution maps of surface targets and terrain. We pointed out that resolution in the slant range to the radar can be obtained by transmitting wideband pulses, usually chirp pulses, and cross-range resolution can be obtained by coherent processing of echo energy returned from the ground as the aircraft or spacecraft carrying the radar travels above and alongside the ground area to be mapped. Figure 7.1 illustrates the commonly recognized form of SAR, called *side-looking SAR*. Synthetic aperture size is the length along the flight track over which coherent integration occurs. As illustrated in the figure, this is limited by range and real antenna beamwidth. Synthetic aperture size shrinks for echoes arriving from distances closer to the aircraft and increases for echoes arriving at distances farther from the aircraft. The effect, after azimuth focusing, is to produce constant cross-range resolution

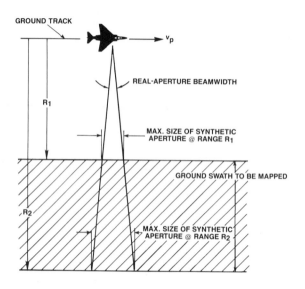

Fig. 7.1 Airborne Side-Looking SAR

independent of range. We saw in Chapter 6 that this cross-range resolution is approximately equal to one-half of the real aperture's cross-range dimension.

A real antenna coherently integrates an incident echo signal distributed across its aperture. Likewise, echo signals collected along a synthetic aperture length must be coherently summed in order to realize the narrow beamwidth associated with a long, synthetically generated aperture. This is achieved by first correcting all forms of platform-to-earth movements that deviate from straight-line motion. What remains is a response for each surface scatterer that varies quadratically in phase with distance along the flight path. The quadratic phase response, as we saw in Chapter 6, was produced by quadratic range change associated with straight-line motion of the radar past the scatterer. Removal of the quadratic phase was called *azimuth focusing.*

In Chapter 6 it was also shown to be possible to achieve a form of SAR called *spotlight SAR,* illustrated in Fig. 7.2. Spotlight SAR is obtained as the radar antenna constantly tracks a particular target area of interest. Here, the cross-range resolution is determined, not by real antenna size as is the case for side-looking SAR, but by target dwell time. ISAR can be explained in terms of SAR by referring to the spotlight form. After correcting for deviation from straight-line motion, a spotlight SAR can be thought of as if the radar were flying a portion $\Delta\phi$ of a circle around the target area, as in Fig. 7.3. We can see from this figure that, although the radar moves about the target, the same data would be collected if the radar were stationary and the target area rotated. This is precisely what occurs with ISAR. The aspect motion of the target relative to the radar is used to generate the target map, which is the *target image*. The ISAR process will now be discussed in more detail. The discussion will be limited to ISAR imagery of targets having dimensions that are small compared with target range to the radar and where the images are obtained from observations made over small segments of viewing angle. This corresponds to applications for long-range imaging of noncooperative aircraft and ship targets.

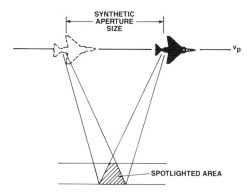

Fig. 7.2 Spotlight SAR

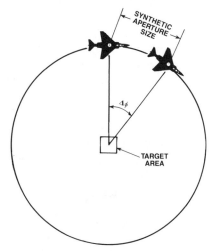

Fig. 7.3 Spotlight SAR—Circular Flight Paths

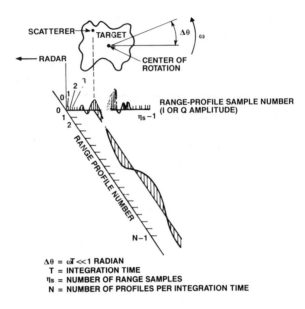

Fig. 7.4 Range-Doppler Sampling of Rotating Target

7.2 BASIC ISAR THEORY FOR SMALL SEGMENTS OF VIEWING ANGLE

Figure 7.4 suggests a series of range profiles produced by a high-range-resolution radar as it observes a rotating target. The signal along one range profile is illustrated, and the response in one range-cell is shown in time history. The response in the range cell corresponding to the scatterer shown in the figure produces a few cycles of Doppler shift during time T, while the target rotates through $\Delta\theta$ rad. Not shown in the figure are Doppler responses produced in other range cells corresponding to other scatterers on the target.

Data for one image is sampled with η_s in-phase and quadrature samples per range profile for each of N range profiles obtained during time T, while the target rotates $\Delta\theta$ rad. Waveforms used to obtain the range profiles and sampling criteria will be discussed later.

Doppler frequency shift produced by a given slant-range resolved scatterer for small $\Delta\theta$ is proportional to target-aspect angular rotation rate as well as cross-range distance between the scatterer and the center of target rotation. One or more Doppler spectral lines can exist for each slant-range cell, one for each Doppler-resolved scatterer. The magnitude of a spectral line is proportional to the reflectivity of the resolved scatterer. The target's reflectivity, therefore, can be mapped in both slant range and cross range with the cross-range scale factor dependent upon target-aspect angular rotation rate. Target track data, if available, can be used to estimate rotation rate and rotation axis alignment. Orientation of the rotation axis relative to the radar line of sight (LOS) establishes the orientation of the image plane. The image is bounded by slant-range and cross-range windows, the significance of which will be discussed later.

7.2.1 Cross-Range Resolution

The basic relationship between target rotational motion, scatterer position, and the resulting Doppler frequency shift can be seen by referring to Fig. 7.5. Neither the radar nor the target has any translational motion in this example. Radar LOS is in the plane of the paper. The target rotates at a constant angular rotation rate ω in rad/s about a fixed axis perpendicular to the plane of the paper. A single scatterer at a cross-range distance r_c then moves with instantaneous velocity ωr_c toward the radar. Doppler frequency shift produced by rotation over a small rotation angle is given by

$$f_D = \frac{2}{c} \omega r_c \bar{f} \qquad (7.1)$$

where $\bar{f}$ is the carrier or center frequency of the radar, and c is the propagation velocity. We will initially assume that f_D is constant during the small viewing-angle change that occurs during integration time T. Later, we will show that image distortion results from the actual sinusoidal vari-

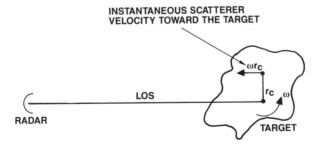

Fig. 7.5 Radial Velocity Produced by a Scatterer on a Rotating Target

ation of f_D that occurs as the target rotates through a finite viewing-angle (aspect) change.

If two scatterers in the same slant-range cell are separated in cross range by a distance δr_c, then the separation between the frequencies of the received signals, from (7.1), is

$$\delta f_D = \frac{2}{c} \omega \delta r_c \bar{f}$$

so that

$$\delta r_c = \frac{c}{2\omega \bar{f}} \delta f_D$$

Let Δr_c denote the cross-range resolution. Then, for a radar that has a Doppler-frequency resolution of Δf_D, we have

$$\Delta r_c = \frac{c}{2\omega \bar{f}} \Delta f_D \tag{7.2}$$

Cross-range resolution Δr_c is thus dependent upon the resolvable difference in the Doppler frequencies from two scatterers in the same slant-range cell. Doppler resolution, in turn, can be related to the available coherent integration time. The approximate relationship, from (2.15b) of Chapter 2, is given by

$$\Delta f_D \approx \frac{1}{T}$$

where T is the integration time, also called the *image frame time,* associated with Doppler filtering.

Cross-range resolution for a small viewing-angle rotation $\Delta\theta$, in radians, occurring during integration time T, is obtained for $\Delta f_D = 1/T$, from (7.2), as

$$\Delta r_c = \frac{c}{2\omega T \bar{f}} = \frac{1}{2} \frac{\lambda}{\omega T} = \frac{1}{2} \frac{\lambda}{\Delta\theta} \tag{7.3}$$

Equation (7.3) is thus the same as (6.12) for SAR, where integration angle $\Delta\theta$ for ISAR corresponds to azimuth integration angle ψ in side-looking SAR and $\Delta\phi$ in spotlight SAR.

Typically, a discrete Fourier transform process is used to convert the set of time-history samples collected in each range cell during the time segment T into a discrete Doppler spectrum. The precise relationship between Doppler frequency resolution and integration time depends upon the type of transform used and the *window* function used to weight the segment of time-history response. Figure 7.6(a) illustrates echo samples available in the same range cell of N range profiles. The discrete Fourier transform of the data is illustrated in Fig. 7.6(b).

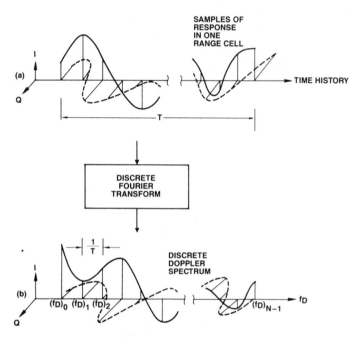

Fig. 7.6 Sampled Time History and Associated Doppler Spectrum in One Range Cell (Illustrated for the Case where One Range Profile is Generated from each Transmitted Chirp Pulse)

7.2.2 Slant-Range Resolution

As for SAR, slant-range resolution for ISAR is obtained by using wideband waveforms. Regardless of the type of waveform, the achievable range resolution is expressed as

$$\Delta r_s \approx \frac{c}{2\beta}$$

where β is the waveform bandwidth. In principle, any of the waveforms discussed in Chapters 4 and 5 would be suitable. Only two are discussed here: chirp-pulse compression and stepped frequency; these are the same two waveforms discussed for SAR in Chapter 6. While pulse compression and stretch waveforms are the most common for SAR, stepped-frequency waveforms have been found to be useful for ISAR when the application requires extreme resolution.

Synthetic processing of stepped-frequency waveforms requires conversion of echo data, collected in the frequency domain, into synthetic range profiles. This is typically carried out by using a discrete Fourier transform process, as illustrated in Fig. 7.7. Resolution for n steps of Δf Hz each is

$$\Delta r_s \approx \frac{c}{2n\Delta f}$$

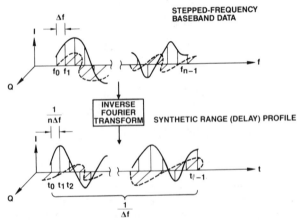

Fig. 7.7 Echo Spectrum and Associated Synthetic Range (Delay) Profile for a Single Burst

Synthetic ISAR involves two dimensions of the Fourier transform: (1) frequency-domain reflectivity into range-delay reflectivity for each burst to resolve targets in range, followed by (2) time-domain reflectivity in each range cell into Doppler frequency-domain reflectivity for each range cell to resolve targets in cross range. The above two-dimensional transformation process, in the most fundamental sense, transforms reflectivity data obtained in the frequency and viewing-angle space into object-space reflectivity estimates.

7.2.3 Slant-Range Sampling

Targets to be imaged using ISAR are usually isolated, in contrast to the large surface areas to be mapped with SAR. For ISAR, therefore, we assume that some type of angle and range tracking is used to collect target reflectivity data from the isolated target. The target is usually immersed in the radar antenna beam. Regardless of waveform, η_s samples from each of N range profiles are required as input data for one image, as shown in Fig. 7.4. The η_s samples from each range profile are directly collected in the time domain upon transmission of chirp pulses or short pulses. When stepped-frequency bursts are transmitted, sampling occurs in the frequency domain. The range profiles are then effectively sampled by the n pulses of each burst so that $\eta_s = n$. A slant-range window will now be defined for each type of waveform.

Sampling of individual range profiles from chirp pulses or short pulses is illustrated in Fig. 7.8. The unambiguously sampled slant-range extent, called the *slant-range window,* is given by

$$w_s = \eta_s \Delta r_s = \eta_s \frac{c}{2\beta} \qquad (7.4)$$

for η_s complex samples spaced by $1/\beta$ in range delay. Bandwidth β for short-pulse or chirp-pulse radars is the pulse bandwidth. Samples are obtained, as described in Chapter 4, by using some form of range tracking that starts the first sample just before the target echo arrives from each pulse. Additional samples are collected during a total delay interval corresponding to the slant-range window given by (7.4). To meet Nyquist's criterion, the sampling rate during this interval must equal or exceed β complex samples per second.

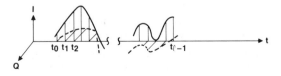

Fig. 7.8 Sampled Range (Delay) Profile

The sampling to obtain individual synthetic range profiles obtained from stepped-frequency bursts requires a sample of the target's reflectivity at each of the n frequencies per burst. In other words, we require one complex sample of the target echo signal produced by each pulse. As discussed in Chapter 3, for unambiguous sampling, a target's reflectivity in the frequency domain requires complex sample pairs spaced by $\Delta f \le 1/(\delta t)$, where δt is the range-delay extent over which the target reflects incident waves. As stated in terms of an unambiguous range window, we write

$$w_s = \frac{c\delta t}{2} = \frac{c}{2\Delta f} \tag{7.5}$$

By comparison with (7.4), the synthetic range window is effectively sampled by $\eta_s = n$ samples with $\beta = n\Delta f$.

Targets that exceed the slant-range window defined by (7.4) for sampling of *real* profiles produced by short-pulse or chirp-pulse radars will be imaged over only that portion of the target for which samples were taken. Targets that exceed the synthetic range window obtained with stepped-frequency waveforms will produce images that are folded over within the range window. The range window for synthetic processing, defined by (7.5), therefore, is actually an *ambiguity window*. By setting pulse duration T_1 equal to $1/\Delta f$, ambiguous responses are eliminated, but only the range extent $cT_1/2$ will be imaged in this case.

7.2.4 Cross-Range Sampling

Cross-range sampling refers to sampling along time history in each resolved range cell. Samples are separated in time by the radar PRI (T_2) for short-pulse or chirp-pulse waveforms and by nT_2 for synthetic stepped-frequency waveforms. Analogous to SAR, a cross-range ambiguity window for ISAR can be defined as the largest cross-range extent that can be unambiguously sampled for a given PRF, viewing-angle rotation rate, and wavelength. For ISAR, the target is usually immersed in the antenna beamwidth so that the ambiguity length refers to the target size in cross-range, rather than to the illuminated cross-range extent of the earth surface as in SAR. From (7.1), which expresses the Doppler frequency produced by a single scatterer on a rotating target, we can show that the Doppler frequency bandwidth produced by scatterers extending over a cross-range window w_c is $2\omega w_c \bar{f}/c$. The PRF required for unambiguous sampling of reflectivity data produced from short-pulse or chirp-pulse radars when viewing a target of cross-range extent w_c, therefore, is

$$\frac{1}{T_2} \geq \frac{2}{c} \omega w_c \bar{f}$$

assuming complex samples are collected; one sample in each range cell for each transmitted pulse.

Synthetic processing of stepped-frequency bursts of n pulses per burst requires a PRF of

$$\frac{1}{T_2} \geq \frac{2n}{c} \omega w_c \bar{f}$$

Later in this chapter, we will estimate PRF requirements for ISAR images of ships and aircraft.

Regardless of waveform, the number of range profiles needed for unambiguous sampling of a target of cross-range extent w_c, based on $N/T \geq f_D$, is

$$N \geq \frac{2}{c} \bar{f} \omega w_c T$$

The unambiguous cross-range length $w_c = N\Delta r_c$ is the maximum cross-range extent of a target that can be examined unambiguously with N stepped-frequency bursts during the viewing-angle change $\Delta\theta$ for synthetic processing, or with N high range resolution pulses for real processing; one profile from each transmitted pulse. For a small aspect change of $\omega T = \Delta\theta$, the unambiguous cross-range window with Δr_c, from (7.3), is given by solving for w_c, which yields

$$w_c = N \frac{\lambda}{2\omega T} = N \frac{\lambda}{2\Delta\theta} \tag{7.6}$$

Wavelength, λ, when referring to short-pulse waveforms, is the wavelength at the carrier frequency. When referring to chirp-pulse or stepped-frequency waveforms, λ is the wavelength at the center frequency. Narrow fractional bandwidth is assumed in both cases.

A summary of the basic image-quality equations using real and synthetic range profiles is given in Table 7.1.

Table 7.1 Summary of Equations for ISAR (for Data Collection over Small Viewing-Angle Segments)

Parameter	ISAR from N Real Profiles	ISAR from N Synthetic Profiles (N bursts of n pulses)
Cross-Range Resolution, Δr_c, for $\Delta f_D = \dfrac{1}{T}$	$\dfrac{1}{2}\dfrac{\lambda}{\omega T}$, Eq. (7.3)	$\dfrac{1}{2}\dfrac{\lambda}{\omega T}$, Eq. (7.3)
Slant-Range Resolution, Δr_s, for $\Delta t = \dfrac{1}{\beta} = \dfrac{1}{n\Delta f}$	$\dfrac{1}{2}\dfrac{c}{\beta}$, Eq. (1.1)	$\dfrac{1}{2}\dfrac{c}{\beta} = \dfrac{1}{2}\dfrac{c}{n\Delta f}$, Eq. (5.8)
Cross-Range Ambiguity Window for $\Delta f_D = \dfrac{1}{T}$	$w_c = N\dfrac{\lambda}{2\omega T}$, Eq. (7.6)	$w_c = N\dfrac{\lambda}{2\omega T}$, Eq. (7.6)
Slant-Range Window for $\Delta t = \dfrac{1}{\beta} = \dfrac{1}{n\Delta f}$	$w_s = \eta_s \dfrac{c}{2\beta}$, Eq. (7.4)	$w_s = \dfrac{1}{2}\dfrac{c}{\Delta f}$, Eq. (7.5)
	(sampled window)	(ambiguity window)

7.3 SOURCES OF TARGET ASPECT ROTATION

So far, we have considered only the viewing-angle rotation produced by rotational motion of the target. Target aspect change is also produced by tangential translation of the target relative to the radar. *Radial translation* (motion along the radar LOS produces no viewing-angle shift. *Tangential translation* (motion normal to the LOS), like target rotation, produces a Doppler gradient associated with scatterers separated in cross range. Figure 7.9 illustrates how a differential Doppler shift is produced between two scatterers of a radar target that has a tangential velocity component relative to the radar. The scale in this drawing has been exaggerated to clarify the relationship between v_{R1} and v_{R2}.

A tangential velocity component v_T of a target relative to a radar at range R produces an apparent component of angular rotation rate as seen by the radar of

$$\omega_T = \frac{v_T}{R} \qquad (7.7)$$

The tangential vector component of the total angular rotation vector of the target as seen by the radar is

$$\omega_T = \frac{\mathbf{v}_t \times \mathbf{R}}{R} \qquad (7.8)$$

where $\mathbf{R}$ is the unit vector along the radar LOS and $\mathbf{v}_t$ is the target-velocity vector relative to the radar. Equation (7.8) reduces to (7.7) when the target's relative velocity vector $\mathbf{v}_t$ is perpendicular to the radar LOS unit vector $\mathbf{R}$.

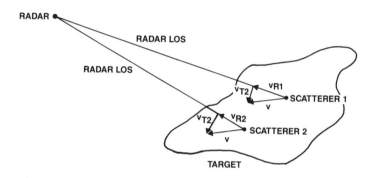

Fig. 7.9 Cross-Range Doppler Produced by Target Translation (*Note:* The exaggerated target size indicates the slight differences that occur between radial velocity components of target scatterers when the target translates relative to the radar and has a non-zero tangential component of translational velocity. For the target velocity v as shown, it is seen that v_{R1} is greater than v_{R2})

Any target aspect rotation relative to the radar produces a Doppler gradient across scatterers that are spread out in the cross-range dimension. Aspect rotation produced by both target translation and target angular motion is indicated in Fig. 7.10. The rotation produced by target angular motion is made up of three sources of rotation: pitch, roll, and yaw (or turn). For aircraft targets at frequencies up to about the X-band region (8.50 GHz to 10.68 GHz), as seen from ground-based radar, translation is likely to be the major contributor to a useful Doppler gradient for

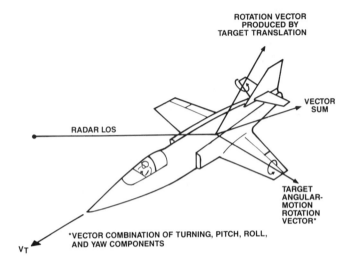

Fig. 7.10 Components of Target Rotation

imaging purposes. For ship targets observed at ranges beyond about 10 nmi, target pitch, roll, and yaw predominate to produce the image.

7.4 TARGET IMAGE PROJECTION PLANE

The image produced from echo signal data collected from a long-range target during the time that it rotates through some small viewing angle can be thought of as a set of reflectivity estimates plotted in a rectangular slant-range *versus* Doppler-frequency coordinate system, which is called the *image projection plane*. This plane contains the radar LOS, and is normal to the *effective rotation vector*. The effective rotation vector is the projection of the actual rotation vector on a plane normal to the radar LOS. Lines of constant slant range lie in the projection plane normal to the LOS. Lines of constant cross range lie in the projection plane parallel to the LOS. We will now discuss the associated vector relationships.

Instantaneous Doppler frequency shift $f_D(t)$, produced at radar frequency f by a single scatterer on a target that is moving with radial velocity v_t toward the radar, is a vector function of v_t and the following time-variable vector quantities: *target rotation vector* $\omega_\Sigma(t)$, *scatterer velocity vector* $\mathbf{v}(t)$, produced by the target's rotation vector, and *target line-of-sight unit vector* $\mathbf{R}(t)$ to the radar.

The line-of-sight unit vector $\mathbf{R}(t)$ for radar range that is large relative to target cross-range extent can be chosen to point toward the radar from some point within the target along its rotational vector ω_Σ as shown in Fig. 7.11(a). Doppler frequency shift produced by the scatterer is

$$f_D(t) = \frac{2[\mathbf{v}(t) \cdot \mathbf{R}(t)]}{c} f + \frac{2v_t}{c} f$$

By dropping the time notation and combining terms, we obtain

$$f_D = \frac{2f}{c} (\mathbf{v} \cdot \mathbf{R} + v_t)$$

If $\mathbf{r}$ is the position vector of the scatterer measured from the intersection of ω_Σ and $\mathbf{R}$, then the Doppler frequency becomes

$$f_D = \frac{2f}{c} (\omega_\Sigma \times \mathbf{r} \cdot \mathbf{R} + v_t)$$

Later in this chapter, we will see that, as part of the ISAR image processing, the target's radial velocity component v_t can be removed, leaving only the Doppler shift produced by target rotation. Then,

$$f_D = \frac{2f}{c} (\omega_\Sigma \times \mathbf{r} \cdot \mathbf{R}) \tag{7.9}$$

Equation (7.9), written to express Doppler shift produced by a scatterer at cross-range displacement r_c, becomes

$$f_D = \frac{2f}{c} [(\omega_\Sigma \times \mathbf{k}r_c) \cdot \mathbf{i}]$$

For angle ϕ between ω_Σ and $\mathbf{R}$:

$$f_D = \frac{2f}{c} (\omega_\Sigma r_c \sin\phi) \tag{7.10}$$

The quantity $\omega_\Sigma \sin\phi$ is the magnitude ω of the effective rotation vector ω, shown in Fig. 7.11(b), that lies normal to the radar LOS in the ω_Σ, $\mathbf{R}$ plane. Equation (7.10), written in terms of the magnitude of the effective rotation vector, becomes

$$f_D = \frac{2f}{c} \omega r_c$$

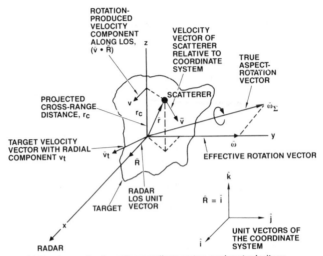

(a) Target geometry viewed in a coordinate system moving at velocity v_t.

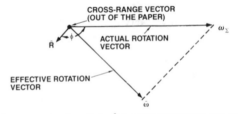

(b) Target geometry viewed in the $\hat{R}$, $\bar{\omega}_{\Sigma}$ plane normal to the cross-range vector $\hat{k} r_c$.

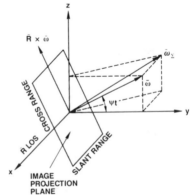

(c) ISAR image plane

Fig. 7.11 Image-Plane Geometry

as given in (7.1).

The image projection plane in Fig. 7.11(a) lies in x, z plane. The image projection plane in a more general x, y, z coordinate system is shown in Fig. 7.11(c). If the z-axis is vertical, the effective rotation axis is tilted at an angle ψ_t from the horizon as viewed by a radar along the x-axis.

The target's actual rotation vector ω_Σ, and hence its effective rotational vector ω, are not directly known from the target echo data. Therefore, the cross-range scale factor and image plane are said to be ambiguous. The effect of the targets' rotation vector on the resulting ISAR image plane can be explained in a qualitative manner by examining Fig. 7.12, where the image plane is illustrated for pitch, roll, and yaw motions of a ship target (no translation). In each case, the actual rotation vector ω_Σ is equal to the effective rotation vector ω, and is normal to the plane of the paper. Radar range is assumed to be large relative to target size.

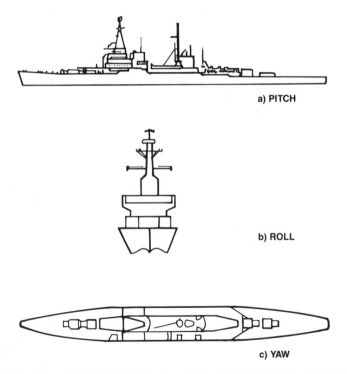

a) PITCH

b) ROLL

c) YAW

THE RADAR LIES ANYWHERE IN THE PLANE OF THE PAPER DIRECTED AT THE TARGET

Fig. 7.12 ISAR Image Views Produced by Target Pitch, Roll, and Yaw Motion

The image planes of the three views of Fig. 7.12 are those which result when the radar LOS vector **R** lies anywhere in the plane of the paper. Figure 7.13 illustrates the image plane of a rolling ship that is resolved in range and Doppler by an airborne radar. The ship and radar are both in the plane of the paper.

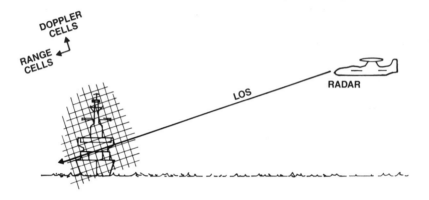

Fig. 7.13 Image Plane with Range and Doppler Cells Indicated for Ship Target with Roll Motion (Fig. 7.12(b) Example)

7.5 PULSE-COMPRESSION ISAR PROCESSING

Real high-range-resolution (HRR) target range profiles for ISAR are obtained (1) by transmitting and receiving very short radar pulses, or (2) by transmitting frequency- or phase-coded pulses for pulse compression in the receiver. Pulse compression is more common. Both the amplitude and phase of the sampled range profiles must be retained for ISAR processing. The target's range profile is produced at the output of the pulse-compression filter, usually at an intermediate frequency. At this point, quadrature detection typically occurs by mixing to baseband. Then, sampling and digitizing follow. The steps leading to the generation of one η_s-element range profile are illustrated in Fig. 7.14. Each range profile is made up of η_s of the I and Q sample pairs. A set of N range profiles, one profile per radar pulse, is processed to form ISAR images as previously illustrated in Fig. 7.4. One complex time-history sample is obtained from each range cell of the range profile. Thus, the number of samples collected in each range cell during one *image frame* of N pulses is $\eta_c = N$. Sequentially generated range profiles are tracked in range. Therefore, range-sampled profiles are in alignment. This is essential to ensure that the $\eta_c = N$ complex samples in each range cell correspond to the same re-range positions of the target. Consider first a fixed target observed with a fixed radar. The range-delay trigger starts the high-speed A/D converter just before the arrival of the range-profile signal. This is the beginning of the range window. Digital I and Q sampling then creates the η_s range samples of the range window. Because the target is at a fixed range position, the ith range sample from each of the successive echo pulses will correspond to the same range position along the target.

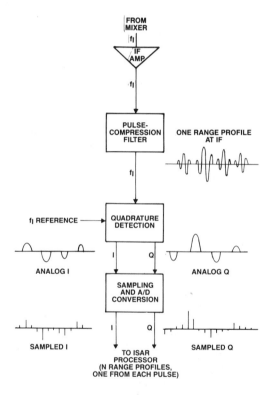

Fig. 7.14 Real Range-Profile Processing for ISAR

Time alignment for a moving target requires range tracking, wherein the delay trigger is continuously adjusted in delay to track the target. In practice, manual range tracking of moving targets cannot be done with sufficient precision for ISAR processing. However, servo loops have been developed to set the range-trigger delay to track a prominent target scatterer. The resulting samples are then equivalent to samples of the same target at a fixed range.

7.6 SYNTHETIC ISAR PROCESSING

The concept of synthetic ISAR imaging radar was originally developed to image air and surface targets in real time at full radar range from a fixed or moving radar platform by using narrowband radar signal processing methods. Synthetic ISAR has also proved to be useful for extremely high resolution imaging of scale models of real targets. The approach, also referred to as *stepped-frequency imaging,* uses the stepped-frequency waveform discussed in Chapter 5. Important elements of the application to ISAR include: (1) the use of stepped-frequency waveforms to obtain a time history of the target's reflectivity sampled in the frequency domain, (2) correction of spectral samples for radar system phase and amplitude ripple, (3) correction of spectral samples for velocity-produced distortion, (4) conversion of the time history of the target's corrected samples of frequency-domain reflectivity into a time history of the target's synthetic range profile, (5) conversion of the target's range-profile history into a slant-range *versus* cross-range image, and (6) moving-window image processing to obtain an animated real-time image display.

The synthetic ISAR technique images air and surface targets by using waveform parameters that are suitable for a wide range of existing and planned radars. With synthetic ISAR, as for pulse-compression ISAR, images are developed from the gradient of Doppler frequencies produced by the target's rotational motion acting on scatterers distributed in cross-range. An advantage of the synthetic technique is that waveforms tend to be compatible with common radar designs, which do not usually provide wide instantaneous bandwidth.

Slant-range locations of the scatterers on a distributed target are obtained, burst by burst, by transforming the discrete echo spectrum acquired from each stepped-frequency burst into a synthetic range profile of the target. The cross-range location of scatterers in each synthetic range cell are then extracted by processing a time history of the bursts. Slant-range and cross-range data are processed together to form the target image, as in pulse-compression ISAR. An ISAR image is generated from N synthetic range profiles obtained from N stepped-frequency bursts, each of n pulses.

When the technique is referred to as stepped-frequency imaging, the term refers to sequences of pulses with the frequency of each successive pulse increased by a constant frequency step. Frequency excursion from the initial frequency to any step, in any case, is harmonically related to the fundamental step size Δf. The total bandwidth required for transmission of all the pulses is much greater than the instantaneous bandwidth of a single pulse. Uniformly increasing pulse-to-pulse frequency stepping is not essential. Hence, pseudorandom, pulse-to-pulse, frequency-coded radars that are designed for improved electronic counter-countermeasures (ECCM) capability could also produce target images. The process of generating images by using the synthetic technique is illustrated in Figs. 7.15 and 7.16.

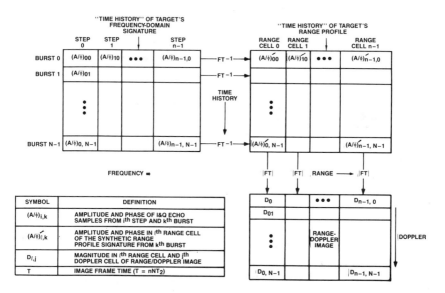

Fig. 7.15 Image Processing Sequence for Synthetic ISAR

In Fig. 7.15, the image processing sequence is illustrated, beginning with a row-column matrix for N bursts (rows) of η_s complex echo samples (columns). This matrix can be thought of as the time history of the target's reflectivity measured at discrete frequencies in the RF domain as the target viewing angle changes due to target aspect rotation relative to the radar. Complex echo samples in the time-history matrix are represented by amplitude and phase $(A/\phi)_{i,k}$. One complex echo sample is collected from each target echo pulse, which corresponds to one sample per transmitted pulse. Thus, $\eta_s = n$. The Fourier transform for each of the N bursts of n frequency samples is taken, row by row, to generate N new rows of synthetic range profiles, each with n synthetic range cells. The result can be represented as a second row-column matrix, called the *corner turn* or *time history of the target's range-profile signature*. Complex values in each synthetic range cell of this matrix are represented by the amplitude and phase $(A/\phi)'_{i,k}$. Finally, the time-history matrix is transformed into a third matrix by taking the Fourier transform of the N complex values in each range cell, column by column. The result, after converting complex values to absolute values $D_{l,j}$, is a range-Doppler matrix, which is the ISAR image. Each set of $n \times N$ original complex data samples is converted to $n \times N$ image pixel brightness values $D_{l,j}$. Figure 7.16 illustrates the same sequence of operations in another way (up to the point of generating a time-history profile in one range cell).

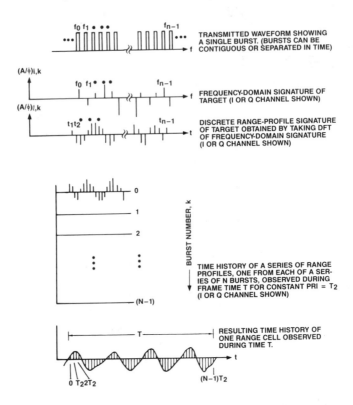

Fig. 7.16 Waveforms Associated with Synthetic ISAR Processing

The presence of a net radial velocity component between radar and target, unless corrected, will produce range walk of scatterers from profile to profile, resulting in misalignment of profiles. This effect, its results, and means for correction will be discussed below for both real and synthetic processing.

The input data matrix of Fig. 7.15, while referred to here as the time history of the target's frequency-domain signature, more fundamentally represents data collected in frequency and viewing-angle space. Indices $k = 0$ to $N - 1$ thus represent discrete aspect positions of the target relative to the radar. The second time-history matrix is then the target's range profile *versus* viewing angle.

7.7 RANGE OFFSET AND RANGE WALK

Generation of an ISAR image from a time history of slant-range profiles, regardless of waveform, therefore requires processing of responses by performing a Fourier transform in each range cell. This can be carried out only if alignment exists along the time history of range profiles. Alignment, however, is disturbed by targets with radial motion relative to the radar. Radial motion can produce both profile-to-profile *range walk* and a constant *range offset*. Range walk results directly from a change in range from profile to profile. Range offset results from range-Doppler coupling inherent to both chirp-pulse and stepped-frequency waveforms. (With nondispersive waveforms, such as short-pulses, or phase-coded waveforms, there is no range offset.) A moving target observed with a frequency-dispersive waveform is offset in range delay from that of a nonmoving target at the same range. Range offset is a fixed offset for constant radial velocity. Range walk, however, accumulates from profile to profile so that range profile alignment is destroyed, even for constant-velocity targets. Velocity correction of some form, therefore, is required to restore the slant-range alignment between adjacent slant-range profiles.

Range walk can be circumvented in real ISAR processing by continuously sampling each new profile at equivalent positions along the range profile. One way is to track a single prominent scatterer. For synthetic ISAR, however, sampling occurs before there is a slant-range profile to track, and hence sample position does not determine the slant-range position of the resulting synthetic slant-range profile. Correction for target velocity, therefore, is required after sampling as part of the processing, as will be described below. First, a single expression will be developed to express range offset and range walk produced by target radial velocity for chirp waveforms. Then, an equivalent expression will be developed for synthetic ISAR processing.

7.7.1 Range Walk and Range Offset (Chirp Waveforms)

Pulse-to-pulse shift in the delay position of the target's range profile is exhibited by both short-pulse and pulse-compression radars when the target moves with radial velocity relative to the radar. This may be observed when the range-sampling position remains fixed. Then, pulse-to-pulse delay shift for pulse repetition interval T_2 and inbound target velocity v_t is $-2v_t T_2/c$. The accumulated number of range-delay cells shifted (called range walk, or *range-cell migration*) due to target translation during the acquisition of k range profiles (one per pulse) is

$$M_w = -\frac{1}{\Delta t} \cdot \frac{2v_t T_2}{c} k$$

$$= -\frac{2kT_2}{c} \beta v_t \tag{7.11}$$

where $\Delta t \approx 1/\beta$ is the range-delay resolution of the radar with bandwidth β.

Range walk, as expressed in (7.11) for real profile processing, only considers the delay shift associated with target translation between radar pulses. Range offset is an additional, but nonaccumulating range-delay shift that occurs with chirp radars for targets of constant speed. Range delay shift $\delta\tau$ from the zero-Doppler response for a linear chirp pulse with frequency slope K Hz/s is coupled to Doppler frequency according to the expression:

$$f_D = -K\delta\tau$$

Delay shift associated with the positive Doppler shift of a target at velocity v_t toward the radar, therefore, is given by

$$\delta\tau = -\frac{f_D}{K} = -f_D \frac{T_1}{\Delta} = -\frac{2v_t \bar{f}}{c} \frac{T_1}{\Delta}$$

where Δ is the chirp bandwidth for chirp-pulse duration T_1 and $\bar{f}$ is the center frequency. The number of range cells shifted for delay resolution $1/\Delta$ is

$$M_s = -\frac{2T_1}{c} \bar{f} v_t \tag{7.12}$$

The total accumulated number of range cells shifted during the acquisition of N echo pulses for ISAR imaging with fixed range sampling, from (7.11) and (7.12), is

$$M = M_s + M_w$$

$$= -\left(\frac{2T_1}{c}\bar{f} + \frac{2NT_2}{c}\Delta\right)v_t \tag{7.13}$$

The first term, range offset, is the number of range cells of fixed delay shift produced by a constant Doppler frequency shift. The second term, range-cell migration or range walk, is the number of range cells of accumulated delay shift due to pulse-to-pulse target translation for the N pulses associated with the ISAR image. Range walk for chirp-pulse processing is usually avoided by employing range tracking, as we discussed above and in Chapter 4. Range offset does not destroy alignment between profiles unless target velocity changes significantly between pulses.

Doppler frequency shift, in addition to producing range shift, produces distortion of the compressed response for a pulse-compression filter matched to the transmitted pulse at $f_D = 0$. Distortion, however, is small until f_D becomes larger than $1/T_1$. This is not likely for ship and aircraft targets viewed by pulsed microwave radars.

7.7.2 Range Walk and Range Offset (Synthetic Processing)

The range shift and range profile distortion described above for real range profile processing becomes more complicated for synthetic range profile processing. Effective transmitted pulse duration for synthetic processing to produce one range profile is nT_2 in length as compared with T_1 for real processing. Thus, even slow targets may produce severe range offset and range profile distortion when employing synthetic ISAR processing. Synthetic range-profile distortion due to target velocity was discussed in Chapter 5. Only the resulting range offset and profile-to-profile range walk will be discussed here.

The processing of stepped-frequency echo signals produces synthetic target range profiles, which appear within an unambiguous range window determined by frequency step size. Delay of a point target seen within the range window is the *group delay* determined by the phase *versus* frequency function $\psi(f, v_t)$ of the stepped-frequency radar system as affected by target radial motion. For a point target moving with velocity v_t, we have

$$\tau = -\frac{1}{2\pi}\frac{d}{df}[\psi(f, v_t)] \tag{7.14}$$

The part of the total delay τ that is associated with target velocity is the delay shift $\delta\tau$. The unshifted component of the delay for the target at range R is $2R/c$. Delay shift due to velocity is given by

$$\delta\tau = -\frac{1}{2\pi}\frac{d}{df}[\psi(f, v_t)] - \frac{2R}{c} \tag{7.15}$$

   The phase function $\psi(f, v_t)$ of (7.14) and (7.15) can be estimated by assuming a linear slope of phase *versus* frequency during each burst (i.e., no dispersion in the propagation media or radar hardware over bandwidth $n\Delta f$). Then, for the kth burst, we have

$$\psi(f, v_t) = \frac{\psi_{n-1,k} - \psi_{0,k}}{(n-1)\Delta f} f \qquad (7.16)$$

The phase of the sampled echo data from one burst of a stepped-frequency waveform, from (5.1) of Chapter 5, is expressed as

$$\psi_i = -2\pi f_i \left[\frac{2R}{c} - \frac{2v_t}{c} S_i \right] \qquad (7.17)$$

where, for sampling at the center of each echo pulse,

$$S_i = iT_2 + \frac{T_1}{2} + \frac{2R}{c}$$

When multiple bursts are to be considered, as for ISAR, we have

$$S_{ik} = (i + nk) T_2 + \frac{T_1}{2} + \frac{2R}{c} \qquad (7.18)$$

The phase advance of echo data sampled according to (7.18) from k bursts is

$$\psi_{ik} = -2\pi f_i \left\{ \frac{2R}{c} - \frac{2v_t}{c} \left[(i + nk) T_2 + \frac{T_1}{2} + \frac{2R}{c} \right] \right\} \qquad (7.19)$$

Equation (7.16), with (7.19) for $f_i = f_0 + i\Delta f$ and $k \gg 1$, becomes

$$\psi(f, v_t) = 2\pi f \left[\frac{2v_t}{c} \frac{f_0 T_2 + \Delta f\left(\frac{T_1}{2} + \frac{2R}{c} + nkT_2 \right)}{\Delta f} - \frac{2R}{c} \right] \qquad (7.20)$$

The total delay, from (7.14) and (7.20), is

$$\tau = -\frac{2v_t}{c} \left[\frac{f_0 T_2 + \Delta f\left(\frac{T_1}{2} + \frac{2R}{c} + nkT_2 \right)}{\Delta f} \right] + \frac{2R}{c}$$

Delay shift due to target velocity, from (7.15), is

$$\delta\tau = -\frac{2v_t}{c\Delta f}\left[f_0 T_2 + \Delta f\left(\frac{T_1}{2} + \frac{2R}{c} + nkT_2\right)\right] \tag{7.21}$$

An approaching target (v_t positive), therefore, has a response shifted to an earlier time, less delay. This was illustrated in Fig. 5.8 and 5.9 of Chapter 5. The number of cells M of range shift for radar delay resolution $\Delta t = 1/(n\Delta f)$ is

$$M = \frac{\delta\tau}{\Delta t} = n\Delta f\delta\tau$$

By substituting $\delta\tau$ from (7.21), we obtain

$$M = -\frac{2n}{c}\left[f_0 T_2 + \Delta f\left(\frac{T_1}{2} + \frac{2R}{c} + nkT_2\right)\right]v_t$$

Because we are interested in the range shift for at least one synthetic range profile:

$$nkT_2 \gg \frac{T_1}{2} + \frac{2R}{c}$$

Then,

$$M \approx -\frac{2nT_2}{c}(f_0 + nk\Delta f)v_t$$

When one entire burst is considered, $k = N - 1$. When N is large, $k \approx N$ so that the accumulated number of range cells shifted due to target velocity during the entire image frame time is

$$M \approx -\frac{2nT_2}{c}(f_0 + nN\Delta f)v_t = -\left[\frac{2(nT_2)}{c}f_0 + \frac{2N(nT_2)n\Delta f}{c}\right]v_t \tag{7.22}$$

Equation (7.22) is plotted in Fig. 7.17 for parameters used in an experimental imaging radar at the Naval Ocean Systems Center (NOSC), San Diego.

The first term of (7.22) is analogous to the Doppler-produced range offset term of (7.13) for chirp-pulse processing with contiguous chirp segments. The stepped-frequency burst length nT_2 corresponds to a chirp

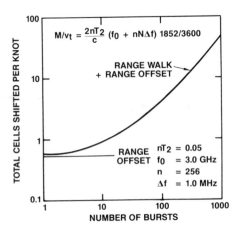

Fig. 7.17 Range Migration Produced by Target Velocity for Synthetic
ISAR

pulse of duration T_1, and the starting frequency f_0 corresponds (approximately, for small percentage bandwidth) to the chirp center frequency $\bar{f}$. The second term of (7.22) is identical to the range walk predicted in (7.13) for $T_2 = nT_2$ and $\Delta = n\Delta f$. For these substitutions, the stepped-frequency waveform required for one ISAR image is approximated in (7.13) by N contiguous chirp pulses of length nT_2, PRI $= nT_2$, and bandwidth $\Delta = n\Delta f$.

Uncorrected range walk will produce distortion in the ISAR image. Echoes from a scatterer at a given cross-range position will "walk" out of the slant-range cell in which the integration process is being carried out by use of the Fourier transform. The result will be less integration of the scatterer's Doppler response, which, in turn, results in less cross-range resolution for that scatterer. In addition, the scatterer's echo "walks" into an adjacent slant-range cell, producing distortion in that cell. We can see from Fig. 7.17 that range walk of about 10 range cells per knot can occur in a 256 × 256 element image for the given parameters. Unless corrected, the image distortion for even very slow targets would be unacceptable. By comparing Fig. 7.17 with Figs. 5.8 and 5.9 of Chapter 5, we can see that range walk distortion produced in a target's ISAR image by radial velocity is more severe for a given target velocity than the resulting distortion within a target's individual synthetic range profile. We account for this through the increase by a factor of N in imaging integration time as compared with range profile generation for a given number of pulses per burst.

7.8 TARGET RADIAL-MOTION CORRECTION FOR SYNTHETIC ISAR

Range walk and range profile distortion occurring with synthetic processing of moving targets cannot be avoided by precise range tracking before sampling as would be the case for pulse-compression radars. Instead, target velocity correction must be carried out on the sampled data. Range tracking before sampling need only be sufficiently precise to obtain samples near the peak of the narrowband pulse, where the signal-to-noise ratio is highest.

Sampled phase, from (7.17), is given by

$$\psi_i = -2\pi f_i \left[\frac{2R}{c} - \frac{2v_t}{c} \left(iT_2 + \frac{T_1}{2} + \frac{2R}{c} \right) \right]$$

Range walk and range profile distortion can be eliminated by multiplying the complex sampled data $G_i = A_i \exp(j\psi_i)$ by a complex exponential ζ that cancels the term containing target velocity v_t. Distortion produced by target radial velocity will tend to be cancelled for

$$\zeta = \exp\left\{ j(-2\pi f_i) \left[\frac{2\bar{v}_t}{c} \left(iT_2 + \frac{T_1}{2} + \frac{2\bar{R}}{c} \right) \right] \right\}$$

where $\bar{R}$ and $\bar{v}_t$ are estimates of the target's range and radial velocity, respectively.

For some applications of synthetic ISAR, the target's radial velocity may be known precisely from auxiliary data of the sampled stepped-frequency echo signals. One example is turntable measurement of target models taken with a fixed radar (zero velocity relative to the turntable). Another example is space-object identification for which precise target range data may be available. When images are to be generated from tactical targets, such as ships and aircraft, however, sufficiently precise target radial velocity data may not be available. Furthermore, the effective radial velocity can vary during the image frame time.

In early tests at NOSC against ship and aircraft targets, a range estimate $\bar{R}$ was obtained from the delay position of the sampling pulse generated by the range tracker. The velocity estimate $\bar{v}_t$ was obtained by calculating the average range rate from the series of sample positions used to collect the N bursts of n echo samples. Application of the correction factor ζ with estimates of range and range rate obtained in this manner was found to be marginal at best, even for slow targets like ships. It was found that the target's effective "instantaneous" velocity varied sufficiently during the image frame time to cause unacceptable image distortion. A velocity-correction process was then sought that would produce a burst-to-burst velocity-correction factor.

Both Hughes Aircraft Company and Syracuse Research Corporation, under US Navy contracts, developed methods for motion compensation that were tested on NOSC data. A burst-by-burst method of velocity estimation (*phase method*) developed by Hughes for NOSC will be described here. In the phase method, the average phase change is determined for each new synthetic range profile. The phase change in each range cell is determined relative to that for the same range cell from the previous profile. The average phase change for the entire new profile is then calculated, and the result is used to correct phase in the frequency domain. The sequence of operations is indicated in Fig. 7.18. Instantaneous target velocity and the range history for a ship target are shown in Figs. 7.19 and 7.20.

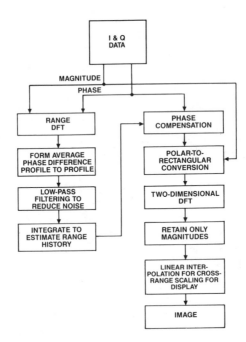

Fig. 7.18 Synthetic ISAR Image-Generation Process

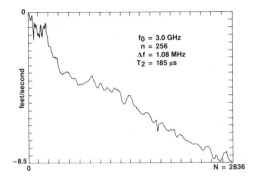

Fig. 7.19 Instantaneous Velocity for Ship Target

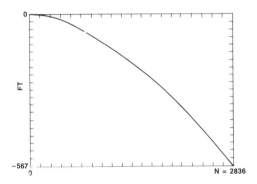

Fig. 7.20 Estimated Range History

Burst-to-burst, two-way phase changes larger than 2π rad are ambiguously related to target velocity. Therefore, the above process for wavelength λ will produce distortion when $2|v_t|nT_2$ is equal to or greater than λ in any range cell. Maximum tolerable uncorrected velocity before phase correction based on this criterion is plotted in Fig. 7.21. To meet this criterion for faster targets, a third method for estimating velocity called the *cross-correlation* method can be employed. The concept is to set up a rough alignment profile to profile before attempting the phase compensation. Here, the synthetic range profile for each burst is cross correlated with the previous range profile to measure the range shift produced by radial velocity. The measured range shift can be removed to set up a rough alignment of the time history of synthetic range profiles. The motion estimate obtained from the cross-correlation process and other smoothing techniques are then applied for velocity correction of the original frequency-domain data before *phase alignment.* The entire range-velocity correction process is further *fine tuned* in several other ways to produce the best images. Other techniques have since been developed for velocity correction of stepped-frequency data.

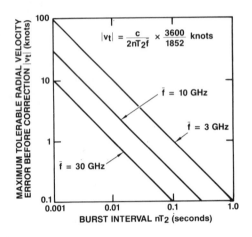

Fig. 7.21 Maximum Tolerable Velocity Error before Phase Correction

7.9   DISTORTION PRODUCED BY TARGET ANGULAR ROTATION

Image distortion is also produced by target rotational motion. Target rotation produces the target Doppler gradient that makes cross-range resolution possible in the first place. However, because the motion of the target's individual backscattering centers is circular, their velocity component toward the radar is not constant and they follow curved paths in range. Conversion of time-aligned profiles into ISAR images using the Fourier transform, range cell by range cell, therefore results in a distorted image. Deviation in Doppler and range, although small during the one to three degrees of target aspect rotation typically required for imaging of ships or aircraft, can severely reduce image quality. Distortion becomes more severe as ISAR resolution cell size is reduced, target size increases, and wavelength increases. The phenomenon is analogous to the effects of quadratic phase error and cell migration produced by range curvature associated with straight-line SAR platform motion past the target area.

Correction for the quadratic phase error is commonly referred to as *focusing.* Correction for cell migration requires two-dimensional processing to integrate the target responses through their curved tracks in data-collection space. Later in this chapter, a polar-reformatting technique will be discussed that produces distortion-free images by reformatting data collected in the polar-frequency *versus* viewing-angle domain into a rectangular frequency *versus* frequency domain. First, we shall discuss the distortion mechanisms and their effect on image quality.

The analysis of cross-range Doppler produced by target rotation, up to this point, has assumed that the target aspect rotation required to form an image was sufficiently small that the Doppler produced by individual scatterers was constant and no significant change in range occurred for any scatterers during the image frame time. Target aspect rotation angles that are sufficiently large to produce significant change in Doppler frequency and range during the image frame time will be examined next. Target geometry is shown in Fig. 7.22, which illustrates a single scatterer at radius *r* from the target's rotation axis. Figure 7.23 is a view seen in the plane of the radar LOS.

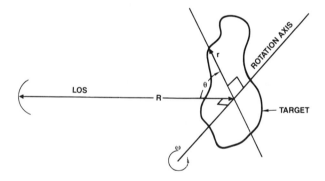

Fig. 7.22 Rotating Target Geometry (*Note:* The radar line of sight (LOS) and rotation axis are orthogonal. Shown is a single scatterer lying on a straight line normal to the rotation axis, which forms an angle θ with the LOS at time $t = 0$)

Physical rotation of the target produces time-dependent echo delay to the scatterer. The resulting distortion of the range profile is not dependent upon the method used to generate the range profile of the target. Distortion will therefore, be analyzed in terms of a real range profile, which permits a more intuitive description of the effect.

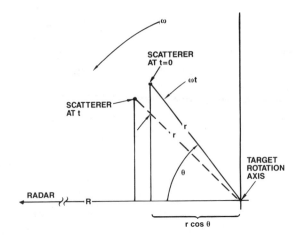

Fig. 7.23 Single Scatterer of a Rotating Target

Range delay to the single scatterer of Fig. 7.23 is

$$\tau(t) = \frac{2}{c} [R - v_t t - r \cos (\omega t - \theta)] \qquad (7.23)$$

where ω is the target's effective aspect angular rotation rate. Following perfect radial-velocity correction, (7.23) becomes

$$\tau(t) = \frac{2R}{c} - \frac{2r}{c} \cos (\omega t - \theta) \qquad (7.24)$$

Phase associated with $\tau(t)$ relative to the transmitted pulse is

$$\psi(t) = -2\pi \bar{f} \tau(t)$$

where $\bar{f}$ is the center frequency of the radar. From (7.24), we have

$$\psi(t) = -2\pi \bar{f} \left[\frac{2R}{c} - \frac{2r}{c} \cos (\omega t - \theta) \right] \qquad (7.25)$$

Doppler frequency shift produced by the scatterer is

$$f_D(t) = \frac{1}{2\pi} \frac{d\psi(t)}{dt}$$

With $\psi(t)$ from (7.25), we have

$$f_D(t) = -\bar{f}\,\frac{2\omega r}{c}\,\sin\,(\omega t - \theta) \tag{7.26}$$

The idealized analysis at the beginning of this chapter assumed $\theta = \pi/2$ at $t = 0$, small aspect change ωT during image frame time T, and constant aspect rotation rate ω. For these conditions, the Doppler frequency shift produced by a scatterer at cross-range distance r_c reduces to

$$f_D = \frac{2}{c}\,\omega r_c \bar{f}$$

where r_c is the component of the radius r seen in the cross-range dimension normal to both the target axis of rotation and the radar LOS. This is the same as expression (7.1), derived at the beginning of this chapter. Our discussion now turns to distortion, which is produced when the actual Doppler phase slope $d\psi(t)/dt$ begins to deviate from a constant during the image frame time T.

7.9.1 Quadratic Phase Distortion

The effect of nonlinear phase slope on ISAR image quality can be analyzed in terms of quadratic phase distortion and cell migration. First, let us consider phase distortion. Delay to each scatterer *versus* time history observed during a small, but significant, segment of aspect rotation is a small segment of the sinusoidal delay function expressed in (7.24). Small segments of either sinusoidal delay *versus* time history or phase *versus* time history are approximately quadratic. Quadratic phase is evident by expanding (7.25) about the argument $\omega t - \theta$ for $\theta = 0$, where the maximum phase nonlinearity occurs. For small ωt, the phase response of a scatterer at radius r normal to the effective rotation axis becomes

$$\psi(t) \approx -2\pi\bar{f}\left[\frac{2R}{c} - \frac{2r}{c}\left(1 - \frac{(\omega t)^2}{2!}\right)\right]$$

The phase function, expressed in terms of wavelength and the scatterer's velocity, becomes

$$\psi(t) = -\frac{4\pi R}{\lambda} + \frac{4\pi r}{\lambda} - \frac{4\pi}{\lambda}\frac{v^2 t^2}{2r} \tag{7.27}$$

where $v = \omega r$ is the cross-range velocity of the scatterer at $\theta = 0$. The first two terms of (7.27) express the total phase advance to the scatterer at $t = 0$. The third term of (7.27) is the quadratic phase. This quadratic phase term is identical to that for SAR, expressed in (6.5), when the scatterer's cross-range velocity v is substituted for the SAR platform's cross-range velocity v_p and the scatterer's radius r from the center of rotation is substituted for the SAR range R. An effect of uncorrected quadratic phase in ISAR, as in the case of SAR, is to reduce the image cross-range resolution. Removal of the quadratic phase, or correction for it, can be thought of as a *focusing* process, as in the case of SAR.

7.9.2   Cell Migration Produced by Target Rotation

Cell migration occurs with ISAR when the data integration angle ωT is large enough to cause scatterers toward the edge of the target to shift by at least one resolution cell. Cell migration for ISAR will be shown to occur in both the range and Doppler-frequency dimensions.

The slant-range between the radar and the scatterer of Fig. 7.23, after target velocity correction, is $R - r \cos(\omega t - \theta)$. Change in slant-range of the scatterer during target rotation is maximum at the cross-range extremes when $\theta = \pi/2$. The number M' of slant-range resolution cells by which the scatterer at r will migrate during integration time T, when rotation begins at $\theta = \pi/2$, is

$$M' = \mathrm{abs}\; \frac{1}{\Delta r_s} \left\{ [R - r\cos(\omega t - \pi/2)]\Big|_{t=0} - [R - r\cos(\omega t - \pi/2)]\Big|_{t=T} \right\}$$

$$= \mathrm{abs}\; \frac{r \sin \omega T}{\Delta r_s}$$

For small rotation angles, the number of cells is

$$M' \approx \mathrm{abs}\; \frac{r}{\Delta r_s} \left[\omega T - \frac{(\omega T)^3}{3!} + \cdots \right] \tag{7.28}$$

Change in cross-range of the scatterer of Fig. 7.23 during target rotation is maximum at the slant-range extremes when $\theta = 0$. The number $\overline{M}$ of cross-range Doppler resolution cells that the scatterer at r will migrate during integration time T, for rotation angles beginning at $t = 0$, is

$$\overline{M} = \mathrm{abs}\; \frac{1}{\Delta f_D} \left(f_D\Big|_{t=0} - f_D\Big|_{t=T} \right)$$

With Doppler resolution given by $1/T$, we have

$$\overline{M} \approx \text{abs} \left(Tf_D \Big|_{t=0} - Tf_D \Big|_{t=T} \right)$$

With f_D from (7.26), for rotation beginning at $\theta = 0$, we obtain

$$\overline{M} \approx \text{abs} \frac{2\overline{f}r\omega T}{c} \sin \omega T$$

For small rotation angles, the number of cells is

$$\overline{M} \approx \text{abs} \frac{2\overline{f}r\omega T}{c} \left[\omega T - \frac{(\omega T)^3}{3!} + \cdots \right]$$

From the approximate expression (7.3) for cross-range resolution:

$$2\overline{f}\omega T \approx \frac{c}{\Delta r_c}$$

so that

$$\overline{M} \approx \text{abs} \frac{r}{\Delta r_c} \left[\omega T - \frac{(\omega T)^3}{3!} + \cdots \right] \tag{7.29}$$

From (7.28) and (7.29), when $\Delta r_c = \Delta r_s$ (square resolution), we have

$$M' = \overline{M}$$

Therefore, for square resolution, first-order slant-range and cross-range cell migration for either M' or $\overline{M}$ becomes

$$M \approx \frac{r}{\Delta r} \omega T$$

From the first expression of (7.3), we write

$$M = \frac{r}{\Delta r} \frac{c}{2\overline{f}} \frac{1}{\Delta r}$$

Consider a target extending from the target rotation axis to a radius r resolved into $n = N = r/\Delta r$ resolution cells in slant range and cross range. The maximum migration is

$$M = \frac{n}{\Delta r}\frac{c}{2\bar{f}} \tag{7.30}$$

Results obtained by using (7.30) for three radar frequency bands are plotted in Fig. 7.24. The quantity n here refers to the number of cells offset from the target's center of rotation, where $f_D = 0$.

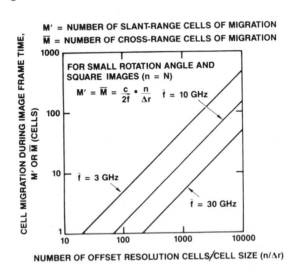

Fig. 7.24 Maximum Slant-Range and Cross-Range Migration Produced by Target Motion

Cross-range cell migration blurs the image in the cross-range dimension at all target slant-range positions, except that position corresponding to zero (corrected) radial velocity. Slant-range cell migration blurs the image in the slant-range dimension at all cross-range positions except at that position corresponding to zero (corrected) Doppler frequency. Only one point is focused in image space. It is at the zero radial-velocity position, which is where Doppler shift is corrected to zero. This position is equivalent to the target center of aspect rotation (centroid). Blur increases with radius as measured from the centroid.

7.9.3 Blur Radius

A practical limit for target size beyond which the unfocused ISAR image becomes blurred at its edges is called the *blur radius*. This is defined as the target radius that results in a maximum of one cell of slant-range and cross-range migration during the required target rotation angle to achieve a given cross-range resolution. In Fig. 7.25, migration approaches one cell when $r\Delta\theta = \Delta r$. To achieve a cross-range resolution of $\Delta r_c = \Delta r$, the required rotation angle from (7.3) is

$$\Delta\theta = \frac{\lambda}{2\Delta r}$$

Target blur radius for one cell of migration is therefore given by

$$r = \frac{2(\Delta r)^2}{\lambda} \tag{7.31}$$

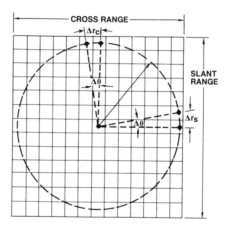

Fig. 7.25 Blur Radius

7.10 POLAR REFORMATTING

Data samples of a target's reflectivity *versus* frequency that are taken as the target rotates is said to be collected in *polar format.* Although such data may be collected at uniformly spaced frequency steps and rotation-angle positions, the samples are nonuniformly spaced in a rectangular format called *frequency space*. The result is that the two-dimensional Fourier transform to target-space reflectivity results in unfocused images for the larger rotation angles needed for high resolution. The notion of a blur radius as discussed above is another perspective on the same effect. The process of resampling from polar to rectangular format produces uniformly spaced data in two-dimensional frequency space. Two-dimensional Fourier-transform processing then produces focused images. Details follow.

7.10.1 Frequency-Space Aperture

Radar target imagery can be explained in terms of Fourier transforms of frequency-space reflectivity data into target-space reflectivity estimates. The term *frequency-space aperture* is sometimes used to refer to the extent of the two-dimensional frequency space over which data are collected. The transformation from frequency space to target space may not be readily apparent from the range-Doppler viewpoint of ISAR imagery discussed up to this point. First, consider data collected by using a pulse-compression radar. Target reflectivity data obtained from a time history of complex range profiles were thought of as range-Doppler data. Range-profile data are in target space. Data collected in each range cell over a limited range of polar viewing angles can be thought of as one dimension of *frequency-space data* to be defined below. Target-space reflectivity estimates in the cross-range dimension in each range cell, as discussed up until now, was obtained from such data by performing a Fourier transform. Data that was used to generate the ISAR image, therefore, existed in both target space and frequency space. The notion of transforming from frequency space to target space becomes more clear in the synthetic ISAR process, whereby the input data can be shown to exist entirely in frequency and viewing-angle coordinates, which for small viewing angles approximate a rectangular frequency-space format.

We will now formalize the concept of frequency space by defining the quantities:

$$f_x = \frac{2f}{c} \cos \theta$$

and

$$f_y = \frac{2f}{c} \sin \theta$$

for polar angle θ, where f_x and f_y are the spatial frequency components (m^{-1}) associated with an RF signal at frequency f as measured at polar angle θ and projected along the horizontal and vertical axes, respectively, of a rectangular frequency-space coordinate system, such as shown in Fig. 7.26.

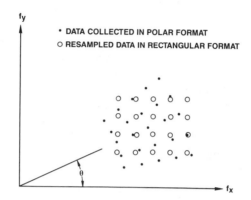

Fig. 7.26 Coordinate System for Frequency-Space Data Collection

Consider a target rotating about a z-axis normal to the paper. Data samples are collected at some signal frequency f at uniformly spaced polar-angle positions. Positions of the data samples, in frequency, appear in Fig. 7.26 as dots along a constant radius. When the radar is shifted to a new frequency, another series of samples is generated at a new radius. Data represented by the dots collected at uniformly spaced polar angles and frequencies are *polar-formatted data*. Stepped-frequency data can be interpreted from Fig. 7.26 as data collected along radial lines that are uniformly spaced at discrete polar-angle positions. This assumes that reflectivity data is collected over the radar's stepped-frequency bandwidth at each polar-angle position. The effect of constant target rotation rate will be discussed later.

To understand the problem associated with polar-formatted data, we should review the nature of the discrete Fourier transform. Any set of complex quantities can be converted by Fourier transform into a second set of complex quantities. However, the discrete Fourier transform, when applied to actual systems, assumes that samples are collected at uniformly spaced intervals in space, time, or frequency. For example, the frequency spectrum of a waveform can be accurately represented by the discrete Fourier transform of a set of samples of the waveform uniformly spaced in time. Conversely, a waveform can be accurately represented by the inverse discrete Fourier transform of a set samples of the waveform's spectrum uniformly spaced in frequency.

The problem posed by polar-formatted data, represented by the dots in Fig. 7.26, is that these data samples are not uniformly spaced in spatial frequency. If, somehow, the frequency-space data could be collected in the rectangular format illustrated by the matrix of small circles, then the requirements for uniformly spaced data sampling would be met in both dimensions of data collection space, and the transformed data would thus produce a focused image. This, however, would require nonuniformly spaced frequency samples at nonuniformly spaced polar angles, where the nonuniformities in both dimensions have been carefully controlled to produce the rectangular spatial-frequency format.

A more convenient process is to reformat data collected at uniform frequency and polar-angle spacings into a rectangular format. The circles in Fig. 7.26 would then represent reformatted samples of the target's reflectivity in two dimensions of spatial frequency: reflectivity *versus* cycles per meter along f_x and f_y. Data samples of this reformatted data set can be transformed into focused target-space imagery in terms of reflectivity estimates *versus* x and y in meters. Discrete values of the complex reflectivity estimates in x and y would be detected to form image pixels.

The need to reformat data increases for a given desired resolution as radar frequency decreases. In Fig. 7.27, a target's sampled reflectivity data appear along discrete polar-angle positions in a single rotation plane. The radar lies in the plane of rotation and along the f_x spatial-frequency axis. The resulting data format is illustrated for two radar bands.

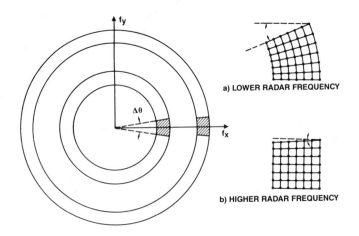

Fig. 7.27 Discrete Frequency Data at Two Radar Bands that Produce the Same Image Resolution

Figure 7.27 (a, b) illustrates how the set of sampled data points deviate from a rectangular format. At the high band, a relatively small angle of rotation may be adequate to produce the needed cross-range resolution. Differences between the polar and rectangular formats are then small. To produce the same resolution at the lower radar band requires that data be collected over a greater angle of target rotation. Data points acquired in polar format over the larger rotation angle can be seen to deviate significantly from uniform spacing in spatial frequency. The blur radius, discussed above, has been exceeded when deviation across the data-collection space exceeds the sampling interval corresponding to one resolution cell in image space. Fourier transforms of the polar-formatted data to produce an image would then result in blur at the edges of the image.

Polar reformatting is a process that can be carried out on SAR or ISAR data collected by using frequency-sampled waveforms such as the stretch waveform or stepped-frequency waveform. Here, reformatting of stepped-frequency ISAR data will be discussed to illustrate the process. The stepped-frequency waveform, because it has been used to provide extremely high resolution, often results in significant scatterer migration through ISAR resolution cells. The dots in Fig. 7.28 illustrate input data samples collected burst by burst, while the target rotated through a range of viewing angles at a constant rotation rate. (We assume that data at this point has been corrected for radial velocity.) The first step is to resample the curved data from each frequency burst into discrete, uniformly spaced polar angles. The resampled data are indicated by the small circles.

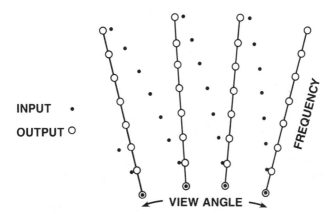

INPUT •

OUTPUT ○

FREQUENCY

← VIEW ANGLE →

Fig. 7.28 Frequency-Stepped Input Data and Resampled Output Data (First Step)

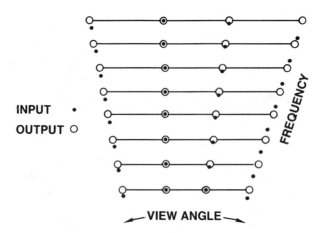

Fig. 7.29 Uniformly Spaced Data along Discrete Polar Angles and Resampled Data along the Central View Angle (Second Step)

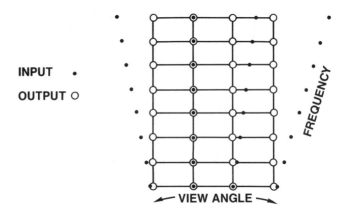

Fig. 7.30 Uniformly Spaced Data along the Central View Angle and Resampled Data in the Direction Normal to the Central Angle (Final Reformatting Step)

The next step, shown in Fig. 7.29, is to resample for uniform spacing in the frequency-space dimension along the central viewing angle. Finally, the data along the discrete polar angles are resampled in the direction normal to the central viewing angle, as shown in Fig. 7.30. At this point, the data can be converted by Fourier transform independently in both dimensions, then detected to form a focused ISAR image.

When ISAR images of targets are to be generated, such as some space objects and turntable models with known motion, the angular rate is known and often it is quite uniform. By contrast, when images of ship or air targets are to be generated, the motion is generally not known, nor is it perfectly uniform. The reformatting process then should be carried out iteratively to produce the best focus. Nearly uniform rotational motion can be assumed for limited rotation angles (e.g., up to 5°) without serious image degradation in many situations. An example of a stepped-frequency image before and after polar reformatting is shown in Fig. 7.31.

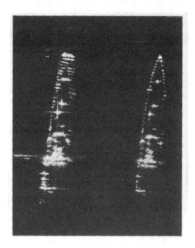

Fig. 7.31 Focused and Unfocused Stepped-Frequency ISAR Image

7.11 PREDICTED CROSS-RANGE RESOLUTION OF SHIP TARGETS

It is possible to estimate image quality based on ship class and sea state when the cross-range Doppler gradient is generated from small segments of a ship's pitch, roll, and yaw angular motion. Pitch, roll, and yaw periods for oceangoing ships are on the order of 5–30 s. Blurring of the target image occurs with ISAR processing methods, described above, when integration time T becomes a significant fraction of the ship's motion period. Blur results from significant change in rotation rate and direction that occurs within the integration angle. Experiments have shown that optimum integration time for ship targets is about 2–3 s at S band

(2.30–2.50 GHz and 2.70–3.70 GHz) and 0.25–0.5 s at X band (8.50–10.68 GHz). Tangential motion of the radar relative to the target is an insignificant source of cross-range Doppler for ship imaging, except for cases of calm seas and short ranges.

Table 7.2 lists computed values of pitch, yaw, and roll amplitudes and periods for two types of ships. Worst-case heading and speed for sea-state-5 wave modeling was used, worst-case heading and speed being those producing the largest ship motion. It is estimated that typical or average heading and speed would reduce rotation-amplitude values by about one-half. The periods would remain relatively constant. Ship rotational motion can be approximated by a sinusoidal function, as shown in Fig. 7.32. Here, the instantaneous angular position of the ship in degrees from vertical is

$$Y = \frac{1}{2} q \sin \left(2\pi \frac{t}{\Omega} \right)$$

where q is the double-amplitude excursion in degrees and Ω is the period of motion in seconds. For this sinusoidal representation, the angular velocity of ship motion in degrees per second is

$$\dot{Y} = \frac{d}{dt} \left[\frac{1}{2} q \sin \left(2\pi \frac{t}{\Omega} \right) \right]$$

$$= \frac{2\pi}{\Omega} \frac{q}{2} \cos \left(2\pi \frac{t}{\Omega} \right)$$

Table 7.2   Computed Worst-Case Ship Motion for Two Ship Types*
(in Sea-State 5)

Ship Type	Double Amplitude q (degrees)		Average Period Ω (seconds)
Destroyer	3.4	pitch	6.7
	3.8	yaw	14.2
	38.4	roll	12.2
Carrier	0.9	pitch	11.2
	1.33	yaw	33.0
	5.0	roll	26.4

*Unpublished Navy hull design data.

The average magnitude of angular velocity is

$$|\dot{Y}|_{ave} = \frac{2}{\Omega} \int_{-\Omega/4}^{+\Omega/4} \dot{Y}\, dt$$

$$= \frac{2q}{\Omega}$$

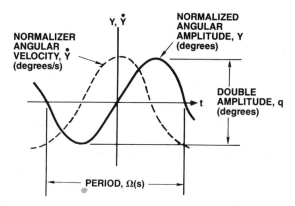

Fig. 7.32 Sinusoidal Representation of Ship Pitch, Roll, or Yaw Motion

Table 7.3 Predicted Cross-Range Resolution Produced by 1.0 s
Integration for Two Ship Types in Sea-State 5 Using an S-Band Radar
($\bar{f} = 3 \times 10^9$ Hz)

Ship Type	Average Angular Velocity $\|\dot{Y}\|_{ave}$ (degrees/second)	Average Angular Excursion in 1.0 s Frame Time $\overline{\Delta\theta}$ (radians)	Average Cross-Range Resolution $\overline{\Delta r_c}$ (meters)
Destroyer	1.01 pitch	.0177	2.82
	0.54 yaw	.0093	5.35
	6.30 roll	.1100	0.46
Carrier	0.16 pitch	.0028	17.83
	0.08 yaw	.0014	35.54
	0.38 roll	.0066	7.56

Table 7.3 lists predicted values of cross-range resolution at a center frequency of 3×10^9 Hz, based on computed ship motions in Table 7.2. Equations used to obtain the results in Table 7.3 are as follows:

(1) $|\dot{Y}|_{ave} = \dfrac{2q}{\Omega}$ °/s, q and Ω from Table 7.2;

(2) $\overline{\Delta\theta} = \dfrac{2\pi T}{360} |\dot{Y}|_{ave}$ rad, where $T = 1.0$ s;

(3) $\overline{\Delta r_c} = \dfrac{\lambda}{2} \dfrac{1}{\overline{\Delta\theta}} = \dfrac{.05}{\overline{\Delta\theta}}$ m, for $\bar{f} = 3 \times 10^9$ Hz.

Results in Table 7.3 must be considered optimistic from an imaging standpoint. For sea-state 3, with wave heights about half those of sea-state 5; for typical rather than worst-case speed and headings, the above resolution values would degrade by about a factor of four. Actual motion during target observation would be the vector sum of the target aspect rotation produced by pitch, yaw, and roll and relative radar-to-target tangential velocity.

7.12 SAMPLE DESIGN CALCULATIONS FOR ISAR

7.12.1 Air Targets

Table 7.4 defines a set of stepped-frequency ISAR parameters that are roughly consistent with use against air targets. Table 7.5 lists calculated values of interest that result when the radar of Table 7.4 is used against aircraft having no significant pitch, roll, yaw, or turning motion. It is assumed that the principal source of target aspect rotation is that produced by the target's 400 kt tangential velocity component relative to the radar. Equations used to generate Table 7.5, including conversion of kts to m/s and nmi to m, are

(1) $\omega = \dfrac{v_T}{R} \cdot \dfrac{1}{3600}$ (rad/s) (Eq. (7.7))

(2) $T = \dfrac{cR}{2v_T \bar{f} \Delta r_c} \cdot 3600$ (s) (from Eqs. (7.3) and (7.7))

(3) $\Delta\theta = \omega T = \dfrac{v_T T}{R} \cdot \dfrac{360}{2\pi} \cdot \dfrac{1}{3600}$ (degrees)

Table 7.4 Hypothetical Radar Design for the Imaging of Air Targets

Parameter	Symbol	Specified	Equation	Value
Slant-Range and Cross-Range Window	w_s, w_c	60 m		
Slant-Range and Cross-Range Resolution	Δr_s, Δr_c	1 m		
Center Frequency	$\bar{f}$	3 GHz		
Bandwidth	$f_{n-1} - f_0$		$\dfrac{c}{2\Delta r_s}$	150 MHz
Pulses per Burst	n		$\dfrac{w_s}{\Delta r_s}$	60
Bursts per Integration Time	N		$\dfrac{w_c}{\Delta r_c}$	60
Frequency Step Size	Δf		$\dfrac{f_{n-1} - f_0}{n - 1}$	2.5 MHz

(4) $\beta_D = \dfrac{2\bar{f} v_T w_c}{cR} \cdot \dfrac{1}{3600} = \dfrac{1}{T}$ (Hz) (from $\beta_D = 2\omega w_c \bar{f}/c$ with Eq. (7.7))

(5) $\dfrac{1}{T_2}\Big|_{\min} = \dfrac{nN}{T}$ (pps)

Actual flight paths of air targets may deviate sufficiently from straight-line motion to permit imaging with less dwell time than indicated in Table 7.5. In general, however, at frequencies below X band (8.50–10.68 GHz), several seconds of dwell time seem to be needed to achieve useful resolution of air targets. Pitch, roll, and yaw motions above X band may be able to generate Doppler gradients that are adequate for useful imaging in a fraction of a second. For example, at Ka band (33.4–36.0 GHz), the target aspect change required to produce the same cross-range resolution (1.0 m) is only about 0.3° as compared with nearly 3° at 3.0 GHz. Above Ka band, a small fraction of a degree of aircraft pitch, roll, and yaw could then produce one meter resolution.

Table 7.5 Sample Calculations for the Radar of Table 7.4
(for an Air Target with Translation Motion Only)

Relative Tangential Velocity v_T (knots)	Radar Range R(nmi)	Effective Angular Rotation Rate $\omega(\text{s}^{-1})$	Required Dwell Time for $\Delta r_c = 1.0$ m T(s)	Target Rotation Angle $\Delta\theta$(degrees)	Doppler Bandwidth β_D (Hz)	Min PRF $\frac{1}{T_2}$ (pps)
400	100.0	1.11×10^{-3}	45.0	2.86	1.33	80
400	50.0	2.22×10^{-3}	22.5	2.86	2.66	160
400	25.0	4.44×10^{-3}	11.3	2.86	5.32	320
400	12.5	8.88×10^{-3}	5.7	2.86	10.64	640

7.12.2 Ship Targets

The situation changes for imaging of ship targets. A ship's tangential motion relative to the radar is small, unless the radar is airborne at close range. Also, pitch, roll, and yaw angular motion of ships during straight-line travel is larger than that for aircraft targets. Thus, the major source of Doppler gradient for ISAR ship imaging is target pitch, roll, and yaw motion. When tangential motion of the radar platform generates a significant part of the total viewing-angle change, the image can be thought of as being generated by both ISAR and SAR processes.

Table 7.6 defines a set of synthetic ISAR parameters that are roughly consistent with use against ship targets. It is assumed that the ship's pitch, roll, and yaw motion is adequate to generate cross-range resolution as fine as two meters.

Table 7.6 Hypothetical Imaging Radar Design for the Imaging of Ship Targets

Parameter	Symbol	Specified	Equation	Value
Slant-Range and Cross-Range Window	w_s, w_c	400 m		
Slant-Range and Cross-Range Resolution	$\Delta r_s, \Delta r_c$	2 m		
Center Frequency	$\bar{f}$	3 GHz		
Bandwidth	$f_{n-1} - f_0$		$\dfrac{c}{2\Delta r_s}$	75 MHz
Pulses per Burst	n		$\dfrac{w_s}{\Delta r_s}$	200
Bursts per Integration Time	N		$\dfrac{w_c}{\Delta r_c}$	200
Frequency Step Size	Δf		$\dfrac{f_{n-1} - f_0}{n-1}$	0.38 MHz
Minimum PRF (for $T < 3.0$ s)	$1/T_2$		$\dfrac{nN}{T}$	13.3 kHz

Recall that a synthetically generated ISAR image is made up of Nn pixels, one pixel on the average for each transmitted pulse. The number of pulses n per burst and number of bursts N per image frame for unambiguous sampling must equal or exceed the number of image resolution cells in slant range and cross range, respectively. The minimum pulse repetition frequency $(1/T_2)_{min}$ is determined by the requirement that N frequency bursts, each of n pulses, must be transmitted and received during the integration time T. For ship targets, integration time will be assumed to be less than about three seconds in order to stay well within the pitch, roll, or yaw periods.

The PRF listed in Table 7.6 could be inconveniently high from a radar design standpoint. The PRF could be reduced without reducing resolution by sizing the window for a better fit to the target shape. For example, if the largest expected ship size were 400 m by 80 m, the PRF for bow, stern, port, or starboard aspects could be reduced to

$$\frac{1}{T_2} = \frac{nN}{T} = \frac{200 \times 40}{3} = 2.7 \text{ kHz}$$

7.13 PULSE-COMPRESSION *versus* STEPPED-FREQUENCY ISAR

Inverse synthetic aperture radar imaging of target models, aircraft, ships, and space objects has been achieved to date mostly by using three basic waveforms:

1. chirp (pulse compression);
2. stretch;
3. pulse-to-pulse stepped frequency.

Pulse-compression and stepped-frequency waveforms, although related, provide the most contrasting performance.

7.13.1 Pulse-Compression ISAR

Pulse compression produces a target range-profile signature for each pulse. This profile must be sampled in real range delay before ISAR processing can proceed. To avoid ambiguity, samples should be spaced in time by no more than the range-delay resolution associated with the chirp bandwidth. Resolution, therefore, can be limited by A/D conversion-rate performance. On the other hand, because an entire target range profile is obtained from each pulse, Doppler sampling for each range cell occurs at the radar's PRF. Even large targets, such as ships at maximum pitch, roll, and yaw rates, are not likely to produce Doppler shift that cannot be sampled adequately.

For example, consider a 10 GHz chirp radar with a PRF of 1000 pps that samples each pulse at 10^8 complex samples per second, which will be assumed to be the maximum sampling rate of the A/D converter. Doppler shift as high as 1000 pps is then unambiguously sampled by I and Q samples in each range cell. In the worst-case under sea-state-5 conditions, the predicted roll rate for the destroyer of Table 7.3 is 6.3°/s. If its exposed height h above the surface is 30 m, the maximum Doppler bandwidth to be sampled following velocity correction to zero at the center of rotation is

$$\beta_D = \frac{2}{c}\, \omega h \bar{f}$$

$$= \frac{2}{3 \times 10^8}\, 6.3 \cdot \frac{2\pi}{360} \cdot 30 \cdot 10 \times 10^9$$

$$= 220 \text{ Hz}$$

This is well below the Doppler sampling rate of 1000 samples per second. The same radar, however, must limit chirp bandwidth to less than 100 MHz to avoid undersampling in range delay. The slant-range resolution is therefore limited to $c/2\beta = 1.5$ m.

7.13.2 Stepped-Frequency ISAR

By contrast, consider a stepped-frequency ISAR, which produces a range-profile signature from each burst of n pulses. Samples can be thought of as being collected in the frequency domain at a spacing equal to the frequency step size. The spacing of the samples in time is at the radar PRF, which does not present an A/D conversion problem, even at extremely high radar PRFs. Range resolution, therefore, is limited only by the radar stepped-frequency bandwidth. On the other hand, because sampling in the Doppler domain effectively occurs at the burst rate, the required PRF is n times as high as an equivalent chirp radar operating against the same target, where n is the number of pulses per burst.

For the example of the destroyer given above, the required PRF in a stepped-frequency mode of 110 steps would be 110×220 Hz $\approx$ 24 k pps. Operation at this PRF at useful ranges means that the echo pulse at each frequency step arrives multiple pulse repetition intervals following the transmitted pulse at that frequency. The frequency synthesizer should then be programmed to set up transmission and local oscillator references that allow measurement of echo signal phase relative to the phase of the corresponding transmission signal at each frequency step. In other words, a transmission phase reference must be recalled at each frequency step after several other pulses were transmitted.

Generally, PRF requirements for synthetic processing can be determined by requiring that the cross-range window w_c equal the number of bursts N multiplied by the cross-range resolution Δr_c provided by target rotation through ωT radians of viewing angle. This requirement, from (7.6), is met for

$$w_c = N \frac{\lambda}{2\omega T}$$

By recalling that $T = NnT_2$, we can write

$$w_c = \frac{\lambda}{2\omega n T_2}$$

When $N = n$, the above expression can be written independently of N and n as

$$w_c = \frac{\lambda}{2\omega} \left(\frac{T_2}{T}\right)^{1/2} \frac{1}{T_2}$$

$$= \frac{\lambda}{2\omega} T^{-1/2} \left(\frac{1}{T_2}\right)^{1/2}$$

The minimum PRF corresponding to this window is

$$\frac{1}{T_2} = T \left(\frac{2\omega w_c}{\lambda}\right)^2$$

For example, to sample a cross-range window w_c equal to the 30 m height of the destroyer during the 6.3°/s roll rate listed for sea-state 5 requires that the PRF of the above 10 GHz radar for $N = n$ and 0.5 s integration time should exceed the value:

$$\frac{1}{T_2} = 0.5 \left(\frac{2 \cdot 6.3 \cdot \dfrac{2\pi}{360} \cdot 30}{.03}\right)^2$$

$$= 24{,}181 \text{ pps}$$

The number of pulses n per burst and number of bursts N per integration time becomes

$$n = N = \sqrt{\frac{T}{T_2}}$$

$$= 110$$

For $T = 0.5$, the burst rate becomes 220 bursts per second, which was shown above to be just adequate to sample the 220 Hz Doppler bandwidth produced by the rolling destroyer. We can see that if cross-range resolution Δr_c produced by target motion is matched by slant-range resolution Δr_s, then (7.6), for $n = N$ and $\lambda/2\Delta\theta = \Delta r$, can be expressed as

$$w_c = \Delta r \sqrt{\frac{T}{T_2}}$$

7.13.3 Summary

Chirp and stepped-frequency waveforms contrast in their technical requirements. Chirp radar design for high resolution requires samples closely spaced in range delay, which translates to a requirement for high-speed and wide dynamic range A/D converters. Stepped-frequency radar design for high resolution requires samples closely spaced in frequency, which translates to a requirement for a frequency synthesizer capable of being programmed to switch rapidly from frequency to frequency while maintaining phase coherence. Figure 7.33 illustrates the general range of operation for the two types of waveforms.

7.14 RADAR RANGE FOR RADAR-IMAGED TARGETS

In this book, we have described wideband radar waveforms and systems that are capable of resolving individual targets into one dimension of slant range (HRR) and the two orthogonal dimensions of slant range and cross range (ISAR). One-dimensional and two-dimensional resolution is illustrated in Fig. 7.34. Ideally, resolution performance of HRR and ISAR is independent of signal-to-noise ratio. Image quality *versus* range is therefore fundamentally determined by the signal-to-noise ratio of re-solved image picture elements (pixels), rather than by resolution *versus* signal-to-noise ratio.

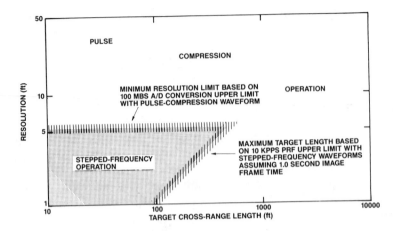

Fig. 7.33 Approximate Target Length-Resolution Limits for Pulse-Compression *versus* Stepped-Frequency Imaging

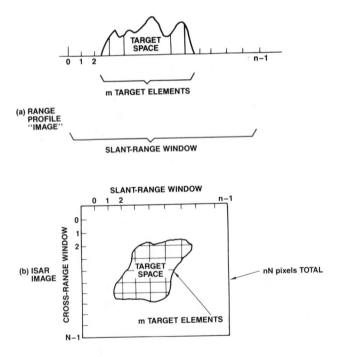

Fig. 7.34 Occupation of Image Space by the Target

The radar range at which targets can be imaged, therefore, may be defined in terms of the signal-to-noise ratio of image pixels following image processing. The term *imaging* as used here will refer to both one-dimensional and two-dimensional target resolution. Because the image process resolves the target into target-space resolution elements, the radar cross section to be considered in the range equation is that of individually resolved target-space elements. This is in contrast to the situation for target detection. Signal bandwidth for target detection is normally narrow so that the echo results from the radar cross section presented by the entire unresolved target. The radar cross section σ_e of resolved target elements will generally be less than the average radar cross section $\bar{\sigma}$ of the unresolved target. The effect is to reduce the signal-to-noise ratio of the target image pixels relative to that for narrowband signal-to-noise ratio. This effect tends to be offset by the image processing gain G_p produced by pulse-to-pulse coherent integration inherent in the imaging process.

7.14.1 Average Signal-to-Noise Ratio

The average output signal-to-noise ratio produced by echo signals from single pulses of a matched-filter radar operating in a narrowband detection mode, from (2.14) of Chapter 2, is

$$\left(\frac{S}{N}\right)_d = \frac{P_t G^2 \lambda^2 L T_1}{(4\pi)^3 R^4 k T_s} \bar{\sigma} \tag{7.32}$$

where T_1 is the transmitted pulse duration.

Now consider a radar operating in a wideband imaging mode. The cross section of resolved target elements, from (2.5) of Chapter 2, is approximated by

$$\sigma_e \approx \frac{\bar{\sigma}}{m}$$

where $\bar{\sigma}$ is the average narrowband cross section of targets resolved into m resolution elements. Average output signal-to-noise ratio of image pixels can be written

$$\left(\frac{S}{N}\right)_{\text{pixel}} = \frac{P_t G^2 \lambda^2 L T_1}{(4\pi)^3 R^4 k T_s} \frac{\bar{\sigma}}{m} G_p \tag{7.33}$$

where G_p is the image processing gain produced by the coherent pulse-to-pulse integration used to produce the target image.

Equations (7.32) and (7.33) apply to either chirp or stepped-frequency waveforms. Chirp radar receivers are said to provide processing gain because the signal-to-noise ratio at the input is increased at the output by pulse compression. For the purpose of this discussion, however, we wish to focus on the processing gain provided by the pulse-to-pulse coherent integration inherent in image processing. By taking T_1 from (7.32) to be the chirp-pulse duration and P_t to be transmitted chirp-pulse power, correct results for output signal-to-noise ratio will be obtained for matched-filter pulse compression of each pulse. Then, processing gain greater than 1.0 for both chirp-pulse and stepped-frequency waveforms can be attributed to the pulse-to-pulse integration provided by image processing.

The minimum image processing gain $(G_p)_{\min}$ occurs when the number of echo pulses integrated is just adequate for unambiguously sampling the slant-range or cross-range windows of the image. As examples, we have $(G_p)_{\min} = nN$ for an nN-pulse synthetic ISAR image frame of nN pixels, $(G_p)_{\min} = N$ for an N-pulse pulse-compression ISAR image frame of nN pixels, $(G_p)_{\min} = n$ for an n-pulse synthetic range profile, and $(G_p)_{\min} = 1$ for a single-pulse pulse-compression range profile. Actual image processing gain G_p will exceed the minimum gain $(G_p)_{\min}$ when the number of radar pulses that have been coherently integrated to generate the image exceeds the minimum required for unambiguous imaging or, in other words, when the target image space is oversampled. For example, if a single range profile is generated by coherently adding the responses from 10 compressed chirp pulses, the summed range profile is then oversampled by a factor of 10 and thus $G_p = 10$.

7.15 FRACTION OF VISIBLE TARGET ELEMENTS

So far, we have discussed only average signal-to-noise ratios. The actual situation is complicated by variations in reflectivity of different scatterers of the target. Real targets consist of individual scatterers of varying reflectivity. The image of a target viewed at high signal level, let us say at close range, will contain visible pixel responses produced by scatterers of both high and low reflectivity. As range increases, the responses of small scatterers will become invisible, but responses from larger scatterers will remain above some *visibility* threshold. The term visibility as used here need not be restricted to the sensory capability of human observation. Automatic radar image *recognizers*, when developed, will also use some visibility threshold criterion to recognize those pixels containing responses produced by scatterers.

The fraction of visible target resolution elements will be defined as the measure of radar target image quality in noise. This fraction can be related to the output signal-to-noise ratio available from the target's ensemble of scatterers as seen in a narrowband mode. Because the target to be imaged and recognized must first be detected, it is convenient to express the fraction of visible target resolution elements in terms of the signal-to-noise ratio required for narrowband detection. This will be done by defining image quality in terms of single-pulse signal-to-noise ratio of the radar in a detection mode. The derivation follows.

The target's average cross section $\bar{\sigma}$, which produces a signal-to-noise ratio $(S/N)_d$ at range R with one narrowband transmitted pulse of length T_1, from (7.32), is

$$\bar{\sigma} = \frac{(4\pi)^3 R^4 k T_s}{P_t G^2 \lambda^2 L T_1} \left(\frac{S}{N}\right)_d \tag{7.34}$$

The quantity $(S/N)_d$ may be considered to be the single-pulse signal-to-noise ratio available for detection of a target of total cross section $\bar{\sigma}$.

Now, consider the same radar in an imaging mode. All radar parameters will be assumed to remain the same except for the substitution of pixel signal-to-noise ratio for $(S/N)_d$. A chirp-pulse radar mode obtains one range profile from each pulse. A stepped-frequency mode obtains one range profile from n pulses. Pulsewidth is T_1 in each case. The visibility threshold cross section γ of a resolved target element, above which the corresponding image pixel will be visible, is

$$\gamma = \frac{(4\pi)^3 R^4 k T_s}{P_t G^2 \lambda^2 L T_1} \frac{1}{G_p} \left(\frac{S}{N}\right)_v \tag{7.35}$$

where $(S/N)_v$ is the pixel signal-to-noise ratio that by some criterion is determined to be required for pixel visibility. The threshold cross section γ can be evaluated from (7.34) and (7.35) by assuming that imaging is carried out at the range where target detection occurs. Target signal-to-noise ratio is $(S/N)_d$, and T_s, G, L, P_t, λ, and T_1 are assumed to remain unchanged from detection to imaging modes. From the ratio of (7.35) and (7.34), we have

$$\gamma = \frac{\bar{\sigma}}{G_p} \frac{(S/N)_v}{(S/N)_d} \tag{7.36}$$

Target elements with cross section above γ will be considered visible. Image quality can be defined in terms of the fraction of visible target elements by using (7.36) together with knowledge of the distribution of radar cross section of resolved scatterers. Little data exist at present concerning the distribution of scatterer reflectivity for ship and air targets. Image quality will therefore be estimated by assuming that target element cross-section is distributed according to the power form of the Rayleigh distribution. The probability density for element cross section σ_e based on this distribution is given by

$$P(\sigma_e) = \frac{1}{\overline{\sigma}_e} \exp\left(-\sigma_e/\overline{\sigma}_e\right) = \frac{m}{\overline{\sigma}} \exp\left[(-m/\overline{\sigma})\sigma_e)\right] \tag{7.37}$$

where $\overline{\sigma}_e = \overline{\sigma}/m$ is the average element cross section.

The probability that σ_e of (7.37) will equal or exceed some threshold value γ is

$$P_e = P[\sigma_e \geq \gamma]$$

$$= \int_{\gamma}^{\infty} \frac{m}{\overline{\sigma}} \exp\left[(-m\sigma_e/\overline{\sigma})\right]d\sigma_e$$

$$= \exp\left[-(m/\overline{\sigma})\gamma\right] \tag{7.38}$$

The fraction of resolved target image elements that are visible can be expressed by substituting γ from (7.36) into (7.38). The result is

$$P_e = \exp\left[-\frac{m}{G_p}\frac{(S/N)_v}{(S/N)_d}\right] \tag{7.39}$$

Equation (7.39) provides a way of roughly evaluating target image quality in terms of single-pulse signal-to-noise ratio produced by the imaging radar operating in a narrowband detection mode at the same range as used for imaging. To make use of this expression, we must assign values of signal-to-noise ratio required for pixel visibility and detection. Figure 7.35 shows (7.39) plotted for three values of m/G_p.

7.15.1   Examples

For illustrative purposes, consider a slowly fluctuating target to be imaged by using a stepped-frequency waveform. From Fig. 2.8(a) of Chapter 2, the required signal-to-noise ratio in the detection mode for a Swerling case 1 target with a single pulse is about +18 dB. Assume that image pixels for the radar image become visible when the pixel signal-to-noise ratio is 6 dB below that for single-pulse detection. Then, $(S/N)_v = 12$ dB versus $(S/N)_d = 18$ dB. For these assumptions, $(S/N)_v/(S/N)_d = 0.25$. The ratio m/G_p is the number of image pixels occupied by the target divided by the number of pulses integrated to generate the image. Assume synthetic ISAR processing with n pulses per burst and N bursts used to create one $n \times N$ element image. Then,

$$G_p = (G_p)_{min} = nN$$

Next, assume that the target occupies one-half of the $n \times N$ element image space. For these assumptions,

$$\frac{m}{G_p} = \frac{0.5\,nN}{nN} = 0.5$$

From Fig. 7.35 or (7.39), the fraction of target pixels containing visible responses is 0.88. In this example, if a 2000-pixel image were generated ($nN = 2000$), the target would be resolved into 1000 resolution elements, of which 880 would be visible at the radar's single-pulse detection range.

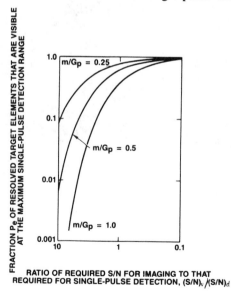

Fig. 7.35 Image Visibility (Fraction of Visible Pixels)

Under the same assumptions, if a second target to be imaged occupies only one-quarter of the image space, $m/G_p = 0.25$. From (7.39), a fraction of about 0.94 of the imaged target pixels would then contain visible responses. The second target would occupy 500 of the 2000 image pixels, of which 470 would be visible at the radar's single-pulse detection range.

SAR maps of the earth's surface often appear to be of photographic quality. By contrast, ISAR images of individual targets, although obtained at much higher resolution, appear to be of much lower quality. The difference is due to the extended surface areas being mapped by SAR as compared with individual targets imaged by ISAR that contain comparatively fewer scatterers. SAR images of nonmoving ships and aircraft are roughly similar to ISAR images of the same targets in motion obtained at the same resolution. Considerable room for improvement in ISAR imagery remains, but photographic-quality imagery does not appear to be likely. Stepped-frequency ISAR images of two commercial aircraft are shown in Fig. 7.36.

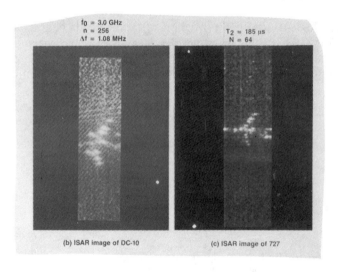

$f_0 = 3.0$ GHz
$n = 256$
$\Delta f = 1.08$ MHz

$T_2 = 185$ μs
$N = 64$

(b) ISAR image of DC-10

(c) ISAR image of 727

Fig. 7.36 ISAR Images of Two Commercial Aircraft

PROBLEMS

7.1 A 300 m ship target in a smooth sea is making a 1.0°/s turn. (a) What is the Doppler bandwidth of the echo signal seen with a 35 GHz shipboard radar viewing the target from broadside at long range assuming no other motion? (b) What cross-range resolution in meters is possible for a target dwell time of 0.1 s?

7.2 The ship target in Prob. 7.1 is viewed from broadside with the same radar during 0.2° of roll in a rough sea. What is the best possible cross-range resolution in meters?

7.3 An aircraft is flying straight with a tangential component of velocity of 200 kts (103 m/s) at a range of 50 nmi (92.6 km) relative to a ground-based radar operating at a wavelength of 0.03 m. What is the best possible cross-range resolution in meters for a five-second target dwell time?

7.4 A chirp radar transmits 0.5 μs RF pulses with dispersion $D = 180$ at a center wavelength of 0.03 m. What is the best possible slant-range and cross-range resolution in meters against a ship target viewed bow on during 0.5° of pitch motion?

7.5 What is the best possible slant-range and cross-range resolution in meters if the radar of Prob. 7.4 transmitted monotone pulses stepped in frequency pulse-to-pulse in repeating bursts of 180 pulses per burst spaced by 2.0 MHz?

7.6 Two-dimensional ISAR images of aircraft are to be produced by a chirp radar operating at 0.03 m wavelength. Resolution capability is to be as fine as 0.5 m in both dimensions and target sizes of up to 75 m in each dimension will be viewed. (a) What is the minimum pulse repetition frequency (PRF) required to image unambiguously targets that have up to 2.0°/s aspect rotation rate? (b) What is the minimum required analog-to-digital (A/D) converter speed in terms of complex sample pairs per second?

7.7 The radar of Prob. 7.6 is to be operated in a stepped-frequency mode. Compute the new requirements for (a) PRF and (b) sampling rate.

7.8 A short-pulse radar is to be used to generate ISAR images containing 128 × 128 pixels (picture elements). (a) What is the minimum number of transmitted pulses required to form a single image? (b) How many complex samples per pulse are required?

7.9 What are the answers to (a) and (b) of Prob. 7.8 if stepped-frequency waveforms are to be employed instead of short pulses?

7.10   Two-dimensional ISAR images are to be obtained of a ship target viewed with a shipboard radar. The ship target has the following dimensions: 200 m long, 20 m wide, and 30 m high out of the water. Assume that by some method the image was calibrated in true slant range and cross range. What would be the image dimensions in meters for the following conditions:

(a) bow view and pitch motion only?
(b) broadside view and roll motion only?
(c) broadside view and yaw motion only?
(d) bow view and yaw motion only?
(e) bow view and roll motion only?

7.11   A stepped-frequency radar has the following parameters: lowest frequency = 3.0 GHz, frequency-step size = 1.0 MHz, pulses per burst = 256, pulse repetition frequency = 5.0 kHz, pulse-width = 3.0 μs, and bursts per image frame = 256. A target is rotating at 1.0°/s in a plane containing the radar line of sight. What, in meters, is

(a) cross-range resolution?
(b) slant-range resolution?
(c) cross-range window?
(d) slant-range window?

7.12   A chirp-pulse radar is to be used to generate ISAR images of a 75 m long air target moving at 200 m/s directly toward the radar. Sampling is carried out on the pulse-compressed signature using a fixed-delay sampling gate through which the target passes. A total of 100 complex samples is collected from each pulse at the rate 150×10^6 samples per second (one complex sample per meter). Slant-range resolution is 1.0 m and pulse repetition frequency (PRF) is 400 pulses per second. (a) How many complete range-profile signatures of the target will be sampled? (b) What is the accumulated number of cells of range walk? (c) How many ISAR image pixels are produced per image following velocity correction?

7.13   What is the target range-measurement error caused by range-Doppler coupling in terms of number of resolution cells for Prob. 7.12 if the chirp pulsewidth is 2.0 μs and center frequency is 9.5 GHz?

7.14   ISAR images of the target of Prob. 7.12 are to be generated using a stepped-frequency waveform. PRF is 10^4 pulses per second, pulses per burst is 100, and processed resolution is the same as for the Prob. 7.12 chirp waveform. A single quadrature pair of samples is collected from each pulse as the target passes through the fixed sampling gate. (a) How many synthetic range profiles will be obtained if the 3 dB width of the sampled pulse is 0.67 μs? (b) What is the accumulated number of range cells of range walk? Neglect samples obtained outside the pulse 3 dB edges.

7.15   A 200 m ship in a 2.0°/s turn is viewed at long range by a 1.3 GHz radar from zero degrees elevation angle. (a) What is the bandwidth of Doppler frequencies observed when the average azimuth aspect angle to the radar is 45° from bow on? (b) Following radial motion correction that corrects to zero Doppler at ship center, what is the change in Doppler frequency during 5.0 s of observation time produced by a scatterer on the bow? (c) What is the resulting cross-range shift in terms of number of resolution cells?

7.16   In Prob. 7.15, what is the number of range cells shifted during the 5.0 s of target dwell time assuming range resolution is 10 m?

7.17   A radar is to be designed to generate ISAR images of 256 slant-range cells by 256 cross-range cells with as fine as 1.5 m resolution. What is the minimum radar center frequency that prevents cell migration due to target rotation from exceeding one cell? Assume that velocity correction centers the image in slant-range and cross-range.

7.18   A target at long range is viewed at 5.4×10^9 Hz. (a) What is the spatial frequency $f_x(\mathrm{m}^{-1})$ at the instant the f_x coordinate axis is aligned with the radar line of sight (LOS)? (b) What is the spatial frequency $f_y(\mathrm{m}^{-1})$ at that instant along an axis at right angles to f_x? (c) If the target then rotates 10°, what are the new values along f_x and f_y?

7.19   A target is viewed over a bandwidth of 300 MHz at a center frequency of 3.0 GHz. (a) What is the spatial-frequency bandwidth (m^{-1}) along the f_x axis when it is aligned with the radar LOS? (b) What viewing-angle change in degrees is required to produce the same spatial-frequency bandwidth along an f_y axis that is in the plane of rotation and perpendicular to the f_x axis?

7.20   Show that the result for Prob. 7.19(b) is also obtained based on expressions $\Delta r_s = c/2\beta$ and $\Delta r_c = \lambda/2\theta$ by requiring $\Delta r_s = \Delta r_s$.

7.21   A stepped-frequency radar is to be designed to provide an ISAR imaging mode with slant-range and cross-range resolution as fine as 0.7 m during an integration time of 5.0 s. The radar PRF is 5000 pulses per second. What is the largest size target in meters that can be handled unambiguously if aspect is unknown? Assume equal slant-range and cross-range windows.

7.22 Air targets are to be imaged while they are flying at up to 600 m/s at ranges as near as 30 km from a 10 GHz ground-based radar. Target length can reach 40 m. (a) What is the maximum received Doppler bandwidth? (b) What is the minimum required pulse-repetition frequency (PRF) for a pulse-compression waveform? (c) What is the minimum required PRF for a stepped-frequency waveform of 128 pulses per burst?

7.23 A target is to be viewed with a radar capable of 0.5 m slant-range resolution. A slant-range (delay) window of 0.5 μs is to be established. What is the minimum processing gain $(G_p)_{min}$ (number of pulses coherently integrated) required to divide up unambiguously the target window in slant-range resolution cells using: (a) chirp waveforms? (b) pulse-to-pulse stepped-frequency waveforms?

7.24 A radar is to be designed for ISAR imaging. A 120 m slant-range by 75 m cross-range image space is to be established with a resolution of 0.5 m in both dimensions. What is the minimum number of pulses $(G_p)_{min}$ required to be integrated to divide up unambiguously the image space using: (a) chirp waveforms? (b) pulse-to-pulse stepped-frequency waveforms?

7.25 A space-based radar in its surface-search surveillance mode obtains a single-pulse signal-to-noise ratio of 18 dB from a 75 m by 10 m ship target. A chirp-pulse compression mode is then selected for ship-target imaging, which involves chirping the transmit pulse used in the surveillance mode. An ISAR image from a 100 pulse look is generated with 1.5 m by 1.5 m resolution. Based on (7.39), how many visible target pixels can be expected for a pixel visibility threshold of 8 dB?

REFERENCES

1. Mensa, Dean L., *High Resolution Target Imaging*, Dedham, MA: Artech House, 1981.

2. Chen, C., and H.C. Andrews, "Multifrequency Imaging of Radar Turntable Data," *IEEE Trans. Aerospace and Electronics Systems*, Vol. AES-16, No. 1, Jan. 1980, pp. 15–22.

3. Walker, J.L., "Range-Doppler Imaging of Rotating Objects," *IEEE Trans. Aerospace and Electronics Systems*, Vol. AES-16, No. 1, Jan. 1980, pp. 23–52.

4. Chen, C., and H.C. Andrews, "Target-motion-induced Radar Imaging," *IEEE Trans. Aerospace and Electronics Systems,* Vol. AES-16, No. 1, Jan. 1980, pp. 2–14.
5. Ausherman, D.A., *et al.,* "Developments in Radar Imaging," *IEEE Trans. Aerospace and Electronics Systems,* Vol. AES-20, No. 4, July 1984, pp. 363–400.

Chapter 8

Three-Dimensional Imaging
with Monopulse Radar

8.1 SHORTCOMINGS OF ISAR

Target imaging by means of ISAR is possible at the full detection range of the radar. From the standpoint of image interpretation, however, there remain the following inherent shortcomings:

1. The cross-range dimension scale is a direct function of the target's aspect angular-rotation rate. Distorted images result, unless the rotation rate can be determined from auxiliary data. Also, defocusing can occur because of a change in aspect rotation rate during the image frame time.

2. The ISAR image plane does not reveal the true aspect of the target, which is unknown because the radar cannot determine the direction of the target's rotation vector that produces the cross-range Doppler gradient.

3. Target dwell time required to produce a given cross-range resolution is dependent upon the target's aspect rotation rate relative to the radar. Therefore, a long-range, nonmaneuvering air target may require tens of seconds to image.

The three above-mentioned problems with ISAR result from its inherent dependence upon the target's changing its aspect to the radar. The magnitude and direction of the target's aspect rotation vector are not determined in the ISAR approach, except from auxiliary data, and the magnitude may be too small.

Despite this limitation, the ISAR technique remains attractive for surveillance problems that require target identification. Consideration has been given to methods by which the above shortcomings associated with ISAR imaging can be resolved in part. A slant-range to cross-range *scale factor* can be estimated from knowledge of target shapes and expected pitch, roll, and yaw rates. Target aspect rotation rate, and thus slant-range to cross-range scale factor, can be estimated from target track data for those ISAR images produced by tangential motion of the target relative to the radar, such as in the case of straight-line flying aircraft targets. The image plane and true aspect angle of imaged targets can be inferred in some cases from the target image itself or its behavior in time during several image-frame times. Finally, the relatively long target-dwell time requirement may be lessened by employing *super-resolution* processing techniques, which obtain cross-range resolution Δr_c corresponding to less than the dwell time $T = \lambda/(2\omega\Delta r_c)$. Target dwell time is also reduced for those applications in which it is practical to operate at shorter wavelengths.

Three-dimensional monopulse radar imaging, described in this chapter, entirely avoids all three of the problems cited above by generating images from monopulse sum-and-difference signals independently of the target's aspect motion. The concept as of this writing remains in the experimental phase. A major disadvantage with respect to ISAR appears to be limited range performance. The basic principle is the extraction of cross-range scatterer position from normalized monopulse error signals along a HRR profile of the target, as indicated in Fig. 8.1 (azimuth only). Figure 8.2 illustrates the general process.

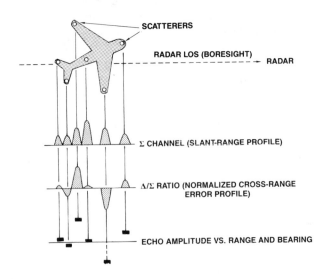

Fig. 8.1 Generation of Cross-Range Error Signals with HRR Monopulse Radar

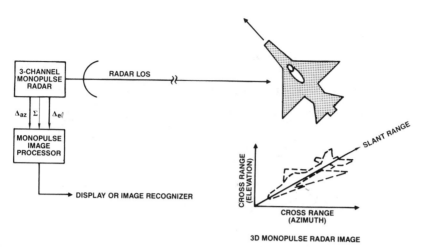

Fig. 8.2 3-D Monopulse Image Generation

8.2 MONOPULSE THREE-DIMENSIONAL IMAGING CONCEPT

Wideband monopulse radar processing makes it possible to measure the position of an isolated point target in two orthogonal dimensions of cross range. When carried out at each resolved slant-range cell of a complex target, the result is a three-dimensional (3-D) image of the target. Orthogonal cross-range dimensions of resolved scatterers are obtained from differential error signals produced in the azimuth and elevation channels of a monopulse radar. Early work at NRL [1] demonstrated cross-range signatures of an aircraft by using short-pulse waveforms. A stepped-frequency waveform with potential for imaging at longer ranges will be discussed in this chapter.

Figure 8.3 is a generic block diagram of a 3-D monopulse radar using stepped-frequency waveforms. Amplitude-comparison monopulse processing is assumed. Bandwidth corresponds to that required for the desired slant-range resolution. Following the three-channel quadrature detection, the signals are digitized for processing into 3-D images. Two alternative types of stepped-frequency processing are indicated in Figs. 8.4 and 8.5. In Fig. 8.4, single bursts, each of n frequencies, are processed to form either 1-D profiles or 3-D images. Stepped-frequency sum-channel signals and error signals from the two difference channels are first corrected in velocity. Each burst of n echo signals from the three channels is then converted by use of the Fourier transform into synthetic range profiles:

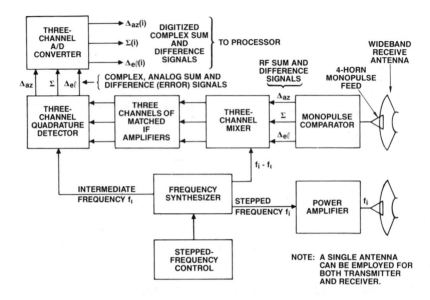

Fig. 8.3 Generic 3-D Monopulse Imaging Radar Using Stepped-Frequency Waveforms

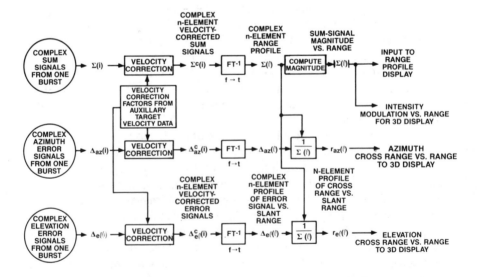

Fig. 8.4 Digital Processing to Generate 1-D Range Profiles and 3-D Images (from Echoes of a Single Burst of *n* Frequency Steps)

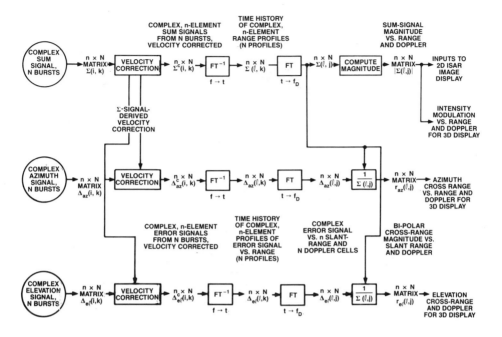

Fig. 8.5 Digital Processing to Generate 2-D and 3-D Images from Echoes of N bursts of n Frequency Steps

sum signals into slant-range profiles and error (or difference) signals into profiles of error signal *versus* range. Error signals in both channels are then normalized, range cell by range cell, by the sum signal to produce bipolar cross-range position data.

A 3-D display format is illustrated in Fig. 8.6. Cross-range positions of resolved scatterers in each slant-range cell are displayed in azimuth and elevation cross-range position. A single display point is shown in the figure. The 3-D image can be displayed isometrically on a conventional 2-D display by using conventional processing techniques. Generic block diagrams for a pulse-compression (real HRR) version of a 3-D imaging radar and the required processing would be somewhat simpler.

The processing in Fig. 8.4 will result in false cross-range estimates of scatterer position where two or more scatterers remain unresolved in a slant-range cell. The resulting error signal in such a slant-range cell will be that produced by the effective phase center of both (or all) scatterers

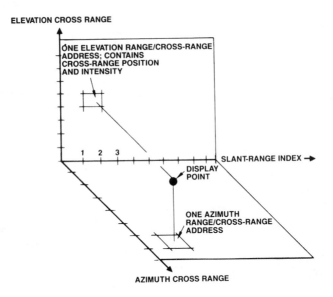

Fig. 8.6 One Frame of 3-D Image Data (from One Burst of n Frequency Steps)

in the cell, and generally it will not correspond to any single scatterer. Increased range resolution tends to overcome the problem. This problem also can be overcome in part while achieving improved range performance by the use of coherent processing of multiple stepped-frequency bursts, as shown in Fig. 8.5. Here, an additional Fourier transform is carried out, similar to that used for stepped-frequency ISAR processing, to separate scatterers in Doppler as well as slant range and cross range. Multiple-pulse processing would achieve the same result for a pulse-compression version. The Doppler frequency, as in ISAR, is that produced by target aspect rotation relative to the radar. Display processing is indicated in Fig. 8.7. Multiple Doppler cells can be seen to exist for each slant-range cell. Therefore, if multiple scatterers exist in a single range cell, they may be separable in terms of Doppler frequency, and therefore displayed separately.

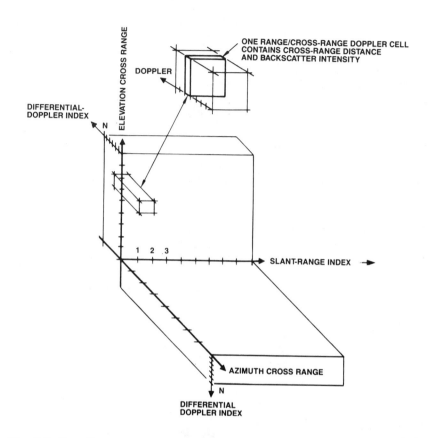

Fig. 8.7 One Frame of 3-D Image Data (from N Bursts of n Frequency Steps)

The capability of the multiple-burst processing of Fig. 8.5 to resolve scatterers is a function of the target aspect motion that occurs during the data-collection time. Thus, the advantage of reduced image frame time associated with monopulse processing as compared with ISAR processing is traded off. Tables 8.1 and 8.2 define terms used in Figs. 8.4 and 8.5. Concept details for the stepped-frequency type of 3-D image processing illustrated in Figs. 8.3 through 8.5 are given later in this chapter (Sec. 8.4).

Table 8.1 Symbols Used in Fig. 8.4
(All Signals are Complex Digital Values Unless Otherwise Noted)

Symbol	Definition
$\Sigma(i)$	Sum signal echo at frequency step i.
$\Sigma^c(i)$	Velocity-corrected sum signal at frequency step i.
$\Delta_{az}(i)$	Azimuth error signal at frequency step i.
$\Delta_{az}^c(i)$	Velocity-corrected azimuth error signal at frequency step i.
$\Delta_{el}(i)$	Elevation error signal at frequency step i.
$\Delta_{el}^c(i)$	Velocity-corrected elevation error signal at frequency step i.
$f \to t$	Transform from frequency domain to synthetic slant-range domain.
$\Sigma(l)$	Sum signal at lth range position.
$\Delta_{az}(l)$	Azimuth error signal at lth range position.
$\Delta_{el}(l)$	Elevation error signal at lth range position.
$r_{az}(l)$	Azimuth cross-range (bipolar) amplitude in lth range position.
$r_{el}(l)$	Elevation cross-range (bipolar) amplitude in lth range position.
$\|\Sigma(l)\|$	Sum signal (magnitude) in lth range position.

8.3 RANGE PERFORMANCE

High resolution monopulse processing makes it possible to measure cross-range positions of target scatterers that are resolved in the slant-range dimension. The position of resolved scatterers is measured in two orthogonal cross-range dimensions. Measurements are relative to scatterers in adjacent resolved slant-range cells. True resolution is not actually achieved in the cross-range dimension; i.e., multiple scatterers in a slant-range cell (or range-Doppler cell) cannot be resolved in cross range. However, the word "resolution" in quotes will be used for convenience to indicate ability to measure range-cell to range-cell differences in cross-range scatterer position.

Slant-range resolution in conventional radar and cross-range resolution in ISAR are independent of target range. For 3-D monopulse imaging, however, we will see that cross-range "resolution" of the target decreases with target range. In Chapter 7, ISAR image performance was estimated in terms of the fraction of resolved target elements that exceeded a radar cross-section threshold value. This threshold value was related to the ratio of the pixel signal-to-noise ratio considered adequate for visibility.

Table 8.2 Symbols Used in Fig. 8.5

Symbol	Definition
$\Sigma(i, k)$	Sum signal echo at frequency step i, burst k.
$\Sigma^c(i, k)$	Velocity-corrected sum signal at step i, burst k.
$\Delta_{az}(i, k)$	Azimuth error signal at step i, burst k.
$\Delta_{az}^c(i, k)$	Velocity-corrected azimuth error signal at step i, burst k.
$\Delta_{el}(i, k)$	Elevation error signal at step i, burst k.
$\Delta_{el}^c(i, k)$	Velocity-corrected elevation error signal at step i, burst k.
$f \rightarrow t$	Transform from frequency domain to synthetic slant-range domain, burst by burst.
$t \rightarrow f_D$	Transform from time-history domain at each synthetic range position to Doppler-frequency domain.
$\Sigma(l, k)$	Sum signal at lth range position of burst k.
$\Delta_{az}(l, k)$	Azimuth error signal at lth range position of burst k.
$\Delta_{el}(l, k)$	Elevation error signal at lth range position of burst k.
$\Sigma(l, j)$	Sum signal at lth range position and jth Doppler frequency.
$\Delta_{az}(l, j)$	Azimuth error signal at lth range position and jth Doppler frequency.
$\Delta_{el}(l, j)$	Elevation error signal at lth range position and jth Doppler frequency.
$r_{az}(l, j)$	Azimuth cross-range bipolar amplitude at lth range position and jth Doppler frequency.
$r_{el}(l, j)$	Elevation cross-range bipolar amplitude at lth slant-range position and jth Doppler frequency.
$\lvert \Sigma(l, j) \rvert$	Sum signal (magnitude) at lth range position and jth Doppler frequency.

Pixel signal-to-noise ratio was based on the radar range equation so that we could calculate image quality *versus* single-pulse detection range. This method is applicable when resolution itself is independent of target range so that the number of visible image elements constitutes the measure of image quality. "Resolution" in cross range for monopulse 3-D imaging, however, is a function of target range. As target range increases, the difference-channel signals, which are measures of cross-range angle, become smaller. Ability to measure changes in scatterer position will degrade as the corresponding changes in signal voltage approach the level of receiver noise. It is, therefore, more appropriate to estimate image quality directly in terms of cross-range "resolution." Therefore, expressions will now be developed for 3-D target imaging range in terms of cross-range "resolution."

The signal-to-noise ratio at the input to the sum channel of a mono-pulse radar, produced by a resolved target scatterer at range R of radar cross section σ, is

$$(S/N)_\Sigma = \frac{S_\Sigma}{N} = \frac{\left(\frac{1}{4\pi}\right)^3 \frac{1}{R^4} G^2\lambda^2 P_t L\sigma}{kT_0\beta_n F} = \frac{V_\Sigma^2/Z_0}{N} \qquad (8.1)$$

where

S_Σ = sum-channel received power out of the comparator,
V_Σ = sum-channel received voltage (rms),
N = thermal noise power,
G = antenna gain,
λ = wavelength,
P_t = transmitted pulse power,
L = radar system and propagation losses ($L \leq 1.0$),
k = Boltzmann's constant,
T_0 = standard noise temperature (290 K),
β_n = noise bandwidth,
Z_0 = receiver input impedance,
F = radar system noise factor.

For a circular monopulse antenna of half-power beamwidth $\phi_{3\text{ dB}}$, an error slope K_m may be defined as the ratio of normalized difference-channel error voltage V_Δ/V_Σ out of the comparator to normalized offset angle $\phi_\Delta/\phi_{3\text{ dB}}$. Thus,

$$K_m = \frac{V_\Delta/V_\Sigma}{\phi_\Delta/\phi_{3\text{ dB}}} \qquad (8.2)$$

where V_Δ is the rms voltage out of the comparator to one of the difference channels.

The error slope defined in this manner is quite independent of antenna beamwidth. Practical values for K_m, according to Barton [2], vary from about 1.2 to 2.0. For $K_m = 1.5$, the rms error voltage, from (8.2), is

$$V_\Delta \approx 1.5 \frac{\phi_\Delta}{\phi_{3\text{ dB}}} V_\Sigma$$

The angular offset from boresight produced by a target scatterer at cross-range displacement y at range R is

$$\phi_\Delta = \frac{y}{R} \frac{360}{2\pi} \text{ (degrees)}$$

By using an approximation given by Jasik [3] for parabolic reflectors, we obtain

$$\frac{1}{\phi_{3 \text{ dB}}} \approx \left(\frac{G}{27,000}\right)^{1/2}$$

for $\phi_{3 \text{ dB}}$ in degrees.

The rms error voltage out of the comparator then becomes

$$V_\Delta = 1.5 \frac{y}{R} \frac{360}{2\pi} \left(\frac{G}{27,000}\right)^{1/2} V_\Sigma$$

The difference in rms error voltage dV_Δ produced by a shift dy in scatterer cross-range position is

$$dV_\Delta = 1.5 \frac{dy}{R} \frac{360}{2\pi} \left(\frac{G}{27,000}\right)^{1/2} V_\Sigma$$

The difference-channel input signal power associated with a cross-range shift dy then is

$$S_\Delta = \frac{(dV_\Delta)^2}{Z_0}$$

$$= 2.25 \left(\frac{dy}{R}\right)^2 \left(\frac{360}{2\pi}\right)^2 \left(\frac{G}{27,000}\right) \frac{V_\Sigma^2}{Z_0}$$

$$= 2.25 \left(\frac{dy}{R}\right)^2 \left(\frac{360}{2\pi}\right)^2 \left(\frac{G}{27,000}\right) S_\Sigma \tag{8.3}$$

The signal-to-noise ratio produced at the input to the difference channel by a scatterer's cross-range shift of $dy = \delta r$, from (8.1) and (8.3), is

$$\left(\frac{S}{N}\right)_\Delta = \frac{S_\Delta}{N} = \frac{\left[2.25\left(\frac{\delta r}{R}\right)^2\left(\frac{360}{2\pi}\right)^2\left(\frac{G}{27,000}\right)\right]\left(\frac{1}{4\pi}\right)^3\frac{1}{R^4}\,G^2\lambda^2 P_t L\sigma}{kT_0\beta_n F} \qquad (8.4)$$

It is convenient to obtain a range expression written in terms of antenna diameter rather than gain. For an antenna aperture A, the gain is

$$G = \frac{4\pi A}{\lambda^2}$$

If we assume 50% antenna aperture efficiency and an antenna diameter of D_a, then the effective area of the antenna is

$$A = \frac{1}{2}\left(\frac{\pi D_a^2}{4}\right)$$

The antenna gain in (8.4) then becomes

$$G = \frac{4\pi}{\lambda^2}\cdot\frac{1}{2}\left(\frac{\pi D_a^2}{4}\right) = \frac{\pi^2 D_a^2}{2\lambda^2} \qquad (8.5)$$

We will assume that targets to be imaged are made up of scatterers that have physical dimensions equal to their cross-range separation δr. The calculation of the radar target range at which scatterers can be separated will be based on the radar cross section of two ideal types of passive reflectors, spherical and flat-plate. In other words, the target is assumed to be made up entirely of scatterers, which are either spherical reflecting surfaces or flat plates facing the radar.

Spheres have the smallest radar cross section for their size of any of the simple geometric shapes. Ideal nonspherical reflectors produce relatively high specular backscattering, which increases with the ratio of their physical dimensions to wavelength. The effect is not expected to occur for most real targets, however, because their normal curved shapes would not present flat regions to the radar over more than a few wavelengths in extent. We therefore conclude that the assumption of spherical scatterers, while appearing conservative, probably roughly represents the expected population of scatterers for real targets. The validity of this conclusion in terms of "resolution" *versus* range remains to be tested experimentally.

Radar cross section of a conducting sphere with diameter δr, for $\delta r \gg \lambda$, is [4]

$$\sigma_s = \frac{\pi(\delta r)^2}{4} \tag{8.6}$$

For specular return from a flat plate of size $\delta r \times \delta r$, the radar cross section is [4]

$$\sigma_f = \frac{4\pi(\delta r)^4}{\lambda^2} \tag{8.7}$$

Signal-to-noise ratio at the input to the difference channels produced by a cross-range shift δr of a spherical scatterer at range R, from (8.4), (8.5), and (8.6), then is

$$\left(\frac{S}{N}\right)_\Delta = \frac{2.25\left(\frac{\delta r}{R}\right)^2\left(\frac{360}{2\pi}\right)^2\left[\frac{\left(\frac{\pi^2 D_a^2}{2\lambda^2}\right)}{27,000}\right]\left(\frac{1}{4\pi}\right)^3 \cdot \frac{1}{R^4}\left(\frac{\pi^2 D_a^2}{2\lambda^2}\right)^2 \lambda^2 P_t L \frac{\pi(\delta r)^2}{4}}{kT_0\beta_n F} \tag{8.8}$$

Equation (8.8) was derived for a single scatterer that changes its cross-range position by δr. The same expression will be assumed to represent the input signal-to-noise ratio:

$$[(S_\Delta)_1 - (S_\Delta)_2]/N$$

associated with any two range-resolved scatterers that are separated by δr. The resulting range to obtain "resolution" δr for the assumption of range-resolved spherical scatterers is

$$R_s = 0.331\left(\frac{\pi D_a^3(\delta r)^2}{\lambda^2}\right)^{1/3}\left(\frac{P_t L}{kT_0\beta_n F(S/N)_\Delta}\right)^{1/6} \tag{8.9}$$

where $(S/N)_\Delta$ is the signal-to-noise ratio at the input of each of the difference channels.

At this point, we have said nothing about the signal waveform. Range is of interest in terms of the signal-to-noise ratio at the output of a receiving system matched to the transmitted waveform. Output signal-to-noise ratio (S/N) from either matched-filter difference channel is $T_1\beta_n(S/N)_\Delta$ for a transmitted pulse of duration T_1. The radar range expressed in (8.9) for spherical scatterers, when written in terms of output signal-to-noise ratio (S/N) of a matched-filter difference channel, becomes

$$R_s = 0.331 \left(\frac{\pi D_a^3(\delta r)^2}{\lambda^2}\right)^{1/3} \left(\frac{P_t T_1 L}{k T_0 F(S/N)}\right)^{1/6} \tag{8.10}$$

The range equation (8.10) differs significantly from the conventional radar range equation for detection (2.14), in Chapter 2. First, the term taken to the one-sixth power in (8.10) contains parameters that formed a term taken to the one-fourth power in (2.14). The key parameters are radar power, transmitted pulsewidth, and required output signal-to-noise ratio. To double 3-D imaging range requires an 18 dB increase in radar transmitter power, compared with 12 dB needed to double detection range. The comparison also applies for changes in transmitted pulsewidth and required output signal-to-noise ratio. Thus, range performance is expected to degrade 6 dB per octave faster for 3-D imaging than for detection. Nonetheless, we can see that 3-D imaging performance in terms of range is directly proportional to antenna diameter while being nearly proportional to radar frequency and desired cross-range "resolution" δr.

8.3.1 Range Performance with Short Pulses and Chirp Pulses

Equation (8.10) expresses range at which the output signal-to-noise ratio produced in the monopulse difference channel by cross-range scatterer separation δr is equal to S/N for a single transmitted pulse of duration T_1. Before applying (8.10) to the stepped-frequency processing outlined in Figs. 8.3, 8.4, and 8.5, consider range performance using short pulses and chirp pulses. Range performance by using (8.10) increases with the pulse energy $P_t T_1$. We obtain increased resolution for uncoded short pulses that are peak-power limited at the expense of range performance because the pulse duration must be reduced in order to increase resolution. The problem is overcome with chirp-pulse waveforms (and other coded waveforms) because resolution is determined by waveform bandwidth, not pulse duration.

8.3.2 Range Performance with Stepped-Frequency Waveforms

Stepped-frequency waveforms have an advantage over both short-pulse and chirp-pulse waveforms in terms of range performance for monopulse imaging because pulse-to-pulse coherent integration is inherent in the processing. Signal-to-noise ratio is increased by a factor of n, following coherent processing associated with the frequency-to-time transformation of each stepped-frequency burst of n echo signals. Pulse-to-pulse coherent processing, in principle, could also be carried out with chirp waveforms, but A/D conversion becomes a problem for wideband signals, as discussed in previous chapters.

Burst-to-burst coherent integration in a stepped-frequency radar provides additional processing gain after application of velocity correction algorithms, which were discussed previously in connection with 2-D ISAR imaging. Velocity correction inputs for 3-D monopulse processing could be derived from the relatively high signal-to-noise data of the sum signal. The resulting phase corrections would be applied to the error signal from each step of each echo burst in the two relatively low-level difference channels, as shown in Fig. 8.5. Burst-to-burst integration, carried out by the second Fourier transform, then produces a signal-to-noise improvement factor equal to the number N of integrated bursts.

The input signal-to-noise ratio of the sum channel, expressed in (8.1) for each pulse, exceeds that of the difference channel, as given in (8.4) or (8.8), by

$$\frac{(S/N)_\Sigma}{(S/N)_\Delta} = \frac{1}{2.25 \left(\frac{\delta r}{R}\right)^2 \left(\frac{360}{2\pi}\right)^2 \frac{\pi^2 D_a^2}{2\lambda^2} \frac{1}{27,000}}$$

Input signal-to-noise ratio in the sum channel associated with an output signal-to-noise ratio (S/N) in the difference channel for N bursts of n steps, assuming $T_1 \beta_n = 1$, is

$$(S/N)_\Sigma = \frac{1}{Nn} \cdot \frac{S/N}{2.25 \left(\frac{\delta r}{R}\right)^2 \left(\frac{360}{2\pi}\right)^2 \frac{\pi^2 D_a^2}{2\lambda^2} \frac{1}{27,000}} \tag{8.11}$$

As an example, consider the hypothetical spaceborne radar parameters of Table 8.3, for which 128 bursts of 128 steps are integrated coherently. The input signal-to-noise ratio in the sum-signal channel for one

Table 8.3 Radar Parameters for Four Hypothetical Radars

Parameter	Symbol	Units	Long-Range Tracking Radar	Airborne Intercept Radar	Spaceborne Radar	Missile Seeker
Antenna Diameter	D_a	ft	8.0 (2.4 m)	3.0 (0.91 m)	50 (15.2 m)	0.9 (0.27 m)
Wavelength	λ	m	.0531	.030	.00857	.02
Peak Power	P_t	kW	2000	50	10	4
Total System Loss	L	dB	−5	−13	−5	−10
Pulses per Burst	n	—	256	128	128	128
Stepped-Frequency Bandwidth	$n\Delta f$	MHz	250	250	100	250
Bursts Integrated	N	—	1	200	128	20
System Noise Factor	F	dB	3.5	3.2	4.0	6.0
Output Signal-to-Noise (Error Signal)	$(S/N)_\Delta$	dB	10	10	10	10
Pulsewidth	T_1	μs	6	4	1	2
PRF	$\dfrac{1}{T_2}$	pps	400	25,000	10,000	2500
Average Power	$(P_t)_{ave}$	W	4800	5000	100	20
Image Frame Time	T	s	0.64	1.024	1.64	1.024
Range Resolution	$\Delta r_s = \dfrac{c}{2n\Delta f}$	ft	2.0 (0.6 m)	2.0 (0.6 m)	4.9 (1.5 m)	2.0 (0.6 m)

pulse per step and a required signal-to-noise ratio of 10 dB in the output cross-range data is calculated from (8.11) and Table 8.3. Results are indicated in Fig. 8.8. Except for very low resolution performance (extreme radar target range), there appears to be an ample signal-to-noise ratio of the sum signal for target detection and application of velocity correction algorithms required for burst-to-burst integration.

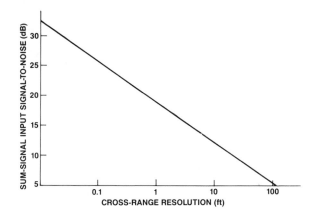

Fig. 8.8 Input Sum-Signal Signal-to-Noise Ratio *versus* Cross-Range "Resolution" for Hypothetical Spaceborne Radar Operating at an Output Difference Signal-to-Noise Ratio of 10 dB

Equation (8.10) for radar-imaging range using a frequency-stepping waveform of N bursts of n frequency steps, therefore, becomes

$$R_s = 0.331 \left(\frac{\pi D_a^3 (\delta r)^2}{\lambda^2} \right)^{1/3} \left(\frac{P_t T_1 L N n}{k T_0 F(S/N)} \right)^{1/6} \tag{8.12}$$

8.3.3 Range Performance Assuming Flat-Plate Scatterers

Equations (8.10) and (8.12) apply for the assumption of spherical scatterers. The range R_f for specular return from flat-plate scatterers is

$$R_f = R_s \left(\frac{\sigma_f}{\sigma_s} \right)^{1/6}$$

Then, with σ_s and σ_f from (8.6) and (8.7), respectively, we have

$$R_f = R_s \left(\frac{\frac{4\pi(\delta r)^4}{\lambda^2}}{\frac{\pi(\delta r)^2}{4}} \right)^{1/6}$$

$$= R_s \left(\frac{4\delta r}{\lambda} \right)^{1/3} \tag{8.13}$$

As an example of the improvement in range performance over that for the assumption of spherical scatterers, the calculated ranges from (8.12) and (8.13) for the tracking radar (parameters listed in Table 8.3) are as follows:

"resolution" $\delta r = 2$ ft: $\begin{cases} R_s = & 16 \text{ nmi} \\ R_f = & 57 \text{ nmi} \end{cases}$

"resolution" $\delta r = 5$ ft: $\begin{cases} R_s = & 29 \text{ nmi} \\ R_f = & 149 \text{ nmi} \end{cases}$

Similar results are obtained by using parameters for other radars listed in Table 8.3.

8.3.4 Range Performance Calculation Examples

Range *versus* cross-range "resolution" was calculated from (8.12) for parameters of each of the four radars of Table 8.3. These radars are representative of three generic types of military radars and a hypothetical spaceborne radar. Plots are shown in Fig. 8.9. Stepped-frequency waveforms were assumed in each case.

Stepped-frequency monopulse radars could generate 3-D images while operating in their tracking modes. A shipboard or ground-based 3-D imaging radar would be required to acquire the target and continue to track. An airborne radar or missile-seeker radar with a track-while-scan (TWS) mode would probably need to switch to a track-only mode on a single target of interest. The spaceborne radar would identify assigned space or air targets from a space platform. Targets of interest would be acquired, then tracked for up to several seconds to obtain the image.

8.4 CONCEPT DETAILS FOR STEPPED-FREQUENCY APPROACH

Figure 8.10 illustrates the stepped-frequency waveform described in Chapter 5 for synthetic processing. Frequency is changed from pulse to

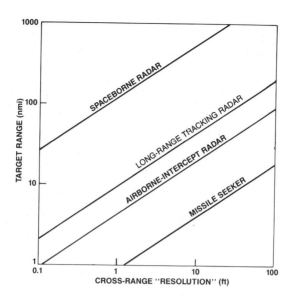

Fig. 8.9 Monopulse Radar Target Range *versus* Cross-Range "Resolution" (Assuming Spherical Scatterers)

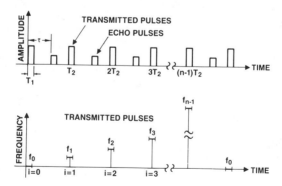

Fig. 8.10 Stepped-Frequency Waveforms

pulse over a burst of frequencies f_0 to f_{n-1}. The frequency of the local oscillator reference signal to the first mixer of Fig. 8.3 is also changed identically from pulse to pulse so that fixed, narrowband, IF echo signals are produced in each of the three channels. The quadrature mixer then mixes the three IF signals with a coherent reference from the synthesizer to produce baseband outputs. These outputs are sampled and digitized, then processed, as in Figs. 8.4 and 8.5, into outputs suitable for 1-D, 2-

D, or 3-D display. The digital processing indicated in Figs. 8.4 and 8.5 includes velocity correction, Fourier transforms, and phase comparison to produce sum-and-difference-channel range profiles. The output magnitude of the sum signal in a given synthetic range cell is proportional to the radar cross section of the resolved scatterer in that cell. The output magnitude of the difference signal in a given synthetic range cell is proportional to the scatterer cross-range distance in that range cell after normalization by the sum-signal output in that cell. Normalization is carried out in the *digital phase comparator* described below.

We will discuss the detailed operation of the stepped-frequency 3-D image processor for a four-feed-horn monopulse radar from the viewpoint of an image produced by echoes from a single point target, illuminated by a single burst of n pulses, stepped in frequency from f_0 to f_{n-1}. The echo signal levels from either the azimuth or elevation pair of monopulse antenna feeds are equal when the target is on boresight. Offset antenna patterns produced by two of the four feeds of a monopulse antenna are illustrated in Fig. 8.11. Difference patterns as seen at baseband are illustrated in Fig. 8.12. Slightly off boresight, the RF signals as seen at the output of feeds 1 and 2 will be unbalanced, as illustrated in Fig. 8.13(a). The cross-range distance of the target from boresight is proportional to the amount of imbalance. The direction, left or right, is indicated by the difference-channel error signal phase, 0 or π, relative to the sum signal, as indicated in Fig. 8.13(b).

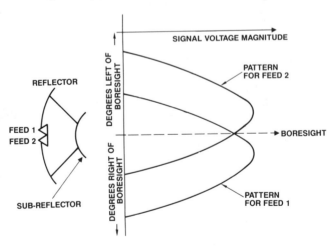

Fig. 8.11 Idealized Antenna Patterns from each of a Pair of Feeds Feeding a Single Reflector

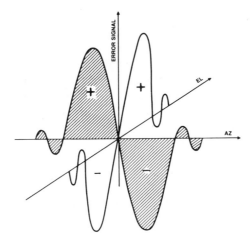

Fig. 8.12 Monopulse Antenna Difference Patterns seen at Baseband from Two Pairs of Feeds

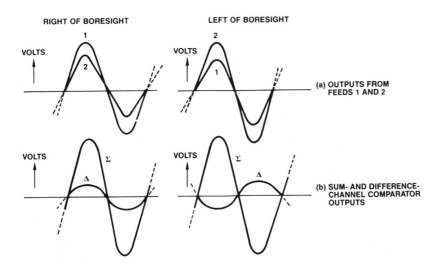

Fig. 8.13 Monopulse Waveforms at One Frequency for Echo from Point Target to the Right and Left of Boresight (Single Cycle of Echo from One Pulse is Shown)

The synthesizer in the block diagram of Fig. 8.3 generates the series of stepped-frequency transmitted pulses of Fig. 8.10, a stepped-frequency local oscillator reference signal, and a fixed IF reference signal. All three signals are assumed to be generated by multiplying up from a fixed master oscillator and, therefore, are all coherently related. The resulting RF sum signal and two difference signals (Σ, Δ_{az}, and Δ_{el} of Fig. 8.3) from the monopulse comparator at each frequency step are the RF signal sum of all four feed antennas and the difference RF signal from each of the two orthogonal pairs, respectively, at each frequency step.

The phase of each of the two difference-channel signals, as stated above, will be either 0 or π radians, relative to the phase of the sum signal. The three channels of echo signal are mixed to a suitable IF, then mixed again to baseband. (Although now at baseband, these signals are still symbolized as Σ, Δ_{az}, and Δ_{el} in Fig. 8.3.) The signals are sampled, then converted to three channels of complex digital data, which are symbolized by $\Sigma(i)$, $\Delta_{az}(i)$, and $\Delta_{el}(i)$, where i denotes the frequency step index. This completes the RF processing.

Figure 8.4 indicated the required digital processing. The first digital process is velocity correction, the methods for which were discussed in Chapter 7. Velocity-corrected data are designated $\Sigma^c(i)$, $\Delta_{az}^c(i)$, and $\Delta_{el}^c(i)$. The quadrature mixer output in the sum channel and either of the difference channels, respectively, at frequency step i for a point target to the right or left of boresight at delay τ, is expressed as

$$\Sigma(i) = |\Sigma(i)|e^{-j2\pi f_i \tau(t)}$$
$$\Delta(i) = \pm|\Delta(i)|e^{-j2\pi f_i \tau(t)}$$

with the plus sign applying to the point target when right of boresight and minus applying to the point target when left of boresight (for the azimuth channel). For velocity corrected signals, we have

$$\tau(t) = \frac{2R}{c} - \frac{2vt}{c} = \frac{2R}{c}$$

The magnitudes $|\Sigma(i)|$ and $|\Delta(i)|$ refer to the sum and difference signal magnitudes, respectively. The sum-channel and the azimuth difference-channel echo responses for one of the frequency steps from a burst of n stepped frequency pulses is illustrated in Fig. 8.14. The symbols $\Delta(i)_+$ and $\Delta(i)_-$ indicate the difference response that would occur at that frequency for the target at each side of boresight, left or right, respectively.

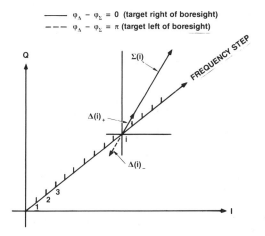

Fig. 8.14 Sampled Sum and Difference Signals Shown for One Frequency
of an *n*-Step Burst (Azimuth Channel)

Next, the resulting range profiles $\Sigma(l)$, $\Delta_{az}(l)$, and $\Delta_{el}(l)$ for each of
the sum and difference channels are generated in the same way as for
single-channel burst data. By using the inverse discrete Fourier transform,
from (5.4) of Chapter 5, the sum and difference range profiles of the point
target at range R respectively become

$$\Sigma(l) = \frac{1}{n} \sum_{i=0}^{n-1} |\Sigma^c(i)| \exp\left[j\left(\frac{2\pi l i}{n} - 2\pi f_i \tau\right)\right] \tag{8.14a}$$

$$\Delta(l) = \frac{1}{n} \sum_{i=0}^{n-1} \pm|\Delta^c(i)| \exp\left[j\left(\frac{2\pi l i}{n} - 2\pi f_i \tau\right)\right] \tag{8.14b}$$

where l is the synthetic range increment and $\tau = 2R/c$. This result is
illustrated in Fig. 8.15 for outputs occurring in one difference channel
when the target being tracked produces a single large response at l_0 and
one smaller response.

The two complex difference signals $\Delta(l)$ at each range position l are
divided by the complex sum signal $\Sigma(l)$ at that range position. The result
is a bipolar amplitude proportional to target distance from boresight, independent of target size. An explanation of this final process follows in
terms of the phase comparison between sum and difference range-profile

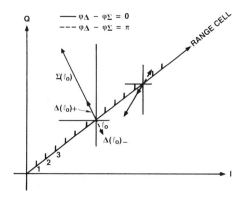

Fig. 8.15 Synthetic Sum and Azimuth Difference-Channel Signals (Shown for a Target Producing Two Responses)

responses to a single point target. The output $r(l)$ of the digital phase comparator for either the azimuth or elevation channel is obtained by dividing (8.14b) by (8.14a); hence,

$$
r(l) = \frac{\Delta(l)}{\Sigma(l)}
$$

$$
= \frac{\dfrac{1}{n} \displaystyle\sum_{i=0}^{n-1} \pm |\Delta^c(i)| \exp\left[j\left(\dfrac{2\pi li}{n} - 2\pi f_i \tau\right)\right]}{\dfrac{1}{n} \displaystyle\sum_{i=0}^{n-1} |\Sigma^c(i)| \exp\left[j\left(\dfrac{2\pi li}{n} - 2\pi f_i \tau\right)\right]}
\tag{8.15}
$$

For a point target at range delay τ, a peak response occurs for some range element l_0 in the n-element synthetic sum and difference range profiles. This peak occurs for the same argument in each exponential of (8.15). For the assumption of a point target, the echo amplitudes are identical at each frequency, so that

$$|\Sigma^c(i)| = |\Sigma|$$

and

$$|\Delta^c(i)| = |\Delta|$$

The phase comparator output expressed in (8.15) at l_0 then becomes

$$r(l_0) = \pm \frac{|\Delta|}{|\Sigma|} \tag{8.16}$$

As we can see from (8.16), the magnitude of the difference response $|\Delta|$ is normalized by the magnitude of the sum response $|\Sigma|$. If referred back to the received rms voltages V_Δ and V_Σ from the comparator, (8.16) then becomes

$$r(l_0) = \pm V_\Delta / V_\Sigma \tag{8.17}$$

where, as before, positive and negative polarities respectively result when the resolved scatterer is to the right and left of boresight. Equation (8.17) can be expressed directly in terms of error slope and normalized offset angle. From (8.2), we have

$$r(l_0) = \pm K_s \frac{\phi_\Delta}{\phi_{3\ \text{dB}}} \tag{8.18}$$

Thus, we can see that the output of the digital phase comparator produces a signal $r(l_0)$, which for a given scatterer is proportional to scatterer offset angle from boresight ϕ_Δ, independent of scatterer size.

8.5 SUMMARY

The monopulse 3-D imaging concept provides a possible means for generating target images dimensioned in two orthogonal cross-range dimensions *versus* slant range. High-range-resolution (HRR) processing, such as pulse-compression or stepped-frequency waveforms, can be used to resolve targets in slant range. Monopulse processing may then be used to measure cross-range position of resolved scatterers in two orthogonal components of cross range. The use of stepped-frequency waveforms provides convenient pulse-to-pulse coherent integration. This may make it possible to estimate cross-range positions of target scatterers from the relatively weak angle-sensitive (error) signals in the difference channels of a monopulse receiver at useful target ranges. The relationship of range resolution and range-window size to radar pulsewidth, step size, and other parameters is identical to that for 2-D stepped-frequency radar. In synthetic 3-D monopulse processing, as for synthetic ISAR processing, successive stepped-frequency echo bursts of data are converted by use of the Fourier transform to obtain synthetic range profiles. Three channels are required for 3-D monopulse processing: a sum channel and two difference channels.

Early results of 2-D monopulse imagery obtained from a short-pulse radar developed at NRL [1] are shown in Fig. 8.16. Preliminary results using a 3.2 GHz stepped-frequency waveform, shown in Figs. 8.17 and 8.18 for a small craft at sea, were obtained at the Naval Ocean Systems Center in 1980. Advantages and disadvantages of 3-D monopulse imaging are summarized below.

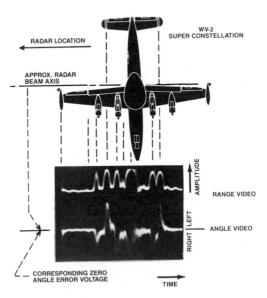

Fig. 8.16 Two-Dimensional Slant-Range and Cross-Range Data Obtained from an Aircraft in Flight with a HRR Monopulse Radar Using a Short-Pulse Waveform (From Howard, D.D., "High Range-Resolution Monopulse Tracking Radar," *IEEE Trans. Aerospace and Electronics Systems,* Vol. AES-11, No. 5, Sept. 1975, p. 753. Reprinted with permission.)

8.5.1 Advantages

- Target aspect change is not required.
- Unambiguous cross-range scale factors are achieved.
- A third dimension of target information is generated.
- 3-D capability can augment ISAR imaging for a monopulse radar.
- Short image-frame time is possible (at high signal-to-noise ratios).
- Compatibility with the normal monopulse tracking function is possible.

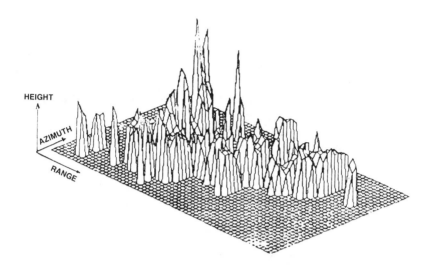

Fig. 8.17 3-D Image of Small Craft (View 1)

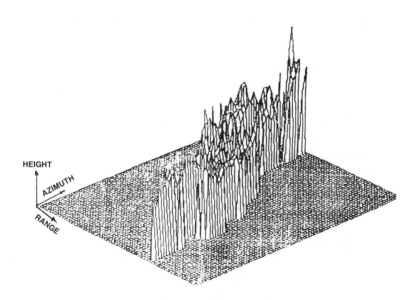

Fig. 8.18 3-D Image of Small Craft (View 2)

8.5.2 Issues

- Good image quality is yet to be demonstrated as of this writing.
- Range limitations are likely.
- Target acquisition may be a problem.
- Required antenna characteristics may be severe (tolerances, bandwidth, and motion stability).
- Multiple unresolved scatterers within individual range cells may distort the image.
- Millimeter-wave frequencies may be essential.

8.5.3 Potential Applications

Three potential future applications are:

- airborne intercept (AI) radar for target confirmation;
- shipboard fire-control for radar target confirmation;
- space and airborne radar for ship and aircraft identification.

Target imaging using monopulse processing is not as yet known to have progressed beyond an experimental stage. Eventual applicability to military or nonmilitary users is speculative.

PROBLEMS

8.1 (a) At what range in nmi will the tracking radar of Fig. 8.9 operating in a 250 MHz chirp-pulse mode obtain 5.0 m of cross-range "resolution" based on one pulse? (b) What would be the range if 256 chirp pulses were coherently summed to form the error signal? Assume all other parameters remain as in Table 8.3.

8.2 Two point targets, each having a radar cross section of 0.1 m^2, are separated by 5.0 m. What is the output signal-to-noise ratio produced by the difference channel of the missile seeker of Table 8.3 at 2.0 km range by one stepped-frequency burst if the point-target separation is cross-range to the radar line-of-sight?

8.3 A ship target having a radar cross section of 2000 m^2 is 90 m in length by 18 m in width. The target is to be imaged from a broadside aspect using the monopulse 3-D imaging method. (a) Based on (2.5) of Chapter 2, what is the average range-resolved radar cross section for a 3.0 m slant-range resolution cell? (b) The target is observed over an azimuth viewing-angle change sufficient to produce 3.0 m cross-range resolution. What is the corresponding radar cross section in the resulting 3.0 m by 3.0 m ISAR resolution cell using the same equation? (c) What is the cross section of a range-resolved spherical reflecting surface of 3.0 m diameter assuming that wavelength is much less than 3.0 m? (d) What is the signal-to-noise ratio out of the difference channel produced by a change of 3.0 m in the cross-range position of resolved scatterers in (a), (b), and (c) above, using the missile-seeker parameters of Table 8.3 at 3.0 nmi (5556 m) from the target? Assume one burst of 128 pulses for (a) and 20 bursts of 128 pulses for (b) and (c).

8.4   Monopulse processing is one method of increasing radar-target angular location accuracy over that associated with the half-power beamwidth of the radar antenna. Sometimes the term *beamsplitting* is used to refer to splitting the radar mainbeam response to a target into fine increments of angular position. A beam-splitting ratio can be defined as the ratio of half-power beamwidth to angular accuracy following beam-splitting. (a) What is the beamsplitting ratio obtained by the airborne intercept radar of Table 8.3 at 10 nmi (18.5 km) when cross-range "resolution" is 1.0 m? (b) What is the beam-splitting ratio associated with an absolute tracking accuracy of ±1.0 mrad for the same radar at the same range in a conventional narrowband angle-tracking mode?

REFERENCES

1.   Howard, D.D., "High Range-Resolution Monopulse Tracking Radar," *IEEE Trans. Aerospace and Electronic Systems,* Vol. AES-11, No. 5, Sept. 1975, pp. 749–755.
2.   Barton, D.K., *Radar System Analysis,* Dedham, MA: Artech House, 1976, p. 275.
3.   Jasik, H., *Antenna Engineering Handbook,* New York: McGraw-Hill, 1961, p. 12-12.
4.   Jasik, H., *Antenna Engineering Handbook,* New York: McGraw-Hill, 1961, p. 13-10.

Chapter 9
Target Imaging with Noncoherent Radar Systems

9.1 COHERENCY REQUIREMENTS FOR TARGET SIGNATURE PROCESSING

Pulse compression, synthetic range-profile generation, and imaging, as discussed up to this point, have implied the use of some type of coherent power-amplifier transmitter. In our discussion of pulse compression, we assumed *intrapulse coherence*. Intrapulse coherence here means that the waveform phase is preserved through the transmitter. In this way, signals for each echo pulse can be compressed on the basis of known phase characteristics of the transmitted pulse.

In our discussion of synthetic HRR, *interpulse coherence* was also implied in that a stable *radar master oscillator* (RMO) existed, from which RF transmission and LO signals were generated, and to which were referenced the PRF and echo sample delay triggers. A radar with interpulse coherence defined in this manner can measure the RF phase difference between the transmitted and echo pulses. We had assumed that echo phase was conveniently measured relative to the RF signal *input* to the transmitter, thus taking advantage of phase coherence through the transmitter.

Thus, up to this point, we have assumed that intrapulse and interpulse coherence, when required, were maintained through the radar transmitter by using RF power amplifiers to amplify the transmitted signal waveform. In this chapter, the possibility of maintaining the required coherence with noncoherent transmitters will be examined: first, briefly, for pulse compression requiring intrapulse coherence; then, in more detail, with respect to pulse-to-pulse coherent integration for synthetic range-profile generation and ISAR image processing that requires transmission-to-reception coherence.

Pulse-compression systems require intrapulse coherence. This is difficult to achieve without a coherent power-amplifier transmitter. However, a power oscillator, such as magnetron transmitter, in principle, could be designed to generate a frequency-coded pulse, such as a chirp pulse, the echo from which would be compressed by a matched filter in the radar receiver. This would require some means for intrapulse control of a magnetron-oscillator output frequency to sufficient accuracy for useful pulse compression. Achievement of this capability in practice is not known to exist.

Synthetic range-profile processing requires coherence from transmission to reception because these techniques depend upon frequency-stepped measurements, pulse-by-pulse, of the echo's relative magnitude and range-delay phase. The received echo phase is measured relative to the transmitted pulse at each frequency. The resulting set of complex values, representing echo amplitude and phase *versus* frequency step, is the target's *reflectivity* sampled in the frequency domain. Synthetic range profiles are generated from these samples. A set of complex samples representing amplitude and phase in each synthetic range cell, taken in time history, is the discrete *Doppler-frequency response* of target scatterers in that range cell. The two-dimensional distribution of Doppler spectrum magnitudes *versus* synthetic range cell is the (unfocused) *range-Doppler ISAR image*. We can thus see that for synthetic range-profile generation and synthetic ISAR it is transmission-to-reception coherence that is required, not intrapulse coherence. As viewed another way, synthetic processing fundamentally depends upon measurements of pulse-to-pulse changes in echo-delay phase and echo amplitude. Therefore, a radar using a pulsed power oscillator as transmitter, while possessing no means with which to retain coherence through the transmitter, can perform coherent interpulse processing if echo delay phase is measured relative to transmitter pulse *output,* rather than transmitter pulse *input,* as is done for convenience in the case of radars using power-amplifier transmitters. Thus, it is conceptually possible to carry out synthetic generation of target range profiles, images, and SAR maps with *noncoherent* radars if their power-oscillator transmitters can be made to be frequency-agile over adequate bandwidth. We will hence see that an important consideration is the required precision of step size.

The most familiar example of a noncoherent radar system is probably that of a pulsed magnetron radar operating at microwave frequencies. The magnetron for these radars oscillates at microwave frequencies upon application of a high-voltage video pulse, and continues to oscillate for the duration of the video pulse, thus producing a high-power RF transmitted pulse. The starting phase and oscillation frequency vary from pulse to pulse. Magnetrons can be made to preserve phase coherence by injection-locking, in which a lower power RF pulse is injected just before and during the high-voltage video pulse. This technique, however, has a disadvantage for high-power radars in that a second, moderate-power coherent amplifier is required as the driver. Injection-locking, therefore, is not commonly found in long-range surveillance and target-tracking radars. However, for most military applications, there remains the possibility of carrying out target signature processing, including ISAR imaging and SAR mapping, with noncoherent, but frequency-agile, pulsed magnetron radars by measuring echo phase relative to transmitter output. This concept will be discussed in more detail in this chapter, starting with background information on frequency agility and *coherent-on-receive* methods for nonimaging radar surveillance functions.

9.2   FREQUENCY-AGILE AND COHERENT-ON-RECEIVE RADARS

Frequency agility generally refers to the ability to change the radar transmission frequency from pulse to pulse by an amount equal to or greater than the pulse bandwidth. Typically, the pulse-to-pulse shift is 2–5 MHz, with total excursions of up to the order of 500 MHz. The advantage, from the viewpoint of surveillance, is improved ECCM or detection performance, as shall be discussed in Chapter 10. Frequency agility in coherent radar systems is achieved by generating a series of transmission and LO signal frequencies such that a fixed IF exists, regardless of the transmission frequency. In this way, the radar's receiver bandwidth remains relatively narrow with a relatively wide frequency-agile transmitter bandwidth. Magnetrons, however, are oscillators. Thus, frequency agility for magnetron radars is achieved by rapid tuning to change the oscillation frequency. This has been achieved in several ways. The most common method is to *dither* the magnetron frequency by an electronically driven tuning plunger, which is part of the magnetron resonance structure (see Fig. 3.20 of Chapter 3).

Magnetron radars, because they are noncoherent, require the receiver to *acquire* the transmitter frequency at each pulse. To do so, a new LO frequency must be generated within a few microseconds following each transmitted pulse. The LO frequency for each pulse, ideally, would be the frequency that resulted in IF echo signals centered in frequency at the band center of the IF amplifier. The minimum requirement is that the resulting IF signals for each pulse should fall somewhere within the radar's IF bandwidth. This is achieved in frequency-agile magnetron search radars by applying a frequency readout voltage from the dither tuning system at the time of each newly transmitted pulse for coarse setting of a *voltage-controlled oscillator* (VCO). A block diagram is shown in Fig. 9.1. Coarse

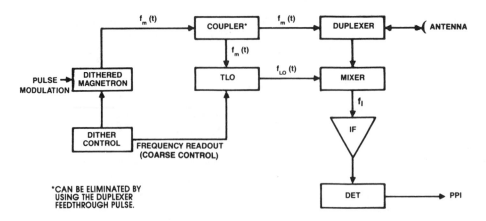

Fig. 9.1 Dithered Frequency-Agile Radar

frequency setting is followed by *automatic frequency control* (AFC) to acquire the frequency of the transmitter. The VCO setting is then held during the interpulse period to serve as the LO until transmission of the next pulse. The term *tracking local oscillator* (TLO) has been used to describe the circuitry that acquires and holds the frequency of each transmitted pulse. We should note that the TLO tracks the transmitted pulse frequency, not the RF phase. A dithered frequency-agile magnetron radar with TLO tracking does not retain coherence between transmitted and received pulses. Furthermore, the resulting transmitted pulses, while spread in frequency, are not stepped with sufficient precision in frequency for synthetic HRR processing. Requirements for HRR, SAR, and ISAR are thus *not* met by conventional frequency-agile radar techniques using dithered magnetrons and a TLO. Frequency-agile magnetron radar techniques are discussed in more depth by Barton [1].

The desired coherence between transmitted and received pulses, while not achieved for conventional frequency-agile magnetron radars, has been possible for many years with fixed-frequency magnetron radars. The technique is called *coherent-on-receive*. This refers to a method of achieving phase coherence between transmitted and received pulses with noncoherent radar systems. The technique was developed during World War II [2] to provide *moving target indication* (MTI) with magnetron radars. Suitable power amplifiers were not available during that time at the microwave frequencies required for many surveillance applications. The coherent-on-receive radar illustrated in Fig. 9.2 works as follows: a *coherent* (local) *oscillator* (COHO) is phase-locked, pulse to pulse, to the difference in frequency between the transmitted pulse and a *stable local oscillator* (STALO). The COHO continues to oscillate at this frequency during the

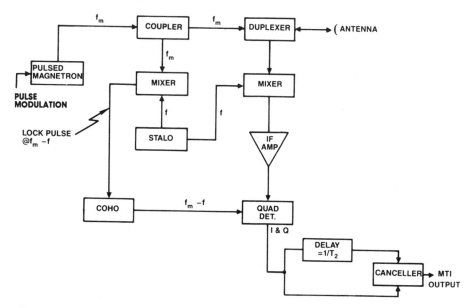

Fig. 9.2 Coherent-on-Receive MTI Radar

interpulse interval associated with each transmitted pulse. The COHO is then relocked to the next magnetron pulse. Echo pulses are mixed with the STALO to produce an IF signal, which is amplified, then mixed with the COHO in a quadrature mixer to baseband. The coherent-on-receive capability can be understood by noting that both the COHO signal for each transmitted pulse and the resulting IF echo signal are down-conversions from the same two signal sources, the magnetron and STALO. Echo IF phase relative to the COHO is ideally determined only by echo delay. Echo IF deviation from the COHO frequency is ideally determined only by target velocity relative to target. MTI is provided by a pulse-to-pulse cancellation loop, illustrated in Fig. 9.2.

Historically, then, magnetron radars have existed for a considerable time that are either frequency-agile or coherent-on-receive, but not both. Nonetheless, both features are required for HRR and image processing. At this point, our discussion will proceed to the techniques that are expected to be required to achieve a stepped-frequency, coherent-on-receive capability when using the available pulsed magnetron oscillator designs. Then, in order to illustrate several of the basic concepts of synthetic processing, we will assess the required magnetron frequency control accuracy *versus* signature fidelity and target size. Finally, some practical design problems associated with synthetic ISAR will be illustrated in terms of available PRF and pulsewidth parameters for pulsed magnetron radars.

9.3 STEPPED-FREQUENCY MAGNETRON IMAGING RADAR

The concept to be discussed here is a technique to measure the delay phase and amplitude of the series of target echoes resulting from precisely controlled, frequency-stepped magnetron pulses. The pulses from the magnetron are controlled so that their frequencies approximate $f_i = f_0 + \Delta f$, $i = 0, 1, 2, \ldots, n - 1$, where Δf is a fixed step size. Two possible methods to achieve magnetron frequency control are (1) by controlling the trigger time of frequency-dithered magnetrons and (2) by rapid tuning of electronically controlled magnetrons. The feedback technique for control used in each method employs a frequency discriminator to produce a frequency-sensing voltage for each frequency step. Methods for controlling the dithered magnetron will be suggested later in this chapter. Echo phase delay at each frequency step is obtained from the difference in phase between each sampled transmitted pulse and the corresponding sampled echo pulse. Transmitted and echo pulses are sampled at a baseband frequency produced by heterodyning down from the received carrier, using signals obtained from a stepped-frequency source. A precise clock, generated from the base frequency of the stepped-frequency source, establishes the range-delay sample position for each pulse. Echo phase delay and amplitude obtained from sampled quadrature data from each of a series of pulses can then be processed to generate target range profiles, SAR maps, and ISAR images. Three-dimensional, stepped-frequency monopulse images of targets could be generated as well. The concept to be discussed in the next section is a means to achieve stepped-frequency coherent processing using noncoherent magnetron radars when transmission starting time, phase, and frequency are not known precisely and there are limited PRF and pulsewidth options.

An earlier approach for obtaining high range resolution from magnetron radars is described by Ruttenberg and Chanzit [3]. In the Ruttenberg-Chanzit approach, a frequency-agile, coherent-on-receive method is used whereby echoes are summed in a recirculating delay line of delay equal to the radar's pulse repetition interval. The summed output is a high resolution response.

9.4 RESPONSE TO A SINGLE FIXED-POINT TARGET

The block diagram of a conceptual coherent-on-receive, frequency-agile radar appears in Fig. 9.3. Waveforms are given in Figs. 9.4 and 9.5. Frequency of the magnetron f_{mi} for each pulse is controlled to approximate the desired frequency f_i for each step. Control methods will be described later in this chapter. Phase of the echo pulse is measured for each frequency

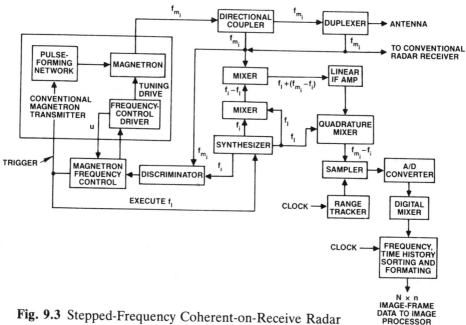

Fig. 9.3 Stepped-Frequency Coherent-on-Receive Radar

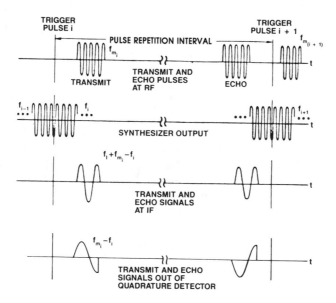

Fig. 9.4 Waveforms of Stepped-Frequency, Coherent-on-Receive Radar

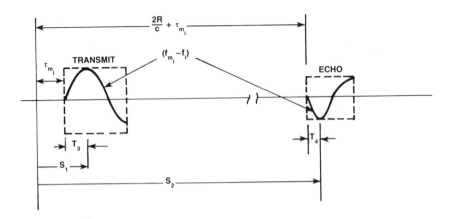

Fig. 9.5 Quadrature-Detected Waveforms for a Single Fixed Target at Range *R*

step from $i = 0$ to $i = n - 1$ of each burst. Echo phase is the phase of the quadrature-detected transmitted pulse signal subtracted from the quadrature-detected echo pulse signal at delay $2R/c$ for a target at range R, where c is the propagation velocity. Quadrature-detected outputs for nonmoving targets are not at zero frequency, as for a coherent transmitter, except for the unlikely situation where $f_{mi} = f_i$. A fixed-range target is assumed, whereas velocity correction would be required for moving targets. Transmission and echo phase are obtained from the two in-phase and quadrature sample pairs produced by two sample gates, which occur at S_1 and S_2 seconds, respectively, from the main trigger pulse. The sample gate at S_1 occurs T_3 seconds after the leading edge of the transmitted pulse. The sample gate at S_2 occurs T_4 seconds after the leading edge of the echo pulse arrives at the radar receiver. The quantity τ_{mi} is the delay from a start pulse to the leading edge of the transmitted pulse, produced by a magnetron at frequency step i. Subtraction of the transmitted phase from the received phase is carried out digitially by a *digitial mixer*. Echo and transmission phase for a point target at fixed range R, as seen by the quadrature detector at sample points S_2 and S_1, respectively, are

$$(\phi_i)_2 = -2\pi f_i S_2 + 2\pi f_{mi} \left[S_2 - \left(\frac{2R}{c} + \tau_{mi} \right) \right]$$

and

$$(\phi_i)_1 = -2\pi f_i S_1 + 2\pi f_{mi} [S_1 - \tau_{mi}]$$

The phase difference at frequency step i is

$$\psi_i = (\phi_i)_2 - (\phi_i)_1 = -2\pi f_i(S_2 - S_1) + 2\pi f_{mi}\left[(S_2 - S_1) - \frac{2R}{c}\right]$$

Sample positions S_1 and S_2 can be expressed as

$$S_2 = \frac{2R}{c} + \tau_{mi} + T_4$$

and

$$S_1 = \tau_{mi} + T_3$$

so that

$$S_2 - S_1 = \frac{2R}{c} + T_4 - T_3$$

where $T_4 - T_3$ is the sampling offset from transmitting to receiving. The measured echo phase relative to transmitted phase then becomes

$$\psi_i = -2\pi f_i\left(\frac{2R}{c} + T_4 - T_3\right) + 2\pi f_{mi}(T_4 - T_3)$$

$$= -2\pi f_i\frac{2R}{c} + 2\pi(T_4 - T_3)(f_{mi} - f_i) \qquad (9.1)$$

where f_i is the synthesizer frequency and f_{mi} is the transmitted frequency, respectively, at each frequency step i. Figure 9.6 illustrates the generation of the transmission and echo phase quantities. Figure 9.7 tracks phase relationships throughout the entire process.

The output of the digital mixer shown in Fig. 9.7 for a nonmoving point target, from (5.3) of Chapter 5, will be the echo function:

$$G_i = A_i e^{j\psi_i} \qquad (9.2)$$

where A_i is the amplitude at frequency step i, and

$$\psi_i = (\phi_i)_2 - (\phi_i)_1$$

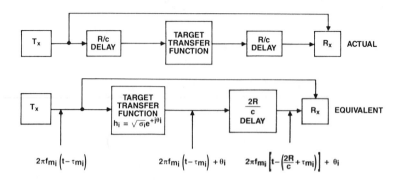

Fig. 9.6 Functional Block Diagram and Phase Relationships for a Stepped-Frequency, Coherent-on-Receive Radar

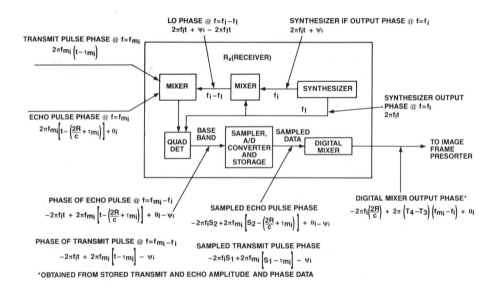

Fig. 9.7 Detailed Phase Relationships for Stepped-Frequency Coherent-on-Receive Radar

With flat amplitude response and a point target, $A_i = A$ for all i. A range-extended target comprised of multiple scatterers will alter the resulting echo phase and amplitude so that the output from the digital mixer is

$$G_i = A \ e^{j\psi_i} \cdot \sqrt{\sigma_i} \ e^{+j\theta_i} \tag{9.3}$$

where $h_i = \sqrt{\sigma_i} \ e^{+j\theta_i}$ is the echo transfer function of the target at frequency step i. Thus, (9.3) for a range-extended target becomes

$$G_i = A \ \sqrt{\sigma_i} \ e^{j(\psi_i + \theta_i)}$$

By substituting ψ_i from (9.1), we obtain

$$G_i = A\sqrt{\sigma_i} \exp j \left[-2\pi f_i \frac{2R}{c} + 2\pi(T_4 - T_3)(f_{m_i} - f_i) + \theta_i \right] \tag{9.4}$$

where $A\sqrt{\sigma_i}$ is the relative amplitude at frequency step i. The echo transfer amplitude $\sqrt{\sigma_i}$ and phase θ_i are independent of range R.

9.5   SYNTHETIC RANGE-PROFILE DISTORTION

Distortion of synthetic range profiles, as we saw in Chapter 5, is produced by random deviation (error) from precise synthesized frequencies $f_i = f_0 + i\Delta f$. Additional distortion is produced in a coherent-on-receive system by random fluctuations in magnetron frequency f_{m_i}. Phase error produced by magnetron frequency deviation $f_{m_i} - f_i$ from (9.1) is the deviation multiplied by $2\pi(T_4 - T_3)$, where $T_4 - T_3 \ll 2R/c$. By contrast, phase error produced by synthesized frequency deviation from f_i is the deviation times $2\pi(2R/c)$ associated with the total range delay extent $2R/c$. Thus, tolerance to random pulse-to-pulse frequency fluctuations of the magnetron is much higher than to random pulse-to-pulse frequency fluctuations of the synthesized frequencies. Distortion due to random frequency fluctuation will now be analyzed, starting with range-profile distortion.

The synthetic range profile H_l *versus* l of a single point target at range R is obtained from the series of n complex echo signals G_i, $i = 0, 1, 2, \ldots, n - 1$. From the inverse discrete Fourier transform, we obtain

$$H_l = \frac{1}{n} \sum_{i=0}^{n-1} G_i \ e^{j(2\pi/n)li}, \ 0 \le l \le n - 1 \tag{9.5}$$

where, from (9.1) and (9.2) with $A_i = 1$ for all i, we have

$$G_i = \exp j \left[-2\pi f_i \frac{2R}{c} + 2\pi(T_4 - T_3)(f_{m_i} - f_i) \right] \qquad (9.6)$$

The synthesizer frequency f_i is stepped Δf in frequency on each pulse, so that

$$f_i = f_0 + i\Delta f$$

9.5.1 Ideal System

In a stepped-frequency system, free of either magnetron frequency fluctuation or sampling offset, (9.6) becomes

$$G_i = \exp j \left[-2\pi(f_0 + i\Delta f) \frac{2R}{c} \right] \qquad (9.7)$$

Phase of the sampled data for the ideal system does not contain the random phase error term $+ 2\pi(T_4 - T_3) \cdot (f_{m_i} - f_i)$.

By substituting (9.7) into (9.5), we can show (see Chapter 5) that the magnitude of the normalized synthetic range profile is given by (5.7):

$$|H_l| = \left| \frac{\sin \pi y}{n \sin \frac{\pi}{n} y} \right| \qquad (9.8)$$

where

$$y = \frac{-2n\Delta f R}{c} + l$$

This is the synthetic range profile of a single point target when frequency and sampling errors are zero. The effect of random frequency fluctuation of the frequency synthesizer on a target's range profile was found in Chapter 5 to be small at radar ranges of common interest for random frequency fluctuation associated with commonly available synthesizers.

Next, we will analyze two additional sources of distortion that are produced by magnetron frequency fluctuation: *random phase error* associated with *target range extent* and random phase error associated with *range-sample delay offset*. First, we will examine distortion for the case of a single point target.

9.5.2 Random Phase Error for Point Targets

To examine the effect of phase error produced by frequency fluctuation on the synthetic range profile of a point target, (9.6) is rewritten in the form of (5.10) as

$$G_i = \exp j \left[-2\pi f_i \frac{2R}{c} - vx_i \right] \qquad (9.9)$$

where vx_i is random phase error produced by frequency error x_i. For random error $(x_i)_s$ in the synthesizer frequency f_i, the resulting random phase error will be $-2\pi(2R/c) \cdot (x_i)_s$. Thus, v is associated with the synthesizer and defined to be $v_s = 2\pi \cdot 2R/c$.

For random error $(x_i)_m$ in the magnetron frequency f_{m_i}, the resulting random phase error will be $2\pi(T_4 - T_3) \cdot (x_i)_m$ for $(x_i)_m \gg (x_i)_s$. Thus, v associated with sampling offset in range delay is defined to be $v_r = -2\pi\delta S$, where $\delta S = T_4 - T_3$ is the range-delay offset.

9.5.3 Random Phase Error for Extended Targets

The third source of phase error is associated with the target itself. This is produced by random changes in the target transfer function term $\sqrt{\sigma_i} \exp (+j\theta_i)$ of (9.4) produced by frequency error of the magnetron pulses. Changes in the transfer function are caused by deviation of interscatterer delay phase from that which occurs when the frequencies are separated by precisely Δf. The effect becomes more severe for targets of large range extent. However, the transfer function is not changed at all if the target contains only one scatterer.

Echo phase error associated with target range-delay extent will be expressed similarly to total range delay. Consider first the delay phase that would be measured for a point target. This phase, from (9.1), is measured relative to the synthesizer signal at frequency f_i, independently of the magnetron signal frequency if samples S_1 and S_2 of Fig. 9.5 are set exactly at the centers of the transmitted and received pulses, respectively. The only phase error is $-2\pi \cdot 2R/c \cdot (x_i)_s$ produced by random frequency error of the synthesizer. Now, consider the delay phase from the sample position to a scatterer near either edge of the target echo pulse in Fig. 9.8. Note that this delay phase is measured with reference to the magnetron's transmitted pulse at frequency f_{m_i}. For random error $(x_i)_m$ of the magnetron frequency, the resulting random phase error will be $2\pi \cdot d/c \cdot (x_i)_m$. Thus, ν associated with target range extent d is defined to be $\nu_d = -2\pi \cdot d/c$.

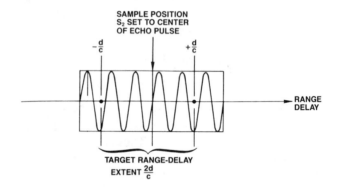

Fig. 9.8 Echo Pulse from a Target of Range-Extent d

9.5.4 Three Types of Random Phase Error (Summary)

Random error in the synthesizer frequency will produce phase errors associated with target range delay $2R/c$. Random error in magnetron frequency also produces a similar type of phase error, but one that is associated only with the range extent of the target itself. A related type of phase error produced by magnetron random frequency error is that associated with the relative sampling delay offset $\delta S = T_4 - T_3$ between transmission and echo pulse sample positions. These three types of phase error are listed in Table 9.1 along with their respective characteristic functions, which are to be discussed below.

It is significant to note that for the design of Fig. 9.3: (1) magnetron random frequency error does not produce any phase error related to total range delay, and (2) if both the transmitted and echo pulses were sampled at exactly the same delay position along the pulse, the only phase error produced by magnetron frequency error would be that associated with target range extent. For a single point target, however, no phase error due to magnetron frequency error would occur at all.

Table 9.1 Summary of Random Echo Phase Error and Resulting
Characteristic Functions

Type of Random Echo Phase Error	Phase Error	Characteristic Function, C_f
Random frequency error $(x_i)_s$, of synthesizer output signal related to target range R.	$-2\pi \cdot \dfrac{2R}{c} \cdot (x_i)_s$	$e^{-\nu_s^2(\sigma_s^2/2)}$ where $\nu_s = 2\pi \cdot \dfrac{2R}{c}$
Random frequency error $(x_i)_m$, of magnetron pulses related to target range extent, d.	$2\pi \cdot \dfrac{d}{c}(x_i)_m$	$e^{-\nu_d^2(\sigma_m^2/2)}$ where $\nu_d = -2\pi \dfrac{d}{c}$
Random frequency error $(x_i)_m$, of magnetron pulses related to relative sampling delay offset δS between transmitted and echo pulse.	$2\pi\delta S(x_i)_m$	$e^{-\nu_r^2(\sigma_m^2/2)}$ where $\nu_r = -2\pi\delta S$

9.5.5   Effect on Peaks and Nulls of the Profile

As we saw in Chapter 5, the synthetic range profile observed when random frequency error is present is the same as for the error-free case, except that the resulting phase errors reduce the peak value of the range profile. If we assume a normal probability distribution of magnetron frequency error, the expected value $E[H_l(x_i)]$ of the peaks is reduced by the factor C_f, which is the characteristic function listed in Table 9.1. Positions of the peaks and nulls remain undisturbed in this case.

9.5.6   Tolerance to Frequency Error

Tolerable values for the standard deviation σ of the frequency error will be calculated on the basis of $\nu\sigma = 1.0$ (-4.3 dB loss) for each type of phase noise. Tolerable values for the standard deviation σ_s of the synthesizer frequency related to target range were discussed in Chapter 5 and found to be easily met for most situations of likely interest. Tolerable values for the standard deviation of the magnetron frequency σ_m related to target range extent d is obtained from the requirement:

$$|\nu_d\,\sigma_m| = 2\pi \cdot \frac{d}{c} \cdot \sigma_m \leqslant 1.0$$

By solving for the tolerable standard deviation, we obtain

$$\sigma_m \leqslant \frac{1.0}{2\pi \cdot \dfrac{d}{c}} \leqslant \frac{1.0}{2\pi \cdot \dfrac{d(\mathrm{m})}{3 \times 10^8\ (\mathrm{m/s})}}$$

Tolerable deviation becomes smaller as the target range extent becomes larger. Tolerable deviation and minimum required frequency step size Δf as a function of slant-range extent d is shown in Table 9.2. Tolerable magnetron frequency deviation is seen to be approximately one-third of the frequency step size.

Table 9.2 Tolerable Standard Deviation of Magnetron Frequency *versus* Target Range Extent

$d(\mathrm{m})$	$\sigma_m(\mathrm{kHz})$	$\Delta f = \dfrac{c}{2d}\ (\mathrm{kHz})$	$\sigma_m/\Delta f$
60	796	2500	.32
200	239	750	.32
300	160	500	.32
600	80	250	.32

Tolerance of magnetron random frequency error related to sampling delay offset δS is computed from the requirement:

$$|\nu_r\sigma_m| = 2\pi\delta S\,\sigma_m \leqslant 1.0$$

so that

$$\sigma_m \leqslant \frac{1.0}{2\pi\delta S} \leqslant \frac{.159}{\delta S\ (\mathrm{s})} \leqslant \frac{159}{\delta S\ (\mu\mathrm{s})}\ (\mathrm{kHz})$$

Tolerable magnetron frequency deviation for several values of sampling delay offset are shown in Table 9.3.

Table 9.3 Tolerable Standard Deviation of Magnetron Frequency *versus* Sampling Delay Offset

δS (μs)	σ_m (kHz)
0.1	1590
0.5	320
1.0	160
5.0	32

Sampling time offset will not likely exceed the transmitted pulsewidth. Assume, for example, a pulsewidth of 1.0 μs. Tolerable magnetron deviation σ_m then is 160 kHz.

9.6 MAGNETRON FREQUENCY CONTROL

Pulse-to-pulse frequency deviation for fixed-frequency magnetrons is typically quoted as about 15 kHz rms for coaxial magnetrons and 100 kHz for conventional magnetrons (σ_m = 15 kHz and 100 kHz, respectively). These values presumably apply for single-frequency operation and modulation pulses having no pulse-to-pulse ripple. If so, the numbers represent inherent frequency deviation expected of magnetrons, independent of modulator and frequency-control characteristics. These deviations are well below the 160 kHz rms tolerable deviation derived above for 300 m targets or 1.0 μs delay offset. For stepped-frequency operation, in Fig. 9.3, random error in magnetron frequency *versus* frequency readout voltage u would introduce an additional source of magnetron frequency uncertainty.

Frequency accuracy commonly quoted for frequency-agile magnetrons is usually several MHz, but such quoted values are likely to be absolute values, which include drift, voltage measurement error, and deviations associated with applications that do not require greater precision. By using constant calibration referenced to precise synthesizer-generated signals, we would expect that magnetron frequency deviation could be held to values near the inherent deviation of fixed-frequency magnetrons.

Illustrated on the left-hand side of Fig. 9.3 is one possible approach for automatically generating an updated readout voltage for each frequency step f_i. These voltages then become new trigger thresholds to the magnetron *pulse-forming network* (PFN) at precise Δf steps in synchronism with the synthesizer. Burst-by-burst correction of trigger threshold is shown in Table 9.4. The magnetron frequency-control unit triggers both the magnetron to fire and the synthesizer to step in frequency to f_i when magnetron frequency readout voltage u reaches the ith stored value of u_i corresponding to f_i. Inaccuracy or drift of frequency readout voltage u *versus* magnetron frequency f_m is automatically corrected by adjusting stored u_i *versus* f_i values from burst to burst. Correction values δf_i are derived from the frequency error voltage of the discriminator. Values of δf_i are converted to the equivalent values of δu_i. The new threshold voltage $u_i + \delta u_i$ will then be used as a threshold for the f_i step when the next burst arrives.

A hypothetical magnetron frequency *versus* readout voltage curve is shown in Fig. 9.9. The data on the curve would be stored in the frequency control unit. Data would be updated for each burst (two bursts, one up and one down for each dither cycle). The stepping action is indicated in Fig. 9.10. For some frequency-agile magnetrons, magnetron frequency is controlled by a free running motor. The synthesizer burst rate* for these magnetrons would require synchronization to the dither frequency. With other magnetrons, frequency is controlled by a control voltage. Control voltage could be set by the synthesizer control to produce a frequency dither in synchronism with the burst rate.

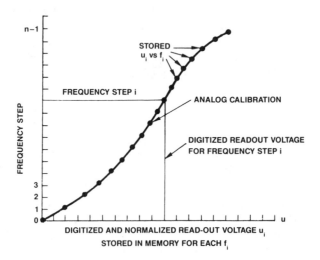

Fig. 9.9 Magnetron Frequency *versus* Readout Voltage (Hypothetical)

---

*Rate of up-burst or down-burst cycling is defined here as the *burst rate*. Each dither cycle produces one upward and one downward frequency burst.

Table 9.4 Burst-by-Burst Trigger Threshold Correction

Initial Trigger Threshold Settings u_i versus f_i	Frequency Errors Measured During First Burst	Equivalent Readout Voltage Errors	New Trigger Threshold Settings	Frequency Errors Measured During Second Burst	Equivalent Readout Voltage Errors	New Trigger Threshold Settings	et cetera
$f_i \quad u_i$	δf_i	δu_i	$u_i = u_i + \delta u_i$	$\delta' f_i$	$\delta' u_i$	$u_i = u_i + \delta u_i + \delta' u_i$	$\cdots$
$f_1 \quad u_1$	δf_1	δu_1	$u_1 + \delta u_1$	$\delta' f_1$	$\delta' u_1$	$u_1 + \delta u_1 + \delta' u_1$	$\cdots$
$f_2 \quad u_2$	δf_2	δu_2	$u_2 + \delta u_2$	$\delta' f_2$	$\delta' u_2$	$u_2 + \delta u_2 + \delta' u_2$	$\cdots$
$f_3 \quad u_3$	δf_3	δu_3	$u_3 + \delta u_3$	$\delta' f_3$	$\delta' u_3$	$u_3 + \delta u_3 + \delta' u_3$	$\cdots$
$\vdots$	$\vdots$						$\vdots$
$f_n \quad u_n$	δf_n	δu_n	$u_n + \delta u_n$	$\delta' f_n$	$\delta' u_n$	$u_n + \delta u_n + \delta' u_n$	$\cdots$

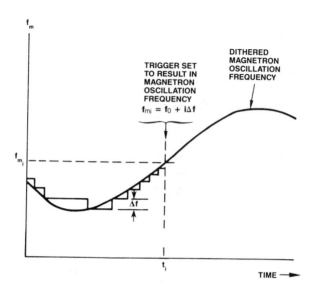

Fig. 9.10 PRF Trigger-Time Determination

9.7 ADDITIONAL SYSTEM CONSIDERATIONS

9.7.1 Intrapulse FM

In the technique described above, the magnetron frequency is changed during each pulse, but constant frequency during the pulse was assumed for calculation of the tolerable frequency error. *Intrapulse frequency modulation* would produce no additional phase error, and thus no additional distortion of the range profile if the FM slope were identical for each frequency step. Were the FM slope to undergo significant random change, restrictions should be placed on the step-to-step sampling timing error $\delta S = T_4 - T_3$. No known data exist on the random characteristics of intrapulse FM slope. The effect is not considered to be significant with respect to performance.

9.7.2 Effect of Frequency Error on Cross-Range Doppler

Cross-range Doppler frequencies are generated by target aspect motion relative to the radar. The cross-range Doppler profile is extracted in each synthetic slant-range cell for ISAR imaging by use of a second transform carried out in each slant-range cell of the series of synthetic range profiles. Any average burst-to-burst phase error produced by frequency error would probably be indistinguishable from error due to target slant-range motion and could be corrected in the velocity correction process. However, remaining uncorrected is burst-to-burst random phase error at any frequency step. Because linear processes are involved, the two series of transforms that produce an ISAR image can be interchanged without affecting the resulting image. Thus, after velocity correction, Doppler spectra could be obtained first, followed by the range profiles. If thought of in this way, the source of cross-range *profile* distortion is random burst-to-burst phase error, rather than random pulse-to-pulse phase error as discussed above for slant-range profile distortion. Unless the random pulse-to-pulse frequency error differs significantly from burst-to-burst error, the cross-range distortion may be expected to be equivalent to range distortion in the ISAR image.

9.7.3 PRF, Frequency, Bandwidth, Pulsewidth, and Dwell Time

The relationship of the PRF, frequency, bandwidth, pulsewidth, and dwell time parameters to image quality and target size was described in Chapter 7. The use of magnetron transmitters does not affect these relationships. Magnetrons, however, are inherently high-peak-power, short-pulse devices. This tends to run contrary to requirements for ISAR imaging of ship targets, where pulse length, when matched by receiver bandwidth, must entirely cover the ship's expected range-delay extent and the PRF must be high enough to produce an adequately large set of n range cells by N cross-range cells during some limited dwell time T. However, we can show that the high-peak-power, short-pulse characteristics of the magnetron do not preclude its use for imaging large targets such as ships. The echo pulses can be *stretched* when they arrive back at the receiver by passing them through a filter of bandwidth equal (matched) to the reciprocal of the desired pulsewidth. In other words, the receiver is deliberately mismatched to the transmitted pulse. The effect would be as if the transmitted pulse were stretched by the same filter response at the magnetron output. Consider operation for a 200 m target. The frequency deviation of the magnetron, from Table 9.2 (based on $v_d \sigma_m \leq 1.0$) must be held to $\sigma_m \leq 239$ kHz for a target of this size to avoid excess phase noise. Receiver bandwidth to pass the echo signal, therefore, can be narrowed to no less than about $2\sigma_m$. For targets of range extent d, the minimum stretched pulsewidth required is given approximately by

$$T_1 = \frac{2d}{c}$$

The receiver bandwidth to match T_1 for a 200 m target is

$$\beta = \frac{1}{T_1}$$

$$= \frac{c}{2d}$$

$$= \frac{3 \times 10^8}{2 \times 200}$$

$$= 750 \text{ kHz}$$

which is adequate bandwidth to cover the expected magnetron deviation of $2\sigma_m = 478$ kHz with very little loss. As another example, a 1.0 μs pulse into a receiver of 500 kHz bandwidth (before sampling) would be stretched to 2.0 μs by the deliberate mismatch, and could then integrate the echo energy from an entire ship up to 300 m in range extent.

The average PRF for N bursts of n pulses must meet the following criteria:

$$\text{PRF} \geqslant \frac{N \times n}{T}$$

and at center frequency $\bar{f}$:

$$\text{PRF} \geqslant n\beta_D = \frac{2n}{c} \omega w_c \bar{f}$$

where T is the target image data-collection time (frame time), β_D is the Doppler bandwidth, ω is the highest angular rotation rate (angular frequency), and w_c is the cross-range window. Optimal frame time to produce good imagery is dependent on target pitch, roll, and yaw motion and the radar frequency. A rule of thumb for ship targets seems to be that $T = 0.5$–1.0 s at 10 GHz and 2.5–5 s at 3 GHz. For a 2000-element image generated from 1.0 s of data, the minimum PRF based on the first PRF criterion is given by

$$\text{PRF(min)} = \frac{2000}{1.0}$$

$$= 2000 \text{ pps}$$

The second PRF criterion sets the minimum PRF that is adequate to sample the maximum expected rotation-produced Doppler spectrum of the signal. With the destroyer target example from Chapter 7, the worst-case sea-state conditions of Table 7.3 produced a roll rate of 6.3°/s. For an exposed height of 30 m above the center-of-rotation axis (rotation axis at or below the surface), the minimum PRF required at a center frequency of 5.4 GHz is

$$\text{PRF} = n\beta_D$$

$$= n\,\frac{2}{3 \times 10^8} \cdot 6.3 \cdot \frac{2\pi}{360} \cdot 30 \cdot 5.4 \times 10^9$$

$$= n \cdot (119)\ \text{pps}$$

for n pulses per burst. When PRF is limited by transmitter duty cycle or other design factors, this worst-case condition can be handled by reducing the number of pulses n per burst, thereby degrading resolution in slant range, cross range, or both for a given slant-range by cross-range window.

A lower PRF at the same resolution and window size may be possible by use of *thinning* (i.e., by skipping some frequency steps). We should also note that range ambiguity associated with a higher PRF for targets at long range might not be a significant problem for ISAR processing. Target location could be determined before imaging at a lower PRF while still in the radar's surveillance mode. For a limited PRF, the available $n \times N$ pixels from the N bursts of n pulses can be set just to cover the target's slant-range by cross-range space. In this way, the available pixels are not wasted on slant-range by cross-range space where there is no target. Note that range-only or 3-D images may be generated from a single burst so that much lower PRFs can be used than in the case of ISAR imaging.

9.7.4 Illustrative Application

Consider conversion of a hypothetical surface-search magnetron radar to incorporate an imaging mode. Conversion could be achieved by replacing an existing fixed-tuned magnetron with a frequency-agile magnetron and the required frequency control, processing, and display. Typical parameters for a converted shipboard surface-search radar system operating in the imaging mode might be as given in Table 9.5.

Table 9.5   Hypothetical Magnetron Radar Parameters
for ISAR Imaging

Lower End of Frequency Band f = 5.4 GHz
Bandwidth (max) $n\Delta f$ = 225 MHz
Average PRF $1/T_2$ = 2000 pps
Pulsewidth T_1 = 0.5 μs (stretched in receiver to ~ 2.0 μs)
Duty Cycle T_1/T_2 = 0.001 μs

Dither Rate (max) $\dot{D}$ = 50 Hz

Step size Δf, number of steps n, bandwidth $n\Delta f$, dither rate $\dot{D}$, and dwell time T in the imaging mode could be varied by the radar operator to provide maximum resolution over the slant-range and cross-range extent of the target for each encountered target type. For example, in an ISAR mode against a long ship target observed from either bow or stern aspect, the target would be observed with many small frequency steps at a low dither rate.* This would provide the best resolution over both the large range extent and the small height extent. This is achieved by avoiding wasted Doppler coverage beyond the relatively narrow height extent of the target by *unsquaring* the range *versus* cross-range coverage. Performance results are predicted in Table 9.6 for operator step size and burst size adjusted for *square resolution* when viewing a large and small ship target for which aspect rotational motion produces 2.0 m and 0.67 m resolution, respectively.

PROBLEMS

9.1   A *radar master oscillator* (RMO) of a coherent radar system provides RF pulses to the input of a traveling-wave-tube amplifier used as a pulse-radar transmitter. The RMO also provides the reference signal to a quadrature detector to mix the echo signal to baseband from a suitable intermediate frequency. The frequency of the RMO shifts by one part in 10^9 during the echo delay associated with a target at 250 nmi (463 km). What is the rms phase error of the quadrature-detected signal produced by the frequency shift if the radar operates at 3.2 GHz?

---

*Actual dither rate might be set at the maximum rate. The effective rate could be reduced by processing samples from two or more dither cycles.

Table 9.6 Example of Operator Settings and Resulting ISAR Performance Against a Ship Target for Hypothetical Surface-Search Radar Parameters, from Table 9.5 ($\Delta r = \Delta r_s = \Delta r_c$)

Parameter	Symbol	Bow or Stern Aspect of Large Ship[1]	Broadside Aspect of Large Ship[1]	Bow or Stern Aspect of Small Ship[1]	Broadside Aspect of Small Ship[1]
OPERATOR SETTINGS					
Target Dwell Time	T	1.0 s	1.0 s	1.0 s	1.0 s
Pixels per Frame	$nN = \dfrac{T}{T_2}$	2000	2000	2000	2000
Number of Frequency Steps per Burst	n (see note 1)	100	20	100	20
Number of Bursts per Dwell	N (see note 1)	20	100	20	100
Required Step Size	$\Delta f = \dfrac{c}{2n\Delta r}$	0.75 MHz	3.75 MHz	2.25 MHz	11.25 MHz
Dither Rate (effective)	$\check{D} = \dfrac{N}{2T}$	10 Hz	50 Hz	10 Hz	50 Hz
Bandwidth	$n\Delta f$	75 MHz	75 MHz	225 MHz	225 MHz

Table 9.6 (cont'd)

Parameter		Symbol	Bow or Stern Aspect of Large Ship[1]	Broadside Aspect of Large Ship[1]	Bow or Stern Aspect of Small Ship[1]	Broadside Aspect of Small Ship[1]
PERFORMANCE	Slant-Range Resolution	Δr_s	2.0 m	2.0 m	0.67 m	0.67 m
	Cross-Range Resolution[2]	Δr_c	2.0 m	2.0 m	0.67 m	0.67 m
	Unambiguous Slant-Range Extent	$\dfrac{c}{2\Delta f}$	200 m	40 m	67 m	13 m
	Unambiguous Cross-Range Extent	$N\Delta r_c$	40 m	200 m	13 m	67 m

Notes:
[1] Length-to-width and length-to-height scale factor both assumed to be 5:1, so that n/N = 5:1 or 1:5 as required.
[2] Assumes target-aspect rotation rates that produce Δr_c = 2.0 m and 0.67 m resolution, respectively, for a large or small ship during the 1.0 s image frame time. Higher rotation rates can produce cross-range fold-over for these settings. Lower rotation rates reduce resolution.

9.2   Target echo pulses from the single-frequency, coherent-on-receive radar of Fig. 9.2 are sampled at the output of the quadrature detector. The MTI canceller is not used. Pulse-to-pulse frequency error in the COHO output is 100 Hz rms. A target detection is based on the output of the discrete Fourier transform of each burst of n samples (one complex sample per pulse). (a) What is the rms phase error of received pulses caused by the COHO frequency error for targets at a range of 150 nmi (277.8 km)? (b) What is the resulting loss in input signal-to-phase noise ratio?

9.3   Standard deviation of the pulse-to-pulse frequency of the magnetron in Fig. 9.3 from the desired uniform frequency steps produced by the frequency synthesizer is 0.5 MHz. (a) If in-phase and quadrature samples are taken at the centers of each transmitted and echo pulse at baseband, without sampling-delay error, what is the attenuation for scatterers seen in the resulting synthetic-range profile ± 50 m from the target center? (b) What is the attenuation for scatterers seen at the center of the target? Assume that the center of the echo pulse corresponds to the target center.

REFERENCES

1.   Barton, D.K., ed.,"Frequency Agility and Diversity," *Radars*, Vol. 6, Dedham, MA: Artech House, 1977.

2.   Barton, D.K., *Radar System Analysis,* Dedham, MA: Artech House, 1976, pp. 191–195.

3.   Ruttenberg, K., and L. Chanzit, "High Range Resolution by Means of Pulse-to-Pulse Frequency Shifting," *IEEE EASCON Record,* 1968, pp. 47–51.

Chapter 10

Applications for Surveillance and Countermeasures

The main emphasis of this book has been the use of wideband, high resolution radar for mapping and imaging. Other benefits and additional applications for improved surveillance in countermeasures environments will be discussed in this chapter. Items to be covered are as follows:

1. Electronic counter-countermeasures (ECCM),
2. Low-flyer detection,
3. Low probability of intercept radar (LPIR),
4. Reduced target fluctuation loss,
5. Small-target detection in clutter.

The importance of radar bandwidth and range-Doppler resolution to achieve these benefits has been well known by the radar community for many years. More recently, the ability to carry out coherent and noncoherent processing at up to 500 MHz of bandwidth and beyond has created new opportunities and renewed interest.

During the 1970s and 1980s, new challenges in terms of surveillance requirements and expected countermeasures environments emerged, which necessitated a re-examination of fundamental approaches to military radar designs. *Jamming,* while always a serious threat, became more formidable. The need for virtually undetectable radar surveillance, called *low probability of intercept radar* (LPIR), after years of controversy, finally became recognized as both necessary and feasible for some surveillance applications. Extremely low flying missiles, difficult to detect with radar, became a trend for some important air-to-surface attack roles, such as antiship attack. Aircraft and missiles with greatly reduced radar cross section became feasible and requirements for reduced signature came to be strongly emphasized for most new designs. Furthermore, surveillance coverage had to be extended for early warning, while retaining high target-revisit rates for close-in surveillance. The role of increased radar resolution and bandwidth, although long recognized as crucial for some of these surveillance tasks, has now become more fully appreciated. To meet these challenges, it is possible that future radar systems will operate over very wide bandwidths with multiple transmitting and receiving beams, which would provide more surveillance information via increased target dwell time without sacrificing target-revisit rate.

By contrast, conventional radar designs today commonly use single-beam scanning, whether the antennas are electronically steered or mechanically scanned, and waveforms are commonly narrowband, although radar operating bandwidth is often quite wide. Performance for conventional designs in the past had been improved by increasing transmitter power, useable antenna gain, and clutter cancellation, or by reducing system noise factor, antenna sidelobes, and system loss. Unfortunately, the improvement made possible by these means has approached its useful limits. On the other hand, there has been limited exploitation of increased resolution and associated information content, which could be produced by processing wideband signal data over extended dwell times. This chapter will illustrate the role of radar bandwidth and resolution for improving surveillance performance to meet some existing and likely future surveillance challenges.

10.1 ELECTRONIC COUNTER-COUNTERMEASURES (ECCM)

The term *electronic countermeasures* (ECM) commonly refers to a broad range of electronic methods used to deny an enemy the full use of its electromagnetic assets. The use of some type of RF jamming signal is the most well known ECM technique. *Electronic counter-countermeasures* (ECCM) usually refers to methods employed to offset ECM so that electromagnetic equipment, in a particular radar, can operate in an expected ECM environment. Antiradar jammers typically attempt to reduce radar sensitivity by radiating energy into the radar receiver via the radar antenna's main-beam, sidelobes, or both. The radar designer has at his or her disposal a number of methods to provide ECCM, including *high radar power, beam agility, sidelobe cancellation* and *sidelobe blanking, special waveforms,* and *power management.* Our discussion will primarily deal with the improved ECCM performance provided by increased radar bandwidth.

Radar designers and users are well aware of the advantage of a wide-bandwidth capability to provide improved resistance to jamming and other countermeasures. An enemy jammer is least effective, all else being equal, when the radar is able to transmit rapidly and randomly over a wide bandwidth of frequencies, while maintaining a very narrow receiver bandwidth. This forces an enemy to spread its available jammer power over the radar's wide transmitting bandwidth, thereby reducing the jammer signal entering the narrowband radar receiver. An ECCM performance factor P_E can thus be defined as follows:

$$P_E(\text{dB}) = 10 \log_{10} \left(\frac{P_t \beta_t}{\beta_n} \right) \tag{10.1}$$

where P_t is the radar's transmitter power, β_t is the transmitter's frequency-agile bandwidth, and β_n is the receiving system's noise bandwidth. As an example, for a hypothetical long-range search radar, $P_t = 100$ kW, $\beta_t = 200$ MHz, and $\beta_n = 10$ kHz (pulsewidth $= 100$ μs). Then,

$$P_E(\text{dB}) = 10 \log_{10} \frac{100 \cdot 10^3 \cdot 200 \cdot 10^6}{10 \cdot 10^3}$$

$$= 93$$

Likely parameters of a hypothetical, long-range, frequency-agile mode for target imaging with the same radar are $P_t = 100$ kW, $\beta_t = 200$ MHz, and $\beta_n = 1.0$ Hz. Then,

$$P_E(\text{dB}) = 10 \log_{10} (100 \cdot 10^3 \cdot 200 \cdot 10^6/1.0)$$
$$= 133$$

As measured by the suggested performance factor, expressed by (10.1), the above radar operating in a frequency-agile imaging mode can be seen to have a 40 dB advantage in ECCM over that in its conventional search mode using the same transmitting bandwidth and transmitter power. The advantage in this case occurs because of the narrow processing bandwidth of the imaging radar. Any complete ECCM evaluation for an actual radar would, of course, involve many other factors, including antenna sidelobe levels and expected jamming strategy.

A more complete, but still idealized, analysis of radar ECCM performance improvement *versus* radar bandwidth can be carried out in terms of an increase in *effective system noise factor* produced by jamming signals entering the radar receiver from a *noise jammer*. The analysis will be idealized by assuming that wideband jamming signals received are indistinguishable from other sources of radar system noise. Jamming equipment to be used against radars can be set up to transmit RF noise power over the radar's entire operating bandwidth, thereby trying to prevent the radar's operation over any portion of its frequency band. This type of jamming is called *noise jamming*. A radar capable of rapid change in operating frequency has the advantage that a countering noise jammer must spread its available power over the radar's entire frequency-agile bandwidth of operation, which will normally be much larger than the radar's receiving system noise bandwidth. The performance of a noise jamming countermeasure is commonly stated in terms of *effective radiated power* (ERP) per unit bandwidth, e.g., W/Hz, W/MHz, kW/MHz, *et cetera*. The ERP term takes into account the jammer *power,* jammer *antenna gain,* and jammer *radiating bandwidth.* Radar ECCM performance in terms of radar bandwidth and jammer ERP can be analyzed as follows by using the concept of effective system noise factor.

The free-space radar range equation, expressed by (2.3) in Chapter 2, can be written as

$$\left(\frac{S}{N}\right)_{in} = \frac{S}{kT_0\beta_n F} = \frac{(P_t G^2 \lambda^2 \sigma L)/[(4\pi)^3 R^4]}{kT_0\beta_n F} \qquad (10.2)$$

where F is the radar system noise factor (without jammer) and T_0 is the standard noise temperature (290 K assumed). The product FT_0 is the radar system noise temperature T_s.

The signal-to-noise ratio at the input to the radar receiver in a jamming environment is expressed as

$$\left(\frac{S}{N}\right)_{in} = \frac{S}{kT_0\beta_n F + N_J} \qquad (10.3)$$

where

S = the received echo signal power;
N_J = the received jammer power;
β_n = the radar's noise bandwidth;
kT_0 = Boltzmann's constant times standard noise temperature;
F = the radar system noise factor with no jamming signal present.

The jammer power received via the radar antenna sidelobes* at jammer-to-radar range R_J is

$$N_J = \frac{P_J G_J G_s \lambda^2 L_r}{\beta_t (4\pi)^2 R_J^2} \beta_n \qquad (10.4)$$

where

$P_J G_J / \beta_t$ = jammer's effective radiated power density (ERP per Hz) for jammer bandwidth matched to radar frequency-agile bandwidth β_t;

P_J = jammer transmitter power;
G_J = jammer antenna gain;
L_r = radar receiving system loss;
G_s = radar antenna sidelobe gain.

For simplicity, any jammer losses are assumed to be included in the terms P_J and G_J, and all radar system loss is assumed to arise from radar receiving system loss. The signal-to-noise ratio at the receiver input, from (10.3) and (10.4), then is

$$\left(\frac{S}{N}\right)_{in} = \frac{S}{kT_0\beta_n\left[F\left(1 + \dfrac{N_J}{kT_0\beta_n F}\right)\right]} = \frac{S}{kT_0\beta_n F_{eff}} \qquad (10.5)$$

where F_{eff} is the effective system noise factor of the radar system, which, using (10.4) with (10.5), is defined as

$$\begin{aligned}
F_{eff} &= F\left(1 + \frac{N_J}{kT_0\beta_n F}\right) \\
&= F\left(1 + \frac{P_J G_J G_s \lambda^2 L_r}{\beta_t(4\pi)^2 R_J^2 kT_0\beta_n F}\beta_n\right) \\
&= F + \frac{P_J G_J G_s}{\beta_t}\left(\frac{\lambda}{4\pi R_J}\right)^2 \frac{L_r}{kT_0} \qquad (10.6)
\end{aligned}$$

---

*Main-lobe jamming is not considered here.

For sidelobe jamming, the radar antenna sidelobe gain is

$$G_s = \begin{cases} G \cdot L_s & \text{(in the sidelobes)} \\ G \cdot L_s \cdot L_c & \text{(in the sidelobes after cancellation)} \end{cases}$$

where G is the main-lobe gain of the radar antenna, L_s is the radar antenna's sidelobe to main-lobe ratio, and L_c is the radar's sidelobe cancellation ratio (for radars employing sidelobe cancellation*). The input signal-to-noise ratio (10.2), written in terms of effective system noise factor, becomes

$$\left(\frac{S}{N}\right)_{\text{in}} = \frac{S}{kT_0\beta_nF_{\text{eff}}} = \frac{(P_tG^2\lambda^2\sigma L_r)/[(4\pi)^3R^4]}{kT_0\beta_nF_{\text{eff}}} \tag{10.7}$$

The radar waveform will be assumed to consist of monotone pulses of duration T_1, which change in frequency from pulse to pulse. Output signal-to-noise ratio, from (2.12) of Chapter 2, is

$$\frac{S}{N} = T_1\beta_n\left(\frac{S}{N}\right)_{\text{in}} \tag{10.8}$$

Free-space detection range R, from (10.7), in terms of required output signal-to-noise ratio (S/N), from (10.8) for detection in jamming, then becomes

$$R = \left[\frac{P_tG^2\lambda^2\sigma L_rT_1}{(4\pi)^3kT_0F_{\text{eff}}S/N}\right]^{1/4} \tag{10.9}$$

The ECCM performance of a hypothetical 3-D (range, azimuth, elevation) air-search radar will now be evaluated in a hypothetical jamming environment as a function of the radar's frequency-agile bandwidth. Radar parameters are listed in Table 10.1. The scanning strategy and coverage are not stated for this example, but 55 and three pulses per dwell are assumed for the high and low PRF modes, respectively. Effective system noise factor *versus* bandwidth is evaluated for the high-PRF mode in Fig.

Sidelobe cancellation refers to a well known method for cancellation of the received jamming signal from the radar's main antenna with the same jammer signal received in an auxiliary quasiomnidirectional antenna. The omnidirectional channel signal is adaptively adjusted in amplitude and phase to effect cancellation, ideally leaving only the echo signal present in the main receiver.

10.1, based on a jammer ERP of 10^6 W located 100 nmi from the radar. The ERP per Hz available from the jammer is assumed to be the ERP divided by the radar's agile bandwidth β_t. Radar range *versus* effective system noise factor with jamming present is evaluated in Fig. 10.2. Finally, radar range *versus* frequency-agile radar operating bandwidth with jamming present is evaluated in Fig. 10.3, using Figs. 10.1 and 10.2. We should note that the effective system noise factor in Fig. 10.1 and the radar range with jamming in Fig. 10.3, although plotted in terms of frequency-agile radar bandwidth, are actually functions of the jammer's frequency spread. A radar with narrow frequency-agile bandwidth would enjoy the same benefits as an otherwise equivalent wideband radar, unless the jammer increased its ERP per Hz by reducing its bandwidth.

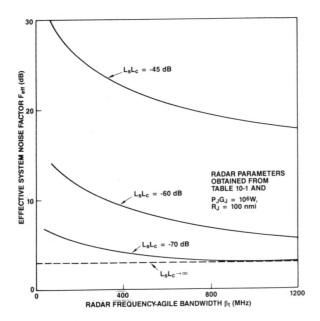

Fig. 10.1 Effective Noise Factor for Radar of Table 10.1 *versus* Radar Transmitter Frequency-Agile Bandwidth (Assuming that the Jammer Spreads its Available Power Uniformly over the Radar Frequency-Agile Bandwidth)

The frequency spectrum of actual jamming signals will not be precisely matched to the radar's transmitter bandwidth. Furthermore, actual jamming signals that appear within the radar's receiver bandwidth will affect radar detection range somewhat differently than thermal noise in the same bandwidth. Equation (10.9), however, is submitted as being useful in two ways: (1) to illustrate the advantage of wide-bandwidth radars against broadband noise jammers, and (2) for ECCM performance comparison of alternative frequency-agile radar and noise-jammer designs.

Table 10.1   Hypothetical 3-D Air-Search Radar Parameters

Parameter	Symbol	Value
Peak Power	P_t	50 kW
PRF	$\dfrac{1}{T_2}$	5000 (high) or 300 (low) pulses per second
Hits* (Pulses) per Dwell	n	55 (high-PRF) or 3 (low-PRF)
Antenna Gain (Radar)	G	10^4 (40 dB)
Average Wavelength	λ	0.1 m
Radar Cross Section	σ	1.0 m^2
Radar Receiving System Loss	L_r	0.5 (-3 dB)
Boltzmann's Constant	k	$1.38 \cdot 10^{-23}$ J/K
Standard Noise Temperature	T_0	290 K
Output Signal-to-Noise Ratio Required for Detection	S/N	1.12 (0.5 dB) for 55 hits, 7.9 (9 dB) for 3 hits, for P_D = 0.5, P_{FA} = 10^{-6}, Swerling Case 1
Radar Pulsewidth Assuming 10% Duty Factor	T_1	20 µs for 55 hits per dwell 333 µs for 3 hits per dwell
Radar System Noise Factor (no Jamming)	F	2 (3 dB)
Transmitter Agile Bandwidth	β_t	variable (Hz)

*Number of pulses transmitted during the dwell time of the radar beam on the target.

Smart jammer designs have been envisioned that can measure radar frequency from each pulse of a frequency-agile radar in sufficient time to jam the radar's receiver before reception of an echo pulse. For situations where this or other smart jammer techniques are feasible and practical, the above analysis does not apply. A wide instantaneous bandwidth radar, in addition to countering *nonsmart* noise jammers, in principle, could defeat a smart jammer. A pulse-compression radar, for example, might be designed to transmit individual pulses containing energy spread over the radar's entire operating bandwidth. In principle, (10.9) may also predict the range performance in a nonsmart, wideband, noise-jammer

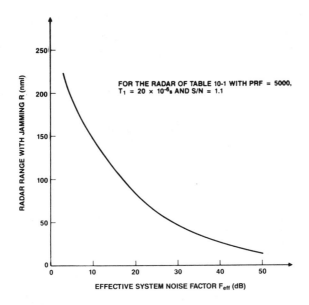

Fig. 10.2 Radar Range with Noise Jamming *versus* Effective Noise Factor
(for Radar of Table 10.1)

environment of a wideband pulse-compression radar. A chirp-pulse compression radar, with chirp bandwidth $\Delta = \beta_t$ and other parameters identical
to those for the frequency-agile radar of Table 10.1, will produce identical
performance.

In practice, however, pulse-compression radars may have serious
potential disadvantages in an ECCM environment. The receiving system's
matched-filter bandwidth of a pulse-compression radar must cover that of
the transmitted pulse from the antenna through detection. The jammer
signal from a narrowband jammer of moderate power operating anywhere
within the radar's bandwidth may exceed the saturation level at some point
in the radar's receiver, thereby desensitizing the receiver to small echo
signals. The same jammer operating against a frequency-agile radar will
have only a small probability of entering the radar's narrowband receiver.
Furthermore, the narrowband receiver's IF amplifiers, which follow the
preamplifier in a frequency-agile system, will be less susceptible to saturation because of their inherently wider dynamic range. *Dynamic range*
can be viewed here as the ratio of maximum output power before saturation
to the thermal noise power *floor*. The thermal noise power floor is proportional to the receiver noise bandwidth so that dynamic range is reduced

as bandwidth increases. In any actual radar design, a major issue is *automatic gain control* (AGC) operation. An AGC system can be designed to protect the receiver against saturation over a large variety of jammer and signal conditions.

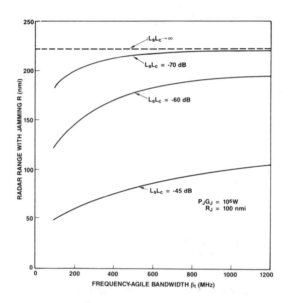

Fig. 10.3 Radar Range with Noise Jamming for Radar of Table 10.1 (Assuming that the Jammer Spreads its Available Power Uniformly over the Radar's Frequency-Agile Bandwidth)

10.2 LOW-FLYER DETECTION

Ability to detect low-flying antiship missiles is of crucial concern to modern naval fleets. Radar detection of low-flying air targets, in general, is a radar problem that dates back to the early days of air-surveillance radar. Two fundamental problems are involved, associated with RF propagation phenomena. First, propagation over the earth's horizon is normally weak. Exceptions are for operation in the 3–30 MHz region, where *skywave* propagation can extend radar detection ranges to beyond 2000 nmi, and for propagation-ducting conditions, which can provide over-the-horizon (OTH) microwave radar range performance up to the equivalent of that for free-space propagation.

A second propagation-related problem associated with low-flyer detection is cancellation of the direct signal in each direction by the indirect signal reflected from the earth's surface. This problem will now be addressed as it affects detection by shipboard radars of extremely low flying targets over the sea surface. We will show why operation at higher microwave frequencies (above 10 GHz) appears to be better than at lower microwave frequencies for detection of these targets at ranges out to the earth's horizon. We will then show, by using two examples, how high resolution radar techniques provide the means to discriminate targets from sea clutter at higher microwave frequencies.

Radar detection range of sea-skimming missiles or aircraft, at the microwave frequencies commonly used for shipboard air surveillance, may be less than the optical horizon (10.6 nmi for a 75-foot radar antenna height). For most operational radars, this is far less than the free-space detection range. The problem of low-flyer detection can be illustrated by using Fig. 10.4. For the low-grazing angles associated with surveillance against low-flying targets, the magnitude of the reflection coefficient at microwave frequencies for reflection from the sea surface approaches unity, regardless of RF polarization [1]. As target height decreases for a given radar height, the difference in length between reflected and direct paths decreases. For low-flying targets, at lower microwave frequencies, the path-length difference may be the equivalent of much less than a wavelength. In this situation, cancellation will occur in both the transmitting and receiving directions. The phase of the reflection coefficient at microwave frequencies is about 180° at near grazing angles for both horizontal and vertical polarization [2]. From the viewpoint of the radar, there are two targets: the *real target* in the direct path to the radar and a *mirror image* of the target below the sea surface, associated with the indirect path reflected from the sea surface.

As target height increases, for a given fixed target range, some height will be reached at which the direct and sea-reflected path difference will approach another half-wavelength. At this point, constructive interference occurs. At high (fixed) frequencies, the familiar *multiple-lobing* phenomenon becomes evident. This results when the phase difference between direct and sea-reflected paths goes through multiple cycles of 2π rad of phase change as the radar or target moves in range or elevation. Figure 10.5 illustrates the relative field strength at the target *versus* radar height for several radar frequencies at a radar range of 15 nmi. Relative field strength, also called the *propagation factor*, is defined as

$$F_p = \frac{\text{Resultant Field at the Target}}{\text{Field at the Target due to Direct Path Only}}$$

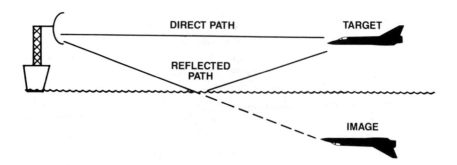

Fig. 10.4 Sea-Surface Reflection

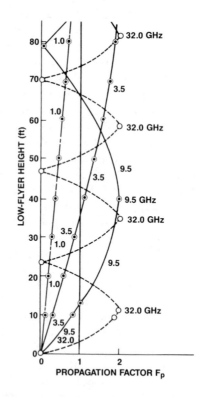

Fig. 10.5 Propagation Factor F_p *versus* Low-Flyer Height for a Range of 15 nmi (From unpublished material produced by T.E. Tice of Arizona State University.)

The propagation factor, together with other propagation effects, determines the range attenuation $g(R)$, defined in Chapter 2.

The received power at the radar is modified by $|F_p|^4$ because of the two-way propagation effects caused by the presence of the reflecting sea surface. We can infer from Fig. 10.5 that at a target height of about 10 feet the range-averaged multipath propagation loss might be reduced near the optical horizon by operating at the higher frequencies. Multiple peaks and nulls of the propagation factor can be seen to appear for targets below 100 feet at frequencies above 9.5 GHz. Peaks and nulls would also be observed at the higher frequencies for low-elevation targets, viewed at constant elevation, but changing range. Low-flyer detection is effectively improved at the higher frequencies by the existence of these lobes because targets moving through multiple lobes in range will present multiple opportunities for detection. By contrast, a 1.0 GHz system will experience severe propagation loss at all ranges out to the horizon. Thus, for targets below 100 feet, detection range is clearly improved by operating at or above X band (8.50–10.68 GHz). Operation at Ku band (13.4–14.0 GHz and 15.7–17.7 GHz) is particularly useful because of the additional advantage of favorable ducting characteristics, which have been found to prevail near the ocean surface at these frequencies.

Unfortunately, detection of small targets flying over ocean surfaces requires *clutter discrimination*. Clutter discrimination historically has been carried out by using narrowband *moving target indication* (MTI) techniques, which are difficult to implement above X band. The two most widely used techniques are high-PRF *pulsed Doppler* and low-PRF *clutter cancellation*. Pulsed Doppler methods are commonly used at frequencies from S band (2.30–2.50 GHz and 2.70–3.70 GHz) to X band. Clutter cancellation methods are commonly used below L band (1.215–1.400 GHz). We will hence show that wideband, high resolution methods may be capable of providing the required clutter discrimination at frequencies above X band, where multipath cancellation is more favorable. First, we will discuss the basic principles of conventional, narrowband, clutter discrimination.

10.2.1 Clutter Discrimination with Narrowband Radars

Narrowband clutter-discrimination radars usually depend upon coherent processing of echo signals to separate moving targets from fixed targets. Conceptually, the simplest type of radar that discriminates moving targets from clutter is probably the *continuous-wave* (CW) radar. By homodyne mixing the received signal with the transmitter reference signal, the output response becomes a steady signal for fixed clutter. Moving targets produce a Doppler frequency given by the expression

$$f_D \approx \frac{2f}{c} v_t$$

for $f \gg f_D$, where v_t is the target radial velocity, c is the propagation velocity, and f is the radar transmitter frequency. At low transmitter power levels, a single antenna can serve as both transmitting and receiving antenna. Highway police use this type of radar to measure automobile speed relative to the radar. In most military applications, the required power precludes sharing a common transmitting-receiving antenna because reflected energy from the antenna or nearby objects for higher power transmission would desensitize or even destroy the receiver. For this reason, a modification of the technique, to be discussed below, called *pulsed Doppler radar,* was developed to allow the use of a single antenna.

Coherent MTI radar systems that use clutter cancellation measure the residual response resulting from the RF subtraction of responses from sequential transmitted pulses. Subtraction is achieved as shown in Fig. 10.6. The cancelled echo response at any instant is the difference between (a) echo signal *versus* range from the previous pulse delayed by the PRI and (b) the echo signal *versus* range from the most recent undelayed pulse. The output of the MTI canceller, ideally, will be zero at range delays for which no moving targets exist. Responses from moving targets will not cancel because there will be a shift in the phase of successive echoes. Blind speeds occur for targets moving so fast toward or away from the radar that the echoes from successive pulses are shifted in phase by 2π rad or multiples of 2π rad.

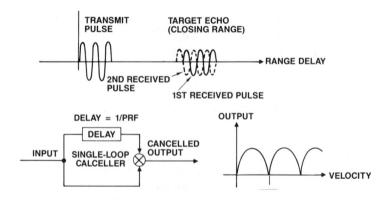

Fig. 10.6 Coherent MTI Canceller

Low-PRF MTI radars usually carry out the MTI process with digitized baseband signals, or at some convenient IF, where quartz delay lines can be used to provide the delay between pulses. Multiple-loop cancellers use additional delay-line loops in series to provide improved cancellation for slowly moving targets. Regardless of design details, however, blind speeds will occur for targets at velocities that produce 0, 2π, 3π, 4π, . . . radians of phase difference between successive received RF pulses. Below about 1.0 GHz, it is possible, for many applications, to operate at sufficiently low PRF rates to avoid range ambiguity associated with target echoes arriving at delays greater than the radar PRI, while at the same time avoiding blind-speed problems. This is possible, below 1.0 GHz, because the change in range between pulses of an air target, at the relatively low PRF associated with long-range air surveillance, is not as likely to be large enough to produce cancellation. Multiple blind speeds, however, may occur at higher radar frequencies for target velocities of interest.

Pulsed Doppler processing at high or medium PRF is commonly employed for clutter discrimination in airborne systems, where the radar frequency is often at S band (2.30–2.50 GHz and 2.70–3.70 GHz) or X band (8.50–10.68 GHz). Here, Doppler filtering is used to separate moving targets from the ground clutter. Note that the ground clutter seen by airborne radars will be spread in Doppler frequency. Whereas the low-PRF MTI system tends to become ambiguous in velocity, the high-PRF pulsed Doppler system is usually ambiguous in range.

Detections with pulsed Doppler radar are normally made from output responses obtained in the Doppler-frequency domain by using various types of Doppler filtering techniques. Target range can be measured after detection by observing the Doppler shift of target responses produced by controlled frequency ramping of the transmitted signal. The high-PRF radar can be thought of as a CW radar that avoids the need for two antennas. While often referred to as being unambiguous in velocity, a single-sideband (SSB) pulsed Doppler radar will produce ambiguous results when a target's Doppler shift exceeds one-half of the radar PRF. To prevent this, the PRF is made at least twice as high as the highest expected Doppler shift of interest. The resulting transmitter switching rates, however, become impractically high above X-band frequencies.

10.2.2　Clutter Discrimination Using High-Resolution Techniques

At frequencies above X band, problems of multiple blind speeds with low-PRF MTI radar and transmitter switching rates with pulsed Doppler radar may be avoided by using high-range-resolution (HRR) methods. One conceptual approach is to employ a high resolution, noncoherent MTI concept based on fiber-optic delay lines [3]. In this approach, subtraction of successive radar video returns from a HRR radar is performed to retain the moving target signals and to reject the stationary clutter signals (see Figs. 10.7 and 10.8). Use of HRR waveforms for MTI reduces clutter cell size and avoids multiple blind speeds. Note that resolution of responses from separate two-way propagation paths would require extreme resolution for low-flyer geometries, and so it is not considered here.

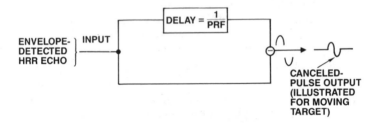

Fig. 10.7 Noncoherent MTI Cancellation

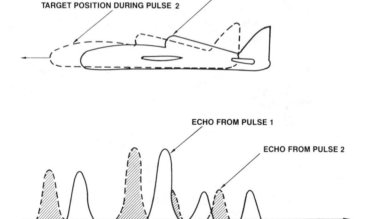

Fig. 10.8 Low-Flyer Detection with HRR (Target Moving toward Radar)

For example, if the radar sends out pulses of 1.0 ns width and 500 μs separation, a moving target with a radial speed of 300 m/s will produce an interpulse range-delay shift of $(2/c) \cdot 300$ m/s $\cdot 500 \times 10^{-6} = 1.0$ ns (i.e., a shift equal to the pulsewidth). This shift would result in an uncanceled response. Fiber-optic delay lines appear capable of providing, at sufficiently low loss, the required time delay and bandwidth. Transducers at the input and output of the canceller convert to and from light and wideband video. As we shall see later, to achieve a given level of signal-to-clutter performance, the noncoherent MTI canceller need not cancel as completely as the coherent canceller.

A second approach is to employ a HRR *track-before-detect* (TBD) concept. Here, the reduced range-cell size resulting from the HRR processing first increases the target-to-clutter ratio by decreasing the *clutter patch,* as indicated in Fig. 10.9. The clutter patch can be defined as the resolved area on the sea surface corresponding to one range-azimuth cell. Then, following a suitable threshold circuit, the threshold crossings are converted to relatively narrowband responses, illustrated in Fig. 10.10. The narrowband responses are tracked by a suitable automatic target-detection algorithm. Input data for TBD processing are illustrated in Fig. 10.11 for threshold crossings over a limited range extent for five antenna scans. Only those threshold crossings which behave like a target track are declared to be targets. Systems have been proposed which would use pulse compression to achieve high resolution. It is likely that a combination of noncoherent cancellation followed by TBD may be optimum. Only two possible means have been suggested above for low-flyer detection with HRR radar. Other high resolution techniques are currently under investigation.

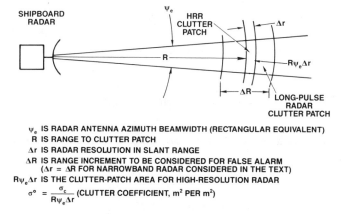

ψ_e IS RADAR ANTENNA AZIMUTH BEAMWIDTH (RECTANGULAR EQUIVALENT)
R IS RANGE TO CLUTTER PATCH
Δr IS RADAR RESOLUTION IN SLANT RANGE
ΔR IS RANGE INCREMENT TO BE CONSIDERED FOR FALSE ALARM
    ($\Delta r = \Delta R$ FOR NARROWBAND RADAR CONSIDERED IN THE TEXT)
$R\psi_e\Delta r$ IS THE CLUTTER-PATCH AREA FOR HIGH-RESOLUTION RADAR

$$\sigma^{\circ} = \frac{\sigma_c}{R\psi_e\Delta r} \text{ (CLUTTER COEFFICIENT, m}^2 \text{ PER m}^2)$$

Fig. 10.9 Clutter Patch on the Sea Surface (Looking Down at the Sea)

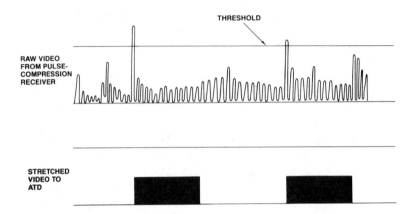

Fig. 10.10 Threshold-Circuit Operation for High Resolution, Track-before-Detect Processing

SCAN 1

SLOW A/C		CLUTTER		FAST A/C							

SCAN 2

	SLOW A/C	CLUTTER				FAST A/C					

SCAN 3

	CLUTTER + A/C							FAST A/C			

SCAN 4

	CLUTTER	SLOW A/C									

SCAN 5

	CLUTTER		SLOW A/C								

⟶ RANGE

Fig. 10.11 Input Data for a Track-before-Detect Processor

10.2.3 Wideband *versus* Narrowband Radar for Clutter Discrimination

Some quantitative comparisons between narrowband and wideband radar will now be discussed for detection of low flyers over rough sea. Figure 10.12 illustrates some relationships between radar sea clutter as characterized for narrowband radar and in terms of amplitude *versus* range and time history for HRR radar. In the three-dimensional sketch of Fig. 10.12,

a series of successive high-range-resolution profiles is indicated with the
clutter sources moving away from a stationary radar. On the left-hand side
of Fig. 10.12, measurements of sea-clutter return are illustrated in terms
of amplitude distribution, power spectrum and correlation in time, radar
frequency, and bandwidth. These characterizations are useful for representing sea-clutter return when individual clutter sources are unresolved
as in the case of narrowband radar.

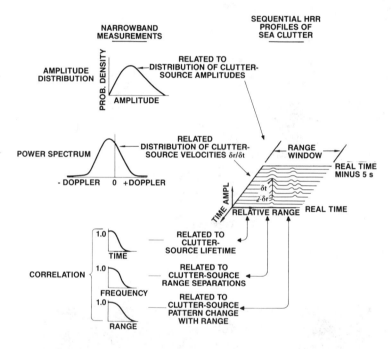

Fig. 10.12 Characterization of Narrowband (Long-Pulse) Sea Clutter
versus High Resolution Sea Clutter

Examples of actual sea-clutter backscatter observed with HRR radar
are shown in Figs. 10.13 and 10.14. The coordinate system and scale factors
are as in Fig. 10.12. Figure 10.13 shows a series of measured, successive
HRR profiles. The radar was fixed and the clutter sources were observed
in open sea. Isolated sources of sea clutter, probably associated with a sea
wave moving toward the radar, are shown in Fig. 10.14. Their lifetime
seems to be about three to five seconds. Range extent appears to be about
10 to 30 feet. It was found that the velocity corresponded approximately
to the wind velocity relative to the radar.

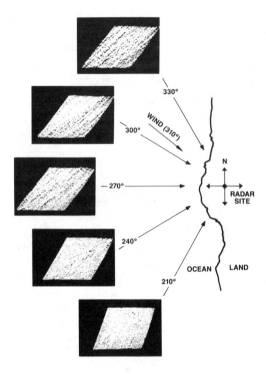

Fig. 10.13 HRR Sea Clutter (Open Sea)

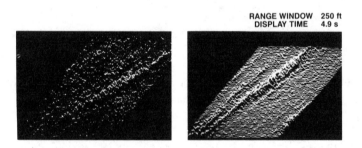

Fig. 10.14 HRR Sea Clutter (Two Typical Views)

With the long pulses associated with narrowband radar, the clutter patch is large. A matched-filter receiving system integrates echo signals from all of the sea-clutter backscatter sources in the patch. The clutter echo signal sampled at any instant at a given range is the phasor sum of the echo signals from all scatterers in the patch at that range. At high sea states, the clutter return, even at the shallow grazing angles associated with shipboard radars, can be much higher than echo signals from low-altitude air targets. For this reason, cancellers have been developed for narrowband radars to provide high cancellation ratios. For HRR, on the other hand, the clutter patch is small. The backscatter sources are resolved for the most part. Highly resolved sea backscatter, therefore, is much smaller than low resolution sea backscatter, even though the clutter coefficient (square meters per square meter of illuminated sea-surface area) is about the same.

The smaller clutter return means that required cancellation ratios for HRR radar are expected to be correspondingly lower than those for narrowband radar. High resolution radar, on the other hand, has many more range cells, each of which can produce a false alarm. Therefore, detection thresholds will be set for a much lower false-alarm probability. The result of these effects will now be analyzed and then illustrated in an example.

The probability P_{FA} that cancelled clutter for cancellation ratio R_c will exceed the radar cross section threshold σ_T is expressed as

$$P_{FA} = P\left(\frac{\sigma_c}{R_c} \geq \sigma_T\right) = P(\sigma_c \geq R_c\sigma_T) \qquad (10.10)$$

From Fig. 10.9, the clutter patch size at range R, beamwidth ψ_e, and resolution Δr_s is $R\psi_e\Delta r_s$. The resulting average sea-clutter cross section is

$$\bar{\sigma}_c = R\psi_e\Delta r_s\sigma°$$

where $\sigma°$ is the *clutter coefficient*.

Sea-clutter fluctuation can be described by a *probability density function*, $p(\sigma_c)$, defined such that $p(\sigma_c)d\sigma_c$ is the probability that the instantaneous sea-clutter backscatter cross section will have values between σ_c and $\sigma_c + d\sigma_c$. The probability that σ_c will equal or exceed some threshold γ is

$$P(\sigma_c \geq \gamma) = \int_{\gamma}^{\infty} p(\sigma_c)d\sigma_c \qquad (10.11)$$

The exponential Rayleigh probability density function has been used to represent the statistics of sea-clutter return. Other density functions used to represent sea-clutter backscatter statistics are the Ricean, log normal, and Weibull densities [4], but here we will assume exponential Rayleigh distribution for simplicity. The Rayleigh distribution applied to sea clutter can be expressed as

$$p(\sigma_c) = \frac{1}{\overline{\sigma}_c} \exp \left(-\sigma_c/\overline{\sigma}_c \right) \tag{10.12}$$

where $\overline{\sigma}_c$ is the average sea-clutter cross section of the illuminated sea-surface patch.

For a detection threshold σ_T with clutter cancellation ratio R_c, the probability of false alarm, from (10.10), (10.11), and (10.12), becomes

$$P_{FA} = P[\sigma_c \geq \gamma] = \int_\gamma^\infty \frac{1}{\overline{\sigma}_c} \exp \left(-\sigma_c/\overline{\sigma}_c \right) d\sigma_c = \exp \left(-\gamma/\overline{\sigma}_c \right) \tag{10.13}$$

where $\gamma = R_c\sigma_T$ with $\gamma \geq 0$.

We can see that for $\gamma = 0$, $P_{FA} = 1$, indicating that there is unity probability that σ_c lies between zero and infinity. The assumed distribution, therefore, is normalized properly.

By solving (10.13) for the ratio $\gamma/\overline{\sigma}_c$, we have

$$\gamma/\overline{\sigma}_c = -\ln \left(P_{FA} \right)$$

The detection threshold, in terms of target RCS, then becomes

$$\sigma_T = \frac{\gamma}{R_c} = -\frac{\overline{\sigma}_c}{R_c} \ln \left(P_{FA} \right)$$

For clutter patch area $R\psi_e\Delta r_s$ and clutter coefficient $\sigma°$, we have

$$\sigma_T = -\frac{R\psi_e\Delta r_s\sigma°}{R_c} \ln \left(P_{FA} \right)$$

The required cancellation ratio R_c for detection of target size σ_T thus is

$$R_c = -\frac{R\psi_e\Delta r_s\sigma° \ln \left(P_{FA} \right)}{\sigma_T} \tag{10.14}$$

The ratio of signal to mean clutter power before cancellation is

$$\left(\frac{S}{C} \right)_1 = \frac{\sigma_T}{\overline{\sigma}_c} = \frac{\sigma_T}{R\psi_e\Delta r_s\sigma°} \tag{10.15}$$

and after cancellation:

$$\left(\frac{S}{C}\right)_2 = \frac{R_c \sigma_T}{\overline{\sigma}_c} = \frac{R_c \sigma_T}{R\psi_e \Delta r_s \sigma°} \tag{10.16}$$

Differences between narrowband radar and HRR radar for detection of targets in clutter will be illustrated next. The two types of radars are compared in Table 10.2 at the same *false-alarm rate* (FAR). Characteristics for two hypothetical radars were chosen to be identical, except for range resolution. A 360° azimuthal search scanning is assumed for each radar. A maximum false-alarm rate is assigned only for a 1.0 nmi surveillance ring to simplify calculations. A different clutter patch area would have to be considered for each range increment if a single false-alarm rate were assigned for the entire area of range coverage. The HRR radar requires four orders of magnitude (40 dB) lower probability of false alarm than that of the narrowband radar, but this disadvantage is offset by requiring almost 40 dB less clutter cancellation. For this reason, a noncoherent canceller (cancellation at video), although inherently less efficient than a coherent canceller (cancellation at baseband or IF), may be appropriate for HRR and could solve the problem of carrying out MTI at frequencies above 10 GHz, where low-flyer detection is easier to achieve.

A more complete analysis would use a better sea-clutter model than the Rayleigh probability distribution, which is known to be optimistic for sea echo as seen with HRR radar. Experimental confirmation of any model, however, would be difficult, if not impractical, for the extremely low P_{FA} values involved with HRR radar. A more complete analysis would also recognize slight differences in $\sigma°$ values for HRR as compared with low resolution radar. Values chosen for the above analysis, $\sigma° = -30$ dB, were for vertical polarization in medium seas at near-grazing angles [5]. More complete analysis indicates that noncoherent HRR-MTI radar used for low-flyer detection will require about 10–20 dB clutter cancellation, instead of 2 dB as calculated in Table 10.2.

One important additional consideration is involved for the above type of noncoherent clutter cancellation. The resolution must be sufficiently high to produce a detectable uncancelled residual for the slowest targets of interest. Target echoes from successive radar pulses will tend to cancel slowly moving targets as well as clutter. The problem becomes more severe as the radar PRF increases. We will try to gain some insight into this consideration by estimating the required resolution for a target moving

Table 10.2   Calculation Sheet for HRR *versus* Narrowband
Clutter Cancellation

Parameter	Symbol	HRR Radar	Narrowband Radar
Radar Range to be Considered	R	10 nmi (18.52 km)	10 nmi (18.52 km)
Incremental Range for which False Alarms are to be Considered (centered at 10 nmi)	δR	1.0 nmi (1852 m)	1.0 nmi (1852 m)
Scanning Rate	ω_s	1 scan/s	1 scan/s
Azimuth Beamwidth (equivalent rectangular)	ψ_e	1.0° (.0175 radians)	1.0° (.0175 radians)
Beam Dwells per Scan	$2\pi/\psi_e$	360	360
Target Size	σ_T	1.0 m²	1.0 m²
Radar Center Frequency	$\bar{f}$	10 GHz	10 GHz
Range Resolution	Δr_s	0.2 m	1.0 nmi (1852 m) (12 μs pulse)
Clutter Coefficient (near grazing, medium seas)	$\sigma°$	10^{-3} m²/m²	10^{-3} m²/m²
Clutter Patch Area at 10 nmi	$R\psi_e\Delta r_s$	65 m²	6.0×10^5 m²
Signal-to-Clutter Ratio before Cancellation, Eq. (10.15)	$(S/C)_1$	12 dB	-28 dB
Alarm Opportunities per Hour in Range Ring $R - \dfrac{\delta R}{2}$ to $R + \dfrac{\delta R}{2}$ $\left(N_a = \omega_s \cdot \dfrac{2\pi}{\psi_e} \cdot \dfrac{\delta R}{\Delta r} \cdot 3600\right)$	N_a	1.20×10^{10} h^{-1}	1.30×10^6 h^{-1}
Required Probability of False Alarm Corresponding to FAR = 1.0 per Hour in Range Ring δR	P_{FA}	8.3×10^{-11}	7.7×10^{-7}
Required Cancellation for $\sigma_T = 1.0$ m², Eq. (10.14)	R_c	2 dB	39 dB

Table 10.2 (cont'd)

Parameter	Symbol	HRR Radar	Narrowband Radar
Signal-to-Clutter Ratio after Cancellation, Eq. (10.16)	$(S/C)_2$	14 dB	11 dB

at a relatively slow radial velocity of 150 m/s toward the radar. For a PRI of 500 μs, the target will travel 150 m/s · 500 · 10^{-6} s = 0.075 m between pulses. For example, video pulses from a 0.15 m resolution radar would then overlap to produce roughly a 3 dB signal degradation in the target response. This is illustrated by the idealized triangular pulses of Fig. 10.15. To handle slower targets without further degradation in target response would require lower PRF, higher resolution, or both. Targets at radial speeds of 150 m/s or higher produce less than the 3 dB degradation for the above example. We should note that R_c in (10.14) is the degraded cancellation ratio.

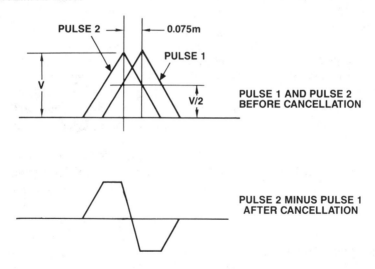

Fig. 10.15 Cancellation of Two HRR Video Pulses

The arguments given above concerning the use of HRR for sea-clutter discrimination also apply, but in a more complex way, to the TBD technique for HRR clutter discrimination. The HRR-TBD concept depends upon reduced clutter-cell size to limit the number of threshold crossings to be sorted out from real targets, while maintaining threshold values sufficiently low to detect small targets.

10.3   LOW PROBABILITY OF INTERCEPT RADAR (LPIR)

One of the most severe problems of military radar is its vulnerability to detection by an enemy. Radars normally emit high-power radiation. Therefore, transmitted signals are easily intercepted by relatively simple receivers at ranges well beyond that of the radar. Problems for the tactical radar user are (1) detection by an enemy of the high-value radar platforms, (2) antiradiation-missile (ARM) attack, and (3) enemy countermeasures. The term *electronic support measures* (ESM) refers to methods and equipment used to carry out surveillance and analysis of emissions from radars or other radiating military equipment.

The development of radars that can carry out useful surveillance, guidance, and tracking functions, while remaining immune to enemy detection, has been pursued, at least sporadically, since the 1960s. This development has been one of the most controversial in radar. It has been claimed by some that it is impossible to ever realize a practical LPIR because the ESM receiver detects the radar over a one-way path, while the (monostatic) radar detects targets over a two-way path. Some proponents argue, on the other hand, that the radar "knows" the exact nature of the waveform it is transmitting and could successfully exploit this advantage. The actual situation, however, is much more complicated than could be inferred by either argument. It is not the intent of this section to resolve the issue, but rather we will assess the role played by radar resolution and bandwidth.

Four generic methods for achieving *low probability of intercept* (LPI) are suggested in Fig. 10.16. First, *spread spectrum,* with echo signal integration carried out over extended time, is probably the most commonly recognized LPI method. Here, the signal transmitted by the radar is spread over a wide band of frequencies, while at the same time there is a relatively long integration time associated with processing the target echo signals. Two example waveforms are illustrated in Fig. 10.17. Both the radar transmitter and the receiver LO in the CW waveform of Fig. 10.17(a) may be shifted in frequency to generate a constant IF. Such a waveform was described in Chapter 4. Various forms of pulse compression, such as that indicated in Fig. 10.17(b), may also be employed to spread the transmitted energy in time, while maintaining adequate range resolution. Practical waveforms, however, are likely to be quite complex.

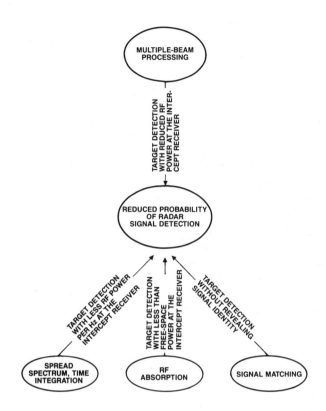

Fig. 10.16 LPIR Techniques

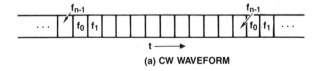

(a) CW WAVEFORM

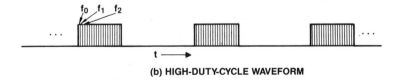

(b) HIGH-DUTY-CYCLE WAVEFORM

Fig. 10.17 Spread-Spectrum, Extended-Time-Integration Waveforms for LPIR

A second LPI method, not involving wideband waveforms at all, is simply to operate at a frequency for which *atmospheric absorption* is relatively high. The lowest of these frequencies is the water-vapor absorption line at 22.234 GHz. This technique is illustrated in Fig. 10.18. For a uniform radar-to-target and radar-to-interceptor environment, the path loss as seen by the radar will just equal that seen by the interceptor when its range to the radar is twice the radar's range to the target. For larger interception ranges, the path loss advantage belongs to the radar. For practical situations, the propagation environments are more complex. Absorption decreases rapidly with elevation so that the radar antenna beam must be shaped in elevation to prevent radiation at high elevation angles, where atmospheric loss would not offer protection. Propagation loss at the water-vapor absorption line also changes with humidity. Operation at this frequency results in problems of reduced radar performance in rain, although this can be countered to some degree by shifting the frequency out of the absorption peak, thereby allowing the rain to provide part of the required path loss. Analysis and experiments have suggested that it may be possible to obtain a radar range of about 15–25 nmi against some low-elevation targets, while maintaining operationally useful signal-interception resistance.

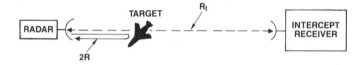

(a) LPIR OPERATION IN A UNIFORM ABSORPTION-LOSS ENVIRONMENT

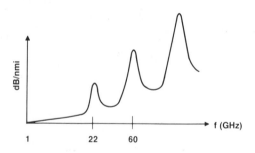

(b) ATMOSPHERIC ABSORPTION LOSS VS. FREQUENCY

Fig. 10.18 Exploitation of RF Absorption to Achieve LPI

A third method for achieving LPI is to operate with *multiple-simultaneous antenna beams* to increase target dwell time without compromising target-revisit time. An example of this method will be given later.

A fourth method to obtain LPI, called *signal matching,* is mentioned for completeness. The concept is to operate the radar with waveforms, beam patterns, and antenna rotation rates that can be confused with radars which are not considered threatening by an enemy. As in the case of the absorption method, wideband waveforms are not necessarily involved here.

10.3.1 Basic LPIR Expressions

The *spread-spectrum, extended-time integration* method will be discussed further to illustrate the role of wide bandwidth to achieve LPI. Combined advantages of high resolution and multiple-beam processing will be considered next. First, we will outline some basic principles involved in analyzing LPIR performance.

The radar transmitter power P_t required to obtain S watts of received echo power from a target of cross section σ at free-space range R for a wavelength λ and radar transmitting-receiving antenna gain G_r is expressed as

$$P_t = \frac{S(4\pi)^3 R^4}{G_r^2 \lambda^2 \sigma L} \tag{10.17}$$

where L is the total radar system loss ($L \leq 1.0$), including two-way propagation loss.

The maximum range R_I at which the radar's transmitted signal can be intercepted with an ESM receiver with sensitivity S_I, through a receiver antenna of gain G_I, is expressed as

$$R_I = \sqrt{\frac{P_t G_r G_I \lambda^2 L_I}{(4\pi)^2 S_I}} \tag{10.18}$$

where L_I is the total ESM receiver system loss ($L_I \leq 1.0$) including one-way propagation loss. By solving (10.18) for the radar transmitter power given by (10.17), with echo power S equal to radar receiver sensitivity S_r, the maximum signal-interception range for a radar that is just able to detect a target of size σ, at up to radar range R, becomes

$$R_I = R^2 \left(\frac{4\pi}{\sigma} \cdot \frac{L_I}{L} \cdot \frac{G_I}{G_r} \cdot \frac{S_r}{S_I} \right)^{1/2} \qquad (10.19)$$

Note that wavelength and radar power do not appear in (10.19). Radar signal-interception range is to be reduced for the following: large target cross section, high ESM receiver loss (low L_I), low radar loss ($L \to 1.0$), low ESM receiver antenna gain, high radar antenna gain, poor ESM receiver sensitivity, and good radar receiver sensitivity.

Equation (10.19), when applied to search radar, contains interrelated terms. Radar receiving system sensitivity depends upon dwell time of the radar antenna beam on the target. Dwell time, in turn, depends upon antenna rotation rate and azimuth beamwidth. The azimuth and elevation beamwidths relate to antenna gain. Despite the interrelated nature of the expression for interception range, it is possible to use it to investigate the effect of radar bandwidth and other parameters on LPI performance. The best radar receiving system sensitivity occurs when the receiving system is matched to the target echo signal that occurs during the available beam dwell time on target. Radar receiving system sensitivity, from (2.13) of Chapter 2, ideally, can reach

$$S_r \approx kT_s \frac{1}{t_d} \frac{S}{N}$$

where t_d is the equivalent rectangular target dwell time and S/N is the signal-to-noise power ratio required at the output of the radar receiving system to declare a target, based on echo energy integrated during the dwell time.

The effect of transmitted bandwidth and resolution for improved radar performance will first be discussed, for purposes of illustration, for two hypothetical single-beam search radar examples. The additional advantages of including multiple-beam processing will be illustrated afterward.

10.3.2 Examples

Single-Beam LPIR Example #1

As a first example, assume a radar having a single antenna, specifically, a rotating antenna operating at 15 rpm (4 s data rate) with an equivalent rectangular beamwidth of 2.0° in azimuth and an antenna gain of 40 dB. The transmitted bandwidth will be assumed to be 2.0 GHz. The periodic, discrete frequency-coded, CW waveform in Fig. 10.17(a), described in Chapter 4, will be assumed to have the capability of lossless coherent signal integration over target dwell time, which is

$$t_d = \frac{2.0}{360} \cdot 4$$

$$= 0.022 \text{ s}$$

Radar receiving system sensitivity for an assumed 15 dB output signal-to-noise ratio requirement for detection and 900 K system noise temperature is

$$S_r = 1.38 \cdot 10^{-23} \cdot 900 \cdot \frac{1}{.022} \cdot 31.6$$

$$= 1.78 \cdot 10^{-17} \ (-167 \text{ dBW})$$

Next, consider the ESM receiver. An operational ESM receiving system, for practical reasons, is not likely to have the sensitivity of the radar receiving system. Further, it is not usually practical to optimize for detecting any particular type of radar. Therefore, the ESM receiver normally can be represented by a wideband predetection amplifier, covering a radar frequency band of interest, followed by a relatively narrowband postdetection video amplifier. The ESM receiver's sensitivity is then dependent upon its selected predetection and postdetection bandwidths. This simple model of an ESM receiver, shown in Fig. 10.19, is convenient for analysis of a radar's interception susceptibility. Actual systems vary considerably, as indicated in Table 10.3.

Table 10.3 Generic ESM Receiver Systems

Receiver Types	Crystal Video Wideband Predetection (Fig. 10.19) Frequency-Tuned Superheterodyne Instantaneous Frequency Measurement (IFM)
Antenna Types	High-Gain Scanning Antenna Omnidirectional (in azimuth)

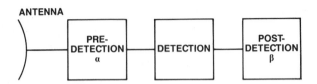

Fig. 10.19 ESM Receiver Model

Assume that interception is possible with an output signal-to-noise ratio (S/N). ESM receiving system sensitivity is then approximated by the expression:

$$S_I = kT_s\beta_I\left(\frac{S}{N}\right)$$

where β_I is a complex function of predetection and postdetection bandwidths, signal level, detection characteristics, and type of signal. The quantity T_s is the system noise temperature of the receiving system. An approximate expression for β_I of the receiver in Fig. 10.19, with square-law detection, is [6]

$$\beta_I = \sqrt{2\alpha\beta}, \text{ for } \alpha \gg \beta$$

for which α is the predetection bandwidth and β is the postdetection bandwidth. Typically, postdetection bandwidth is set to correspond to expected pulsewidths of pulsed radars likely to be encountered. For purposes of illustration, assume a predetection bandwidth matched to the CW radar's transmission bandwidth of 2.0 GHz and a postdetection bandwidth of 1.0 MHz. Then,

$$\alpha = 2.0 \text{ GHz}$$

and

$$\beta = 10^6 \text{ Hz}$$

thus,

$$\beta_I = 63 \text{ MHz}$$

Assume further that $T_s = 5000$ K and $S/N = 20$ (13 dB). The receiver's sensitivity for these parameters becomes

$$S_I = 1.38 \cdot 10^{-23} \cdot 5000 \cdot 63 \cdot 10^6 \cdot 20$$

$$= 0.87 \cdot 10^{-10} \ (-101 \ \text{dBW})$$

A value of $S_I = 10^{-10}$ W (-100 dBW) will be assumed here. Typical antenna gain for an ESM receiver may be about 10 dB to obtain nearly omnidirectional coverage in azimuth. Table 10.4 summarizes radar and ESM parameters for this first LPIR example. Radar LPI performance will be examined for 100 nmi and 20 nmi free-space radar range against a 1.0 m² target.

Table 10.4 Hypothetical ESM Receiver and Radar Parameters

ESM Receiver	*Radar*
$G_I = 10 \ (10 \ \text{dB})$ $S_I = 10^{-10}$ W (-100 dBW) $L_I = 0.10 \ (-10 \ \text{dB})$	$G_r = 10^4 \ (40 \ \text{dB})$ $S_r = 1.78 \times 10^{-17}$ W (-167 dBW) $L = 0.25 \ (-6 \ \text{dB})$ $\sigma = 1.0 \ \text{m}^2$ $R = 185{,}200$ m (100 nmi)

With the parameters of Table 10.4, using (10.19), the free-space range within which the main beam of the radar could be intercepted is

$$R_I = (185{,}200)^2 \sqrt{\frac{4\pi}{1.0} \cdot \frac{0.10}{0.25} \cdot \frac{10}{10^4} \cdot \frac{1.78 \cdot 10^{-17}}{1 \cdot 10^{-10}}}$$

$$= 1026 \ \text{km} \ (554 \ \text{nmi})$$

If the radar power were reduced so that it would just detect the same sized target at 20 nmi, the range at which the main lobe could be intercepted is 22 nmi.

Single-Beam LPIR Example #2

As a more complex example, consider the LPI potential of the hypothetical long-range, 3-D, air-search radar as described earlier in our radar ECCM performance example. The LPI potential of this radar will be calculated from its parameters given in Table 10.1, except for peak power, which will be a dependent variable to be calculated. Assume that the radar has an antenna with an equivalent rectangular azimuthal beamwidth of 1.0°, which uniformly scans in azimuth at 15 rpm. For this example, assume the same ESM receiver parameters as in the first example. Performance for the 3-D air-search radar example is calculated in Table 10.5 and the results appear in Table 10.6.

Detection of the radar's main beam in its short-range surveillance mode can be seen to occur when the ESM receiver platform approaches to within 56 nmi of the radar. For long-range area defense (100 nmi) against 10 m^2 air targets, main-beam interception can occur at free-space ranges of up to 441 nmi. For higher PRF, the radar requires more peak power for the same range and target size, which results in greater signal-interception ranges.

The radar peak power required to achieve these results when operating in the low-PRF mode is obtained from (10.17) with $S = S_r$. By using the parameters of Table 10.5, (10.17) is evaluated in Table 10.7 for $\lambda = 0.1$ m.

Multiple-Beam LPIR Example

A potentially powerful, but highly complex, approach to achieving LPI performance is to transmit and receive through multiple simultaneous antenna beams with high resolution waveforms. In this approach, the multiple-beam processing allows increasing dwell time without compromising surveillance revisit time. High resolution processing converts fluctuating targets into highly resolved, steady responses. Coherent processing over the increased target dwell time can then produce useful detection performance for extremely low radiated RF power densities at the target. The advantage of multiple-beam processing is illustrated in Fig. 10.20 for a hypothetical 10-beam azimuth-scanning antenna *versus* a single-beam system. In this idealized illustration, the beams are instantaneously shifted from one dwell to the next. For a revisit time of four seconds, the 10-beam system is thus capable of achieving 10 times the target dwell as the single-beam antenna.

Implementation of *multiple simultaneous beam surveillance* will refer here to transmission and reception through n_b separate RF connections to a single aperture. An example of a simple multiple-beam antenna is a parabolic reflector type of antenna with several closely spaced feeds near the focal point. A separate transmitting or receiving beam then exists for each feed. When operated as a radar, each beam dwells on its own solid angle of coverage so that during a given dwell the radar surveys n_b times as much solid-angle coverage as the same aperture fed by a single feed. A single transmitter could supply RF power to the entire array of feeds, but an independent receiver, processor, and detector function would be

Table 10.5 LPIR Performance Calculation Sheet

Parameter	Symbol	ESM Receiver	Radar
Antenna Scan Rate	ω_s	nonscanning	15 rpm = 90°/s
Azimuth Beamwidth	ψ_e	omnidirectional (360°)	1.0° (equivalent rectangular)
PRF	$1/T_2$	NA	300 or 5000 pps
Hits per Dwell	n	NA	$\frac{\psi_e}{90}\frac{1}{T_2}$ = 3 or 55 hits
Required Receiver Output Signal-to-Noise Ratio	S/N	20 (13 dB)	1.12 (0.5 dB) for 55 hits 7.9 (9.0 dB) for 3 hits Swerling Case 1 ($P_D = 0.5$, $P_{FA} = 10^{-6}$)
Predetection Bandwidth Postdetection Bandwidth	α β	$2 \cdot 10^9$ Hz 10^6 Hz	NA
Radar Pulsewidth (10% duty factor)	T_1	NA	20 μs for 55 hits per dwell 333 μs for 3 hits per dwell
Receiver Bandwidth	β_I	$\sqrt{2\alpha\beta}$ = 63 MHz	NA
Receiving System Noise Temperature	T_s	5000 K	600 K
Boltzmann's Constant	k		$1.38 \cdot 10^{-23}$ J/K
ESM System Sensitivity, Calculated from $kT_s\beta\,(S/N)$	S_I	$0.87 \cdot 10^{-10}$ W (−100 dBW)	NA
Radar System Sensitivity, Calculated from $kT_s(1/T_1)\cdot(S/N)$*	S_r	NA	$4.64 \cdot 10^{-16}$ W, $n = 55$ (−153 dBW) $1.96 \cdot 10^{-16}$ W, $n = 3$ (−157 dBW)
Target Radar Cross Section	σ	NA	1, 10 m²
System Loss	L_I, L	0.1 (−10 dB)	0.5 (−3 dB)
Antenna Gain	G_I, G_r	10 (10 dB)	10^4 (40 dB)

*Equation (2.13) of Chapter 2.

required for each independent beam. Electronic beam steering would likely be required in a practical design.

Discussion of practical approaches for achieving high resolution multiple-beam radar surveillance is beyond the scope of this book. Rather,

Table 10.6 Calculation of Interception Range R_I for Two Values of Free-Space Detection Range R by Using Eq. (10.19) with the Results of Table 10.5

σ	R	R_I for Low PRF (n = 3)	R_I for High PRF (n = 55)
1 m²	20 nmi	56 nmi	86 nmi
10 m²	100 nmi	441 nmi	678 nmi

Table 10.7 LPIR Transmitter Power Calculations by Using Eq. (10.17) with the Results of Table 10.5 (Low PRF)

		P_t	
R	σ	Peak	Average (for 10% duty)
20 nmi	1 m²	1.5 W	0.15 W
100 nmi	10 m²	92.0 W	9.2 W

advantages and potential performance will be assessed for idealized processing. High resolution processing in each beam will be assumed to convert each fluctuating target in the beam into a group of point-target power responses that are randomly distributed in range delay, which can be summed to form a nonfluctuating signal. The average cross section of a target consisting of an ensemble of random scattering elements is approximately equal to the sum of the cross sections of the individual elements [7]. Therefore, the sum of the received signal power from resolved, nonfluctuating target scattering elements can be treated as equal to the signal power produced by the target's average cross section. This idealization allows LPI performance to be expressed in terms of a nonfluctuating, but conventionally specified, target RCS, rather than in terms of the RCS of resolved scatterers, which is more difficult to specify.

In practice, some target fluctuations would remain. All reflection sources of actual targets would likely not be resolved. Those that would be might not resolve into point scatterers, but rather into reflection sources that produce range-extended echoes. Even those that are resolved into point scatterers would produce range-extended responses because of time sidelobes associated with the radar. As the target changed aspect to the radar, interference among unresolved reflection sources and the range-extended responses of resolved and unresolved sources would produce

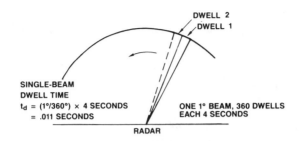

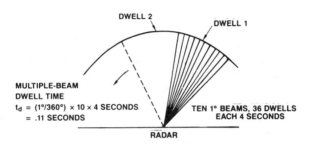

Fig. 10.20 Single-Beam *versus* Multiple-Beam Scanning (each with 4 s Revisit Time)

fluctuating responses to be summed noncoherently. The resulting summed response would then also fluctuate, but mildly it is hoped, as compared with the single-frequency response.

Echo signals from resolved scatterers of the target, regardless of radar waveform, will be assumed for this analysis to be steady signals that can be coherently integrated during the entire target dwell time t_d. The receiving system can then be assumed to be matched to nonfluctuating signals of duration t_d. Target detection is based on the sum of the signal power produced by individual resolved scatterers. The resulting signal-to-noise ratio (S/N) can then be assumed to be that produced by a nonfluctuating target of cross section $\bar{\sigma}$, which is the average cross section of the unresolved target. Sensitivity of the receiving system when written as the minimum required signal power for detection of power averaged over duration t_d is expressed as

$$\bar{S}_r = kT_s \frac{1}{t_d} \frac{S}{N}$$

where S/N is the signal-to-noise ratio required for detection. The receiving system sensitivity, when written as the minimum required signal power averaged over pulse duration T_1, is expressed as

$$S_r = kT_s \frac{1}{t_d} \frac{S}{N} \frac{T_2}{T_1}$$

The quantity T_2/T_1 is the reciprocal of the radar's duty cycle. Average dwell time on target during n_d beam dwells of the array of beams is

$$t_d = \frac{T_r}{n_d}$$

where T_r is the surveillance revisit time. If the half-power beamwidths in elevation and azimuth are $\theta_{3\,dB}$ and $\phi_{3\,dB}$, respectively, the number of beam dwells required to scan a solid-angle surveillance coverage of Ω steradians, assuming $4\pi \gg \theta_{3\,dB} \cdot \phi_{3\,dB}$, is given by

$$n_d = \frac{1}{n_b} \frac{\Omega}{\theta_{3\,dB}\phi_{3\,dB}}$$

for n_b simultaneous beams arranged so that adjacent beams and beam dwell positions cross at the half-power points in azimuth and elevation. The average dwell time on target then becomes

$$t_d = \frac{n_b T_r \theta_{3\,dB}\phi_{3\,dB}}{\Omega}$$

so that the sensitivity in terms of peak echo power is expressed as

$$S_r = kT_s \frac{\Omega \; S/N}{n_b T_r \theta_{3\,dB}\phi_{3\,dB}} \frac{T_2}{T_1}$$

Antenna gain and half-power beamwidth are related by the expression:

$$G_r = \frac{4\pi}{\theta_{3\,dB}\phi_{3\,dB}} F_g^2$$

where F_g is typically quoted as having values between about 0.65 and 0.9. By substituting for $\theta_{3\,dB}\phi_{3\,dB}$, the radar receiving system sensitivity becomes

$$S_r = kT_s \frac{G_r \Omega(S/N)}{4\pi n_b T_r F_g^2} \frac{T_2}{T_1}$$

and the interception range, from (10.19), becomes

$$R_I = R^2 \left(L_I \cdot \frac{G_I}{S_I} \cdot \frac{kT_s \Omega(S/N)}{L\, n_b T_r F_g^2 \bar{\sigma}} \cdot \frac{T_2}{T_1} \right)^{1/2} \qquad (10.20)$$

Interception range for the radar and ESM receiver combination specified in Table 10.5 was calculated by using (10.20) for an elevation coverage of 16° (0.28 rad). Results are plotted in Fig. 10.21. Bandwidth, while not an explicit parameter of interception range as calculated by (10.20), was assumed adequate to resolve targets into nonfluctuating scatterers and to force the enemy to operate with a wide (2.0 GHz) predetection bandwidth. Potential improvement over that of the single-beam version of the Table 10.5 radar system can be dramatically shown by comparing results in Fig. 10.21 with those in Table 10.6. An actual multiple-beam system will fall short of providing the equivalent of lossless coherent integration (perfect matched-filter processing), and we would not achieve the idealized result of eliminating target fluctuation. An estimate of the associated losses can be included in the total radar loss term L.

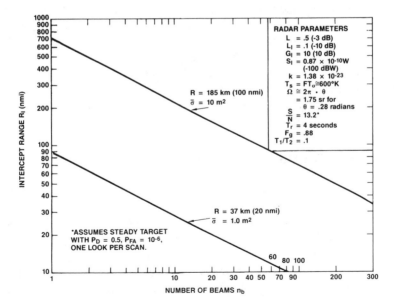

Fig. 10.21 Interception Range *versus* Number of Beams (Radar and Interceptor Receiver Defined in Table 10.5)

10.3.3 Some Final Remarks Regarding LPIR

Factors that would enter into a more complete evaluation of radar LPI performance are as follows:

1. atmospheric propagation loss and ducting;
2. radar horizon relative to target and ESM receiver;
3. potential for highly sensitive, special-purpose, multichannel ESM receivers;
4. ESM receiver platform type (surface or air).

An ESM receiver could use a high-gain scanning antenna to search for radar sidelobes, but probability per scan of intercepting radar main-beam radiation for practical scanning rates would then be very low. To achieve the same interception ranges as for omnidirectional main-lobe interception, the gain of the scanning antenna, all other factors being equal, would have to be increased with respect to that of the omnidirectional (azimuthal) antenna assumed above. In fact, the gain increase required is equal to the radar antenna's peak-to-sidelobe ratio. For example, if that ratio is 33 dB, the interceptor antenna of Table 10.5 with a gain of 10 dB will have to be increased in size to produce a gain of 43 dB. In the example of Table 10.5, this happens to be greater than the radar antenna gain, and would require something on the order of 20-foot diameter aperture. This aperture size is not likely to be practical for most applications. Therefore, we may conclude that main-lobe interception is probably the *worst case* that the radar will encounter in LPI operation.

We should note that radar bandwidth and resolution are but two factors that determine LPI capability. Other important factors have been shown to be the number of simultaneous beams and the required surveillance revisit time. A more complete discussion of radar signal interception is given by Wiley [8].

10.4   REDUCED TARGET FLUCTUATION LOSS

10.4.1   Sources of Fluctuation Loss

As discussed in Chapter 2, a *fluctuation loss* is associated with detection of most moving targets of interest. The source of this loss is the target's fluctuating reflectivity as seen by the radar as the target is viewed at continuously changing target aspects. A target's reflectivity observed at some typical surveillance frequency, antenna scanning rate, and target dwell period, is relatively steady during a single beam's dwell, but varies significantly from scan to scan. Figures 2.9 and 2.10 of Chapter 2 illustrate that the RCS of aircraft targets can be expected to vary significantly, even for small aspect changes on the order of a degree or less. Therefore, a target's pitch, roll, yaw, turn, and tangential translations relative to the radar produce large scan-to-scan variations in target reflectivity. The effect is even greater for ship targets, which are more complex and normally experience more pitch, roll, and yaw motion than aircraft.

One common mathematical description of target fluctuation is referred to as the exponential form of the Rayleigh probability density, which we used earlier in this chapter to represent sea-clutter reflectivity statistics. The probability density of the instantaneous cross section for a target of average cross section $\bar{\sigma}$, when represented by this form, is expressed as

$$p(\sigma) = \frac{1}{\bar{\sigma}} \exp\left(-\sigma/\bar{\sigma}\right)$$

The single-pulse probability of detection computed for this representation and that for a Swerling case 3 representation, given by

$$p(\sigma) = \frac{4\sigma}{\bar{\sigma}^2} \exp\left(\frac{-2\sigma}{\bar{\sigma}}\right)$$

are compared [9] in Fig. 10.22 with respect to target fluctuation loss. Fluctuation loss L_f is defined as the ratio by which the required average signal-to-noise ratio produced by a fluctuating target must exceed that produced by a steady target to achieve a given probability of detection. Fluctuation loss plotted in Fig. 10.22 applies for a wide range of false-alarm probabilities, centered about $P_{FA} = 10^{-8}$ [9]. Note that loss exists only for values for detection probability above about $P_D = 0.33$. Below this value, upward fluctuations of the target echo enhance rather than reduce detection relative to a steady target. Only high values of P_D will be considered in our discussion of fluctuation loss reduction to follow.

Figure 10.22 applies only for single-pulse detection. Fluctuation loss also occurs when target reflectivity is sampled (at a single frequency) with multiple pulses per beam dwell. Multiple-pulse fluctuation loss was illustrated in Fig. 2.8 of Chapter 2 for the Swerling case 1 model of a fluctuating target with $P_{FA} = 10^{-9}$. Here, we can see that loss is about -5.2 dB for $P_D = 0.8$ and -1.5 dB for $P_D = 0.5$, regardless of the number of pulses integrated before detection.

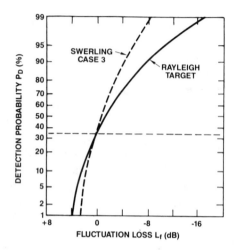

Fig. 10.22 Fluctuation Loss *versus* Detection Probability (From Barton, D.K., *Radar System Analysis,* Dedham, MA: Artech House, 1979, p. 24. Reprinted with permission.)

10.4.2 Frequency-Agility Method

A search-radar design that exploits pulse-to-pulse frequency-agile waveforms to improve ECCM or LPI performance also may potentially possess the necessary processing for improved target detection performance relative to an otherwise equivalent design operating at a single frequency. The result is improved detection for high probability-of-detection requirements when multiple pulses transmitted during a dwell period are sufficiently spaced in frequency to produce independent measures of target reflectivity. In other words, there is a reduction in the loss of detection performance associated with target fluctuation. Reduction in detection loss by this means becomes significant for slowly fluctuating targets, as represented by the Swerling case 1 model, and when the single-scan detection probability criterion is greater than about 50%.

Target fluctuation as seen by a scanning search radar is illustrated in Fig. 10.23. The target's echo signal, due to aspect motion relative to the radar, changes rapidly relative to a scan period (typically, 2–10 s), while very little change occurs during a beam dwell (typically, 5–50 ms). A single-frequency radar then sees a steady target during a beam dwell. In other words, target echo pulses obtained during a beam dwell tend to be of equal amplitude, rather than independent samples of the fluctuating echo response. The average echo signal level in Fig. 10.23, necessary to obtain a reasonably high probability of detection on each dwell, must be quite high relative to noise or clutter to prevent excessive false alarms. However, if the individual pulses available during a dwell could be converted into independent measures of target reflectivity data, then a lower average signal level could result in the same probability of detection and false alarm. The result would be higher sensitivity.

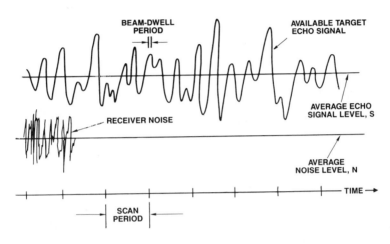

Fig. 10.23 Single-Frequency Target-Echo and Receiver-Noise
            Characteristics

Independent samples of a slowly fluctuating target can be obtained during the short interval of a typical dwell by changing the transmitted frequency from pulse to pulse during the dwell. The frequency change between pulses alters the phase relationships among interfering echo signals reflected by the multiple scatterers of the target. A set of such echo pulses obtained during a single dwell, therefore, will vary in amplitude from pulse to pulse, as though we were observing a fast fluctuating target. Thus, a slowly fluctuating target is converted into a fast fluctuating target by employing frequency agility. If a slowly fluctuating target were represented by the Swerling case 1 fluctuation model, it may be converted into the equivalent Swerling case 2 target, as is illustrated in Fig. 10.24. In this figure, the number of predicted echo pulses per dwell that are integrated before detection is 30 and 300. For single-scan detection probabilities below about 33%, Swerling case 1 target characteristics are shown to be more favorable. Above 33% detection probability, Swerling case 2 characteristics have the advantage. For a single-scan detection probability of $P_D = 90\%$, the input signal-to-noise ratio per pulse required for detection is reduced by about 8 dB due to pulse-to-pulse decorrelation. The relationships illustrated are only weakly related to the number of pulses integrated or the probability of false alarm P_{FA}. An approximate analysis will now be carried out by viewing frequency agility as a means for conversion from Swerling case 1 to Swerling case 2 statistics.

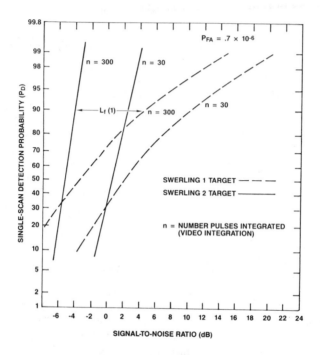

Fig. 10.24 Single-Scan Detection Probability *versus* Signal-to-Noise Ratio for Swerling Cases 1 and 2 Targets (From unpublished material supplied by Tom Lund of Teledyne Ryan, San Diego, CA.)

It has been shown [10] that decorrelation occurs when the frequency change between pulses is greater than a critical difference frequency Δf_c, defined as

$$\Delta f_c = \frac{c}{2l}$$

where c is the velocity of light and l is the range depth of the target's ensemble of scattering elements. For example, assume a minimum target dimension in the range direction of 20 m. The critical difference frequency

Δf_c necessary to obtain pulse-to-pulse independence is then 7.5 MHz.

Barton [10] discusses an approximate relationship between the number of independent frequency samples integrated n_e and the reduction in fluctuation loss* L_f. Frequency-agile gain $G(n_e)$, obtained by video integration of n_e independent samples, is defined by Barton in terms of reduction in single-frequency fluctuation loss $L_f(1)$, to be

$$G(n_e) = [L_f(1)]^{1 - 1/n_e}$$

which in dB form becomes

$$10 \log G(n_e) = \left(1 - \frac{1}{n_e}\right) 10 \log L_f(1) \qquad (10.21)$$

The quantity $L_f(1)$ from Fig. 10.24 for $P_D = 0.9$ is about 8 dB. The effective number of independent samples is related to the total frequency-agile bandwidth β_t and critical bandwidth Δf_c by the expression:

$$n_e = 1 + \frac{\beta_t}{\Delta f_c} \qquad (10.22)$$

Plots of frequency-agile gain (reduction in signal-to-noise ratio) required for detection, compared to that required for a Swerling case 1 target, as a function of the number of independent frequency samples integrated, are given in Fig. 10.25. Results plotted in Fig. 10.25 are obtained from (10.21) by using values of $L_f(1)$ *versus* P_D obtained from Fig. 10.24. Also shown in the figure is the Swerling case 2 limit for each plot. This limit is the gain that can be achieved with complete pulse-to-pulse independence among the total number of pulses received per dwell. The greatest gain is obtained from the first few independent samples. Improvement achieved for more than about six samples is quite small. These results change only about 0.5 dB when the number of pulses integrated n_e varies between 10 and 300. In the above example, where $l = 20$ m, six independent samples correspond to six pulses spaced 7.5 MHz apart for a total frequency-agile bandwidth, from (10.22), of

$$\beta_t = (n_e - 1)\Delta f_c = (6 - 1)7.5 = 37.5 \text{ MHz}$$

---

*For the Barton analysis, $L_f \geq 1.0$.

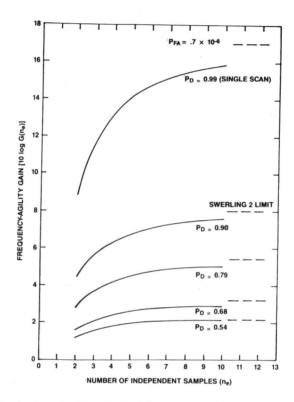

Fig. 10.25 Frequency-Agility Gain *versus* Number of Independent Samples (From unpublished material supplied by Tom Lund of Teledyne Ryan Electronics, San Diego, CA.)

Frequency agility for detection improvement is a well known technique that is used with a number of existing radar systems. Frequency-agile magnetrons provide an inexpensive means to achieve wideband frequency agility for common search-radar applications. Video pulse integration is usually provided by luminosity addition on the *plan-position-indicator* (PPI) display and by the human observer.

10.4.3   High-Resolution Method

Frequency agility, as described above, reduces fluctuation loss by noncoherent integration of multiple echoes produced by transmitted pulses that are dispersed in frequency. A second method will now be described for reducing detection loss by using high resolution processing to resolve targets into individual scatterers before detection. If complex targets could be resolved into point-target scatterers, then fluctuation for each scatterer would be reduced to zero. Ideally, as described above for multiple-beam LPIR, a detection could then be made on the basis of the nonfluctuating sum of predetected (video) responses from the resolved scatterers of the target. Then, as for the LPIR case, the radar range equation can be conveniently expressed in terms of the required signal-to-noise ratio (S/N) at the receiver output produced by a nonfluctuating target of cross section equal to the average target cross section.

Dwell time for a single-beam scanning radar with elevation and azimuth beamwidths $\theta_{3\,dB}$ and $\phi_{3\,dB}$, respectively, is approximately given by

$$t_d = \frac{T_r \theta_{3\,dB} \phi_{3\,dB}}{\Omega} \tag{10.23}$$

where T_r is target revisit time and Ω is the solid angle of surveillance coverage.

Transmitter power to be used in the radar equation to compute single-dwell echo power is the transmitter power averaged over dwell time t_d, regardless of whether we assume pulsed or CW transmission. Residual fluctuation loss produced by unresolved scatterers will be considered as part of the total radar system loss L along with other processing losses. The radar range equation (2.14) of Chapter 2 can then be written as

$$R = \left[\frac{(P_t)_{\text{ave}} G^2 \lambda^2 L \, \bar{\sigma} \, t_d}{(4\pi)^3 k T_s (S/N)} \right]^{1/4}$$

where dwell time t_d is substituted for signal duration T_1. With t_d from (10.23), the radar detection range becomes

$$R = \left[\frac{(P_t)_{\text{ave}} G^2 \lambda^2 L \, \bar{\sigma}}{(4\pi)^3 k T_s (S/N)} \frac{T_r \theta_{3\,dB} \phi_{3\,dB}}{\Omega} \right]^{1/4}$$

This expression can be simplified by relating antenna gain and beamwidth using the substitution:

$$\theta_{3\,dB} \phi_{3\,dB} = \frac{4\pi}{G} F_g^2$$

where, as before, F_g is an antenna factor that typically varies between about 0.65 and 0.9. The expression for radar range based on detection of the summed predetected power responses from resolved targets then becomes

$$R = \left[\frac{(P_t)_{\text{ave}} G \lambda^2 L \; T_r F_g^2 \bar{\sigma}}{(4\pi)^2 k T_s (S/N) \Omega} \right]^{1/4} \qquad (10.24)$$

Waveform bandwidth does not appear explicitly in (10.24), but the assumption of resolved scatterers implies a bandwidth on the order of 500 MHz.

Assumptions regarding summation of predetected responses and aspect-averaged RCS were chosen here to result in an idealized closed-form expression. An actual system would probably employ more sophisticated and superior detection methods. Potential detection improvement for the idealized concept is illustrated by comparing the respective performance of the radar specified in Table 10.8 for high resolution and low resolution processing. Performance for high resolution processing will be predicted by (10.24). Performance for low resolution processing will be predicted for comparison by the more common form of the radar equation, given by

$$R = \left[\frac{P_t G^2 \lambda^2 L \; T_1 \bar{\sigma}}{(4\pi)^3 k T_s (S/N)} \right]^{1/4} \qquad (10.25)$$

where P_t is peak power. In each case there are about four pulses per dwell. For the high resolution mode, HRR echo data in each resolved range cell from the four transmitted pulses per dwell are first coherently summed, then predetected to form a set of HRR video responses. Each video response is proportional to echo power from a resolved scatterer. High resolution video responses extending over a selected coarse range cell, centered at range R, are then summed to form a *single look*. This single look is then treated as a single echo pulse for establishing the required signal-to-noise ratio. For low resolution processing, the four narrowband output pulses per dwell are first predetected to form a set of low resolution video responses, which are summed before making a detection decision.

The signal-to-noise ratio in (10.24) for high resolution processing will be assumed to be that required to meet the P_D and P_{FA} criterion in Table 10.8 for a steady target observed by a single echo pulse. The signal-to-noise ratio in (10.25) for low resolution processing will be assumed to be that required to meet the P_D and P_{FA} criterion in Table 10.8 for a fluctuating target (Swerling case 1) with integration of four predetected pulses. Detection parameters for each type of processing are summarized in Table 10.9 and results are plotted in Fig. 10.26. A range improvement of nearly

Table 10.8 Surveillance Radar Parameters

Parameter	Symbol	Value
Azimuth Beamwidth	$\phi_{3\,dB}$	.017 rad (1.0°)
Elevation Beamwidth	$\theta_{3\,dB}$	0.28 rad (16°)
Average Power	$(P_t)_{ave}$	3600 W
Peak Power	P_t	10^5 W
Center Frequency	f	1.0×10^9 Hz ($\lambda = 0.3$ m)
Antenna Gain	G	2000 (33 dB)
Solid Angle of Surveillance	Ω	$2\pi\theta_{3\,dB} = 1.76$ sr
System Noise Temperature	T_s	500 K
Total System Loss	L	0.25 (-6 dB)
PRF	$1/T_2$	360
Average Azimuthal Rotation Rate	ω_s	2π-radian azimuth scans each 4.0 s
Target Revisit Time	T_r	4.0 s
Pulsewidth	T_1	100×10^{-6} s
Duty Cycle	T_1/T_2	.036
Probability of Detection (each dwell)	P_D	0.9
Probability of False Alarm (each dwell)	P_{FA}	10^{-8}
Antenna Factor	F_g	0.88

Table 10.9 Low Resolution *versus* High Resolution Detection Parameters for the Design of Table 10.8

Parameter	Expression	Low Resolution Design	High Resolution Design
Looks per Dwell	n	4 pulses	1 look
Assumed Target Fluctuation Model	—	Swerling case 1	steady target
Required Signal-to-Noise Ratio	S/N	55 (17.4 dB)	26 (14.1 dB)

2:1 with high resolution is predicted for this example. This improvement results from (1) the assumption of a steady target for high resolution processing *versus* a fluctuating target for low resolution processing, and (2) the advantage of single-look processing over four-look processing.

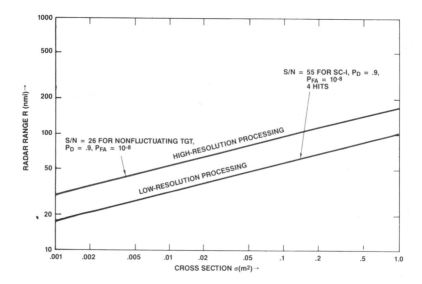

Fig. 10.26 Radar Range for High Resolution *versus* Low Resolution Processing (for Radar Defined in Table 10.8)

10.5 SMALL, SLOWLY MOVING TARGET DETECTION IN CLUTTER

Targets are separated from sea, land, weather, and chaff clutter by narrowband radars using velocity separation. If the target has higher radial velocity relative to the radar than that of the clutter sources, the clutter can be separated from the target by use of MTI processing.

However, if there is a requirement to detect small, slowly moving or small stationary targets in clutter, then MTI cannot provide clutter discrimination. High resolution methods have proved to be useful for this application. Clutter cell size associated with high resolution radar is reduced relative to the range extent of the target. A threshold criterion can then be selected to produce false alarms on only very high clutter spikes. A typical design will declare a detection based on a selected number of threshold crossings during a given number of scans. For example, a detection criterion may be set to require one crossing in five scans.

PROBLEMS

10.1 The radar of Table 10.1 operates over a 150 MHz pulse-to-pulse frequency-agile bandwidth. A jammer having an effective radiated power of 10^6 W toward the radar is operating at 50 nmi (92.6 km) range to the radar with a uniform noise bandwidth of 250 MHz. (a) What is the effective system noise factor of the radar? (b) What is the radar range against a 1.0 m^2 target? Assume that the radar antenna sidelobe levels are expected to be -40 dB relative to the peak antenna gain. Assume the high-PRF mode and no sidelobe cancellation.

10.2 The duty cycle of the radar of Table 10.1, in a *burn-through* mode, can be increased briefly to 25% in critical coverage areas when jamming is severe. Assume 35 dB antenna sidelobe levels and 25 dB sidelobe cancellation. What is the burn-through range performance against a 1.0 m^2 target for the standoff noise jammer considered in Fig. 10.1 if jammer power is spread uniformly over the radar's 200 MHz transmitter bandwidth? Assume the high-PRF mode.

10.3 Self-protection noise jammers onboard attacking aircraft attempt to deny range information to radars on the defending target. Show that range information is first obtained by the defending search radar at a closing range of

$$R \approx \left[\frac{P_t G \sigma T_1 L \beta_t}{4\pi \dfrac{S}{N} P_J G_J L_r} \right]^{1/2}$$

where S/N is the signal-to-noise (jamming) ratio per pulse required for ranging. Assume that receiving-system noise is predominately due to noise jamming. (The terms L and L_r represent total radar system loss and radar receiving system loss, respectively. Other parameters correspond to those of Table 10.1.)

10.4 The radar of Table 10.1 is performing shipboard air surveillance in its high-PRF mode. A standoff jammer is not present, but the ship is under attack from an aircraft ($\sigma = 5.0$ m^2) equipped with self-protection jamming equipment. The jammer transmits 50 W over a frequency band covering the radar's 200 MHz frequency-agile bandwidth through a 12 dB gain antenna directed at the ship. From Prob. 10.3, at what closing range does the radar first obtain range information on the attacking aircraft? Assume range information is obtained at the same signal-to-noise ratio as for target detection. Also assume that all radar losses arise from receiving system losses so that $L = L_r$.

10.5   A high-PRF radar is to be designed to operate at 9.4 GHz for airborne intercept of other aircraft. What is the minimum required PRF to avoid ambiguous velocity responses for closing speeds of up to 2500 m/s? Neglect clutter.

10.6   A low-PRF MTI radar is to be designed to operate at 425 MHz for airborne early warning against air targets. (a) What is the PRF that results in the first blind speed for a target at a velocity of 500 m/s? (b) What is the maximum unambiguous range at this PRF? Assume a single delay-line canceller.

10.7   The Rayleigh density of x for $x \geq 0$ is defined as

$$f(x) = \frac{x}{\sigma^2} e^{-(x^2)/2\alpha^2}$$

where α is a constant. Show that when the *amplitude* of the echo from sea clutter is said to be Rayleigh distributed, the sea clutter cross section itself has the probability density given by (10.12). This is sometimes referred to as the log form or exponential form of the Rayleigh density. (*Hint:* Let the instantaneous sea-clutter cross section $\sigma_c = x^2$ and let the average sea-clutter cross section $\bar{\sigma}_c = 2\alpha^2$, which is the expected value of x^2.)

10.8   If the clutter coefficient $\sigma°$ of sea clutter is 10^{-3} for low-flyer geometry, what is the probability at any instant that clutter return from a range of 10 km will exceed that of a target of 1.0 m^2 cross section observed with a shipboard radar having 0.5 m resolution? Assume a fan-beam antenna of 1.0° azimuth beamwidth and assume a Rayleigh probability density for the clutter statistics.

10.9   Assuming sea-clutter decorrelation times of 0.05 s, how much data collection time is required to confirm a clutter-statistics model at threshold value γ for which $P[\sigma_c \geq \gamma] = 10^{-5}$. Assume the following conditions: the number of measurements required to produce 100 threshold crossings above γ will be adequate for confirmation; only one range gate exists at the range position for measurement; and the clutter statistics are stationary.

10.10   Low-flyer detection is to be carried out with a noncoherent MTI radar design by using a wideband delay-line canceller (e.g., by using the fiber optics line described in the text). The compressed pulsewidth is 2.0 ns. Radar PRF is 1000 pps. What is the minimum detectable target radial velocity based on the criterion that the pulse-to-pulse delay difference must be greater than one-half the compressed pulsewidth?

10.11 Show that the ratio of radar received echo power to power received by an ESM receiver in a target at range R is given by $(4\pi/\lambda^2)(G_r/G_I)g(R)\sigma$, where $g(R)$ is the one-way propagation path loss between the radar and target for isotropic transmitting and receiving antennas, G_r is the radar antenna gain, G_I is the gain of the ESM receiver antenna, and σ is the target's radar cross section.

10.12 A shipboard LPI radar is to be developed at 22.234 GHz center frequency with the objective of providing 15 nmi detection range against a 0.1 m^2 target while remaining immune to signal interception beyond 50 nmi by an ESM receiver of -70 dBm sensitivity and 10 dB antenna gain (when system loss is included). This requirement is to apply for both target and ESM receiver at zero degrees elevation and for standard atmospheric conditions. What is the minimum required radar antenna gain if the receiving system is to be matched to a target dwell time of 10 ms? Required radar signal-to-noise ratio per dwell is 16 dB, system noise temperature is 1500 K, and radar system loss is -6 dB. (The *two-way* propagation loss at zero degrees elevation under standard conditions at 22.2 GHz is -9 dB and -32 dB for 15 nmi and 50 nmi, respectively, at sea level.)

10.13 An ESM receiver uses an omnidirectional antenna. Total system loss is -6 dB. Predetection bandwidth is 4.0 GHz and postdetection bandwidth is 0.25×10^6 MHz. The system noise temperature is 2500 K. At what free-space range are -45 dB sidelobes of the radar in Table 10.1 detectable, assuming that a signal-to-noise ratio of 16 dB per pulse is adequate for signal-interception confirmation? Assume negligible atmospheric loss.

10.14 The radar evaluated in Table 10.5 is modified for improved LPI performance by operating with a low-power, frequency-coded periodic waveform (100% duty) to permit lossless coherent integration of the target echo signal for each dwell. What is the new free-space signal-interception range with the same ESM receiver if power is adjusted just to detect a 1.0 m^2, Swerling case 1 target at 20 nmi with $P_D = 0.5$ and $P_{FA} = 10^{-6}$ for each dwell? Assume that the target is steady during each dwell (i.e., equivalent to one pulse integrated per dwell).

10.15 A radar with a PRF of 400 pps scans at 30 rpm in azimuth searching for sea-surface targets. Effective rectangular beamwidth is 2.0°. What is the maximum possible frequency-agile gain with $P = 0.8$ and $P_{FA} = 0.7 \times 10^{-6}$ for each dwell over that for a single-frequency radar? Use Fig. 10.25.

10.16   What minimum frequency-agile bandwidth is required for the radar of Prob. 10.15 for optimum detection of ship targets of expected range extent of 50 m?

10.17   A fast-scanning (180 rpm) airborne ASW radar is designed to detect small, slowly moving targets in sea clutter at low grazing angles. Range resolution is 0.3 m, effective rectangular beamwidth is 2.0° and $\sigma°$ is -30 dB. (a) What is the signal-to-clutter ratio per scan against a 5.0 m^2 target at 40 km range assuming one pulse per dwell? (b) How many scan-to-scan noncoherent integrations are required and what is the required surveillance time to produce a probability of detection of 0.8 and a probability of false alarm of 10^{-6} based on the signal-to-clutter ratio per pulse for Swerling case 1 target statistics? This corresponds to assuming that the target slowly fluctuates from scan to scan and that the sea clutter is noise-like and decorrelated from scan to scan.

REFERENCES

1.   Long, M.W., *Radar Reflectivity of Land and Sea,* Second Edition, Dedham, MA: Artech House, 1983, Fig. 4.4, p. 102.
2.   Long, M.W., *Radar Reflectivity of Land and Sea,* Second Edition, Dedham, MA: Artech House, 1983, Fig. 4.5, p. 103.
3.   Chang, C.T., *et al.,* "Noncoherent Radar Moving Target Indicator Using Fiber Optic Delay Lines," *IEEE Trans. Circuits and Systems,* Vol. CAS-26, No. 12, Dec. 1979, pp. 1132–1135.
4.   Long, M.W., *Radar Reflectivity of Land and Sea,* Second Edition, Dedham, MA: Artech House, 1983, p. 42.
5.   Skolnik, M.L., ed., *Radar Handbook,* New York: McGraw-Hill, 1970, Fig. 3, p. 26-7.
6.   Boyd, J.A., *et al., Electronic Countermeasures,* Ann Arbor, MI: Institute of Science and Technology, University of Michigan, pp. 9-41, 9-42, 1961.
7.   Berkowitz, R.S., *Modern Radar,* New York: John Wiley and Sons, 1965, p. 567.
8.   Wiley, R.G., *Electronic Intelligence: The Analysis of Radar Signals,* Dedham, MA: Artech House, 1982.
9.   Barton, D.K., *Radar System Analysis,* Dedham, MA: Artech House, 1979, p. 23.
10. Barton, D.K., "Simple Procedures for Radar Detection Calculations," *IEEE Trans. Aerospace and Electronic Systems,* Vol. AES-5, No. 5, Sept. 1969, pp. 837–846.

Solutions

ANSWERS TO EVEN-NUMBERED PROBLEMS

Chapter 1:
1.2. 1.33 μs; 1.4(a). one sample; 1.4(b). 1000 samples; 1.6(a). 50 MHz; 1.6(b). 20 ns.

Chapter 2:
2.2. 146 W; 2.4(a). 1.93°; 2.4(b). 624 m; 2.8. 149 km; 2.10. 50 pulses; 2.12. $s(t) = B \exp j2\pi f(t - 2R/c)$; 2.14(a). -177 dBW; 2.14(b). -107 dBW; 2.18. 50.3 mi/h; 2.20. 600 m.

Chapter 3:
3.2. -1257 rad, 66.7 ns; 3.4(a). 10.0000200 GHz at $t = 0$, 10.0000233 GHz at $t = 10$ s; 3.4(b). 20 kHz at $t = 0$, 23.33 kHz at $t = 10$ s; 3.6. 10 ns; 3.8. -20 dB at -0.2 μs and -20 dB at $+0.2$ μs; 3.10(a). 5; 3.10(b). 30 dB; 3.12(a). zero; 3.12(b). zero; 3.12(c). 6.4°; 3.18. 0 to 50 MHz; 3.22. 3 dB; 3.24. 1.10 to 1.60 GHz; 3.26. 24 dB; 3.28(a). .027 Hz; 3.30. 1000; 3.32. 6.6 ns.

Chapter 4:
4.4. 0.664 s; 4.6(a). 32; 4.6(b). 23.4 m; 4.6(c). 6.4 MHz; 4.12(a). 15 MHz; 4.12(b). 0.5 MHz; 4.12(c). 30, 4.12(d). 60 μs; 4.14. 1.0 MHz; 4.16. 5.0 MHz; 4.18. 0.086 dB; 4.20(a). 100 MHz; 4.20(b). 0.50 dB; 4.20(c). 10 ns; 4.20(d). 20 dB; 4.24. 15; 4.26. 116 m; 4.28. -28.5 m.

Chapter 5:
5.2(c). 24 dB; 5.4. 0.22 m/s; 5.6. 4361 Hz.

Chapter 6:
6.2. $\beta = 6.0$ MHz, $\bar{f} = 36$ GHz; 6.4(a). 0.208 s; 6.4(b). 17.3 m; 6.8(a). 1.29 m; 6.8(b). 360 pps; 6.8(c). 417 km; 6.10. 772 m; 6.14(a). 5.61 m; 6.14(b). 1070 m; 6.16. $+3$ dB; 6.18. ℰ′/7 pps; 6.20(a). 5; 6.20(b). 5.12 km.

Chapter 7:
7.2. 1.23 m; 7.4. Δr_s = 0.417 m, Δr_c = 1.72 m; 7.6(a). 175 pps; 7.6(b).
300 megasamples/s; 7.8(a). 128; 7.8(b). 128; 7.10(a). 200 × 30; 7.10(b).
20 × 30; 7.10(c). 20 × 200; 7.10(d). 200 × 20, 7.10(e). 200 × 0;
7.12(a). 50; 7.12(b). −25; 7.12(c). 5000; 7.14(a). 50; 7.14(b). −100;
7.16. 1.24; 7.18(a). 36 m^{-1}; 7.18(b). 0 m^{-1}; 7.18(c). 35.4 m^{-1}; 7.18(d).
6.25 m^{-1}; 7.22(a). 53 Hz; 7.22(b). 53 pps; 7.22(c). 6827 pps; 7.24(a).
150; 7.24(b). 36,000.

Chapter 8:
8.2. 10.0 dB; 8.4(a). 537; 8.4(b). 29.

Chapter 9:
9.2(a). 1.16 rad (rms); 9.2(b). −5.8 dB.

Chapter 10:
10.2. 319 km; 10.4. 23.8 km; 10.6(a). 1417; 10.6(b). 106 km;
10.8. 1.05 × 10^{-5}; 10.10. 150 m/s; 10.12. 48 dB; 10.14. 27 km; 10.16.
9 MHz.

List of Symbols

A	Antenna aperture; amplitude.
$\mathcal{A}$	Physical area.
$A(f)$	Amplitude *versus* frequency.
A_i	Amplitude of mixer output at frequency step i.
A_r	Radar receiving system antenna aperture.
$(A/\phi)_{i,k}$	Amplitude and phase of sample from ith frequency step of kth burst.
$(A/\phi)'_{l,k}$	Amplitude and phase in the lth range cell of the synthetic range profile produced by the kth burst of a stepped-frequency waveform.
$A_r(\phi)$	Radar antenna aperture *versus* azimuth angle.
$A(\omega)$	Amplitude *versus* angular frequency.
$ABCD$	Transmission line matrix.
B, B'	Amplitudes.
B_i, B'_i	Amplitudes of received signal at frequency step i.
$C(z)$	Fresnel cosine integral.
C_f	Characteristic function.
$C_f(-\nu)$	Characteristic function at $t = -\nu$.
D	Dispersion factor.
$\dot{D}$	Magnetron frequency dither rate.
D_a	Antenna diameter.
$D_{l,j}$	Magnitude of ISAR image in lth Doppler cell of jth range cell.
E	Received signal energy.
E_I	Incident electric RF field.
E_s	Scattered electric RF field.
$E[(\sigma)_s^2]$	Expected value of sampled variance.
$E(x)$	Expected value of x.

$E(x^2)$	Expected value of x^2.
$E[H_l(x_i)]$	Expected value of H_l associated with frequency error x_i.
F	Radar system noise factor.
$\mathscr{F}$	Optical focal length.
$\mathscr{F}_a, \mathscr{F}_r$	Optical focal lengths of SAR data film in the azimuth and range dimensions, respectively.
F_{eff}	Effective system noise factor.
F_g	Factor relating antenna beamwidth and antenna gain.
F_n	Effective noise factor of a receiver.
F_p	Propagation factor.
F_T	Transmission-line factor.
G	Gain.
G_i	Sampled output at frequency step i.
$G_{i,k}$	Sampled output at frequency step i of burst k.
G_I	Interceptor-receiver antenna gain.
G_J	Jammer antenna gain.
G_p	Pulse-to-pulse processing gain.
G_T	Transmission-line transfer function.
G_t	Transmitting antenna gain.
G_r	Radar antenna gain (transmitter-receiver) or radar receiving antenna gain for separate transmitting receiving antenna.
G_s	Antenna sidelobe gain.
$G(\phi)$	Antenna gain *versus* azimuth angle.
$(G_p)_{min}$	Minimum pulse-to-pulse processing gain.
$(G_T)_m$	Transmission-line transfer function in the matched condition.
$G(n_e)$	Frequency-agility gain produced by integration of n_e independent echo pulses.
H_l	Synthetic range-profile response at range increment l.
$H_{l,k}$	Synthetic range-profile response at range increment l of burst k.
$H(f)$	Transfer function.
$H(\bar{f})$	Transfer function at carrier or center frequency.
$H(i\Delta f)$	Transfer function at frequency $i\Delta f$.
$H(\omega)$	Transfer function in terms of angular frequency.
I	Current.
I_1, I_2	Input current and output current, respectively, of a transmission line.
$I(1)$	Pixel intensity produced by one SAR look.
$I(n_e)$	Pixel intensity produced by n_e independent SAR looks, noncoherently added.

$\bar{I}(1)$	Mean SAR pixel intensity, one look.
$\bar{I}(n_e)$	Mean SAR pixel intensity, n_e looks.
$J_0(b_1),$ $J_1(b_1),$ $J_2(b_1),$ $\ldots$	Bessel functions of the first kind.
K	Chirp rate (Hz/s).
K_m	Normalized error slope of a monopulse antenna.
L	Loss ($L \leq 1.0$).
$\mathscr{L}$	Synthetic aperture length.
L_c	Antenna sidelobe cancellation ratio ($L \leq 1.0$).
L_f	Target fluctuation loss ($L_f \geq 1.0$).
$L_f(1)$	Single-frequency target fluctuation loss ($L_f \geq 1.0$).
L_l	ESM-receiver system loss ($L_l \leq 1.0$).
L_r	Radar receiving system loss ($L_r \leq 1.0$).
L_s	Antenna sidelobe-to-main lobe ratio ($L_s \leq 1.0$).
M	Number of cells of range or cross-range migration.
M'	Number of cells of range migration.
$\overline{M}$	Number of cells of cross-range migration.
M_s	Number of cells of range shift caused by Doppler shift.
M_w	Number of cells of range walk.
N	Noise power; a positive integer.
N_a	Alarm opportunities per hour.
N_J	Received power from a noise jammer.
N_0	Single-sideband noise power per Hz.
P	Delay slope (s/Hz).
P_D	Probability of detection.
P_E	ECCM performance factor.
P_e	Fraction of visible pixel elements.
P_{FA}	Probability of false alarm.
P_J	Jammer transmitter power.
P_t	Radar transmitter power.
$(P_t)_{ave}$	Radar average transmitter power.
$P(x \geq y)$	Probability that any variable x is greater than some threshold y.
R	Radar range; minimum range to a scatterer in side-looking SAR; range to target rotation axis in ISAR.
$\tilde{R}$	Estimated range.
$\mathbf{R}$	Unit vector directed to the radar along the radar LOS.
$\mathbf{R}(t)$	Instantaneous unit vector.
R_c	Cancellation ratio ($R_c \geq 1.0$).
R_f	Monopulse imaging range based on flat-plate reflectors.
R_I	Radar signal interception range.

R_J Jammer range from radar.

R_s Monopulse imaging range based on spherical reflectors.

R_1, R_2 Range to near and far edges, respectively, of range data-collection interval.

S Signal power.

$\hat{S}$ Peak signal power.

S_I Signal power sensitivity of ESM receiver.

S_r Signal power sensitivity of radar receiver system.

$\overline{S}_r$ Radar receiver sensitivity as a function of signal power averaged over target beam dwell.

S_Δ Signal power out of the difference channel of a monopulse comparator.

S_Σ Signal power out of the sum channel of a monopulse comparator.

S_i Sampling time of frequency step i.

$S_{i,k}$ Sampling time of frequency step i of burst k.

S_1 Sampling time of magnetron pulse.

S_2 Sampling time of received pulse of a magnetron radar.

$S(f)$ Spectrum of signal $s(t)$.

$S_i(f)$ Spectrum of input signal $s_i(t)$.

$S_o(f)$ Spectrum of output signal $s_o(t)$.

$S_r(f)$ Spectrum of real signal $s_r(t)$.

$S_1(f)$ Spectrum of waveform $s_1(t)$

$S_1(f_1)$ Spectrum of point target response $s_1(t_1)$ in range delay.

$S_1(f_2)$ Spectrum of point target response $s_1(t_2)$ in azimuthal delay.

$S(f_1)$ Spectrum of range delay response $s(t_1)$.

$S_i(\omega)$ Angular frequency spectrum of input signal $s_i(t)$.

$S_o(\omega)$ Angular frequency spectrum of output signal $s_o(t)$

$S(i\Delta f)$ Value of discrete signal spectrum at $i\Delta f$.

$S_1(i\Delta f)$ Value of discrete waveform spectrum at $i\Delta f$.

$S(z)$ Fresnel sine integral.

S/N Power ratio of output signal to noise.

$(S/N)_d$ Power ratio of signal to noise of a radar in a detection mode.

$(S/N)_{in}$ Power ratio of signal to noise at the input to a receiver.

$(\hat{S}/N)_{out}$ Ratio of instantaneous peak power to average noise power out of a matched filter.

$(S/N)_{pixel}$ Average power ratio of signal to noise of an image pixel.

$(S/N)_v$ Required power ratio of signal to noise to provide a visible response.

$(S/N)_\Delta$	Power ratio of signal to noise out of the difference channel of a monopulse comparator.
$(S/N)_\Sigma$	Power ratio of signal to noise out of the sum channel of a monopulse comparator.
$S/N(n_e)$	Power ratio of signal to speckle noise following non-coherent integration of n_e looks.
S/C	Power ratio of signal to clutter.
$(S/C)_1$	Signal-to-clutter ratio before cancellation.
$(S/C)_2$	Signal-to-clutter ratio after cancellation.
T	Integration time; sample spacing.
T_a	Antenna noise temperature.
T_e	Effective noise temperature of a receiving system.
T_0	Standard noise temperature (290 K).
T_0^2	Quadratic phase error constant.
T_r	Surveillance revisit time.
T_s	System noise temperature.
T_1	Pulsewidth; duration of a waveform frequency segment.
T_2	Pulse repetition interval (PRI).
T_3	Delay from leading edge to sample position of magnetron transmitted pulse.
T_4	Delay from leading edge to sample position of received echo signal from magnetron transmitted pulse.
U_s	Scattered radiation power per unit solid angle toward the radar.
V	Voltage.
V_s	Source voltage at input to a transmission line.
V_Δ	Root mean square voltage out of difference channel of a monopulse comparator.
V_Σ	Root mean square voltage out of sum channel of a monopulse comparator.
V_1	Input voltage to a transmission line; voltage of first of two inputs to a mixer.
V_2	Output voltage from a transmission line; voltage of second of two inputs to a mixer.
Y	Instantaneous angular position in ship pitch, roll, or yaw.
$\dot{Y}$	Angular velocity of ship pitch, roll, or yaw.
$\|\dot{Y}\|_{ave}$	Average magnitude of angular velocity $\dot{Y}$.
Z_0	Characteristic impedance; load impedance.

Z_1, Z_2 Source and load impedances of a transmission line.

$Z(y)$ Response at position y.

$Z(\phi)$ Response at azimuth angle ϕ.

$Z(0)$ Response at zero.

a dimension of geometric shape; acceleration; a constant.

$a_0, a_1,$ $a_2, \ldots, a_i$ Fourier series coefficients of amplitude term of a transfer function.

$a(t)$ Amplitude *versus* time

b A constant.

$b_0, b_1,$ $b_2, \ldots, b_i$ Fourier series coefficients of phase term of a transfer function.

c Propagation velocity; a constant.

d A constant; distance.

d_k Relative radar range of kth scatterer.

e Exponential, 2.718.

f Frequency.

$\bar{f}$ Carrier frequency; average frequency; center frequency.

f' Frequency of a spurious signal.

f_D Doppler frequency.

f_{D2}, f_{D1} Doppler frequencies associated with scatterers 1 and 2, respectively.

f_I Intermediate frequency.

f_{LO} Local oscillator frequency.

f_c Cut-off frequency of waveguide.

f_e Band-edge frequency.

f_i The ith frequency.

f_{in} Frequency of input signal to a frequency synthesizer.

f_m Magnetron frequency.

f_{mi} Magnetron frequency at frequency step i.

f_{n-1} Last frequency of n frequency steps.

f_s Sampling rate.

f_x The x-component of spatial frequency.

f_y The y-component of spatial frequency.

f_0 *Zero*th frequency.

f_1, f_2 Frequencies of signals 1 and 2, respectively.

$\bar{f}(t, \tau)$ Average frequency deviation during the interval from t to $t + \tau$.

$\bar{f}(iT, \tau)$ Samples of average frequency deviation at ith time interval T.

$\bar{f}(T, \tau)$ Second of two samples of average frequency deviation.

$\bar{f}(0, \tau)$ First of two samples of average frequency deviation.

$f_D(t)$	Instantaneous Doppler frequency.
$f_{LO}(t)$	Local oscillator frequency *versus* time.
$f_m(t)$	Magnetron frequency *versus* time.
$g(R)$	One-way range attenuation.
h	Echo transfer function of a target.
h_i	Echo transfer function of a target at the ith frequency.
h_k	Echo transfer function of the kth scatterer of a target.
h_1	Radar height; antenna height.
h_2	Target height.
$h(t)$	Impulse response.
$h(t_1)$	Impulse response in range delay.
$h(t_2)$	Impulse response in azimuthal delay.
$h(\tau - t)$	Impulse response of $\tau - t$.
$h(l\Delta t)$	Discrete value of impulse response at time $l\Delta t$.
i	Positive integer.
$\mathbf{i}$	Unit vector along x coordinate.
j	$\sqrt{-1}$; positive integer.
$\mathbf{j}$	Unit vector along y.
k	Boltzmann's constant (1.23×10^{-23} J/K); a positive integer.
$\mathbf{k}$	Unit vector along z.
l	Length; positive integer; range depth.
l_0	Discrete range delay position of peak response.
m	Positive integer.
m_D	Number of Doppler-resolved cells of a target.
m_i	Sampled output from a mixer at frequency step i.
m_r	Number of range-resolved cells of a target.
m_{rD}	Number of range-Doppler resolved cells of a target.
$m_i(t),$ $m_i'(t)$	Outputs from I and Q channels, respectively, of a quadrature mixer at frequency step i.
$m_{i,k}(t)$ $m_{i,k}'(t)$	Outputs from I and Q channels, respectively, of a quadrature mixer at frequency step i of burst k.
n	Positive integer.
n_b	Number of beams of a multiple-beam antenna.
n_d	Number of beam dwells.
n_e	Number of noncoherently added pulses or SAR looks.
n_r	Delay-trigger reset count.
n_t	Main-trigger reset count.
p	Positive integer.
$p(x)$	Probability density of x.
$p(x_i)$	Probability density of random frequency error at frequency step i.

$p(y)$	Chi-square density of y.
$p(\sigma)$	Probability density of radar cross section.
$p(\sigma_c)$	Probability density of sea-clutter radar cross section.
$p(\sigma_e)$	Probability density of resolved target-element cross section.
$p[I(1)]$	Probability density of pixel intensity for one SAR look.
$p[I(n_e)]$	Probability density of pixel intensity for n_e SAR looks.
q	Double amplitude excursion in ship pitch, roll, or yaw.
r	Scatterer distance from target rotation axis.
r_c	Cross-range distance.
$\mathbf{r}$	Position vector of a scatterer.
$\mathbf{r}_c$	Cross-range distance vector.
$r(l)$	Normalized monopulse output signal at range index l.
$r(l_o)$	Normalized monopulse output at position of peak response.
r_1, r_2	VSWR at input and output, respectively, of a transmission line.
s	Variable of integration.
s_e	Echo power density.
s_I	Power density incident on a radar target.
$s(t)$	Complex representation of a waveform or signal.
$s(t_1)$	Range delay response.
$s(t - \tau)$	Signal delayed by τ.
$s'(t - \tau)$	Baseband signal delayed by τ.
$s(l\Delta t)$	Response at time $l\Delta t$.
$s_i(t)$	Input signal.
$s_i(\tau)$	Input signal at delay τ.
$s_i(-t)$	Time-reversed input signal.
$s_i(t - \tau)$	Input signal delayed by τ.
$s_i(\tau - t)$	Time-reversed input signal delayed by τ.
$s_o(t)$	Output signal.
$s_i(l\Delta t)$	Input signal at time $l\Delta t$.
$s_o(t, f_D)$	Output signal at Doppler frequency f_D.
$s_r(t)$	Representation of real waveform or signal.
$\hat{s}_r(t)$	Hilbert transform of $s_r(t)$.
$s_1(t)$	Waveform expressed in the time domain; point target response.
$s_1(t_1)$	Waveform; point target response in range delay.
$s_1(t_2)$	Waveform; point target response in azimuthal delay.
$s_1(t - \tau)$	Waveform delayed by τ.
$s_1(l\Delta t)$	Waveform at time $l\Delta t$.
t	Time.
t_d	Dwell time.

t_1	Waveform code bit length; short pulsewidth; compressed pulse width.
t_1, t_2	Fast time and slow time; range delay and time history; range delay and azimuthal delay.
u	Readout voltage.
u_i	Readout voltage at frequency step i.
v	Velocity.
$\mathbf{v}$	Velocity vector.
v_a	SAR film transport velocity.
v_p	Radar platform velocity.
v_r	Range sweep velocity of SAR CRT scanner.
v_{R1}, v_{R2}	Radial velocity of target scatterers 1 and 2, respectively.
v_t	Target radial velocity.
v_T	Tangential velocity.
v_{T1}, v_{T2}	Tangential velocity of target scatterers 1 and 2, respectively.
$\bar{v}_t$	Estimated target velocity.
$\mathbf{v}_t$	Target radial velocity vector.
$\mathbf{v}(t)$	Instantaneous velocity vector.
v_1, v_2	Scatterer velocity at beam edges 1 and 2, respectively, relative to side-looking SAR.
w_c	Cross-range window.
w_s	Slant-range window.
x	Random variable; linear displacement; abscissa.
x_1, x_2	Range and azimuth cross-axis dimensions of SAR film; I, Q amplitudes.
x_i	Amplitudes of I and Q outputs; frequency error at frequency step i; random sample of variable x.
$x_i(t)$	Stepped-frequency transmitted waveform at frequency step i.
$(x_i)_s$	Synthesizer frequency error of frequency step i.
$(x_i)_m$	Magnetron frequency error of frequency step i.
y	Linear displacement; sum of squares of n random variables in chi-square density; ordinate.
$y_i(t)$	Stepped-frequency received signal at frequency step i.
z	The z-axis.
$z_i(t)$	Stepped-frequency reference signal at frequency step i.
z_1, z_2	Respective arguments of sine and cosine Fresnel integrals.
α	Variable; predetection bandwidth.
β	Bandwidth; phase constant; variable; postdetection bandwidth.
β_I	ESM-receiver bandwidth.

β_n	Noise bandwidth.
β_D	Doppler bandwidth.
β_t	Transmitter bandwidth.
γ	Threshold; integer.
γ_m	Land-clutter return.
γ_p	Propagation constant.
δf_D	Doppler frequency separation.
δI	Current deviation.
δf	Change in frequency.
δf_i	Change in frequency at frequency step i.
$\delta' f_i$	Change in frequency at frequency step i of second burst.
δR	Range increment; deviation from SAR minimum range to a scatterer.
δr	Slant-range or cross-range displacement.
δr_c	Cross-range separation of scatterers.
δS	Range-delay sample offset.
δt	Range delay extent; time shift.
δu	Change in readout voltage.
δu_i	Change in readout voltage at frequency step i.
$\delta' u_i$	Change in readout voltage at frequency step i of second burst.
δV	Voltage deviation.
$\delta \tau$	Delay shift.
$\delta \phi$	Difference between matched and mismatched insertion phase.
$(\delta \phi)_{max}$	Maximum deviation from linear insertion phase.
ζ	Complex exponential for velocity correction; part of argument of Fresnel integral (unfocused SAR).
η	Part of argument of Fresnel integral (unfocused SAR).
η_s	Number of slant-range samples or stepped-frequency samples.
η_c	Number of cross-range samples.
θ	Rotation angle; polar angle; elevation angle; phase angle.
θ_d	Incident angle.
θ_i	Phase at frequency step i.
$\theta(t)$	Phase *versus* time.
$\theta_{3\,dB}$	Half-power beamwidth in elevation.
λ	Wavelength.
λ_l	Optical wavelength.
ν	Phase delay associated with frequency error.

v_d	Phase delay for frequency error associated with target range extent for a magnetron radar.
v_r	Phase delay for frequency error produced by sampling offset in a magnetron radar.
v_s	Phase delay for frequency error produced by the radar's frequency synthesizer.
π	3.1416.
σ	Radar cross section; standard deviation.
σ°	Clutter coefficient.
$\bar{\sigma}$	Average radar cross section.
σ^2	Variance.
σ_c	Clutter cross section.
$\bar{\sigma}_c$	Average clutter cross section.
σ_e	Radar cross section of resolved target element.
$\bar{\sigma}_e$	Average radar cross section of resolved target element.
σ_f	Radar radar cross section of a flat plate.
σ_i	Target cross section at frequency step i.
σ_k	Radar cross section of kth scatterer of a target.
σ_m	Standard deviation of frequency error of a magnetron.
σ_s	Radar cross section of a conducting sphere; standard deviation of frequency error of a frequency synthesizer.
σ_T	Target detection threshold in terms of RCS.
σ_y^2	Fractional Allan variance of frequency deviation.
$(\sigma_e)_D$	Radar cross section of Doppler-resolved scattering element.
$(\sigma_e)_r$	Radar cross section of range-resolved target scattering element.
$(\sigma_e)_{rD}$	Radar cross section of range-Doppler resolved element.
$(\sigma)_s^2$	Sample variance.
$\sigma_c(t)$	Instantaneous clutter cross section.
$\sigma[I(1)]$	Standard deviation of SAR single-look pixel intensity.
$\sigma[I(n_e)]$	Standard deviation of SAR pixel intensity, n_e looks.
$\sigma^2[n, T, \tau]$	Allan variance.
$\sigma^2[2, T, \tau]$	Allan variance for two samples of frequency deviation.
τ	Delay; time interval.
τ_{m_i}	Delay from start pulse to leading edge of transmitted pulse of a magnetron.
$\tau(t)$	Delay at time t.
$\tau_d(\omega)$	Delay error at $\pm\omega$ rad/s from center frequency.
$\tau_g(f), \tau_g(\omega)$	Group delay *versus* f and ω, respectively.
$\tau_p(f)$	Phase delay.

ϕ	Azimuth angle; phase angle; insertion phase.
ϕ_i	Phase at frequency step i.
ϕ_k	Phase associated with echo signal from kth scatterer of a target.
ϕ_Δ	Angle off-boresight.
ϕ_{3dB}	Half-power beamwidth in azimuth; half power beamwidth of circular antenna.
$\phi(f)$	Phase *versus* frequency.
$\phi(t)$	Instantaneous phase deviation at time t.
$\phi(t + \tau)$	Instantaneous phase deviation at time $t + \tau$.
$\phi(\omega)$	Phase *versus* angular frequency.
$\phi(\omega_e)$	Quadratic phase deviation at band edges.
$\chi(\tau, f_D)$	Ambiguity function.
ψ	Antenna beam segment over which coherent integration occurs.
ψ_e	Equivalent rectangular beamwidth.
ψ_i	Phase at frequency step i; phase at code-bit position i; input phase.
$\psi_{i,k}$	Phase at frequency step i of burst k.
ψ_t	Tilt angle of effective rotation axis.
ψ_1, ψ_2	Phase of input signals 1 and 2, respectively.
$\psi(f, v_t)$	Phase *versus* frequency and target velocity.
$\psi(t)$	Phase *versus* time; pre-envelope or analytic signal.
$\psi(t_1)$	Range-delay phase.
$\psi(t_2)$	Azimuthal delay phase.
$\psi(x)$	Phase *versus* x.
$\psi_i(t)$	Phase *versus* time at frequency step i.
$\psi_1(t)$	Two-way phase advance *versus* time of the echo signal from a point target at boresight.
$\psi_2(t, y)$	Two-way phase advance *versus* time of the echo signal from a point target displaced y from boresight.
ω	Angular rotation rate; angular frequency.
$\overline{\omega}$	Center value of ω.
$\boldsymbol{\omega}$	Effective target aspect rotation vector.
ω_A	Vector component of target aspect rotation produced by target rotation.
ω_e	Band edge in angular frequency.
ω_s	Antenna scanning rate.
ω_T	Component of target aspect rotation rate produced by tangential motion of the target.

ω_T	Vector component of target aspect rotation produced by target tangential rotation.
ω_Σ	Magnitude of actual target aspect rotation rate.
ω_Σ	Actual target rotation vector.
$\omega_\Sigma(t)$	Instantaneous target rotation vector.
$\Gamma(i + 1)$	Gamma function of $i + 1$.
$\Gamma\left(\dfrac{n}{2}\right)$	Gamma function of $n/2$.
$\Gamma(n_e)$	Gamma function of the number n_e of SAR looks.
Δ	Chirp-pulse frequency excursion; monopulse erorr signal.
Δ_{az}	Azimuth error signal.
$\Delta_{az}(l)$	Azimuth error signal at range index l.
Δ_{el}	Elevation error signal.
$\Delta_{el}(l)$	Elevation error signal at range index l.
Δf	Frequency step; frequency spacing.
Δf_c	Critical frequency shift to produce an independent sample of reflectivity data.
Δf_D	Doppler frequency resolution.
ΔR_I	Illuminated range extent.
$(\Delta R)_f$	SAR range depth of focus.
Δr	Slant-range or cross-range resolution.
Δr_c	Cross-range resolution.
$\overline{\Delta r_c}$	Average cross-range resolution.
Δr_s	Slant-range resolution.
Δt	Time resolution; sample time spacing.
$\Delta\theta$	ISAR integration angle.
$\overline{\Delta\theta}$	Average excursion in rotation angle of target during ISAR image frame time.
$\Delta\phi$	Azimuth integration angle for spotlight SAR.
$\Delta(i)$	Monopulse difference signal at frequency step i.
$\Delta^c(i)$	Velocity-corrected monopulse difference signal at frequency step i.
$\Delta(l)$	Monopulse difference signal at range index l.
T	Azimuth delay.
$\Sigma^c(i)$	Velocity-corrected monopulse sum signal at frequency step i.
Σ	Sum-channel signal out of a monopulse comparator.
$\Sigma(l)$	Monopulse sum signal at range index l.
$\Sigma(i)$	Monopulse sum signal at frequency step i.

Ψ_i	Phase of H_l at frequency step i.
$\Psi(f)$	Spectrum of analytic function $\psi(t)$.
ψ_i	Phase at frequency step i.
Ω	Period of ship pitch, roll, or yaw motion; solid angle of coverage.
∞	Infinity.
!	Factorial.

Index